The New York Times Presents

SMARTER BY SUNDAY

The New York Times

SMARTER

BY SUNDAY

52 Weekends of Essential Knowledge

for the Curious Mind

ST. MARTIN'S PRESS ⌇ NEW YORK

ISBN 978-0-312-57134-4

First published in the United States by St. Martin's Press.

First Edition: October 2010

10 9 8 7 6 5 4 3 2 1

For The New York Times:
Michael S. Greenspon, General Manager, News Services; Nancy Lee, Editor of the Syndicate, Vice President of Licensing; Alex Ward, Editorial Director, Book Development

Contributors: This book was assembled and edited by the staff of Elizabeth Publishing and by a group of academic and professional writers.

Elizabeth Publishing
  General Editor: John W. Wright
  Executive Editor: Matt Fisher

Senior Writers and Editors
Ellen Chodosh, Lisette Johnson, George L. Seibel IV

Principal Writers: Andrea Galyean, Ellen Garrison, Terry Golway, John Major, Johanna Stoberock, Jenny Tesar

Contributors: Herb Addison, Christopher Anderson, Ariana Brookes, Susan Doll, Philip Francis, Michael Kaufman, Anna Kelman, David Major, Michael Miller, Lisa Parmelee, David Sobel, Mike Tanier, Meline Toumani, Philip Turner

Design and Layout: Virginia Norey, Matt Fisher

Chief Copyeditor: Jerold Kappes

CONTENTS

Foreword   x

Weekend 1:   The Birth of Western Literature   1

The Iliad and *The Odyssey* | Origins of Theater: Greek Drama

Weekend 2:   The Most Violent Century in History   11

World War I: The War to End All Wars
World War II: Tens of Millions Killed

Weekend 3:   American Popular Music I   21

The Great American Songbook | The Origins of Rock

Weekend 4:   Japan: A Brief History   31

Ancient Civilization through 1868 | 1868–Present

Weekend 5:   Ancient Egypt   41

A Political History | A Cultural History

Weekend 6:   A History of Classical Music   51

Classical Music to the Romantic Period
Beethoven and the Romantic Era

Weekend 7:   The American Civil War   61

Slavery and the Road to Civil War
A House Divided: The American Civil War

Weekend 8:   The Computer Revolution   71

The History of Computing
The Internet and the World Wide Web

Weekend 9:   The World on the Brink   81

The Cold War | Nuclear Weapons

Weekend 10: The Universe   91

The Big Bang, Stars, and Galaxies | The Sun and Its Family

Weekend 11: The United States After the Civil War   101

The Gilded Age | The Progressive Era

Weekend 12 : The Bible   111

The Hebrew Bible, The Old Testament | The New Testament

Weekend 13: The World in Your Living Room   121

The Radio Music Box | The Revolution Will Be Televised

Weekend 14: The Religions of Asia   131

Hinduism | Buddhism, Confucianism, and Taoism

Weekend 15: The Written Word   141

Writing and Printing | Newspapers and Magazines

Weekend 16: Medicine: A Brief History   151

Medicine From the Ancients to the Enlightenment
Modern Medicine

Weekend 17: Islam   161

The Religion of Islam | The Expansion of Islam

Weekend 18: The Renaissance   171

Literature and Ideas | Renaissance Art

Weekend 19: "The World Turned Upside Down"   181

The American Revolution | The Creation of the U.S. Constitution

Weekend 20: The Environment   191

Global Warming and Climate Change
Pollution and the Rise of Environmentalism

Weekend 21: William Shakespeare   201

His Life and Work | Shakespeare's Major Plays

Weekend 22: *Homo sapiens* **and the Birth of Civilization**   211

The Peopling of the World | The Rise of Civilization

Weekend 23: Physics: A Brief History   221

The Basics | Matter, Energy, and Einstein

Weekend 24: The Reformation of the Christian World   231

The Protestant Revolution
The Counter-Reformation and the Wars of Religion

Weekend 25: Opera and Dance   241

Opera: A Brief History | The History of Dance

Weekend 26: The French Revolution and the Napoleonic Era   251

To Kill a King: The French Revolution
Napoleon Bonaparte: Emperor of Europe

Weekend 27: Energy   261

Oil | Nuclear Power

Weekend 28: The Art Instinct   271

Prehistoric and Ancient Art
Art in the Middle Ages and Early Renaissance

Weekend 29: The European Novel   281

The French, German, and Russian Novel | The English Novel

Weekend 30: The Sixties   291

The Civil Rights Movement | The Vietnam War

Weekend 31: Forms of Life   301

The Animal Kingdom | The Kingdoms of Life

Weekend 32: The Jazz Age and New Deal   311

The Roaring Twenties | The Great Depression and New Deal

Weekend 33: English Poetry: An Overview   321

From *Beowulf* to *Paradise Lost*
Romantics and Victorians

Weekend 34: Great American Writers   331

American Prose | American Poetry

Weekend 35: The Human Story   341

Evolution: The Theory and the Evidence
Genetics: The Blueprint of Life

Weekend 36: China   351

The Mandate Of Heaven
Modern China: From Foreign Rule to World Power

Weekend 37: Europe Conquers the World   363

The Age of European Expansion | Europe Colonizes the World

Weekend 38: Judeo-Christian Religions   373

Judaism | Christianity

Weekend 39: American Popular Music II   383

From the Blues to Hip-Hop | Folk and Country Music

Weekend 40: Philosophy: The Life of the Mind   393

Rational Thought in the Ancient World | From Faith to Reason

Weekend 41: The Law   403

Law in the Ancient World | The American Constitutional System

Weekend 42: Modern Thought   415

Modern Philosophy | Psychology: Science and the Human Mind

Weekend 43: Modernism in Art and Music   427

The Shock and the New: 20th Century Art
20th Century Classical Music

Weekend 44: The Earth and Its Elements   437

The Earth | The Elements

Weekend 45: The Industrial Revolution   447

Origins of the Modern Economic World
Marx and the Challenge to the New Order

Weekend 46: Poetry: An Introduction   457

Poetry from the Greeks to the Middle Ages | How Poetry Works

Weekend 47: Languages of the World   467

Languages of the World | The English Language Today

Weekend 48: Painting in the 19th Century   479

American Painting | Impressionism and After

Weekend 49: Marvels of Modern Technology   489

Electricity | Planes, Trains, and Automobiles

Weekend 50: Ancient Rome   501

From Republic to Empire | The Empire

Weekend 51: American Film   513

American Film: A Brief History | Great American Film Directors

Weekend 52: Mathematics   525

A History of Mathematics | Branches of Mathematics

Index   533

FOREWORD

As the editors of this book, we had a simple objective: to present our readers with essential information on a variety of subjects that together make up the basic elements of what is commonly called a "well-rounded education." We have organized the information in such a way that each subject can be read casually over a weekend, hence the title, *Smarter by Sunday*. The format is based on the 52 weekends in a calendar year. Each weekend is centered on a single topic ("The Universe," "Rome," "The Renaissance," "The Novel," "American Popular Music," etc.) with each of the two days covering different aspects of the main theme. This arrangement allows readers to dip into any topic they find interesting, or perhaps feel somewhat ignorant about. Several weekends are devoted to each of the following subjects: Art, Music, Literature, History, Religion, Economics, Philosophy and Science.

We acknowledge that the contents of the book are overwhelmingly devoted to matters that concern Western history, art, literature, and even science. Our editorial decisions have been based on the fact that our readership lives in North America where educational traditions have been established for several centuries. So while we devote several weekends to the histories of China and Japan, as well as the Islamic world and to the major religions of those regions, the heart of this book is firmly planted in Europe and the United States.

Of course, space considerations had a good deal to do with the end results. We hope an examination of the table of contents will help to exonerate us from a charge of provincialism, since we were hard-pressed to cut any topic presently included. We believe the information presented here will be useful to many different kinds of readers who wish to explore a variety of subjects that we hope will stimulate interest in the wider world of learning.

The Editors

Weekend 1: The Birth of Western Literature

Day 1: *The Iliad* and *The Odyssey*

The tradition of Western literature flows from two primary sources: Homer and the Bible. The two epic poems attributed to Homer, *The Iliad* and *The Odyssey*, both concern the Trojan War, a central event in Greek history and brilliantly rendered into myth in Homer's works. The seed of the Trojan War was planted when the Trojan prince Paris judged a beauty contest between the three goddesses Hera, Athena, and Aphrodite. Each attempted to bribe Paris; Hera with land, Athena with the skills of a warrior, and Aphrodite with the love of the most beautiful woman in the world, Helen of Sparta. Paris chose Aphrodite, and when Paris whisked Helen away from her Greek husband, King Menelaus, the Greek armies banded together to besiege Troy and recapture Helen.

The Iliad and *The Odyssey* have given the world some of the most memorable characters in literature; the mighty but temperamental warrior Achilles; Odysseus the crafty storyteller; the wife of Odysseus, faithful Penelope; and the enigmatic beauty, Helen of Troy. The Greek gods are also described in similar ways. Zeus, Athena, Hera, and Apollo all bicker and seduce with as much zest as the human characters, but their ability to determine the fate of human lives gives them power within both the poems and the culture from which they emerged.

Many of the themes in Homer's work have become central in Western literature. Achilles' choice between the tranquil, domestic life and that of a warrior is part of the larger struggle of choosing between mortal peace and immortal glory. Odysseus survives his decade-long trip home due to his extraordinary storytelling skills, thereby elevating narrative itself to the highest virtue.

♦Homer The supposedly blind poet Homer is the alleged author of both *The Iliad* and *The Odyssey*, along with other ancient writings. Ancient Greeks believed he was the genuine author, but modern scholars are skeptical. No verifiable biographical information is known, but most dates of his birth range from around 950–850 B.C. in the region of Ionia, now a part of modern Turkey. This range coincides with the establishment of a Greek alphabet and the introduction of writing in ancient

Greece and has been determined by clues within the poems themselves. Homer's epics were meant to be sung, and there is evidence to support the theory that what Homer recorded was the detailed narrative that had been accumulated over several hundred years as the stories became foundational myths within Greek culture. Homer's phraseology and meter, known as dactylic or "heroic" hexameter, influenced other ancient poets—such as Sappho, Callinus, and Tyrtaeus. The 33 "Homeric Hymns" celebrating Greek deities are named so because they were anonymously written in this form.

•*The Iliad* Homer's epic poem is about the 10-year war between the ancient Greeks and the Trojans, that may have been waged around 1000–1100 B.C. The war began when the Greek armies sailed to Troy to avenge the abduction of Helen, the wife of the Greek king Menelaus, by the Trojan prince Paris. The central figure is the young Greek warrior Achilles, who must choose between death with immortal glory on the battlefield and a long life of domestic tranquility ending in an unremarked death.

After nine years of attempting to siege the walled city of Troy, frustration plagues the Greek warriors. Their leader, Agamemnon, angers Achilles, who then withdraws from the battle and threatens to return to his homeland. Menelaus (brother to Agamemnon) decides to engage the Trojan hero Paris in one-on-one combat to determine the war's outcome. Menelaus wins, but the goddess Aphrodite saves Paris, and the war's status appears in doubt. The gods intervene frequently in the Trojan War, with factions and rivalries as rampant on Mount Olympus as among the mortals below. The gods decide that the war must continue, despite Menelaus' victory against Paris.

Troy's best warrior is Hector, brother of Paris and son of Priam, the Trojan king. As the war continues, Hector prepares himself for battle and shares a tender farewell with his wife, Andromache, and their frightened son, Astyanax. Hector knows that the longer the war lasts the more likely it is he will never return to his family.

With the gods agreeing not to interfere, the Greeks begin to lose ground. Odysseus and Ajax beg Achilles to return. He rejects them and their offerings, expressing his hatred for Agamemnon and claiming he would not rejoin the fight unless Hector and the Trojans were at the beaches, about to burn the Greek ships.

After Agamemnon is wounded in battle, Hector and his forces fight against the weakened Greeks. The Trojans reach a moat and a wall that the Greeks have built to protect the ships. A portent—an eagle flying with a snake in its talons—causes hesitation until Hector dismisses its importance. They advance to the seemingly impenetrable wall, and the Trojan hero Sarpedon eventually breaches it, allowing the Trojans to force the Greeks back to the ships.

The god Poseidon intervenes on behalf of the Greeks to encourage them to reengage the battle. He succeeds, and Hector and his troops are halted. Meanwhile, Zeus favors the Trojans. However, his wife, Hera, uses all her charms to soothe Zeus into a deep sleep to aid Poseidon's intervention. The deceit is successful, and the Greeks push the Trojans back, wounding Hector in the process. Zeus awakens and is enraged. He berates Hera and has Poseidon abandon his effort; he also has Hera send Apollo to rejuvenate Hector and send him back to battle. The Trojans take control and drive the Greeks back to the ships, which they heroically defend, although they realize the tide of battle has again changed.

Still Achilles stays away, but his beloved companion, Patroclus, wishes to fight, and with Achilles' blessing dons Achilles' famous armor and leads his men to drive the Trojans away from the ships. Patroclus slays Sarpedon, thereby enraging Hector, who leads a charge against the Greeks and kills Patroclus in revenge.

Achilles is overwhelmed with grief. His desire to avenge Patroclus sends him back into battle. At an assembly of the army, Achilles and Agamemnon reconcile. The Greek army, Achilles in the lead, takes to the battlefield. With Achilles back in the battle, Zeus assembles the gods and permits them to side with their favorite mortals. Achilles and the Trojan Aeneas (the future founder of Rome) face off, but Poseidon saves Aeneas. Achilles then encounters Hector, and each is saved in turn by Athena and Apollo. Achilles then goes on a bloody rampage through the ranks of the Trojans, forcing the Trojans to retreat to their city walls.

Hector alone remains outside to battle Achilles. Priam begs him to reconsider, but Hector insists. Achilles approaches, and fearing for his life, Hector runs around Troy's walls three times as Achilles chases him. They finally fight, and mighty Hector is killed. Achilles ties his feet to a chariot and drags Hector toward the Greek ships as Hector's wife and parents look on in grief.

Achilles mourns for Patroclus, whose body is cremated, and elaborate funeral games take place. Priam remains disconsolate without even the comfort of honoring Hector's body. The gods offer a solution: Thetis tells Achilles to accept a ransom for the return of Hector's body, and Iris convinces Priam to approach Achilles with valuable gifts. *The Iliad* closes with Hector's funeral, signaling impending doom for the city of Troy.

◆*The Odyssey* Homer's epic tale covers the period following the Trojan War and recounts the travels of the Greek warrior Odysseus in the 10 years he takes to return to his homeland, Ithaca. As the story begins, it has been seven years since the end of the war, and Odysseus is trapped on the island of the goddess-queen Calypso. Back home in Ithaca, a group of rowdy suitors have gathered to try to win the hand of Odysseus's wife, Penelope. His grown son, Telemachus, is visited by the disguised Athena and advised to dismiss the suitors and seek the whereabouts of his father.

Accompanied by the disguised Athena, Telemachus sails to Pylos, home of wise old Nestor, a survivor of the Trojan War, and then to Menelaus and Helen at Sparta. Menelaus tells several tales of the war, including Odysseus's ploy of the Trojan Horse. He also relates Agamemnon's fatal homecoming and the imprisonment of Odysseus by Calypso.

Odysseus is still with Calypso, longing to return home. After Athena's intervention, he builds a raft and sets off, but wrathful Poseidon drives Odysseus into the sea. He washes up on the island of the Phaeacians, where he is received as an honored guest. The following day, King Alcinous' men prepare a ship for Odysseus' return, and a great feast is held in the palace, where Odysseus is asked to recount his adventures.

He relates his encounter with the giant one-eyed Cyclops, who devoured several of his men before Odysseus lulled him to sleep with wine. He and his men then gouged out his eye and retreated to their ship. (The Cyclops was Poseidon's son, and his murder is the reason for Poseidon's anger toward Odysseus.) Odysseus tells how he approached Ithaca but was blown back by the winds and landed on the isle of the Laestrygonians, cannibals who killed most of his men. They then landed on Aeaea, the home of the goddess Circe, who turned many of his men into swine and convinced Odysseus to stay with her in luxury. He eventually leaves with instructions from her to visit Hades and consult the seer Teiresias about his future.

Odysseus obeys and confronts Teiresias, who predicts he will have a difficult journey home but will live long and die in comfort in his home-land. He returns to Circe's island and then sails by the spell-inducing Sirens and the rocks and whirlpool of Scylla and Charybdis, losing six of his men. He lands on the island of the sun god Hyperion, where his men disobediently devour the god's sacred cows, resulting in their death in a storm and leaving Odysseus alone to float to shore on Calypso's island.

Alcinous and his court are amazed at Odysseus's tale, but soon Athena appears to inform him of the trouble at home. She changes his appear-ance into that of an old beggar and sends him to his former swineherd, Eumaeus, at Ithaca. Odysseus proceeds to Eumaeus's hut, where he is gra-ciously greeted as a stranger. Athena also sends Telemachus to Eumaeus's hut. He obeys, and when Eumaeus leaves to tell Penelope of Telemachus's return, Athena returns Odysseus to his natural form, and he identifies himself to his son. They conceive plans for Odysseus's return to the palace and for the disposition of the suitors. Telemachus alone knows his true identity.

In the palace, Penelope sits with the disguised Odysseus, and he as-sures her that her husband will return shortly. She doubts him, but her aged maid, Eurycleia, who nursed Odysseus, notices a familiar scar on his feet, and recognizes him but is forced to secrecy. Odysseus is enraged as he observes the household with the suitors continuing to waste his re-sources while they discuss murdering Telemachus.

Penelope reluctantly announces to the suitors that whoever can string Odysseus's great bow and shoot an arrow through the openings of 12 axe handles will have her hand in marriage. They each try, but none can string the bow. Odysseus, still a disguised beggar, asks to try and success-fully shoots the arrow through the axe handles to the amazement of all. Odysseus and Telemachus together kill the suitors one by one.

Eurycleia wakes Penelope to tell her that the aged beggar is Odysseus and that he has killed the suitors. Penelope has doubts and meets with Odysseus, who proves himself by describing their marital bed, built from an olive tree, a fact unknown to others. He recounts the tales of his re-turn, and they are finally reunited.

Day 2: Origins of Theater: Greek Drama

Legend has it that Western drama began in 534 B.C., when the Greek poet Thespis first stood apart from the chorus to speak as a separate actor, giving birth to the term *thespian*. Thespis was most likely performing in a *dithyramb*—a choral hymn and dance—that was performed in honor of Dionysus, the god of fertility and wine. Thespis was the first recorded entrant in the Great Dionysia, a playwriting competition in honor of Dionysus, held each year in Athens, which drew all the great playwrights of the day. Tragedy emerged as a dramatic form before comedy, and the earliest competitions were between cycles of three tragedies followed by a satyr play, a kind of whimsical burlesque. The tragedies dealt with stories of the gods or tales of historical Greek heroes. Though playwriting was likely a popular pastime, the works of only three Greek tragedy writers survive: those of Aeschylus, Sophocles, and Euripides.

✦**Aeschylus** Historians believe that Aeschylus was born around 525 B.C. in Eleusis, a city just west of Athens. Democracy was burgeoning in Athens, and when Aeschylus was about 35 years old, he participated in the Battle of Marathon—the Greeks' first successful victory over the invading Persians. Aeschylus entered the Great Dionysia every year, winning for the first time in 472 B.C. with *The Persians*, which was based on his military experience. It is the oldest of his surviving works.

In 458, Aeschylus wrote his best known cycle, *The Oresteia*, which is the only surviving complete ancient trilogy. The first play, *Agamemnon*, tells the story of the return of Agamemnon, king of Argos, from the Trojan War. His wife, Clytemnestra, having entered into an affair with his cousin, Aegisthus, has planned his assassination. She kills him in the bath with an axe, in a style similar to that of animal sacrifice. The play ends with the chorus foreshadowing the return of Orestes, Agamemnon's son, to avenge his father's death.

In *The Libation Bearers*, Orestes is reunited with his sister, Electra, at Agamemnon's grave. Once Orestes convinces Electra of his identity, he and his sister devise a plan to kill their mother and Aegisthus, now her husband. After deceiving his mother so that she will receive him, Orestes reveals himself to Aegisthus and kills him. Orestes then struggles over the opposing calls of familial duty, but eventually decides to go through with the murder of his mother. As he flees the palace, he is haunted by the Furies—fierce female deities thought to be the personification of the anger of the dead.

The Eumenides presents the judgment of Orestes. The Furies chase Orestes to the temple of Apollo in Delphi, where Apollo holds off the Furies and sends Orestes to Athens. The Furies later find Orestes in Athens clutching a statue of Athena. Smelling the blood of his mother in the air and seeing blood soaking the ground around his feet, they surround Orestes. However, Apollo convinces Athena to acquit Orestes. The Furies are renamed the Eumenides and charged with ensuring the prosperity of Athens. Mercy, Athena claims, is always preferable to vengeance.

Before Aeschylus, drama was limited in form to one actor, the protagonist. This actor could play different roles, but could only have dialogue with the chorus. Thematic and aesthetic possibilities were opened by Aeschylus's addition of a second actor. In his writing, Aeschylus also advanced the idea of *hubris*—the extreme arrogance of a character, and usually justification for the character's downfall. For all his textual innovations, Aeschylus was more than just a writer. He also mastered set and costume design, employed scenic effects, and both choreographed and trained his chorus. Because the standard practice was for dramatists to act in their own plays, Aeschylus was also most likely a performer.

♦**Sophocles** The next of the revolutionary Greek playwrights was Sophocles, who, as an undiscovered novice, became a legend when he beat Aeschylus at the Dionysian festival of 467. Sophocles was born around 496 B.C. near Athens. In 442, he served as one of the treasurers managing money flowing in and out of the Delian League, and in 440 he was elected one of the executive officials in command of the armed forces. By 413, in his old age, Sophocles was one of 10 commissioners entrusted with rebuilding Athens following its defeat at Syracuse.

Sophocles wrote 123 dramas for the Great Dionysia. Historians believe that he competed about 30 times and claimed as many as 24 victories. Despite his prolific output, only seven of his plays are extant. His works, unlike those of Aeschylus and Euripides, which deal primarily with religious and intellectual matters, revolve around the folly of human existence. Most of Sophocles' characters lack basic wisdom, and plots generally feature flaws of character or matters of confusion—rumors, ruses, madness, and quick judgment.

Most of Sophocles' influential work cannot be traced to a specific year, though *Ajax* is generally considered the earliest surviving play. *Electra* and *Philoctetes* are among his more famous, but his best-known works are the three Theban plays. These plays are considered the premier achievement of high Greek drama, both for complexity of plot and psychology of character.

Oedipus Rex, or *Oedipus the King*, was the second of the Theban plays to be produced (first performed in 429 B.C.; the first was *Antigone*) though it comes first in the trilogy's internal chronology. Before the first scene of *Oedipus Rex*, Oedipus has left his hometown of Corinth, having heard an oracle prophesy that he will kill his true father and marry his mother. While journeying to Thebes, Oedipus is nearly run off the road by an old man. He kills the old man and proceeds. He saves Thebes from the Sphinx, and as a reward becomes king of the city, and husband to Jocasta, the widow of Thebes's former king. King Oedipus is told that to quell a plague in Thebes, he must avenge the death of Laius, Jocasta's first husband. The majority of the play's tense and ominous action revolves around this investigation: it is revealed that Laius was the old man whom Oedipus killed; that Laius and Jocasta gave up their son after the oracle told them of the same prophecy that Oedipus has heard; and that Oedipus, having been raised by foster parents, is their son. In killing Laius and marrying Jocasta, he has unwittingly fulfilled the prophecy. Upon learning the truth, Jocasta hangs herself, and Oedipus stabs his eyes with needles to enter a life of retributive introspection.

In *Oedipus at Colonus*, the old and blind former king wanders in exile, rejected by his sons, and cared for by his daughters, Antigone and Ismene. Oedipus comes upon the sacred grove of Colonus, where Theseus, king of Athens, guarantees him protection. Oedipus's son, Polyneices, is bent on attacking Thebes. Oedipus puts a curse on him, which eventually results in Polyneices's early death. Oedipus dies when he is swallowed into the earth at Colonus, where he becomes a mysterious protector of the land that has given him refuge.

Part three, *Antigone*, deals with the conflicting issues of civic versus familial and religious obligations. It opens just after Creon, new king of Thebes and brother to Jocasta, has declared that anyone who buries Polyneices—whose body has been left just outside Thebes after his failed attempt to attack the city—will be punished by death. Ignoring the threat and instead adhering to familial loyalty and love, Antigone buries her brother's corpse, and is then condemned to die. The blind prophet Tiresias convinces Creon to commute her sentence, but Antigone has already killed herself in prison. Creon's son is so distraught by the event that he kills himself, and Creon's wife, in a fit of depression, kills herself as well.

Like Aeschylus, Sophocles was a master of all theatrical trades. He is credited with inventing "scenic paintings," backdrops meant to establish location or mood. Sophocles's main textual innovation was to bring a third actor onstage, which allowed the playwright to add more characters and the actors to broaden their interactions. In 406, Sophocles led a public chorus of mourning for Euripides, a contemporary 16 years his junior, and died the same year at the age of 90.

◆**Euripides** Euripides was the third of the great Greek tragic dramatists. He entered the dramatic festival for the first time in 455 B.C. and won his first festival in 441. He was controversial for his rationalization of ancient Greek religion—the myths and legends that formed the basis for most other classical dramas.

About 19 of Euripides' 92 plays survive, the best known being *Medea*, first performed in 431. Medea, princess of Cochia, marries the hero Jason and bears him two sons before Jason leaves her and takes the princess of Corinth as his wife. Medea decides her best revenge is to leave Jason to grow old alone, with neither wife nor children, and kills both the princess of Corinth and her own sons. She then disappears in the chariot of the sun god Helios, her grandfather, and Jason is unable to avenge his family's death.

◆**Comedy** Comedy has its moments in the great tragedies of Aeschylus, Sophocles, and Euripides, but the comedic form emerged slightly later. Greek comedies became audience favorites for their bawdy and topical humor used to skewer politicians and the wealthy. Historians pinpoint three phases of the genre—Old, Middle, and New—the first characterized mainly by the works of Aristophanes, author of the sole surviving Old Comedic plays. Burlesque, pantomime, and the chorus were assigned important functions in the plays of Aristophanes, and his plots were marked by fantasy, satire, sexual humor, political critique, and invective against public figures—such as Euripides, seen notably in Aristophanes' *The Frogs*.

◆**Aristophanes** Most facts about Aristophanes' life are gleaned from the text of his roughly 40 plays. He was born about 450 B.C., and wrote his first play, *The Banqueters*, in 427. The oldest of his plays to survive intact is *Acharnians*, first performed in 425. Aristophanes is known for the witty dialogue and episodic parodies that make up his plays, which, though their plots are often fractured or incomplete, have managed to transcend thousands of generations. Some are still performed today.

Two of Aristophanes' best-known works are *The Birds* and *Lysistrata*. Some scholars regard *The Birds* as a fantastical comedy, but others see it as a political satire on the failed expedition of Athens to conquer Syracuse. The protagonist of *The Birds*, Peisthetaerus, persuades birds to help him build a new, perfected city to be suspended below heaven. Peisthetaerus and his helpers are then charged with keeping undesirable humans out of their new home, Cloudcuckooland. *Lysistrata* was written after the defeat of the Athenian expedition to Sicily in 413; it is generally read as a commentary both on gender issues and the Peloponnesian War. In the play, the title character convinces all the women of Greece to refuse sex until men have drawn up a peace agreement between Athens and Sparta, after which the women of each city are reunited with their husbands.

The last play of Aristophanes' career, *Wealth*, is a marked transition into the era of Middle Comedy, which was followed by the New Comedy of ancient Greece. These traditions moved away from parodying public figures and events, and instead featured characters that were average Greek citizens. The chorus also further receded. The New Comedy playwright Menander is credited with having introduced stock characters (the catty barmaid, the arrogant warrior, the wise king, etc.) in about 320 B.C. By the beginning of the fourth century, Greek drama had been roughly defined by its star playwrights, but it wasn't until Aristotle (384–322) published his *Poetics* that the ideals of drama were formally defined—ideals that would inform Western drama for centuries to come. Aristotle introduced the term *catharsis*—the purging of spectator's emotions through pity and fear—and insisted that playwrights create a unified sense of time, place, and action. For Aristotle, characters were second to plot, a conviction that was standard until the modernist dramas of the 20th century.

Weekend 2:
The Most Violent Century in History

In the history of human conflict, no century has been as deadly and destructive as the 20th century. Two world wars and numerous other large-scale conflicts led to tens of millions of casualties from the tropical islands of the South Pacific to the frozen streets of Moscow. An estimated 10 million died in the First World War, and 60–70 million in the Second. Unlike the hundreds of earlier wars, most of the dead were not soldiers. In the 20th century, the battlefield broadened to include urban neighborhoods, factories, and other civilian targets. Gone forever were the days when armies faced each other on wide-open spaces far from civilian homes and farms. Modern technology delivered weapons of mass destruction from the air, across hundreds and eventually thousands of miles, bringing destruction to densely populated cities.

At the turn of the century, the instability of European imperial rule in Africa and Asia became evident during an uprising against British rule in South Africa, known as the Boer War (1899–1902). The ambitions and military capability of Japan, especially on the sea, were revealed in 1905, when the Japanese defeated Russia's far larger army and navy in a brief war, establishing itself as a power in Asia and exposing Russia as a power in decline.

Day 1: World War I: The War to End All Wars

Europe's imperial powers had been engaged in economic and military rivalries for decades, but these became increasingly virulent during the first part of the 20th century. Great Britain's dominance of the seas came under aggressive challenge from Germany. Brooding over a defeat at the hands of Prussia in 1871, France aligned itself with Great Britain, its traditional enemy, against Germany. Britain, France, and Russia formed an alliance that pressured Germany on both its east and west borders. Germany, in turn, aligned with the ancient kingdom of Austria-Hungary and with the Turkish-ruled Ottoman Empire to its south. The world's great nations were in position for a fight, a single incident away from catastrophe.

On June 28, 1914, the heir to the Austro-Hungarian throne, Archduke Franz Ferdinand, was murdered—along with his wife—while touring the city of Sarajevo in the Austro-Hungarian province of Bosnia-Herzegovina. The assassin, Gavrilo Princip, acted on behalf of Serbian nationalists who sought to expel the Austrians from the Balkans and to create a larger Serbian state.

The assassination did not immediately lead to hostilities, but because Serbia was aligned with Russia, larger alliances were called into play and tensions were immediately heightened. When Serbia refused to investigate links between the assassins and members of the Serbian government, Austria-Hungary declared war on the Serbs in late July. Russia began to mobilize its enormous army to defend its ally, Serbia; Germany felt threatened and declared war on Russia soon after and then, on August 3, it went to war with France as well. The German army crossed into neutral Belgium on its way to France, prompting Britain to enter the war on France's side.

On one side were the Central Powers, made up of Germany, Austria-Hungary and, before long, the Ottoman Turks. Opposing them were the Allies: Britain, France, and Russia, along with Belgium and Serbia. The German attack on France through Belgium met with initial success, but the French regrouped at the Battle of the Marne and prevented a successful march on Paris. Tens of thousands lost their lives in a series of battles near the Belgian town of Ypres as both sides sought to command the continental coastline along the English Channel. The battles ended without a clear result but with massive casualties, establishing a terrible pattern for the war's western front.

With German forces engaged in France and Belgium to the west, Russia launched an offensive against Germany's eastern flank. Although the Russians outnumbered them, the Germans, under the command of Paul von Hindenburg and Erich Ludendorff, were able to outmaneuver and decisively defeat the Russians at the Battle of Tannenberg in early September 1914. A quarter million Russians were killed or wounded, while the Germans lost just over 10,000. Russia's defeat and losses foiled the Allies' plans for a holding action in the west to be accompanied by a massive Russian onslaught in the east. The Russian commander, Alexander Samsonov, committed suicide when he learned of his army's losses.

Most of the war took place in Europe, but battles also took place in Africa and Asia as the contending forces attempted to strip their rivals of colonial possessions. Intense fighting in German East Africa (present-day Tanzania) broke out when the Allies sought to expel German power there, and in Syria, Palestine, and present-day Iraq between the British and the Turks.

◆**The Western Front** The combatants on the western front dug miles of trenches to provide shelter from artillery shells. The trench came to symbolize the war on the western front, where progress was measured in yards and neither side seemed able to take the offensive without suffering devastating casualties. The weapons of war had changed more quickly than tactics. Now, a generation of generals and other senior officers failed to understand the power of well-placed machine guns. Troops in the trenches of the western front were periodically ordered "over the top" to charge enemy emplacements, and they died by the tens of thousands.

The British changed their strategy at the suggestion of Winston Churchill, who was First Lord of the Admiralty, Britain's supreme naval commander. However, their effort to get at Germany through an invasion of Turkey led to further disaster at Gallipoli, followed by ignominious retreat in late 1915. In another effort to break the deadlock, Britain and Germany engaged each other on the seas in the Battle of Jutland in the spring of 1916. The battle took place in the North Sea as the Germans attempted to break a British naval blockade of German ports. Twice during the battle, German warships outmaneuvered the vaunted Royal Navy, firing devastating broadsides. The British took heavy casualties but remained an active presence on the North Sea. Germany then decided to conduct its naval war from below the sea, using the newly perfected submarines to attack warships and merchant vessels alike.

Meanwhile, the fighting on land became more intense. In February 1916, the Germans attacked the French city of Verdun near the Meuse River in hopes of smashing the French defenders and demoralizing the civilian population. The French, despite being outnumbered, rallied under the leadership of General Philippe Pétain and stopped the Germans cold. Meanwhile, the British launched an offensive of their own. The Battle of the Somme began when British soldiers came out of the trenches on the morning of July 1 to face heavily defended German positions along the River Somme. By the time night fell, nearly 20,000 were killed and 40,000 wounded in a single day of combat. The battles of Verdun and the Somme raged for months, resulting in 620,000 British casualties, 375,000 French, and more than 750,000 German. Very little ground changed hands, despite this unprecedented loss of life.

◆**The Eastern Front**   The war was more fluid but no less bloody in the East. Russia took the offensive with new ally Romania, but the Germans thwarted the measure. The Russian czar, Nicholas II, was in personal command of his country's forces on the eastern front, leaving his wife, Queen Alexandra, to deal with an increasingly dissatisfied national legislature and a war-weary population. A rebellion against czarist rule broke out in St. Petersburg in March 1917, and the czar abdicated the throne on March 15. A new provisional government under Alexander Kerensky took power but continued the czar's war policy. Kerensky was overthrown in November when the Bolsheviks seized power under Vladmir Lenin and Leon Trotsky. The Bolshevik regime declared a truce and began peace negotiations with Germany, signing the Treaty of Brest-Litovsk and ending the war on the eastern front.

With Germany able to focus exclusively on the western front, the already brutal combat escalated to unimaginable levels in the spring of 1917, which saw hundreds of thousands more casualties at Ypres and Passchendaele in the Flanders region of Belgium.

◆**America Enters the War**   Good news for the Allies arrived in April 1917, when the United States, which had been neutral, declared war on the Central Powers after German submarines attacked American commercial ships in the Atlantic Ocean. President Woodrow Wilson proclaimed that this was "a war to make the world safe for democracy." By June 1917, the first American troops landed in France and saw action at Château-Thierry, helping to halt a German offensive. In March 1918, the Germans attacked the British near the French town of Amiens, but their offensive sputtered to a halt. They then turned their attention to the French capital Paris. The French rallied, however, at the second Battle of the Marne in the summer of 1918, shutting down the German offensive.

With the reinforcement of American troops, the Allies launched a major offensive in September 1918. American troops saw intense combat in multiple battles in the Argonne Forest, ultimately forcing Germany into retreat. German soldiers and civilians had become increasingly demoralized seeing the American involvement as a devastating development. Political and social unrest broke out at home due in large part to food shortages caused by a British naval blockade. The discouraged German government asked for peace terms with the Allies, and an armistice brought the war to an end on November 11, 1918.

In 1919, the victors presided over a peace conference in Paris. President Woodrow Wilson took center stage as a self-appointed honest broker, pushing hard for self-determination of all peoples. His "Fourteen Points" presented a plan for a League of Nations that would prevent future wars and included no punitive damages against the losing combatants. The European leaders, having suffered such enormous casualties, had different ideas. The French president Georges Clemenceau sniffed, "Mr. Wilson bores me with his 14 Points; why God Almighty has only 10!" Although they embraced Wilson's ideas publicly, behind closed doors, the British prime minister David Lloyd George and Georges Clemenceau drew up their own plans that essentially called for Germany to be treated as a conquered nation that was responsible for the war. The Treaty of Versailles forced Germany to pay reparations, return the regions of Alsace and Lorraine to France, and demilitarize the Rhineland, Germany's industrial heartland.

The humiliation of Germany was so complete that many Germans concluded their government had betrayed them. A young corporal named Adolf Hitler fanned the flames of discontent, declaring in 1922, "It cannot be that two million Germans have fallen in vain... No, we do not pardon, we demand—vengeance!"

Day 2: World War II: Tens of Millions Killed

In 1919, the Treaty of Versailles formally ended World War I and, spearheaded by Woodrow Wilson, the League of Nations was created to help prevent another large-scale conflict. The United States Senate, however, refused to ratify the treaty, greatly diminishing the League's influence. A defeated Germany was faltering under the weight of economic depression and experienced massive political upheaval throughout the 1920s, mostly related to socialism and communism. Adolf Hitler, an Austrian-born veteran of the war on the western front and one of the founders of the National Socialist Party ("Nazi") was appointed chancellor of the German state in January 1933. Hitler promised to restore order and German dignity, contending that the people and the army had been "stabbed in the back" by their military leaders when they surrendered in 1918.

Hitler's rise mirrored the success of Italy's Benito Mussolini, a journalist and founder of the Fascist Party, who 10 years earlier became the country's prime minister. Within three years, Mussolini crushed all opposition and established a totalitarian state, adopting the title of Il Duce ("the leader"). Aggressive leaders also came to power in Japan, which emerged as the dominant military force in Asia after defeating Russia in 1906. In 1931, Japanese troops invaded the Chinese territory of Manchuria and seized a valuable supply of raw materials needed for further expansion. Japanese and Chinese troops fought sporadically over the next five years, leading to a full-scale invasion by Japan in 1937.

Upon taking office, Hitler immediately began to rebuild Germany's armed forces despite prohibitions written into the Treaty of Versailles. In 1936, German troops marched into the industrial Rhineland region, demilitarized under terms of the treaty, but oddly did not provoke an armed response from Britain and France. Although appeasement was a popular policy in both Britain and France, at least one member of the British Parliament, Winston Churchill, warned that both countries were deluding themselves. Churchill demanded that Britain take similar measures to match Hitler's dramatic military buildup. Churchill was denounced as a warmonger and an alarmist.

In early 1938, Germany invaded Austria unopposed, and Hitler demanded the annexation of the German-speaking Sudetenland region of Czechoslovakia. Believing that appeasement of Hitler could ward off another general war, Britain and France agreed to Hitler's demand at a conference in Munich in September 1938. The British prime minister Neville Chamberlain announced that the agreement guaranteed "peace in our time" because Hitler had assured him that he sought no further territory in Europe.

Civil war in Spain and Japan's invasion of China saw the widespread use of air power to target civilian populations and munitions factories far from traditional battle lines. Witnessing the full terror of air power and scarred by their losses in World War I, Britain and France were desperate to avoid another conflict with Germany.

While Hitler remained a threat to his neighbors, his domestic policies proved even more insidious. He and other Nazi leaders stirred up resentment against Germany's Jewish population, leading to a murderous rampage against Jewish-owned businesses on November 9–10, 1938. The oceans of shattered glass in the street gave the incident the nickname "Kristallnacht" (Crystal Night). Stepping up its campaign of anti-Semitism, Germany forced Jews to identify themselves in public by wearing yellow Stars of David and forcing Jewish doctors, lawyers, and university professors to resign. By 1940, concentration camps were created, and literally millions of Jews from Germany, Austria, Poland, France, Italy, the Balkans, and other places were transported to them, where they would be systematically murdered or die from forced labor.

Hitler now turned his attention to Poland on its eastern frontier, with designs to acquire the port city of Danzig. Danzig was a "free city" under League of Nations protection, but an increasingly aggressive Hitler signaled that he was prepared to use force to bring Danzig under German control. As Britain and France considered how it would respond to a German invasion of Poland, Hitler signed an alliance with Italy and Japan and opened diplomatic negotiations with the Soviet Union. On August 23, 1939, Germany and the Soviets signed a secret nonaggression pact, clearing the way for a German move to the East. The agreement allowed the Soviets to claim a part of eastern Poland once the German invasion began.

On September 1, 1939, German forces crossed into Poland, and Britain and France announced they would come to Poland's assistance, marking the beginning of a new worldwide war. The Poles were overwhelmed, however, especially when the Russians invaded from the East; the Polish capital of Warsaw fell in less than a month. Once Poland fell, the conflict lapsed into a period of inaction that became known as the "phony war." A large British expeditionary force was deployed in France, but the Germans made no move in that direction. The eerie calm was shattered on May 10, when Germany simultaneously attacked Belgium, the Netherlands, and Luxembourg, beginning its march toward France. The British prime minister Neville Chamberlain resigned, and Churchill entered the war cabinet as First Lord of the Admiralty and Britain's head of government. In a memorable speech to the House of Commons, Churchill said he had nothing to offer but "blood, toil, tears, and sweat."

The battle for France was short-lived; by the end of May, the Germans declared victory, and the British Expeditionary Force was forced to retreat to the British mainland using a hastily organized fleet of warships and pleasure craft, which transported more than 200,000 troops from Dunkirk, France, to the English coast. France surrendered on June 22, meaning Hitler was master of western Europe from Norway to the south of France, from Normandy to Warsaw.

President Franklin Roosevelt now ramped up American war efforts while managing to walk a fine line between official neutrality and sympathy for Britain's defiance of the Nazis. Germany prepared an invasion force to bring the war to the British Isles and dispatched heavy bombers to attack airfields and munitions factories. Throughout the summer of 1940, the Royal Air Force successfully fought the Germans in a spectacular battle high above Britain. Casualties in these engagements were so tremendous that Germany changed its strategy in September, focusing on civilian targets and urban areas, instead of Britain's military infrastructure. Known as the Battle of Britain, this early example of air combat led Hitler to postpone plans for a cross-Channel invasion.

In early 1941, British land forces engaged Italy, Germany's ally, in North Africa. A string of British successes pushed Hitler to deploy one of his most capable commanders, Erwin Rommel, to Libya in February. The British continued to fight alone, save for some of its Commonwealth allies, against the united German and Italian forces. The United States assisted Britain through a policy called "lend-lease," which allowed the U.S. to both maintain neutrality and offer support. Under the policy, Roosevelt sent arms and ammunition to cash-strapped Britain in exchange for leases on British bases around the world. Hitler launched a surprise attack on the Soviet Union on June 22, 1941, a violation of the nonaggression pact he signed with Moscow in 1939. The Germans moved relentlessly toward Moscow throughout the summer.

✦**America Joins the Allies**   Throughout the 1930s, the United States had criticized Japan's continuous aggressive behavior against China and Indochina, including its invasion of China and the establishment of a puppet regime. In October 1941, Japan's war minister, Hideki Tojo, was named prime minister. Tojo supported a more aggressive stand against the United States, and on December 7, 1941, Japanese warplanes attacked the U.S. naval base at Pearl Harbor, Hawaii.

The surprise attack led the United States to declare war on Japan on December 8. Japan's allies, Germany and Italy, declared war on the U.S. on December 11. Churchill met with Roosevelt later in the month and agreed that the two powers would concentrate on Germany first in their two-front war against the Axis.

Having delivered a stunning blow to the U.S. Pacific Fleet, the Japanese rolled up victories throughout Asia. They captured the supposedly invulnerable British garrison in Singapore in February 1942, and then the Philippine Islands in April, forcing the U.S. commander Douglas MacArthur to flee to Australia. But the U.S. responded in surprisingly quick fashion. In mid-April, General James Doolittle led a bombing raid over Tokyo, and in June, U.S. carriers and Navy planes decimated the Japanese fleet at the Battle of Midway. American Marines landed in Guadalcanal in August, taking the offensive against Japan less than a year after the attack on Pearl Harbor.

In North Africa, British forces under the command of General Bernard Montgomery defeated the seemingly invincible General Erwin Rommel, the "Desert Fox," at the Battle of El Alamein in Egypt in October. The following month, U.S. forces landed in Algeria and Morocco, squeezing Rommel on both flanks.

At the end of 1942, an epic struggle unfolded outside of Stalingrad in Russia. The German army became bogged down as winter approached, and in late November, the battered Red Army launched a huge offensive to free the city. The battle ended on January 31, 1943, with a stunning German defeat. The Germans, like their allies the Japanese, would never truly take the offensive again.

The Anglo-American offensive in North Africa cleared the region of German forces in March 1943, setting in motion a successful Anglo-American invasion of Sicily in July, and an attack on the Italian mainland beginning in September. Mussolini was deposed even before the Allies invaded, and the new Italian government surrendered to the Allies and declared war on Germany.

As the war began to go badly for Hitler, he put into motion his plan for a "final solution" to "the Jewish problem." Throughout the regions held by the Nazi forces and in the concentration camps, Jews were murdered at an appalling rate. By the war's end, an estimated 6 million would die, the worst slaughter of innocent people in human history.

◆**D-Day and Allied Victory**   U.S. forces continued to press Japan in the Pacific, landing on the island of Tarawa in the Gilbert Islands on November 20. With momentum on their side, the leaders of the three major allied powers—America's Franklin Roosevelt, Britain's Winston Churchill, and the Soviet Union's Joseph Stalin—met in Tehran, Iran, to plan common strategy, including the opening of a second front in France. That front became reality on the morning of June 6, 1944, "D-Day," when the largest armada in history—commanded by the U.S. general Dwight Eisenhower—crossed the English Channel to deliver tens of thousands of American, British, and Canadian troops to the beaches of Normandy. Nazi Germany now was pinned between the Red Army to the east and a growing Anglo-American offensive in the west. A group of German officers, including Rommel, devised a plot to assassinate Hitler in July, but it failed. Rommel commited suicide, and other officers were executed.

The Japanese continued to sustain heavy losses in the Pacific, leading to the ouster of Prime Minister Tojo, as the U.S. moved closer to Japan's home islands. American forces returned to the Philippines on October 20, and a U.S. fleet sank 34 Japanese ships in the Battle of Leyte Gulf in late October. The year ended with a desperate German counteroffensive in the Ardennes Forest beginning on December 16. Known as the Battle of the Bulge, it was Hitler's last stand.

Within days after the German offensive sputtered out, the Soviets launched a massive attack through Poland beginning on January 12, 1945. The Allied air offensive over Germany continued to wreak massive casualties, especially during the firebombing of Dresden in mid-February. As the Allies closed in on Berlin, an ailing Franklin Roosevelt died on April 12, succeeded by Harry Truman. Hitler and several of his top aides committed suicide on April 30 as the Red Army approached Berlin. The new German government surrendered on May 7.

The war in Asia became even more ferocious as the Americans approached the Japanese mainland. Tens of thousands died in the U.S. assault on Okinawa as the Japanese fought to the last man. Japanese pilots engaged in suicide attacks on U.S. naval vessels off Okinawa. On August 6, 1945, the U.S. dropped an atomic bomb over the Japanese city of Hiroshima, killing tens of thousands. Another nuclear weapon fell on Nagasaki on August 9. The Japanese surrendered on August 14. The most catastrophic war in human history had come to an end, leaving more than 60–70 million dead.

Weekend 3: American Popular Music I

Day 1: The Great American Songbook

The period from 1900 to 1950 is known as the Golden Age of the American popular song. It was an era that gave us Irving Berlin, Cole Porter, and George Gershwin, three giants among the many talented songwriters and lyricists composing during those years. Some 300,000 compositions were copyrighted in the first half of the 20th century, and the best of them make up what is called the "Great American Songbook."

♦**Tin Pan Alley** From approximately 1880 to 1940, the American music publishing industry was concentrated in New York City, on West 28th Street between Broadway and Sixth Avenue. Writer Monroe Rosenfeld likened the cacophony of so many songwriters pounding on so many pianos to the sound of beating on tin pans, and coined the moniker "Tin Pan Alley." The name has since been applied to popular songs written there.

In the case of Tin Pan Alley, geographic convergence was more than a simple convenience. Songwriters, "song pluggers," and other functionaries worked in close proximity to the major sheet music publishers who first set up shop in the neighborhood. But in Tin Pan Alley, as in Vienna during the Classical era and Detroit during Motown's heyday, great art came from a concentration of talented people who settled in the same geographic "pocket."

The lyricists and composers who worked in Tin Pan Alley created some of the most memorable popular songs of the day. It was an interesting environment; songwriters, alone or in teams, churned out their compositions in factory-like style. The best of these songs were sold to music publishing companies and then issued as sheet music (before the explosion of the record business) or picked up by one of the major singers of the day. Sometimes these tunes ended up in vaudeville productions, Broadway plays, or Hollywood movies. The best of the best endured and became classics.

♦**The Great Composers** The first great Tin Pan Alley songwriter was a legendary vaudeville and Broadway song-and-dance man, playwright, actor, and producer. **George M. Cohan** is considered the father of American musical comedy. Along with partner Sam H. Harris, Cohan produced more than three dozen Broadway shows between 1906 and 1926. For these and other plays, Cohan wrote more than 1,500 original songs, noted for their hummable melodies, clever lyrics, and, during the World War I era, patriotic themes. Cohan's best-remembered songs include "Give My Regards to Broadway," "The Yankee Doodle Boy" (commonly known as "Yankee Doodle Dandy"), "Forty-five Minutes from Broadway," "Mary's a Grand Old Name," "You're a Grand Old Flag," "Harrigan," and "Over There."

The American popular song became more sophisticated over time, and one of the first innovators in terms of style and sophistication was **Jerome Kern**. Kern was the first true master of 20th-century musical theater, writing from the turn of the century through the 1940s. He composed for various lyricists, including Dorothy Fields, Ira Gershwin, and Oscar Hammerstein II. During the course of his career, Kern wrote more than 700 songs and 100 scores for plays and films, including the ground-breaking 1927 musical *Show Boat*, which featured lyrics by Hammerstein. Kern's most notable songs include "Lovely to Look At," "A Fine Romance," "Never Gonna Dance," "Pick Yourself Up," and "The Way You Look Tonight," all with Fields; "Can't Help Lovin' Dat Man," "Ol' Man River," and "All the Things You Are," with Hammerstein; "Smoke Gets In Your Eyes," with Otto Harbach; and "Till the Clouds Roll By," with Guy Bolton and P. G. Wodehouse.

The most prolific and successful of all the Tin Pan Alley songwriters was **Irving Berlin**, who had a long career creating some of America's best-loved songs. He was responsible for popularizing ragtime music with "Alexander's Ragtime Band," a tremendous hit in 1911. In the 1920s and 1930s, Berlin created a jazzy swing style in numbers like "Blue Skies" (1926) and in his famous score for the Fred Astaire/Ginger Rogers film *Top Hat* (1935), which featured "The Continental," "Cheek to Cheek," and the title tune. Then, in 1938, Berlin captured a growing sense of patriotism by re-releasing his song "God Bless America" (first written in 1918). Two years later, he penned the perennial holiday favorite "White Christmas," which won the Academy Award for best song in 1942. Unlike other Tin Pan Alley songwriters who specialized in either lyrics or music (and hence worked as part of a two-person team), Berlin was responsible for both these components in all his works. His output comprised more than 3,000 songs, as well as the scores for 21 films and 17 Broadway shows.

If Irving Berlin is the father of the American popular song, his favored son is **George Gershwin**, an innovative composer whose work ranged from pop songs to classical pieces like *Rhapsody in Blue* and *An American in Paris*. Not only were his songs several notches above the competition in terms of melodic and harmonic structure, he also was one of the first composers to incorporate jazz-influenced rhythms and harmonies into his music. More often than not, George's brother, Ira, collaborated on lyrics. Together, the Gershwins composed music for more than a dozen Broadway shows as well as the 1935 opera *Porgy and Bess* which combined elements of jazz, blues, and folk. Their most famous songs include "Swanee," "Fascinating Rhythm," "Someone to Watch Over Me," "I Got Rhythm," "But Not For Me," "Embraceable You," "'S Wonderful," "Summertime," "They Can't Take That Away from Me," "A Foggy Day," "Let's Call the Whole Thing Off," "Nice Work If You Can Get It," "Shall We Dance," "They All Laughed," and "Our Love is Here to Stay."

Cole Porter was a contemporary of Berlin and the Gershwins. He blended complex melodies and harmonies with witty, sophisticated lyrics and clever rhymes. Porter composed numerous Broadway and Hollywood musicals. His vast songbook includes "Love for Sale," "Night and Day," "It's Bad for Me," "Anything Goes," "I Get a Kick Out of You," "You're the Top," "Begin the Beguine," "I've Got You Under My Skin," "It's De-Lovely," "In the Still of the Night," "Ev'ry Time We Say Goodbye," and "All of You."

The next generation of Tin Pan Alley songwriters included **Harold Arlen**, who wrote for both Broadway and Hollywood musicals, most notably *The Wizard of Oz*. His songs include "That Old Black Magic," "One for My Baby (and One More for the Road)," and "Come Rain or Come Shine," all with Johnny Mercer; "Last Night When We Were Young" and "Over the Rainbow," with Yip Harburg; "It's Only a Paper Moon," with Harburg and Billy Rose; "I've Got the World on a String" and "Stormy Weather," with Ted Koehler; and "The Man That Got Away," with Ira Gershwin.

Hoagy Carmichael was a talented songwriter in the Tin Pan Alley tradition, even though he didn't live or write in New York City—like

Porter, Carmichael hailed from Indiana. Carmichael's easygoing compositions reflect his love of the jazz music of the 1920s, and his songs employ jazz-like harmonies and rhythms. His most famous songs include "Lazybones" and "In the Cool, Cool, Cool of the Evening," with Johnny Mercer; "Star Dust," with Mitchell Parrish; "Georgia on My Mind," with Stuart Gorrell; "I Get Along Without You Very Well," with lyrics from a poem by Jane Brown Thompson; "Lazy River," with Sidney Arodin; "Ole Buttermilk Sky," with Jack Brooks; and "Two Sleepy People" and "Heart and Soul," with Frank Loesser.

In the later years of Tin Pan Alley, lyricist **Frank Loesser** began composing his own songs. Loesser was an extremely versatile songwriter; each of his Broadway shows had its unique flavor. The best known of these were *Guys and Dolls*, Danny Kaye's heartwarming movie musical *Hans Christian Andersen*, and the sweetly satirical *How to Succeed in Business Without Really Trying*. Loesser's notable songs include "Baby It's Cold Outside," "Luck Be a Lady Tonight," "Inch Worm," and "I Believe in You."

Richard Rodgers was not technically a Tin Pan Alley writer, but he is considered the dean of 20th-century musical theater, having created more than 40 Broadway musicals (including *Oklahoma!*, *Carousel*, *South Pacific*, and *The Sound of Music*) and hundreds of popular songs. Working originally with lyricist Lorenz Hart and later with Oscar Hammerstein II, Rodgers's compositions were known for their consistent inventiveness and sophistication. Rodgers's songbook includes "Mountain Greenery," "Thou Swell," "Spring Is Here," "Isn't It Romantic?," "Blue Moon," "My Romance," "The Lady Is a Tramp," "My Funny Valentine," and "Bewitched, Bothered and Bewildered," all with Hart; and "Oh What a Beautiful Mornin'," "People Will Say We're in Love," "You'll Never Walk Alone," "If I Loved You," "Some Enchanted Evening," "My Favorite Things," and "Climb Every Mountain," all written with Hammerstein.

◆**The Great Singers**   One of the earliest singers of the popular song was **Bing Crosby**. It may be hard for a modern audience to think of him this way, but in his day Crosby was a jazzy innovator. He had a laid-back, crooning style that was perfectly suited to interpretation of songs from the Great American Songbook.

In addition to being one of the century's great dancers, **Fred Astaire** was a sympathetic interpreter of the classic song. His movie musicals with partner Ginger Rogers were used to introduce new tunes from the likes of Berlin, Porter, Kern, and the Gershwins—and Astaire's renditions of these classic songs remain among the most definitive.

Ella Fitzgerald was the premier female interpreter of the popular song. Best known as a big band vocalist and jazz singer, Fitzgerald also released a series of critically acclaimed Songbook albums, each featuring songs from a specific great American songwriter. Her interpretation of these standards was hip and jazzy yet respectful of the original tunes.

Frank Sinatra started out as a skinny kid singing vocals for the Harry James and Tommy Dorsey big bands, but he came into his own with his solo recordings for Capitol Records in the 1950s, concept albums built around popular standards. In these albums, Sinatra almost single-handedly rescued the Great American Songbook from obscurity—and forged his position as the dean of American popular song.

◆**The End of An Era** The golden age of Tin Pan Alley ended after World War II, when the movie and stage musical went into decline and rock 'n' roll began to dominate the charts. Short-playing 45 RPM records ("singles") became the major means of selling songs, and individual performers became more important than the songwriters.

During the late 1950s and particularly the 1960s, these factors contributed to a decline in sheet music sales, and it became less common for music publishers to hire their own stables of songwriters. Composers started to perform their own songs, and singers started to write their own music. The music publishing industry eventually dispersed from Tin Pan Alley, first taking up residence in the Brill Building farther uptown in Manhattan and later moving west to California.

Despite the demise of Tin Pan Alley as a place, the Great American Songbook remains fixed in the musical firmament. These are songs that will live forever in our memory and on the lips of talented singers of all generations.

Day 2: The Origins of Rock

To no small degree, rock 'n' roll resulted from a collision between the black and white musical worlds. From the dawn of the recording era to well after World War II, the music industry was highly segregated; records by black artists were marketed separately from those by whites and typically labeled as "race records." After the war, however, black music started to move onto the pop charts, under the new name of rhythm & blues.

◆**Rhythm and Blues** R&B has its roots in the ensembles of the late 1940s and early 1950s, most notable of which was the band led by saxophonist Louis Jordan. Jordan's music, dubbed "jump blues" or "jump jazz," blended jazz, blues, a shuffle beat, and lighthearted lyrics. The music proved as popular among whites as blacks, opening the door for other black artists with similar crossover appeal.

An important R&B artist of the 1950s was Ruth Brown, known as "Miss Rhythm." Ruth introduced the fledgling R&B style to a wide audience of both blacks and whites and served as the inspiration for subsequent generations of female soul singers. She recorded for the newly formed Atlantic Records, which became known, in a play on Yankee Stadium's slogan, as "The House That Ruth Built." Atlantic was founded in 1947 by Ahmet Ertegün and Herb Abrahamson, who were later joined by the famed producer Jerry Wexler. The label became home to the industry's top R&B and soul artists, including Solomon Burke, Ray Charles, Aretha Franklin, and the Drifters.

Of these later Atlantic artists, Ray Charles was arguably the most influential. After signing with Atlantic Records, Charles transformed himself from a jazz-influenced pianist into a soul-stirring R&B performer with his first major hit, 1954's "I Got a Woman." His intense, gospel-influenced vocals, along with his pounding piano accompaniment, set the pattern for later hits, including "What'd I Say" and "Hit the Road, Jack."

Other influential R&B hit-makers that crossed over onto the white charts during the 1950s were the vocal groups the Coasters and the Drifters. These two groups had the distinction of being produced by the team of Jerry Leiber and Mike Stoller, two early Brill Building songwriters and producers who brought "uptown" sophistication to "downtown" R&B—and inspired the birth of rock 'n' roll.

◆**Enter the King** Rock 'n' roll's first true superstar was Elvis Presley. Record producer Sam Phillips famously described Elvis as a "white man who sounds black." And, indeed, Elvis's first release in 1954 paired an R&B hit ("That's Alright, Mama," originally recorded by Big Mama Thornton) with a country song ("Blue Moon of Kentucky," by Bill Monroe). Both spoke to Elvis's unique sensibility.

As the musician most responsible for popularizing rock 'n' roll on an international level, Elvis was one of the most important figures in 20th-century popular music. A country boy from Tupelo, Mississippi, Elvis got his first guitar at age nine. His family moved to Memphis two years later, where Elvis started playing with other musicians, as well as singing gospel in his church choir. He grew up listening to a mix of "hillbilly" music on the radio and blues music performed live in Memphis clubs.

Elvis made his first recording in 1953, at the age of 18, as a present for his mother. That recording was made at the now-famous Sun Records studio in Memphis, and it caught the ear of Sun's boss, Sam Phillips. Phillips, who was already in the business of recording Memphis blues artists such as Howlin' Wolf, was on the lookout for a crossover artist to deliver black music to a white audience. Elvis fit the bill.

Presley was the first performer to fuse country and blues music into the style known as rockabilly, and he also was the first rock artist to inspire a mania among his fans, thanks to his sneering good looks and hip-swiveling style. His records sold millions of copies and almost single-handedly established rock 'n' roll as a viable musical form.

Elvis's most important early recordings include "Heartbreak Hotel," "Hound Dog," and "Love Me Tender," all in 1956, as well as the later "All Shook Up" and "Little Sister." After a stint in the army and as an actor, Elvis had a late-1960s resurgence with the 1969 hits "Suspicious Minds," "In the Ghetto," "Kentucky Rain," and "Burning Love." In his final years, Elvis was almost a parody of his former self, giving lethargic and often shortened performances. He died of apparent drug misuse in 1977.

◆**Black Artists in a White Man's World** Despite the segregation practiced by the music industry, many black artists succeeded in the early years of rock 'n' roll. First of these was Fats Domino, who combined a relaxed New Orleans backbeat with pop-flavored material on songs like "Ain't That a Shame" and "Blueberry Hill." Also from New Orleans was Little Richard, a manic performer who combined gospel fervor with piano-pounding theatrics in his mid-1950s hits "Tutti Frutti," "Long Tall Sally," and "Good Golly Miss Molly."

Arguably the most influential black musician during the formative years of rock 'n' roll, however, was Chuck Berry. Berry defined the instrumental voice of rock 'n' roll, in particular its guitar sound and the straight-ahead 4/4 rock beat. He was also a key shaper of the rock 'n' roll song form and an sharp lyricist. Berry was able to craft songs that ad-

dressed classic topics from a teenage perspective in the teenage vernacular. His key recordings were made between 1955 and 1965, including "Maybellene," "Roll Over Beethoven," "Rock 'n' Roll Music,"
"School Day," "Sweet Little Sixteen," "Johnny B. Goode," "Memphis,
Tennessee," and "No Particular Place to Go."

◆**The Day the Music Died** The classic era of rock 'n' roll is generally defined as lasting from about 1954 through 1959. At the turn of the
decade, Elvis Presley was drafted into the army, Chuck Berry was imprisoned for transporting an underage woman across state lines for "illicit purposes," and on February 3, 1959, Texas rocker Buddy Holly died
in a Wisconsin plane crash that also killed performers Ritchie Valens
and J. P. "The Big Bopper" Richardson. The coup de grâce for the first
generation of rock 'n' roll, however, was the music industry's ability to co-
opt the surface appeal of the music by offering up stars who combined
teenage good looks, snappy songs, and just enough rebelliousness to
please the growing teen audience—without scaring away their parents.

The most successful purveyor of the new teen pop was businessman,
promoter, and TV host Dick Clark. Clark's enormously popular *American Bandstand* television program became a launching pad for numerous
teen singers, including several native to the program's hometown of
Philadelphia. Clark had ties with several local record labels, who in turn
released the recordings of his latest "discoveries." This led to the brief
careers of a number of cookie-cutter teen idols, such as Paul Anka,
Frankie Avalon, and Bobby Vee.

◆**Girl Groups and the Wall of Sound** During the early 1960s,
New York City's Brill Building was home to some of the most talented
songwriters in the business. Many of these songwriters fed songs to a
succession of female vocal groups. These "girl groups" were groups of
teenage girls who sang songs about puppy love, problems in school, and
other topics relevant to the youth of the day. Many of these groups were
formed spontaneously by the girls themselves, and then were discovered and promoted through an independent label owner or producer.
Popular girl groups included the Shirelles, the Ronettes, the Crystals,
and the Shangri-Las.

One of the leading teen pop producers was Phil Spector. He hoped
to create what he called "teenaged symphonies"—recordings that em-

ployed a large stable of professional Los Angeles studio musicians (known collectively as the "Wrecking Crew") to create a dense sonic style that became known as the Wall of Sound.

To create his Wall of Sound, Spector used multiple guitars, drums, strings, and vocalists, all packed together and playing live in a small, reverb-soaked recording studio. He used this production technique for recording many of the most popular girl groups of the time, including the Ronettes and the Crystals, and also performers such as the Righteous Brothers and Ike and Tina Turner.

♦**Surf Music and the Beach Boys**   Also popular in the early 1960s was surf music: guitar-based rock songs about girls, cars, surfing, and other California-based youth activities. The primary purveyors of the surf sound were the Beach Boys, led by composer/singer Brian Wilson.

Wilson, an untrained but naturally brilliant composer and arranger, was a flawed genius who expanded rock's vocabulary to include complex harmonies, sophisticated chord progressions, and an overriding spirituality. While Wilson's early tunes were simple three-chord constructions extolling the joys of surfing and hot rods, his later compositions with the lyricists Tony Asher and Van Dyke Parks explored more adult themes and were more musically complex.

Wilson's crowning achievement was the 1966 album *Pet Sounds*, considered among the greatest rock albums of all time. Wilson's innovative arrangements and production techniques (learned at the knee of Phil Spector), influenced and inspired John Lennon and Paul McCartney in their expanding body of work. Wilson's most memorable tunes from this period include "In My Room," "Surfer Girl," "Don't Worry Baby," "The Little Girl I Once Knew," "Caroline No," "God Only Knows," "Good Vibrations," "Heroes and Villains," and "Wouldn't It Be Nice."

♦**The Beatles and the British Invasion**   American popular music in the early 1960s was considered tame. That all changed in 1964, when the British group the Beatles arrived on American shores. The "Fab Four," as they were known, livened up the music scene with their perky blend of American country, R&B, and early rock 'n' roll. It also didn't hurt that they were smart, funny, and terribly photogenic.

The Beatles had the good fortune to be fronted by two Brill Building–caliber songwriters, John Lennon and Paul McCartney. Unlike the previous generation, Lennon and McCartney were skilled songwriters who performed their own songs, leading subsequent popular performers to likewise eschew outside songwriting. To be "like the Beatles" was to be both songwriters and performers, even if an artist had little or no formal musical training.

From the start, the Beatles had a unique sound, understanding that the recording of a song was at least as important as the composition itself. Their compositions progressed over the course of the 1960s from simple melodic constructions to more harmonically complex experiments, all the while maintaining a keen sense of melody. By the mid-1960s, the group began experimenting further in the studio, producing unique effects using backwards tape loops, double and triple tracking, experiments with vocal processing, and feedback. They also pioneered the "concept album" with 1967's *Sgt. Pepper's Lonely Hearts Club Band*. This creation of a "group within the group" was also a first and would influence future artists to create musical alter egos. Groundbreaking tracks such as "The Inner Light" and the *musique concréte*–inspired "Revolution 9" helped paved the way for avant-garde, postmodern experiments of the 1970s and '80s in pop music.

The Beatles' success led to a "British Invasion" of similar-sounding groups riding on the Fab Four's coattails. Though most of these groups were "one-hit wonders," one group that did have lasting success was the Rolling Stones. In contrast to the teen-friendly Beatles, the Stones were cleverly marketed as the "bad boys" of rock 'n' roll. Originally a blues band playing covers of American material, band members Mick Jagger and Keith Richards eventually started to write their own material. The Stones' more aggressive sound and lyrics, in songs such as "(I Can't Get No) Satisfaction," "Paint It Black," and "Let's Spend the Night Together," influenced other British bands, including the Animals, the Kinks, and the Who.

Weekend 4: Japan: A Brief History

Day 1: Ancient Civilization through 1868

The earliest phase of human occupation of Japan is known from numerous sites dating back to around 16,000 B.C., in the waning millennia of the last Ice Age. Beginning around 10,000 B.C., the Neolithic Jomon people made sophisticated stone tools but practiced little agriculture, relying instead on abundant resources of shellfish and other seafood, as well as various wild plants. Village dwellers, they produced some of the earliest pottery known from anywhere in the world.

Beginning in the third century B.C., a wave of new settlers arrived from Korea or southern Manchuria, displacing, absorbing, or eliminating the earlier Jomon people. These invaders, people of the Yayoi culture, brought with them characteristic features of the East Asian Bronze Age, including metallurgy, bronze swords and other weapons, horse-riding, rice agriculture, and silk. From initial settlements on the southwestern island of Kyushu, they spread eastward and northward throughout Japan (excluding northernmost Honshu and the island of Hokkaido) wherever arable land was available. The Yayoi culture had a clan-based social structure dominated by a military aristocracy. By the fourth century A.D., leaders of the Yamato clan based in the Kansai region (near today's cities of Nara, Osaka, and Kyoto) began to achieve a dominant position within the military class. Deceased Yamato rulers were buried in large mounded tombs containing distinctive figural ceramic sculptures (haniwa), visual symbols of their power and authority. The later Yamato rulers claimed the title of emperor, founding the imperial family that remains on the Chrysanthemum Throne of Japan to the present day.

Buddhism was introduced into Japan from Korea in the mid-sixth century, gradually winning acceptance despite the hostility of adherents of the native animist religion, Shinto. The regency of Prince Shotoku (r. 574–622) saw a surge of continental influence at court. The prince founded several Buddhist temples and promulgated a 17-article "constitution" that reflected both Buddhist and Confucian principles. Further reforms in the mid-seventh century shaped the Japanese monarchy still more closely on the Chinese model, establishing an elaborate administrative apparatus; unlike China, however, the upper ranks of Japan's civil service were reserved for members of the aristocracy.

Japan's first permanent capital was built at Nara in 710. The city was built on a grid pattern, in Chinese style, but without a city wall— Japan's rulers had neither internal nor foreign enemies. The city soon became dominated by several large and powerful Buddhist temples; partly to escape their influence, the imperial court moved from Nara to a new capital, Heian-kyo (today's Kyoto), built in 794. During the Nara Period, teams of official scholars wrote two important historical texts: the *Kojiki* (*Record of Ancient Matters*) and the *Nihongi* (*History of Japan*), both of which asserted the divine ancestry and ancient lineage of the imperial clan. In the eighth century, the *Man'yoshu* (*Book of Ten Thousand Leaves*), the first anthology of Japanese poetry, was compiled.

The following Heian Period (794–1185) was the golden age of the Japanese aristocracy. Enriched by revenues from rural agricultural estates, aristocratic families built sumptuous mansions and indulged in aesthetic pursuits. Upper-class men and women dressed in elaborate and fashionable silk robes and were expected to be adept at poetry, calligraphy, music, incense blending, and other polite arts. Japanese literature flourished with poetry, diaries, and works of fiction, including the landmark novel *The Tale of Genji* by Lady Murasaki (early 11th century). Emperors reigned but did not rule; Heian political power was firmly under the control of members of the aristocratic Fujiwara clan.

During the latter part of the Heian Period, a new social class emerged outside the capital. The *samurai* ("servants") were a rural military class that began to challenge the aristocracy's dominance and control of wealth. A military clan from western Japan, the Taira, seized the capital in 1156. They in turn were ousted in 1185 by the Minamoto clan, based at Kamakura, far to the east of Heian-kyo. There they established a capital city that they termed a *bakufu* ("tent government," supposedly a military encampment) and bestowed on its generals the title of *shogun* ("barbarian-subduing generalissimo"), to signify that they wielded power on the emperor's behalf. This institution of military government, which endured until 1868 (with several changes of ruling clan), left the emperor an isolated and powerless figurehead.

The Minamoto regime was weakened in 1274 and 1281 by two attempted invasions by Kublai Khan, the Mongol emperor of China.

Timely typhoons—*kamikaze* ("divine winds")—wrecked the Mongol fleets. New forms of Buddhism, including the Pure Land and Lotus sects, took root during this period. In 1333, a retired emperor made an unsuccessful attempt to restore the authority of the imperial throne; a new military strongman, Ashikaga Takauji, emerged from the turmoil and established a shogun-led government in the Muramachi district of Kyoto, ending Kamakura's tenure as capital.

The Ashikaga shoguns proved to be ardent patrons of culture but inept military rulers. The Zen sect of Buddhism flourished, along with Zen-related arts such as Noh theater, painting, temple architecture and gardening, and the tea ceremony. The Onin Wars (1467–77), pitted various *daimyo* (military clan leaders) against one another and ushered in a century of civil war that left both the country and its samurai ruling class battered and exhausted.

In the 16th century, a series of three vigorous military leaders accomplished the long and difficult process of ending these civil wars and reunifying the country. Oda Nobunaga was the first Japanese military leader to make effective use of firearms, introduced into Japan by Portuguese merchants in 1543. He managed to subdue most of his daimyo rivals before being assassinated in 1582. The second unifier, Toyotomi Hideyoshi rose from very humble beginnings to become Japan's leading military figure in the late 16th century. His spectacular castle in Kyoto gave its name to the Momoyama Period, a time of extravagant creativity in such decorative arts as ceramics, screen-painting, and ceremonial arms and armor. Hideyoshi sapped his own power with an ill-advised and unsuccessful invasion of Korea in the 1590s, emboldening several rivals to challenge him. Forces loyal to his son were disastrously defeated at the Battle of Sekigahara (1600) by the army of Tokugawa Ieyasu, the third and most successful unifier.

Ieyasu established the Tokugawa shogunate at Edo (today's Tokyo) in 1601 and set about consolidating his power to protect against potential domestic and foreign threats. The remaining Hideyoshi loyalists were wiped out in a siege of Osaka Castle that ended in 1615. Land was redistributed to Tokugawa clansmen and loyal daimyo; in a system of "court attendance by turns," all daimyo were required to have a house at Edo, reside there either six months of every year or in alternate years, and to leave sons permanently in Edo as hostages. Ieyasu and his successors cleverly impoverished potential daimyo rivals by forcing them to contribute lavishly to the construction of a Tokugawa clan temple and tomb complex at Nikko. The ruling privileges of the samurai were confirmed, and individual samurai were encouraged to adhere to a code of *bushido* ("military conduct"), emphasizing honor, loyalty, austerity, skill at arms, and Zen religious discipline.

During this period, foreign influence was sharply curtailed. Portuguese and other European missionaries had some success in spreading Christianity in the late 16th and early 17th centuries, especially in the southwestern island of Kyushu. Ieyasu and his successor Iemitsu viewed Christians as disloyal and suppressed them ruthlessly. The desperate Shimabara Uprising of Christians in Kyushu (1636) ended with the massacre of thousands, forcing the Christians for the next two and a half centuries to cling to a tiny and precarious underground existence. After the 1630s, foreigners were prohibited under penalty of death from entering Japan, and Japanese who went abroad were forbidden to return.

With domestic peace and effective government, the Tokugawa Period was an era of prosperity for the military upper class and for a growing class of urban merchants, although peasants remained exploited and impoverished. Trade in commodities such as rice, copper, and timber enriched rulers and merchants alike. Wealth created a demand for consumer and luxury goods such as textiles and clothing, ceramics, lacquer, paper, brushes, as well as swords and armor (possession of which was strictly limited to the samurai class). All of these goods and more were produced and sold in the burgeoning cities that grew up around ports of domestic trade and near the castles of regional daimyo.

Prohibited by class distinctions from participating in government affairs or having any hope of rising to samurai status, prosperous merchants and artisans created their own distinctive "townsman culture." Sumptuary laws regulated the display of wealth by non-samurai, so town-dwellers devoted energy to evading and subverting such restrictions. Lavish entertainment districts grew up in cities, offering new theatrical entertainments such as Kabuki drama and Bunraku puppet theater, tea-houses staffed by female entertainers talented in dancing and musical arts, as well as expensive restaurants, gambling rooms, and other opportunities for conspicuous consumption. Samurai who (illegally) participated in such activities often fell into debt to merchant-class bankers, contributing to a subtle shift in economic power from the military to the commercial class.

As European and American trade with China and other Asian countries grew in the early 19th century, Japan's policy of isolation became increasingly difficult to sustain. Western nations demanded that Japan supply munitions and fuel to passing vessels, and open its ports to trade. Several attempts at direct diplomacy failed before; in 1852, Commodore Matthew Perry of the U.S. sailed for Japan with orders not to take no for an answer. His squadron of heavily armed ships anchored in Uruga Bay, near Edo in 1853, and he insisted on delivering a letter from President Millard Fillmore to the emperor. It was, of course, diverted to the shogun. Perry's second visit to Japan, in 1854, resulted in the Treaty of Kanegawa, which established diplomatic and trade relations between Japan and the United States. Agreements with Great Britain and other Western powers soon followed. The first American consul, Townsend Harris, took up residence in Japan in 1856.

Conservatives in the military aristocracy were outraged by the shogunal government's capitulation to the foreigners' demands. More openminded samurai, however, soon realized that calls to "expel the barbarians" were futile; attacks on Western ships, diplomats, and merchants led the West to demand further concessions. A new slogan of "enrich the state, strengthen the military" signified a desire to understand and imitate the sources of Western strength so as to avoid China's fate of imperialist exploitation. A group of relatively young samurai— Ito Hirobumi, Saigo Takamori, Yamagata Aritomo, and others—began calling for a return of power to the imperial throne as a first step toward reform. In November 1867, the 15th Tokugawa shogun resigned and was not replaced; on January 3, 1868, the Meiji Emperor formally declared the restoration of imperial rule. This largely peaceful revolution, under the leadership of a self-appointed group of men willing to undertake far-reaching reforms to preserve Japan's independence, marks the beginning of the modern era of Japanese history.

Day 2: 1868–Present

The abolition of the shogunate in 1867 and the restoration of direct imperial authority in early 1868 did not mean that the Meiji Emperor— a 15-year-old boy at the time—actually ruled Japan. Rather, these developments empowered a small group of unelected, self-appointed men, acting in the emperor's name, to undertake far-reaching changes aimed at strengthening Japan and preserving its independence. The commitment of the new government to a program of comprehensive reform was affirmed in a key document, known as the Charter Oath, issued in the emperor's name in March 1868.

Widespread change had already come to Japan with the legalization of foreign trade in the mid-1850s, but the pace of change accelerated sharply in 1868. Innovations included Japan's first Western-style school (1868), telegraph service (1870), new national currency and postal service (1871), as well as railway service and mechanized silk mills (1872). In 1869, the formal class structure of the old regime was abolished and samurai became ex-samurai (with small public stipends), and daimyo were reappointed as governors of their former fiefs. The Iwakura Mission, a high-level fact-finding delegation, went on a two-year (1871–73) tour of Europe and America, looking for the best possible models to follow in education, politics, the military, industry, and other important fields. Many Western advisers found employment in Japan and contributed to a wide range of modernization programs. In Japan's new capital at Tokyo (formerly the shogunal capital of Edo) and in other major cities, adventurous citizens began to develop a taste for innovations such as Western food and fashionable clothing. Fukuzawa Yukichi and other prominent intellectuals urged educational and cultural reform as the basis of modern nationalism.

Not everyone was pleased. In 1877, Saigo Takamori, one of the original Meiji reformers, feeling that change had gone too far, led a rebellion of disaffected samurai based in the province of Satsuma, on the island of Kyushu. His movement proved no match for the new national army, equipped with modern weapons; the rebellion collapsed with Saigo's death on the battlefield in September. (Saigo subsequently became a popular symbol of noble adherence to principles.)

The process of setting up a modern social and political system continued in the 1880s and 1890s, with the enactment of the Peace Preservation Law (1887), giving the government strong police powers; the establishment of a privy council (1888); the promulgation of the Meiji Constitution (1889), the fundamental framework of the new constitutional monarchy; and the Imperial Rescript on Education, which portrayed public education as both the gift of the emperor and the duty of citizens. A comprehensive framework of laws was established with the enactment of the Meiji Civil Code in 1898.

Conscious of how the Western nations had dominated or colonized China, India, and the nations of Southeast Asia, Japan's new leaders were anxious to avoid a similar fate. Accordingly, they pursued an aggressive foreign policy aimed at making Japan a member of the imperialist "club." In 1885, the statesman Ito Hirobumi conducted the Tianjin Convention with China, which ended Korea's longstanding subservience to China and established Korean neutrality. When Chinese troops entered Korea in 1894 to aid the new monarchy in putting down a rebellion, Japan termed that a violation of the convention and sent troops also. In the ensuing Sino–Japanese War of 1894–95, Japan emerged the easy victor. The spoils of war in the Treaty of Shimonoseki included the island of Taiwan, Japanese occupation of Korea, and a substantial indemnity. Bolstered by the Anglo–Japanese Alliance of 1902, which kept France and Germany at bay, Japan felt free to provoke hostilities with Russia. A treaty provision granting Japan concessions in the Liaodong Peninsula of southern Manchuria was dropped under pressure from Russia, France, and Germany; their so-called Tripartite Intervention was received with great hostility in Japan. Japan's sense of unfinished business led to the Russo–Japanese War of 1904–05. To the surprise of many, the Japanese defeated the forces of the czar both on land and at sea. The war ended in 1905 with the Treaty of Portsmouth, through the good offices of President Theodore Roosevelt; Japan achieved its aim of acquiring all of Russia's claims in Manchuria. Japan incorporated Korea into the Japanese empire—its first full-fledged colony—in 1910.

The Meiji Emperor, a mere boy in 1868, had grown up to be an active and intelligent monarch and a full participant in the councils of the country's elder statesmen. He died in 1912 and was succeeded by the weak-minded Taisho Emperor, whose incapacity led to a change in the country's political climate. Political parties, organized early in the Meiji Period, had competed for public office under the constitutional monarchy, but now came into greater prominence. Parties, differing little in policy and acting as coalitions of interest groups, dominated the political atmosphere. The 14 years of the Taisho Period were marked by a sense of normality, heightened by the emergence of a new Japanese popular culture outstanding for the fiction of Natsume Soseki and other modern writers, as well as theater, cinema, and recorded music. The Taisho Period was in some respects a Japanese version of the Jazz Age. At the same time, government continued to be conservative and defensive; labor unions and other signs of leftist aspirations were vigorously suppressed.

Japan continued to pursue foreign ambitions. In 1915, the Japanese government delivered to the young and weak Republic of China a set of Twenty-One Demands, giving Japan a privileged economic and territorial position in China; the Chinese government had little choice but to agree. Later in the decade, China and Japan were on the same side in World War I, but the war's end and the Treaty of Versailles affirmed Japan's gains on the Asian mainland at China's expense.

The Taisho Emperor was succeeded in 1926 by his son the Showa Emperor (widely known abroad by his personal name, Hirohito, which was, however, taboo in Japan). Many of the leaders of Japan, seeing their country as small, vulnerable, and resource-poor, regarded an empire as a necessity both for economic security and for international prestige.

Japan's large army in Manchuria began acting independently of Japan's own government in pursuing an aggressive mainland policy. In 1928, army officers assassinated the Chinese warlord of Manchuria, Chang Tso-lin (Zhang Zuolin) and on September 18, 1931, staged a fake "terrorist incident" on the Manchurian Railway that was used as an excuse for the military takeover of all of Manchuria. The civilian government at home had little choice but to go along with a military adventure that many party leaders opposed. The effects of the worldwide Great Depression, especially the collapse of the silk industry, hit Japan hard and strengthened the hands of extremists. The 1930s became an era of "government by assassination" as a series of prime ministers paid with their lives for their caution in foreign affairs. The most extreme incident occurred in February 1936, when a mutiny of young officers, declaring their loyalty to the emperor, sent tanks into the streets of Tokyo. The rebellion managed to seize government buildings and killed several leading politicians before it was suppressed. The emperor angrily demanded that the conspirators be punished, but the incident had the effect of strengthening the hands of the military high command as the only guarantor of public order.

A skirmish with Chinese troops at the Marco Polo Bridge near Beijing on July 7, 1937, gave Japan an excuse to begin full-scale hostilities in China; by the end of the year, Japanese troops had occupied all of coastal China as well as its central river valleys. Japan allied itself with Nazi Germany and fascist Italy in 1940 and began pushing south to occupy French Indochina. The United States (still at that point not involved in World War II) declared an embargo on shipments of scrap metal and oil to Japan to protest this aggression. The Japanese government viewed this as cause for war (which many welcomed in any case). The coordinated attacks of December 1941 on Pearl Harbor, Hong Kong, Singapore, Java, and other targets ensued.

Japan's failure to destroy the American Pacific fleet of aircraft carriers, and its strategies to wage protracted war with limited resources and to occupy huge hostile territories in China, Southeast Asia, and the Pacific Islands, meant its doom was certain in World War II (though at very great cost to its adversaries). The atomic bombing of Hiroshima and Nagasaki in August 1945 quickly brought about Japan's surrender.

The American occupation, under General Douglas MacArthur, rejected suggestions of a highly punitive postwar policy in favor of a largely successful effort to rebuild a Japan that would be democratic, economically viable, and purged of militarism. Those values were worked into a new constitution written for Japan by the occupying authorities and adopted by the Diet (legislature) in 1946. The new policy included retaining the institution of the emperor as a nonpolitical "symbol of the state," land reform, breaking up large industrial corporations, and attention to the rights of women. Some top wartime leaders were tried as war criminals and executed; many others were rehabilitated.

The invasion of South Korea by North Korea on June 25, 1950, abruptly turned Japan from an occupied, defeated enemy into a vital ally; U.S.-led United Nations forces fighting in Korea absolutely required base areas in Japan to pursue that conflict. With the Korean War in stalemate, American occupation of Japan ended on April 28, 1952, replaced by a treaty in which the U.S. guaranteed the security of a demilitarized Japan. The treaty, despite public demonstrations that forced the cancellation of a planned visit by President Eisenhower, was renewed in 1960 and, with modifications, remains in effect today.

The newly organized Liberal Democratic Party dominated Japanese politics in the immediate postwar period. Political disputes have tended to involve factions within the L.D.P. rather than serious challenges from Socialist, Communist, and other opposition parties, and with rare exceptions the L.D.P. has controlled Japan's government throughout the postwar period. A series of lackluster prime ministers amid the economic difficulties of the first decade of the 21st century led to the end of L.D.P.'s era of dominance in 2009.

•**Japan's Economy** In the 1950s, Japan began to rebuild its shattered infrastructure and based its economic recovery on international trade and export-oriented manufacturing. This trend continued in the 1960s as the Ministry of International Trade and Industry steered investments into such industries as automobile manufacturing, ship-building, and consumer electronics. Domestic demand also grew, despite such economic shocks in the early 1970s as a striking rise in the price of oil and a drastic revaluation of the yen. Large corporations offered employees lifetime employment in return for loyalty and hard work. In sum, Japan had built a postwar society that was conformist, middle-class, economically secure, and largely homogeneous.

A property bubble that fueled the economy in the 1980s and early 1990s collapsed in 1997. Recovery took several years, and the economy sank once again in the worldwide recession of 2008–09, though Japan's economy remains the world's third largest.

Japan in the early 21st century finds itself with a strong and innovative economy, but also with concerns about its declining influence in world affairs, as well as political torpor and an uncertain future. Long-term concerns include a low birthrate, severely limited immigration, and increased longevity, all of which lead to a declining population, shrinking workforce, and increased demand for social services for the elderly.

Weekend 5: Ancient Egypt

Day 1: Political History

Ancient Egypt was one of the world's great early civilizations, a nation and culture that dominated northern Africa for nearly 3,000 years and saw hundreds of kings rule over some 30 dynasties. Factors like climate and geography, together with innovative leadership and bureaucratic organization, made possible a legacy that continues to fascinate scholars and amateurs alike: the pyramids, with their staggering scale and mathematical ingenuity; mummies and tombs that provide modern researchers with an enormous body of material to examine; and innumerable carvings of pictures and writing, made decipherable by the Rosetta Stone. The unusually high status of women, the worship of gods of sun and nature, and a fixation on the afterlife are some of the themes that make ancient Egypt alluring to modern students.

As the Ganges was to India and the Yangtze to China, the Nile River was the mother of Egyptian civilization, spurring the rise of agriculture, trade, and one of the most successful societies in the ancient world. Flowing northward out of Burundi into Lake Victoria then through Uganda and Sudan on its way to the Mediterranean Sea, the Nile is the longest river in the world, traversing more than 4,000 miles of the African continent.

Although the Nile flooded wildly during the postglacial period, by 6000 B.C. it was stable enough to support permanent settlements of migrants from the Near East or elsewhere in Africa. By about 4000 B.C., the descendants of those prehistoric settlers had built a network of farming villages along the 660-mile-long Nile River Valley. Over the next thousand years, the Nile River tribes consolidated into small kingdoms, and then into two large groups—one occupying the lower delta and another in the upper valley. The Nile River peoples traded throughout the Near East and especially borrowed many agricultural and cultural ideas from the thriving Sumerian society across the Red Sea. However, while Sumer was organized into 12 autonomous city-states, the Nile groups finally united under one leader, known to legend as Menes, who founded his capital at Memphis around 3100 B.C. and began the first dynasty of the Old Kingdom (ca. 3100–2200 B.C.). From then until the Roman conquest more than 3,000 years later, a total of 30 dynasties, each with a succession of kings known as pharaohs, ruled ancient Egypt. Unlike Sumerian kings who ruled on behalf of the gods, the Egyptian pharaoh was regarded as a divine being in his own right, and much wealth and time was spent building an appropriate tomb to help him reenter the land of the gods after his death. The pharaoh employed an array of officials to organize all aspects of society, and the tightly ordered Egyptian state promoted the implementation of technological and artistic advances throughout the Nile villages. Egyptian farmers perfected many tools originally invented in Asia; these improved production techniques made Egypt the wealthiest state in the ancient Middle East, and the forbidding desert to the south ensured relative freedom from invasion. With these advantages, the population of the region rose from about 1 million in 3000 B.C. to about 3 million by 1000 B.C.

As the temporal and religious leader, the pharaoh theoretically owned all the land in ancient Egypt, although private citizens were able to buy and sell some property. Farmers were obligated to pay a portion of their output to high-ranking officials. Old Kingdom inhabitants grew crops such as wheat and barley—used for both bread and beer—and probably domesticated cattle and donkeys. They kept cats, dogs, and monkeys as pets, and raised sheep, goats, pigs, and fowl for meat. Hunting, however, was a pastime for the elite, and the hunting of lions and wild cattle was reserved for royalty alone. True slavery was uncommon, although slaves were often conscripted as construction workers for tombs or other state buildings.

The oral language of ancient Egypt shared similarities with the Semitic languages of the Near East—Hebrew, Arabic, and the Hamitic languages of Africa. But Egyptians were among the first to develop a comprehensive written language, as they began using their system of hieroglyphic symbols about 3000 B.C., soon after the Sumerians invented cuneiform writing. Hieroglyphics evolved from pictures used on tomb paintings and were used to tell stories about the deceased, but they also allowed a permanent record of laws, rituals, and business transactions. Scribes wrote religious and administrative texts on papyrus, a form of paper made from reeds that grew along the Nile.

The prosperity of the Old Kingdom produced a burst of creativity in architecture and the arts. For the Egyptians, this cultural expression served the twin goals of organizing earthly existence and guaranteeing smooth entry into the afterlife. Architects mastered stone-working techniques for massive tombs. Painters and sculptors created realistic portraits and life-sized statues of the dead. Scribes developed the tradition of tomb writing into the art of biography. Others wrote *Sebayt* ("instructions") to preserve important teachings, like the *Ipuwer* papyrus, a poem about natural disasters, including the Great Flood.

Beginning around 2181 B.C., this stable society collapsed as northern and southern leaders clashed when an old pharaoh outlived his heirs, causing a rift over succession. As the fighting dragged on, provincial officials became more powerful, further splintering rule. Meanwhile, low river levels brought widespread famine, and factional fighters destroyed monuments and artwork. These "dark ages" are known as the First Intermediate Period.

However, around 2030 B.C., Nebhepetre Mentuhotep II reunited Egypt and established a new capital at Thebes. During the subsequent Middle Kingdom (ca. 2030–1640 B.C.), a cultural revival restored much of the Old Kingdom architecture and sculpture. Artists created impressive new works, and a court official compiled the *Story of Sinuhe*—a classic of Egyptian literature that recounts the life of a nobleman in the aftermath of the assassination of Amenemhet I. Despite such attainments, the warlike Hyksos invaded Egypt from Syria-Palestine with fast-moving chariots, which gave them a unique advantage in battle. The Hyksos ruled Egypt during the century-long Second Intermediate Period (ca. 1640–1550 B.C.). They brought a variety of technological advances to Egypt, including new weapons and tools and techniques for metalwork and pottery. The Eighteenth Dynasty drove out the conquerors and, from their capital at Thebes, reestablished royal authority throughout the valley.

Almost immediately after they expelled the Hyksos, the pharaohs of the New Kingdom (1550–1070 B.C.) began to expand northward into Syria. Thutmose I (d. 1495 B.C.) sent an invading army as far as the Euphrates River, but Thutmose II (r. ca. 1495–1490 B.C.) could not sustain his father's conquests and lost power to his half sister and wife, Hatshepsut (r. ca. 1473–58 B.C.). Upon the death of Thutmose II,

Hatshepsut initially served as a regent to his son, Thutmose III. But as the stronger ruler, and possibly due to Thutmose III's youth, she eventually assumed the position of pharaoh. Some monuments from the period dedicated by Hatshepsut portray both as rulers. Hatshepsut maintained her control over the throne during the first 20 years of the reign of Thutmose III until her death around 1458 B.C.

Hatshepsut's reign was primarily peaceful; she expanded trade and developed natural resources, including mining at Sinai. She also supported construction, restoring numerous monuments and adding to the famous mortuary complex at Deir-el-Bahri. In reliefs and statuary, Hatshepsut was often depicted as male, including a false beard, although texts usually indicated her female gender in some way. Hatshepsut was not the only female ruler of ancient Egypt; she was one of several women, including Nefertiti and Cleopatra, who each reigned for brief periods. Less is known about their ascents to power and subsequent reigns, due to limited records.

After Hatshepsut died, Thutmose III became a powerful ruler, sending armies to the east and establishing an Egyptian empire in Palestine and Syria. These colonies were ruled by local princes, while Egyptian bureaucrats and garrison commanders oversaw imperial interests and collected tribute payments. Thutmose III also pushed Egyptian control southward into Sudan and Nubia and built more than 50 new temples throughout the thriving empire. However, Pharaoh Amenhotep IV (r. ca. 1372–1354 B.C.), husband to Queen Nefertiti, instigated radical religious reforms that disrupted these political gains. The pharaoh changed his name to Akhenaton and relinquished all the Egyptian gods except for a sun god named Aton and his incarnation on Earth, the pharaoh. This quasi-monotheistic revolution did not fully succeed, but it absorbed the attention of the monarchy to such an extent that the empire crumbled. Akhenaton's young son-in-law, Tutankhamen (r. 1361–52 B.C.), returned the country to the older religious traditions and began an arduous recovery period. During his 10-year reign, Tutankhamen (whose almost-intact tomb was discovered in 1922, shedding great light on the culture of the Eighteenth Dynasty) reestablished the rule of law and sponsored new buildings in the capital at Thebes. But by 1200 B.C., a series of invasions by Hittites and others forced the Egyptians to abandon the outposts of their empire and defend the Nile

Valley. Still, the Eighteenth Dynasty may have been the height of culture in ancient Egypt. It was also better recorded than most; a set of tablets called the Tell el Amarna yielded information on the reigns of Amenhotep III and his son, Akhenaton.

Egyptian rule splintered again after the death of Ramses XI and, during the Third Intermediate Period (1065–525 B.C.), the priesthood gained influence over a series of ineffective monarchs. The state, weakened by invasions of Libyans from the western desert and Nubians from the Upper Nile, finally fell victim to conquest by the Assyrians (671 B.C.), who had already absorbed Syria and Palestine, and later the Persians (525 B.C.) under Cambyses II. Cambyses II was succeeded by Darius I, who was held in higher esteem by Egyptians for his attempts to improve temples and codify earlier laws. The centuries under Persian rule were a difficult period, however, as Egypt faced true foreign domination for the first time. In 332 B.C., Alexander the Great invaded Egypt with an army of Greeks and Macedonians. Alexander faced little resistance from Egyptians, who regarded his takeover as their liberation from Persian rule. His general, Ptolemy I, founded the last Egyptian dynasty as an essentially Greek state in which Greek language and culture dominated. After Ptolemy I, there followed a succession of kings also called Ptolemy. When Ptolemy XI sought help from the Roman leader Pompey, the Romans were able to establish a foothold in Egypt. Later, Cleopatra, daughter of Ptolemy XI, tried to retain power for Egypt, calling on the Roman emperor Julius Caesar for help. But the Roman Octavian (the future Emperor Augustus) annexed Egypt for Rome, putting Cleopatra's son, Ptolemy XIV, to death. Egypt became a Roman province in 30 B.C.

◆The Israelites To Jewish and Christian cultures, Egyptian history is closely intertwined with the story of the Israelites, a Semitic people who trace their origins to the ancient city of Ur in Mesopotamia. The Israelites, united by a covenant between their patriarch, Abraham, and their god, Yahweh, migrated to the Canaan region of Palestine sometime after 1900 B.C. According to the Hebrew Scriptures, Joseph, a son of the Israelite patriarch Jacob, was exiled from Canaan and moved to Egypt, where he became a trusted confidant to the pharaoh. By this account, Joseph's descendants lived comfortably among the Egyptians until "there came to power in Egypt a new king who knew nothing of Joseph." The Israelites were then enslaved until Moses, a divinely designated liberator, petitioned the pharaoh for their freedom. The pharaoh refused and, after a protracted struggle, a "mixed multitude"—possibly including others in bondage—fled the Egyptian kingdom into the desert of Sinai and eventually back to Canaan. While no independent archaeological evidence has been discovered for Moses or the other patriarchs, substantial evidence suggests that the Israelites did enter Egypt sometime around the Hyksos period, lived in the Egyptian delta until about 1280 B.C., and occupied parts of Canaan during the decline of Egyptian power there.

Day 2: A Cultural History

Architecture, writing, religion, and burial rituals are some of the most fascinating areas of ancient Egyptian culture. The tombs of pharaohs are noteworthy not only for their architecture but also for the rich materials and records they have preserved, allowing scholars to learn about particular rulers or dynasties, and, as thousands of mummies have been unearthed, to examine unique Egyptian techniques for burying the dead. Following the discovery of the Rosetta Stone, a tremendous body of hieroglyphics became decipherable. Egyptian religion, although it changed sporadically at the whims of the pharaohs, was centered on a deep attachment to nature, including the sun and the waters of the Nile, the most important resource in the life of a civilization that bordered the Sahara.

♦**Architecture** The most notable surviving examples of architecture in the Mediterranean world are the tombs and temples of ancient Egypt. Most of these buildings were identified solely with the pharaoh who commissioned them, but the first architect known by name, Imhotep, worked during the height of the Old Kingdom and is credited with designing King Zoser's tomb complex, built about 2680 B.C. in Saqqara. There is no historical precedent for the tomb's remarkable six-stepped pyramid, and Imhotep is also believed to have invented building in stone—an accomplishment so important that later Egyptians deified him as the son of the creator god Ptah.

Egypt had an abundance of sandstone, limestone, and granite, which permitted larger and more detailed structures than in nearby civilizations. Under order of the pharaoh, builders commanded huge numbers of laborers and artisans and invented ingenious engineering techniques to manipulate massive stones into precise arrangements.

Egyptian temples and tombs were usually made with thick, tapering walls and round columns supporting flat stone roofs. The most famous examples are the complex of pyramids and the Great Sphinx at Giza. The largest and oldest of this group, the pyramid of Cheops (2589–2566 B.C.), was originally 482 feet high by 760 feet square, and occupied about 13 acres. Also known as the Great Pyramid, it was built for the pharaoh Khufu. According to legend, the pharaoh began building his pyramid as a "house of eternity" immediately upon taking power. It was built on the west bank of the Nile, as most cemeteries were, because the sun set, or died, in the west. Builders, who were usually farmers put to labor during the seasons when their fields were flooded, worked for about 20 years, setting layer after layer and building ramps to reach higher levels as they went. The pyramid was topped with a shining golden block. Later pharaohs were buried in more modest tombs furnished with sculptures and painted reliefs. The tombs of Mentuhotep (built ca. 2050 B.C.) and Hatshepsut (ca. 1458 B.C.) at Deir el-Bahri are considerably smaller than the pyramids at Giza. Lesser citizens constructed even simpler tombs according to their means. By the time of the New Kingdom, temples replaced tombs as Egypt's dominant architectural achievements. Among the most impressive was the temple complex of Karnak (in the modern city of Luxor) built in stages between about 1525 B.C. and 1350 B.C. The complex at Karnak includes the great hypostyle hall, a spread of 5,000 square meters lined with 134 carved columns ranging from 30 to over 60 feet in height that would later influence the Greeks and Romans.

◆**Writing** The ancient Egyptians created two main systems of writing: the hieroglyphic, in which pictures were used to represent meanings, and the closely related hieratic, a form of cursive. In the First Dynasty (3110–2884 B.C.) the hieroglyphic system was already well developed and used on monuments and other forms of display. But hieroglyphics were more than simply self-referent pictures. Some symbols represented a specific object or idea, some stood in for a syllable or sound, and others gave clues as to how the preceding symbols should be interpreted—such as an eye to indicate that the previous hieroglyph had something to do with seeing. By the time of the Middle Kingdom, hieroglyphics fell out of use, and the hieratic script became more common, used for private documents and administrative matters. In the late

B.C. centuries, demotic script, a developed form of the hieratic, took precedence over the others.

A major development in the understanding of these forms of writing came with the discovery of the Rosetta Stone, a slab of black granite about three and a half feet long and two and a half feet wide, found in 1799 by a Frenchman near the city of Rosetta, northeast of Alexandria. The stone was inscribed in Egyptian and Greek, using three writing systems: hieroglyphics, demotics, and the Greek alphabet. Within a few decades, scholars had deciphered the ancient Egyptian scripts, making possible the translation of a vast body of hieroglyphic inscriptions.

◆**Literature** The most important work of early Egyptian literature is the *Book of Going Forth by Day* (earliest portions ca. 2300–2100 B.C.; also known as the *Egyptian Book of the Dead*), a collection of incantations and spells (in many different versions) placed in tombs as guides for the dead in their journey to the afterlife. Ancient Egyptian literature is also rich in poetry, including love poems, hymns to the gods, and evocations of daily life, written over a period of many centuries from the late third millennium to the early first millennium B.C. The story of "The Sailor and the Wonder Island," from the Middle Kingdom (2022–1850 B.C.) has some parallels with the later Greek myth of Atlantis.

◆**Religion and Mythology** At the start of the Old Kingdom around 3000 B.C., the newly united Egypt, having brought together many local cultures that had lived separately along the Nile River Valley, contained great cultural and religious diversity. This is reflected in the complex and often contradictory myths that survive in written Egyptian sources. Despite internal differences, much of Egyptian religion was concerned with life, death, renewal, and the afterlife. The sun plays a large role in Egyptian mythology, with four major deities representing different aspects of the sun (such as its rising and setting): Atum, Amon, Aton, and Ra.

The two most important Egyptian cosmogonies are identified with two principal cities, Heliopolis and Hermopolis. In the Heliopolitan cosmogony, the primordial waters give birth to Atum (the sun). From his mucus (or semen) comes Shu (air) and Tefnut (moisture). Shu and Tefnut beget Geb (earth) and Nut (sky), who beget two gods, Osiris and Seth, and two goddesses, Isis and Nephthys. These nine deities are the core pantheon, joined by other gods such as Horus, son of Isis and Osiris. The Hermopolitan cosmogony features four god-goddess pairs: Kuk and Kauket (darkness), Huh and Hauhet (limitlessness), Amon and Amaunet (invisibility), and Nun and Naunet (primordial waters). When the pharaoh Menes (also called Narmer) united Upper and Lower Egypt to found the Old Kingdom (ca. 2575–2130 B.C.), he joined together the two pantheons. In his system, Ptah spoke the eight Hermopolitan gods into existence, and then created the nine Heliopolitan deities.

The role of the pharaoh in religion   The pharaoh was generally understood as an earthly representative of the gods. He communicated the will of the gods and administered it according to the concept of *maat*, or justice. Some pharaohs instituted major changes in religion—such as when Akhenaton decreed that the sun god Aton was the only god, and that he, the pharaoh, was Aton's earthly son. To enforce this shift to monotheism, Ikhnaton destroyed monuments to Amon, who had been regarded as the most powerful of the gods before, and abolished traditions connected to the old religion. After Akhenaton's death, an angry priesthood destroyed his mummy and erased many references to him. Egypt returned to its earlier, polytheistic religious traditions. Some scholars argue that Akhenaton's religious fanaticism hastened the decline of Egypt, as the pharaoh neglected his provinces, weakening the empire that later kings would govern.

Polytheistic Egyptian religion, although it varied over the dynasties and was remarkably flexible in its adjustments to need and circumstance, included gods that oversaw many aspects of nature and life, such as the sky, the waters of the Nile, love and fertility, truth and justice, wisdom, war and vengeance, and of course the afterlife, which was a major focus of Egyptian culture.

♦Funerary Practice   Egyptian religion stressed the importance of the afterlife and so, instead of cremating their dead, ancient Egyptians developed a sophisticated embalming process to preserve the body for its journey to the underworld. First, they purified the body by washing it with palm wine and water from the Nile. They then removed essential organs such as the stomach, liver, and intestines, using natron, a mineral salt, to dehydrate them before putting them back into the body. The heart was not removed from the body, as it was needed to navigate the afterlife. The cadaver was dehydrated and preserved with bitumen, honey, and gum resin, then wrapped in linen. Individual body parts, including fingers and toes, were wrapped separately and layered with amulets that served specific purposes in guiding the body on its path. After the ritual "opening of the mouth," permitting the mummified body to breathe and eat, the mummy was entombed with food and cherished keepsakes—including pets who were mummified and placed alongside their former masters. Royalty received elaborate tombs, double coffins, and sarcophagi decorated with their likenesses, as well as scenes of their lives and burials. Even simple coffins, though interred in cemeteries rather than tombs, usually bore at least both the name of the deceased and paintings of eyes to help show the deceased the way out.

Weekend 6: A History of Classical Music

"Classical music" takes its name from the Classical era of 1750–1820, but refers more commonly to the sacred, concert, and chamber music produced throughout history. Although classical music no longer attracts the crowds it once did, it has influenced everything we hear. The musical forms, theories of composition, and even the instruments used today were created over centuries, and can be heard in the works of today's rock performers, hip-hop artists, and Broadway composers. Even listeners unfamiliar with the subject are likely to recognize classical pieces in movie soundtracks, commercials, or television programs.

Day 1: Classical Music to the Romantic Period

Classical music emerged in the Christian Church during the Middle Ages. In the early medieval period (ca. A.D. 500) music was almost exclusively monophonic, meaning that there was a single melodic line without any harmony or accompaniment. Monks in early Christian church services performed the first examples of this music, known as *plainsong* or *plainchant*. It consisted of Latin words derived from the Roman Catholic Mass, set to a simple unharmonized melody, using eight tones with set intervals between them. This sequence of notes—called modes—eventually evolved into today's modern scales (do, re, mi, fa, sol, la, ti, do). Plainsong ultimately became known as Gregorian chant, after Pope Gregory I, who encouraged a ritualized use of music by the church in the late sixth century.

This type of music held sway until around A.D. 1100, when sacred musical forms were supplemented by a developing folk music tradition. This music was essentially poetry set to music, performed on simple string instruments. The new form of secular singing originated in southern France, played and sung by roving poet-minstrels. Known as troubadours, they went from castle to castle singing songs, telling stories, and otherwise entertaining the lords and ladies of the upper class.

Around the same time, monophony slowly gave way to polyphony, in which multiple melodic lines are sung simultaneously. Polyphony even found its way into the Latin Mass. One of the most prolific composers of the late Middle Ages was Guillaume de Machaut (b. 1300). He not only composed some 100 songs, he also wrote several masses and *motets* (a sacred vocal form for two to four voices), and was one of the first known composers to explore polyphonic forms.

◆**The Renaissance** Music, like all the arts, flourished during the Renaissance (1400–1600). With the rise of the middle class, more people moved to cities and spent their leisure time attending plays, concerts, and other forms of entertainment. Music became part of the common education, and, thanks to the invention of the printing press (ca. 1455), sheet music and method books (for lute, recorder, and guitar) were made available to the general populace.

The music of the Renaissance took the form of simple, smooth-flowing melodies and harmonies, and many new instruments came to prominence, including the viol (predecessor to the modern violin), guitar, harp, recorder, sackbut (predecessor to the trombone), harpsichord, and clavichord.

The most important musical form during the Renaissance was the Latin Mass, which inspired many great vocal works. In the 15th century, composers began to incorporate melodies from secular songs into the Mass, and by the end of the 16th century, composers became more ambitious, using more voices and instruments and adding more elaborate ornamentation to the music. During the Renaissance, the Mass became a significant musical genre, as important in its time as the symphony would be in the 19th century. The master of the Renaissance-era Mass was the 16th-century composer Giovanni Pierluigi da Palestrina, whose 104 masses are considered the epitome of the Renaissance Mass style.

The *madrigal*, a new secular song form that set poetic text in an arrangement for four to six voices, became popular during the Renaissance. The first madrigals were sung in Italy at the end of the 13th century as a form of social activity in the homes of cultivated aristocrats; by the 16th century, the form had become more complex in its polyphony and had spread across Europe to England.

Other key Renaissance composers included Guillaume Dufay, who composed in almost every available musical form of the time, and Josquin Després, who wrote 18 masses and nearly 100 motets. Claudio Monteverdi bridged the Renaissance and Baroque eras, writing both sacred and secular vocal music. Monteverdi was the first composer to make the words of a song the starting place for each composition. Whatever mood the words conveyed was reflected in the music, especially in his operas.

◆**The Baroque Period**   The music of the Baroque era (1600–1750) echoed the dramatic styles of the period's art, architecture, and fashion. The term itself was originally used in a derogatory sense by the supporters of the Renaissance ideals of symmetry and simplicity in music. The simple melodies of the Renaissance evolved into flamboyant airs, full of trills and turns and other ornamentation. Elaborate melodies were layered on top of one another, and the concept of *chordal accompaniment*— with three or more notes played simultaneously under the melody—gained favor. *Harmony* and *counterpoint*, in which two or more simultaneous musical lines are played together, replaced simple polyphony, and rich orchestral sound was heard for the first time.

Composers also began to work with harmony, and they explored new compositional techniques such as *dissonance* (the jarring quality of two close pitches played simultaneously) and *chromaticism*, which utilizes all 12 tones within a musical scale, rather than the limited eight tones found in sacred chants. The dominant musical forms reached an almost excessive degree of elaborateness, and musical expression became more formal, if not somewhat mechanical in its construction.

Several new musical forms came into prominence during the Baroque era: the *oratorio*, an unstaged opera with sacred text; the *sonata*, an instrumental piece composed in four movements; and the *opera*. These new forms made use of more and different combinations of instruments—and, in the case of opera, encouraged the interplay of voices and instruments.

The most influential Baroque composers were those of the later period—notably Antonio Vivaldi, George Frideric Handel, and Johann Sebastian Bach, all of whom composed in the first half of the 18th century.

Antonio Vivaldi was born in Venice, and although he was ordained as a priest, he was employed for most of his working life at the Ospedale della Pietá, an orphanage for girls that developed a highly regarded conservatory of music. Vivaldi wrote 46 operas, most of which are lost, but he is remembered in the annals of music for bringing the concerto to its mature state. The *concerto* is a form in which one or more solo instruments is supported by a large orchestra. Vivaldi, a violin virtuoso himself, wrote close to 500 concertos, intended for use by his students. These were inventive and musically challenging, and allowed soloists to fully display their talents. The best known of his concertos are *The Four Seasons* (1723).

George Frideric Handel, though German by birth, spent most of his career in England. An accomplished organist and violinist, Handel performed on concert stages in Italy and London. He composed in all genres, writing chamber music and orchestral works such as *Water Music* and *Music for the Royal Fireworks* (commissioned by King George I), but he was primarily a vocal composer, writing 40 operas and 20 oratorios. The "Hallelujah Chorus" of his masterwork, *Messiah*, is one of the most recognizable pieces of music in the Western world.

Johann Sebastian Bach, foremost among the Baroque composers, was a true musical genius and the most important member of a large musical family, which included 20 children, most notably Carl Philipp Emanuel (C. P. E.) and Johann Christian, influential composers in their own right. J. S. Bach produced an astounding variety of chamber and orchestral works, including the *Brandenburg Concertos*, as well as a large number of organ and keyboard works. His *Well-Tempered Clavier*, a collection of solo keyboard works is regarded as one of the most important compositions in Western music. It has been used by generations of piano students in developing their technique. Bach wrote most of his great church music when he was cantor of St. Thomas's Church in Leipzig. These include sacred and secular cantatas, motets, and other large choral pieces, including *St. Matthew Passion*, written for Good Friday vespers services at the church.

What makes Bach central to the history of music was his absolute mastery of the strict compositional techniques of his day. He combined expressive melodies with the rigorous intricacy of counterpoint—most notably in his suites for solo violin and solo cello—as well as in much of his harpsichord music. His musical genius perfectly balanced technical mastery, intellectual control, and almost limitless inventiveness.

Bach and the other composers of the Baroque era were often employed by persons in the wealthy ruling class, in what was called the patronage system. In this system, the patron paid the composer for each work and usually decided what kind of piece the composer should write. These patrons tended to favor dances, preludes, and suites, and though working within these genres could be creatively limiting, the best of the

Baroque composers were able to thoroughly explore, and in some cases expand, these and other Baroque-era forms.

◆**The Classical Period** The Classical era (1750–1820) is widely regarded as an exceptional period in terms of musical achievement. It represented a clean break from the Baroque, as younger musicians rebelled against the heavy ornamentation and perceived restrictions of Baroque-era counterpoint, replacing them with simplicity, balance, and strong emotion. Compared to Baroque music, the music of the Classical era is lighter, clearer, and less complicated, and the melodies themselves are more graceful and lyrical. As the patronage system of the Baroque era died out, it was replaced by public concerts, which gave composers a newfound freedom of choice in terms of compositional inspiration and the forms it would take. It was a period that included the most celebrated composers of all time, who created some of the best known works in musical history.

Much of the great music of the Classical period came from a single city. By the mid-1700s, Vienna, Austria, had become a magnet for musicians from throughout Europe. This confluence of talent resulted in a convergence of musical styles and a melting pot of ideas, out of which emerged the full-blown Classical style. This new style was forged by the three giants of the period, all of whom lived in Vienna at the time—Franz Joseph Haydn, Wolfgang Amadeus Mozart, and Ludwig van Beethoven.

Franz Joseph Haydn was the most celebrated composer of the early Classical period. Often referred to as "Papa Haydn," he was a key figure in the development of the string quartet, but he is best known as the "father of the symphony," composing an astonishing 104 symphonic works. Haydn spent the early years of his musical career in Vienna, as Kapellmeister for the wealthy House of Esterházy, a noble Hungarian family. His most famous works were written during his two long visits to London. The 12 "London symphonies" (Nos. 93–104) were grander than anything he'd composed in Vienna. The second of these, No. 94 in G—nicknamed "Surprise" because of a sudden loud chord appearing after the tranquil beginning of the second movement—is among the most popular symphonies of the Classical period.

Wolfgang Amadeus Mozart made his own impressive contributions to the symphonic tradition, but was greatly influenced by Haydn's symphonic works. Mozart was a master in every form in which he chose to work. A child prodigy born into a musical family, Mozart was the most sought-after composer and performer of his day. He produced at least 626 nearly flawless works including 41 symphonies, 27 piano concertos, 27 string quartets, and five violin concertos, and is regarded as the world's greatest natural musical genius. During his travels as a performer, he assimilated and refined all the musical styles he encountered, developing a love for the singing voice. His mature compositions are distinguished by their melodic beauty, formal elegance, and richness of harmony and texture. He had a rare gift for memorable melodies, which many consider the hallmark of his style.

Mozart is regarded as the originator of the piano concerto, composing most of these works for occasions when he would play the solo part. He transformed the concerto into a conversation between a solo instrument and the orchestra, and these works contain the same dramatic spirit that is evident in his operas. Of his 27 piano concertos, perhaps the most recognized is *Piano Concerto No. 21* (1785), anachronistically known as "Elvira Madigan" following its use in the soundtrack of the 1967 Swedish film of the same name. Among his other familiar and beloved works are *Serenade No. 13 in G for Strings* (*Eine Kleine Nachtmusik*, 1787), *Symphony No. 41 in C* (*Jupiter*, 1788) and the operas *Le Nozze de Figaro* (*The Marriage of Figaro*, 1785–86), *Don Giovanni* (1787), *Così Fan Tutte* (*Women are Like That*, 1790), and *Die Zauberflöte* (*The Magic Flute*, 1790–91).

Haydn and Mozart played an important role in the development of the modern orchestra, helping to standardize the instrumental makeup of that musical body. During the Baroque period, the orchestra was dominated by the string section, but by the late 18th century, wind instruments were regarded as equal to the strings in terms of playing the melody, as well as supplying harmony.

Day 2: Beethoven and the Romantic Era

Ludwig van Beethoven is claimed by both the Classical and Romantic periods—a musical giant whose work was uniquely innovative and influential. Beethoven moved from Germany to Vienna in 1787 when he was 17, in hopes of studying with Mozart. Rather than working for a church or noble court, as was common earlier in the Classical period, Beethoven struggled to support himself through a combination of individual gifts and annual stipends from members of the aristocracy, income from subscription concerts, and private lessons. Because he wasn't under constant pressure to deliver compositions to patrons, his musical output was smaller than that of Haydn and Mozart. But he had considerable freedom as to what and how he composed. In Beethoven's hands, several musical genres—most notably the symphony—reached new heights, featuring longer and more ambitious movements within each piece.

Despite his steady hearing loss beginning at age 28, Beethoven radically transformed every musical form in which he worked, composing his most important pieces when he was totally deaf. He introduced a new level of emotional expression, accompanied by bold harmonies and tonal relationships, and did much to raise the stature of the piano sonata, writing 32 such pieces, famously *No. 14* ("Moonlight") and *No. 13* ("Pathetique"). All his sonatas incorporate dramatic elements usually found in symphonies. His concertos, notably the *Fifth Piano Concerto* ("Emperor") allowed the solo instrument to soar over orchestral parts written in symphonic proportions.

Like many of his generation, Beethoven was attracted to the ideas of the Enlightenment, and this is reflected in his music. Beginning with his third symphony, the *Eroica* (1804), Beethoven bridged the cultural divide separating the 18th and 19th centuries. The *Eroica*, originally intended as a work dedicated to the heroic ideal embodied by Napoleon, is double the length of any Mozart symphony and requires an expanded orchestra. The composer's expressions of idealism, agony, and triumph are immediately evident, even to a listener approaching the work for the first time. Another resonating example of emotion in Beethoven's work is the famous four note opening theme to his *Symphony No. 5 in C Minor*. This simple motif ("ba ba ba bom") is worked into a cascading wall of sound, building large blocks of chords with massive power. Beethoven's *Ninth Symphony*, twice the length of his earlier symphonic works, adds a large choir to the orchestra, and features an elaborate choral setting of Schiller's "Ode to Joy," an optimistic hymn championing the brotherhood of humanity.

Beethoven's mastery of structure and tonal key relationships established him as the dominant musical figure of the 19th century. He was so admired by the public that an estimated 20,000 people attended his funeral in 1827.

◆**The Romantic Period 1820–1900** A central characteristic of
the composers of the Romantic period was their desire to follow the inspiration of literature, history, visual arts, and other nonmusical sources. They
emphasized personal expression of emotion and the freedom of form. There
were great variations among the length of pieces, the number of movements in these pieces, and the types of instruments or voices used.

This new movement resulted not in revolution, but in the evolution
of established musical forms and the creation of new forms, all typified by
the use of unusual chord progressions, sophisticated harmonies, and unexpected *modulations* (the changing from one key to another). While Romantic music was more technically complex than anything that came
before, it was also infused with sweeping and truly romantic melodies.

The Industrial Revolution brought with it the final evolution of most
of the musical instruments used in symphonic orchestras today. Stan-
dardization in the manufacture of instruments and new technical developments made instruments easier to play and produced a more
reliable sound, allowing composers and performers to produce musical
effects that had not been possible before.

Franz Schubert, a Viennese-born composer, established the German
art song, or *lieder*, as a new art form. In his short life, he wrote more
than 600 songs inspired by the lyric poetry written in the late 18th century by Goëthe, Heine, Schiller, and others. His two song cycles are
miniature music dramas. *Die Schöne Mullerin* (*The Fair Maid of the Mill*,
1823) is a narrative cycle representing the courtship of a miller's daughter. *Winterreise* (*Winter's Journey*, 1827), is a more contemplative piece
that portrays in music nearly every conceivable emotional state. Schubert's instrumental works were not fully appreciated during his lifetime,
but his *Piano Quintet in A Major* (the "Trout"), and *Symphony No. 8* (the
"Unfinished," so-called because it consists of only two movements) remain standards in the classical repertory.

The Romantic symphony bears a close resemblance to that of the
Classical era, building upon the grandeur suggested in Beethoven's later
works. Romantic-era symphonies tend to use larger orchestras than
those from the Classical period, and they often incorporate more than
four movements. Johannes Brahms is one master of this new breed of
symphony and considered the true successor to Beethoven, writing
sweeping, lush scores with strong personal aspects to them. His four sym-

phonies and his majestic *Violin Concerto* are emblematic of the work of this period. Other key symphonic composers of the Romantic era are Anton Bruckner, whose nine symphonies are comparable to those of Beethoven, complete with soaring melodies and rich chromatic harmony, and Felix Mendelssohn, whose *String Octet, Italian Symphony* and *Scotch Symphony* are now standards in the classical repertory.

In the 1820s and '30s, much of the intellectual activity in Europe was centered in Paris, which was filled with poets, painters, and composers. Franz Liszt came to Paris from Hungary in 1823, Frédéric Chopin arrived from Poland in 1830, joining the French-born composer Hector Berlioz. This confluence of talent led directly to the development of "programme music," described by Liszt as music that tells a story, illustrates a literary idea, or evokes a pictorial scene.

Hector Berlioz, broke new ground with his *Symphonie Fantastique*, inspired not only by Gothic fiction and Shakespearean drama, but by a Shakespearean actress, Harriet Smithson, for whom he had an uncontrollable passion. The *Symphonie* was the first to use a melodic motif, an *idée fixe* (fixed idea) that recurs in each movement, connecting a large and varied piece into a unified whole. This *idée fixe* scheme was also used by Franz Liszt.

The best-known type of programme music is the symphonic poem, a single-movement orchestral work on a symphonic scale—essentially a short symphony. Liszt was the most prolific proponent of this new genre, composing 13 symphonic poems that dealt with subjects taken from classical mythology, Romantic literature, and imaginative fantasy. Among these are *Les Préludes* (1848), the *Dante Symphony* (1857), based on the *Divine Comedy*, and the *Faust Symphony* (1857) based on Goëthe's masterwork.

On the world stage, the period following the Napoleonic wars gave rise to nationalism, as ethnic groups in many countries struggled for self-determination. Likewise in music, composers in eastern Europe, Russia, and Scandinavia broke away from French and German influences and began to draw on local folk songs, national epics, and peasant dances for their inspiration. The Czech composer Antonín Dvorák incorporated folk songs and rhythms into symphonic works such as *Slavonic Rhapsodies* and *Slavonic Dances*, and he challenged American composers to develop their own national music when he incorporated African-American folk music and Native American rhythms into his *Symphony No. 9* (*From the New World*, 1893). The spiritual, "Goin' Home", written by William Arms

Fisher, one of Dvořák's students, is based on the "Largo" movement of this beautiful symphony. Frédéric Chopin, who composed more than 200 technically demanding yet highly lyrical piano works, contributed to the nationalist movement with his polonaises and mazurkas.

Russian composers also sought to establish a uniquely nationalist style. Their contributions include Modeste Mussorgsky's tone poem *Night on Bald Mountain*, and Nikolai Rimsky-Korsakov's *Scheherazade*. The fourth, Pyotr Tchaikovsky, incorporated folk material into his work when it fit into his larger designs. He did, however, continue to follow the musical traditions of the Continental countries. He wrote seven symphonies, but Tchaikovsky is most remembered as setting new standards for the role of music in the classical ballets, "Swan Lake" (1877), "The Sleeping Beauty" (1890), and "The Nutcracker" (1892).

Gustav Mahler, the Czech-born Austrian composer, was the transitional artist between the Romantic and Modernist periods. Mahler was a renowned conductor, leading orchestras throughout Europe as well as the Metropolitan Opera Orchestra and New York Philharmonic in the United States. In this role, he championed and preserved the music of the earlier musical periods, and at the same time, encouraged new composers like Arnold Schoenberg, whose work would have a tremendous influence in the 20th century.

Although Mahler drew on the fundamentals of the Romantic period, his work is often considered part of the expressionist movement, in which composers sought to depict extreme states of mind, creating music that could be alternately harsh, violent, dissonant, or passionate and poignant. In this, Mahler was inspired by the German composer Richard Wagner, who was a master at conveying love and emotion in his music. Wagner set the benchmark for Mahler and other composers, with the opening chord of the opera *Tristan und Isolde*, known as the "Tristan chord," whose lack of resolution intensifies the dramatic tension of the music. Mahler's symphonies were enormous, both in length—often running more than 90 minutes—and in the size of the orchestra. His *Symphony No. 8* (*Symphony of a Thousand*, 1906) calls for a gigantic orchestra, five vocal soloists, a boy's choir, and an adult choir. Mahler didn't live to hear his *Symphony No. 9* (1908–09) performed. It is considered to be his farewell to the world, and at the same time marks the end of the Romantic movement.

Weekend 7: The American Civil War

Day 1: Slavery and the Road to Civil War

The long, torturous path leading to the American Civil War began in Virginia in 1619, when about 20 African men were brought to the English settlement of Jamestown to work as indentured servants. Many workers in the colonies were indentured servants, that is, in return for paid passage to America, they agreed to work for no wages for a set period, usually about seven years. Within a generation, however, thousands of Africans were taken involuntarily from their homes, transported across the Atlantic, and sold as slaves to white settlers in England's American colonies. The economy of the southern colonies, based on labor-intensive agriculture in an unforgiving climate, grew dependent on an ever-increasing number of slaves to harvest crops such as tobacco and cotton. Many leading members of the nation's founding generation, including George Washington and Thomas Jefferson, owned slaves.

Slavery was legal in the North until the early 19th century, but the institution never caught on, in part because the region's soil did not allow for the system of large plantations that took hold in the South. Northern political and religious leaders began to develop misgivings about slavery during and after the American Revolution, especially as the nation began to expand westward. The Northwest Ordinance, which Congress passed in July 1787, prohibited slavery in new states as they formed in the region now called the Midwest. As northern states began to abolish slavery, the Northwest Ordinance had the effect of creating a large regional bloc where slavery was prohibited.

Differences over slavery were played out even during the Constitutional Convention in 1787 as southern delegates sought implicit recognition of slavery in the nation's basic set of laws and warned their colleagues from the North that they would not support a document perceived to contain antislavery language. The convention chose not to confront slavery but to evade it through compromises. For example, slaves were counted as three-fifths of a person for purposes of electoral representation and taxation, and the Constitution included a provision calling for the return of escaped slaves. Northern interests, however, were ambiguously addressed in the Constitution as well, establishing a ban on the slave trade within 20 years of ratification.

In 1820, tensions rose over the prospective statehood of Missouri, which was carved out of the Louisiana Territory, purchased in 1803 by President Thomas Jefferson. With Congress evenly divided between free states and slave states, the Speaker of the House of Representatives, Henry Clay of Kentucky, worked out a compromise in which Maine was admitted as a free state and Missouri as a slave state, adding that slavery would be banned in the Louisiana Territory north of Missouri's southern border, parallel 36°30' north (Missouri was exempted from the prohibition). While the Missouri Compromise maintained the balance of power between free states and slave states in Congress, the debate itself prompted fear for the nation's future. As he followed this debate, Thomas Jefferson described sectional differences over slavery as a "fire bell in the night...the death knell of the Union."

In 1828, Jefferson's nightmarish vision of a divided Union moved closer to reality when political figures in South Carolina led by John C. Calhoun began to argue that they had the power to declare federal laws null and void in their state. Senators Daniel Webster of Massachusetts and Robert Hayne of South Carolina engaged in a famous debate over states' rights and the nature of the American Union in 1830.

South Carolina objected to high federal tariffs, which many Southerners believed favored the industrial North over the import-dependent, agricultural South. When President Andrew Jackson signed a new tariff policy in 1832, Calhoun, his vice president, resigned and became a national spokesman for its nullification. South Carolina declared that the tariffs did not have the force of law within its borders. Jackson threatened the use of force against the dissidents, and South Carolina backed down as Washington reduced the tariff. Although the issue of the moment had been resolved, sectional differences were at a fever pitch, and the state of the Union was very unstable. Adding to the tension was the slaveowner's worst fear—a slave revolt. Some 60 white people died in Virginia in 1831, when a slave named Nat Turner led an uprising of slaves and free blacks. The rebellion was crushed quickly, and dozens of African Americans, including Turner, were killed or later executed.

As the North became more urban, more industrial, and more heterogeneous, southern slaveholders developed a narrative to justify the region's continued dependence on slavery. As the slave population neared 4 million (in an overall U.S. population of 31 million), southern whites drew a favorable contrast between enslavement, which they argued was beneficial for blacks, and industrial wage labor in the North, which they saw as demeaning and inhumane work performed by alien immigrants who supported corrupt political machines. The growing antislavery movement in the North saw southern plantation culture as decadent and immoral, an institution with which there could be no compromise.

A Boston-based journalist named William Lloyd Garrison became a leading spokesman for the abolitionist cause through his newspaper, *The Liberator*, which he published for 34 years, 1831–65. Garrison and other abolitionists, inspired by evangelical Christianity, became zealous critics of slavery and denounced not only slaveholders, but those in the North who sought compromise rather than outright abolition. In 1844, Garrison burned a copy of the U.S. Constitution, which he called "A Covenant With Death" for its compromises over slavery. Northern abolitionists and their newspapers became objects of hate and scorn in the South. The abolitionists were vocal and eloquent, but they had a narrow base of support, centered in Boston and led by elite clergy and journalists.

•**The Union in Peril** American expansion collided with Mexico's claim to Texas, which had been admitted to the Union as a slave state in 1845, leading to war in 1846. Southern politicians were particularly enthusiastic about the war, for they saw the possibility of new slave states in the vast territories of the Southwest then under Mexican rule. Some Northerners, however, opposed the war, in part because they feared victory would foment the growth of slavery. Among the conflict's opponents were a congressman from Illinois named Abraham Lincoln and a writer in Massachusetts, Henry David Thoreau, who refused to pay his taxes in protest of what he saw as an unjust war. The U.S. victory over Mexico in 1848 added territory that included the future states of California, Utah, and Nevada, as well as portions of Colorado, New Mexico, and Arizona.

In anticipation of these vast territorial gains, a Pennsylvania congressman named David Wilmot introduced a clause in an appropriations bill in 1846 that sought to ban slavery from any land won from

Mexico. The measure, known as the Wilmot Proviso, violated a tacit agreement in Congress to avoid discussion of slavery on the House and Senate floors. The bill, with the proviso attached, won narrow approval in the House; Northerners supported it regardless of party affiliation, and Southerners were unanimously opposed. During this time, American politics were not dominated by the two major political parties, Democrat and Whig; instead they were dictated by the real division, that of North and South. The proviso never passed the full Congress, but it inspired debate over the future of slavery as never before. A later version of the proviso called for a ban on slavery in all new territories, not just those acquired from Mexico. With southern Democrats seeking to stop the antislavery moment, some northern Democrats left the party and formed the Free Soil Party, which formally opposed the extension of slavery.

As slavery continued to threaten the Union's stability, politicians desperately sought to postpone, or perhaps avoid altogether, a day of reckoning. Under the legislative leadership of Henry Clay, Congress constructed what became known as the Compromise of 1850. It granted admission of California as a free state, banned the internal slave trade from Washington, D.C., allowed for slavery to be decided by popular vote in the new territories of New Mexico and Utah, and enforced a stringent new Fugitive Slave Law, which required all U.S. citizens to assist in the return of escaped slaves. Southern slave owners were adamant about the return of escaped slaves, a response to the success of former slaves like Harriet Tubman, who fled bondage in Maryland for freedom in Pennsylvania. Tubman, assisting the flight of other slaves, was one of the guiding lights of the Underground Railroad.

The Compromise of 1850 eased political tensions, but the publication of the antislavery novel *Uncle Tom's Cabin* by Harriet Beecher Stowe in 1852 created an uproar in both North and South. The book's portrayal of slavery's cruelty won new recruits to the abolitionist movement, but southern whites saw the tale as yet another northern assault on their distinctive way of life.

The political consensus engineered in 1850 broke down after just four years, when Congress passed the Kansas–Nebraska Act. The legislation repealed the Missouri Compromise by permitting the new territories of Kansas and Nebraska, both of them north of the old Missouri Compromise line, to decide for themselves whether they would be free or slave states. Democrats, most prominently Senator

Stephen A. Douglas of Illinois, saw this exercise in popular sovereignty as a justifiably democratic solution to the issue of slavery's expansion. The abolitionist movement, however, was horrified. Debate over the act in Congress was vicious, even leading to threats of physical violence. When it passed, even more violence erupted as pro-slavery forces and abolitionists converged on Kansas, which was nearing a vote on slavery. Among the combatants was a passionate abolitionist named John Brown. As Kansas bled, a Democratic congressman from South Carolina, Preston Smith Brooks, assaulted Massachusetts senator Charles Sumner, a leading abolitionist, with a cane on May 22, 1855. Sumner nearly died in the attack—it took him three years to recover.

As the nation moved closer to the abyss, the Supreme Court ruled in 1857 against a slave named Dred Scott, who had sued for his freedom because he had lived for a short time in Illinois, where slavery was illegal. The Court ruled that Scott had no right to sue in the first place because he was not and could never be a citizen. The ruling went much further, however, asserting that Congress could not prohibit slavery in any territories. The decision provoked outrage in the North and satisfaction in the South.

Two years later, in 1859, John Brown and a band of militant abolitionists attacked a federal armory in Harpers Ferry, Virginia, hoping to provoke a slave revolt. The attempt failed, and Brown was hanged for treason, becoming a martyr in the eyes of fellow abolitionists.

The Whig Party, hopelessly divided between its northern and southern wings, broke up, and many of its northern members formed the Republican Party. The presidential election of 1860 saw the emergence of Abraham Lincoln as the Republican Party's nominee. He had gained national fame two years earlier when he challenged Stephen Douglas for the Illinois senate seat and bested him in seven public debates. Although Douglas won the election, Lincoln's fame spread, helping him earn the Republican presidential nomination in 1860. Lincoln, who was not on the ballot in nine southern states, opposed the extension of slavery and had argued against slavery as immoral, but he said he would not support its abolition in states where it already existed. In a four-way race that included Stephen Douglas, Lincoln won the presidency with just 39.8 percent of the vote.

Day 2: A House Divided: The American Civil War

Abraham Lincoln's strong yet reasoned approach to slavery distinguished him from rivals in the 1860 election. His most famous speech on the subject took place in Springfield, Illinois, in June 1858, when he was running for the Senate. Paraphrasing a famous passage from the New Testament's Gospel of St. Matthew, he said, "A house divided against itself cannot stand. I believe this government cannot endure, permanently, half slave and half free. I do not expect the Union to be dissolved—I do not expect the house to fall—but I do expect it will cease to be divided. It will become all one thing or all the other."

On December 20, 1860, weeks after Lincoln's election, South Carolina officially "dissolved" its bond with the Union, seceding from the United States of America. Six more slave states—Florida, Alabama, Georgia, Mississippi, Louisiana, and Texas—quickly followed. Within months, Virginia, North Carolina, Tennessee, and Arkansas joined with them to form a new nation, the Confederate States of America.

Determined to maintain federal authority, Lincoln attempted to resupply Fort Sumter in South Carolina's Charleston harbor. On April 12, 1861, Confederates shelled the Union garrison, which surrendered the next day. On April 15, Lincoln declared the lower South to be in state of "insurrection" and called for 75,000 volunteers to suppress the rebellion.

Many on both sides believed the conflict would be over within a few months, but when Confederates routed the undisciplined Union Army in their first major battle at Bull Run, Virginia (July 21, 1861), it became clear that the war would be protracted and costly. The loss was deeply embarrassing to the Lincoln administration and greatly boosted morale in the Confederacy.

♦**1862** The Union's original plan (Winfield Scott's "Anaconda" Plan) was to blockade Confederate ports and control the Mississippi River, thus encircling and constricting the South like a snake. In February 1862, a then-unknown Union general, Ulysses S. Grant, seized Forts Henry and Donelson on the Tennessee River. His victory at Shiloh, Tennessee, (April 6–7) meant the Union controlled the Mississippi River to Memphis. At the river's mouth, Union Navy Flag Officer David G. Farragut captured New Orleans (May 1). Union forces then moved to take the Confederacy's last stronghold on the Mississippi: Vicksburg, Mississippi.

The Union Army in Virginia (called the Army of the Potomac), under the leadership of Major General George B. McClellan, sought to take the Confederate capital of Richmond, Virginia. McClellan postponed the attack to drill his soldiers, then slowly moved them up the James River from the south and across the Virginia Peninsula. During this stage, the first ironclad vessels, the *Virginia* (Confederate) and the *Monitor* (Union), fought to a draw near Hampton Roads (March 9). The Confederacy's Army of Northern Virginia dealt a blow at the Battle of Fair Oaks/Seven Pines (May 31–June 1), although their commander, Joseph E. Johnston, was wounded and replaced by Robert E. Lee. A series of battles from June 25 to July 1 forced McClellan back to the James River, where the campaign had begun.

Thoroughly frustrated, Lincoln ordered McClellan to abandon the Peninsular Campaign, unite with a new army under Major General John Pope, and attack Richmond from the north. The Confederate army under Lee and Thomas Jonathan "Stonewall" Jackson moved north to Manassas and checked Pope's forces in the Second Battle of Bull Run (August 28–30).

Lee then moved across the Potomac River into Maryland. McClellan attacked at Antietam Creek, near Sharpsburg (September 17). In one day, 6,000 died and 17,000 were wounded, making it the bloodiest single day of the war. Lee withdrew his tattered army to Virginia, handing McClellan, who opted not to pursue, a technical victory.

Lincoln used the victory to issue a preliminary Emancipation Proclamation. Unless the seceded states returned to the Union by January 1, 1863, Lincoln said, their slaves "shall be then, thenceforward, and forever free."

On November 7, Lincoln replaced McClellan with General Ambrose E. Burnside, who immediately formulated plans for an offensive against Richmond. Burnside's impulsiveness proved almost as ruinous as McClellan's timidity. At Fredericksburg (December 13), he ordered 16 attacks on fortified Confederate positions with disastrous results, losing nearly 13,000 men compared to Lee's 5,300.

The Army of the Potomac was unable to take Richmond, and Grant's assault on Vicksburg (December 26–29), led by Lieutenant General

William T. Sherman, was a failure. However, the Union successfully defended Kentucky from General Braxton Bragg's "Heartland Offensive" with victories at Perryville, Kentucky, (October 8), and Stones River near Murfreesboro, Tennessee in late December.

•1863 In April, a 120,000-strong Army of the Potomac, now under General Joseph Hooker, once again set out to defeat Lee and take Richmond. Lee nearly destroyed the force at Chancellorsville (April 30–May 6, 1863). However, Lee's stunning victory cost more than 20 percent of his force, including "Stonewall" Jackson, killed accidentally by his own men.

Lee now gambled on a risky offensive into Union territory in June, figuring he could feed his army on northern farms and gather supplies, and that victory might also lead to a negotiated end to the war. "Peace Democrats" in the North were already calling for a settlement with the Confederacy. The Army of the Potomac, now 83,000 strong and under the command of General George C. Meade, faced Lee's 75,000 troops near Gettysburg, Pennsylvania (July 1–3). Three days of Confederate assaults culminated in "Pickett's Charge," when General George Pickett led 15,000 troops against the heavily fortified Union center at Cemetery Ridge. Half were killed or wounded in the failed rush across a mile of open field. Having lost one-third of his men (28,000 casualties), Lee retreated toward Virginia on July 4. That same day, Grant accepted the surrender of Vicksburg, meaning the Union had taken the entire Mississippi River and thereby severed the South in two.

That fall, Union Major General William S. Rosecrans pursued General Bragg to Chickamauga, Georgia (September 18–20), where his army suffered a devastating loss. Rosecrans retreated to Chattanooga, and Bragg, in pursuit, surrounded the city. Grant and the general he increasingly counted on, William T. Sherman, successfully dislodged the Confederates (November 23–25) and Bragg retreated to Georgia.

•1864 In the beginning of 1864, Lincoln called on Grant to take command of all Union armies. He ordered simultaneous assaults by every Union army and left Sherman in Tennessee to command an attack on Atlanta, an industrial hub.

Grant, after joining forces with General Meade, planned a quick overland march of 120,000 troops through the thickets and scrub brush of north-central Virginia toward Richmond, aiming to draw out and destroy Lee's army of 66,000. Lee moved faster than Grant anticipated. Using the rough, wooded terrain of the wilderness between the Rapidan and James Rivers (May 5–7) to his advantage, Lee forced a costly face-off, leading to 18,400 federal and 11,400 rebel casualties. Grant withdrew but continued his advance on Richmond. It stalled at Spotsylvania Court House, where a two-week engagement (May 8–21) between the armies was equally inconclusive and bloody (18,000 federal casualties to 12,000 for the rebels). One Union attack at "Bloody Angle" (May 12–13) stretched for 20 hours in some of the war's most horrific fighting.

Grant neared Richmond, hoping to draw Lee out for a final, decisive battle. A massive assault at Cold Harbor on June 3 ended up as the worst Union rout since Fredericksburg as upward of 7,000 federals fell, compared to fewer than 1,500 Confederates. Grant changed his strategy, moving south past Richmond to seize the vital railroad junction at Petersburg in an attempt to cut the capital's supply line. On June 9, Grant's army settled into a siege outside Petersburg, digging trenches, intercepting rebel supplies, and slowly whittling away at Lee's line.

General Sherman's advance on Atlanta faced far less resistance. He had double the forces of his opponent, General Joseph Johnston (110,000 to 55,000), who chose to backtrack toward Atlanta, picking at Sherman's army in a series of strategically executed stands. Johnston repulsed Sherman's only direct assault at Kennesaw Mountain (June 27), but the Confederate president Jefferson Davis nonetheless replaced him with General John B. Hood. Hood's botched assaults around Atlanta in July allowed Sherman to cut the city's supply line, prompting Hood to evacuate on September 1. It was a crushing blow that all but doomed the Confederacy, boosting the North's morale and helping reelect Lincoln in November.

Shortly after seizing Atlanta, Sherman's army embarked on an epic journey across Georgia to deprive the Confederate Army of badly needed supplies and demoralize its people. Less than a week after troops ended Hood's invasion of Tennessee at Nashville (December 15–16), Sherman's army took Savannah. His 285-mile "March to the Sea" left a 60-mile-wide swath of destruction in its wake.

◆1865 In January, Grant called Sherman's army north to help pinch Lee at Petersburg. Sherman chose to continue his destructive march through the Carolinas. By then, Grant's siege of Petersburg had stretched into its ninth month. Lee's men, nearly completely cut off from supplies, were starving. Thousands deserted. In a final attempt to break through Grant's line, Lee took Fort Stedman (March 25) but couldn't hold it. On April 1, General Philip Sheridan's cavalry and a large force of infantry attacked Lee's right flank under General Pickett at Five Forks, cutting off the only remaining railroad line into Petersburg. An all-out attack the next day forced Lee to retreat from both Richmond and Petersburg.

Lee's one remaining hope was to somehow slip his ragged army west and south to join forces with Johnston in North Carolina. To prevent this, Grant dispatched Sheridan's cavalry, which headed them off at Appomattox Courthouse, Virginia. Lee made one last attempt to break out but failed. On April 9, 1865, Lee surrendered. Almost four years to the day after the first shots were fired at Fort Sumter, the Civil War was over. More than 600,000 American soldiers died in the conflict. Both Grant and Lincoln hoped to lead the country to a peaceful healing after the war; Lincoln pledged to "bind up the nation's wound," and Grant refused punitive measures by allowing Lee's army to simply disperse and return home.

In the end, these efforts toward peaceful reconciliation would fail, so bitter was the hatred the war had engendered on both sides. One of the first casualties was President Lincoln himself, who was murdered in Ford's Theatre by a crazed southern sympathizer, John Wilkes Booth, just a few days after Lee's surrender. A short time later, Union troops would be dispatched throughout the South as a vindictive "reconstruction" was imposed for nearly a decade.

Weekend 8: The Computer Revolution

Day 1: The History of Computing

In the most basic sense, computers are complex calculators. Everything that happens onscreen, whether typing, drawing, or streaming media, is translated from a mathematical computation that the computer solves with blazing speed. Computers began, in fact, as 19th-century machines to help scientists with mathematical computations.

The British mathematician Charles Babbage is often referred to as the "father of computing," due to his development of two separate computing machines, the Difference Engine and the Analytical Engine, in the 19th century. The Difference Engine was conceived as a steam-powered, fully automatic machine, capable of printing the results of its computations on paper; the Analytical Engine could operate on numbers of up to 50 decimal places and was capable of storing 1,000 such numbers. The Analytical Engine also included conditional control that enabled the machine to execute instructions in a specific order. These instructions were entered into the machine on punch cards, a technique used to input information into computers until the 1970s.

The American scientist Herman Hollerith constructed the first electromechanical adding and sorting machine in 1886. This machine, which he dubbed a "tabulator," was put to its first commercial use in 1890 for the U.S. Census Bureau. Based on this success, Hollerith formed the Tabulating Machine Company in 1896, which by 1924 had become International Business Machines (I.B.M.).

In 1936, the German scientist Konrad Zuse began construction of the Z1, the world's first programmable binary computer. The Z1, built in Zuse's bedroom, was controlled by perforated strips of discarded movie film. His most important contribution was the adoption of the binary system, in which numbers are converted into 0s and 1s—also called digital computing.

The next major leap in computing technology involved the use of vacuum tubes as on/off valves. This enabled calculations to be made electronically rather than mechanically, which resulted in a significant increase in calculating speed. The first use of the vacuum tube in a computing device was in 1938, when Joseph Desch and Robert Mumma built a machine they called the Electronic Accumulator. This machine primed the world for true computers and would be the dominant switching technology for the next 20 years.

◆Notable early computers

The Turing Machine In 1937, the English mathematician Alan Turing, in a paper on the mathematical theory of computation, conceived of the idea for a "universal machine" capable of executing any describable algorithm (set of instructions). Although never built, this theoretical machine, dubbed the Turing Machine, formed the basis for the concept of "computability," separate from the process of calculation.

Colossus Commissioned to crack the secret code used by German Enigma cipher machines during World War II, Colossus was completed in December 1943 by Thomas Flowers at London's Post Office Research Laboratories. Ten Colossus machines were built over the course of the war, but all were destroyed immediately after completing their work to keep the design from falling into enemy hands.

ENIAC The Electronic Numerical Integrator and Computer, or ENIAC, was developed to quickly compute firing and bombing tables for military use, and was completed in 1946. Compared with today's computers, ENIAC was a monster. Composed of 30 separate units (plus power supply and forced-air cooling), it weighed over 30 tons and contained more than 18,000 vacuum tubes, 1,500 relays, and hundreds of thousands of resistors, capacitors, and inductors. Later, ENIAC was put into service for calculations involved in the design of the hydrogen bomb. It served as the nation's main computational workhorse until 1952.

◆The growth of business computers

The transistor—short for transfer resistor—was developed at AT&T Bell Laboratories in 1947 by Walter H. Brattain, William Shockley, and John Bardeen, who were awarded the 1956 Nobel Prize in Physics for their work. The transistor's small size, high yield, low heat production, and low price helped to make the next generation of computers run 1,000 times faster than the previous generation. The first completely transistorized computer, named TRADIC, was developed by Bell Laboratories in 1953.

Transistorized computers were both powerful and affordable enough to be adopted by large corporations around the world. From the mid-1960s on, formerly manual tasks were automated by large mainframe computers; the most popular uses of computers included inventory management, payroll management, file management, and report generation. During this period, the computer landscape was dominated by one company: I.B.M. At one point in the 1960s, 90 percent of the installed computers in the European market were I.B.M. models.

The next leap forward was the invention of the microprocessor or computer chip—a computer processing unit (CPU) contained in an integrated circuit on a tiny piece of silicon—which ushered in the era of modern computers. Nearly all computers in use now have CPUs of varying power and size. Since computer manufacturing shifted from transistors to microprocessors, improvements in computing have come from increases in speed and power, not from entirely new technology. Since the manufacturing technology required to create CPUs is stable, refining the techniques for printing microprocessors allowed for quick reduction in the cost of computer parts, which allowed for new kinds of smaller, portable computers, including machines for home use.

•**Home computing** In 1975, New Mexico–based company MITS (Micro Instrumentation and Telemetry Systems) released what is generally regarded as the world's first true personal computer, the Altair 8800. The Altair was based on Intel's 8080 microprocessor, contained 256 bytes of memory, and sold for $395 in kit form, or $498 assembled. Two thousand Altair 8800s were sold in the first year of release.

I.B.M. released its first personal computer—called, simply enough, the I.B.M. PC—in August 1981. The standard model had 64Kb of RAM (a Kb or *kilobyte* is a thousand bytes; a byte is a small group of 0s and 1s used for computation; RAM is random access memory, used by computers for temporary calculations and storage) and a single 160Kb single-sided floppy disk drive, and sold for $1,565 (without the green-on-black monochrome display). I.B.M. hoped to sell 240,000 units in a five-year period. It received that many orders in the machine's first month of release. In fact, the I.B.M. PC was so successful that its hardware technology and operating system became the industry standard.

Microsoft Microsoft Corporation was founded in 1975 by Bill Gates and Paul Allen. Their first product was a version of the BASIC programming language, which they sold to MITS for use in its Altair computers. The key to their long-lasting success, however, was their contract with I.B.M. to supply an operating system for the original I.B.M. PC. Whereas earlier operating systems were text-based, Windows was graphical—and supported the click-and-drag operation of a mouse. The first version of Windows, launched in November 1985, required more power than machines of that era could deliver and had little effect on the market. A more fully functional version, Windows 2.0, was released in 1987. But it was version 3.0, released in 1990, that introduced true multitasking to the personal computing environment.

Apple Apple, Inc. was founded in 1976 by Steven Jobs and Steven Wozniak, two former game programmers at Atari. They built their first computer (the prototype for the Apple I) in Jobs's garage.

The first computer from Apple, dubbed the Apple I, was released in 1976. It was based on the MOS 6502 microprocessor and sold for $666.66. Apple's second computer, the Apple II, was introduced in April 1977. Like the Apple I, the Apple II used the MOS 6502 chip, but it included an integrated keyboard and color graphics. The selling price was $1,295. The next iteration, the Apple III, was released in 1980 but was less successful than its predecessors. This was partly due to the unit's higher price and business focus; depending on configuration, the Apple III sold for between $4,340 and $7,800

Apple released the first Macintosh computer in January 1984, supported by an advertisement during that year's Super Bowl broadcast. Based on Motorola's 68000 microprocessor, it incorporated an icon-driven screen interface and mouse input. Priced at $2,495, it was an immediate success and in various incarnations remains the core of Apple's line of computers. By the mid-1980s, Apple had become the fastest-growing company in history, generating at its peak (in 2000) almost $8 billion in revenues

◆**Industry consolidation** As the 1990s started, there were dozens of PC manufacturers, including Acer, I.B.M., Compaq, CompuAdd, Dell, Gateway, Hewlett Packard, Northgate, and Zeos. With the market growing at annual rates in excess of 10 percent, there seemed to be room for everyone. But as the decade progressed, competition became fierce. Minor players dropped by the wayside, and many major players consolidated—one example was the acquisition of Compaq by Hewlett Packard.

As dominant as Microsoft was in the operating systems arena, it was never fully without competition. In the early days of the PC era, that competition came from DOS clones such as Digital Research's DR DOS; in the late 1990s, competition came from an offshoot of the UNIX operating system, called Linux. Linux, first introduced in 1991, is an open source variant of the established UNIX operating system, which was developed by Ken Thompson and Dennis Ritchie in 1975. The Linux operating system was developed by (and named for) Linus Torvalds, a second-year student of computer science at the University of Helsinki. Torvalds permitted his operating system to be distributed free; as a result, it provided a viable alternative to Windows.

◆**Supercomputing** Although the personal computer was the technology story of the 1980s and 1990s, larger computers continued to evolve—into faster, more powerful machines called supercomputers. Used by universities, governments, and corporations, modern supercomputers are actually made up of dozens or hundreds of linked computers that work together on extremely complex mathematical or physics problems such as global climate modeling and weather forecasting.

Seymour Cray was the inventor behind the first commercial supercomputer. Finished in 1976, his Cray-1 contained 200,000 integrated circuits and could perform at 160 million flops (*flops* means floating point operations per second, a measure of computational speed; a million flops is called a megaflop; a billion, a gigaflop; a trillion, a teraflop). Its price was approximately $8.8 million. Throughout the 1980s and 1990s, Cray delivered faster and more powerful supercomputers, including the Cray XMP (1982, 500 megaflops), the Cray-2 (1985, 1.9 gigaflops), and the Cray C90 (1991, 16 gigaflops). Cray Research merged with Silicon Graphics, Inc., in 1996.

I.B.M. Corporation has long been at the forefront of supercomputer development. I.B.M.'s supercomputers include Deep Blue (1996, 1 teraflop), ASCI White (2000, 12.3 teraflops), the ASCI Purple (2005, 100 teraflops), Blue Gene/L (2005, 290 teraflops), and RoadRunner (2008, 1700 teraflops), currently the world's fastest computer.

Day 2: The Internet and the World Wide Web

There are over one and a half billion people connected to the Internet today, and yet before 1990, most people had never even heard of it. People born after 1980 have never known a time when school and work were not affected by this extraordinary technology, one so pervasive that for those who can remember long enough, it is common to refer to the time "before the Internet" as a separate period in history.

For the generation of computer users who first went online after 1995 (and that's most of us), the Internet appeared fully formed, an ever-expanding landscape of information, messages, and distraction. For most people, it has become commonplace to think of the Internet as if it were a single huge entity, a body of information and devices that connects most of the humans on the planet. Few people realize that the Internet had its beginning in the late 1960s, and strictly speaking, the Internet is not information. Actually, the Internet is the remarkable framework that enables us to move information around, an open system designed over several decades to support many kinds of networks and applications, although most people recognize only two of those networks: the World Wide Web and e-mail.

The first incarnation of the Internet, called ARPANET, was proposed in 1967 as a research project by the U.S. Department of Defense. The main aim of the project was to enable reliable communication between two computers by using *packet switching*, the relay of information bundled into chunks or packets. The first two nodes of this network were at UCLA and the Stanford Research Institute, then part of Stanford University. It became operable in 1969. E-mail was first conceived in 1972 and quickly became the main service provided by ARPANET. As the single main network of the day, ARPANET was seen as a communication and research tool meant for a limited number of sites; the original specification described a maximum of 256 host mainframes. The protocol TCP/IP—a standard for packet transfer, particularly how to handle smooth data flow if transfer was interrupted—was proposed, and the word *Internet* first used in 1974. For many in the computer industry, the two things are synonymous, as the term *Internet* referred to the ability of TCP/IP to enable communication between separate networks, "inter-networking" them.

By 1981, more than 200 host computers were connected to ARPANET, with new hosts being added every 20 days. In 1983,

ARPANET formally adopted TCP/IP as its official protocol, and the federal government began requiring that network-related contracts support TCP/IP, helping to promote it as the de facto engine of the Internet. Also that year, a new service allowed for the use of *domain names*, unique and meaningful identifiers for networked devices and files. Still in use, the domain name system matches up a computer's network address (a long complex number that describes its location in the network) to an arbitrary name. This allows users to remember a Web address as www.nytimes.com, for example, instead of a seemingly meaningless string of numbers.

ARPANET was not the only network active in the 1980s; many government and private networks were created, serving dedicated and often isolated research and academic communities, all transferring information via TCP/IP. In 1985, the National Science Foundation founded (and funded) NSFNET to serve the broader academic community regardless of discipline, with a significant caveat—no commercial activity allowed. With universities eager to take advantage of government-funded infrastructure improvements, NSFNET grew quickly, while the commercial restriction had two important effects on the development of the Internet: it helped foster an environment of open collaboration, planting the idea that information should be free, and it also spurred private commercial interests to develop competing infrastructural networks.

◆**The World Wide Web**   Although most people use the terms *Internet* and *World Wide Web* interchangeably, they are actually different entities. In the same way that television broadcasting is different from television programming, the Internet is the structure or medium, while the World Wide Web is one of the kinds of content that the Internet makes possible. The World Wide Web was invented in 1989 at Switzerland's CERN Particle Physics Library by Tim Berners-Lee. The Web applies the concept of hypertext linking, originally developed to interconnect bibliographic citations for academic papers, to Internet documents. The concept of hypertext was very simple: every online computer and file has a unique location in the network, so any networked document can contain one or more references (called *hyperlinks*) to any other by simply indicating the location or URL—the address that shows the name of the server and the precise virtual location of the document on that server—of the other document. Along with the idea of finding documents by URL, a simple markup language called HTML (hypertext markup language), made creating new hyperlinked documents easy. The number of hyperlinked pages making up the Web quickly mushroomed.

ARPANET was decommissioned in 1990, and the NSF lifted the ban on commercial traffic in 1991, clearing the way for the commercial Internet. Still, until Netscape shocked the financial world with its 1995 IPO (first day of trading saw the stock close at $75/share, inaugurating the first Internet stock market boom), most people thought of the Internet as a purely academic curiosity, a tool for trading research papers. Most activity over the Internet was text-based, and Web browsers were unfamiliar to many, mostly limited to terminals at university campuses and large libraries.

In 1995, there were 25 million users connected to the Internet worldwide. The number of users exploded to 527 million by the end of 2001, and has grown to over 1.6 billion by 2009. According to the U.S. Census Bureau, 190.6 million American adults (85 percent) had access to the Internet in 2008, either from home or work. The rapidity of this growth can be attributed to several factors: private commercial investment in infrastructure gave incentive for companies to develop high-speed access for homes and offices; a generation of students graduated from college with expectations of chatting, e-mailing, and browsing online; and businesses migrated many internal and external communications to e-mail and set up company presences online. Also, during the 1990s, the increased power and lower prices of desktop and laptop computers encouraged people to buy them for uses beyond the office, both widening the context and environments for going online, and providing market incentive to Internet service providers (ISPs) such as AOL, CompuServe, and Earthlink. For many people, access to the Internet helped to make the decision whether to buy a home computer, since an Internet connection was now a means of corresponding and socializing.

◆**Organizing the Web**   Calculating the precise size of the Web is extremely difficult, but according to the analytic firm Netcraft.com, there are were at least 231 million unique Web site domains in early 2009, though the total number of visitable pages is likely to be several times higher, since any domain contains some uncounted number of pages or blogs. For example, the social network Facebook reports more than twice that many members, each having a unique page, so the number of individual Web pages is vast.

Since its earliest days, the building blocks of content on the Internet and WWW have been people's thoughts and writings sent out into cyberspace, and many pages on the Web are still created by individuals and small groups. In the late 1990s, sophisticated tools and services made creating new Web pages simpler, often removing the need to know any HTML, fueling the rapid expansion of the Web. Added to this was the growing number of companies that realized that a Web presence was a requirement for any business. As the Web grew, directory sites such as Yahoo! became increasingly important. As businesses realized that the Web was too large and too crowded to expect that customers would find them by browsing alone, an entire economy related to Web advertising was born, and this helped to launch an early Internet giant, Google.

Google, a search engine launched in 1998 by a pair of Stanford students, Larry Page and Sergey Brin, dispensed with the idea of a managed directory altogether. Instead, they developed their service around search, with automated programs scouring the Web link by link and indexing everything they found. Thanks to a proprietary system for ranking search results, Google was able to deliver more accurate results than its numerous competitors. In 1999, Google handled 3 million searches a day, but by 2004 that number had risen to 200 million. Today, analysts estimate that 2 billion searches are done on Google each day.

Google went public in 2004, raising more than $1.6 billion in an initial public offering, and today has more than 10,000 employees. From its beginnings in search and search advertising, Google has quickly expanded and offers an evolving group of free utilities, applications, and services, all under the grandly stated company mission to organize the world's knowledge.

That mission statement, when mixed with the company's imperative to mind its bottom line, typifies both the paradoxical nature of business on the Web and also the main tension of the commercial Web itself. The complexity lies in the business requirement to make money from information and services that most people expect for free. Additionally, the copying and sharing of online content has complicated businesses' relationships to their own intellectual and commercial property. Google has run afoul of the book publishing industry repeatedly in this regard during its effort to reproduce scans of copyrighted works online as part of Google book search. That compromises have been reached thus far point to both the disruptive, game-changing nature of the Internet for traditional businesses like print publishing, and also to Google's importance to the Internet. In that sense, Google is one of the keystone online businesses that demonstrate the power of the Internet to affect industries outside of cyberspace. Along with challenges to traditional commerce models that have come from sites like ebay.com, craigslist.org, and amazon.com, Google continues to expand its reach beyond just search.

Online search is as important as ever, as one of the most common uses of the Web is finding answers or explanations quickly. While search is still the cornerstone of finding information online, there are significant alternative efforts to organize and present information. The most notably successful example is wikipedia.org, a free, multilanguage, volunteer-written encyclopedia. Since it began in 2001, wikipedia.org has already amassed over 2.7 million volunteer-submitted articles—over 1 billion words—in English alone. Wikipedia is the best known example of a *wiki*, a Web site that greatly simplifies creation of new, linked pages by way of a special syntax. Also, wikis generally are configured to allow for large numbers of writers and editors; wikipedia.org reports having over 9 million registered users and an unknown number of additional anonymous contributors.

The large number of contributors, the ease of editing or creating a page, and the wild success of wikipedia.org, has led to significant controversy regarding whether any information found there can be considered as authoritative as a traditional encyclopedia. Critics say that wikipedia.org and sites like it offer too much information with too little authority, and many educational institutions forbid citing Wikipedia as a source in formal writings. Advocates point to the rapidity and enthusiasm with which questionable points in articles are identified, flagged, and dissected. And for many people, the Web is a vast, free, interlinked encyclopedia of facts and explanations on every conceivable topic, an idea that has shaped the Internet since the ARPANET days.

Weekend 9: The World on the Brink

Day 1: The Cold War

The partnership among the British Empire, the United States, and the Soviet Union during World War II was uneasy in the best of times. But as victory neared and the three powers began planning in earnest for a new world order, ideological differences and conflicting agendas frayed the bonds that had held the coalition together for four years.

In February 1945, the U.S. president Franklin Roosevelt, British prime minister Winston Churchill, and Soviet leader Joseph Stalin mapped out their vision of a postwar world. The Soviets claimed a sphere of influence over Eastern Europe and joined the British, Americans, and French in a joint occupation of Germany.

Roosevelt died suddenly on April 12, so when the victors next convened in the German city of Potsdam in July 1945, Harry Truman had replaced Franklin Roosevelt while Britain had changed prime ministers in the middle of the proceedings, with Clement Attlee taking over from Churchill. Only Stalin remained from the original Big Three, giving him a stronger hand at the negotiating table. Anglo-American concerns over the future of a democratic Poland strained relations with Stalin, who opposed the Polish government-in-exile based in London. After the Soviets installed a pro-Soviet Communist government in Poland, Churchill, now leader of the opposition in the House of Commons, traveled to the United States to deliver a speech in which he declared that an "iron curtain" had fallen in Europe, dividing east from west. The speech, given in March 1946, could be viewed as the formal declaration of what became known as the "Cold War."

Maps all over the globe were adjusted to account for geopolitical realities of the new conflict. The Korean peninsula was divided into a Communist north and a pro-Western, democratic south. The occupation of Germany hardened into what appeared to be a permanent division of the country into an American-aligned West Germany (formally known as the Federal Republic of Germany) and pro-Soviet East Germany (or the German Democratic Republic). The former capital of Germany, Berlin, was split into east and west, serving as a lonely pro-Western outpost in the heart of Communist East Germany.

As East–West relations grew more tense, a young American diplo-mat in Moscow, George Kennan, dispatched an 8,000-word telegram arguing that the Soviets were intent on expansion. The United States and the West, he wrote, could outlast the Soviets by containing it within its already established sphere of influence. Kennan's influential telegram provided the framework for President Truman's announcement, in early 1947, that Washington would oppose the spread of communism throughout the world. The strategy, known as the Truman Doctrine, was put into place immediately in Greece and Turkey, both of which were battling Communist insurgencies.

The first close encounter between the two superpowers took place in Germany in 1948, when the Soviets closed roads leading to West Berlin, thus denying vital supplies to civilians and Allied soldiers in that portion of the city. The United States responded by resupplying the city by air until the Soviets backed down and reopened access. The success of the Berlin airlift was a huge propaganda victory for the U.S., but it also hard-ened attitudes between the two superpowers.

The Berlin crisis helped set the stage for the foundation of a new anti-Soviet, transatlantic alliance known as the North Atlantic Treaty Organization. Founded in 1949, NATO consisted of the United States, Canada, and the nations of western Europe. Members declared that an attack on one of its signatories would be considered an attack on all. The Communist equivalent of NATO was called the Warsaw Pact, signed in Poland in 1955.

The U.S. and its allies had a key advantage over the Soviets and their allies in the immediate postwar years: America's uncontested control of nuclear weaponry. But that changed in August 1949, when the Soviets stunned America and the world with news that it successfully tested its own atomic bomb. That same year, the Western effort to contain com-munism suffered a tremendous shock when Chinese Communists led by Mao Zedong drove the pro-West nationalist movement out of power. Mao's success, coming on the heels of the Soviets' successful nuclear effort, inspired a wave of political finger-pointing in the United States. A number of Americans were arrested on charges of passing nuclear technology to Moscow, raising the specter of Communist traitors in the highest ranks of the U.S. government.

On June 25, 1950, Communist forces in North Korea launched a surprise attack on pro-Western South Korea. The United States argued that the United Nations ought to come to South Korea's defense because of the North Korean aggression. When the Soviet Union boycotted a U.N. session during the debate, the U.S. motion to defend South Korea passed. With the United States supplying the bulk of the troops under the leadership of General Douglas MacArthur, the U.N. operation pushed North Korean troops from the deep south to the Yalu River, which divided the two Koreas. But when MacArthur continued to push further north, Communist China entered the war on North Korea's side. The war bogged down in a stalemate, and MacArthur was removed from command by Truman. Combat ceased with an uneasy truce in 1953.

Fear of communism helped the Republicans win the presidency for the first time since 1928 with war hero Dwight Eisenhower at the top of the ticket. Eisenhower's choice for vice president spoke to the nation's concerns about the Soviet threat—he selected a young senator from California named Richard Nixon, who had made his name as one of Capitol Hill's strongest anticommunists.

Communism's string of advances and the possibility of Americans serving as Soviet agents inspired a wave of public concern that the United States was losing the Cold War. Senator Joseph McCarthy, a Republican from Wisconsin, fanned the flames of anxiety with accusations that he had information about the existence of Soviet agents within the U.S. government. McCarthy rose from political obscurity to become the country's leading anticommunist zealot. His policy of innuendo and guilt by association set the stage for a larger congressional campaign against suspected Communists in Hollywood as well as in government. The senator's smear tactics led to the coining of a new word—*McCarthyism*. His career came to a crashing end in 1953, however, when he accused the U.S. Army of harboring Communists. The subsequent Army–McCarthy hearings, broadcast live on television, led to sharp public criticism of the Senator's reckless accusations. The Senate formally censured McCarthy in 1954. He died, ravaged by alcohol, in 1957.

The Soviets and Americans continued to develop, test, and deploy a huge and widely scattered stockpile of nuclear weapons, enough to destroy the world several times over. The most frightening arms race in human history followed as both sides sought to maintain superiority over the other.

Politicians and military planners looked for strategic openings through surrogate wars outside of Europe. Korea was the first of several conflicts between the Soviets and the United States. In the late 1950s, both superpowers looked to gain strategic advantage as the old European imperial powers began to withdraw from their colonial possessions in Southeast Asia and sub-Saharan Africa.

Power changed hands in Moscow for the first time since the 1920s when Joseph Stalin died in 1953 and was succeeded by Nikita Khrushchev, a former coal miner. Khrushchev stunned members of the Soviet Communist Party in 1956, when he delivered a long speech denouncing Stalin's murderous regime. The "secret speech" was a milestone in Cold War history, for it marked the first time that a high Communist official acknowledged the brutality of Stalin's rule.

 Khrushchev was well aware of the significance of the "secret speech." In 1961, he met with the young, newly elected president of the United States, John F. Kennedy, in Vienna. During their summit, the older, more experienced Khrushchev dominated the talks with a litany of criticism of American policy and capitalism. The Vienna summit heightened Cold War tensions as both sides prepared for a conflict over continued Western control of West Berlin. That portion of the city became an oasis for East Germans looking to escape Communist rule. In late summer, 1961, the East Germans began construction on a wall that divided the city, stopped the flow of refugees, and served as a symbol of the Cold War.

Khrushchev, believing Kennedy was weak and ineffective, upped the great power ante in 1962, when the Soviets began building nuclear missile sites on Cuba, 90 miles off the coast of Florida. U.S. intelligence provided President Kennedy with evidence of the buildup, leading the president to order a blockade of the island in October 1962. The tense standoff ended when Soviet vessels turned away rather than confront the U.S. naval blockade. The Soviets agreed to dismantle the sites, while the U.S. secretly agreed to remove missiles from Turkey.

The Cuban missile crisis was the closest the Cold War ever came to a nuclear confrontation. During the ensuing years, however, the two superpowers engaged in surrogate wars in Asia and Africa. America's attempt to halt a Communist insurgency in South Vietnam, an extension of its involvement in the Korean conflict, lasted more than a decade, and ended with a Communist victory in 1975. An estimated 3 million Vietnamese died, as did 58,000 American troops.

During his presidency (1969–74), Richard Nixon, who had made his name as an anticommunist, initiated a new strategy of engagement with the Soviets, called détente. The policy led to bilateral talks aimed at reducing nuclear arsenals. However, cooperation gave way to renewed confrontation when the Soviets invaded Afghanistan in 1979. Nixon's 1972 trip to China to meet with Mao and other Chinese leaders was much more successful, at least from the point of view of trade and economic growth.

President Jimmy Carter led a widespread boycott of the 1980 Summer Olympics in Moscow to protest the invasion. Carter lost a reelection bid in November 1980, when Ronald Reagan captured the White House after promising to take a tougher stand against the Soviets. In 1983, during a speech in Florida, Reagan described the Soviet Union as an "evil empire." He deployed a new generation of intermediate-range nuclear missiles in Europe and increased defense spending by hundreds of billions of dollars. The Soviets were hard-pressed to react, in part because of instability at the top. Three Soviet leaders, Leonid Brezhnev, Yuri Andropov, and Konstantin Chernenko, all died between 1982 and 1985.

Mikhail Gorbachev emerged from the chaos to become general secretary of the Soviet Communist Party—the nation's de facto leader—in March 1985. He instituted new policies of *glasnost* ("openness") and *perestroika* ("reform"), which impressed Western leaders. Reagan and Gorbachev engaged in a series of four remarkable summit meetings from 1986 to 1988 that produced historic reductions in nuclear arsenals.

The Soviet-dominated nations of Eastern Europe began to dislodge themselves from Moscow's grip. In November 1989, East Germany announced an end to travel restrictions to the West, making the Berlin Wall superfluous. The wall came down, and so did Communist regimes in Czechoslovakia, Hungary, Romania, Bulgaria, Poland, and East Germany itself. The momentum carried all the way to Moscow. On Christmas Day 1991, Mikhail Gorbachev signed an order formally dissolving the Soviet Union. The twilight struggle between East and West had come to an unexpected end.

Day 2: Nuclear Weapons

In 1939, physicist Leo Szilard met with his former teacher Albert Einstein on Long Island, New York, to discuss two startling developments taking place in Europe. The German physicists Otto Hahn and Fritz Strassman had published their discovery of nuclear fission, the process of splitting off neutrons from an atomic nucleus. Moreover, the German military had seized uranium mines in Czechoslovakia and halted the sale of uranium ore. It was obvious to Szilard that the Germans had discovered both the process and the fuel to make a nuclear weapon. He convinced Einstein to write to President Franklin D. Roosevelt to inform him of the threat.

In response to Einstein's letter, President Roosevelt set about formulating and implementing a massive, secret program to develop nuclear technology, and in less than six years nuclear weapons went from obscure theory to dreadful reality. In the United States, the project to develop a nuclear bomb was called the Manhattan Project and was staffed by hundreds of scientists in 30 secret locations, the most famous of which was the laboratory complex at Los Alamos, New Mexico. The Manhattan Project was headed by J. Robert Oppenheimer, often called the "father of the bomb."

Between 1939 and 1945, a constant stream of innovations in physics and chemistry proved the practicality of nuclear fission research for both power and weapons. Much of the experimental hands-on work took place in the three-year period between 1942 and 1945. Enrico Fermi created the first working nuclear reactor at the University of Chicago in December 1942. Two months later, construction of a uranium enrichment plant in Oak Ridge, Tennessee, began. Two months after that, the Los Alamos team began to assemble. By mid-1944, Los Alamos scientists were testing fissile properties of enriched uranium.

By the time the first prototypes of the bomb were being readied in the end of June 1945, Hitler had already committed suicide, the Germans had surrendered, and the Allied powers were busy dividing the country. Meanwhile, nuclear tests at Los Alamos continued. The first bomb test on July 16, 1945, code-named Trinity, released 20 kilotons of force, the equivalent of 20,000 tons of TNT. The following day, 70 Los Alamos scientists signed a petition urging President Harry S. Truman not to use the bomb on Japanese targets unless Japan first had been given the chance to surrender. Ten days later, Truman issued an ultimatum to Japan, which was ignored. Meanwhile, two bombs were readied for deployment.

"Little Boy," the 15-kiloton uranium bomb dropped on Hiroshima, Japan, on August 6, 1945, was detonated in the air over the city at a height that would maximize the explosion's reach. It released a fireball 1,200 feet in diameter of unimaginable heat—7,200 degrees Fahrenheit. The bomb instantly vaporized thousands of people and sent out a shockwave that shredded much of the city. What was left caught fire. More than 80,000 people were killed immediately. Radiation poisoning killed some of the survivors and debilitated more. In all, as many as 140,000 people were killed by the Hiroshima bomb. "Fat Man," with improved design and more volatile plutonium fuel, was dropped three days later on Nagasaki and released 21 kilotons, though, as Nagasaki sits in a protected valley, killed fewer—40,000. Japan surrendered six days later.

The debate over Truman's decision to unleash such a devastating attack on civilian populations has not abated even today. Supporters argue that the lives of hundreds of thousands of soldiers were saved by avoiding an invasion of Japan. Opponents contend that the first bomb should have been dropped on an unpopulated area.

◆**Nuclear Weapons after Hiroshima**   The speed and urgency of wartime development of the theoretical physics, experimental knowhow, and military infrastructure needed to make the United States a nuclear power reflected the widely held belief that first Germany and then the Soviet Union were developing a nuclear weapon. Subsequent historical research, however, casts doubt on any of these powers as early innovators in the area; paradoxically, most of the early innovations in the Soviet nuclear weapons program could be traced to stolen secrets delivered by Klaus Fuchs, a Los Alamos scientist who delivered intelligence to Soviet agents between 1944 and 1946.

Even before World War II ended, the U.S. had become wary of Stalin's U.S.S.R. and knew that the Soviet scientists were racing to develop comparable nuclear technology. It was only a matter of time before the Soviet Union would "have the bomb," even though it did not become clear until later how much Soviet progress was due to espionage. The timing of Fuchs's stay at Los Alamos is crucial to the nuclear arms race, since he was not able to deliver any detailed information about new, improved bomb designs that were developed after his tenure there had ended.

Both "Little Boy" and "Fat Man" got their explosive force from a fission-derived chain reaction. At the time, these were misleadingly called "atomic bombs" or "A-bombs," though they are now referred to as "single-stage nuclear weapons." At Los Alamos, scientists discovered that bombs could be augmented by including a mixture of deuterium and tritium gases in the weapon's core. This led to work on a new kind of nuclear bomb design that used a second stage, a *fusion* reaction initiated by the X-rays generated by the initial *fission* reaction. These fission-fusion weapons are dramatically more powerful than single-stage fission weapons. In the 1950s, these were referred to as "hydrogen bombs" or "H-bombs," though we now know them as "two-stage" or "*thermo*nuclear weapons." Many Los Alamos scientists were opposed to development of the H-bomb, saying that such weapons would only be useful against targets such as civilian cities and towns, not military troops.

The U.S.S.R.'s first successful A-bomb test had taken place in 1949, much sooner than U.S. predictions, and citing the seemingly inevitable Soviet discovery of the new weapon, work on the H-bomb continued. U.S. scientists conducted tests of increasingly refined and destructive bombs, magnifying their yield from kilotons to megatons, while suspecting that Soviet work was close behind. In the 1950s, most U.S. nuclear weapons tests were performed either at U.S.-controlled Pacific islands or in Nevada testing facilities. According to the Department of Energy, a total of 106 tests were conducted on or near Bikini, Christmas, Johnston, and Enewetak Islands, before the dangers and extent of fallout radiation were well understood. (Those islands remain radioactively "hot" today.) The first successful two-stage thermonuclear weapon test, code-named "Mike," was off Enewetak Island in the South Pacific on November 1, 1952. It released 10.4 megatons of force, nearly 1,000 times the explosive yield of "Little Boy," and completely destroyed the island it was on, leaving only a crater in the ocean floor. The first Soviet thermonuclear detonation took place the following year, on August 12, 1953.

Rocket technology was improving, and nuclear-armed rockets began testing in the early 1950s, but rocket range was limited. Military strategy of the time relied on the assumption that an enemy's weapons would have to be housed in silos or carried by large planes. In the early 1950s, the reasoning behind military nuclear strategy was to prepare a large, overwhelming force that could eliminate an enemy's weapons with a single, indefensible "first strike."

When newly elected President John F. Kennedy appointed Robert McNamara as secretary of defense in 1961, U.S. military strategy underwent a dramatic shift. McNamara was a proponent of the doctrine of "mutually assured destruction," which stated that the best way to deter an enemy was to stockpile such an overabundance of weapons and keep them readied in such a variety of places that a retaliatory "second strike" would be unpreventable. To this end in 1961, the Air Force's Strategic Air Command began mission Looking Glass, in which one of a fleet of modified, nuclear-armed Boeing EC-135Cs remained in the air continuously for over 29 years, to provide an airborne base of military command in the case of a large-scale attack on ground posts. The global nuclear picture now looked complicated and precarious, as the two superpowers tried to locate ever-increasing numbers of weapons in locations all over the planet.

The nuclear arms race reached its crisis point in 1962, when a Soviet missile base was discovered under construction in Cuba, prompting what was to be called the "Cuban missile crisis." The U.S. Navy quarantined Cuba, prompting a duel between President Kennedy and Prime Minister Nikita Khrushchev that put the world at the precarious edge of a nuclear conflict. In the end, Khrushchev agreed to remove the weapons, and Kennedy secretly ordered U.S. missiles removed from Turkey.

In the wake of the near-cataclysm, both the U.S. and U.S.S.R. began a period of nuclear détente, gradually limiting the scope of nuclear weapons testing. In 1963, the U.S. and U.S.S.R. agreed to halt all aboveground and airborne nuclear tests. (Since 1963, all U.S. tests have been underground, and almost all have taken place in Nevada testing facilities.) Strategic Arms Limitation Talks (SALT) held between the U.S. and U.S.S.R. between 1969 and 1972 resulted in the Anti-Ballistic Missile Treaty, which limited the number of ballistic missiles in either nation's stockpile. In 1976, the U.S. and U.S.S.R. agreed to limit tests to fewer than 150 kilotons. SALT II talks, held between 1972 and 1979, resulted in agreements to limit the total number of strategic weapons for either nation, though the treaty was never ratified by the United States and President Reagan withdrew from SALT II in 1986.

♦**Arms reduction after the Cold War**   At the end of the Cold War, the U.S. and U.S.S.R. had a combined stockpile of more than 40,000 nuclear warheads, down from the Cold War peak of 70,000.

Building on détente-based agreements from the 1970s, two international agreements in 1995 and 1996 banned further nuclear weapons testing outright; the 1995 Nuclear Nonproliferation Treaty was a U.N. initiative to limit nuclear weapons to those states that had them already, and the 1996 Comprehensive Nuclear Test Ban Treaty prohibited any nuclear testing by any state. In 2002, the Strategic Offensive Reductions Treaty (SORT, also known as the Moscow Treaty) was signed between the U.S. and Russia; it contained agreements to reduce the number of active warheads to between 1,700 and 2,200 by 2012.

In the United States, there is a publicly known process for dismantling old nuclear weapons, but in the case of the old Soviet stockpile, the process is much less regulated, and there is widespread international concern regarding the state of the Russian/Soviet stockpile amid speculation of nuclear weapons smuggling and theft in Eurasia. Although Russian officials deny that any nuclear materials have been stolen, fairly numerous anecdotal accounts, including those from former military, black marketeers, and smugglers suggest otherwise.

✦**New nuclear powers** The various treaties and agreements aimed at reducing the number of thermonuclear weapons worldwide have not prevented other nations from researching nuclear weapons production. When the Nuclear Nonproliferation Treaty was signed in 1995, three nations declined to sign and a fourth acceded and then violated the treaty. Perhaps unsurprisingly, those nations—India, Israel, Pakistan, and North Korea respectively—all subsequently became nuclear weapons powers. The current list of nuclear weapons states contains these four plus the United States, Russia, the United Kingdom, France, and China. In addition, current international scrutiny focuses on Iran's suspected nuclear weapons program.

The emergence of two rogue groups—the global Islamic terrorism network and the global arms black market—complicates the picture considerably. Much of the suspected resources of these two groups is thought to originate in stolen Russian or Soviet materials (referred to as "loose nukes"). Moreover, due to the affinity between Islamic terrorist groups and radical Islamic factions inside Iran, there is great concern about Iran's potential participation (willing or not) in augmenting the striking capabilities of rogue groups.

Weekend 10: The Universe

Day 1: The Big Bang, Stars, and Galaxies

In the winter of 1610, the Italian scientist Galileo Galilei, using a telescope he had designed, saw the night skies as they had never been seen before. He observed the face of the Moon, identified sunspots, and puzzled over the changing illumination of Venus over a period of weeks. He saw moons of Jupiter that vanished and reappeared periodically. He saw that the Milky Way is not merely a whitish band across the sky but consists of a vast number of stars, far more than the few thousand visible to the naked eye. Though human beings had been studying the sky for centuries, Galileo was the first to observe its elements at high magnification—and the conclusions he drew from those observations would change the way human beings understand both the universe and our place in it.

Astronomy is unique among the sciences because most of the objects it studies are not directly accessible; huge distances separate Earth from even nearby astronomical objects. With the exception of bodies in our own solar system, all the objects are too far away for direct sampling or spacecraft reconnaissance (techniques in use for only a few decades). Instead, information about distant objects is gleaned from the collection, analysis, and interpretation of electromagnetic radiation—light, X-rays, and other forms of energy given off by all objects in the universe. Collection of data is done through the use of a variety of telescopes far more powerful and sophisticated than the device used by Galileo some 400 years ago.

No single astronomical instrument has changed the way we perceive the universe more than the Hubble Space Telescope, launched into space by the United States in 1990. Named after the great 20th-century astronomer Edwin Hubble, the telescope sent back images that were like nothing ever seen. Since it observes from a low orbit in space, the Hubble telescope captures images undistorted by Earth's atmosphere and is able to record more clearly very faint amounts of light from the farthest and darkest parts of the universe. More than 6,000 articles based on data from the Hubble have been published, including a more accurate dating of the age of the universe (14 billion years), information on how galaxies form, the discovery of numerous extrasolar planets, as well as new theories about the nature of energy and gravity. In 2013, the Hubble will be replaced by the even more powerful James Webb Telescope, which will be sent deeper into space.

◆**The Universe** The contents of the universe range in size from individual gas atoms and dust grains to enormous clusters and superclusters of galaxies. As Galileo began to observe, these contents are in a constant state of flux in relation to one another: planets orbit stars, stars collapse or explode, galaxies expand and contract.

The Sun and all other stars are massive bodies of gas that undergo fusion reactions in their core. As a result of these reactions, stars emit visible light as well as electromagnetic radiation at other wavelengths. Temperature, mass, and luminosity are properties of all stars: the brightest stars are also the highest in both mass and temperature. Small stars are called *dwarfs*—the brightest are blue dwarfs, the dimmest are red dwarfs. Brown dwarfs are bodies too small to be classified as stars, but too large to be planets, at between 13 and 80 times the mass of Jupiter. They glow dimly as a result of energy released by gravitational contraction.

Almost half the stars in the visible universe are actually part of a binary system—pairs of stars that orbit each other. Astronomers can sometimes see both stars, but more commonly they identify binaries by observing the influence of the dimmer star's gravitational pull on the other. Sometimes material from one star in a binary collides with the other, causing a phenomenon called a *nova*, in which the luminosity of the star system dramatically increases.

A *supernova* occurs when old stars explode, resulting in a phenomenon many times brighter than an ordinary nova. In fact, Chinese astronomers in A.D. 1054 reported a supernova that was visible in the daytime. The remnants of these explosions are usually termed *nebulas*, interstellar clouds of dust, hydrogen gas, and plasma that emit light as a result of energy from stars ionizing the gas. Some patches of dust reflect the light of nearby stars and seem to glow. The most striking nebulas consist of glowing gas surrounded by opaque dust or vice versa, which gives the nebula a definite shape.

At the center of many nebulas is a neutron star, sometimes called a *pulsar*. A neutron star is one that has collapsed in a violent explosion so powerful that the gravity compacting the star's atomic matter is stronger than the nuclear forces that normally keep individual subatomic particles from touching. All the star's neutrons and protons can touch, forming the equivalent of a giant atomic nucleus. The star is electrically neutral because of the charge of the collapsed electrons. Such a star may be only a dozen miles in diameter but may have a mass twice that of the Sun. Pulsars are neutron stars that emit electromagnetic signals from their magnetic poles in a direction that reaches Earth. As the star rotates, the light appears to "pulse" from the star, in an effect similar to the rotation of a lighthouse beacon.

Another possible result of a supernova explosion is the creation of a *black hole*. This occurs when a stellar body becomes so dense for its size that not even light can escape its powerful gravitational pull. Black holes have been observed at the center of many galaxies, including our own.

Young stars like our Sun "burn" hydrogen in a nuclear fusion process resulting in helium. When a star has consumed all the hydrogen in its core, new fusion reactions begin, changing the helium to carbon. The new reactions are much hotter than the earlier fusion of hydrogen to helium, and this added energy causes the relatively cool outer layers of hydrogen and helium to expand and turn red, creating what's known as a *red giant*. When the Sun becomes a red giant in the distant future, it will expand almost to the orbit of Earth, completely engulfing Mercury and Venus, and charring Earth to a cinder.

Until 1995, our Sun was the only star known to have planets. Since then, however, hundreds of planets have been detected orbiting other stars. Many of these extrasolar planets orbit their star at very close distances, but astronomers have also found systems similar to ours, with Jovian-sized planets at large distances from their stars.

There are also objects called *quasars* that produce far too much energy to be stars. No one knows for sure what they are, but there is some evidence that quasars are energy torrents from black holes in the center of distant galaxies, so distant their light has not yet reached Earth.

◆**Galaxies** Ordinary matter is believed to form only 5 percent of the universe by mass. Galaxies—systems of many stars separated from one another by largely empty space—rotate in a way that indicates they must be embedded in a gravitational field caused by undetectable matter (missing mass, more commonly called "dark matter"), while all galaxies are flying apart with increasing speed caused by some unknown force that opposes gravity (dark energy). There are a number of competing theories as to the nature of these entities. The missing mass may consist of slow-moving unknown subatomic particles, while dark energy might be a cosmological constant inherent to the vacuum of empty space.

Galaxies are classified into several types. A spiral galaxy has a bright, flattened disk of stars, gas, and dust with spiral arms, along with a central bulge and diffuse halo. Elliptical galaxies, on the other hand, are roughly ovular or spherical in shape, with stars orbiting the galaxy center in random directions. Elliptical galaxies contain mostly old stars, have little gas or dust, and show no evidence of ongoing star formation. Galaxies that do not fit the spiral or elliptical descriptions are classified as irregular galaxies. These tend to be smaller than the other types of galaxies and have asymmetrical shapes.

◆**The Milky Way** The galaxy to which our Sun and its planets belong is a spiral galaxy called the Milky Way. It is estimated to contain at least 200 billion stars as well as star-forming material and other matter. The Sun is located about halfway between the center of the galaxy's flattened disk of stars and its edge. The disk contains most of the stars in the galaxy and nearly all of the interstellar gas and dust. The common name Milky Way dates to antiquity and refers to the white "spilled milk" appearance of the night sky when one's vision is directed toward the galactic core.

Clusters and superclusters are groups of galaxies associated in space. There may be just a few members of a cluster or as many as thousands, but they are recognizable by the proximity of galaxies (within clusters) or clusters of galaxies (within superclusters). About 30 galaxies form the Local Group (our cluster), including the Milky Way, the Andromeda galaxy, and the Large and Small Magellanic Clouds. The Local Group is a member of a cluster of galaxies called the Virgo Cluster, which contains over 1,000 galaxies. On an even larger scale, the Virgo Cluster is just one cluster in the Virgo Supercluster, which is a collection of over 1 million galaxies.

◆**The Big Bang**   The Big Bang is the generally accepted theory derived from the observation that as the universe ages, it is rapidly expanding outward in all directions. If the universe is expanding over time, then it must have been smaller as we travel backward in time. The origin of the universe is thought to have been an initial moment when all observable matter was compressed into a tiny space of unimaginable heat and mass, followed by an explosive expansion. Data collected through various astronomical observations support the idea that the universe began in a hotter, denser state than we currently find it. Cosmic expansion is the most direct byproduct, as space continues to stretch outward, carrying galaxies along with it and away from one another. The abundance of hydrogen and helium is naturally explained as having formed during the first extremely hot moments after the Big Bang, when the universe was hot enough to produce matter from energy and fuse hydrogen into helium. The radio glow seen in all directions, known as cosmic background radiation, is the remnant of heat from the Big Bang, weakened by the stretching of space since that time.

The speeds of galaxies combined with their distances from one another allow scientists to estimate how long they have been receding from one another—therefore estimating the time elapsed since the Big Bang. Careful measurements of the recession rate and the cosmic background radiation combine to give an age of the universe of 13.7 billion years. For comparison, the Sun and solar system formed in the Milky Way 4.5 billion years ago.

Day 2: The Sun and Its Family

"We shall place the Sun himself at the center of the Universe," wrote Nicolas Copernicus in his great work *On the Revolutions of the Heavenly Spheres*, published in 1543. This conclusion by the Polish polymath—he was an astronomer, mathematician, physician, diplomat, governor, translator, and Catholic cleric—contradicted the widely held belief that Earth was at the center of the universe. Copernicus was the first to correctly attribute the daily motions of the Sun and stars to the rotation of Earth, annual changes in the appearance of the sky to the orbital motion of Earth around the Sun, and retrograde motion to the relative speeds of planets as they orbit the Sun. His model wasn't entirely correct, however, because it still relied on the perfect circular orbits of planets described by Aristotle. It took 30 years of careful observations by the Danish astronomer Tycho Brahe (1546–1610), and the interpretation of Brahe's data by the German mathematician Johannes Kepler (1571–1630), to show that planets orbit the Sun on elliptical paths, moving faster along their orbits when closer to the Sun, and that there is a precise mathematical relation between a planet's distance from the Sun and the time it takes to complete an orbit.

Today, of course, we know that the star we call the Sun isn't the center of the universe, but rather the center of our solar system, which comprises the Sun and all the objects that orbit it. The Sun, which provides the energy that allows life on Earth to exist, is believed to have been formed out of a molecular cloud some 5 billion years ago and is composed primarily of hydrogen and helium. The temperature of the Sun is approximately 28,280,000 degrees Fahrenheit (15,710,000 Celsius) at its core. By itself it comprises about 98.6 percent of the solar system's mass.

◆Planets The largest objects that orbit the Sun are referred to as planets. These are grouped broadly into two categories: the terrestrial planets and the Jovian planets. The terrestrial planets are the four closest to the Sun: Mercury, Venus, Earth, and Mars. These are composed primarily of silicon-based rock and metals. The Jovian planets include Jupiter, Saturn, Uranus, and Neptune. Jupiter and Saturn are composed mostly of hydrogen gas, whereas Uranus and Neptune are composed of icy cores surrounded by hydrogen atmospheres.

Mercury As the planet closest to the Sun, Mercury has the shortest orbit. Its view from Earth is usually obscured by the Sun's glare, but it is sometimes visible on the horizon just after sunset, when it is called the Evening Star, or just before dawn, when it is called the Morning Star. About 14 times each century, Mercury can also be seen crossing directly in front of the Sun.

It is a waterless, airless world that alternately bakes and freezes as it orbits the Sun. The high temperatures on the sunlit side mean that the planet cannot retain a substantial atmosphere. Its surface is scarred with hundreds of thousands of craters, probably formed during the early history of the solar system, when large numbers of asteroids and comets slammed into planetary surfaces. Many craters have been smoothed over by ancient lava flows. The surface is also crisscrossed by huge cliffs, or scarps, probably formed as Mercury's surface cooled and shrank.

Venus In Earth's night sky, Venus is second only to the Moon in luminousity, as it passes closer to Earth than any other planet. Since it orbits between Earth and the Sun, Venus, like Mercury, can be seen either just before sunrise or just after sunset.

The Venusian atmosphere consists almost entirely of carbon dioxide. Thick clouds shroud the planet's surface from direct view, and droplets of sulfuric acid and water have been identified in the clouds. The clouds and high level of carbon dioxide have combined to trap heat in the lower atmosphere where temperatures are hot enough to melt lead.

More than a thousand geographical features have been identified on the surface of Venus, including mountains, volcanoes, rifts, basins, and impact craters. About 10 percent of the planet's surface is highland terrain, 70 percent rolling uplands, and 20 percent lowland plains. Volcanic activity dominates Venusian geology; the planet is covered with volcanic domes and lava channels.

Earth Third from the Sun, Earth is the only one in the solar system known to harbor life, the result of its distinct atmosphere and the presence of an ozone layer that, together with Earth's magnetic field, blocks deadly radiation. From space, our planet appears as a bright blue-and-white sphere—blue because some 70 percent of the surface is covered by water, and white because clouds cover about half the planet's surface.

Earth's only natural satellite, the Moon, is over one-quarter the size of Earth in diameter. The Moon's rotation and revolution are synchronized, meaning the same side of the satellite always faces Earth. Analysis of Moon rocks brought back to Earth by astronauts has led to the hypothesis that the Moon formed when the collision of a large protoplanet stripped material from Earth's crust.

The Moon is airless and devoid of life. A mixture of fine powder and broken rock blankets the surface. The near side (the side seen from Earth) also has large regions of solidified lava. The surface is pockmarked with craters and larger impact basins and is broken by huge mountain ranges.

Mars The distinctive coloring of the "Red Planet" comes from iron oxide in the soil. The surface is heavily cratered, and there is extensive evidence of once-active volcanoes. Ice caps cover both poles, which advance and recede with changes in the seasons. There are also spectacular features such as Olympus Mons (an extinct volcano three times as high as Earth's Mt. Everest), mammoth canyons, one of which is four times deeper than the Grand Canyon and as wide as the U.S., and a gigantic basin that is larger than Alaska. The two irregularly shaped satellites of Mars are Deimos and Phobos. They are the only satellites besides the Moon that orbit a terrestrial planet; neither Mercury nor Venus have moons.

The big question of whether there is (or was) life on Mars has yet to be answered with certainty. Water once flowed there in great quantities, and the soil is similar to that found in many backyards here on Earth, so the possibility cannot be ruled out.

Jupiter The largest planet in the solar system, Jupiter has 2.5 times more mass than all the other planets of the solar system put together. It has a faint but extensive ring system and more than 60 moons, many of them quite small.

The most prominent feature of Jupiter is its colorful cloud layers. Because the planet spins so fast, its clouds tend to form bands that give the planet a striped appearance. There are numerous eddies and swirls in Jupiter's atmosphere, most famously the Great Red Spot, a massive hurricane located in the southern hemisphere near the equator.

The interior composition of Jupiter is largely a mystery. Its density is only about one-fourth that of the terrestrial planets, indicating that it is composed of light atoms, more than 90 percent of them hydrogen. Although hydrogen normally takes the form of a gas on Earth, it exists in more exotic states at the high pressures inside Jupiter: below a gaseous cloud layer, the hydrogen is compressed into a liquid and then a liquid metal. At the very center of the planet there may be a small core of rocklike and icelike material.

Saturn The sixth planet from the Sun, Saturn is the second largest. It has a pale yellowish color and a spectacular ring system consisting of more than 1,000 rings, which are composed mostly of ice particles and a smaller amount of rocky debris and dust. Some of the rings are circular, others are elliptical, and at least two are intertwined, or "braided." The planet has more than 30 known moons, most of them relatively small and pockmarked by meteor craters. Titan, Saturn's largest moon, is one of the few moons in the solar system known to have an atmosphere. Saturn's atmosphere consists of densely compacted hydrogen, helium, and other gases. Scientists believe there is a solid core of rock about two times the size of Earth at its center.

Uranus The seventh planet in the solar system and the third of the Jovian gas giants, Uranus is a faintly greenish color, perhaps because its atmosphere contains methane. It has a system of faint rings and at least 21 moons. Uranus's atmosphere is very cold, though scientists theorize that, as on Jupiter and Saturn, temperatures and pressures increase dramatically below the outer layer of atmosphere. At some pressure the hydrogen and helium might be sufficiently compressed to form a liquid or slushy surface "crust." Underneath this crust is thought to be a mantle of solidified methane, ammonia, and water, and inside this mantle is a rocky core of silicon and iron.

Neptune The last of the Jovian planets, Neptune is the eighth planet in the solar system. It is a pale bluish color but has a clear atmosphere. Scientists believe Neptune has a three-layered structure similar to that of Uranus: a crust of solidified or liquid hydrogen and helium, a mantle of solidified gases and water, and a hot, rocky core.

•The Planet That Wasn't From 1930 through the end of the 20th century, the solar system was thought to contain nine planets, the ninth being Pluto. In recent years, however, several objects similar to Pluto were discovered in the outer solar system. This caused a rethinking of what makes a planet a planet.

In 2006, the International Astronomical Union (I.A.U.) for the first time defined the term *planet*. In this new definition, a planet is a celestial body that is in orbit around a star, has sufficient mass so that it assumes a nearly round shape, and has cleared its orbit of planetesimals (embryonic planets) and similar debris. Pluto meets only the first two of these criteria. It was thus removed from the rank of major planets and reclassified as a dwarf planet. The I.A.U. classifies a dwarf planet as a celestial body that is in orbit around the Sun, has sufficient mass so that it assumes a nearly round shape, has not cleared its orbit of planetesimals, and is a not a satellite of another similar object. Today, there are five recognized dwarf planets: Pluto, Eris, Ceres, Haumea, and Makemake. Ceres is the largest asteroid in the main asteroid belt between Mars and Jupiter. The other four orbit the Sun on the frozen fringes of the solar system.

◆**Smaller Objects in the Solar System** Asteroids are small objects with compositions similar to the terrestrial planets. They are found primarily in the asteroid belt, a band lying between the orbits of Mars and Jupiter. Smaller numbers are found in orbits that cross those of the terrestrial planets, including Earth's orbit, and others lead or trail a planet along its journey around the Sun. More than 200,000 asteroids are known.

Comets are icy bodies, composed mostly of water ice and carbon dioxide ice. When far from the Sun, comets are essentially in deep freeze, but if a comet's orbit carries it closer to the Sun than Jupiter, significant amounts of the ice evaporate and trail away from the main body of the comet. This forms the comet's distinctive tail. As the ice evaporates, small, solid, grainlike particles mixed in with the ice are also released. The main body of a comet may be only a few kilometers in diameter, but upon close approach to the Sun, the tail may extend for millions of kilometers.

Weekend 11: The United States After the Civil War

Historians date the Gilded Age from the end of the Civil War in 1865 until 1893, when a financial panic led to a steep recession and growing dissent in the nation's cities and on the prairies. Demands for social justice, a more active government, and new protections for working people inaugurated the Progressive Era, which dominated American politics and culture from 1896 until the U.S. entered World War I in 1917. The Progressive agenda, which led to greater government regulation of the marketplace, women's suffrage, and broad political reforms, provided the foundation for Franklin Roosevelt's New Deal beginning in 1933.

Day 1: The Gilded Age

As he surveyed the American social, cultural, and political landscape less than a decade removed from a catastrophic civil war, author Mark Twain coined a descriptive phrase that remains part of the nation's historiography—the Gilded Age. Twain's book, *The Gilded Age: A Tale of Today*, was written in 1873, when federal troops occupied the shattered states of the former Confederacy, when workers in the nation's factories and coal mines chafed under difficult working and living conditions, and when a fledgling domestic terrorist group, the Ku Klux Klan, rode through the Southern night in search of black victims.

The Gilded Age, as Twain described it, was a time when enormous wealth was in the hands of a few American industrialists who built ostentatious mansions—they called them "cottages"—in places like Newport, Rhode Island. It soon became a period of searing social conflict, radical attempts at political and social reform, internal warfare in the West, and great demographic changes in the nation's cities. Labor unrest led to violent confrontations in Chicago and in the coal patches of northeastern Pennsylvania. So-called "radical Republicans" pushed for a true reconstruction of Southern society after the abolition of slavery, while Native Americans in the Great Plains found themselves in the path of a westward rush of pioneers in Conestoga wagons, and people from southern and eastern Europe poured into the nation's seaports, bringing with them alien customs, languages, and traditions.

The narrative of the Gilded Age, then, consists of more than the stories of great fortunes and famous families like the Rockefellers, Vanderbilts, and Carnegies. It includes immigrants, workers, African Americans, women, and union organizers for whom the Gilded Age was a term rich in irony, precisely how Twain meant it.

◆**Fortunes Are Made**   The Gilded Age was born of the transformative Civil War years, during which northern cities, filled with cheap immigrant labor, became industrial behemoths, due in part to Washington's need for armaments. Industrial output continued to grow in the postwar years as the country returned to building its cities and expanding its reach from coast to coast. Completion of the transcontinental railroad in 1869 meant that goods and materials could be moved cheaply and rapidly from one ocean port to another. The following year, 1870, a 31-year-old businessman named John D. Rockefeller sought to capitalize on the country's emerging new source of energy and fuel, forming a company called Standard Oil of Ohio.

Joining Rockefeller as icons of the Gilded Age were a Scottish immigrant named Andrew Carnegie, who made a fortune in the production of steel, and Cornelius Vanderbilt, who invested first in steamships and then in railroads, to create fabulous wealth for himself and his family. All three, along with lesser-known industrialists, were self-made men whose fortunes were derived not from inheritance but from impeccable timing, good luck, shrewd investment, and a ruthless business plan. Rockefeller sought the outright elimination of competitors. Carnegie followed a different model for the Carnegie Steel Company—he bought up his suppliers and the companies that distributed and sold finished products, so the company, which was renamed U.S. Steel when Carnegie sold it to J. P. Morgan, controlled every aspect in the production, distribution, and sale of its steel.

The fortunes made in steel, oil, railroads, and finance led to conspicuous displays of wealth in northern cities, especially in New York, home of Wall Street and many of the nation's new millionaires. Newspapers reported on lavish parties, including one in which the hostess's dog sported a diamond collar said to cost $15,000. Mark Twain summarized the ethos of the age when he asked, rhetorically, "What is the chief end of man?" It was, he wrote, "to get rich. In what way? Dishonestly if we can; honestly if we must."

In fact, dishonesty was not uncommon. In 1869, the financiers Jay Gould and Jim Fisk hatched an audacious scheme to buy up the nation's gold supply in an attempt to manipulate wheat prices and drive up grain traffic on the Erie Railroad, in which they had an investment. The plot reached from Wall Street to the White House, as Gould enlisted the help of President Ulysses S. Grant's son-in-law. The scheme unraveled when the president realized what Fisk and Gould were doing and ordered the government to sell gold on the open market, which depressed prices and foiled the plans of speculators. Gould and Fisk became symbols of a class of industrialists known as "robber barons." Undeterred, Gould sought to win complete control of the Erie Railroad four years later, in 1873, by bribing a fraudulent British aristocrat who promised to bring European investors into the deal. Once again the deal collapsed, but Gould continued to operate as one of the age's most notorious financiers, obtaining control of four railroads and other ventures that helped him compile a fortune of more than $70 million.

◆**Political Corruption** Dishonest wealth, it seemed, was everywhere, including the halls of government. In New York, a powerful political boss named William Tweed and several associates were accused of shaking down contractors and other officials for millions of dollars. Tweed, the boss of New York's Tammany Hall political machine, was arrested, indicted, and imprisoned on corruption charges, and when he died in prison in 1877, his name was linked, and would continue to be linked, with the corrupt excesses of the Gilded Age. He also was the only one of the era's widely known wheeler-dealers who actually served time in prison for his shady dealings.

What Tweed was to municipal politics, the administration of Ulysses S. Grant was to the national scene. Although he was never accused of plotting to enrich himself, Grant presided over an administration that became enmeshed in the financial and corporate scandals of the era. The Credit Mobilier scandal, which broke in 1873, involved efforts by directors of the Union Pacific railroad to enrich themselves through a fictitious corporation, Credit Mobilier. Thirteen members of Congress were implicated in a plot to cover up the payments through Credit Mobilier, but all except two escaped censure. The president's private secretary, Orville Babcock, was indicted in 1875 on charges that he assisted whiskey distillers in their attempt to avoid paying federal taxes. Also, Grant's secretary of war, William Belknap, was impeached on charges that he took bribes from traders on Indian posts. He resigned immediately and so avoided forced removal in a Senate trial. Historians generally regard the Grant administration as one of the most corrupt in U.S. history.

Whatever Grant's failings as an administrator, he does earn high marks from some historians for his willingness to confront a guerrilla counter-revolution in the South as unreconstructed Confederates engaged in terrorism and intimidation to prevent freed slaves from assuming a role in political and civic life. Postwar amendments to the U.S. Constitution granted equal protection to all citizens, native-born and naturalized, and guaranteed the right to vote without regard to color or creed (Gilded Age women, including activists such as Victoria Woodhull, Elizabeth Cady Stanton, and Susan B. Anthony, sought to break the male monopoly on suffrage as well). Grant aggressively sought to protect freedmen from the depredations of the Ku Klux Klan, viewing white violence as a continuation of the Civil War. Grant supported measures to enforce federal election laws and civil rights measures, and he aggressively enforced the Ku Klux Klan Act, passed in 1871, making it a crime to wear disguises—Klan members famously wore white sheets and hoods to hide their identities—and to foment political conspiracies. In 1874, he ordered 5,000 federal troops to New Orleans to crush a white supremacist group called the "White League."

While thousands of federal troops supervised Reconstruction in the South, others were deployed in the West, particularly in the Plains states, as American settlers and railroads continued their inexorable march toward the Pacific coast. The discovery of gold in the Dakotas in 1874 and improved methods of enclosure, which allowed pioneers to graze cattle, increased demand for Native American lands. Just a few weeks before the nation celebrated the 100th anniversary of the Declaration of Independence, General George Armstrong Custer and more than 250 troops were killed fighting the Sioux at the Little Bighorn River in Montana. The following year, the U.S. cavalry routed the Nez Perce tribe in Oregon. The tribe was forced to march from its homeland to a reservation in Oklahoma. But even the reservations were not sacrosanct: in 1887, the Dawes Act split up reservations into individual plots of land. Those plots deemed "surplus" were turned over to white settlers, who purchased them from the government.

•**Financial Failures** As industrialists created great fortunes and entrepreneurial pioneers followed rutted paths through the Plains and across the Rocky Mountains, wage earners in the North and Midwest struggled to earn a living during a long and deep economic recession. Hard times followed the collapse of the Philadelphia-based banking firm Jay Cooke & Company in 1873. The Cooke failure created a financial panic on Wall Street, leading to years of economic contraction or at best, sluggish growth. Thousands of businesses failed, driving the unemployment rate to nearly 15 percent by the mid-1870s. Railroad workers suffered as dozens of rail companies went bankrupt, leading to a series of strikes that crippled rail shipping in the summer of 1877. The new president, Rutherford B. Hayes, dispatched federal troops to break the strike, but workers resisted. More than 100 strikers and soldiers were killed in violent clashes before rail service returned to normal.

Hayes had the manpower to send to the railyards because he was removing troops from the South and ending federal supervision of the former Confederate states. He promised to do so as part of the deal that made him president, after he and his Democratic opponent, Samuel Tilden, fought to an indecisive conclusion in 1876. Tilden won the popular vote, but the electoral vote was contested. Democrats in the South agreed to support Hayes's election if Republicans promised to end the military occupation of their region.

The rail strikes of 1877 signaled the beginning of a tense, often violent relationship among labor, management, and the government through the 1890s. In 1886, hundreds of thousands of workers throughout the country marched on May Day (May 1) to demand an eight-hour work day. Four days later, as workers assembled in Chicago's Haymarket Square to rally support for thousands of strikers in the city, a bomb exploded, killing seven police officers. The police fired into the crowd, killing four demonstrators. Dozens more were wounded. Seven anarchists were convicted of setting off the bomb, and four were hanged.

The age's violence and sense of dread were compounded even before the Haymarket affair, when President James Garfield was shot in July 1881 while walking to Union Station in Washington, D.C. Garfield survived for weeks, but died in September in Long Branch, New Jersey.

His assassin, Charles Guiteau, was a disappointed office-seeker. His crime and motive brought new demands for an end to widespread political patronage at all levels of government.

Other voices began to question the age's embrace of laissez-faire economics, which held that government should stand aside and allow market forces to dictate social, cultural, and political order. The nexus of railroad magnates and political figures led to recurring scandals—and the accumulation of great fortunes—prompting Congress to pass the Interstate Commerce Act in 1887 to regulate the railroads. In 1890, Congress passed the landmark Sherman Antitrust Act, named for Senator John Sherman, brother of the famous Union general William Tecumseh Sherman. The law gave Washington the power to prevent monopolies, often referred to as "trusts."

The Gilded Age economic bubble burst in 1893. The nation's railroads, one of the era's great job-creating machines, were over-leveraged and bitterly competitive. When the Philadelphia and Reading Railroad collapsed in early 1893, investors feared the worst. Bank depositors made a run for their money, leading to a series of bank failures, which led to more failures in credit-starved businesses. As railroads failed, markets for coal and other products became inaccessible, leading to further bankruptcies and closures. The unemployment rate jumped from about 3 percent in 1892 to more than 10 percent in 1893, then worsened to nearly 20 percent, by some accounts, in 1894. The crisis began as President Grover Cleveland took office for the second time, having been turned out of office in 1888, becoming the only U.S. president to serve two nonconsecutive terms. An orthodox politician who enjoyed the support of the business community, Cleveland had no response as the nation plunged into the worst economic depression of its history. Jobless workers under the leadership of Jacob Coxey marched on Washington in 1894, while rail workers in Pullman, Illinois, walked off their jobs in May of that year. The American Railway Union, under the leadership of the socialist Eugene V. Debs, called a nationwide rail strike of about a quarter-million workers. President Cleveland sent federal troops to Chicago, the nation's key rail hub, to break the strike. But the severity of the economic downturn would soon result in dramatic changes in the dynamics of American politics, just as it would in 1932.

Day 2: The Progressive Era

A new era began, unexpectedly, on the platform of the Democratic National Convention in Chicago in 1896. A 36-year-old congressman from Nebraska named William Jennings Bryan delivered a spellbinding speech that advocated a looser government monetary policy based on silver, not gold. Eastern bankers supported the gold standard, but farmers and small merchants wanted a more inflationary monetary policy that would allow them to settle their debts more quickly. Bryan said he spoke for "the producing masses" and "toilers everywhere" who supported silver-backed currency. Addressing supporters of the gold standard, he concluded his speech with a brilliant final phrase: "You shall not press down upon the brow of labor this crown of thorns. You shall not crucify mankind upon a cross of gold." Delegates spontaneously nominated him as the party's presidential candidate. Although Bryan went on to lose to William McKinley, his nomination and alliance with the Populist Party, which advocated radical change in the nation's political and economic relations, marked the formal beginning of the Progressive Era in U.S. politics.

Historians continue to debate the significance of the Progressive Era, which extended from the 1890s to the end of World War I in 1918. The era was once traditionally associated with greater government regulation of the marketplace, a vast array of political and moral reform movements, new ideas of social justice, early ideas about conservation and environmental preservation, and a rejection of the Gilded Age's excesses. More recent scholarship, however, notes that Progressives in the South imposed Jim Crow legislation in the region (leading the Supreme Court to rule, in *Plessey v. Ferguson* in 1896, that segregation was constitutional), and others embraced race-based ideologies to justify American expansion in the Caribbean and Pacific. While Progressives led the fight to win the vote for women, they also supported Prohibition as part of an effort to reform the morals of immigrants and city dwellers.

Progressivism grew out of the populist movement of the early 1890s, as farmers and laborers organized to protest working conditions, corporate mergers, monopolies, and economic inequality. The Populist Party ran an independent candidate, James K. Weaver, for president in 1892. In addition to silver coinage, the party supported government ownership of railroads and telegraph and telephone systems, a graduated income

tax, secret ballots, enforcement of an eight-hour work day, direct election of U.S. senators, and a one-term limit for president and vice president. Weaver received a million votes in the presidential election of
1892, and won Colorado, Idaho, Kansas, and Nevada. Bryan's candidacy in 1896 brought the Populists and Democrats together, adding momentum to fledgling efforts at wholesale reform.

The movement found its man in 1901, when President McKinley, the
last Civil War veteran to serve in the White House and symbol of a dis-
appearing age, was shot and killed in Buffalo, New York. The killing was
a reminder of 19th-century anxieties; the assassin, Leon Czolgosz, was a
Polish-born anarchist, precisely the sort of dissident who incited fear during the labor unrest of the 1880s. With McKinley's death, his brash, 42-
year-old vice president, Theodore Roosevelt, became the nation's
youngest-ever chief executive. Roosevelt, a Republican, consciously saw
himself as a product of his progressive-minded generation. "We Progressives stand for the rights of the people," he said, adding that Progressives
supported regulation of interstate commerce, opposed creation of corporate monopolies, and resisted the influence of business in politics.

While the Populists looked to the Democratic Party as a partner for
change, the Progressive movement found allies in both parties. Republicans, like young Wisconsin governor Robert LaFollette, led campaigns to
curb corporate power and make local politics less corrupt. At the national
level, Roosevelt expanded Washington's reach at a dizzying pace, creating
a new cabinet agency, the Department of Labor and Commerce, to implement and monitor the government's new role as a regulator and medi-
ator. Roosevelt's Justice Department used the Sherman Antitrust Act to
prosecute monopolies in industries ranging from banking to meatpacking.
The Roosevelt administration broke up more than 40 trusts from 1901 to
early 1909, and Roosevelt himself became known as the "Trust-buster."

Roosevelt signed the Pure Food and Drug Act in 1906, requiring government inspection of food and drug supplies on behalf of consumers.
The creation of national monuments at the Grand Canyon and Mount
Olympus (1902), and the designation of game preserves in Montana
and Alaska (1909), preserved vast lands from commercial development.
Roosevelt supported expanded government regulation of railroads and
presided over the first-ever conference on the conservation of natural
resources and treasures.

The young president also enthusiastically embraced a more aggressive role in world affairs. He won a Nobel Peace Prize for mediating an end to the Russian–Japanese war in 1905, and he dispatched a muscular U.S. naval armada, dubbed the "Great White Fleet," around the world to show off the nation's new military might. American expansion under Roosevelt included overt support for a rebellion in Panama in 1903, which led to the installation of a friendly government willing to allow the U.S. to build and control a canal within Panama's borders. When completed in 1914, the Panama Canal linked the Atlantic and Pacific Oceans, allowing trade and naval vessels traveling around South America.

At a local level, Progressives fought with the political machines founded during the Gilded Age in many U.S. cities, especially those with large immigrant populations. Journalists like Lincoln Steffens uncovered municipal corruption in New York, Philadelphia, St. Paul, and other cities, while Ray Stannard Baker condemned ties between corporate power and the U.S. Senate, and Ida B. Wells crusaded against the widespread lynching of African Americans in the South. Progressives demanded many of the same reforms that Populists had supported in the early 1890s, including the direct election of U.S. senators, party primary elections to choose nominees for office, and the income tax. They also supported the efforts of social reformers, including Jane Addams of Chicago, to ameliorate conditions for the urban poor, as well as feminists such as Carrie Chapman Catt and Alice Paul, who campaigned for women's suffrage. Ironically, however, many progressive social reforms were achieved through legislation written by or approved by machine politicians. For example, after a fire killed more than 140 female workers at the Triangle Shirtwaist Factory in New York in 1911, the state passed aggressive labor laws and workplace regulations, thanks in part to the leadership of two members of the Tammany Hall political machine, Alfred E. Smith and Robert F. Wagner.

The constitutional legacy of the Progressive movement was perhaps its greatest achievement. Not since passage of the Reconstruction amendments (the 13th, 14th, and 15th) were so many changes made to the Constitution in such a short time. Two changes were approved in 1913; the 16th Amendment, which created a federal income tax, and the 17th, which instituted the popular election of U.S. senators. The 18th Amendment, approved in 1919, instituted Prohibition, and the 19th, approved in 1920, gave women the right to vote.

The ideas of progressivism became so widespread that in the presidential election of 1912, three nominees—Woodrow Wilson, incumbent William Howard Taft, and former president Theodore Roosevelt—all cast themselves as Progressives. Indeed, the election became a three-way affair when Roosevelt, who had retired from office in 1909, challenged his hand-picked successor, Taft, for the Republican nomination because he believed Taft was insufficiently progressive. When Taft managed to retain the G.O.P.'s nomination, Roosevelt and his allies formed a new entity, the Progressive (or Bull Moose) Party. While Taft was considered more conservative than both Wilson, a former president of Princeton University and one-term Democratic governor of New Jersey, and Roosevelt, his administration actually initiated more prosecutions against corporate trusts than Roosevelt. But as the era moved to the left, it was Roosevelt, not Taft, who articulated an even greater expansion of government power in the marketplace. He formed alliances with labor unions, advocated for stricter workplace safety regulations, supported the removal of tariffs designed to protect American industries, and emphasized environmental concerns.

Wilson took advantage of the split in Republican ranks and won the presidency with just 42 percent of the popular vote (although he won the Electoral College vote with ease, accumulating 435 votes). Wilson's two terms (1913–21) saw another burst of progressive activity at the national and local level. Wilson called his program the "New Freedom" plan, and it included the creation of the Federal Trade Commission to encourage competition, passage of the Federal Reserve system to govern the banking industry, child labor restrictions (which the Supreme Court declared to be unconstitutional), strong support for labor unions, and government-sponsored plans to make farming more efficient. Wilson also segregated the federal workforce, a measure consistent with the Jim Crow laws that Southern Progressives had implemented in the late 19th century.

The Progressive Era wound down when the U.S. entered World War I in 1917 as military and foreign affairs took priority over domestic policies. Wilson's progressive ideas included a visionary plan to convene a League of Nations to settle international disputes, but U.S. isolationists blocked U.S. membership in the League. Wilson suffered a stroke and was incapacitated during his final few months of office, and the election of Republican Warren Harding as president in 1920 signaled the end of the Progressive Era in Washington.

Weekend 12 : The Bible

The Bible (Greek *biblia*, book) contains the fundamental texts of the Jewish and Christian religions, and is an inseparable part of the background of Islam as well. It has been translated into several hundred different languages, and is one of the most influential books in history, having shaped the religion, literature, and politics of much of the world for two millennia.

The Hebrew Bible dates, in its earliest parts, to before 1000 B.C. and includes material composed as late as the second century B.C. In Jewish contexts, this work is often referred to as the *Tanakh*, an acronym for the Hebrew Bible's three parts: Torah ("Law"), Nevi'im ("Prophets"), and Ketuvim ("Writings"). With the rise of Christianity in the early first millennium A.D., new writings were created and added to the original Hebrew Bible. The resulting two-part Bible came to be called, by Christians, the Old Testament and the New Testament, reflecting the Christian belief that humankind's relationship to God was fundamentally changed by the life, ministry, death, and Resurrection of Jesus Christ. The term *Old Testament* is rejected by adherents of Judaism, however, who regard the Hebrew Bible as complete.

The relationship between the Hebrew Bible and the Old Testament is complicated by the fact that not all Christian Old Testaments are the same; their contents vary by sect and denomination. Generally speaking, the Protestant Old Testament follows the Tanakh, with the same books, but not in exactly the same order. The Old Testament recognized by the Catholic and Orthodox Churches derives from an early (ca. 300 B.C.) translation of the Hebrew Bible into Greek. This translation, known as the Septuagint (a shortening of a Latin phrase meaning "translation of the seventy," after the number of scholars said to have been involved in producing it) included, or later incorporated, additional books—known collectively as the Apocrypha—that were accepted as canonical in the Catholic and Orthodox traditions, but were rejected both by Jewish scholars and most Protestant reformers.

Day 1: The Hebrew Bible, The Old Testament

The Hebrew Bible consists of 24 books divided into three sections: the Law (Torah), including the first five books of the Bible; the Prophets (Nevi'im); and Writings (Ketuvim). In their present form, these books are believed to have passed through a long history of oral tradition before being written down in Hebrew, with a few passages in Aramaic. Moses began the texts in the early 1400s B.C., but it was not until centuries later that the Torah and other writings were completed by a council of rabbis and were "canonized" (recognized officially as the sacred authority of God). Modern scholars date the canonization of the biblical text between 200 B.C. and A.D. 200. The standard Hebrew Bible is called the Masoretic or "transmitted" text.

♦**Torah (The Books of Moses)** "In the beginning God created the heavens and the earth." So begins Genesis, the first of the five books that make up the Torah. Along with Exodus, Numbers, Leviticus, and Deuteronomy, the narrative tells the story of the world and of the Jewish people, from the Creation to Moses' rescue of the Hebrews from slavery in Egypt. There are fundamental disagreements within both Judaism and Christianity over whether this narrative is literally true in all respects, or whether parts of it are true only in a metaphorical or spiritual sense.

Genesis and Exodus contain some of the best-known stories in the world: Adam and Eve, Noah and the Great Flood ("I will cause it to rain upon the earth for forty days and forty nights"), Abraham's migration to the Holy Land, Jacob's Ladder, Joseph's coat of many colors. Exodus describes the story of the Israelites' bondage in Egypt and their escape from slavery. Moses, Israelite by birth but raised in Pharaoh's household, is commanded by God to seek freedom for the Israelites. When Pharaoh refuses, God sends 10 plagues upon Egypt (water turned to blood, infestations of lice, frogs, wild beasts, and locusts, pestilence, boils, hail, darkness, and the slaying of the first born). The final plague takes the life of Pharaoh's son and convinces him to free the Israelites.

After wandering in the desert for 40 years, God gives Moses the Ten Commandments on two stone tablets. The commandments outline the rules of religious observance and morality by which God expected his people to live, and they remain a fundamental part of the Jewish and

Christian religions. Although the language of the commandments varies according to denomination and translation, the content is the same:

> "You shall have no other gods before Me.
> You shall not worship graven images.
> You shall not take the name of the Lord in vain.
> You shall remember the Sabbath and keep it holy.
> Honor your father and mother.
> You shall not commit murder.
> You shall not commit adultery.
> You shall not steal.
> You shall not bear false witness against your neighbor.
> You shall not covet your neighbor's goods."

Leviticus sets out detailed rules governing Jewish life, including forms of sacrifice, laws of purity, the code of holiness, and teachings on rituals, festivals, and social matters. Leviticus explains the woes that have befallen Israel as a result of the people's sins, and stresses atonement.

Numbers describes legal matters as well as priestly and temple duties; it also narrates the story of the rebellion against Moses' leadership and preparations for the conquest of Canaan, or the "Promised Land."

Deuteronomy is composed of the sermons and discourses of Moses, summarizing the events at Mt. Sinai and calling for faithfulness to God. It concludes with the final words and instructions of Moses linking the people to God, their past, and their future in the new land.

◆**Historical Narratives**   The books of **Joshua, Judges, Ruth, 1 and 2 Samuel, 1 and 2 Kings, 1 and 2 Chronicles, Ezra, Nehemiah, and Esther** provide a historical and genealogical narrative of the Jewish people. They begin with the Israelites' entry into the promised land of Canaan under the leadership of Joshua, then range through the formation of the Jewish state and its vicissitudes: the monarchies of David, Solomon, and their successors; the building of the First Temple; the destruction of the Temple and the resultant Babylonian occupation; and the return from exile and the rebuilding of Jerusalem and its temple under the leadership of Ezra and Nehemiah. This section of the Bible includes the only canonical narratives named for women (the Apocrypha includes the book of Judith). The book of Ruth is a tale of love and loyalty in which Ruth leaves her home in Moab to return to Judah with her beloved mother-in-law, Naomi. ("Whither thou goest, I will go; and where thou lodgest, I will lodge; thy people shall be my people; and thy God my God"). The story of Esther provides the basis for the traditional Jewish feast of Purim, which celebrates Esther's foiling of the plot of Haman to kill all the Jews, saving her family and her people.

◆Books of Spiritual Guidance The books of **Job, Psalms, Proverbs, Ecclesiastes, and the Song of Solomon** deal with the relationships of the human to the divine, the nature of righteousness, the problem of suffering, and the importance of wisdom. Job addresses the question of why the righteous suffer and challenges the benevolence of God. The Psalms are works of poetry ("The Lord is my shepherd, I shall not want"), many of which praise God, while others ask for his aid and guidance. This text was attributed to King David but is now known to have been written by multiple authors over a long period of time. Proverbs is a compilation of sayings that offer advice on a range of matters, usually with a moral point. A key theme of Proverbs is the virtue of wisdom as opposed to folly. Ecclesiastes seeks to grasp the elusive meaning of human existence. The Song of Solomon, ostensibly a collection of erotic poetry, is interpreted by religious scholars as an allegory of God's love for His people.

◆The Major Prophets The books of **Isaiah, Jeremiah, Lamentations, Ezekiel, and Daniel** deal generally with the rise of Babylon, the destruction of Jerusalem and the Temple, the Israelites' slavery in Babylon, and the return of the Jewish people to their homeland by permission of the Persian emperor Cyrus. The prophets warn of the consequences of disobedience to God, but hold out the promise of a return to his favor. Christians interpret much of the prophecy in these books, particularly Isaiah, as foretelling the life and mission of Jesus. Jeremiah, one of the greatest prophets, made enemies throughout his career with his ominous predictions. His core message is a stern call to true repentance, warning that ceremonies and confessions are inadequate in God's sight. The book of Daniel includes narratives set in the Babylonian and Persian courts. The best known of these stories is one in which King Darius was tricked into sentencing his favorite adviser, Daniel, to a night in a sealed den of lions. Because of his piety, God saves Daniel from the mouth of the beasts, and Darius sends the men who accused Daniel to the grisly fate from which Daniel was spared.

◆**The Minor Prophets** The books of **Hosea, Joel, Amos, Obadiah, Jonah, Micah, Nahum, Habakkuk, Zephaniah, Haggai, Zechariah, and Malachi** (sometimes collectively known as "the Twelve") contain warnings against wickedness, idolatry, unacceptable sacrifices, and other sins and shortcomings, and tell of the terrible wrath of God they will provoke, declaring that people must leave their sinful ways in order to gain God's mercy. Of the Minor Prophets, perhaps the best known is Jonah. God tells Jonah to go to the Assyrian capital of Nineveh and denounce its wickedness, but instead Jonah sails to Tarshish. En route, the ship is threatened by a God-sent storm. As propitiation for his disobedience, God besieges the ship by means of a great storm, during which Jonah is thrown into the water and swallowed by a whale. After he is freed by God, Jonah goes to Nineveh, where he preaches with success and is instructed by God on the need for mercy.

◆**Translations of the Old Testament** The Septuagint was created to serve the needs of Greek-speaking Jews in parts of the ancient world beyond the borders of Israel. It also introduced some non-Jews, called Gentiles, in the region to Jewish ideas of monotheism. The Greek version was later rejected by rabbinical Judaism, however, and many Jews believe that the Tanakh is authentic and authoritative only in its Hebrew version (as most Muslims regard the Koran as authoritative only in Arabic). Christian tradition, on the other hand, encourages the translation of Scripture. Important translations of the Old Testament into Latin (the "Vulgate" translation from the Hebrew by St. Jerome) and Syriac (the main language of Christian churches throughout Asia) were in circulation by the fourth century A.D.

Day 2: The New Testament

The New Testament includes 27 books: four Gospels (Old English, "good news"), the Acts of the Apostles, 21 letters (called Epistles), and the Book of Revelation. These books were written in Greek over a period of about a century, from ca. A.D. 50 (the earliest of Paul's letters) to the mid-second century A.D. The arrangement of the books is roughly chronological according to events, rather than composition: the story of Jesus (Gospels), the beginning of the Church (Acts), advice to churches and the beginnings of Christian theology (Letters), and the end of the world and final salvation of believers (Revelation). Little is known about the actual authors of the books, apart from some letters genuinely attributable to Paul.

♦**The Gospels** There are four Gospels, each attributed to one of Jesus' disciples: **Mark, Matthew, Luke, and John.** The central story in all of the Gospels is the suffering and death of Jesus, who was executed by Roman soldiers for claiming to be the Son of God, and thereby gravely threatening the authority of Jewish scholars called Pharisees. The earliest Gospel is that of Mark, written around A.D. 70, the time of the fall of Jerusalem and the destruction of the Second Temple by the Romans. Luke and Matthew were written during the late first century, using the Gospel of Mark, already well known, as a source. Matthew, Mark, and Luke are called the Synoptic ("seen together") Gospels because they tell essentially the same story of Jesus' life, ministry, Crucifixion, and Resurrection in complementary fashion.

The author of Mark gathers the sayings of Jesus and stories of his life and ministry from the oral traditions of the early church. Beginning with John's baptism of Jesus, he goes on to tell of the miracles Jesus performed, such as calming the waters and feeding the multitudes with loaves and fishes, and then proceeds to detail the circumstances surrounding Jesus' journey to Jerusalem, death, and Resurrection. According to Mark, only after the Crucifixion are Jesus and his mission fully understood by the people, and he is recognized as the son of God.

Unlike Mark, Matthew states at the outset that Jesus is the Messiah. He describes the story of his birth in Bethlehem, the adoration of the Magi, the wrath of Herod, and the flight of Mary, Joseph, and Jesus to Egypt. The narrative of Jesus' ministry includes the Sermon on the Mount and the recognition of Jesus as the Messiah by his disciples. The author of Matthew contrasts the Old Testament time of prophecy with the era of God's fulfillment in Jesus: the believer needs to receive Jesus to be part of God's eternal kingdom.

Luke begins with the birth of John the Baptist and then relates the story of Jesus' birth. He goes on to describe the conflicts with the Pharisees, the journey to Jerusalem, Jesus' death, Resurrection and appearances to his disciples, and his Ascension to Heaven. Luke emphasizes Jesus' concern with the poor and the duties of the rich to the poor.

The stories of the Good Samaritan and the Prodigal Son are found only in the Gospel of Luke.

The Gospel of John was written later than the Synoptic Gospels, around A.D. 90–120, but was composed without their reference. Its approach to the story of Jesus is distinctively different. It begins with the assertion that the eternal Word is embodied in Jesus, but the focus is not on the everyday moral and religious implications of Jesus' teaching, but rather on his claims to be the Messiah. John omits the parables, the Sermon on the Mount, and other narrative elements that characterize the three earlier Gospels, and instead focuses on the conflict between Jesus and the Pharisees, and more broadly, Jesus versus the Jews. The Gospel ends with Jesus' death, Resurrection, and appearances to the disciples.

•**The Acts of the Apostles** Written about A.D. 80–85, the Acts of the Apostles (often referred to simply as "Acts") is by the same author as Luke. It begins where Luke ends, with the Ascension of Jesus to Heaven, and recalls Jesus' injunction to preach the Gospel to "the ends of the earth." Thus liberated from its origins as a local Jewish sect, Christianity began spreading widely in the Mediterranean world, the Middle East, and beyond. Acts describes the earliest years of the church, its rapid growth among both Jews and Gentiles, doctrinal controversies, the conversion of Paul, and his apostolic travels. It ends with Paul's final preaching and imprisonment in Rome.

•**The Letters** Though less familiar to laypersons than the Gospels, the Letters give the clearest sense of the emergence and early character of Christianity. Letters are the dominant form of literature in the New Testament. They are diverse in content, but collectively they give a vivid picture of the early Christian church struggling to understand the teachings of Jesus correctly, to distinguish between true and false doctrines, to create a congregational life that lived up to Christ's vision of Christian brotherhood, and to deal with scorn and abuse from nonbelievers and the secular authorities.

Collections of letters by (or attributed to) Paul circulated among Christian churches by the end of the first century. A major theme of the Pauline letters is the relationship between Christianity and Judaism. Of the 21 letters in the New Testament, the first 13 are ascribed to Paul;

nine are to churches (ordered by length, longest first), and four are addressed to individuals. Of these, only Romans, 1 and 2 Corinthians, Galatians, Philippians, 1 Thessalonians, and Philemon are now generally regarded as authentically by Paul.

Romans was written to the church in Rome between A.D. 55 and 58. In these letters, Paul defends the Gospel to the Gentiles, answering questions and challenges raised by Jewish Christians in Rome.

1 Corinthians was written about A.D. 54. Here, Paul gives advice on problems that were endangering the congregation's communal life, claiming that Christians must behave in a worthy manner and that whatever is done should be done in love, with an awareness of the grace bestowed on them by their faith, both in the present and for eternity.

2 Corinthians is thought to be a composite of at least two letters by Paul to the church in Corinth, in which he assures the Corinthians of his devotion and writes of the need for generosity in supporting other congregations.

Galatians, written between A.D. 50 and 55, provides the earliest statement of gentile Christian theology as distinct from Judaism. Paul admonishes Christians in Galatia (present-day Turkey) not to stray from the gospel of faith in favor of laws advocated by competing Jewish-Christian missionaries. Insisting that the New Covenant through Jesus completely supersedes the Old Covenant between God and the Hebrews, Paul declares that Christians are saved by faith, not by adherence to the laws of the Torah.

1 Thessalonians was written to the church in Thessalonica (northeastern Greece). Written about A.D. 50, it is the earliest book in the New Testament. In it, Paul affirms that Christians who die prior to the Second Coming of Christ, as well as those who are then alive, will share in the new life in Christ.

The Pauline letters are followed by the anonymous letter to the **Hebrews**, probably a sermon addressed to a Jewish audience, giving Old Testament justification for Christian beliefs.

Three letters (**1 and 2 Timothy, and Titus**) are considered non-Pauline, and opinions vary on 2 Thessalonians, Ephesians, and Colossians. The remaining seven letters, traditionally attributed to James, Peter, John, and Jude, are by unknown authors writing near the end of the first century.

◆Revelation Written about A.D. 95 and ascribed to John the Divine (not the same person as the author of the Gospel of John and the Letters of John), this book consists of visions revealed to the author by Christ about the end of the world and the salvation of the faithful. The text was accepted as prophetic by the early Church Fathers and thus included in the New Testament. It describes allegorically the struggle between good and evil, reflecting the actual struggle of the time between Christians and the authorities of the Roman Empire. Its vivid images include angels, a scroll with seven seals, savage beasts and plagues, the Battle of Armageddon, and John's final vision of a new heaven and earth: a New Jerusalem, the rule of God, and the salvation of his faithful people.

◆Translations of the New Testament The New Testament was written in Greek, and together with the Septuagint Greek translation of the Old Testament, was the Bible of the early Christian church. It is still in use in the Orthodox tradition. St. Jerome's fourth-century Latin Vulgate ("common tongue") translation of the Hebrew Old Testament and the Greek New Testament met demands for a Latin Bible for the European world, remaining standard in the Catholic Church until modern times.

Thereafter, few translations were undertaken, and in the Latin-speaking world they were officially discouraged. Pope Innocent III banned unauthorized versions of the Bible in 1199. John Wycliffe (1324–84) produced the first complete English Bible in 1382; William Tyndale published his translation of the New Testament in 1536. Both men were executed for producing translations without authorization. Meanwhile, Martin Luther published his German translation of the New Testament in 1522, and translations into Dutch (1526) and French (1530) soon followed. In 1604, King James of England authorized a commission to produce a new Standard Edition of the Bible, which became one of the most widely used of all Bibles, and a founding work of English literature, known as the King James Version (KJV).

In modern times, the Bible has been translated into hundreds of languages, and many new English translations have appeared. Notable ones include the Revised Standard Version (published in 1946–57) and the New English Bible (a new translation from original sources, rather than a revision of earlier English versions), published in 1970. The same year saw the publication of the New American Bible, which met the need for an English-language Bible for use in Catholic churches, replacing the Latin Vulgate Bible, in the wake of the Vatican II reforms. A recent trend has emerged for new versions of the Bible designed to appeal to specialized audiences. Illustrated, children's, and searchable online editions are now widely available.

◆**The Apocrypha** The Apocrypha, originally Scriptures of the Septuagint, were part of the early Christian Bible. They remain part of the Roman Catholic Old Testament and, with some additional books, of Orthodox Old Testaments. While they are of historical interest, they are noncanonical in Protestant churches. Of Jewish origin, they were written in Hebrew, Aramaic, and Greek during the period 300 B.C. to A.D. 100. Their content is quite diverse, from supplements to the Tanakh, to prophetic warnings against evildoing, to prayers and ritual texts, to apocalyptic visions. They do not form part of the standard Hebrew Bible.

Weekend 13: The World in Your Living Room

Day 1: The Radio Music Box

Radio and television today are so much a part of everyday life in literally every corner of the globe that it is difficult for us to believe that what we call broadcasting is less than a century old. Although the evolution of radio's technological elements stretch back into the 19th century, the first primitive radio stations didn't appear until about 1905. These "ham-radio" stations grew so rapidly that in 1912 the U.S. government required them to obtain licenses.

In 1916, David Sarnoff, a young engineer at Marconi and soon to be an executive at RCA, wrote what would become a famous memo outlining the basic structure of broadcasting:

> I have in mind a plan of development which would make radio a "household utility" in the same sense as the piano or phonograph…the receiver can be designed in the form of a simple "radio music box," and arranged for several different wavelengths…The box can be placed on a table in the parlor or living room…the same principle can be extended to numerous other fields, for example, receiving lectures at home…also events of national importance…baseball scores can be transmitted…

So even before radio had been born, broadcasting's essential characteristics could be clearly seen—entertainment and information brought into the home.

It was not until 1920 that a station in Pittsburgh, KDKA, was able to reach a wide audience of 2,000 listeners by broadcasting the returns of the Harding–Cox presidential election. The effect of that broadcast was so powerful that business leaders, government officials, religious zealots, baseball teams, in fact anyone who had a message to send or a product to sell, saw immediately what this new technology could accomplish. By this time, all of the important patents related to radio had been bought up by large corporations, notably Westinghouse, General Electric, and AT&T, so the question of how to finance broadcasting became of the utmost importance. Some advocated the British approach of placing a tax on purchases of the receiving sets; a few even proposed that the wealthy fund it, as they did libraries and museums. The possibility of having advertising was unanimously rejected since everyone objected to "salesmanship in the home." AT&T first expressed its belief that radio should be financed in the same way as the telephone where the sender of the message pays the bill. But this idea was quickly abandoned as they realized it was not possible to earn any money under that plan.

In 1922, the AT&T-owned station in New York, WEAF, began offering to sell time on its broadcasts, and the station's first commercial message aired in August 1922. It was a talk about how wonderful life was in a suburban Queens apartment complex. These were followed by talks on gasoline, greeting cards, cosmetics, and automobiles, but there was no aggressive selling or mentioning of price. But these brief speeches did little to stir up business, and in 1923, AT&T took the radical step of broadcasting popular music, including live vaudeville acts such as The Happiness Boys, from a Broadway theater. The public responded immediately, and the future of radio as the provider of popular entertainment had begun, followed quickly by rapid growth in the sales of radios.

By 1930, there were radio sets in 12 million homes, and by 1936 over 24 million homes had a private set. On the eve of World War II, 90 percent of American homes (51 million) owned a radio.

◆**The Networks**   The emergence of NBC and CBS as "national networks" in the late 1920s transformed radio into the central cultural medium of American society. In September 1926, the Radio Corporation of America (RCA), led by David Sarnoff, formed the National Broadcasting Company (NBC) and debuted nationally with a live gala broadcast from the Waldorf-Astoria Hotel in New York, which reached 21 stations as far west as Kansas City. By 1927, NBC offered full-time coast-to-coast programming on their two networks, christened "NBC Red" (primarily entertainment and music), and "NBC Blue" (primarily news and culture). Soon independent stations rushed to join the networks as affiliates that could purchase programming from NBC and sell time to local advertisers. By 1933, NBC owned 52 full-time and 36 part-time affiliates—15 percent of all radio stations in the country.

The Columbia Broadcasting Company (CBS) was small when Sam Paley, a wealthy cigar manufacturer, bought controlling interest in it in September 1928 and put his son, William, in charge. Young Paley offered more generous contracts to affiliates than did NBC and provided basic program services free of charge. In exchange, CBS asked for "option time," in which affiliates guaranteed slots in their evening schedules. CBS thereby assured sponsors that their advertisements would reach a national audience. By 1933, CBS surpassed NBC with 91 affiliates. Now, for any station to compete in the market, it was necessary to affiliate with either of the two networks.

By the late 1930s, Congress began to pressure the Federal Communications Commission (F.C.C.) to investigate the monopolistic practices of the networks. As a result, in 1943, NBC sold its Blue network for $8 million to the candy tycoon Edward J. Noble. Noble called his new network the American Broadcasting Company (ABC), and it eventually became the third viable radio network.

Programming Local stations offered programming for 12 to 18 hours a day, filling those hours with shows and musical recordings that appealed to regional tastes. These stations embraced the networks because only they had the financial resources to supply fresh, live programs on a daily basis, including such favorites as *The Grand Ole' Opry* and *National Barn Dance*. Radio helped listeners maintain their local and regional identities but also addressed them as members of an American national audience eager for news, entertainment, sports, and brand-name products.

♦The Advertising Agencies The credit for the invention of almost all forms of radio programs, most of which were reincarnated for television, belongs to the advertising agencies whose employees handled the production of nearly all programs during the era of network radio. The agencies hired writers, contracted for studio facilities, and presented a finished product rife with commercials integrated into the program itself.

The origins of the morning talk show are found in programs aimed primarily at housewives, employing cheerful hosts who spoke directly to the American woman about recipes, health issues, and domestic advice. Similarly, the "soap opera" was invented to serve the needs of companies like Procter and Gamble that wanted to market cleaning supplies to homemakers. "Soaps" involved characters in entanglements that ran in daily 15-minute installments. Irna Phillips, an advertising executive, is credited with creating the first of these, *Painted Dreams*, in 1930, and *The Guiding Light*, which ended its five-decade run in 2009.

Prime Time The evening hours were dubbed "prime time" because radio's largest audiences tuned in then, and networks could charge higher rates for advertising. In the evenings, networks created a new cultural experience for Americans to enjoy with their families and fellow listeners. Vaudeville morphed into "musical-variety," and since almost all of the programs were produced by advertising agencies, they carried the sponsor's name in the title: *The Kraft Music Hall* (with Bing Crosby), *The Jell-O Program* (with Jack Benny), *The Fleischmann Yeast Hour* (with Rudy Vallee), *The Camel Caravan* (with Eddie Cantor), and *The Shell Chateau* (with Al Jolson) are just a few. George Burns and Gracie Allen also had great triumphs, as did the big band orchestras of Benny Goodman, Glenn Miller, and others.

The enduring genre of situation comedy—also born from vaudeville—became popular and influential in the first decade of radio. The most popular was *Amos 'n' Andy*, a show about two African-American friends from the South who find themselves in an all-black neighborhood in the North, operating the Fresh Air Taxi Company. From 1928 until 1943, it aired six nights a week and had 40 million listeners. In ensuing years, many other situation comedies followed with huge success; *The Goldbergs*, the *Fibber McGee and Molly Show*, and *The Adventures of Ozzie and Harriet*. Dramatic series like *The Lone Ranger*, *Dragnet*, and *Gunsmoke* were also well represented on the radio. Anthology dramas on radio were prestigious, and the stories generally consisted of adaptations of renowned novels, plays, or movies.

◆**News** In 1933, President Franklin D. Roosevelt used radio to speak directly to America with his "fireside chats," a series he implemented to address fears and concerns as the country dealt with the Great Depression and later, the beginning of World War II. Radio also brought an intimacy to the news, as demonstrated by the response to coverage of the 1935 trial of Bruno Hauptmann, the convicted kidnapper of the baby of aviation idol Charles Lindbergh.

Radio also enabled reporters to comment on world events directly from the scene. From 1939 to 1941, CBS and NBC covered the war in Europe using short wave radio to transmit live reports across the Atlantic. CBS's Edward R. Murrow brought the war to life for American listeners with his show *I Can Hear It Now*, by sharing his encounters with Londoners whose city was under siege during Germany's bombing campaign.

With the advent of television in 1948, advertisers began to shift budgets, and radio networks were forced to eliminate programs throughout the 1950s. Radio adapted by introducing the "disc jockey"—record spinners whose personalities became a station's identity. With the "Top 40" format, one that relied heavily on popular music, radio and the recording industry established a powerful link. This fueled the growth of rock 'n' roll, attracting radio's most lucrative audience to date: teenagers. The car radio, which was a luxury before World War II, became standard. Japanese corporations mass-marketed portable transistor radios, and by the mid-1960s radio was used like never before; it was now mobile, and not only in automobiles. Nonetheless, with the automobile in mind, advertisers began to target listeners commuting to and from work, and radio reclaimed its local roots with news, weather, and traffic reports.

◆**Modern Radio**   The emergence of FM radio greatly expanded the kinds of programs available. There were fewer than 1,000 FM stations in the early 1960s, but by 1976 there were roughly 4,000. FM offered an alternative to AM, which largely followed repetitive commercial formulas, by playing obscure tracks or entire albums by artistically ambitious musicians. AM reinvented itself to retain listeners by creating the "all news, all talk" format. By the late 1990s, there were nearly 1,000 stations devoted to this new formula, creating celebrity hosts like Howard Stern and Rush Limbaugh, who were syndicated to hundreds of stations. After the Telecommunications Act of 1996, deregulation removed limits on the number of radio stations a corporation could own, and conglomerates such as Clear Channel Communications set the pace for consolidation. A backlash followed, and critics continue to argue that an autonomous local media is essential for participation in a democratic society.

Satellite networks have become new players early in the 21st century, broadcasting directly to consumers who buy specialized receivers and pay a monthly fee, and offering an advertising-free alternative to traditional "terrestrial" radio. Two major companies in this venture, Sirius and XM, merged in July 2008 after posting huge losses.

Day 2: The Revolution Will Be Televised

On the foggy morning of September 7, 1927, in a small house at 202 Green Street in San Francisco, an obscure young inventor named Philo T. Farnsworth transmitted the image of a triangle across a crowded laboratory, where it appeared on a receiver placed behind a partition on the far side of the room. Farnsworth's invention, registered with the U.S. Patents Office as an "Image Dissector" tube, scanned the image electronically, using a focused electronic beam, and sent the signal through the air to the awaiting receiver. At the age of 21, Farnsworth had invented electronic television, an achievement that had eluded scientists at America's greatest corporations.

From a wood-paneled office in a New York skyscraper 3,000 miles away, RCA commercial manager David Sarnoff was also attempting to create a workable television system. In 1929, he brought the Russian-born scientist Vladimir Zworykin from Westinghouse to supervise television research at RCA. Starting with an annual budget of more than $100,000, Zworykin and his staff worked feverishly to develop a proprietary television system for which RCA would control all underlying patents. But RCA trailed Farnsworth badly because Zworykin had not succeeded in creating a television camera. In the end, RCA resorted to infringing Farnsworth's patents and was forced to pay a licensing fee after a protracted lawsuit. But RCA would win eventually.

The key to establishing RCA's dominance depended on providing a program service through the NBC network. On April 30, 1939, NBC became the first network to launch regular television service with its inaugural telecast of the opening-day ceremonies at the New York World's Fair. The following day, RCA television sets went on sale in New York department stores; a set with a 7-by-10-inch screen sold for $1,000. NBC followed its debut with daily broadcasts and highly promoted live events beamed to a few thousand receivers in the New York area. A Columbia–Princeton baseball game in May and a Giants–Dodgers game from Ebbets Field in June are considered to be the first sports telecasts in America. The onset of World War II postponed further developments, but the delay only helped to build up excitement for its eventual audience.

◆The Rise of Commercial Television, 1948–1959   In the fall of 1948, the television networks had introduced regular prime-time sched-

ules, and by the end of 1949, 1 million American households, or about 2 percent of the population, had a television set. By 1954, however, more than half of all Americans had TV sets, as the number of households with television jumped to 26 million. By 1959, the television set was as common as a refrigerator; 44 million households, or 86 percent of the population, had TV sets, and the average household had one switched on for nearly six hours a day.

The comedy-variety format represented by television's first breakout hit, *The Texaco Star Theater* (1948), starring Milton Berle, kept the traditions of vaudeville alive into the television era. The raucous comic sketches and musical numbers, the performances of acrobats, magicians, pantomimes, and plate-spinners on *Texaco Star Theater*, *The Colgate Comedy Hour* (1950), *The Red Skelton Show* (1951), and the critically acclaimed *Your Show of Shows* (1950), starring Sid Caesar and Imogene Coca, brought astonishing, original comic entertainment into American homes. The most durable of these series began in 1948 as *Toast of the Town* and, after taking on the name of its host in 1955, continued until 1971 as *The Ed Sullivan Show*. Jackie Gleason is best remembered as Ralph Kramden from the situation comedy *The Honeymooners* (1955), but he became a star playing a range of hilarious characters on his comedy-variety series, *The Jackie Gleason Show* (1952).

The most popular television series of the early 1950s was *I Love Lucy*, starring Lucille Ball and Desi Arnaz, which debuted on CBS in October 1951 and spent four of its six seasons as the highest-rated series on television. The remarkable popularity of *I Love Lucy* established the family sitcom as television's essential genre for decades to come.

◆**The Network Era**   The chief beneficiaries of television's explosive growth during the 1950s were the networks, which expanded by turning virtually every new television station into a network outlet. As with radio, local stations joined the national TV networks to get access to network programs and to share in the income from national advertising. Four networks introduced regular prime-time schedules in 1948, but a Federal Communications Commission (F.C.C.) decision ensured that NBC and CBS would hold an insurmountable lead over the smaller networks, ABC and Du Mont.

By 1960, American television had become synonymous with network television. Of the 515 television stations licensed by the F.C.C. to serve the "public interest" of its community, 96 percent were affiliated with a national network. Over the next two decades, on any given evening, nearly 95 percent of those watching television were tuned into one of the three networks. By monopolizing television in America, the networks set the terms that governed virtually every aspect of the television industry. In creating a national audience for commercial broadcasting, the networks controlled the largest advertising market in history. Many Americans watched the growing network monopoly with alarm. The airwaves were supposed to be a public domain, licensed by the F.C.C. on behalf of the American people, but they had become nothing more than an advertising medium.

In commercial terms, the network news divisions were a "loss leader"— not a source of income, but one of prestige and network identity—an effort to serve the public service mandate. The debates between Richard Nixon and John F. Kennedy during the 1960 presidential campaign were a milestone, giving television a central role in the electoral process.

The regular evening news programs didn't play a truly prominent role at the networks until they were expanded from 15 to 30 minutes in 1963. *The CBS Evening News* with Walter Cronkite and NBC's *The Huntley-Brinkley Report* with Chet Huntley and David Brinkley became flagship programs for their networks. Network news coverage of desegregation efforts in the South and the war in Vietnam provided unexpected momentum to the civil rights and antiwar movements during the 1960s by bringing shocking or emotionally charged pictures of these events into American homes.

One of the defining achievements of this period was the ability to create a mass audience on a scale that had never been achieved before. When the Beatles first appeared on *The Ed Sullivan Show* in February 1964, the event drew 73 million viewers, more than 40 percent of the total population. It's an astonishing figure—and a good measure of the band's popularity—but it's less astonishing when weighed against the fact that a routine episode of *The Beverly Hillbillies* aired two weeks earlier drew 70 million viewers.

Television also covered major historical events that attracted enormous audiences, including the assassination and funeral of President Kennedy and the first Moon landing in July 1969.

Some entertainment programs in which there was intense viewer involvement in the story and characters could have a single episode of a series turn into a national event. The first of these involved the final episode of *The Fugitive*, which aired in August 1967 and was viewed by 51 million people, or 27 percent of the population. A decade later, 69 million people (32 percent of the population) tuned in for the final episode of the miniseries *Roots* (1977), and in 1980, 83 million people (38 percent of the population) watched the episode of *Dallas* that answered the previous season's cliffhanger question, "Who Shot J. R.?"

On February 28, 1983, a record 106 million people—47 percent of all Americans—watched the final episode of M*A*S*H, which concluded its 10-year run on CBS. At the time, the average American home received 14 television channels; the same home today has more than 50. The M*A*S*H finale represents the end of the era of network monopoly because for the last time almost half of all Americans gathered to watch a single television program.

◆**The Cable Era** Cable television began in the 1940s and 1950s as community antenna television (CATV), a solution to reception problems in geographically isolated towns. The answer was to erect a large antenna tower in a high location and distribute the signal to subscribers using coaxial cable. Because a large community antenna could receive distant signals and amplify the weaker UHF channels, it created a situation in which cable viewers received more channels than those typically available over the air, and each channel arrived with a strong, clear signal.

The turning point for cable television came during the 1970s when several corporations began to distribute program services by satellite, making it possible to reach audiences on a national—and eventually international—scale. Time, Inc. was the first to launch a satellite-based service when it premiered Home Box Office (HBO) in 1975. By the end of the decade, other subscription-based movie channels, including Showtime and HBO's own spin-off network, Cinemax, had followed suit.

Between 1976 and 1981, several cable networks emerged to offer an alternative to the major networks. C-Span (introduced 1979) provided commercial-free coverage of the U.S. Congress. The Christian Broadcasting Network (CBN) was the most successful of many networks devoted to religious programming. Black Entertainment Television (BET) aimed at young African-American viewers who had rarely been served well by the broadcast networks. ESPN attracted an audience of adult males by delivering a steady stream of sporting events and sports news. Nickelodeon offered programs for children.

In 1980, Ted Turner launched the Cable News Network (CNN), directly challenging the broadcast networks by delivering national and international news on a round-the-clock basis. The premiere of MTV in 1981 was a godsend for the music, advertising, and cable television industries. In essence, everything on MTV during its early days was an advertisement. Music videos were supplied to the network by the music industry, which saw an unprecedented opportunity to promote record sales. The introduction of the highly profitable Home Shopping Network in 1985 and its competitor, QVC, in 1986, showed that cable networks could eliminate programs and commercials entirely by selling directly to customers.

In 1984, the Big Three still claimed 80 percent of the nation's TV audience, but that was already a sharp drop from the days when they could count on more than 90 percent of the audience. As competition has increased, the broadcast networks' share of the total audience has spiraled downward each year. In 2008, there were six broadcast networks, and together they account for just 28 percent of the total audience.

By 1981, a majority of American households now contained more than one television set. The availability of multiple sets in the home changes the dynamic of television viewing by freeing family members to make choices based on their individual tastes.

Videocassette recorders, which became a common feature in American homes during the 1980s, allowed users to tape TV programs and watch them at their convenience, a practice that came to be known as "time-shifting," a development continued by DVR and TiVo devices today. The remote control device became popular during the 1980s, and it remains a significant influnce on the manner in which people experience television. Many viewers use the remote control to avoid watching commercials, while others scan restlessly through the channels, not watching entire programs.

Weekend 14: The Major Religions of Asia

Day 1: Hinduism

Hinduism is a modern term applied broadly to mean "the religion of India." The term encompasses myriad sects, cults, and schools of philosophy and theology that are united by certain core beliefs and practices.

Modern Hinduism derives from the ancient religion of India, known as Vedism or Brahmanism. Originating in prehistoric times, this was a highly formalistic religion in which ceremonies, sacrifices, and purifications were carried out by a priestly class in accordance with sacred texts. In the first millennium B.C., a new body of literature proposed that spiritual mastery is not limited to a priestly caste but is available to anyone who has sufficient discipline and devotion.

After about the fourth century A.D., Hinduism spread from India to Southeast Asia, especially in what is now Indonesia, where it was later replaced by Islam. Most Hindus now live in India or are part of the worldwide Indian diaspora.

Hindu worship today is largely an individual or family matter, stressing individual devotions rather than collective worship (except during festivals, in which tens of thousands of people might participate). There are striking regional and sectarian differences in the relative importance accorded to various gods, the ways in which they are worshipped, and in other practices.

◆**Scripture** The Vedas, which date to about 1500 B.C., are collections of hymns, chants, and rituals that guided the practices of the ancient priestly class. Foremost among them is the *Rig Veda*, which contains a large body of hymns sung to accompany sacrifices and other ceremonies. The religion of the Vedas was modified by the *Upanishads*, texts (usually in dialogue form) from the mid-first millennium B.C. that explore basic religious and philosophical concepts and expand the scope of religious belief and practice. Religious ideas are also expressed in the historical texts and mythology that form the foundation of Indian culture, especially the *Ramayana* (ca. 300 B.C.), an account of the struggles and triumph of the paragon of virtue, Lord Rama; the *Mahabharata* (ca. 200 B.C.), which tells of a titanic war between two royal clans; and the

Bhagavad Gita—originally an independent text later incorporated into the *Mahabharata*—a classic exploration of issues of *karma* and *dharma*. A huge body of philosophical and theological literature has grown up over the centuries in the form of commentaries to these early texts.

◆**Core Beliefs**   *Atman* and *brahman* are often translated simply as "soul" and "divine spirit," but they carry more complex meanings. Brahman is both the source and substance of all existence; atman is brahman manifested as the individual "self" of a living being. The key spiritual insight of Hinduism is that there is fundamentally no dividing line between atman and brahman, between the "self" and the universe.

Maya, usually translated as "illusion," refers to the impression, gained through the senses, that the differentiation of things in the universe is real and stable. Maya implies that the apparent differentiation of substance into individual things is illusory, and that the world ultimately is of a singular spiritual nature in a constant state of flux.

Karma refers to the moral consequences of every act committed by an individual in life, carried over from one lifetime to the next. Karma in itself is neither good nor bad, but on an individual level the experience of its consequences might be perceived as good or bad.

Dharma means both "duty" and "truth." It refers to an individual's duty as determined by life circumstances (such as caste status, sex, wealth, and power) and the actions that proceed from that duty. A person's individual dharma might include devotion to a particular god. Thus, acting appropriately in accordance with one's station in life is itself a form of worship, and a path to oneness with the universe.

Moksha means "liberation." The primary goal of Hindu belief and practice is the spiritual liberation that comes from a realization that there is no distinction between brahman and atman. Having moksha as a spiritual goal (in part through dharma or appropriate religious duty) does not preclude the pursuit of worldly goals, such as *arrha*, wealth and power, and *kama*, pleasure.

Castes   Caste determined the fundamental structure of traditional Indian society and remains important today despite legal prohibitions of discrimination according to caste status. There are four main castes: *Brahmins* or priests; *kshatryas* or warrior-aristocrats; *vaishyas*, including merchants, landowners, and skilled artisans; and *shudras*, laborers. There are hundreds of sub-castes, based on occupation, region, and other factors. Below the caste system are *dalits*, "untouchables" who perform ritually unclean occupations. Caste forms the basis of religious practice through the concept that one's dharma varies according to caste. Hinduism is generally not a proselytizing religion, and many Hindus deny the possibility of conversion because converts would have no caste.

Yoga is widely understood in the West as meaning a system of exercise and breath control; in Hinduism that is only one meaning of a much broader term. A yoga (also called *marga*, "way") is an active path to spiritual growth and perfection; yogas can focus on meditation and study, social duty and the performance of good works, devotion to a deity, or other paths such as the hatha yoga of physical culture.

Deities in Hinduism manifest themselves in a variety of forms and receive many different types of devotion, but three fundamental forms predominate. Brahma represents the creative force; Vishnu preserves and sustains the universe; and Shiva will bring about its ultimate destruction. Many other gods are understood as particular manifestations of these three: for example, the widely revered Rama and Krishna are both incarnations of Vishnu; the popular elephant-headed god, Ganesh, patron of auspicious beginnings, is the son of Shiva and his wife, Parvati. Many of the (mostly male) gods have consorts and animal companions, and each god has vivid stories of their lives and actions. Individual worship of these deities through prayer and offerings is known by the general term *puja*.

Hinduism teaches a deep respect for living things; many Hindus are vegetarians. Cows are especially revered as exemplars of maternal goodness and divine bounty.

The diversity of Hindu holidays reflects the religion's regional and sectarian variety. Some of the more important and widespread holidays are Dipavali, a festival of lights celebrating Lakshmi, goddess of prosperity; Holi, a spring festival; and Dashara, a harvest festival.

◆History The oldest Hindu writings are Vedic texts associated with a group of invaders (probably from southeastern Europe or somewhere in the region between the Black and Caspian Seas) known as the Aryans, who conquered much of India early in the second millennium B.C. (Hindu fundamentalists associated with the Hindutva movement regard Vedic civilization as wholly indigenous to India, and they deny that any invasion took place, despite significant archaeological and linguistic evidence to the contrary.) The invaders also brought with them the caste system, the Sanskrit language, and a family of gods with obvious ties to other European deities (the Aryan father of the gods, Dyaus Pitr, was clearly the same figure as the Roman Jupiter or the Greek Zeus). Over many centuries, the Vedic religion assimilated local customs and folk religions, including the ideas of karma and reincarnation.

The mid- to late first millennium B.C.—the time when many of the *Upanishads*, along with the *Ramayana*, the *Mahabharata*, and the *Bhagavad Gita* were composed—marked a major transformation in Vedism, as ascetics challenged the religion and the power of the priests. Prominent among these reformers were Vardhamana, the founder of Jainism, and Siddhartha Gautama, later known as the Buddha. During this volatile period some Brahman priests propounded the doctrine that there is a dharma (duty) for each stage of a person's life. This was an argument, in effect, for social responsibility; among other things it inveighed against the increasingly widespread phenomenon of men abandoning society for a life of religious rigor and austerity. To become a hermit, in this view, was contrary to dharma unless the person had reached an "appropriate" stage of life.

Between the second century B.C. and the fourth century A.D., the classic epics (probably initially composed for oral performance) became standardized in written form; cults of Vishnu and Shiva grew in power; and Hinduism spread to Southeast Asia. From the fourth to the ninth century, bhakti ("devotional") Hinduism grew rapidly in popularity as religious leaders adapted their practices to vernacular languages, such as Tamil, rather than the traditional Sanskrit. Beginning with the establishment of the Delhi Sultanate in 1206, a succession of Muslim regimes dominated northern India, and many Hindus in areas that are now Pakistan, Bangladesh, and Kashmir, as well as in northern India itself, willingly or forcibly converted to Islam. Christianity, which had existed in India since the early centuries A.D., became more widespread in the subcontinent in the 19th century, especially under the influence of the British East India Company.

The 19th and 20th centuries also brought the struggle for Indian independence. Many major new leaders and reformers linked the struggle for independence to a revival of Hindu religion and culture. The best known of these leaders was Mahatma Gandhi, who brought the Hindu ascetic tradition and the principle of *satyagraha* ("passive resistance") to bear on the social and political reform movement in India.

After independence and the separation of Pakistan from India in 1947, the gulf between the Hindu majority and the large Muslim minority in India widened. Violent clashes continue into the 21st century, especially in the disputed territory of Kashmir. In India, two contradictory trends exist at the same time. On the one hand, Hindu nationalism, inspired in part by fear of and opposition to Islam, has emphasized the links between Hinduism and Indian identity. On the other hand, secularization and urbanization have led to the decline (though by no means the disappearance) of many traditional Hindu practices and a diminution in the importance of the traditionally privileged priestly class.

Day 2: Buddhism, Confucianism, and Taoism

◆**Buddhism** The central tenets of Buddhism were developed by Siddhartha Guatama in the fifth century B.C. Siddhartha Guatama, the Buddha ("awakened one"), began his religious practice and exploration in ancient Indian Vedic traditions, and thus Hinduism and Buddhism share many religious concepts. However, Buddhism offers its own unique prescription for escaping from life's grim cycle of birth, death, old age, sickness, and death.

History Siddhartha Gautama was brought up in the wealthy, sheltered palace of his father, the ruler of a small kingdom in northeastern India, and upon leaving the palace was shocked to learn of the suffering of ordinary people. Embarking on years of travel, austerity, and meditation, he eventually experienced enlightenment, becoming the Buddha. Preaching his new insights on the causes of suffering (the Four Noble Truths), and the means for escaping it (the Noble Eightfold Path), he gathered a group of disciples who formed the first Buddhist community. Later, followers wrote down the Buddha's teachings and spread the faith, in part through the establishment of monastic communities. Promoted by King Ashoka of the Maurya dynasty (r. 269–232 B.C.), Buddhism was firmly established in India and spread to Southeast Asia, then to the Silk Road kingdoms of Central Asia, and finally to China, Korea, and Japan. Hinduism eventually supplanted Buddhism in India.

As it spread, Buddhism divided into the three major sects that continue to characterize it today. Buddhism differs from other world religions in that its sects have developed around central teachings and texts. *Theravada* ("The Teachings of the Elders") sees the quest for enlightenment as primarily a matter of individual spiritual cultivation in a monastic environment. The *Theravada* ideal is the *arhat*, a fully enlightened person who will enter Buddhahood in his or her next rebirth.

Mahayana ("The Greater Vehicle") stresses the role of *bodhisattvas*, beings of perfect compassion, who have postponed their own Buddha-transformation in order to assist ordinary people along the path to salvation and enlightenment. Many Mahayana Buddhists believe that the souls of those helped by bodhisattvas wait in a paradise-like setting until the time all sentient beings simultaneously achieve nirvana, and the world of illusion comes to an end.

Vajrayana or *Tantric* ("Esoteric") Buddhism, also called Lamaism, is sometimes considered a branch of Mahayana Buddhism. It stresses the interpretation of cosmic forces of good and evil through images, sacred diagrams, rituals, dance, and other means.

Theravada Buddhism today is prominent in Southeast Asia, particularly Thailand, Laos, Cambodia, Myanmar, and Sri Lanka. In those countries, it is customary for young boys to take temporary vows and experience monastic life for a period of several weeks or more; some pursue permanent religious vocations. Mahayana is the main form of Buddhism in China, Korea, and Japan. Prominent East Asian Mahayana sub-sects include Pure Land, which gives special prominence to the bodhisattva Amitabha, the great savior Buddha; the Japanese sect of Nichiren, named for its 13th-century founder and which stresses the *Lotus Sutra*, one of the earlier Mahayana texts; and Chan (Japanese Zen), which emphasizes monasticism, self-discipline, and meditation over scriptural authority. Vajrayana practitioners are found primarily in Tibet and Mongolia.

Scripture　Buddhist scriptures amount to thousands of volumes, organized into the *Tripitaka* ("Three Baskets"), comprising three types of teaching: *sutras*, considered the authentic word of the Buddha (though some sutras were not written until centuries after the Buddha's lifetime); *vinayas*, rules of monastic life; and *abhidharmas*, commentaries and systematizing treatises on Buddhist doctrines.

Core Beliefs Because of their common roots in ancient Indian religion, Buddhism and Hinduism share many concepts. These include *ahimsa* (doing no harm to living creatures); *samsara*, the cycle of birth and rebirth; *karma*, the accumulated consequences of an individual's actions over the course of multiple lifetimes; and *dharma*, which in Buddhism is expanded to mean not only "truth" and "duty," as in Hindu tradition, but also the doctrine proclaimed by the Buddha.

Nirvana The Buddhist nirvana, escape from the cycle of rebirth, is conceptually similar to the Hindu moksha. Buddhism, however, rejects the key Hindu belief in the unity of the individual soul and the universal soul ("atman is brahman") in favor of *anatman*, a denial that any phenomenon, even the soul, has ultimate reality, thus extending the doctrine of *maya*, "illusion," to include the entire universe. Buddhism also differs from Hinduism in explicitly rejecting the concept of caste.

The Four Noble Truths encapsulate the basic doctrine of Buddhism. Formulated by the Buddha in the course of achieving enlightenment, they are: all life is suffering; suffering stems from desire or attachment, a futile wish for the illusions of the world to be real; desire can be overcome; the means for overcoming desire is the Noble Eightfold Path.

The Noble Eightfold Path consists of eight steps, practiced simultaneously (not sequentially), to guide the spiritual life of the Buddhist. They are: right views, right intentions, right speech, right conduct, right livelihood, right effort, right mindfulness, and right concentration. Right views and intentions produce morality; right speech, conduct, and livelihood produce wisdom; and right effort, mindfulness, and concentration produce spiritual development. *Right* in all these instances means "in conformity with the individual's dharma."

The Three Jewels of Buddhism constitute the foundations of Buddhist communities: Buddha, dharma, and *sangha* (the community of Buddhist monks and nuns). A key point of Buddhist doctrine is that the Buddha is not a deity (Buddhism is sometimes described as "a religion without a god"), but a being who has attained a state of full enlightenment and thus nirvana, liberation from illusion and therefore from the cycle of rebirth and suffering. Buddhahood is a state to which all sentient beings can aspire.

Buddhist monastic life revolves around communal study, performance of rituals (such as chanting the sutras), and ministering to the religious needs of the laity. Lay Buddhist worship is largely an individual affair, with few or no occasions involving the laity as a whole. Some sects of Buddhism celebrate holidays that vary from sect to sect; there are no universally celebrated Buddhist holidays or festivals.

◆**Confucianism** Confucianism takes its name from the sixth-century B.C. scholar and civil servant Kong Qiu or Kongzi ("Master Kong"; sometimes written as Kung Fu-Tzu and latinized as "Confucius" by 17th-century Jesuit missionaries in China), but he is not the "founder" of Confucianism in the same sense that the Buddha was the founder of Buddhism. Rather, Confucius was responsible for systematizing and teaching a scholarly tradition and code of ethical conduct that had its roots hundreds of years in the past, particularly in China's ancient cult of ancestor worship. The teachings of Confucius, as recorded in the *Analects* (the collected teachings of Confucius, written down by disciples over a long period after the Master's death) advocate a humanitarian ethical system focused on five values: *ren* ("reciprocal human-feeling"); *yi* ("righteousness"); *li* ("propriety, including ritually correct behavior"); *zhi* ("knowledge"); and *xin* ("trustworthiness"). Collectively these values contribute to the paramount Confucian virtues of *xiao* ("filial piety"); and *wen* ("culture or civilization; also civil as opposed to military power").

Confucianism remained primarily a philosophical school of thought and a political ideology for many centuries, but it began to develop into more of a religious system, complete with ceremonies, festivals, and temples, in the first century A.D., partially in response to the growing influence of Buddhism in China. Today, it is widely viewed in China as an equal part of a religious triad with Buddhism and Taoism (below); Confucius is often portrayed in religious images next to Laozi and the Buddha. There are about 6.3 million self-identified Confucianists in various countries around the world, but in a sense anyone who is culturally Chinese is to some degree a Confucianist.

The Analects of Confucius The *Analects* is one of the 13 works that form the Confucian canon of classical Chinese literature and philosophy. The Chinese title, *Lunyü*, can be translated as "Discussions and Conversations" or "Assessments and Conversations." The term *analects* (from the Greek, meaning "literary gleanings") is now conventional; it was first used by Jesuit missionaries in China in the 17th century.

The 20 chapters of the *Analects* purport to record the conversations of the teacher and philosopher Confucius (Kongzi) with his disciples. Traditionally it was thought that these conversations and teachings were written down from memory by a group of disciples shortly after Confucius's death. Recent scholarship has shown that the chapters are so diverse in both language and doctrine that they cannot have been composed in a short period of time by a small group of collaborators. The current view is that the chapters were composed over a period of more than two centuries, approximately 479–250 B.C., and that the present order of the chapters within the book does not reflect the order in which they were written.

The chapters of the *Analects* can be considered in groups, reflecting their approximate date of composition.

Chapters 4, 5, and 6 These are the work of Confucius's original disciples, dating to about 479–460 B.C. They emphasize the cardinal virtue of *ren* ("reciprocal human feeling"), the *dao* (the "Way," the natural order of things), the concept of the gentleman (*junzi* or "son of a prince," but in Confucius's radical reformulation, defined by conduct rather than by aristocratic birth), and the importance of putting one's cultivation of virtue into practice by holding public office. These chapters begin to define Confucianism as a coherent "school" of teachings.

Chapters 7, 8, and 9 These derive from the disciples' disciples and date to the last half of the fifth century B.C. They continue to define the school's doctrines and portray Confucius as a "transmitter, not an innovator," guided by the enlightened example of the sage-rulers of antiquity and emphasizing the internalization of values and virtuous conduct.

Chapters 2, 3, 10, 11, 12, and 13 The mid-fourth century (roughly 380–320 B.C.) chapters introduce ritual (*li*, a word covering meanings from the correct conduct of religious rituals to ordinary social etiquette) as a key Confucian virtue, and speak, as the earlier chapters do, about Heaven and the realm of spirits. Individual passages specifically engage in debate with other philosophical schools of the time.

Chapters 1, 14, 15, 16, 17, 18, 19, and 20 Dating to the late fourth to mid- third century B.C., these final chapters depict a world of escalating warfare, in which the *Analects* struggle to define the role of the public official. By the mid-third century B.C., it appeared that the Confucian school had been soundly defeated; but not much more than a century later, early in the early Imperial era, Confucianism made a decisive recovery, becoming the basis for China's official ideology for the next two millennia.

   ♦**Taoism** The legendary founder of Taoism (also spelled Daoism) is Laozi (old spelling Lao Tzu; probably a wholly mythical figure but traditionally dated ca. 600 B.C.), whose name means "old master." According to tradition, he is the sole author of the core Taoist text, the *Daodejing* (*The Way and its Power*). Modern scholarship has established, however, that the book is a work of anonymous, and probably multiple, authorship from the late fourth century B.C. The *Daodejing*, also known as the *Book of Laozi*, is a collection of 81 brief, poetic chapters that discuss, often through challenging paradoxes, the nature of the Dao (Tao), the source and essence of all being. An eponymous collection of writings by Zhuangzi (old spelling Chuang Tzu; ca. 300 B.C.) is another important Taoist text. From the beginning, Taoism included elements of both religion and philosophy. It advocated a political ideal of simplicity and austerity, with the state being ruled by a sage-king empowered by his complete oneness with the Dao itself to act with *wu-wei*, or nonintentionality: effortlessly effecting his actions while seeming to do nothing. Self-cultivation was central to early Daoist practice, with sagehood and immortality its religious goals.

   Beginning in the third century A.D., undoubtedly under the influence of Buddhism, Taoism took on more of the overt trappings of organized religion and gave rise to various sects through divine revelations granted to their founders. The two most important sects, the Heavenly Masters Sect and the Highest Clarity Sect, organized networks of temples, ordained clergy, and were governed by hereditary leaders. These sects remain a vital part of religious life in Taiwan and in many overseas Chinese communities, and they are experiencing a dramatic revival in post-Mao China, where thousands of active priests are serving hundreds of temples.

Weekend 15: The Written Word

Day 1: Writing and Printing

The advent and subsequent development of writing can be considered a landmark of human history, the main catalyst of most human progress since its appearance 6,000 years ago. But it would take more than 5,400 years for easy and rapid transmission of written thought and ideas to develop in the form of the printing press, the source of yet another revolution.

In Mesopotamia, traders in the thriving Sumerian culture were among the first in the world to see a practical use for writing and, by about 4000 B.C., professional scribes were recording business transactions and legal rulings by cutting pictograms and numerals in horizontal rows on round, handheld clay tablets. The scribes developed a stylus, a small triangle-tipped tool that allowed them to approximate the necessary symbols with a few quick stamps rather than more tedious drawing. Known today as "cuneiform" (from Latin for "wedge-shaped") writing, this Sumerian innovation spread throughout the Middle East between 2900 and 2600 B.C.

Meanwhile in Egypt, starting around 3000 B.C., a complex system of pictograms was combined with more traditional representational artwork to tell narrative stories about events or people. Many of the pictograms were painted or carved on temples, tombs, or items with religious importance; these characters were later called "hieroglyphics" (from Greek for "priestly writing"). Egyptian scribes also used ink and brushes to write less formal (often historical and legal) documents in cursive script called "hieratic" on scrolls made from papyrus, a lightweight sheet made from the stem of a water plant from the Nile.

♦**The Alphabet** Egyptian hieroglyphics and Sumerian cuneiform writing were familiar to the well-traveled traders of Phoenicia, and by 2000 B.C. Phoenician writers had borrowed elements of both systems to create their own written alphabet. The Phoenicians did not use pictograms to represent objects, but instead developed a series of 22 written letters that corresponded to each of their consonant sounds. While other phonetic alphabets existed, including one with 30 symbols used in Ugarit in northern Syria, the Phoenician system spread to almost every culture that encountered it.

Across the Mediterranean, the Greeks adopted the Phoenician alphabet by about 1300 B.C., although they modified some of the letter-forms and added vowels. (The word *alphabet* comes from the first two letters—alpha and beta—of the Greek lettering system.) Greek writers wrote with reed pens on papyrus and with styluses on tablets coated with black wax. Their early writing copied the Phoenician orientation from right to left, but Greeks began writing in both directions, creating a flow of letters back and forth. By the fifth century B.C., however, they had standardized their writing in rows of left to right and oriented all of their letters accordingly.

The nearby Etruscans used the Greek alphabet and writing style as a model for their own and, by 700 B.C., Roman writers had borrowed and further modified the Greek and Etruscan alphabets to create the Latinate alphabet now in use throughout most of Europe and the Western world.

✦**The Book** Egyptian, Greek, and Roman societies all developed literary cultures that used writing not just for commercial record keeping but to preserve histories, poems, plays, songs, and legends. Rulers and wealthy citizens built libraries for storing vast collections of books, almost all of which were written on papyrus or parchment scrolls. To stock these libraries, scribes were hired or enslaved to copy scrolls by hand. Since books could then be accessed by common people, censorship occurred, and individual scrolls or whole libraries were burned in order to suppress new ideas or to punish enemies.

Around 250 B.C., the Romans began using parchment, a thin writing material made from animal skin, which was easier to write on and less expensive than papyrus imported from Egypt. Instead of forming the parchment sheets into long scrolls, some parchment makers cut the sheets into rectangular leaves, which they folded in half along the left edge to form a folio of four pages. Four leaves folded together formed a *quarto*, and longer manuscripts of several quartos were stacked and bound into a book form, known as a *codex*.

By the second century A.D., the codex form had been adopted by early Christians seeking to spread their new religion because it was easier to use and store than a scroll. The written Gospels proved very useful in acquiring and teaching new converts and, by the fourth century A.D., the Roman Catholic Church had created scriptoriums in monasteries where literate monks could copy Bibles and other works for use in devotional and missionary work.

Although Viking raids and the collapse of the Roman Empire slowed the spread of literacy, and many libraries were destroyed during the early medieval period, book-copying centers in Constantinople and in religious centers across Europe still produced thousands of manuscripts. The high cost of parchment sometimes forced copyists to wash the ink off older texts and reuse the material for new works, and in order to further conserve parchment, many scribes slowly altered the large capital letters of Roman script to smaller forms. Each scriptorium developed a distinctive style of script. Celtic monks, for example, commonly added a larger, ornately decorated letter at the beginning of each paragraph.

In A.D. 780, the Holy Roman Emperor Charlemagne charged the English scholar Alcuin with oversight of clerical education, which included a massive production of new books. In order to standardize the much altered Roman alphabet across the Empire, Alcuin devised the Carolingian script, which for the first time formally distinguished between capital (majuscule) and lowercase (minuscule) letters. Monastery scribes then spread this new script throughout Europe between 800 and 1200.

♦**Paper and Printing** While writers and scribes in Europe wrote primarily on parchment or higher-quality *vellum* (parchment made from fine animal skin), by A.D. 100 the Chinese had invented an excellent and inexpensive writing material made from scraps of cloth and fiber. This invention, paper, was first introduced in Europe when Arabian merchants brought it to Italy in 1150. Italian manufacturers learned the technique and began making paper in the 13th century, and over the next two centuries it was adopted throughout Europe for use in books and letters.

During the Renaissance, the low cost of paper combined with a rising interest in learning created an unprecedented demand for books. Newly founded schools and universities required textbooks and literary works, and booksellers hired copyists to produce thousands of manuscripts. These professional scribes further altered the elegant but labor-intensive Carolingian script to form several regional versions of the more efficient black letter or Gothic script.

In the early 14th century, European artisans imported the Chinese method of using carved wooden blocks and pigmented ink to print multiple copies of an image—including words—onto paper. The carving was laborious and the blocks wore out quickly, so block printing was generally restricted to short books, pamphlets, and playing cards.

•Johannes Gutenberg and the Printing Press Johannes Gensfleisch was born about 1397 in Mainz, Germany, and later adopted the name of his family's ancestral city, Gutenberg. He trained as a goldsmith but extended his metalworking knowledge to printing. However, instead of *xylography*, using single woodblocks to print each page, he began experimenting with the idea of *typography*, using moveable blocks for each letter of text.

By 1444, Gutenberg was finally able to produce calendars and other small works. In 1450, the financier Johann Fust loaned Gutenberg additional money, and Gutenberg soon perfected his combination of moveable cast metal type, oil-based ink, and a lever-operated printing press. Between 1452 and 1455, Gutenberg produced the first major printed book in history, a massive two-volume Latin Bible of over 1,280 pages with 42 lines of type and two columns per page. He printed 200 copies, with lettering designed after the Gothic script then used for manuscripts and hired an illustrator to hand-decorate them.

By the time Gutenberg died in 1468, his inventions had been copied by dozens of other entrepreneurs. Many books were still hand-copied or block-printed, and some book collectors shunned the new machine-produced texts, but the technology spread swiftly. In 1461, Albrecht Pfister published *Der Edelstein*, the first illustrated printed book, and by 1500 printing presses had been established in 282 cities and 20 countries throughout Europe. Between 8 and 24 million individual books were in print, representing more than 30,000 titles.

Books printed in the 15th century are now known as the "incunabula" (from the Latin for "swaddling clothes," indicating something in its infancy), and they include Chaucer's *Canterbury Tales*, produced by William Caxton, the first English printer, as well as many Bibles and the *Peregrinatino in terrum sanctum*, the first illustrated travel-book, produced in 1486 in Mainz by Erhard Reuwich, a Dutch artist and printer. The incunabula varied widely as printers chose texts likely to appeal to their nearby constituents and designed typefaces based on local writing styles.

•The Reformation and the Power of Print The power of the written word grew exponentially with the printing press. In 1517, supporters of Martin Luther used the new technology to print and distribute copies of his "95 Theses" against the Catholic Church, and within weeks Luther's radical ideas had reached beyond Germany to help spur the Protestant Reformation.

This new power, however, revived old methods of censorship. Following the publication of Luther's German-language "September Bible" in 1522, William Tyndale printed 3,000 copies of his own English translation of the New Testament in 1526, but Catholic authorities seized and burned almost all of the books as soon as they arrived in London. Although Tyndale himself was later executed as a heretic, his translations served as the basis for English Bibles published under the reign of King Henry VIII.

The rapid and inexpensive production of printed matter promoted secular thought as well, and the ideas of 17th-century writers such as René Descartes and Thomas Hobbes reached far more people more quickly than had those of earlier philosophers. The proliferation of books fueled scientific discoveries, literary creation, and political upheavals.

In the New World, printing presses were established almost as soon as colonists arrived. Benjamin Franklin began his printing career at age 12, founded America's first circulating library in 1731, and built his reputation with *Poor Richard's Almanack*, which spread Franklin's thrift-promoting adages throughout the colonies. Thomas Paine used the press to an even more dramatic end with *Common Sense*, a short essay that greatly influenced the Declaration of Independence and stoked enthusiasm for the American Revolution.

◆**Technological Advances in Printing** In the first three centuries following the invention of the printing press, the design and durability of moveable type was improved by new metal formulation and casting techniques. Typeface design became a minor art form, but the press itself was changed only modestly. Then, in rapid succession, several innovations of the Industrial Revolution broadened the ease and accessibility of printing.

In 1796, Alois Senefelder invented the technique of lithography, which uses prepared etched plates rather than individual moveable type. The lithographic process proved ideal for full-color printing and remains a popular publishing method for high-quality text, illustrated books, and magazines.

The steam press came along in 1801, operating like a standard press but much faster, making 1,100 impressions per hour. In 1843, the American Richard March Hoe replaced the flatbed printing plate of the steam press with a revolving print cylinder that could produce millions of pages a day.

These changes and later developments, such as offset lithography (invented in 1903) and the digital printing popularized in the late 20th century, have all increased the speed of publication since Gutenberg's day. In the early 21st century, eBooks, which exist only in digital form, have gained increasing popularity. Few ideas, however, have had the impact of the printing press itself. Perhaps only written language—starting as a few scratches on a cave wall—has offered as great a power to expand the human mind.

Day 2: Newspapers and Magazines

Newspapers have played an integral role in American life ever since the colonial period, a time when they were established and circulated in every region. Magazines came to prominence in the middle of the 19th century in the U.S. and quickly acquired a large, literate audience eager for good writing on important issues, new fiction, as well as poetry. The print media would hold a preeminent place in the cultural life of the nation for two centuries until the full development of the Internet, which now threatens the very existence of newspapers and magazines alike. In the last decade, publications across the country have faced massive layoffs, dwindling circulation, and bankruptcy, leaving the fate of printed versions decidedly uncertain as pressure mounts to publish online.

♦The Origin of News News-writing dates back to ancient times. Sheets called *tipao* were passed among government officials during China's Han dynasty (206 B.C. to A.D. 220), while in the Forum of Ancient Rome, daily reports called *acta diurnal* contained noteworthy items. Gutenberg's printing press arrived around 1450 and made the idiom more popular, accessible, and affordable.

During the 16th and 17th centuries, news was largely published in pamphlets produced in response to a single, significant event. Venice was the first city to have a regularly printed news sheet, or gazette. Gazettes were distributed weekly as early as 1566 and were carried by merchants to ports in the Mediterranean and beyond. The new form caught on quickly; weekly publications appeared in European cities throughout the 17th century. The oldest surviving weekly was created in Strasbourg, France, in 1609, and the first daily newspaper appeared in Leipzig, Germany, in 1650. The first English daily, *The Daily Courant*, followed in 1702.

Newspapers flourished in America. When the Revolutionary War began, most colonies had weekly papers. Boston had four, and New York City had three. The first American newspaper, Boston's *Publick Occurrences*, printed only one issue in 1690 before being suppressed by the governor of Massachusetts for inflammatory content. This battle between the press and the government had begun in England 50 years earlier, but the ideals of the American Revolution made freedom of speech and of the press a priority. Congress is prohibited from making laws that "abridge the freedom of the press" in the First Amendment of the United States Constitution.

This freedom was not without controversy. The young government and the press clashed over how the news should be conveyed to the public—especially political news. President John Adams endorsed the Sedition Act in 1798, which prohibited "false, scandalous and malicious writing" and was aimed at censoring government scrutiny. Though the act lapsed under President Thomas Jefferson, the issue of defamation would continue to cause controversy throughout American history.

♦**Media for the Masses**   In September 1833, *The Sun* went on sale for one cent in New York City. It was the first of the "penny papers." The invention of the steam press had led to more effective printing practices, and by 1835 *The Sun* was selling 15,000 copies daily. Penny papers soon emerged in other cities. Quick turnaround reporting benefitted from Morse's telegraph and the completion of the transatlantic telegraph cable in 1866.

By the 1880s, there were approximately 7,000 papers in the U.S., including *The New York Times* (1851) and *The Washington Post* (1877). Circulation grew as literacy increased and more people could afford to buy the news. The Linotype, which set entire lines of text at once, made printing much more efficient, and improvements in color printing and photography made papers visually interesting. Sensationalist stories, startling images, and bold headlines were used to sell papers. Much like today, crime, violence, war, and politics dominated the news.

Nowhere was the newspaper boom more evident than in New York City, where newspaper publishers Joseph Pulitzer and William Randolph Hearst battled for readers at the close of the 19th century. Pulitzer purchased the *New York World* in 1883, quickly making it a success. He incorporated color comic strips and bold layouts and reached out to working people with games, contests, and illustrations. The *New York World* featured solid, investigative reporting, yet it also sought to entertain with violence, sports, women's fashion, comics, and special Sunday editions. In California, William Randolph Hearst, who had made *The San Francisco Examiner* a success, was watching closely. In 1896, he purchased *The New York Morning Journal* (shortened to *The New York Journal*), sparking the most legendary "circulation war" in America's history. The weapon of choice was "yellow journalism."

Yellow journalism—which most historians agree is named for the "Yellow Kid" character in a popular comic—is the practice of using sensationalism to sell newspapers. In the late 19th century, this included "scare" headlines, fake pictures and interviews, and unnamed sources. Local crime and pseudoscience was often given preference over hard news. Because the *New York World* sold for two cents, Hearst dropped the price of *The Journal* to a penny. In 1896, he recruited most of Pulitzer's Sunday staff, as well as Richard F. Outcault, the inventor of the color comic. By the time America entered the Spanish–American War in 1898, the papers each sold more than 1 million copies per day.

Pulitzer grew to disdain "yellow" tactics and founded both the Columbia School of Journalism and the Pulitzer Prize. Hearst went on to head a media empire that by the mid-1920s included 28 newspapers as well as magazines such as *Cosmopolitan, Good Housekeeping,* and *Harper's Bazaar.*

◆**Magazines** Magazines first appeared in the coffeehouses of early 18th-century London. Single sheets of paper, they were covered on both sides with gossip, opinion, and shipping news. Joseph Addison and Sir Richard Steele, who collaborated on *The Tatler* (1709–11) and *The Spectator* (1711–14), were the most successful of the early magazine editors, and they also wrote most of their publication content (called "copy" in industry jargon).

Magazines emerged as a popular form of entertainment in the United States after 1850 and contributed in large part to the prevalence of print in the 20th century. Because of inventions such as the Linotype and Eastman's film (1884), magazines were able to take their place as color-

ful, inexpensive dissertations on politics, women's fashion, and literature. *Harper's Weekly* (which began as *Harper's Monthly* in 1850) was one
of the first modern magazines. Initially known for serials by Dickens and
Thackeray, *Harper's* became a powerful political force, largely due to the
political cartoonist Thomas Nast, who helped to elect three presidents
and destroy New York City's Boss Tweed. *The Atlantic Monthly* (1857)
published Julia Ward Howe's "The Battle Hymn of the Republic" and
stories by Mark Twain. *Harper's Bazaar*, (1867), the first modern fashion
magazine, was aimed at middle- and upper-class women, containing illustrations (and later, photographs) of European fashion. Other early
magazines included *Vanity Fair* (1868), *Cosmopolitan* (1886), *Vogue*
(1892), *Time* (1923), *Fortune* (1930), and *Life* (1936).

Not surprisingly, the advent of magazines and the magazine format
coincided with the development of the advertising industry. In the
1850s, early advertisements sold cough drops and soap using bold and
colorful images. Over the next few decades, products like Ivory Soap,
Singer Sewing Machines, Coca-Cola, and Eastman's Kodak Film were all
given national exposure—but for a price. This price was proportional
to the popularity of the magazine, and periodicals competed to draw
more advertising dollars.

This relationship, which made publishers dependent on advertising
for survival, remains strong today, and has expanded to include radio
and television. Despite current troubles, 19,532 different magazine titles
were published in America in 2007, and more than 650 new magazines
launched in 2008. Magazines showcased a variety of literary talent
throughout the 20th century. Gay Talese, Norman Mailer, Joan Didion,
Tom Wolfe, and Hunter S. Thompson helped to found a new, unconventional form of journalism known as "New Journalism" in the 1960s.
Their work, which applied fiction techniques to nonfiction material,
was presented in such magazines as *Esquire*, *New York*, and *Playboy*. *The
Saturday Evening Post* featured 321 cover paintings by painter and illustrator Norman Rockwell between 1916 and 1963, and photojournalism
emerged as film technology improved. The magazine industry continued
to expand, targeting youth and niche markets, but the number of newspapers steadily decreased. Papers were absorbed and discontinued as
control of the news fell into the hands of a few, and with a declining
readership publishers could no longer support multiple dailies.

◆**Digital News: The Future of Newspapers and Magazines**   Television and the Internet are largely responsible for the endangered state of modern print journalism. The number of Americans who read a daily newspaper dropped below 50 percent in 2007, and in 2009 the Pew Research Center found that for the first time the Internet topped newspapers as the leading news source. Sixty percent of respondents under the age of 30 said they viewed most of their news online. According to Nielsen Online, newspaper Web sites grew in unique visitors in 2008, and some spiked in net worth up to $450 million.

The Internet has forced publications to find new ways to stay profitable. Newspapers today compete with well-funded Web sites such as *Politico*, *Slate*, and *Salon*, as well as blogs such as *The Huffington Post*, which by 2007 outranked all but six online newspapers in visitor counts, even though the site itself creates little of its own content. Most major papers now have free online versions, but some are considering the idea of charging a subscription fee. Many magazines now also offer free online access to select content, though magazines have survived the Internet revolution better than newspapers.

In 2007, six companies accounted for nearly half of all newspaper circulation. There were massive job cuts in the print industry throughout 2008 and 2009, and papers across the country cut content, filed for bankruptcy, and in some cases printed their final editions. In the March 11, 2009, *New York Times* article, "As Cities Go From Two Papers to One, Talk of Zero," Mike Simonton, a senior director at Fitch Ratings stated, "In 2009 and 2010, all the two-newspaper markets will become one-newspaper markets, and you will start to see one-newspaper markets become no-newspaper markets." The article also noted that advertising revenue dropped by about 25 percent in 2007 and 2008, with no signs of leveling off in 2009.

As print media wanes, online news continues to attract new readers. According to Nielsen Online, by 2009 print circulation of newspapers had dropped from a peak of 62 million a few decades ago to just 49 million. Yet online readership has grown at an even faster rate, reaching almost 75 million American readers and 3.7 billion page views in January 2009. In the words of the *Times*, "Industry executives who once scoffed at the idea of an Internet-only product now concede that they are probably headed in that direction."

Weekend 16: Medicine: A Brief History

Day 1: Medicine From the Ancients to the Enlightenment

Organ transplants, high-tech prosthetic devices, and powerful vaccines that have all but eradicated devastating illness around the world are commonplace in the 21st century. But the origins of all of this amazing technology go back to prehistoric times. The history of medicine is the story of innovation emerging from the human desire to extend life and eliminate physical suffering.

In 1991, a corpse was discovered in the Italian Alps. An autopsy revealed that among other ailments, the dead man suffered from parasitic whipworm, most likely the result of the accidental ingestion of the parasite's eggs along with beans or grain. His possessions—buried with him in the ice—included a birch fungus known to contain oils toxic to whipworm, suggesting that the man, or someone he knew, was treating the infestation with a natural antibiotic. What makes this discovery particularly remarkable is that the corpse—nicknamed Ötzi the Iceman—was over 5,000 years old. The practice of medicine, the art and science of healing, began long before the advent of written records. Prehistoric people had ideas on the causes of illnesses and developed remedies, ranging from magical incantations to rational strategies.

At the time the Iceman lived, civilizations had begun to form in the Middle East, and people started to record information in symbols, words, and pictures. The scientific study of medicine—as opposed to the application of folk remedies—was born as that information was passed from one healer to another and from one civilization to the next. Clay tables from the second century B.C. in Mesopotamia contain diagnostic treatises with subsections covering gynecology, pediatrics, and convulsive disorders. Skin lesions, venereal disease, and fevers are described, and some of the treatments prescribed resemble the modern approach to these same conditions. Surgeries were performed, and the earliest known legal code, the Code of Hammurabi, composed by the ruler of Babylon around 1700 B.C., included laws pertaining to the liability of physicians who "used the knife."

Papyri from ancient Egypt, dating from 3000 B.C. to 1200 B.C., in-

clude methods for recognizing pregnancy and the sex of a fetus, accurate descriptions of diseases, and scientific treatment of various ailments.
The Ebers Papyrus (ca. 1550 B.C. but possibly based on earlier papyri)
describes a wide range of diseases along with more than 700 remedies.

In Greece, the practice of medicine based on empirical knowledge
emerged around 500 B.C. The physician Hippocrates (ca. 460 B.C.–370
BC.) is credited with establishing medicine as a scientific undertaking.
He wrote the first clinical description of diphtheria, recognized that tuberculosis occurs most commonly between the ages of 18 and 35, and
observed "those naturally very fat are more liable to sudden death than
the thin." The Hippocratic Oath, dating from around the time of Hippocrates, pledges physicians to do their best for patients, to avoid doing
harm, and to keep information about their patients confidential; it continues to serve as a code of conduct for physicians today.

By the beginning of the Christian era, the Romans had created a
widespread empire, but their capital city, Rome, was crowded, dirty, and
frequently plagued by epidemics. The Romans adopted important public health measures, building aqueducts to bring freshwater into the city,
and sewers to carry away waste. Public baths were established to encourage personal hygiene, and special buildings were set aside to care for
the sick. The treatment of injured soldiers advanced surgical expertise
as Roman surgeons learned to reduce limb fractures, tie ligatures around
blood vessels, and cauterize wounds to stop bleeding. The most influential physician of ancient Rome was a Greek, Galen of Pergamum
(129–ca. 216), who made his name by using pulse readings in diagnosing problems, demonstrating how different parts of the spinal cord control different muscles, and proving that arteries contain blood, not air.
Though he was a prolific writer, author of about 300 known titles (about
half of which have survived), Galen wasn't right about everything. For
one thing, he believed that the liver was the main organ of the blood system. Nevertheless, for more than 1,400 years, his theories were considered infallible and served as the basis of medical education throughout
Europe.

Following the collapse of the Roman Empire in the fifth century,
medical knowledge was essentially lost throughout Europe as religious
teachings about the cause of disease held sway. Questioning the teachings of the church led to charges of heresy and blasphemy. Dissection of
human corpses was forbidden, and experimental investigations were

suppressed. The great pestilences of the period were considered the will of God. Infirmaries were built, but they were crowded, unsanitary places where care consisted of little more than kindness to the dying.

Fortunately, Arab physicians in the Middle East preserved, adopted, and expanded on the rational ideas of the ancient Greeks and Romans. In the Islamic Empire, medicinal plants were avidly collected; the number of drugs used to treat illness increased greatly, and pharmacy became a distinct vocation. The Persian scholar ar-Rāzī, or Rhazes (ca. 860–ca. 925), wrote the first description of smallpox and measles; he used opium as an anesthetic, plaster of Paris for casts, and animal guts for sutures. His multivolume *Comprehensive Book* contained all the medical knowledge of the time. Beginning in the late eighth century, hospitals providing both medical care and medical apprenticeships were opened in major cities in the empire. Early in the 11th century, another Persian polymath named Ibn Sīnā, known as Avicenna, recognized that tuberculosis is contagious, and that some diseases are spread through water or soil. His greatest contribution was undoubtedly the publication of the *Canon of Medicine*, a vast encyclopedia of medical knowledge, which remains one of the most famous books in the history of medicine.

In the 12th century, the first medical school in Europe was established in Salerno, Italy, and was so influential that the Holy Roman Emperor Frederick II decreed that anyone who wanted to practice medicine had to be approved by the masters of Salerno. A revival of learning took place in Europe beginning in the early 13th century, as classical medical texts as well as works by Islamic scholars were translated into Latin, and major centers for the study of medicine opened in Paris and Montpellier in France and Bologna in Italy. The invention of the printing press in the mid-15th century led to books on surgery and medicinal plants.

In the 16th century, as religious prohibitions against human dissection were lifted, the modern study of anatomy began, allowing scientists to distinguish between abnormal and normal anatomical features. Andreas Vesalius, a Belgian physician, dissected human and animal cadavers and proved that the structure of human anatomy differs markedly from that of animals; his discoveries were published in *On the Structure of the Human Body* (1543), the first work to accurately illustrate human anatomy. Soon after, Gabriele Falloppio described the tubes between the ovary and the uterus, subsequently named for him, as well as previously unknown structures in the skull and inner ear. Bartolomeo Eustachio (1513–74) identified the tube that connects the middle ear to the back of the throat, today known as the Eustachian tube. Hieronymus Fabricius compared the anatomy of embryos of dogs, cats, horses, and humans, and he provided detailed descriptions of the semilunar valves in blood veins. His work was the basis for the discovery of blood circulation by his student William Harvey, who published his findings in 1628 in *An Anatomical Study of the Motion of the Heart and of the Blood in Animals*, proving, for the first time, that the heart pumps blood into arteries, the arteries carry the blood throughout the body, and the veins return the blood to the heart.

This new understanding of human anatomy allowed surgery to emerge as a separate discipline. Previously, surgery was performed by barber-surgeons and was considered a less dignified occupation than medicine. This perspective was changed by Ambroise Paré, a leading surgeon in the 16th century, who served four kings and earned the reputation as the "father of modern surgery." Using the experience he gained on the battlefield, Paré pioneered the use of ligatures and dressings to stop bleeding instead of the painful practice of cautery. Paré is credited with originating the use of prostheses—artificial replacements for a missing part of the body—and popularized the use of the truss for treating hernias, which were previously often "cured" by castration.

One of the most important medical tools, helping physicians understand anatomy and identify signs of disease, was the compound microscope, invented in 1590 by Zacharius Janssen, a Dutch optician. Using single-lens microscopes he made himself, Antoni van Leeuwenhock (1632–1723) later became the first person to see blood capillaries, cells, sperm, and one-celled organisms.

Understanding normal anatomy led to the scientific study of diseased organs. An interest in the causes of disease (epidemiology) became more urgent in this period because of the epidemics of plague and other diseases that were killing huge numbers of Europeans. Paracelsus (1493–1541), a German-Swiss physician and alchemist, attacked the widely held belief, handed down from ancient Greece that disease results from internal disturbances of four bodily "humors" (blood, phlegm, yellow bile, and black bile), stating that external agents caused disease. In the mid-16th century, Girolamo Fracastoro proposed that epidemic diseases are spread by tiny particles, with contagion occurring by either direct contact, indirect contact via infected items, or even without contact.

People with a technical bent looked for ways to detect organ abnormalities in living patients. Traditionally, physicians mainly used a collection of basic tools—scalpels, forceps, and catheters—to deal with patients. In the 1620s, the Paduan scholar Santorio Santorio developed the pulsilogium, originally conceived by Galileo, to measure the beats of a man's pulse. In 1761, Leopold Auenbrugger introduced percussion—tapping on a patient's chest and listening to the resulting sounds—as a way of determining if the lungs were filled with fluid. New medical practices also emerged during the 18th century. Dominique Amel invented the fine-point syringe. James Lind discovered that ingesting lemon juice could prevent and cure scurvy, and William Withering discovered the value of digitalis in treating edema and heart disease.

In 1796, Edward Jenner developed a vaccination against the virus that caused smallpox. Subjects were inoculated with a serum containing material from cowpox—the bovine form of the disease—and were found to be immune from smallpox when they were exposed to it later. Although it took another 50 years to find an effective method of producing this antiviral medication in volume, Jenner's early work was responsible for eradicating the disease.

In the 18th century, physicians created the foundation for modern hospitals, where treatment and restored health, rather than containment and death, were attainable goals, and the first medical school in the United States was established at the University of Pennsylvania. At the same time, Philippe Pinel, a French physician, pioneered the humane treatment of the mentally ill, discarding the long-held belief that mental illness was caused by demonic possession.

Day 2: Modern Medicine

In the 19th century, sound scientific thinking and new medical technologies led to advances in every area of medicine, particularly the eradication of many of the world's worst diseases. Of fundamental importance was the discovery of a connection between filth and disease, and public acceptance of the theory led to improved sanitation and other public health measures. Independently established by Louis Pasteur and Robert

Koch in the 1870s, the germ theory of disease, which holds that bacteria and other microbes cause and spread infectious diseases, enabled scientists to isolate the causative agents of diphtheria, tuberculosis, and other scourges, leading to the development of vaccines. In 1879, Pasteur accidentally discovered that bacteria could be weakened, which prevents them from causing disease but still enables them to trigger immunity in infected individuals. Using weakened anthrax bacteria taken from the blood of diseased animals, Pasteur developed the first artificially produced vaccine in 1881. Vaccines for rabies (1885), cholera (1893), plague (1897), and typhoid (1897) soon followed.

Many new drugs were developed at this time, including acetylsalicylate, a derivative of the active ingredient in willow bark, a remedy used for combating fever for more than 2,000 years. Now known as "aspirin," it went on the market in 1899 after development by the German pharmaceutical company Bayer. Other drugs to appear in the physician's medicine cabinet included digitalis for heart ailments, amyl nitrate for angina, quinine for malaria, and sedatives such as chloral hydrate and paraldehyde.

Scientists of the era discovered that all organisms are composed of cells, determined the functions of nerves and certain parts of the brain, showed the role of the liver in carbohydrate metabolism, and carefully described numerous diseases for the first time. In 1819, the French physician René Laënnec invented the stethoscope, which was used to listen to the lungs and heart, allowing physicians to hear for the first time "the cry of the suffering organs." Until the 1860s, doctors used long thermometers to take a patient's temperature, a process that took almost 20 minutes. In 1866, Thomas Allbutt introduced the short, clinical thermometer, the use of which was advanced by Carl Wunderlich, who showed that fever is a symptom, not a disease. In 1895, Wilhelm Conrad Röntgen made the first "medical" X-ray, named for a then unknown type of radiation, which for the first time enabled doctors to see inside the body without surgery.

Modern surgery emerged in the 19th century as well. Physicians recognized the three major obstacles to successful surgery—pain, infection, and bleeding. Two American dentists, Horace Wells and William Morton, discovered anesthesia in the 1840s. By reducing the trauma of surgery for patients, anesthesia allowed doctors to take more time over their work and to apply surgery to more ailments. In 1867, the British surgeon Joseph Lister popularized antiseptic surgery and sterilized equipment, and the practice dramatically reduced infections in surgery patients and improved the odds of survival. Around 1890, William Halsted introduced the practice of wearing sterilized rubber gloves during surgery. By the end of the 19th century, the age-old practice of bloodletting was finally abandoned. The modern blood-type classification system, used to replenish a patient's blood through transfusions, began with the 1900 discovery of the ABO blood groups by the Austrian scientist Karl Landsteiner.

Not all medical milestones were achieved in laboratories and operating rooms. In 1889, William Osler was appointed the first physician-in-chief at John's Hopkins Hospital in Baltimore, where he revolutionized the way the medical curriculum was taught. Osler insisted that students learn at the bedside, implementing his belief that "the good physician treats the disease; the great physician treats the patient who has the disease." Students took patient histories, conducted physical examinations, and studied laboratory results, leading to a more interactive and humane treatment of medical conditions. Osler established the medical residency, in which doctors in training make up much of a hospital's medical staff. This system remains in place today in most teaching hospitals.

In the 20th century, advances in medicine came rapidly, changing the nature of death's threat. When the 20th century began, life expectancy in the United States was 47 years. In 2000, the average life span had increased to almost 77 years. The dramatic decline in the mortality rate is in large part due to the advancement of medicine, as well as the development of drugs to combat infectious diseases.

In 1901, Walter Reed, a U.S. Navy pathologist, discovered that viruses could cause disease in humans. His experiments proved that yellow fever was caused by a virus transmitted by mosquitoes. Development of electron microscopes in the 1930s gave scientists their first glimpse of viruses, and tissue culture techniques enabled researchers to grow viruses in the laboratory for drug testing, preparation of vaccines, and other purposes. Another type of disease-causing agent, distinct from viruses, was first isolated in 1982. Called prions, these particles consist of a single protein; they can be transformed into abnormal shapes capable of destroying cells. Prions cause spongiform encephalopathies, fatal diseases characterized by the breakdown of brain tissue—the most famous of which is commonly known as mad cow disease.

Hormones were isolated in 1901, and the therapeutic use of hormones began 20 years later when insulin, a hormone produced by certain pancreatic cells, was injected into a person with diabetes, a disease that slows or stops the body's natural production of insulin. Perhaps the most significant contribution in the field of endocrinology came 50 years later, with the creation of the birth control pill. In the early 1950s, Gregory Pincus, an American biologist and researcher, discovered that injections of the hormone progesterone would inhibit ovulation and prevent pregnancy. Seed money for this effort was provided by Margaret Sanger, a lifelong advocate for women's rights. At the same time, Carl Djerassi created an orally effective form of synthetic progesterone. It was another decade before "the pill" received F.D.A. approval and became commercially available, ushering in both a medical and social revolution.

In the first decade of the 20th century, scientists realized that certain "accessory food factors" are essential to good health. In 1911, Casimir Funk (1884–1967) found the first of these factors, B, and in a 1912 paper proposed the factors be called vitamins. Soon after the discovery of vitamins A (1913), D (1922), E (1922), C (1928), and K (1934), these substances soon became widely available.

Paul Ehrlich (1854–1915), a German scientist, helped found modern chemotherapy—the use of chemicals to fight disease—a treatment that proved effective against diseases that did not respond to serum therapy. He began to work with substances that killed or inhibited the growth of parasites, and in 1910 he successfully synthesized Salvarsan, the "magic bullet" used to cure syphilis.

Medicine was revolutionized in 1928, when Alexander Fleming discovered the antibiotic properties of penicillin, but he was unable to produce it in a form pure enough to use on patients. Ten years later, Howard Florey and others at Oxford University solved this problem, and by World War II techniques were developed in the United States for the commercial production of the drug. Its disease-fighting potential was recognized in the early years of World War II, and it saved the lives of countless wounded soldiers. Today a number of penicillins are available, and they are among the most widely used antibiotics. In 1900, pneumonia and tuberculosis were the leading causes of death in the United States, but by

2000 these and most other common bacterial infections had been brought under control, although scientists now recognize that microorganisms have the ability to develop a resistance to these medications.

Genetics, as a distinct field of study, came to prominence in 1900, when three botanists independently rediscovered the basic laws of heredity published by Gregor Mendel in 1866. By 1911, Thomas Hunt Morgan (1866–1945) had discovered that mutations could occur in genes, and by the 1940s scientists had established that all organisms as well as viruses can mutate. (See Weekend 35, "The Human Story.")

In the early 20th century, surgeons began to specialize and new fields emerged, building on the efforts of a few extraordinary individuals. Not for the first time, the theater of war made an enormous contribution to the progress of medicine. Harold Gillies, a New Zealand-born, British Red Cross doctor in World War I, saw that while soldiers could survive their battle wounds, surgeons had neither the skill nor the time to deal with their often dramatic disfigurements. Gillies devoted himself to the study and practice of plastic surgery, founding Queen's Hospital in Kent, England, where more than 10,000 reconstructive surgeries were performed. The techniques he invented, including skin grafts, were adopted by surgeons around the world and ushered in the era of reconstructive and, ultimately, cosmetic surgery.

Working in some of America's finest hospitals, including John's Hopkins Hospital in Baltimore and Peter Bent Brigham Hospital in Boston, Harvey Cushing emerged as the first true neurosurgeon in the early 20th century. Among his many innovations, Cushing created a way to stem the flow of blood with clamps and cuffs, minimizing the possibility that the patient would bleed to death. He pioneered the use of the "electric scalpel" and demanded that his team work with masks and gloves to minimize infection. His patients were the first to receive around-the-clock nursing care after surgery, and this type of postoperative treatment was the forerunner of intensive care units. Taken together, Cushing's contributions made brain surgery safer and more effective.

Other surgical milestones during this period included the first successful appendectomies, performed in Davenport, Iowa, in 1885 by Dr. William West Grant, and at roughly the same time by Dr. H. Hancock in England. In 1932, the American surgeon Michael E. DeBakey developed a roller pump that became an essential component of the heart-lung machine, which enabled the first open-heart surgery, performed by John H. Gibbon, Jr. in 1953. In 1966, DeBakey implanted the first mechanical heart in a human, and the successful transplantation of the liver (1963), lung (1963), pancreas (1966), intestine (1966) soon followed. In 1967, Dr. Christiaan Barnard performed the first successful human heart transplant. Bone marrow transplants began in 1964, and today stem cell transplants represent one of the most exciting—and controversial—frontiers in modern surgery. In 1990, the so-called laparoscopic technique was perfected, allowing surgeons to make much smaller incisions in the patient's abdomen to remove small organs through the navel.

Twentieth-century technologies such as computers, electronics, fiber optics, lasers, and ultrasound were all incorporated into medicine, making diagnosis more accurate and treatments safer. Mammography for diagnosing breast cancer was introduced in 1913 and the electroencephalograph (EEG) for recording brain waves in 1929. The heart can be monitored by recording electrical activity via skin electrodes with an electrocardiography (EKG) machine; magnetic resonance imaging (MRI) greatly improved the imaging provided by X-rays. A CAT scan combines X-ray equipment with computers that create detailed images of body tissue, allowing for greater ease in tough diagnoses. Great advances also occurred in the construction of artificial body parts: aluminum, titanium, plastic resins, and three-dimensional computer modeling are used to build sophisticated limbs and joints.

Through the past millennia, the human life span has increased as people have learned how to prevent and treat illness, although in spite of medical advances, humans continue to face major health challenges. While many infectious diseases have been brought under control, AIDS, Lyme disease, and other emerging diseases discovered only in recent decades have created new medical battlefields. As people live longer, there is a growing incidence of arthritis, Alzheimer's disease, and heart failure. However, a better understanding of human biology, genetics, and psychology has led to improved preventive measures, diagnostic tools, and therapies.

Weekend 17: Islam

Day 1: The Religion of Islam

Islam (literally, "submission to God"), was founded by the prophet Muhammad (ca. 570–632), to whom, Muslims believe, God revealed his complete and final message to humankind.

Muhammad was a merchant in Mecca, a cosmopolitan Arabian trading city with a local polytheistic cult, as well as Jewish and Christian communities. In his middle age, he received a commandment from God to recite God's holy word. Gathering a steadily widening circle of believers, Muhammad preached a message of uncompromising monotheism, peace, and justice on Earth, and salvation in the world to come. Opposed by powerful local clans, he withdrew with his followers to Medina in 622. This event, the *hijira*, marks Year 1 of the Muslim calendar. By 627 (in the Gregorian calendar), Muhammad had consolidated his leadership in Medina, and in 628 the Treaty of Hudaybiyah permitted Muslims to make the sacred pilgrimage to Mecca. It wasn't until 630 (two years before his death) that Muhammad and his followers were able to occupy Mecca, after eight years of desert warfare.

Islam spread rapidly, in part by military conquest, to become within a century the dominant religious and political force in the Middle East, North Africa, and Persia. It later spread to South Asia, parts of Southeast Asia, and by the 15th century had a significant influence on the cultures of Spain and what would become modern Turkey. Today, with 1.3 billion adherents in 184 countries, Islam is the world's second-largest religion, after Christianity. Indonesia has the largest Islamic population of any country in the world, followed by Pakistan and India.

•**Scripture** The Koran (Arabic for "recitation") is the sacred scripture of Islam, believed by adherents to be the authentic and verbatim word of God, spoken in Arabic to the Prophet Muhammad by the Angel Gabriel beginning in A.D. 610 and continuing throughout the Prophet's lifetime. The Koran emerges from the biblical traditions of Abraham and bears some similarities and parallels to both the Hebrew Bible and the Christian New Testament, placing Muhammad in the line of biblical patriarchs and prophets, including Moses and Jesus.

The Koran also includes some of the stories of Adam and Eve, Abraham, Moses, and David and assumes that these stories will be familiar to the reader. Yet the Koran focuses on the significance of these events rather than their historical details.

Muslims trace their descent to the lineage of Abraham through his son Ishmael. The Koran accords Jews and Christians special status as "people of the Book" and heirs to the tradition of Abraham, even though they remain nonbelievers in Islam. Muhammad, however, is seen as the "Seal of the Prophets," beyond whom no further revelations will be given. The divine words were recited by Muhammad to his followers and preserved by them, first in oral form. According to traditional accounts, they were written down beginning around the time of the Prophet's death in 632. Several years after they were recorded, the third Caliph, 'Uthman, ordered copies to be made and distributed throughout the Islamic world to ensure their preservation. The 114 written chapters or sections ("suras") were subsequently collected to form the Koran.

Each sura (except, for reasons that are unclear, Sura 9) begins with the formula, "In the name of God, the Lord of Mercy, the Giver of Mercy." The titles of the suras reinforce the Koran's status as primarily an oral document for recitation rather than a written book for silent reading. They are more mnemonic devices than descriptions of the contents of the sura. For example, the title of Sura 2, "The Cow," is not about cows; the title serves as a brief reminder to the reader that this is the sura that makes a reference to a cow. Many suras are rather diverse in content, and brief summaries can give only a general idea of what each is about.

Generally speaking, the focus of the Koran is on the life of the Islamic community, with its commitment to justice, equality of believers before God, humility, and piety. Many suras refer to specific instances or circumstances in the life of Muhammad as he struggled to make his prophecy understood and accepted by his community. Muhammad's mission was to warn the people of God's plan for the salvation of believers and assure that disbelievers will be condemned to eternal punishment on the Day of Judgment. Others emphasize the torments of hell that await those who do evil or deny God. God's warning as delivered by Muhammad is directed at those who hear and reject the word of God, rather than those who have not heard it. In the suras, God provides Muhammad with arguments to use to reassure believers and to persuade disbelievers to change their minds, and Muhammad himself is often counseled to be patient in delivering his message and not to lose heart. The first sura, or "The Opening," is a brief summary of the entire content of the Koran, memorized in Arabic by Muslims and recited as part of the obligatory daily prayers. It reads, in its entirety (in the translation of M.A.S. Abdel Haleem, 2004):

> "In the name of God, the Lord of Mercy, the Giver of Mercy!
> Praise belongs to God, Lord of the Worlds, the Lord of
> Mercy, the Giver of Mercy, Master of the Day of Judgment.
> It is You we worship; it is You we ask for help. Guide us to the
> straight path: the path of those You have blessed, those who
> incur no anger and who have not gone astray."

Following "The Opening," the suras are arranged in order of length, from longest to shortest.

The Koran, also sometimes referred to as *al Kitab* (Arabic for "The Book"), is the ultimate religious authority in Islam. Other written authorities exist, such as *hadith* (traditions concerning the Prophet), *ijma* (consensus of Islamic jurists), and *qiyas* (analogy, such as a ban on intoxicating drugs, considered analogous with the Koran's ban on alcohol), but nothing in these conflicts with or contradicts the Koran. It is the fountainhead of Islamic scholarship, often said by believers to contain everything in the world.

The Koran remains in large part a recited text, and skillful recitation of Holy Scripture is a highly esteemed art. All Muslims memorize at least some parts of the Koran for use in daily prayers, and memorization of the entire text is a prerequisite for further training as an Islamic scholar or jurist. The Koran has been translated into many languages, but because the original Arabic version is considered to be the verbatim word of God, no translation can be considered to have religious authority.

◆**Belief and Practice** Muslims affirm the oneness of Allah (Arabic for "the God"), creator and sustainer of the universe, explicitly rejecting the Christian doctrine of the Trinity. Muhammad is understood to be the last and greatest of God's prophets, but he is not regarded in any way as a divinity or object of worship.

Believers by definition subscribe to the Five Pillars of Islam:

Profession of Faith "There is no God but God, and Muhammad is His Prophet." These are the first words spoken to a newborn Muslim, and they are recited daily throughout a person's life.

Prayer Most Muslims pray five times daily: before dawn, midday, mid-afternoon, sunset, and nighttime. Muslims perform ritual purification before prayer and pray in the direction of Mecca.

Charity Devout Muslims are obligated to give a portion of their wealth to the poor. The actual percentage varies, but is usually about 2.5 percent yearly, and is based on all of a person's possessions, not only their annual income.

Fasting During the holy month of Ramadan Muslims are required to abstain from food, liquid, tobacco, and sex between dawn and dusk during the ninth month of the Muslim calendar, Ramadan.

Pilgrimage (Hajj) Every Muslim is expected to visit Mecca once in his or her lifetime, unless prevented by poverty or illness, and only Muslims may enter the city. About 2 million people make the journey each year. Completing the pilgrimage gives a Muslim the status of *hajji* or *hajjiyah* ("male or female pilgrim").

Jihad, "struggle," is sometimes called the "sixth pillar of Islam." A term with a wide range of meanings, it can refer to anything from an individual's struggle to lead a righteous life, to a "holy war" against enemies of the faith.

Muslims divide the world into the Dar al-Islam ("world submissive to God") and the Dar al-Harb ("world at war with God"). The former is, ideally, a society of peace and justice that makes no distinction between secular and sacred matters. Islamic law and government are designed to apply to all aspects of Muslim life.

◆Schools and Sects Islam is divided into two great sects, a large variety of subsects that reflect ethnicity, local cultures, and degrees of fundamentalism or latitude (among other factors) as well as a trans-sectarian mystical movement. The break between the two main sects originally reflected a dispute about the line of prophetic succession after Muhammad's death, but over time the split has also come to reflect deeper differences of faith and practice.

Sunni Islam, followed by a great majority of Muslims, emphasizes the Sunna (Arabic for "tradition") of Muhammad as found in the Koran and the hadiths. It relies on learned jurists to pronounce authoritatively on doctrinal issues. Sunni Islam prevails throughout most of the Muslim world, with centers of authority in Saudi Arabia and Egypt.

Shi'ite Islam, found mainly in Persia (Iran), Iraq, Syria, and as a minority sect elsewhere in the world, descends from the faction that supported Muhammad's nephew and son-in-law Ali, Ali's son Husayn, and their heirs as the legitimate line of succession. Ali and Husayn are revered by Shi'ites as great martyrs who were assassinated in the succession crisis. Shi'ites emphasize struggle and sacrifice as signs of faith, and they look for the return of a long-lost *imam* (religious leader) from the line of Muhammad.

Sufism is Islamic mysticism, in which adepts use various techniques (breath control, music, drumming, spin-dancing, etc.) to achieve a trancelike state of transcendence and a sense of oneness with God. Sufism exists throughout the Islamic world but is sometimes suppressed by both Sunni and Shi'ite authorities for its supposedly heterodox beliefs and practices.

◆**Holidays**   The Islamic calendar consists of 12 lunar months totaling about 354 days. It is not synchronized with the solar year.

Id al-Adha (Day of Sacrifice) commemorates Abraham's sacrifice of a ram in place of his son. It is celebrated in the 12th month and is considered the most suitable month for the hajj (pilgrimage to Mecca). Id al-Fitr (Day of Breaking the Fast) marks the end of the holy month of Ramadan. In the Shi'ite world, Muharram, in the first lunar month, commemorates the martyrdom of Husayn and is celebrated with great passion.

Day 2: The Expansion of Islam

Because Islam divides the world between Dar al-Islam ("world submissive to God") and the Dar al-Harb ("world at war with God"), the conversion of the world has been a religious imperative for many adherents of Islam, as of course it was for Christianity at the time. Within two years of Muhammad's death, the armies of Islam were on the march. Over the next decade, they detached Syria, Mesopotamia, Egypt, and Libya from remnants of the Roman Empire, and then conquered Persia.

In 661, the internal struggle for power between Muhammad's family and the old tribal aristocracy first arose and would occupy Islam's leaders for the next 50 years. The caliphs ("successors") of the Umayyad dynasty ruled for a century from their capital at Damascus, but not without challenges from those who remained loyal to the family of the Prophet (Shi'a Muslims), and looked for the return of the "hidden Imam" to restore the rightful successor. Those who accepted the legitimacy of the caliphs were known as Sunni Muslims.

♦**Islam in Europe** By the beginning of the eighth century, the Umayyad rulers were in complete command and conquest soon returned as their objective. In 711, Muslim expansion to Europe began in Hispania (modern-day Spain), as the Moors—peoples of North Africa, of both Arab and Berber descent—invaded under the flag of the Umayyad caliphate. During the eight-year campaign, they managed to bring a majority of the Iberian Peninsula under Islamic control. They called the conquered region al-Andalus, and it was here, during the 11th and 12th centuries, that Islamic influence peaked in Europe. The area is home to some of the best-preserved artifacts of Islamic domination, notably the Alhambra Palace in Granada (completed in the 14th century). The region also served as a gateway through which the Christian world learned of agricultural techniques such as irrigation, as well as the cultivation of sugar, oranges, and lemons. Islam would remain a powerful influence in Spain for seven centuries, until the reign of King Ferdinand II of Aragon and Queen Isabella of Castile when, in 1492, Muslims were expelled from Spain along with Jews.

Islamic conquests were less successful in other parts of Europe, notably those in the Frankish kingdom during the mid-eighth century. In 732, the Umayyad leader Abd-ar-Rahman led a Muslim army toward

Tours, his troops enriching themselves with the spoils of war as they made their way north. The Frankish king, Charles Martel, formed a hasty alliance with an old enemy, Eudo of Aquitaine, and prepared to challenge the Muslim forces. After a weeklong standoff between the towns of Tours and Poitiers, the Muslims attacked, but the disciplined Franks held their position. Sensing defeat, some of ar-Rahman's men retreated. After ar-Rahman was killed, the retreat became a rout, and Islamic influence in Western Europe would never spread farther.

♦**Expansion into India and Southeast Asia** The Abbasid dynasty employed Turkish auxiliaries (in the same way that Romans had utilized Germanic tribes) in their Near Eastern armies; one such army, under chieftain Mahmud of Ghazni (r. 997–1030), moved out of Afghanistan into the Punjab (the area straddling India and Pakistan) about the year 1000, and by 1030 had established a Muslim dynasty there. Over the next 200 years, they spread their influence over the Rajputs, the Hindu rulers of India, eastward into the plain of the Ganges River, establishing their capital at Delhi about the year 1200. Many of the rich Hindu temples were plundered and destroyed by the invaders. Under the sultan Ala-ud-din (r. 1296–1316), most of the subcontinent was brought under one rule.

Unable to break the caste tradition, the ruling Turks became a casteless minority of warrior-aristocrats extracting heavy taxes but relying upon the Hindu princes for administration. Although the Hindu temples had been devastated, they were rebuilt, as the Muslim Turks had to exercise a practical tolerance for Hinduism. After the death of Ala-ud-din, his empire dissolved into a medley of warring kingdoms ruled by Muslim generals or Hindu princes over whom the sultans at Delhi exercised varying degrees of control.

In the archipelago of Indonesia and curving north into the Philippines, Muslim traders and missionaries spread the Islamic faith. By A.D. 1500, 20 Islamic states had been established as many rulers converted, though many of the inhabitants of those states continued to follow indigenous religious beliefs. The Hindu aristocracy of Java took refuge on the island of Bali, which still preserves elements of pre-Islamic Indonesian culture and where a unique form of Hinduism is still practiced.

◆**Expansion into Africa** By the year 800, Muslim traders from Morocco were in contact with the Kingdom of Ghana. Camel caravans crossed the Sahara to the grasslands between the upper Niger and Senegal Rivers, bearing salt and goods from the Mediterranean basin, and returning with gold and ivory from Ghana. Extracting import and export taxes and monopolizing the gold supply, the kings of Ghana exercised an imperial control over the trading cities of the region, growing wealthy and powerful, yet by 1076, the caliphs in Morocco were able to conquer the region.

Muslim expansion occurred in western Africa as well. In 1050, Muslim Arabs crossed the Red Sea and annexed the Somali coast from the ancient Christian kingdom of Ethiopia. The conquest of Ghana by Muslim Berbers in 1076 led to a series of successor states. Under Mansa Musa (r. ca. 1312–37), Islam spread through the western savanna, and the king himself made a pilgrimage to Mecca in 1324. Farther east, the king of the Songhay people on the great bend of the Niger River had already converted to Islam in the 11th century; thus, Islam dominated not only the northern coast of Africa but almost the entire belt of savanna south of the Sahara as well.

◆**The Battle of Manzikert** In the middle of the 11th century, Byzantium faced a new Muslim threat in Alp-Arslan, leader of the Seljuk Turks. The Seljuks were originally from Central Asia, but they converted to Islam as they moved west and conquered Baghdad and Persia.

After Alp-Arslan conquered the capital of resource-rich Armenia, the emperor, Romanus IV Diogenes, decided to block the Seljuk Turks' expansion into his territory. Romanus won several early battles, but in 1071 Alp-Arslan captured Manzikert in eastern Turkey, marched back to Persia, and then to Syria. Romanus recaptured the city in short order, but after marching out of the city, he found himself face-to-face with Alp-Arslan's main army. Romanus had the initial advantage after a day of fighting, but when the Seljuks regrouped, many of the Byzantine troops continued to retreat toward their camp rather than stand and fight. Romanus himself was captured. The Seljuks took most of Anatolia (the Asian portion of Turkey), and then later conquered Syria (1084), creating an empire that stretched from Egypt to India and endured in some form until 1243. In addition, the holy city of Jerusalem was also taken by them, a significant event as it turned out.

◆**The Crusades** In the years following the defeat at Manzikert, the Byzantine emperors realized they needed the help of Western Christendom if the forces of Islam were to be held in check. The capture of Jerusalem and the despoiling of the Holy Sepulchre (where Jesus was supposed to have been buried and where he rose from the dead) by Muslims aroused Pope Urban II to begin urging Christian leaders to launch a holy war to regain control of the Holy Land and the sacred places of Christendom. By 1097, the First Crusade, led by Frankish and German noblemen, had achieved several military victories in the Middle East, culminating in the capture of Jerusalem in 1099 and the establishment of several Christian fiefdoms in the region.

In 1144, the Turks struck back, recapturing the key city of Edessa and causing the Christian leaders of France and the Holy Roman Empire to launch the Second Crusade. Before their armies reached the Holy Land, the soldiers pillaged at will through Byzantine territory. In 1148, they were defeated at Damascus by the Turks, and the Crusade ended in failure. In 1176, the great Muslim military leader, Saladin, won control of Egypt and Syria, prompting the Europeans to agree to a truce in 1180. In 1187, they broke the truce by attacking a Muslim caravan, and Saladin launched a fierce attack, badly defeating the Crusaders and forcing them to surrender not only themselves, but a relic they believed to be the True Cross on which Christ was crucified. Known as the Battle of Hattin, this victory marked the beginning of firm Muslim control of the Holy Land for 500 years.

Six more Crusades would be launched between 1189 and 1272, none of them successful in any serious way. In the Third Crusade, the legendary Richard I "The Lion Heart" of England, secured several cities but not Jerusalem. The Fourth Crusade proved a disgrace to the cause as Venice insisted on attacking Byzantium and looting the city (1204) so the armies never reached the Holy Land.

In 1212, in the so-called Childrens' Crusade, mobs of enthusiastic French children led by a charismatic 12-year-old boy, Stephen of Cloyes, vowed to succeed in the Holy Land where their elders had failed. Stephen brought several thousand children and some young adults together to sail from Marseilles, but in fact the sailors had arranged to sell them into slavery in the Middle East. In Germany, a group of 20,000 children marched from Cologne to Genoa under the guidance of a boy named Nicholas, but despite the pope's meeting with them, they could find no one to sail them across the Mediterranean. The fate of many of them was death from exhaustion, while many others never returned home.

Crusades five through nine (1217–1270) resulted in a few victories for the Europeans, but soon the Muslim forces would regain what they had lost. In 1268, Jaffa and Antioch fell to the Muslims, and the Christians finally proved willing to end their foolish adventure in 1272. Muslims captured Tripoli in 1289 and Acre, the last Christian stronghold, in 1291, effectively ending the Crusades' presence in the East, except for Cyprus, which was captured by the Ottoman Turks in the 16th century.

No Crusades were ever again launched toward the Holy Land, although Crusader-like campaigns were undertaken against Muslim incursions in Europe. The most famous of these was the victory of the Christian fleet under the command of John of Austria over the Turks at the Battle of Lepanto, off Greece, in 1571. The Crusades to the Holy Land, although ultimately a failure, led to a wide range of influences on the West through contacts with other civilizations, increased commerce, and improved geographical knowledge. They also strengthened monarchs against the pope, who lost the power to direct these great Christian enterprises.

Weekend 18: The Renaissance

Day 1: Literature and Ideas

The European Renaissance sprang from the chaos of the Late Middle Ages, as the final Crusades, the Great Famine, the Black Death, the Hundred Years War, and the Ottoman capture of Constantinople disrupted the relative stability of medieval society. However, the resulting flow of Eastern trade and refugees also brought scientific advances from the Islamic world and the rediscovery of ancient Greek and Roman texts, which had been lost in the West but preserved by Byzantine scholars.

In Florence, scholars inspired by the return of Greek and Roman writings, instigated a humanist revival of art and literature during the 14th century. Humanists, like their classical predecessors, espoused the power of the individual, the value of empirical observation, and the divine virtue of beauty. Artists and intellectuals began to look back past the Christian era to ancient ideals in literature, philosophy, and art. Some writers and artists tried to imitate Greek and Roman examples, while others borrowed merely the underlying principles of order, harmony, and grace. The wealthy and powerful Medici family fueled this creative resurgence by building libraries and giving financial and personal support to artists, architects, and scholars. This Renaissance (literally "rebirth") soon spread from Florence to Siena, Venice, and Rome.

By the early 1500s, the Renaissance had moved into northern Europe, aided by the 1455 invention of the printing press, new universities, and increased trade throughout the Continent. However the Italian Renaissance quest for perfection was modified by northern scholars and religious reformers, who applied its humanist ideals to more pragmatic ends.

Although some Renaissance principles conflicted with Catholic doctrine, the movement was not antireligious, and many of its major works were on Christian themes or even commissioned by the church. However, the Renaissance emphasis on individual potential, direct knowledge, and earthly experiences broke with the church-dominated medieval era to form the basis of modern cultural values. Advanced learning—especially in multiple fields—was encouraged, and talented architects, painters, and sculptors established themselves as individual creators with specific aesthetic goals rather than simply as craftsmen for hire. The contemporary understanding of the visionary "artist" is itself a Renaissance idea, formed under a belief in the limitless ability of the human mind. By the 17th century, the original impulses of Renaissance innovation had faded, but the spirit of creative possibility and the aesthetic achievements of the era remained central to Western culture.

•Renaissance Ideas

Humanism In Florence, the Catholic cleric and poet Francesco Petrarch collected ancient Greek and Roman texts and admired the classical commitment to logic and direct understanding. Petrarch argued that earthly knowledge and experience could actually be a pathway to God, rather than a barrier to faith. His humanist philosophy of human potential encouraged centuries of artistic and scientific innovation, as it revived the idea that people could understand and improve the world around them rather than simply accept it as a creation of God. As defined by Count Giovanni Pico della Mirandola in his influential *Oration on the Dignity of Man* (1486), humanism recognized a hierarchical natural world in which humans could claim pride of place only by exercising their superior faculties of reason.

While most humanists tried to encourage human achievement within the dominant framework of Christianity, later Catholic humanists took a skeptical view of church organization and materialism and applied classical textual criticism to religious works. The Dutch priest Desiderius Erasmus urged believers to read the Bible for themselves and to develop a personal relationship with God. Although Erasmus disapproved of the radical Protestant Reformation, he urged institutional reform of the church in his satirical book *The Praise of Folly* (1509).

Renaissance Political Theorists As secular state powers displaced the Catholic Church in Europe and feudal chieftains tried to consolidate power, many scholars turned from theology to social morality and political statecraft. The classical scholar and Florentine civil servant Niccolò Machiavelli is regarded as a founder of modern political science for his incisive examinations of power and government. In *The Prince* (published posthumously in 1530), Machiavelli suggested that the authority and maintenance of the state were more important than individual morality or liberty, and that civic life could be improved only through the effective application of power. Machiavelli's cynical realism was in direct opposition to Erasmus, whose *Education of a Christian Prince* (1516) urged benevolent and just leadership. The idealistic Sir Thomas More of England portrayed a perfectly ordered and harmonious society in *Utopia* (1516), which implicitly criticized the inequality and disorder of European political structures.

The medieval image of a God-driven universe was further challenged by scientific and philosophical descriptions of a world that obeyed only mechanical and mathematical rules. Nicolaus Copernicus helped launch the Scientific Revolution when he used decades of careful observation to produce his startling theory that the Sun was the center of the universe, not the Earth as was commonly believed. In philosophy, the influence of scientific empiricism had a profound effect on late 16th-century thinkers such as Francis Bacon. (See Weekend 40, "Philosophy: The Life of the Mind.")

Late Renaissance Theology While skeptical of blind faith, the devout French mathematician Blaise Pascal found both empiricism and rationalism insufficient for comprehending the universe. Pascal's eloquent *Penseés* (published posthumously in 1670) explores several philosophical and theological paradoxes—including the notion of infinity—but concludes that one should "wager" as if God does exist even though such existence cannot be proven.

Baruch Spinoza, however, resolved the question of God's existence by declaring that everything that exists is, in fact, God. Spinoza claimed that different forms of matter are simply local and finite "attributes" of an infinite God—just as the body and the mind are the same thing, with the mind simply the "idea" form of the physical body.

◆Renaissance Literature

Classics Rediscovered in Italy The rediscovery of classical literary works in the 13th and 14th centuries shifted the scope of Italian literature from religious allegories and courtly novels to profound explorations of the breadth of human experience. In Florence, Petrarch and Giovanni Boccaccio translated ancient texts and revived the methods and forms of the originals—including the classical tradition of textual analysis and criticism.

While Petrarch wrote primarily in Latin, he used the local Tuscan dialect for composing his *Canzoniere*, a collection of 300 sonnets dedicated to his lost love, Laura. Boccaccio used the same dialect for *The Decameron*

(1350–53)—100 allegorical novellas about love. Their works—with Dante's *Divina Commedia* (*Divine Comedy*, 1308–21)—established Tuscan as the Italian standard and helped to popularize the use of vernacular language for serious literature. The invention of the printing press soon spread new and classical works across Italy and beyond.

While lyric poetry—especially the sonnet form—dominated Italian Renaissance literature, many Italian writers also composed narrative poems inspired by Homer and Virgil. The most successful was Ludovico Ariosto's lengthy humanist epic poem, *Orlando Furioso* (1516), a clever and extravagant imagining of the adventures of a lovesick knight. The poet Torquato Tasso was best known for *La Gerusalemme Liberata* (*Jerusalem Delivered*, 1580), a fanciful version of the First Crusade. Michelangelo Buonarroti, the great painter and sculptor, was also a prolific poet who composed hundreds of sonnets.

In prose writing, Baldassare Castiglione adopted the dialogue form for *The Courtier* (1528), a primer on courtly behavior that described the humanist concept of the "uomo universal"—a well-educated and diversely knowledgeable individual who would later be called the "Renaissance man." The Greek theatrical traditions inspired others, like Machiavelli, author of *The Prince*, who further illustrated his ruthlessly pragmatic view of society in the satirical comedy *La Mandragola* (*The Mandrake*, 1518).

Renaissance Literature in France Italian Renaissance poetry became so popular in early 16th-century France that a group of poets known as the Pléiade, led by Pierre de Ronsard, dedicated themselves to establishing French as a suitable language for original verse. Adapting the sonnet and the classical ode, they produced love poems and works on mythological themes and the virtues of nature.

The French prose writer François Rabelais composed four extended comic, socially incisive tales about father-and-son giants in *Pantagruel* (1532) and *Gargantua* (1534), and Boccaccio's *Decameron* inspired many French writers to create short stories or novellas. Michel de Montaigne, the first great modern essayist, applied classical commentary techniques and a skeptical, humanist perspective to a range of contemporary subjects.

The Golden Age in Spain Under the artistic patronage of the Hapsburgs, the Italian lyric tradition reached Spanish poets such as Garcilaso de la Vega, who modified the sonnet to better suit the Spanish language.

The witty Francisco de Quevedo and his rival, the erudite Luis de Góngora, also expanded the poetic potential of Spanish.

Religious writing flourished in Spain during the Counter-Reformation; St. Teresa of Avila and San Juan de la Cruz produced deeply mystical works on the nature of prayer and the growth of the soul.

The prolific playwright Lope de Vega organized Spain's loose dramatic traditions into a distinctive three-act commedia with established character types and poetic forms. But the masterpiece of Spanish literature is still *Don Quixote de la Mancha* (1605–15), Miguel de Cervantes's parody of the chivalric genre novel. The all-encompassing *Don Quixote*—considered the first modern novel—alternates between illusion and reality to recount the adventures of an idealistic old gentleman so addled by romances that he fancies himself a knight and undertakes a richly and hilariously imagined journey across Spain with his peasant "squire," Sancho Panza.

(For Renaissance literature in England, see Weekend 21, "William Shakespeare" and Weekend 33, "English Poetry: An Overview.")

Day 2: Renaissance Art

Sculptors and painters in Florence in the early 15th century made a series of achievements that fully established Renaissance ideas and techniques in art. The sculptor Donatello created statues employing the *contrapposto* pose, similar to those from the Classic Greek period, that depicts the figure in a relaxed stance; his *St. Mark* (1411–13), for example, leans at ease on one leg, assuming a naturalistic stance. Donatello's unclothed bronze statue of a youthful *David* (ca. 1425–30) revived the tradition of the classical nude, which had no place in the Christian art of the Middle Ages.

Donatello and his teacher Lorenzo Ghiberti also made important developments in relief sculpture. They created the illusion of three-dimensional depth on a two-dimensional surface by employing the scientific method of linear perspective devised by the Italian architect Filippo Brunelleschi.

Combining linear perspective with painting techniques like modeling, the Tuscan painter Masaccio produced solid-looking figures that seemed to exist in real spaces, such as the fresco *Holy Trinity* (1425–28, Santa Maria Novella, Florence) a drastic change from the flat medieval aesthetic. Fra Angelico, a Dominican monk, merged scientific precision with spiritual reverence in his religious panel paintings and frescoes at San Marco monastery, which combine a serene mood with realistically rendered figures and background elements. The multitalented Piero della Francesca published three treatises on mathematics and geometry, and his paintings demonstrate an exacting attention to composition and perspective. Piero's masterwork, *The History of the True Cross* (ca. 1447–1460), is also the first nocturnal scene in Western art.

Archaeological discoveries of ancient art and architecture inspired Renaissance painters to incorporate pagan elements into their work, and secular subjects and portraits became increasingly popular in the 15th century. Domenico Ghirlandaio placed New Testament characters in settings as detailed as Roman *trompe l'oeil* paintings and combined contemporary domestic trappings with ancient architecture, as in the Tornabuoni Chapel (1485–90). Sandro Botticelli risked the ire of the church with such pagan works as *The Birth of Venus* (ca. 1480), which depicts a voluptuous nude woman rising from the sea on a seashell.

♦**High Renaissance Art** During the period between 1495 and 1520, a rapid progression of artistic accomplishments occurred in Italy. While religious themes were still important, harmonious forms, unified composition and skillful execution—including smooth, nearly invisible brushstrokes—became more important than thematic or moral content. Painters aspired to be faithful to nature through careful observation and life-studies, and a more tolerant attitude from religious leaders allowed a revival of the nude figure.

Leonardo da Vinci, the first great master of the High Renaissance, exemplified the "Renaissance man" interested in everything from mathematics to botany to music. His gesture studies along with his extensive study of human bodies gave his figures great liveliness, and his knowledge of mathematics allowed him to develop a convincing atmospheric perspective exemplified by his *Last Supper* (1492/4–98). He developed new techniques, including a method of shaping figures by imitating the effects of light and shadow rather than with outlines. He also perfected *sfumato*, in which tiny dots in delicately varied shades create a hazy, indistinct atmosphere. These techniques created the poetic qualities of Leonardo's most famous work, the thoughtful *Mona Lisa* (1503–05), whose enigmatic smile is softened by the shadows around her eyes and mouth.

Michelangelo Buonarotti, as diversely talented as Leonardo, was an engineer, poet, architect, and artist. While primarily a sculptor—his *Pietà* (1499) and *David* (1501–04) are considered among the finest sculptures of all time. Michelangelo apprenticed with Ghirlandaio and used his knowledge of anatomy to create a muscular and awe-inspiring painting style. His frescoes for the Sistine Chapel in Rome (1508–12) cover the ceiling with monumental figures in such dramatic Old Testament scenes as "The Creation," in which a gray-bearded God reaches out his finger to impart the spark of life to Adam.

Raphael completed the trinity of High Renaissance masters. Unsurpassed in his technical perfection and in the visual harmony of his works, Raphael's frescoes, especially for the Stanza della Segnatura in the Vatican Palace in Rome (1509–11), are more serene and delicate than those of Michelangelo, seamlessly blending classical composition with devoutly Christian themes. Although Leonardo and Michelangelo were admired for their originality, Raphael's formal symmetry and graceful, expressive figures—as in his *Sistine Madonna* (1512–1514), with its pair of winged cherubs at the bottom—epitomize Renaissance style.

While southern Italian painters focused on composition and form, Venetian artists experimented with the sensuous colors and new effects made possible by oil paints. Giorgione employed sfumato to create moody, poetic paintings with glowing light and realistic landscape backgrounds. Titian mastered tonal color and developed a rich, painterly approach that made him the most famous Venetian painter of the Renaissance. For decades, Titian operated a large studio where assistants would fill in the less important parts of his paintings and was an exceptionally versatile and prolific artist. Over his long career, Titian painted altarpieces—including the bold and dynamic *Assumption of the Virgin* (1516–18)—as well as portraits, religious subjects, and classical scenes such as the *Bacchanal* (ca. 1518). The luminous colors, controlled lighting, and subtle brushwork of Titian's paintings influenced generations of Western painters.

◆Northern Renaissance Painting

Italian Renaissance advancements spread to northern Europe during the 16th century, although for most northern painters, content still took precedence over form. Albrecht Dürer, the foremost northern artist of his time, traveled to Venice to learn Italian techniques and brought elegance and careful observation to his many religious paintings and self-portraits. Dürer's detailed wood-cut prints, such as *St. Jerome in His Study* (1514), were much admired in Italy, and his watercolor paintings were probably the first landscape studies in Western art. Further from Renaissance delicacy, the eccentric Dutch painter Hieronymous Bosch promoted Christian morality with grotesque imagery, disturbing perspectives, and apocalyptic violence. Bosch's complicated religious triptychs, including *The Garden of Earthly Delights* (ca. 1503–04), presented dark allegories about human folly that would later inspire 20th-century Surrealists.

The Northern Renaissance was a product of intellectual and artistic influences from the Italian Renaissance, strongly modified by the work of northern intellectuals such as the humanist Desiderius Erasmus and religious reformers, including Martin Luther and John Calvin. After 1517, the Protestant Reformation curtailed the German tradition of religious paintings, although it still flourished in southern Europe and the Catholic realms of Germany. Luther was indifferent to religious art, but Calvin was actively hostile toward it, so in the Calvinist Netherlands portraiture and secular scenes flourished instead. Hans Holbein the Younger, a German artist working in Switzerland and England, became famous for his monumental, intensely detailed portraits of King Henry VIII and Erasmus. Lucas Cranach painted several portraits of Erasmus as well as pagan-themed works. Pieter Bruegel the Elder made finely delineated documentaries of peasant life that also suggest symbolic meanings, as in *Hunters in the Snow* (1565), which shows empty-handed men returning with their dogs to a wintry town.

✦**Mannerism**   After 1520, as artists strove for increasingly virtuosic effects, a new style emerged in Rome and Florence. Reacting against the idealized naturalism of the High Renaissance, several artists began to intentionally distort the perspectives, figures, colors, and objects in their paintings. The term *Mannerism* was initially used to criticize such works as being artificially "mannered" after certain aspects of Raphael and Michelangelo; however, recently some art historians have considered some of Michelangelo's later work to be of the Mannerist style.

One of the earliest Mannerist paintings, Rosso Fiorentino's *Descent from the Cross* (1521), abandoned Renaissance balance and harmony for a dizzying composition of discordant colors and sharp angles. Parmigianino presented otherworldly figures with elongated bodies, improbably smooth skin, and contrived poses in paintings such as *Madonna with the Long Neck* (ca. 1535). Agnolo Bronzino became famous for rigidly elegant portraits with precisely rendered clothing. Tintoretto emulated Titian's color and light but traded naturalism for dynamic and emotional compositions such as his *Last Supper* (ca. 1594), going to great lengths to give the event an everyday setting to contrast with the supernatural aspects of Christ and the angels.

Domenico Theotocopolous, known as El Greco, was a controversial artist who worked in both Venice and Spain. His paintings—which include perceptive portraits, turbulent landscapes, and eccentrically iconographic religious scenes—feature elongated figures, vivid and sometimes grotesque colors, and jumbled compositions. However, El Greco's human figures—especially in devotional paintings such as The *Adoration of the Shepherds* (1612–14) and *The Burial of the Count Orgaz* (1586)—seem to glow from an inner light, and his interweaving of form and space greatly influenced Paul Cézanne and Pablo Picasso three centuries later.

◆**Renaissance Architecture** During the Renaissance, architects emerged from the near anonymity of the Middle Ages. As they rose from the level of builder to designer, architects sought distinctive forms of aesthetic expression and looked for an alternative to the Gothic style. Italian architects found inspiration in the archaeological discoveries of ancient Roman buildings and soon borrowed the classical models of building design—including rounded arches, symmetrical floor plans, and ordered columns.

The remaining challenge for 15th-century architects was to adapt classical elements to buildings that did not exist in ancient times. One of the most successful was Filippo Brunelleschi, who won a 1418 competition to complete the long-delayed cathedral of Florence, Santa Maria del Fiore. Brunelleschi's masterly design, elegantly blended a Renaissance dome, the first of its size constructed without the aid of a supporting formwork, with the original Gothic-style cathedral begun in 1296.

One of the best examples of Renaissance architecture is the small classically inspired chapel by Donato Bramante Tempietto (early 1500s). This small chapel, which marks the site of St. Peter's crucifixion, is the perfect union of illusionist painting with architecture, for while the exterior carries a monumental weight, the inside of the building is only 15 feet in diameter, too small to hold any congregation.

But the Renaissance designer who most influenced the subsequent history of architecture was Andrea Palladio. Palladio applied the elements of classical design to a series of elegant country villas outside of Venice, including the Villa Capra (1560s)—also known as the Rotonda—in Vincenza. The Villa Capra exemplified the Palladian design idiom with symmetrical rooms under a low dome and a refined exterior with tall columns. Palladio also wrote the authoritative *Four Books on Architecture* (1570), an encyclopedic illustrated work of idealized buildings. In it, he summarized Renaissance attitudes toward the Romans who, he said, "...in building well, vastly excelled all those who have [lived] since their time."

Renaissance Architecture Outside Italy The principles of Renaissance architecture spread from Italy to France and inspired a number of châteaux in the Loire region, including Chambord, with its complicated roofline of elaborate towers and chimneys designed by several architects. Renaissance palaces like the Palais de Fountainebleau (1528) also featured interior decorations and frescos by Italian artists.

Spain's wealth and power grew rapidly during the Renaissance, and its architects had ample opportunities to design major works. King Philip II built the imposing palace of San Lorenzo de El Escorial near Madrid between 1559 and 1584. The imposing royal complex enclosed the palace, a church, a monastery, and a college organized around two courtyards and flanked by arcades and porticoes.

The English architect Inigo Jones studied architecture in Italy, where he focused on Palladio's buildings and theories, and his subsequent work spread Palladian design throughout England and eventually to the United States. Jones's Banqueting House in London (1619–21) exemplified his work, with Ionic and Corinthian columns inside and out, and decorative stone swags on the grand façade.

In the late 17th century, Christopher Wren turned to architecture after training in mathematics and sciences. The Great London Fire of 1666 gave Wren the opportunity to replace more than 50 parish churches with new buildings of ingeniously differing designs. His greatest work, Saint Paul's Cathedral (1675–1710), employs all of the grand features of classical Renaissance building with its monumental western façade, splendid dome, and barrel-vaulted interior.

Weekend 19: "The World Turned Upside Down"

Day 1: The American Revolution

When the vaunted British army surrendered to George Washington in October 1781 at Yorktown, Virginia, their band is said to have played the popular tune "The World Turned Upside Down." This appraisal could not have been more apt. In the space of only 25 years, from 1765 to 1789, the people in the 13 English colonies in North America moved inexorably from being devoted servants of King George III to becoming revolutionaries determined to be free of British rule, and finally to becoming citizens of a new nation, the first ever to be established by a written constitution. For well over a century, the colonies had developed traditional institutions of self-government that the Crown never disparaged nor interfered with in any manner.

Throughout the 18th century, the king and Parliament had run up huge debts fighting wars in Europe, and soon they were looking for revenues from any possible source. With peace restored following the French and Indian War (1754–63), the British authorities looked to recoup their losses. Leaders in London believed the colonists ought to pay for their own defense and saw colonial trade as a practical way to raise the money. There were already laws, called "Navigational Acts," giving Britain exclusive trade rights with America, but they were long neglected. Parliament ended this period of "salutary neglect" by revising and creating a series of taxes on products imported by the colonies. The Quartering Act of 1765 also required colonies to provide supplies and shelter for British troops stationed in America.

Leaders of the opposition in Massachusetts organized the first boycott of British goods. Agitation heightened in 1765 with the passage of the Stamp Act, which imposed a tax on a wide range of products, including newspapers, legal documents, licenses, and even dice. Colonists were outraged over what they viewed as "internal" taxes imposed by Parliament in which they had no representation. Some formed organizations such as the Sons of Liberty that staged riots against the agents in charge of collecting the taxes and marking the articles with a special stamp.

Parliament repealed the Stamp Act but continued to search for ways to generate revenue through taxes; first through a variety of imports

(Townshend Acts) and then just through tea. A serious clash in New York between the Sons of Liberty and soldiers (January 1770) was followed by the "Boston Massacre" (March 5), when panicky British soldiers opened fire on a rowdy crowd, killing five.

England caused further agitation when it tried to save its debt-ridden East India Company by selling its surplus tea to the colonies, where tea was the only import still taxed. Protests against its arrival culminated with the Boston Tea Party (December 16, 1773) when a group of colonists dressed as Indians dumped hundreds of chests of British tea from a merchant ship into Boston Harbor. Parliament reacted by passing the Coercive Acts (called the "Intolerable Acts" in the colonies) in 1774. The legislation closed the port of Boston, drastically altered the colonial charter of Massachusetts, and suppressed town meetings.

In response, 10 colonies elected delegates to a Continental Congress, which met in Philadelphia that September. This body issued a "Declaration of Rights and Grievances" that pledged obedience to the king but denied the right of Parliament to tax the colonies. It also renewed the embargo on all trade with England.

•**The War Begins** Colonial militias proliferated in anticipation of a clash with British troops. In Boston, the wary British general Thomas Gage sought to thwart the militarization by seizing a large cache of arms and ammunition at Concord. As he moved his troops on the night of April 18, 1775, Boston patriots including Paul Revere raced ahead to warn the colonists. In the early morning hours of April 19, armed citizens at Lexington known as "minutemen" confronted the British troops. A violent skirmish ensued, but the British continued their march toward Concord. There, more minutemen waited. Resistance was better organized, forcing the British to retreat back to Boston. American militants gathered in the hills outside the city, besieging Gage's men.

On May 10, a joint expedition led by Ethan Allen and Benedict Arnold seized the neglected British stronghold of Fort Ticonderoga on Lake Champlain in New York without a shot fired. That same day, a second Continental Congress convened in Philadelphia, and, reacting to Lexington and Concord, delegates voted to prepare "a state of defense," though they still sought peace. On June 15, they authorized George Washington to command an army of 20,000. In July, they wrote a petition of reconciliation to the king.

Before Washington arrived in Boston, British forces assaulted patriot positions on Breed's Hill and Bunker Hill (June 17). The furious battle ended when the patriots ran out of ammunition and retreated. The British, though victorious, suffered more than a thousand casualties— no battle of the coming American Revolution would cost them more. News of the battle convinced King George III to proclaim America in a state of rebellion on August 23. He replaced General Gage with General William Howe. By then, Washington had laid siege to Boston with a hodgepodge of colonial militia men numbering around 14,000.

♦**1776** On January 1, 1776, the enlistments of thousands of colonial militiamen expired. Many went home. Washington proposed an assault on Boston in February, but his fellow generals opposed the plan. Undeterred, he secretly fortified Dorchester Heights with artillery and bombarded Boston. Howe withdrew his troops by sea to Halifax, Canada, and the Americans took Boston on March 17. Anticipating a British assault on New York City, Washington's army marched south to set up a defense on Long Island.

By May 1776, the Continental Congress had urged every colony to establish an independent government. Thomas Paine's pamphlet *Common Sense* popularized the idea of complete separation between America and Great Britain. As General Howe and some 20,000 British troops prepared to sail to New York, the Second Continental Congress was in Philadelphia finalizing the colonies' Declaration of Independence from England. The final draft was unanimously agreed to on July 4, although New York abstained.

British forces sailed into New York City in August and began their attack on Brooklyn troops during the night of August 26. The Americans were outflanked and suffered high casualties, barely escaping across the East River to Manhattan on the night of August 29. They subsequently withdrew from lower Manhattan in early September. Howe continued his rout of the American army, forcing Washington to retreat again after the Battle of White Plains on October 28. Fort Washington, the last American outpost in Manhattan, fell on November 16. Its garrison of 3,000 soldiers surrendered.

The bedraggled Americans withdrew through New Jersey and into Pennsylvania, with the British hot on their heels. Both armies retired to winter quarters, following the custom of the day, but the Americans launched successful surprise attacks on two outposts in New Jersey, at Trenton on December 26, and at Princeton on January 4, 1777.

❖**War on Two Fronts** In the summer of 1777, Britain launched two campaigns to split New England from the rest of America: one in northern New York, and the other at Philadelphia. The British general John Burgoyne failed in an offensive from Canada to take New York's capital, Albany. They captured Fort Ticonderoga without a fight on July 6, but American morale surged after a militia checked a British detachment at Bennington, Vermont, on August 16. American troops under Horatio Gates inflicted huge casualties on September 19 at Bemis Heights, and a new American assault, on October 7, led to Burgoyne's surrender of 5,000 troops at Saratoga on October 17.

Meanwhile, Howe advanced toward Philadelphia, defeating Washington at the Battle of Brandywine on September 11. Members of Congress began to flee Philadelphia, which the British occupied on September 23. Washington countered with an elaborate attack on Howe's main force on the city's outskirts, at Germantown, on October 4. It failed, but the bold move impressed the courts of Europe.

The Continental Congress, having reconvened at York, Pennsylvania, approved the Articles of Confederation on November 15, 1777. Fearing centralized power, its architects created a weak national government that left most power with the individual states.

Washington's battered army had established winter quarters in Valley Forge, Pennsylvania. The snowy winter proved harsh. American soldiers lived in desperate conditions with few supplies, though they received valuable military training from the Prussian officer Baron Friedrich Wilhelm von Steuben.

❖**War in the South** February brought news that France had agreed to ally with America. The British, expecting a French invasion at Philadelphia, withdrew to New York, where it had better access to its fleet. Along the way, Washington attacked at Monmouth Courthouse (June 28). This last major engagement in the North was a draw, but proved the Americans were still strong enough to fight.

Confined to New York in the north, the British shifted the war south to the Carolinas and Georgia, where they believed there were more loyalists. They captured Georgia's main port, Savannah, and capital, Augusta, by early 1779. On May 12, 1780, the Americans suffered their worst defeat of the war and surrendered at Charleston, South Carolina. The British, under Generals Henry Clinton and Charles Cornwallis, captured nearly 5,000 prisoners. Congress ordered Horatio Gates, hero of Saratoga, to rally the Americans in the South, but he, too, was defeated at Camden, South Carolina (August 16). More terrible news followed in September when Washington discovered that Benedict Arnold had betrayed the cause and tried to hand over the garrison at West Point to the British.

On October 7, the American militia defeated loyalist American troops at the battle of Kings Mountain, South Carolina. Nathanael Greene, chosen to reorganize the American army in the South, split it in two; a detachment under Daniel Morgan stunned the British at the Battle of Cowpens, South Carolina (January 17, 1781). Then Greene and Morgan reunited, gathered militia reinforcements in Virginia, and returned to fight Cornwallis at Guilford Courthouse, North Carolina (March 15). Though technically a British victory, Cornwallis suffered high casualties and withdrew to Wilmington, North Carolina. Planning to unite his forces with Clinton's in Virginia, he settled into camp at Yorktown, Virginia, on August 5. Sensing an opportunity to attack by land and sea, Washington and his French allies marched and sailed from the North. Pinched between the Franco-American armies and the French Navy, the British surrendered on October 19. Though hostilities continued, in essence the war ended with the surrender of Yorktown.

•**A New Nation** The final peace treaties were signed on September 3, 1783, in Paris. The British evacuated New York, their last outpost, on November 25, and Washington bade farewell to his officers in New York's Fraunces Tavern on December 4.

The new nation emerged from the war with severe economic problems. The chaos caused by having 13 different trade, tariff, and tax policies established by the individual states added to the difficulties. The instability led to protests such as Shays Rebellion (August 1786– February 1777) in Massachusetts, instigated by debtors who faced foreclosure on their farms. Moreover, major threats loomed from foreign powers such as Spain, which still controlled Florida and the lower Mississippi. Concerned leaders at the Annapolis Conference (September 1786) called upon the states to send representatives to a convention and discuss changes to the Confederation government.

Dependent on state legislatures for funds, Congress had a difficult time financing the needs of the Continental Army during the American Revolution. The army's top officers, including George Washington, Nathanael Greene, and Henry Knox, went on to become strong advocates for a more powerful central government, based on their wartime experiences with a weak Congress.

Day 2: The Creation of the U.S. Constitution

The Constitutional Convention gathered in Philadelphia in May 1787 and remained in session through September, despite the onerous summer heat and the often bitter nature of the debates. Fifty-five delegates attended the convention, although not all at the same time. New Hampshire's two representatives did not arrive until July, some delegates left in the middle of the proceedings, and Rhode Island never sent a delegate. All 55 were white men, most of them well educated and wealthy. More than 30 were trained in law, and many had served in the Continental Congress or the Continental Army. Almost half of them owned slaves, including George Washington and James Madison.

The delegates elected George Washington as the convention's president, a logical choice given his heroic role during the Revolution. Washington, however, was not a disinterested, neutral figure. His army experience had soured him on the idealistic notion of widely dispersed power, which had been made popular by figures such as Patrick Henry.

James Madison of Virginia, a 36-year-old bachelor, was a student of political theory and, like Washington, was convinced the young country needed a strong central government. He arrived in Philadelphia two weeks before the convention opened and spent the time outlining his argument in support of a new, strong national government.

◆**The Virginia Plan** Just a few days into the proceedings, after the delegates established rules governing debates, the convention voted to meet in secret. Delegates wished to speak candidly and to settle their differences without the influence of public opinion. On May 29, 1787, Governor Edmund Randolph of Virginia introduced a series of resolutions, the careful handiwork of his colleague, Madison. Known as the Virginia Plan, it was in essence not a revision of the Articles of Confederation, but an entirely new document, one that called for (among other things) the creation of a two-house national legislature with membership determined by the size of each state's population. Members of the lower house would be chosen in a popular vote, while the upper house would be selected by members of the lower house. The plan also empowered Congress to create an executive and judicial branch, as well as the power to override state laws that it believed conflicted with national law. Shrewdly, the plan also called for its own ratification not by state legislatures, which would see it as an attenuation of their powers, but by special state conventions.

The Virginia Plan established the framework for the debate to come. The full convention took up debate in mid-June, with William Paterson of New Jersey presenting an alternative plan calling for a one-house legislature, like the Continental Congress, where each state was represented equally regardless of population. Paterson's plan included an executive branch of several executives, each appointed by Congress. The executives would in turn appoint the national government's judges. It was a more conservative document, designed as a revision of the Articles rather than a fresh start.

♦Small States vs. Large States   Paterson's plan won some support, until Madison took the floor and pointed out that New Jersey's insistence on equal representation meant any new states formed out of territories west of the Appalachians, despite having fewer people than New Jersey and the other small states, would be on an equal footing with them. Paterson soon found himself a lonely man. His proposal won support from only his home state and New York.

Nevertheless, the small states—most prominently New Jersey, Delaware, and New York (a small state in population, if not in size)— refused to go along with Madison's plan, which had the support of Virginia, Massachusetts, and Pennsylvania.

Debate between the large and small states grew intense through June. A delegate from Connecticut, Roger Sherman, tried to break the deadlock with a compromise: a two-house Congress, but with a lower house based on population and an upper house in which all states would have equal representation. The plan was voted down almost immediately, infuriating the small states and threatening to bring the convention to an abrupt, and unsuccessful, end. In early July, delegates voted to form a committee to reconsider the issue of representation.

The committee brought back a recommendation that many historians call the "Great Compromise"—in essence, the plan that Connecticut's Sherman had proposed weeks earlier: a two-house legislature, a
lower house based on population and an upper house with equal representation. The compromise also recognized that a portion of the population were slaves, so for purposes of representation and taxation in the
lower house, slaves would count as three-fifths of a person. The final
language, however, did not use the word *slave*, which historians interpret
as a reflection of the founders' discomfort with slavery. Instead, the final
version referred to persons "bound to service for a term of years." Furthermore, Native Americans were explicitly excluded from the population count.

The so-called Great Compromise passed, despite the objections of
Pennsylvania, Virginia, South Carolina, and Georgia (the smaller south-
ern states had big ambitions as they staked claims to territories in the
West). Delegates, at last, could get on with other business.

♦**The Separation of Powers**   Delegates knew from experience that
Congress under the Articles lacked the power to enforce its will, chiefly
because it lacked the power to tax. The long list of powers delegates
chose to assign to Congress included the power of taxation, as well as to
declare war, coin money, establish a post office, regulate foreign commerce, and establish naturalization procedures. This very specific list
ended with a surprisingly vague phrase—Congress could pass any laws
"which shall be necessary and proper" to execute its enumerated powers.

The idea of an executive branch eventually won favor, although some
delegates believed in multiple executives as a check against too much
power in one person's hands. One delegate called the idea of a powerful president "the foetus of monarchy." In the end, however, the convention did give executive authority to a single president, an official
chosen by electors selected by state legislatures. Although the president
was given authority over the nation's armed forces, the financial power
to create an army and wage war remained with Congress.

Intent on distributing power as widely as possible, the convention
also created a judiciary branch to check and balance the two other
branches. Chief Justice John Marshall established the principle of judi-

cial review in the case of *Marbury v. Madison* in 1803, which provides for the authority of the Supreme Court to overturn any laws passed that conflict with the Constitution. The defendant in the case was James Madison, who had gone on to become President Thomas Jefferson's secretary of state. Marshall ruled that the Judiciary Act of 1789 was unconstitutional, the first time the Court overturned a federal statute.

While the delegates cobbled together a framework for a new national government based on values such as freedom, liberty, and compromise, the institution of slavery persisted as the antithesis of these values. Many delegates from the North opposed the slave trade. Southern delegates, led by Charles Pinckney of South Carolina, were intent on defending slavery, with some threatening to withhold their support for the new document if it barred the slave trade.

The three-fifths compromise was just one way in which the convention sought to deal with slavery by, in essence, not dealing with it. Southerners went along with a compromise that gave Congress the authority to ban the slave trade in 20 years, which it did, effective January 1, 1808. Northerners agreed to provisions requiring that escaped slaves be returned to their owners, although again, the authors resorted to euphemism, referring to slaves as persons "held in service or labour."

After many long weeks of deliberations, delegates signed the new document, the Constitution, on September 17. It began with a preamble, famously stating that "We, the People," had drawn up a new government in order to "form a more perfect Union."

♦**Ratification** The campaign for ratification was waged state by state. Madison, Alexander Hamilton, and John Jay argued for ratification in New York in a series of brilliant essays referred to as the Federalist Papers, the first of which was published in October 1787. But some opponents, such as Patrick Henry and his fellow Virginian, Richard Henry Lee, were equally eloquent in arguing that the Constitution was a betrayal of the Revolution; the very phrase "We, the People," set off alarm bells among critics like Patrick Henry, who believed the states, not the people, were sovereign. The question of ratification became entwined with local politics in each state, leading to political horse-trading and arm-twisting. For example, John Hancock of Massachusetts was won over by a whispered promise that if he voted to approve the Constitution, he might become the nation's first vice president.

The Constitution's advocates were forced to acknowledge concerns that they had created a strong central government without enumerating guarantees of personal liberty. Those concerns led to promises that the Constitution would be revised immediately to include a list of individual rights over which no government could trample, at least not in theory. The subsequent Bill of Rights—the first 10 amendments to the Constitution—was proposed in 1789 and ratified in 1791. The Bill of Rights effected laws such as the separation of church and state, freedom of the press, freedom of speech, the right of militias to bear arms, and the right to peacefully assemble.

The Constitution became law when New Hampshire became the ninth state to ratify it on June 21, 1788. But several states—including New York and Virginia—remained in doubt. Virginia ratified and joined the Union on June 25, 1788, and New York followed suit on July 26, but the votes in both states were extremely close. Virginia's convention voted 89–79 in favor, and in New York, the vote was 30–27. Rhode Island was the last to ratify, on May 29, 1790, more than a year after George Washington took the office of president.

Weekend 20: The Environment

Day 1: Global Warming and Climate Change

The temperature of the Earth has fluctuated throughout the planet's history, causing both ice ages and periods of intense heat. However, beginning with the Industrial Revolution in the late 18th century, human activities began to change the composition of the atmosphere and the Earth's climate. While some people disagree that humans are having a significant effect on global climate, the Intergovernmental Panel on Climate Change (I.P.C.C.), a group of several thousand scientists commissioned by the United Nations, reported in 2007 that "the evidence of global warming is now unequivocal" and said that human activity is the major contributor. The terms *climate change* and *global warming* are often used interchangeably, although global warming is only one factor in the larger issue of climate change.

The essential differences between historical climatic change and human-caused global warming include both the rate of the change, which is faster than that to which many plant and animal species can adapt, and also the sizable human population of the Earth, which could cause serious shortages of land, water, and food in the event of a major climate shift. Most climatologists agree that the Earth warmed by 1.1 degrees Fahrenheit between 1850 and 1990, an alarming rate considering that worldwide temperatures rose only 9 degrees Fahrenheit since the end of the last ice age, 12,000 years ago. In fact, the eight warmest years recorded since 1850 occurred between 1998 and 2009. At its current rate, the Earth is likely to warm by an additional 3 to 7 degrees Fahrenheit by the year 2100. According to the I.P.C.C., such warming would cause both drought and rising sea levels, and destroy water supplies, forests, and agriculture in many parts of the world.

Global warming occurs when certain atmospheric gases prevent the Earth from reflecting excess sunlight, instead trapping heat in the Earth's atmosphere, oceans, and land. Some of these "greenhouse gases" occur naturally and are necessary to keep the Earth's surface warm enough for human life, but the higher concentrations produced over the last two centuries are trapping more heat than the Earth can release.

Carbon dioxide, or CO_2, is the most prevalent greenhouse gas. Its presence in the atmosphere has increased by 36 percent since before the Industrial Revolution, when people began to burn fossil fuels including oil, coal, and natural gas, and burn trees for deforestation. Methane, the second-biggest contributor to global warming, is now at 148 percent of preindustrial levels and is emitted primarily by decomposing landfill waste, large-scale cattle raising, natural gas leaks, rice paddies, and coal mining.

Many climatologists predict that global warming will also change weather patterns. There is evidence that heat waves, storms, and droughts have already increased in frequency and intensity, and the U.S. National Climatic Data Center reports that extreme extra-tropical cyclones over the North Atlantic have increased since 1988. However, temperature increases and weather changes are not uniform, and some places will, theoretically, experience more severe effects than others.

Increasing temperatures expand the volume of ocean water and melt glacial ice, and, as a result, climatologists expect the sea level to rise between 3.4 inches and 3 feet above 1990 levels by the end of the 21st century. In the U.S., a 3-foot rise would flood 7,000 square miles of dry land—mostly in the Southeast—and would destroy a comparable area of coastal wetlands, erode recreational beaches, exacerbate coastal flooding, and increase the salinity of aquifers and estuaries. Industrialized continental nations like the United States could probably sustain the population shifts caused by such changes, but globally, about 1.75 billion people live within 40 miles of the sea, mostly along low-lying islands, flood plains, and estuaries.

There are two principal ways of responding to climate change: mitigation and adaptation. Mitigation involves measures that will reduce human contributions to climate change. An example of this approach is the "cap-and-trade" system designed to reduce CO_2 emissions by giving companies that produce large quantitites of CO_2 financial incentive to reduce their emissions.

Whereas mitigation deals with the causes of climate change, adaptation addresses its effects. To deal with changing levels of precipitation, for example, water supply systems can be linked and expanded. However, adaptations can have adverse environmental consequences themselves; extra air conditioning requires more electricity, for example, and seawalls can prevent natural wetland formation. Furthermore, poor nations have few adaptive options because they do not have the necessary social, political, or financial resources to implement them. Bangladesh, for example, cannot afford flood protection for its low-lying coastal areas, and subsistence farmers in Africa may not be able to survive even a brief drought.

One of the first international efforts to manage global warming was the 1997 conference in Kyoto, Japan, where representatives of more than 150 countries reached a tentative agreement to reduce greenhouse gases by an average of 5 percent worldwide (from 1990 levels) by 2010. By 2009, 187 countries had ratified the Kyoto Protocol, though the agreement expires in 2012. World leaders met in Copenhagen in December 2009 in an effort to reach a new agreement, which called on developed nations to start work immediately; the U.S. agreed to reduce emissions by 14–17 percent below 2005 levels by 2020.

Emissions reduction strategies include: reducing electricity use through energy-efficient factories and appliances; replacing coal-fired power plants with solar, hydroelectric, or wind power; raising fuel efficiency standards for automobiles and reducing automobile use; insulating buildings to reduce heating and cooling needs; and regulating major fossil fuel suppliers and greenhouse gas producers. Although scientists cannot definitively predict what amount—if any—of greenhouse gas reductions would curtail global warming, most agree that a large-scale international effort could reduce the severity of the consequences.

•**Biodiversity** While pollution and global warming have obvious effects on human health, ecologists also define environmental health according to biodiversity. Biodiversity measures the variety of living things and their interactions on three levels: genetic, species, and ecosystem diversity. The number of known species—characterized by scientific analysis and description—is more than 1.7 million, including nearly 1 million species of insects, about 14,000 species of amphibians and reptiles, and 5,400 mammalian species. However, there are many other species living on Earth, including trillions of microscopic organisms like bacteria. These species interact to form sustainable check-and-balance networks like the food chain.

Human population growth, deforestation, pollution, and global warming have caused a rapid loss of biodiversity. Today's extinction rate is estimated to be 1,000 to 10,000 times higher than the natural rate, and some scientists believe we are in the midst of a mass extinction. For example, the International Union for Conservation of Nature reported in 2008 that 30 percent of amphibian species are critically endangered or vulnerable. This number increased 2,588 percent between 1996 (18 species) and 2010 (484 species).

◆**Environmentalism in the U.S.**   The first federal environmental act was the establishment of Yellowstone National Park in March 1872 in the territories of Montana and Wyoming. Instead of promoting the land for development, Congress and President Ulysses S. Grant declared that it should be preserved "as a public park or pleasuring ground for the benefit and enjoyment of the people." As the first such preserve in the world, Yellowstone inaugurated an international national park movement that currently includes some 1,200 parks or preserves in 100 countries, including 391 in the United States.

The Scottish naturalist John Muir became an early advocate for preservation after his travels and scientific work convinced him that some natural areas need protection from human exploitation. Muir founded the Sierra Club in 1892 to that end and urged President Theodore Roosevelt to join the cause. Roosevelt, himself known as an ardent outdoorsman, eventually dedicated more than 150 million acres to national parks and forests, and founded the U.S. Forest Service, which manages forests for water and timber resources while protecting them for wildlife and recreation. The first chief of the Forest Service, Gifford Pinchot, promoted a "wise use" strategy of wilderness management that proposed, in contrast to Muir, that nature could be safely commercialized.

Another early American environmentalist, Aldo Leopold, called for a "land ethic" that recognized the value of the natural world as beyond financial. In 1924, due to Leopold's efforts as a Forest Service employee, the Gila National Forest in New Mexico became the world's first designated wilderness. This designation allows travel only by foot or horseback and bans any commercial activity except grazing in order to protect the usefulness of the wilderness for cleaning air and reducing climate change, as well as providing clean water, wildlife habitat, and natural recreational experiences.

Interest in environmental issues escalated again in the late 20th century due to the increasingly visible effects of human behavior on the environment. "Going green" is now an international movement address-ing land and water conservation, air and water pollution, solid waste disposal, global warming, and biodiversity.

◆**Renewable Energy** The first wind turbines actually predate the electric power grid, with two near-simultaneous developments in the late 19th century. The Scottish engineer James Blyth constructed a 33-foot electricity-generating wind turbine in 1887, and the following year the American engineer Charles Brush built the first automatic wind tur-bine, wiring the first electrically powered building in Ohio. Likewise, throughout the 1800s, scientists were experimenting in the various tech-nologies that make photovoltaic solar panels possible; the first solar-powered steam engine was built in 1861.

Since then, the use of wind and solar power has grown steadily, with a surge in recent years. Wind power, while still providing a small total percentage of U.S. power, is growing much more rapidly than solar power. From 1990 to 2008, U.S. production of wind power grew from 300 trillion Btu annually to 510 trillion; solar has increased modestly from 60 trillion Btu to 90 trillion. Shipments of solar photovoltaic cells and modules continues to expand, however. From 2000 to 2008, U.S. manufacturers increased shipments of photovoltaic components from 20,000 modules in 2000 to 524,000 modules in 2008. Production of hy-droelectric power, the nation's largest renewable energy source, has re-mained more or less steady since 1990, declining somewhat from 3.05 quadrillion Btu to 2.45 quadrillion Btu in 2008.

In 2008, the United States overtook Germany as the world's biggest producer of wind power. In the United States, Texas generates the most wind power, with more than double the capacity of the number two pro-ducer, Iowa. The state with the fastest-growing wind power industry is Michigan.

The 2009 federal stimulus package has helped spur development in both the wind and solar industries, with $16.25 billion earmarked by the U.S. Department of Energy for energy efficiency and renewable en-ergy projects. The American Wind Energy Association reported a record year in 2009, installing equipment with over 10,000 megawatts of pro-ducing capacity that year. Overall, consumption of all renewable energy increased from 6.2 quadrillion Btu in 1990 to 7.3 quadrillion Btu in 2008.

Day 2: Pollution and the Rise of Environmentalism

Today's powerful environmental movement originated during the 1960s and 1970s. The 1962 publication of *Silent Spring*, by the biologist and nature writer Rachel Carson pioneered the idea that human health is dependent on the health of the local and global environment. The popularity of the book, which linked industrial and agricultural chemical pollution to both human and ecological health risks, eventually led to a nationwide ban on DDT and other pesticides. Before 1970, the U.S. didn't require pollution controls on cars, all gasoline contained lead, and cities dumped untreated sewage into rivers—some of which, like Cleveland's Cuyahoga, became so saturated with chemical waste that they actually caught fire. Carson's book, combined with the growing evidence of smog-filled cities, trash-filled rivers, and a 1969 oil spill off the California coast, suggested to Americans that unchecked waste procedures might not be wholly desirable.

Against this backdrop, President Richard Nixon signed the first major piece of modern environmental legislation on January 1, 1970, the National Environmental Policy Act, which asserted governmental authority over environmental issues. In July, Nixon established the National Oceanic and Atmospheric Administration (N.O.A.A.) to protect and develop marine resources. In December, he launched the Environmental Protection Agency (E.P.A.) to set, monitor, and enforce national environmental guidelines. The Clean Air Act of 1970 required the E.P.A. to develop regulations to protect citizens from airborne contaminants, and the Clean Water Act of 1972, which was the first strong and enforceable water pollution control act, established specific goals for eliminating toxic substances from surface water. Both laws were later expanded. By the end of 1974, the Pesticide Control Act, the Endangered Species Act, and the Safe Drinking Water Act had all become law.

During the 1980s, the E.P.A. pushed through a law to deal with hazardous waste, which gave the states power to run their own hazardous waste programs and put procedures in place to deal with environmental accidents such as oil spills. Great strides were made in the 1990s, among them the Pollution Prevention Act, which changed the way the E.P.A. handled waste and emissions, and fostered markets for recycled materials. Amendments to both the Clean Air Act and the Clean Water

Act were passed during the 1990s.

The E.P.A. is responsible for setting pollution emission standards. In 2009, the E.P.A. formally declared that greenhouse gases endangered public health and began the process of regulation of these gases for the first time.

◆**Water Pollution** In 1854, the English physician John Snow first linked water quality with human health when he traced London's cholera epidemic to contaminated public water pumps. Great Britain began purifying water supplies with chlorine, and soon cholera, typhoid, and dysentery were nearly eliminated. In the United States, New Jersey adopted the practice in 1908, and within a few years, most major U.S. cities provided treated water to their residents.

The 20th century brought new, more complicated forms of water pollution. Agricultural expansion led to the introduction of synthetic fertilizers, herbicides, pesticides, and concentrated animal wastes from large-scale livestock operations. All of these pollutants eventually wash into rivers, streams, and lakes, contaminating drinking water supplies and endangering aquatic life. Manufacturing plants have released persistent toxins such as PCBs, dioxins, and mercury into rivers across the country, and hospitals discharge large amounts of hazardous waste. Many of the most polluted rivers and lakes have been cleaned up since the 1970s, but a 1999 E.P.A. water quality index reported that 21 percent of the nation's 2,111 watersheds had serious problems, including pollution and loss of wetlands. Advisories were issued on fish consumption and water use across America.

Pollution also damages marine ecosystems and the people who depend on them for food, employment, and recreation. Contaminants including raw sewage and oil spread into the ocean through storm drain overflows. Although most dramatic when an oil well or cargo ship leaks oil as a result of an accident—like the catastrophic 2010 BP Deepwater Horizon explosion in the Gulf of Mexico—most oil enters the ocean incrementally from municipal and industrial runoff, the cleaning of ships' bilges or tanks, and other routine occurrences. Because oil floats, it accumulates in large slicks on the water surface and on beaches. Although some of the most volatile components evaporate, the remaining oil is still toxic and can suffocate plants, birds, and animals.

Plastic is a serious danger in the ocean because it takes hundreds of years to decompose in water. Plastic bottles, bags, and nets are pushed by wind and ocean currents into massive floating waste clumps that kill animals like jellyfish, sea turtles, and seals who become entangled. The two largest of these clumps are known as the Western and Eastern Pacific Gyres—together they are known as the Great Pacific Garbage Patch. Floating in a remote area of the Pacific Ocean, each is bigger than Texas and contains an estimated 3.5 million tons of trash. Since plastic particles can outnumber zooplankton by six to one, birds and fish mistake the smaller pieces for food. An international treaty prohibits disposal of plastic wastes in the ocean, but the treaty is very difficult to enforce, and the majority of plastics in the ocean are washed there from land.

•Air Pollution   Air pollution is another side effect of industrial development, as smoke and other emissions are released into the atmosphere from power plants, home furnaces, factories, oil refineries, motor vehicles, trains, and other sources. The effects of air pollution are sometimes painfully obvious, as in 1952, when smoke from coal furnaces created a deadly "pea soup fog" that killed 12,000 Londoners. Other kinds of pollution, such as the microparticles produced by automobile exhaust, or the hazardous gases used in solvents and dry cleaning, are less visible, but nonetheless harmful. Some pollutants are relatively innocuous at low levels, but in many areas, air pollution can cause or aggravate health conditions such as asthma, heart disease, and immune system deficiency.

In the U.S., the E.P.A. monitors air quality at thousands of sites for six pollutants: particulate matter, sulfur dioxides, carbon monoxide, nitrogen dioxide, lead, and ozone. The E.P.A. then presents their findings to the public through the daily Air Quality Index (AQI), which measures the levels of these pollutants (except lead) on a scale of 0–500. Ratings of 0–50 generally represent good air quality, while higher values indicate greater levels of air pollution and greater health concerns. From 1990 to 2008, overall air quality in the U.S. improved for each of the six pollutants, though most major cities still experienced unhealthy air quality days. All areas monitored by the E.P.A., however, experienced fewer unhealthy days in 2008 than in 2001.

An important part of cleaning the air is controlling emissions. Most states and companies are given a "cap" on the amount of each pollutant that they are allowed to emit. States can then allow companies that reduce their emissions below that cap to sell their extra pollution credits to other companies—this practice is known as *emissions trading* and is used nationally and internationally to control several kinds of pollutants.

◆**Waste Disposal** In 2008, Americans produced more than 250 million tons of household trash, also known as municipal solid waste (MSW), which does not include wastes from mining, agricultural or industrial processing, demolition and construction, sewage sludge, junked autos, or obsolete equipment.

There are four primary methods of dealing with solid waste: source reduction, recycling, landfills, and incineration. The first two methods prevent or divert materials from entering the waste stream; the last two are disposal methods.

Source reduction is the use of fewer materials in manufacturing, packaging, and transporting commodities. Simple examples of source reduction include buying reusable rather than disposable products, or buying juice concentrates rather than reconstituted juice. These practices reduce the amount of packaging material and the number of boxes and vehicles required for shipping.

Recycling involves collecting used materials like glass and aluminum, which are then remanufactured into new products. Recycling saves energy and raw materials and reduces waste. One form of recycling is composting, in which food and yard wastes decompose into healthy soil. Recycling recovered more than 33 percent of MSW generated in the U.S. in 2008. Since 1980, many municipalities have enacted laws to reduce solid waste in landfills, and in 2008 there were 8,659 curbside recycling programs in the U.S., serving 59 percent of the population. Since food and yard waste account for about 25 percent of MSW, many municipalities also encourage composting, and there were 3,510 community composting programs across the country in 2007.

Landfills are the cheapest method of waste disposal, and in 2008 they received 54 percent of MSW—totaling some 135 million tons. However, landfills pose environmental problems themselves, including the release of methane gas and contamination of groundwater supplies. They also may contain toxic wastes that require regular monitoring. In 2008, there were 1,812 active landfills in the continental U.S. As urban areas run out of space, they often pay to send their garbage to rural areas, where residents must balance the potential revenue with environmental risks, offensive odors, and declining property values.

In 2008, 12.6 percent of MSW in the U.S. was burned. Incineration was once a more common disposal method, but despite its efficiency, it produces odors, particulate matter, and toxic gases. However, combustion also generates energy that can supplement other energy sources. At present, there are more than 85 energy-recovery combustors in the U.S., able to incinerate nearly 100,000 tons of MSW per day.

Wastes that are dangerous to people and the environment must be separated from MSW and designated hazardous waste, which includes substances that cause cancer, reproductive and neurological disorders, or other health problems. The U.S. produced 47 million tons of hazardous waste in 2007, mostly from chemical manufacturers, electroplating companies, petroleum refineries, dry cleaners, auto repair shops, hospitals, exterminators, and photo-processing centers. As of 2007, there were 1,395 authorized disposal facilities for hazardous wastes.

Additionally, the E.P.A.'s Superfund program investigates, controls and cleans up sites that have been heavily contaminated by hazardous wastes. Out of nearly 50,000 Superfund sites identified since 1980, 12,228 were active in 2007, with 1,279 on the National Priorities List pending cleanup in 2010.

Concerns have emerged during the last 30 years over nuclear waste, which can remain radioactive for possibly thousands of years, posing risks of cancer and radiation poisoning. Most nuclear waste comes from nuclear weapons production facilities, nuclear power plants, medical radiation equipment, industrial X-ray alternatives, and residues from uranium mining. Nuclear waste in the U.S. is regulated by the Nuclear Regulatory Agency and is classified as either high- or low- level depending on the amount of radiation it emits. Developing safe disposal methods and acceptable sites for nuclear waste remains a challenge—as illustrated by the 20-year-long standoff over proposals to store U.S. nuclear waste in Nevada's Yucca Mountain—and waste from power plants and other facilities often remain in "temporary" sites.

Weekend 21: William Shakespeare

The works of William Shakespeare enjoy virtually universal popularity, his plays translated and performed around the world. The reasons for his reputation as the greatest writer of the English language are many, including the poetic beauty of his imagery and the narrative drive and complex themes he employs. But for most readers and playgoers, Shakespeare's greatest appeal is found in his creation of memorable characters and the many roles actors long to play—haunted, brooding Hamlet; madly jealous Othello, old, deluded Lear; violently ambitious Macbeth and his murderous wife, Lady Macbeth; the fascinating evildoers, Iago and Shylock, one ingenious, the other sympathetic; lovesick Romeo and Juliet; clever Portia; spunky Rosalind; conscience-stricken Brutus. These characters jump off the page and emerge on the stage as real people in as many interpretations of motive as there are actors who play the roles. Beyond the stage, the characters become us, or we become them. Indeed, Shakespeare's many unforgettable characters are the mirrors the playwright holds up to human nature so we can truly see ourselves.

Day 1: His Life and Work

Shakespeare was born in Stratford-upon-Avon on about April 23, 1564, to John and Mary Arden Shakespeare, noted citizens of the town. He married Anne Hathaway in 1582, when she was 26 and he was 18; their daughter Susannah was born six months later. In 1585, Hathaway gave birth to twins, son Hamnet and daughter Judith. But in 1586, Shakespeare left his family in Stratford and traveled to London to pursue a career in the theater. At the time, theater companies were beginning to establish permanent buildings and operated under the patronage of wealthy gentlemen, but still relied on the public for money. The men in the troupes often had multiple responsibilities, including playing female roles, as women were not allowed to perform in public.

Shakespeare was originally just one of several Renaissance Era playwrights who worked in and around London during the reign of Queen Elizabeth I. In the 1580s, the "University Wits," a group of six highly educated writers influenced by the classical models of ancient Greece and Rome began to create theatrical productions more elevated in subject, tone, and language than those of the popular mystery and morality plays of medieval times. These playwrights, the most famous of whom was Christopher Marlowe, wrote dramas and comedies based on historical and literary subjects rather than biblical themes or stock characters, used a highly poetic style rather than ordinary speech, and revived devices such as soliloquies, ghosts, and confidantes. While the Wits defined early Elizabethan drama, other playwrights also thrived in this new style, including Ben Jonson, who did not actually have a university education but was one of the most ardent followers of classical models, and William Shakespeare.

In London, Shakespeare joined an acting company and, between 1589 and 1591, wrote his first plays—a trilogy chronicling the reign of King Henry VI. But an outbreak of the plague in 1592 forced the closure of all central London theaters for two years. Despite the rarity of theatrical performances, Shakespeare continued to write plays, including *Richard III* and *The Taming of the Shrew*. He also turned to poetry and eventually wrote 154 sonnets as well.

A friendly competition for audience favor arose between the newcomer Shakespeare and the more established Marlowe, but it ended abruptly when Marlowe was killed in a bar fight in 1593. When the theaters reopened in 1594, Shakespeare joined Lord Chamberlain's Men, a troupe that had been recently formed by several performers of the defunct Lord Strange's Men, who worked from 1588 to 1594. The group soon produced Shakespeare's *Romeo and Juliet* and *A Midsummer Night's Dream* as well as plays by Jonson, Marlowe, and others. In 1599, the Globe Theatre, a new permanent public theater, opened for the exclusive use of the Lord Chamberlain's Men.

A production of Shakespeare's *Richard II* in 1601 was implicated in a failed rebellion attempt by Robert Devereux, the earl of Essex, against Queen Elizabeth I because of its subversive themes and the political leanings of some of the Lord Chamberlain's Men, but the playwright was not charged in the ensuing investigation. The queen died in 1603 and was succeeded by James I, who was a great supporter of the theater and of Shakespeare's work in particular. After King James saw a production of *As You Like It*, he issued a royal order to change the name of the Lord Chamberlain's Men to the King's Men. Shakespeare would write for the King's Men for the rest of his career, sometimes in collaboration with other troupe members, and he produced a total of 38 plays before his death on April 23, 1616, his 52nd birthday.

In those 52 years, Shakespeare's artistic achievements displayed deep levels of insight into human character and a brilliant mastery of the English language. He is often called simply "the Bard" or "the Poet" to attest to his poetic supremacy; he originated hundreds of now-common English phrases and quotations such as "with bated breath," "salad days," and "foregone conclusion." Four centuries after his death, Shakespeare's works are still produced as traditional plays, as movies, and in adaptations such as *West Side Story*, Jerome Robbins's and Leonard Bernstein's 1957 musical version of *Romeo and Juliet*.

Of Shakespeare's plays, 10 are tragedies, 10 are historical dramas, and 18 are comedies. His works make frequent use of such Elizabethan dramatic devices as prologues and epilogues delivered directly to the audience, double entendres, comic interludes to relieve the tension in the tragedies, and improbable instances of mistaken identity. Shakespeare, like Marlowe, wrote in blank verse, mostly unrhymed *iambic pentameter*, the poetic meter that uses five consecutive pairs of alternating unstressed and stressed syllables in each line. This convention gives the plays a distinctive and even quaint sound today, but was not unusual for the time in which they were written. Shakespeare, like most of his contemporaries, borrowed plots and ideas from existing stories, legends, and historical incidents. But the deeply felt psychological portraits of his characters, his sensitivity to the cruelties and absurdities of life, his alternately structured and playful approach to plot, and his extraordinary use of imagery are the elements that give his works their lasting power and vitality.

◆**Shakespeare's Sonnets** So much has been written about Shakespeare's plays that we often forget he also wrote some of the most beautiful love poetry in English, mostly in the sonnet form. Sonnets (literally "small sounds") originated in Renaissance Italy. They are 14-line poems that can express strong emotions and profound thoughts. Shakespeare wrote his sonnets relatively early in his career, sometime during the years 1592 and 1596. His sequence of 154 sonnets, aside from the last two, divide into two groups: those addressed to or about a Young Man (1–126) and those addressed to or about a Dark Lady (127–152). In the past, much attention was given to the sonnets as if they are a story, as in a novel or play. While a narrative element is surely present, Shakespeare's sonnets are now generally viewed by critics as technical "verbal contraptions" pointing to underlying moral questions behind their wordplay of metaphor, images, and rhyme.

The format found in the Shakespearean sonnet—three-quatrains with a closing couplet—lends itself to a logical progression: "When…then…and then…so…" As a matter of fact, some of the best sonnets begin with the word *when*, (e.g. 15, 29, 30, 106). Many of the sonnets are about the fleeting nature of love and life.

Sonnet 30

When to the sessions of sweet silent thought
I summon up remembrance of things past,
I sigh the lack of many a thing I sought,
And with old woes new wail my dear time's waste:
Then can I drown an eye, unused to flow,
For precious friends hid in death's dateless night,
And weep afresh love's long since cancell'd woe,
And moan the expense of many a vanish'd sight:
Then can I grieve at grievances foregone,
And heavily from woe to woe tell o'er
The sad account of fore-bemoaned moan,
Which I new pay as if not paid before.
But if the while I think on thee, dear friend,
All losses are restored and sorrows end.

♦**The Shakespeare Controversy** Since the middle of the 19th century, several studies have appeared asserting that Shakespeare was not a real person, but the pseudonym of another author of the Elizabethan era. Others say that because the works are so brilliant, they cannot possibly be the work of one man, and therefore bear the mark of many writers. Behind these theories are the bare facts of Shakespeare's life, which would indicate that he was not highly educated, so therefore incapable of writing such magnificent works. Mark Twain and Sigmund Freud helped lend credence to this idea.

Some theories suggest that Francis Bacon wrote much of what we attribute to Shakespeare, since Bacon possessed the range of cultural knowledge exhibited in Shakespeare's works and was often seen in the royal court. Another popular contender for the real identity of Shakespeare is the 17th earl of Oxford, Edward de Vere, whose life seems to be reflected in a number of Shakespeare's works. An obvious candidate for Shakespeare's identity has been the playwright, poet, and translator Christopher Marlowe, Shakespeare's rival. Marlowe and Shakespeare always competed with each other to turn out popular plays, all of which followed a similar poetic style—a blank verse version of iambic pentameter.

These theories notwithstanding, several local government and church documents from Stratford-upon-Avon in the 16th century mention John Shakespeare and his various business and government dealings, in addition to the births of his children. Today, virtually every serious scholar of Shakespeare believes that Shakespeare did exist and wrote all of his own dramatic and poetic works. But the controversy endures; the Calvin Hoffman Prize, worth almost one million British pounds, is still offered as an incentive to investigate and uncover a concrete answer to the question of Shakespeare's identity.

Day 2: Shakespeare's Major Plays

◆**Romeo and Juliet** A prologue tells of the titular doomed "star-crossed lovers" and their feuding families, the Montagues and Capulets in Verona, Italy. In Act I, after a brawl between servants of these families, Romeo, a Montague, sneaks into the Capulet ball, where he and Juliet fall in love at first sight. In the famous balcony scene in Act II, they declare their love for each other and later secretly marry, hoping their marriage will pacify the feud. In Act III, Tybalt, a Capulet, challenges Romeo to fight, but now secretly married to Juliet, he refuses. Romeo's friend Mercutio takes up the challenge and is killed by Tybalt. Enraged, Romeo slays Tybalt and is punished by exile. Before he leaves, he spends a rapturous night with Juliet, who, in marrying Romeo, has spurned her parents' desire that she marry Count Paris. In Act IV, Juliet obtains a potion from Friar Laurence that will make her appear dead until Romeo returns. When the Nurse fails to awaken Juliet, she is presumed to have actually died. In Act V, at Juliet's tomb, a distraught Romeo encounters Paris, whom he slays, then (believing Juliet has died) poisons himself. Juliet awakes, sees Romeo's dead body, and stabs herself with his dagger.

The two families arrive and are moved to end the feud.

This early tragedy features literature's most famous lovers and expresses the dangers of their impulsiveness, using rich poetic language contrasted with ribald humor. It is one of the fullest expressions of romance in the English language.

◆**Julius Caesar** Set in 44 B.C. Rome, this play shows how the fear of a power-hungry dictator led to betrayal and self-sacrifice. In Act I, Cassius and Brutus agree that Caesar's tyranny must be forestalled. Caesar ignores a warning about the Ides, or 15th, of March and refuses Mark Antony's offer of a crown. In Act II, Brutus joins the conspiracy to assassinate Caesar, who in Act III continues to ignore warnings, goes to the Senate on the Ides of March, and is stabbed to death by conspirators. Among them is Brutus, and shocked by this betrayal, Caesar asks with disbelief, "Et tu, Brute?" ("and you too, Brutus?"), as he falls dying. Brutus and Cassius speak to the angry citizens and try to justify the murder, but Mark Antony's famous "Friends, Romans, countrymen" speech stirs the crowd to fury, forcing Brutus and Cassius to flee. In Act IV, Mark Antony and his allies plan to attack the armies of Brutus and Cassius. On the night before the battle, Brutus is haunted by Caesar's ghost. During the battle in Act V, Cassius and Brutus both commit suicide. Mark Antony declares Brutus the "noblest Roman of them all" because he did not act out of envy but rather "honest thought" for the good of Rome.

This political play abounds in powerful speeches that display a high level of rhetoric appropriate to its subject matter.

◆**Hamlet, Prince of Denmark** Considered the most complex of Shakespeare's tragedies, this revenge drama begins with the line "Who's there?" A ghost on the ramparts of Castle Elsinore has appeared to friends of Hamlet, whose father, the king, has died under mysterious circumstances. Hamlet's mother hastily married Hamlet's uncle Claudius, now the de facto king. The ghost, Hamlet's father, reveals to his son that Claudius was responsible for his death, and instructs Hamlet to seek revenge. In Act II, Hamlet feigns madness with Ophelia, once his lover, in order to confuse Claudius and his counselor, Polonius, who is Ophelia's father. Hamlet also engages a troupe of actors to perform a scene mimicking his father's murder to trick Claudius into revealing his guilt. During the "play within the play," Claudius runs from the room, thereby convincing

Hamlet of his guilt. In Act III, Hamlet contemplates suicide in the famous "To be, or not to be" monologue. On his way to see Gertrude, Hamlet spies Claudius praying and passes up the opportunity to kill him, believing that if killed during prayer, Claudius's soul would ascend directly to heaven. In conversation with Gertrude, Hamlet senses someone hiding behind a curtain. Thinking that it is Claudius, he now seizes the opportunity for revenge, but stabs Polonius instead. In Act IV, Claudius sends Hamlet to England in a plan to have him killed. Distraught Ophelia loses her mind and is found drowned, covered in flowers. Having outwitted his executioners, Hamlet returns to Elsinore in Act V and encounters jolly gravediggers who have dug up the skull of Yoric, the king's jester whom Hamlet remembers fondly. The gravesite is for Ophelia, and Hamlet confronts her grieving brother, Laertes, who blames Hamlet for her death. Claudius arranges a duel between them, giving Laertes a poisoned sword, and preparing a poisoned chalice for Hamlet should he survive the duel. In the duel, the swords get switched and both are fatally wounded. Gertrude mistakenly drinks from the poisoned chalice and confesses her and Claudius's guilt. Hamlet then stabs and kills Claudius. Hamlet dies, and an invading Norwegian force conquers Denmark.

The complex motives, emotions, action—and inaction—of a hero tormented by duty, grief, and conscience make a compelling theatrical experience that delves deeply into the mystery of human existence.

•**Othello, the Moor of Venice** This compactly structured play reveals the pernicious power of jealousy and self-delusion. In Act I, the diabolical Iago declares revenge on Othello, the black Moor who is military commander in Venice, for promoting Cassio over him. He reveals the secret marriage of Othello to Desdemona, angering her father, to whom Othello defends himself nobly. As Othello is ordered to Cyprus to fight the Turks, Iago plots to make him suspect an affair between Desdemona and Cassio. In Act II, Iago provokes a drunk Cassio into a fight and Othello demotes Cassio for the incident. Iago then urges Cassio to appeal to Desdemona for reinstatement. In Act III, Iago has Othello secretly listen to a conversation between Cassio and Desdemona, furthering Othello's jealous suspicions. Iago conceals a handkerchief Desdemona has dropped, a memorable gift from Othello, telling him he has seen Cassio carrying it. Othello asks his wife for the handkerchief, but she says she has lost it. In Act IV, Iago provokes Othello's "green-eyed monster" of jealousy further, and Othello resolves to kill his wife. In Act V, Iago attacks Cassio, wounding him. Othello confronts Desdemona, declaring his love and yet the need to kill her because of the implications of the lost handkerchief. He smothers her in the marriage bed. When Emilia, Iago's wife, reveals Desdemona's fidelity and Iago's villainy, Othello, "one that lov'd not wisely, but too well," wounds Iago, then stabs himself and dies. Fiendish Iago lives to face torture for his crimes.

♦**Macbeth** This swift and bloody tragedy explores the conflict between fate and overpowering ambition. In Act I, King Duncan of Scotland awards Macbeth the title Thane of Cawdor after he is victorious in battle. Three witches tell Macbeth he will one day be king, and so he hesitates to usurp Duncan until resolute Lady Macbeth urges him to action. In Act II, Macbeth murders Duncan, and Lady Macbeth plants the bloody dagger on the king's guards. Macbeth is crowned king. In Act III, Macbeth orders the death of Banquo, whose descendants the witches had prophesied would be future kings. Banquo's ghost appears to the overwrought Macbeth at a banquet celebrating his kingship. In Act IV, the witches give Macbeth new prophecies, which he misinterprets as favorable. Malcolm, Duncan's son, and his ally, Macduff, plan to attack Macbeth's forces. In Act V, Lady Macbeth sleepwalks and is driven mad and dies, presumably a suicide. Macbeth, when told of his wife's death, famously reflects that life is "full of sound and fury, signifying nothing." He now realizes the witches' prophecies have fated Macduff to defeat him. Macduff beheads Macbeth, and Malcolm is proclaimed king.

♦**King Lear** Many consider this tragedy of greed and madness as Shakespeare's finest. In Act I, the aging King Lear divides his kingdom among his three daughters. Two of them, Goneril and Regan, try to outdo each other in winning their father's favor, but Cordelia, the youngest, is unwilling to participate in the insincere flattery and so is disinherited. Edmund, bastard son of Gloucester (Lear's ally) tricks his father into believing that his legitimate son, Edgar, is plotting against him. In Act II, Lear and Gloucester, attended by the all-knowing Fool, begin to realize their children's treachery. Lear agitatedly wanders onto the stormy heath. In Act III, Lear, now mad, curses the storm, then finds shelter with his Fool. Regan and her husband attack Gloucester, ripping out his eyes. In Act IV, Edgar helps his blind father to safety. Goneril and

Regan battle for power, and for the love of Edmund. In Act V, as the opposing armies prepare for battle, the jealous treachery of Goneril and
Regan is fully revealed and they kill each other. Edgar wounds Edmund
fatally, but not before the latter has ordered Cordelia hanged. Lear carries her body onstage, momentarily believing she lives, and he dies saying, "Never, never, never, never, never."

This profound drama, dense in themes and poetic imagery, explores
with shattering power the boundaries of human capacity for good and evil.

◆**A Midsummer Night's Dream** In this charming comedy set on
Midsummer Night (June 23), the follies of the play lend themselves to
staging for both existential spareness and theatrical spectacle. In Act I,
on the eve of the wedding of the duke of Athens, young Hermia and
Helena are kept away from their respective lovers, Lysander and
Demetrius. In the woods outside Athens, they cross paths with Nick
Bottom and other rustics who are bumbling through the rehearsal of a
play to celebrate the duke's wedding. In Act II, Oberon and Titania, the
king and queen of the woods, quarrel, and the king commands Puck, the
jester, to create a love potion to make the sleeping queen fall in love
with the first person she sees upon waking, whom he hopes will be himself. Puck also anoints the sleeping Lysander, who sees Helena upon
waking and is struck with love. In Act III, Demetrius is also given the
love potion and wakes to see Helena, falling in love. Puck transforms
Bottom's head into a donkey's, but when the queen awakens and sees
him, she is nonetheless infatuated. In Act IV, the queen realizes that
she has become "enamour'd of an ass," and the mismatched lovers are
restored to their original choices. In Act V, a triple wedding feast is celebrated as the rustics present their hilarious version of Ovid's "Pyramus
and Thisby" to entertain the lovers.

◆**The Merchant of Venice** This dark comedy about love and revenge presents one of Shakespeare's most complicated characters, the
comically vengeful, but legitimately wronged, Jewish moneylender Shylock. In Act I, the Christian merchant Antonio borrows money from
Shylock to help Bassanio woo the heiress Portia. Shylock agrees but on
condition that Antonio forfeit a pound of his flesh if he cannot repay the
debt on time. In Act II, Shylock's daughter, Jessica, steals Shylock's gold
and runs away with Lorenzo, her secret love. In Act III, Bassanio wins
Portia, but Antonio is unable to repay his debt. Portia and her maid,

Nerissa, disguise themselves as men to witness Antonio's trial. In Act IV, Shylock demands his pound of flesh, and Portia (as "Balthazar" the judge) rules in his favor but invokes the "quality of mercy," allowing Shylock to take exactly one pound of flesh, but with not a drop of blood, and furthermore requiring Shylock to become a Christian. In Act V, Jessica and Lorenzo compare themselves to storied lovers from literature, and Portia and Nerissa reveal their roles in the judgment against Shylock.

◆**As You Like It** Composed alternately in verse and prose, this comedy is also an earnest exploration of the nature of love, social classes, cruelty, and redemption. In Act I, Oliver plots to have his brother Orlando killed in a wrestling match, but Orlando wins. Rosalind, daughter of banished Duke Senior, observes the match and falls in love with Orlando and he with her. Frederick, brother to the duke, orders Rosalind to join her father in the Forest of Arden, where she decides to disguise herself as a man, "Ganymede." In Act II, the duke finds comfort in the forest, away from court, and a place where shepherds philosophize. As Oliver continues to threaten him, Orlando also flees to the forest, where he is welcomed by the duke. The melancholy courtier Jaques entertains the men with a cynical speech on the "seven ages" of man. In Act III, Frederick orders Oliver to find and kill Orlando, who has been hanging love poems on trees in the forest, hoping to find Rosalind. Instead, he finds "Ganymede," who poses as Rosalind so Orlando can practice courtship, and with whom he trades witticisms about love. In Act IV, "Ganymede" and Orlando continue courting as Rosalind, still in disguise, realizes she truly loves Orlando. Later, Oliver encounters "Ganymede" with news that Orlando has been wounded, and the sight of a bloody cloth causes her to faint. In Act V, Oliver and Orlando reconcile, and "Ganymede" assures Orlando he will marry Rosalind, who finally reveals herself, and wedding blessings are bestowed on several joyous couples.

Weekend 22: *Homo sapiens* and the Birth of Civilization

Day 1: The Peopling of the World

Scientists today estimate that the Earth is 4.6 billion years old, but that number has shifted more than a few times over the last century. The earliest signs of human activity did not appear until 2.7 million years ago, in the early Stone Age (or Lower Paleolithic era), which lasted until 200,000 years ago, although the species called Australopithecus dates back more than 4 million years ago. Africa is often referred to as "the cradle of humanity," and all the fossil discoveries were made there.

The earliest human ancestors—called hominids—walked upright on two legs and were scavengers. *Homo erectus*, another early hominid dating from 1.5 million years ago, evolved in Africa but migrated to Eurasia, the first human species to do so. These very early humans used fire (but probably could not make it), created stone weapons and tools, and were successful in occupying a wide range of habitats. Nevertheless, all non-African populations of *Homo erectus* eventually died out without leaving descendants.

Our own species, *Homo sapiens*, evolved from *Homo erectus* through various transitional stages in the savannah lands of eastern Africa about 150,000 years ago. *Homo sapiens* is a highly social and adaptable species, fully capable of using complex language. Modern humans moved out from the original species' homeland on the eastern plains of Africa to occupy much of eastern, northern, and southern parts of the continent. The special challenges of the rain forest environment slowed the movement of humans into the western regions of Africa.

Around 105,000 years ago, modern humans migrated northward through Egypt and out of Africa via the Sinai Peninsula to the Middle East. There they apparently met and coexisted with humans of a different and older species—Neanderthals (*Homo neandertalensis*)—that had a simpler, less flexible culture and technology.

Following the coast of southern Asia, modern humans were in India and Southeast Asia by 90,000 years ago. (Ocean levels were generally much lower at the time because a vast amount of water was locked up in the glaciers of the Ice Age, so much of Southeast Asia was dry land, part of an exposed continental shelf. Any traces of these people and their coastal migrations would now be submerged off the present-day coastlines of Asia.) Sometime between 65,000 and 40,000 years ago, humans crossed miles of open ocean (probably on rafts) to reach New Guinea and Australia. No later than 50,000 years ago, other populations migrated from the Middle East across the plains of Central Asia to China and northeastern Asia, eventually making it to the islands of Japan. As *Homo sapiens* spread to East and Southeast Asia, remnant populations of *Homo erectus* were displaced and became extinct.

Humans made their way into Europe beginning around 40,000 years ago, challenging the existing populations of Neanderthals there. Whether from superior social organization and technology, outright extermination of the Neanderthal competitors, or some other cause (or combination of causes), the last Neanderthals became extinct around 30,000 years ago, and *Homo sapiens* was in complete control of the Eurasian continent. The early human occupants of Europe and northern Asia of the Late Paleolithic period, roughly 40,000 to 12,000 years ago, devised highly sophisticated means of dealing with the cold glacial environment, including the efficient hunting of large animals, the processing of hides and the creation of cut-and-sewn hide and fur garments, the use of fire (for heating, cooking, and light), and the creation of warm shelters from the elements.

The earliest known structures built by archaic humans were excavated at Terra Amata in southern France, dating to about 380,000 years ago. The site consisted of some 20 huts built of branches held in place by large stones arrayed in oval rings. Beginning around 40,000 years ago in Europe, early humans began to create domestic and ceremonial spaces in caves that were often elaborately decorated with wall paintings. A typical example is the cave at Lascaux in southwestern France, which was inhabited between 10,000 and 20,000 years ago. Not only does it contain evidence of daily life, but its walls are painted with exquisitely sensitive pictures of animals and humans; these paintings are assumed to have had religious or magical significance.

The "tool kit" of these Paleolithic *Homo sapiens* was far more elaborate than that of earlier human species, and it included not only a wide range of edged tools and projectile points, but also important devices

such as spear-throwers, needles, and hammers, all made of carefully chosen materials (such as antler and bone) and skillfully crafted.

Using this technology, some humans moved to northeastern-most
Eurasia, and from there across a broad plain of open land connecting
Eurasia with North America (a "land bridge" where the Bering Strait
now separates the two continents), introducing humans to the Americas around 15,000 years ago. Some scholars adhere to a conservative
view that dates the event to around 13,500 years ago, based on the archaeological record of the Clovis Culture complex (originally identified
in New Mexico, but found widely in North America), characterized by
distinctive and finely made projectile points. Other scientists point to se-
curely dated sites that predate the Clovis Culture by at least several
thousand years, including some in South America, which suggest a considerably earlier migration. With this migration, or series of migrations,
all of the continents of Earth except for Antarctica had become human
habitats. Settlement of the Indo-Pacific archipelagoes soon followed,
with the ancestors of the Austronesian-speaking peoples setting out
from the Fujian coast of China around 7000 B.C. to settle Taiwan, the
Philippines, Indonesia, Melanesia, Micronesia, and Polynesia.

Over the course of these migrations, humans became adapted to specific habitats (hot, cold, sunny, light-deprived, and so on), and widely
separated populations developed in genetic isolation from one another.
These two factors caused the evolution of superficial traits such as skin
color, hair color and texture, eyelid shape, and so forth, which came to
be the external defining characteristics of what is now called "race." All
humans during the millennia of the great migrations also demonstrated
the human capacity for the creation of culture and art. Art from this
period showed great diversity and refinement, from the cave paintings
and ivory sculptures of prehistoric Europe to the equally ancient rock art
of Australia.

All humans at that time shared the basic lifestyle of hunting and
gathering. Animals, birds, and fish were hunted and trapped for food,
shellfish were gathered in oceans and rivers, and great numbers of plants
were identified and harvested for use as food, fiber, medicine, dyes, and
for other purposes. It was a potentially rich and abundant way of living,
but one that depended on low population density and little population
growth, probably resulting from prolonged nursing of children (which

suppresses maternal fertility), as well as from high infant and child mortality rates. Even very slow growth in population density was probably a significant impetus for the migration, as bands of migrants left populated areas in search of new hunting and gathering grounds. The end of the last ice age 11,000 to 12,000 years ago led to unprecedented population growth in some places, which had momentous consequences for human history.

◆The Neolithic Revolution (ca. 8000–5000 B.C.)   Beginning about 10,000 B.C., a strong global warming period began to melt the huge glaciers that had covered much of northern Eurasia and North America for thousands of years. Some results of this warming trend, which lasted for several millennia, included the creation of vast steppes or prairies south of the retreating glaciers that were the ideal habitat for huge herds of horses, bison, and other food animals. Further south, warmer, wetter conditions encouraged the growth of food plants and the animals (such as antelope and wild goats) that grazed on them. Humans quickly took advantage of these new food sources, and human population and population density began to climb.

At this point, some people in crowded environments began to take a more active role in managing food resources—encouraging certain crops, for example, through seeding, weeding, and harvesting plants in certain locations that were well known and over which some form of ownership may have been asserted. This led to the development of a wide range of domesticated plants, including wheat and legumes in Mesopotamia and northwestern India; millet in North China, and rice in South China and Southeast Asia; and corn (maize) and beans in Mesoamerica. Neolithic hunters began following, directing, managing and culling herds of horses or wild cattle, protecting them from wild predators to save them for human use. In this way, the first steps toward the domestication of plants and animals were taken. With food management came a tendency to travel less and to settle down more, to guard and enjoy the resources that were under management. Camps became villages, or at least season-long settlements. Animals that acted as scavengers at these settlements (wolves, swine, fowl) were seen to be useful, selected for docility (the fiercer ones were killed), and eventually domesticated (as dogs, pigs, and chickens). A more sedentary life made obsolete the hunter-gatherer nomad's requirement that possessions be light and portable. Pottery was perhaps the most significant example of this change; it greatly improved the possibilities for storing and cooking food in a proto-village environment. These changes are collectively referred to as the "Neolithic Revolution."

The full-scale Neolithic ("new stone") culture, evident in the Middle East by 8000 B.C. and found in many parts of the world over the course of time, involved agriculture, particularly the raising of grain crops, and a sharply reduced reliance on wild plants; the domestication of animals for various purposes, and a reduced reliance on wild game; settled life in villages; water management; the production and use of cloth and pottery, and of a wide range of well-made stone tools; evidence of belief systems, including ceremonial burial of the dead; and a range of other adaptations to a settled lifestyle. Life for Neolithic villagers may have been harder than it had been for their hunter-gatherer ancestors. Raising, harvesting, storing, and processing grain for food took unremitting toil, as did the work of animal husbandry. Crowding together in villages, as well as living in close proximity to domestic animals, exposed farmers to many more diseases than had affected hunter-gatherer bands. The payoff, as population burgeoned and opportunities for migration to unpopulated areas dwindled, was that the same land that had supported a few hundred hunter-gatherers could now support several thousand of Neolithic farmers.

The earliest surviving evidence of one of these towns is Jericho on the Jordan River, where settlement began around 7500 B.C. Built largely of mud bricks in successive waves of construction, the settlement already showed traits that would characterize later cities: a population much larger than prehistoric villages, a perimeter wall to defend against enemies, and public buildings set among private dwellings.

Day 2: The Rise of Civilization (ca. 3000–1500 B.C.)

The transition from prehistoric Neolithic culture to civilization seems to have involved in every case a combination of two things: first, a culture founded on settled agricultural communities; second, the development of urban centers with literate religious and social hierarchies, whose members asserted control over such matters as irrigation and water control, ritual and religious observances, and the application of military power or legitimized violence, as well as the right to appropriate for their own use a portion of the goods produced by ordinary farmers and workers.

Agricultural communities came into being over time in many parts of the prehistoric world, including Mesopotamia (the "land between the rivers," i.e. the Tigris and the Euphrates), several of the large river valleys of China, parts of India and Southeast Asia, the Nile Valley and the great bend of the Niger River in Africa, the Danube Valley in Europe, parts of Central America and Mexico, the Mississippi Valley, and the Amazon Basin in the New World, the highlands of New Guinea, and throughout the islands of the Pacific Ocean.

Urban centers eventually appeared in some, but not all, of these Neolithic cultures. It happened first in Mesopotamia in the fourth millennium B.C., but other areas, such as Egypt and the Indus Valley, soon followed. Across Eurasia, the invention and spread of the technologies of metallurgy (by the early third millennium B.C. in Mesopotamia and Egypt, but not until a thousand years later in China) gave the Bronze Age its name.

♦**Mesopotamia**   The 600–mile-long plain of the Tigris and Euphrates river valleys stretching from Anatolia to the Persian Gulf is the site of the earliest known civilization, which takes its name from the city-state of Sumer. The first of a succession of Mesopotamian civilizations, Sumerian culture first blossomed around 3500 to 3000 B.C. Each of the cities within the Sumerian area was a sacred temple city, the realm of a god whose regent on Earth was the priest-king. Sumerian culture gave rise to a number of important innovations, including a calendar, the invention of writing (cuneiform, written with a stylus on tablets of soft clay), the plow, the potter's wheel, and wheeled carts. The development of writing, in particular, was an important element in the commercial and administrative success of the Sumerian city-states.

Separate and frequently warring city-states such as Lagash, Nippur, and Ur came under the control of the more northerly Empire of Akkad, whose greatest king was Sargon (ca. 2250 B.C.). The Akkadian Empire fell to the Babylonian Empire, whose king Hammurabi (ca. 1750 B.C.) conquered all of Mesopotamia, going on to establish the first known Code of Laws. Shortly before 1500 B.C., this empire fell to the Kassites, northern invaders who relied on a new military shock weapon, the horse-drawn chariot.

The Indus Basin, stretching from the Himalayas to the Arabian Sea, had become by about 3000 B.C. another locus of settled agriculture. The emerging Indus culture showed signs of Sumerian influence. The great cities of Harappa and Mohenjo-Daro have been excavated, along with many small villages. Small statuary and cylinder seals demonstrate a rich religious, artistic, and commercial life. Some evidence of writing has been discovered, but it remains undeciphered. This Indian civilization flourished from about 2500 to about 1500 B.C., when it was conquered by Central Asian ("Aryan") tribesmen who used chariots and arrows.

Around 2000 B.C., three centers of civilization influenced by Mesopotamia and Egypt began to develop: the Canaanites in Syria and Palestine, the Hittites in Asia Minor, and the Minoan civilization on the island of Crete. It is not clear whether Minos was a name or, like *pharaoh*, a title. The palace of Minos, called the Labyrinth, dominated the trading city of Knossos, center of a "sea empire" whose ships were in contact with Italy, Egypt, Asia Minor, and mainland Greece. Yet by about 1500 B.C., the Minoan economy was in decline, possibly because of overexploitation of the Cretan environment as well as the damage wrought by a series of earthquakes. Not long after, a Greek prince was ruling at Knossos.

◆**India and China** Around 1950 B.C., the millet-based agricultural villages of the North China Plain gave rise to the semi-legendary Xia Dynasty, which ushered in the Bronze Age in East Asia. The Xia were overthrown around 1550 B.C. by Tang the Victorious, who established the Shang dynasty, which endured for 500 years. The Shang dynasty is noted for its sophisticated bronze vessels, used in worship of the royal ancestors, and for oracle bones inscribed with an early form of Chinese script that asked questions of the gods. Shang culture was enriched after 1350 B.C. by new technologies from western Eurasia, including the chariot, the cultivation of wheat, and sheepraising. Roughly contemporary with the Shang state was the separate Bronze Age culture of the Ba people, characterized by large, highly stylized bronze human statues and masks, with sites in the Sichuan Basin near the present city of Chengdu.

•**The Iron Age**   In the millennium from about 1500 to about 500 B.C., civilized life continued to spread as civilizations took on their classic form in the "heroic age" of the ancient world. By the mid-first millennium B.C., iron had begun to replace bronze, first for tools and later for weapons, ushering in the Iron Age. The impact of the chariot warriors from the Eurasian steppes, a huge area of grassland stretching from the Black Sea almost to the Pacific Ocean, altered the earliest civilizations in different ways and to different degrees—least in the Near East, most in India.

•**The Middle East**   The Kassite conquest of the First Babylonian Empire shortly before 1500 B.C. did not lead to substantial changes, as the northern conquerors adopted the culture and political structure of the conquered. The Assyrians retained their own rulers, under Kassite domination. Those rulers eventually took advantage of a series of incursions by other northern horsemen against the Kassites and gained their independence as the First Assyrian Empire (ca. 1150–728 B.C.). The Assyrians were fierce warriors, and in the course of establishing the Second Assyrian Empire (728–612 B.C.) they launched attacks on southern Mesopotamia, Syria, Palestine, and even, briefly, on Egypt. The great Assyrian capital of Nineveh was destroyed, however, in 612 B.C. by the cavalry of the Medes, an Indo-European people. The Medes proceeded to conquer the Assyrian territory east of the Tigris as well as Armenia and eastern Iran, forming a short-lived empire (625–559 B.C.). Assyria's fall permitted the Second Babylonian Empire (625–538 B.C.) to arise in Mesopotamia.

Both the Medes and the Assyrians fell victim to the Persian Empire (559–331 B.C.). Cyrus the Great (r. 550–533 B.C.) overturned his Median overlord, conquered King Croesus of Lydia in Asia Minor, and overthrew King Nebuchadnezzar III of Babylon. In the next generation, a war of succession threatened the empire; unity was restored when Darius I (r. 521–485 B.C.), grandson of Cyrus, came to the throne.

Darius brought the empire to its greatest extent, consolidating the conquest of Egypt and expanding eastward beyond the Indus by 519 B.C. Dividing his empire into 20 "satrapies" (administrative offices), Darius improved communications by building good roads, and he was farsighted enough to commence the construction of a Mediterranean war fleet, which eventually would be destroyed by the Athenian navy at the battle of Salamis in 480 B.C., ending the Persians' decades-long attempt to conquer the Greek city-states.

◆**The People of Israel** Tracing their origin to the ancient city of Ur in Mesopotamia and the covenant between their patriarch, Abraham, and their god, Yahweh, the Israelites migrated to Canaan sometime after 1900 B.C. Entering Egypt, probably in the Hyksos period, they dwelt in the Egyptian delta until about 1280 B.C., when, against strong resistance from the pharaoh, Moses led the Hebrews out of Egypt into the desert of Sinai, where, according to the Old Testament, they became God's chosen people in the Sinai covenant. Shortly before 1200 B.C., they occupied parts of Canaan during the decline of Egyptian power there. (This account is based upon biblical narratives; no independent archaeological evidence has yet been discovered for Abraham, Moses, and the other patriarchs.)

The league of religious clans was transformed into the Kingdom of Israel (ca. 1020–922 B.C.), which flourished under the kings Saul (r. ca. 1028–1013 B.C.), David (r. 1013–973 B.C.), and Solomon (r. 973–933 B.C.) largely undisturbed by the neighboring great powers of Egypt and Assyria. After the death of Solomon, the kingdom divided into Israel in the north and Judah in the south. The northern kingdom fell to the Assyrians under Sargon II (r. 722–705 B.C.) in 721 B.C. Judah held on until the Second Babylonian Empire under Nebuchadnezzar II (r. ca. 605–562 B.C.) destroyed the capital, Jerusalem, in 587 B.C. After the establishment of the Persian Empire, the Jews were permitted (538 B.C.) to return to Palestine.

◆**The Americas** The domestication of plants and the creation of Neolithic cultures began in Mexico as early as 7000 B.C. and led to settled village cultures by 2500 B.C. based on the cultivation of squash, beans, chilies, and maize (corn). The earliest civilization in the Americas was that of the Olmec, whose cities lay in the Valley of

Mexico, on the coast in the vicinity of Veracruz, and in the highlands around Oaxaca. The Olmec cities are marked by large square step-pyramids, and by carvings of enormous stone heads. Olmec culture appears to have begun around 1200 B.C. and to have persisted for some 800 years before being supplanted by the Zapotec.

Meanwhile, to the south, the great civilization of the Maya was beginning to take form in what is known as the late Preclassic Period, beginning around 300 B.C. in the Yucatán Peninsula and adjacent areas of southern Mexico, Belize, Guatemala, and parts of Honduras and El Salvador. Some ancient Mayan villages had by this time begun to evolve into cities marked by plazas flanked by pyramids, temples, and palaces.

With the late Olmec, the Zapotec, and the Preclassic Maya, all the hallmarks of Mesoamerican civilization were in place: pyramids and other monumental architecture, a calendar, ritual ballgames, bar-and-dot numbers, and hieroglyphic inscriptions, as well as personal blood sacrifices by members of the ruling elite, together with ritual human sacrifice to nourish the maize goddess and other deities.

Weekend 23: Physics: A Brief History

Day 1: The Basics

A baseball pitcher stands on the mound. He holds the ball in his hand by his side, then lifts it, extends his arm behind his body, and, with as much energy as he can muster, brings his arm forward. When his hand is as far in front of his body as possible, he releases the baseball. It hurtles through the air toward a bat positioned several feet above the surface of the Earth and moving at a slower speed toward the ball. The two meet with a loud crack, and the ball changes its course and its speed. This moment, repeated in fields and stadiums countless times every summer day, displays all the basic laws of physics as they unfold one by one. The same rules of the universe that keep the Earth spinning determine the path of that baseball in flight: the laws of motion, the laws of conservation, and the law of gravity.

•**Laws of Motion** Sir Isaac Newton's three laws of motion described in his *Principia* (1687) describe theoretical objects in a vacuum, though they are easily observable in the real world, even where forces like friction and air drag tend to overwhelm the natural motion of objects. To obtain realistic solutions to problems, physicists and engineers begin with Newton's laws and then add in the various forces that also affect motion—for example, a strong wind on game day.

Newton's first law of motion, the law of inertia, states that any object at rest tends to stay at rest. But that's just one side of the coin—the logic of the law means that any object in motion tends to stay in motion unless it is acted upon by an external force (like gravity). Not just the motion that is affected by this law; velocity (how an object changes position over time) and acceleration (how an object changes velocity over time) also remain the same without influence from an external force. Once a baseball is released by the pitcher, it will move with constant velocity in a straight line, at a constant acceleration (except for the influence of gravity and other outside forces). Even a curve ball doesn't curve on its own; it merely obeys the first law of motion while external forces like air pressure and gravity do their work.

The second law of motion is often simplified as "Force equals mass times acceleration (F = ma)": the net force on an object is equal to the mass of the object multiplied by its acceleration. Mass is a measure of the amount of matter in an object, and near the Earth's surface it is roughly equivalent to weight. The implication of this law is that when a constant force is applied to an object, that object will accelerate, or increase in velocity. Thus, a rocket, which is propelled by a constant force as long as its fuel is burning, constantly increases in velocity. A thrown baseball, however, does not have constant force behind it, so in order to maximize its velocity a pitcher must alter either the force of the pitch or, if he's not a particularly ethical pitcher, the mass of the ball.

The third law of motion is "For every action there is an equal and opposite reaction," meaning forces that bring about action and reaction always occur in pairs. Our pitcher must direct as much force behind him as he plans to direct toward home plate—this is why when the ball collides with the bat, at the velocity and acceleration determined by the force of that pitch, the third law of motion demands that the bat react in an equal and opposite direction to the ball that hit it.

◆**Conservation Laws**   The conservation laws are rules stating that a certain entity must not change in quantity during a certain class of operations. All such conservation laws treat only closed systems, where nothing is being added from the outside.

The Conservation of Momentum principle, which states that momentum in a closed system stays constant, is equivalent to Newton's third law. Momentum is the product of mass times velocity, so if the mass of a system changes, then the velocity must change. For example, a hot air balloon carrying a girl and a dog has a certain mass and a certain velocity provided by helium. The product of these is a certain momentum. If the dog jumps out of the balloon, the mass changes, and conservation of momentum demands that the velocity change in an equal and opposite reaction: the balloon accelerates on its upward path. If the girl follows the dog, the momentum is altered once again, the balloon's acceleration increasing in direct proportion to the change in mass.

A similar conservation law applies to an object moving in a circle, like a twirling ice skater. She has a special kind of momentum, called angular momentum, which combines mass and velocity with acceleration. In order to determine the acceleration, we must know the speed with which the body is traveling in its circular path (for example, the skater's rotations per second), and the radius of that circle (defined by the distance of the outermost part of the skater's body—the tip of an extended hand, say—to the center of her body). The product of this speed, the mass of the object and the square of the circle's radius gives us the body's angular momentum. Conservation of angular momentum is the law stating that in a closed system angular momentum, just like its linear counterpart, must stay the same. Thus, the angular momentum is defined when the skater's arms are outstretched, and it will be conserved when she draws her arms into her body; the rate of rotation has to increase to compensate for the decreased radius, and because the rate depends on the square of the radius, it increases exponentially.

Conservation of mass simply means that in a closed system the total amount of mass appears to be conserved in all but nuclear reactions and other extreme conditions. Without this constant, momentum would be impossible to determine. Conservation of energy applies the same rule to energy. Energy comes in many forms: mechanical, chemical, electrical, heat, and so forth; as one form is changed into another (excepting nuclear reactions and extreme conditions), this law guarantees that the total amount of energy remains the same. These two laws differ somewhat from other conservation laws in that the conservation only appears to be constant. This qualifier is the result of Einstein's special theory of relativity, which implies that energy and mass are related. Consequently, mass and energy by themselves are not conserved, since one can be converted into the other. In ordinary situations, where the effect of Einstein's discovery is usually negligible, mass and energy each appear to be conserved.

In some situations, however, one can be converted into the other. In both nuclear fission (splitting of the atomic nucleus) and nuclear fusion (the joining of atomic nuclei, producing the energy of a hydrogen bomb), mass is converted into energy, but the overall sum of mass and energy is conserved according to the general law. The more general law, then, is the law of conservation of mass-energy: the total amount of mass and energy must be conserved.

◆**Law of Gravity** Newton's Law of Universal Gravitation, described along with his other laws in his *Principia*, is a mathematical formula that can determine the gravitational force between any two objects. That force is proportional to the product of the objects' masses and inversely proportional to the square of the distance between them. If F is the force, G is the number that represents that ratio (the gravitational constant), m and M are the two masses, and r is the distance between the objects, then the equation is F = (GmM) divided by r2.

This law implies that all objects falling near the surface of Earth will fall with the same rate of acceleration (ignoring drag caused by air): thus, a brick falls with the same rate of acceleration as a feather—but only if they are dropped from the same height. Acceleration increases—the falling object gathers speed—over time. Close to the surface of the Earth, the rate of acceleration is 32.174 feet per second per second (ft/sec2), or 9.8 m/sec2, and is conventionally labeled g. Applying this in the equation that describes the rate to falling objects gives the velocity, v, and distance, d, after any amount of time, t, in seconds. If the object starts at rest and 32 ft/sec2 is used as an approximation for g, then v=32t and d=16t2. For example, after 3 seconds, a dropped object that is still falling will have a velocity of 32x3=96 ft/sec2 and will have fallen a distance of 16x32=144 feet. This is why an object dropped from a great height is more likely to break on impact than one dropped only a short distance—the increase in velocity means it hits the Earth with greater force.

Albert Einstein's general theory of relativity introduced laws of gravity more accurate than those discovered by Newton, but Newton's gravitational theory is extremely accurate for most practical situations.

◆Laws of Thermodynamics   There are two laws of thermodynamics, the study of the relationship between energy and heat. All bodies contain heat as energy no matter how cold they are, although there is not much heat at temperatures close to absolute zero. The first law of thermodynamics is the same as the law of conservation of energy: in a closed system, the total amount of energy, including heat, is always conserved. If energy is transferred from chemical form to heat form, for example, the amount of energy remains constant.

The second law indicates that heat in a closed system can never travel from a low-temperature region to one of higher temperature in a self-sustaining process. Self-sustaining in this case describes a process that does not need energy from outside the system to keep it going.

◆Laws of Electromagnetic Radiation   Electromagnetic radiation is a phenomenon that takes the form of waves made of electric and magnetic fields, which travel through space. There are several different types of electromagnetic radiation, including visible light, infrared, and radio waves. The velocity of a wave is how fast the wave travels as a whole; the wavelength is the distance between one crest of the wave and the next crest; the frequency is how many crests pass a particular location in a unit of time.

The Law of Electromagnetic Energy determines the energy of an electromagnetic wave using a small number known as Planck's constant, units of energy per frequency. Using E for energy, h for Planck's constant, and f for frequency, the law is summarized in the equation $E = hf$.

◆**Laws of Quantum Physics** Quantum physics is the application of the laws of physics to the subatomic realm—systems, such as electrons and protons, too small to be seen. A quantum is a discrete, indivisable unity of energy. Quantum physics is considered a distinct branch of physics because at that subatomic level objects behave differently than they do at larger, visible sizes. A quantum changes in steps, instead of continuously, and small masses sometimes act like particles, sometimes like waves. Among the laws that describe the behavior of small masses, two are basic and easily stated.

Heisenberg's Uncertainty Principle states that it is impossible to specify the position and momentum of a particle, such as an electron, at the same time. If the position can be ascertained, the momentum cannot be, and vice versa.

Pauli's Exclusion Principle states that two particles of matter cannot be in the same quantum state: the specific physical system involving quanta. Particles of matter include the electron, neutron, and proton. (Bosons, particles of force, do not obey Pauli's exclusion principle.)

◆**Subfields of Physics** Because physics is a fundamental underpinning of most other sciences, it is often studied in subfields as an integral component of another branch of science. Three notable examples are combinations of physics with astronomy, earth science, and biology.

Astrophysics is the study of stars, gas clouds, and other astronomical bodies, based on the application of the laws of physics—including energy production, composition, and evolution—to the field of astronomy. While a broad view of astrophysics would include virtually all of astronomy, the discipline was originally concerned primarily with energy production and the development of stars from gas clouds, through several stages of stellar evolution, to explosions as supernovas and collapse as burned-out cinders or black holes. In recent years, the evolution of the universe as a whole (cosmology) has become a central focus of many astrophysicists.

Geophysics is the study of the structure of Earth based on the application of physical laws to Earth's shape, seismology, electromagnetic properties, oceans, and atmosphere. The methods of geophysics have revealed Earth's layered structure, consisting of inner and outer cores, mantle, and crust, as well as provided the theoretical basis of plate tectonics. The definition of geophysics has been stretched to include the physical properties of planets other than Earth.

Biophysics is the study of such physical processes as transport of materials in living organisms, growth of such organisms, and their structural stability in terms of the laws of physics. Of particular concern are the transport of ions across cell membranes and the mechanisms of protein folding; the field is also interested in the physics of such imaging techniques as CT, MRI, and PET scans.

Day 2: Matter, Energy, and Einstein

For more than 200 years, Sir Isaac Newton's equations, based on his laws of gravity, stood unchallenged in the scientific world. They could predict and explain the orbits of the planets on their elliptical paths, down to the very moment when a planet would be at its closest point to the Sun. Only one exception baffled astronomers: the planet Mercury was measured to be moving at a rate considerably faster than the most finely calibrated Newtonian equations could account for. Ad hoc explanations for this inconsistency were offered, but no supporting evidence of Mercury's unique behavior could be found. None, that is, until 1905, when a 26-year-old patent clerk in Bern, Switzerland, published a study that would revolutionize physics and astronomy, as well as force scientists to reexamine some of their most fundamental concepts.

Einstein's theories of special relativity and general relativity explained, among other things, why astronomers on Earth perceived the movement of Mercury quite differently than they would if they could somehow stand on that planet's surface: all measurements of space and time, he showed, are relative. Neither Mercury nor anything else can accurately be said to have an "absolute speed" or exist in "absolute time."

Special relativity, first introduced in a German science journal in 1906, was a brilliant resolution of two seemingly contradictory ideas:

1. The laws of physics are the same for all observers in uniform motion relative to one another.

2. The speed of light in a vacuum is the same for all observers, regardless of their motion or the motion of the light source.

Instead of attempting to disprove one theory or modify the other, Einstein accepted them both as true and predicted the consequences of that coexistence. In doing so, he unified the concepts of space and time into a single four-dimensional structure called "spacetime." Combined with other laws of physics, the two postulates of special relativity predict the equivalence of mass and energy. Einstein's famous equation $E=mc2$, where E is energy, m is mass, and c is the speed of light in a vacuum, is the mathematical representation of that equivalence. A definition of modern physics, then, might be "the study of matter-energy in space-time."

The general theory of relativity, published in 1915, is a description of gravity in terms of spacetime. It combines special relativity and Newton's law of universal gravitation to describe gravity not as a force but a curvature of space and time. Its implications, too, were vast and promised to revise the Newtonian understanding of the universe.

Almost as soon as it was published, it became clear that the theory as originally formulated predicted an expanding universe, as well as the existence of what we now call black holes, stars that have collapsed into points with such a strong gravitational force that light cannot escape. Both concepts have been debated, discarded, and revisited since Einstein's time, but neither has been disproved. In 1919, one consequence predicted by the theory of general relativity, the "lensing effect" caused by the gravitational force of an entire galaxy, was observed for the first time. That fall, *The Times* of London ran a banner headline that announced: "Revolution in Science—New Theory of the Universe—Newtonian Ideas Overthrown."

◆**Atoms and Energy** Einstein's special theory of relativity predicted that a great deal of energy is released when an atom is split. It had only been in the late 1890s that J. J. Thomson identified the first subatomic particle and proved that atoms are divisible. Previously, in an idea held since the time of ancient Greek philosophers, it was thought that atoms are the tiniest, most basic units of matter. Another important discovery of the late 1890s, radioactivity (the emission of radiation energy from certain atoms), was made by Henri Becquerel. Decades would pass before scientists succeeded in releasing the energy in atoms, ushering in the age of atomic weapons and nuclear power plants.

Today, physicists have a standard model of the particles that make up atoms or that are smaller than atoms. This model incorporates three of the four fundamental forces in nature: the strong and weak nuclear forces and the electromagnetic force (the other force is gravity). A current challenge to physicists is to develop a "theory of everything" that would account for all the fundamental forces, including gravity.

Here are the most important subatomic particles, with the dates of their discovery:

Electron (1897) The electron is a low-mass particle that can be found in the outer reaches of the atom. One property of the electron is charge, the response to electric or magnetic fields. The charge of a single electron is always the same and is identified as -1 (negative one). Each atom consists of a cloud of electrons around a center of positive charge, which is called the nucleus.

Proton (1911) At least one proton is always found in the nucleus of every atom. The proton has a charge that is the same in strength as that of the electron, but it responds in the opposite direction to an electric or magnetic field. This charge is $+1$ (positive one).

Neutron (1932) The neutron is very much like a neutral proton, with just slightly more mass. Neutrons are stable when they are found in atoms but decay into other particles when left to themselves.

Neutrinos (1955) Neutrinos are thought to be among the most common particles in the universe, but they interact with ordinary matter so weakly that they are very difficult to observe and have a very small mass.

Quarks (1964-95) Physicists have determined that a way to explain the properties of subatomic particles is to think of them as heavy particles made from combinations of light ones, just as the atom is made from combinations of electrons, protons, and neutrons. These smaller particles are called quarks, and there are six varieties. Two quarks, known as up and down, form protons and neutrons. The rest are only produced in high-energy collisions, such as in particle accelerators and cosmic rays.

J/psi particle (1974) J/psi particle is a heavy particle that appears at high energies. It is produced by another kind of quark called the charm quark.

Antiparticles (1930) In 1930 Paul A. M. Dirac observed that one solution to his equations predicted a particle that would be a mirror image of the electron, exactly the same as the electron but with a positive instead of a negative charge. The particle, discovered two years later, was named the positron. The same equations predicted mirror images for all subatomic particles. These particles are called antiparticles (another name for positron is antielectron).

Antiatoms (1995) Since antiparticles have all the properties of ordinary particles, it is possible to create an antiatom by combining subatomic antiparticles. This was accomplished in 1995 with the production of a few antiatoms of antihydrogen were produced by causing an antielectron (positron) to orbit an antiproton.

Bosons (1924) While matter is made from subatomic particles, so are the forces that act on matter. The particles that create these forces are collectively called bosons because the mathematics of the behavior of this type of particle was worked out originally by Satyendranath Bose in 1924, although it was put into final form by Einstein. The observed bosons are the photon, pions, gluons, W particles, and Z particles. Bosons that are predicted, but that have not been observed, include Higgs particles and gravitons.

Photon (1905) The photon is the particle that possesses the electromagnetic force. Although we usually think of the photon as the particle of light, it is also the particle form of radio waves, X-rays, or gamma rays. The mass of the photon is 0.

Fermions (1926) All the particles that make up matter are called fermions, including leptons and quarks, and the particles made from quarks. They all obey the Pauli Exclusion Principle; that is, they occupy a definite space, and as such two fermions cannot be in the same place at the same time.

Muon (1935) The muon is now recognized as a high-energy analogue to the electron, with a mass about 200 times that of the electron.

Pion (1947) Predicted in 1935, a pion possesses the strong force that holds the nucleus of atoms together. However, since each pion appears and disappears almost instantly, the pions are not usually counted as part of the nucleus.

Gluons (1965–73) The eight different bosons that produce a force between quarks known as the color force are called gluons. The color force is also the basis of the strong force that holds the nucleus together.

W and Z particles (1983) The particles that produce the weak force are called W and Z. At high energies, however, the weak force merges with the electromagnetic force, so that W and Z are to some extent analogues to the photon; however, they could not be more different, since the photon has a 0 rest mass and both W particles and the single Z particle are very massive.

Graviton and Higgs particle (not yet observed) A particle that produces gravitational force by its exchange between all kinds of particles is known as the graviton, but so far exists only in theory. The Higgs particle is the main undetected particle of the standard model of subatomic particles; it is believed to confer mass on all other particles.

Strange particles (1950) Starting in 1950, experimenters observed a number of previously undetected particles that did not behave as particles were expected to. Because these particles have masses greater than that of the proton and neutron, they were called hyperons. Other unexpected particles, about the size of the pion, were classed as mesons.

✦Stimulated emissions of radiation In 1917, Einstein described the concept of a process known as the stimulated emissions of radiation, a process now used in lasers. A laser is a device that produces an intense and focused beam of light waves. In a laser, one photon of light absorbed in an energized molecule releases two or more photons that are exactly the same as the first. By reflecting such photons back and forth inside the laser, but allowing some to escape in one direction, the energy of the laser emerges as a beam of identical photons.

Theodore Maiman built the first working laser in 1960, that used the molecules of a ruby to create its beam. Improvements in design started quickly, and by 1965 a laser was built that could be adjusted to different wavelengths of light. In 1970, the first carbon-dioxide lasers could cut through metals or be used for welding. Applications proliferated. As early as 1962, a laser was used in eye surgery, where lasers have become a common tool. Perhaps the most common uses of lasers today are in barcode scanners, CD and DVD players, and fiber-optic communications. Special tools for farmers and carpenters use lasers as aids in leveling, surveying, or measuring distances.

Weekend 24: The Reformation of the Christian World

Day 1: The Protestant Revolution

In the world today, the number of people who claim Christianity as their religion number approximately 2 billion. More than 1.1 billion are Roman Catholics; the rest are generally known as Protestants, a term coined in 1528 during the struggle of European Christians seeking a new way to salvation different from the one established and enforced by the Catholic Church for over 1,000 years. Given the fact that the power of the Catholic Church was so deeply entrenched, the success of Protestantism was a landmark event in Western history. Even more extraordinary is the rapidity with which it took hold. In less than 40 years (1517–55), most of Europe was segregated into Catholic and Protestant towns, cities, and kingdoms. The roots of popular discontent with the church were rooted in a history riddled with corruption and overt sinfulness on the part of the clergy, the bishops, and even the pope himself.

•**Luther, Calvin, and the Protestant Revolution** From the time Emperor Constantine converted to Christianity and granted it toleration throughout the Roman Empire in the early fourth century A.D., the organizational structure of the church became intimately entwined with secular governments. As the church spread throughout Europe, its power to enforce laws, both religious and secular, was carried out by the bishops and local pastors and soon accepted as the norm by the people and the rulers. Central power was concentrated in the city of Rome and embodied in one man, the pope, whose pronouncements about church doctrine were deemed infallible. Over the centuries, any person or group deviating from official doctrines were declared heretics and severely punished, often by being burned at the stake.

Although the central mission of the papacy was spiritual—to save souls—its ever increasing temporal power and vast material wealth resulted in the kind of arrogance and corruption that can infect all human institutions. As early as the late 11th century, Pope Gregory VII felt obliged to crack down on clergymen who married, kept concubines, and caused scandal by fathering children. He also fought to end the buying and selling of church offices, and the undue influence of the nobility on choosing bishops for their own benefit. Such reform movements arose several times over the next few centuries. At the end of the 14th century, the papacy itself lost all its influence and much of its dignity when, largely as a result of a desire for temporal power, three popes held that office at the same time. The "Great Schism" lasted for an entire generation (1378–1417), and its legacy of undermining the pope's claims of being "God's Vicar on Earth" has never abated.

Despite the shame of the papal schism, the popes of the later 15th century and early 16th century continued to pursue the trappings of temporal power, including the development of a military force that was used in wars against other Italian city-states. But it was an elaborate plan to rebuild the city of Rome, including the basilica of St. Peter (built on the Apostle's Tomb by Constantine in the mid-fourth century) that would eventually cause the revolt that shattered the once-unified world of Christendom. Today we see in this rebuilding project the glorious works of Michelangelo, Bramante, Raphael, and others, but to those bent on church reform at the time, it was just another example of the church's vanity as it pursued prestige and adulation rather than addressing the needs of the faithful. As the costs of the rebuilding grew ever larger, the papacy resorted to the dubious practice of selling indulgences, allowing people to buy a reduction of future time spent in Purgatory for one's sins.

This idea enraged Martin Luther, a young, learned Augustinian monk in the university town of Wittenberg, in Saxony. On October 31, 1517, he posted 95 "theses," challenging the leaders of the church on the efficacy of indulgences, asserting that "money clinking into the money chest" does not save a soul from Purgatory. By the spring of 1518, the debate over indulgences had spread across much of Europe as the printing press revealed its full power to affect political and cultural change. Between 1517 and 1520, Luther would write 30 theological tracts that had 300,000 copies printed. Over the next two years, Luther expanded his attacks to several core beliefs of the church, most notably in his assertion that each person has a direct relationship with God and that the mediation of the clergy has no effect on salvation. Moreover, good works on Earth mattered not at all, only faith in a merciful God could lead a soul to heaven. In 1520, after Pope Leo X condemned his teachings,

Luther published *On the Babylonian Captivity of the Church*, which challenged the church's doctrine that Christ was actually present in the Eucharist (known as transubstantiation) and in January 1520 he was formally excommunicated.

Luther immediately went into hiding and was given protection by the Duke of Saxony, thereby preventing his arrest and likely execution. During this time, he translated the New Testament into German, a key development in the Protestant movement. All future sects would follow suit, making God's revelation through the Bible available to all Europeans in their native languages and resulting in the rapid growth in literacy rates throughout Europe.

Many of Luther's followers seized the moment and confiscated church lands, attacked the clergy, and smashed and burned religious statues and paintings. In 1524, thousands of German peasants revolted against their lords, citing Luther's teachings. Luther disparaged them publicly, but thousands were slaughtered in the ensuing repression.

Over the next 20 years, Luther continued to write tracts attacking church leaders and their practices. He also translated the Old Testament into German and wrote many hymns, all in German. He was married to a former nun in 1525, fathered five children, and lived a quiet domestic life until his death in 1546. By that time, northern Germany, the Netherlands, and Scandinavia had embraced his religious beliefs, but the emergence of new and powerful preachers with different religious views did not allow Luther to die a contented man.

•**The Rise of Calvinism** Luther's rebellion against the established religious authority would inspire others to follow suit. In fact, Protestantism was almost immediately divided theologically and politically. In 1519, only two years after Luther had posted his 95 theses, another learned Catholic priest, Ulrich Zwingli, began to preach in Zurich, Switzerland. Zwingli contended that the Bible, including the Old Testament, was the center of Christian salvation. He also married and in 1520 began attacking indulgences, penitential works, and the worship of saints. By 1525, the Roman Mass under Zwingli became only a communion service with both bread and wine given to the faithful as it is in the Bible. All images were removed from churches, and marriage became a civil ceremony.

Luther had serious disagreements with some of the tenets Zwingli and other Protestant leaders were promulgating, and in 1529 a group of them met in the city of Marburg to find common ground. By the following year, at the Diet of Augsburg, they realized that several of their differences were irreconcilable, and they have remained divided ever since.

By 1540, however, a new, very popular sect would arise, again in a Swiss city, Geneva, under the leadership of another highly educated priest, John Calvin. In 1534, at age 25, he fled his native France out of fear that the new religious ideas he was preaching in Paris would lead to his execution. In 1536, he settled in Geneva, where his powerful preaching immediately won him a devoted following. However, when he attempted to convince the city magistrates that they should submit to God's law rather than the civil law, he was banished and spent several years in Strasbourg, where he attracted a large following of French Protestants fleeing Catholic repression.

In 1541, the elders of Geneva asked Calvin and his congregation to return. Geneva soon became the home of Reformation scholars seeking a safe refuge. In 1557, John Knox joined Calvin's congregation and would later found the Church of Scotland on Calvinist beliefs. In 1559, Calvin established his Academy to teach his doctrines to future generations of scholars and also published the third and last edition of his theological text, *The Institutes of the Christian Religion*, consisting of 80 chapters in four books. Like Luther, he insisted on publishing in both Latin and in the vernacular French.

Calvin's theology embraced the basic ideas of the Reformation— the truth of the Bible and its central place in the Christian's life, the rejection of the need for clerical mediation between God and men, stripping churches of images and statues, and reducing the Mass to a service stressing the symbolic nature of Holy Communion. Dividing Protestant sects even further, Calvin held the belief that after the Fall of Adam and Eve, humankind became so depraved that God decided only a few could achieve salvation and were therefore "predestined" to be saved. Their identity could be discovered by their strict adherence to the Ten Commandments and their participation in a religious congregation. Historically, predestination proved less influential than Calvin's insistence that the civil state and religious authorities act in concert, making the Bible the basis of law and government. These ideas took hold in Geneva, parts of Germany, France, the Netherlands, and later in Scotland, England, and the New World (where the Puritans held sway).

◆**The Reformation in England** Unlike almost all of the Reformation movements on the Continent, which were essentially popular uprisings, it was the monarchy in England that led one of the most Catholic peoples to turn on their church and embrace their king, Henry VIII, as their religious leader. For the first 20 years of Henry's reign, no one would have predicted this turn of events.

Shortly after ascending to the throne at age 18 in 1509, Henry married his brother's widow, Catherine of Aragon, the daughter of Ferdinand and Isabella of Spain. He did this after receiving a papal dispensation based on Catherine's testimony that her first marriage had not been consummated. Although at first a diplomatically advantageous marriage, the couple appeared compatible, and when Henry was away at war, Catherine proved a most capable leader. In 1516, she gave birth to a daughter, Mary, but Catherine was at that time 31 and increasingly unlikely to produce a male heir to the throne.

When Luther attacked the church and the papacy in 1517, Henry wrote a powerful public rebuttal that earned him the accolade "Defender of the Faith" from the pope himself. Over the next decade, England's political fortunes faltered, and Henry grew anxious about his legacy. In the late 1520s, he began an affair with a young, beautiful woman, Anne Boleyn, and began to petition the pope for a divorce from Catherine. As the pope continually refused, Henry's frustration grew and he married Anne anyway, severed all ties with Rome, and gained control of the English Church. Between 1531 and 1534, Parliament, almost without objection, passed a series of acts that resulted in the total subjection of bishops and clergy to the monarchy. In 1533, Anne was made queen and soon gave birth to a daughter (Elizabeth I), and the pope excommunicated Henry.

In 1534, the Reformation in England was completed by the Act of Supremacy, which gave legal underpinning to Henry's claim that the monarch is "the only supreme head of the Church of England" with unlimited power to direct its affairs. Government officials were required to swear an oath acknowledging Henry as head of the church. Only a handful refused, including St. Thomas More, who had earlier been Henry's adviser, chancellor, and staunch supporter. In 1536, Henry consolidated his power by seizing numerous monasteries and in many cases selling off their lands to wealthy noblemen who, of course, gladly endorsed the new order. In that same year, Anne was accused of adultery and incest, and beheaded. Henry soon married Jane Seymour, and in 1537 she bore the king his male heir (Edward VI). Henry declared his two daughters to be illegitimate so the boy could succeed him without difficulty.

Unlike the reform movements begun by Luther and Calvin, the English approach favored the retention of many of the theological tenets of the Catholic Church. However, the Mass did become a communion service, all devotionals were now conducted in English rather than Latin, and a Bible in English was approved. Only a century later, England would be torn apart by religious struggles having to do with the decisions made at this time. In the middle of the 16th century, Europe was caught up in the violent political and military aspects of the Reformation as the papacy and Holy Roman Empire launched a major counterattack against the forces of Protestantism.

Day 2: The Counter-Reformation and the Wars of Religion

Despite the upheaval caused throughout Europe by Luther's attack on church authority, a formal response was not issued from the Vatican until 25 years after Luther's excommunication. In part, this was because the papacy remained in control of those millions who opposed serious reforms, and in addition, the Reformation had moved too swiftly for any military action or easy containment.

Many supporters of the church did take action, and over the years the reformers would gain control of the papacy. In 1528, a preaching order called the Capuchins were founded to go into the rural areas to instruct people in the "true" church doctrine. In 1534, Spanish nobleman and soldier, Ignatius of Loyola, left the military with six of his followers and took vows of poverty, chastity, and obedience, in Paris. In 1540, Pope Paul III granted them permission to form a religious order, the Society of Jesus (Jesuits) with Ignatius as their leader. They quickly attracted many men devoted to the church and soon founded schools and universities in major cities throughout Europe. Later, they would also establish missions in far-off lands, including India, Japan, China, and the Americas.

In 1545, Pope Paul III finally succeeded in calling a General Council of all the bishops to meet in Trent, a small city in the Alps. Two years of political wrangling overshadowed any discussions about reform. In 1547, however, Emperor Charles V finally launched a successful military campaign against a coalition of German Protestant states. After several years of attempting to impose Catholicism on the defeated regions, Charles was forced to admit defeat. In 1555, peace was established at the Diet of Augsburg, which proclaimed that each state determined its own religion.

The council of bishops continued to meet sporadically until 1563, and after much debate and negotiation, presented a unified front on most of the crucial issues. The bishops categorically rejected both the doctrine of salvation by faith alone and the idea that only the Bible contains God's truth. The council also reiterated the validity of all seven sacraments, including the "real presence" of Christ in Holy Communion. Some serious reforms were finally embraced: simony (including the selling of indulgences) was banned outright, the moral lives of bishops and priests were to be scrutinized, and the education of the clergy much enhanced.

In the decades that followed, the new spirit energizing the church's faithful would lead to violent conflicts between Protestants and Catholics, as both sides claimed that God had shown them the truth, and the other's beliefs were heresy. While Spain and England would play the most conspicuous roles in the last half of the 16th century, much of Europe would experience the scourge of warfare over religious belief for more than a century, as powerful leaders on both sides seized the moment to blend religion and politics to their own advantage.

In France, for example, the Protestant movement had attracted a large following soon after Luther's first salvos against the church. King Francis I quickly repressed those known as Huguenots, and many fled to settle in Strasbourg, then a free city. Here they came under the influence of Calvin's doctrines, and by 1560 there were 2,000 religious communities in France organized on his principles. Their need to proclaim their religious beliefs publicly led to serious outbreaks of violence in many cities and towns, culminating in March 1562 with the slaughter of 50 Protestants worshipping in a barn in Champagne. Protestant leaders declared war, and over the next 35 years, eight separate religious wars were fought. One of them began in Paris on August 24, 1572, when Catholic loyalists attacked Protestant nobility gathered for a wedding. Some 3,000 would die in what is known as the St. Bartholomew's Day Massacre. Over the next few months, an estimated 7,000 Huguenots were slaughtered outside of Paris.

In 1593, peace was established for a short time while the Protestant claimant to the French throne, Henry IV, converted to Catholicism in order to become king ("Paris is worth a Mass," he said). In 1598, he issued the Edict of Nantes, which granted the Huguenots a degree of religious freedom and a guarantee of royal protection.

♦**England and Spain**   Since the English Reformation was driven for over 20 years by the king's demands, his successors claimed the same power. When Henry VIII died in 1547, his only male heir (by Jane Seymour), Edward VI, was nine years old. A regent was appointed who supported the new Church of England. Edward died in 1552, and his half sister, Mary Tudor (Henry's daughter by Catherine of Aragon) became queen. A devout and unwavering Catholic, she quickly married the Spanish prince, Philip, who was the Roman Church's most loyal defender. Mary launched a fierce attack on the supporters of the English Church, earning her the nickname "Bloody Mary." More than 300 people, including bishops, nobles, and ordinary people, were deemed heretics and burned at the stake during her brief six-year reign.

When Mary died in 1558, Elizabeth I, daughter of Henry and Anne Boleyn, was crowned queen, and by the following year England was once again a Protestant nation. After consolidating her power by selecting shrewd advisers and gaining popular support by her commitment to the Church of England, Elizabeth was able to restore stability to the monarchy. The pope excommunicated Elizabeth in 1570. With the help of Philip of Spain and several Jesuits, a series of plots against the queen's life were set in motion, only to be discovered and their leaders tortured to death.

In 1585, Elizabeth reluctantly took up the Protestant cause against Mary's widower, now Philip II of Spain, who was waging war in the Netherlands against the enemies of the church. Spain's power was far superior to England's, and Philip now devised a plan to invade England, depose Elizabeth, and place the people under Spanish rule. In 1588, a great fleet of 130 ships was prepared in Spain, but English naval raids and bad weather forced several delays. In July of 1588, however, the Spanish Armada, now carrying 20,000–30,000 soldiers, entered the English Channel, but were driven back by the smaller, faster English ships. Days later, another battle ensued, and this time the Armada was seriously defeated. Because of bad weather, the fleet was forced to sail around Scotland, then to land in Ireland, where they were attacked by English foot soldiers. More than half the ships were lost, and only 5,000 men returned to Spain.

Over the next 15 years, Elizabeth would reign in relative peace, although she continued to aid Protestants struggling to resist Catholic attacks. During this time, the great voice of English literature, William Shakespeare, would emerge, but so too would the first signs of religious conflict among several Protestant groups. To the Presbyterians, and their stricter offshoot, the Puritans, the English Church retained too many vestiges of Catholicism, such as liturgical music, statues, and paintings. They sought a government based on religious tenets found in the Bible, pursuant to their Calvinist theological beliefs.

After Elizabeth's death in 1603, a Scottish family, the Stuarts, became the ruling dynasty, with James I its first ruler. Over the next 50 years, the Presbyterians, having steadily gained political power in Parliament, continuously confronted the monarchy's assertions of divine right prerogatives. At first the king's government resorted to serious repression of those who advocated for change, leading many Puritans to flee to America.

From 1629 to 1640, James's successor, Charles I, refused to call Parliament into session and persecutions of religious nonconformists and political opponents were increased. When financial necessity forced the king to summon Parliament, the Presbyterian faction demanded concessions from the monarchy that prevented the king from dismissing Parliament without its permission, and even insisted on having control of the army. After Charles attempted to have the opposition leaders arrested, civil war soon became all but inevitable. Sporadic, occasionally fierce fighting lasted from 1642 to 1649 and resulted in the king's defeat and subsequent beheading in January 1649. The monarchy was dissolved, and a Protectorate established under the ruthless but brilliant military leader Oliver Cromwell, who brought peace through violence to Ireland and Scotland, as well as England. For 10 years, Puritan religious ideas were rigorously applied, including the suppression of theater, music, and all forms of popular entertainment.

The restoration of the monarchy in 1660 effectively ended the political power of the Presbyterians and the Puritans in England, but the role of religion in its politics arose again in 1688, when fears that a Catholic monarch, James II, would restore "popery." This resulted in his forced exile, and a firmly Protestant Dutch prince, William of Orange, was crowned king by order of the now all-powerful Parliament. Known as the "Glorious Revolution," it was the English Protestants' final blow against Catholic rule, 154 years after Henry VIII's revolt against papal authority.

•The Thirty Years War, 1618-48 The most destructive wars fought between Catholics and Protestants over the struggle for political power and theological supremacy began with a dispute between the Holy Roman Empire and the German principality of Bohemia. When the emperor's son Ferdinand, an ardent Catholic, was made king of Bohemia, the Protestant nobles there rejected him, and in 1618 threw the emperor's emissaries out of a window (known as the "Defenestration of Prague"). They then chose a Calvinist king, but Imperial forces quickly defeated him and began to impose Catholicism throughout Bohemia.

Protestant states grew fearful that this Hapsburg Empire would soon attack them, so Denmark, with aid from England and the Netherlands, entered the war in 1625, but was quickly defeated. In 1629, the emperor issued the Edict of Restitution, which restored all lands taken from the Catholic Church since 1552. This assertion of power by the Hapsburg dynasty on behalf of the church alarmed the Protestant states, now including Sweden, which entered the war in 1630 and won several victories under the king Gustavus Adolphus. Peace appeared to be restored in 1635 when the Edict of Restitution was annulled, but now the French, also fearing the power of the Hapsburgs, openly supported the Swedes in the last phase of the war. Soon France and Spain, both Catholic states, were at war with each other in what was a war for political power, independent of religion.

Finally, in 1644, peace negotiations began with all the contending states participating. In 1648, the Peace of Westphalia brought the war to an end, but not before the total devastation of Germany and the end of the power of the Holy Roman Empire. The Protestant states won a complete victory regarding annexed church lands. France gained territory, including Alsace and Lorraine, and emerged as the most powerful kingdom in Europe.

Weekend 25: Opera and Dance

Most opera lovers would agree that beautiful singing by highly trained artists, accompanied by the musical creations of the greatest composers, produces a theatrical experience unmatched in its emotional intensity by any other art form. Still, the imminent death of opera has been predicted for more than 30 years. Today, however, modern technology is bringing live opera to people around the world as the Metropolitan Opera in New York has launched a highly successful venture to show its performances in high definition in nearly 1,000 theaters worldwide. These performances are often sold out, helping to convince European opera houses to do the same. The future of opera may then be far brighter than anyone thought possible.

Day 1: Opera: A Brief History

◆**Baroque Origins** The operatic form originated in Florence, Italy, during the Baroque era (1600–1750). It grew out of attempts to recreate the effect of ancient Greek and Roman dramas in a more modern context. The first opera is generally considered to be *Daphne*, composed in 1597 by Jacopo Peri. Early operas were referred to as "drama per musica" (drama through music), and their plots were typically based on myth, much like their inspiration, the classic dramas of ancient Greece and Rome. *Daphne* is a perfect example, telling the story of the god Apollo and his courtship of a nymph named Daphne.

Many of these formative works were only half-sung, as vocal passages alternated with orchestral interludes and choruses commenting on the events. During this time, a new style of solo singing developed that was used for dramatic purposes, a blend of spoken word and singing called recitative. In this style, the music was subservient to the words. By the 1620s, however, a different type of vocal style gained prominence. In contrast to the recitative, the style of singing known as aria was more expressive and melodious, with the music taking precedence over the words. Over time, the aria became a showcase for virtuoso singing, and it eventually became a self-contained piece for solo voice with orchestral accompaniment.

The aria style was used prominently in the later operas of Claudio Monteverdi (b. Italy, 1567–1643), especially *Il ritorno d'Ulisse in patria* (*The Return of Ulysses*, 1640) and *L'incoronazione di Poppea* (*The Coronation of Poppaea*, 1642). Monteverdi was also known for using multiple musical forms in his operas, for example *Orfeo* (*Orpheus*, 1607), which was one of the first works to combine choruses, dances, madrigals, and duets. In addition to developing the aria, Monteverdi also introduced a larger and richer-sounding orchestra, and he was the first to reflect the emotions of the libretto in his music.

While opera was born in Italy, it quickly spread throughout all of Europe. By 1700, Vienna, Paris, Hamburg, and London were all centers of operatic activity. Due to public demand, most composers worked at least partly in the operatic form. Even the great Antonio Vivaldi, more known for his concert works, wrote hundreds of operas.

In London, George Frideric Handel composed a series of 42 powerful operas, including *Ariodante*, *Alcina*, *Guilio Cesare* (*Julius Caesar*), and *Orlando*. He was the first composer to write an Italian opera for the London stage, and in 1719 Handel joined with a group of English nobles to found the Royal Academy of Music, a company dedicated to the production of Italian operas. Handel's operas, like his other compositions, were praised for their high quality of orchestral and vocal writing; he was known for introducing new, relatively uncommon instruments into his works.

◆**Classical Opera**   Opera underwent many important changes during the Classical era (1750–1820). Italian opera had become a series of overly wrought arias designed to display the talents of the public's favorite singers. New composers cut back on the ornamentation, reintroduced instrumental interludes and accompaniments between arias, and made greater use of choral singing. They also combined groups of recitatives, arias, duets, choruses, and instrumental sections into unified scenes. The Classical period saw the decline of *opera seria* and the rise of lighter forms, such as *opera buffa* and *opera comique*. These new forms used more realistic spoken dialogue interspersed with songs, and the music was of a simpler style.

The most important figure in this movement was Wolfgang Amadeus Mozart. In Mozart's operas, the music for each character is distinct in tone and style from the other characters, and the action is reflected in the structure of the music. Mozart brought the orchestra to the fore-front of the opera. He was a prolific composer, writing 20 operas before his premature death at age 35. His most notable works include *Così fan tutte*, *Idomeneo*, *Le nozze di Figaro* (*The Marriage of Figaro*, 1786), *Don Giovanni*, and his final work, *Die Zauberflöte* (*The Magic Flute*, 1791).

Many of Mozart's operas are known for their hilarious comic aspects, with twisting, farcical plots set to witty music that brought clever characters to life. His mature compositions are distinguished by their melodic beauty, formal elegance, and richness of harmony and texture. His operas incorporated sophisticated orchestral techniques perfected in his other instrumental works.

◆**Romantic Opera** Even with the development of the symphony, concerto, and sonata, opera remained the most popular music of the Romantic period (1820–1900). During this era, grand spectacles and spectacular singing were characteristic of the longer, bigger, and more majestic works, typified by the French grand opera. Hector Berlioz's epic *Les Troyens* (*The Trojans*, ca. 1856) was not only longer in duration than previous French operas, but also employed more musicians, more artists, more technicians, and more stagehands.

In Italy, Gioachino Antonio Rossini introduced a new style known as *bel canto* (literally, "beautiful singing"). This new style of opera featured complex and ornate melodic lines (which vocalists could ornament at will), simple harmonic structure, and musical numbers that combined to make composite scenes. In the history of opera, Rossini is a transitional figure. His early operas are more Classical in nature, while his later ones are definitively Romantic. His most famous opera, *Il Barbiere di Siviglia* (*The Barber of Seville*) was written during a single two-week period in 1816. Rossini's other famous opera is *Guillaume Tell* (*William Tell*), composed in 1829, with its memorable overture, the finale of which was popularized as the theme music for the Lone Ranger.

Later in the 19th century, Rossini's fellow countryman Giuseppe Verdi introduced a new realism and intensity of expression to the form. His operas combined rhythmic vitality with superbly crafted melodies to great popular acclaim. Verdi eschewed the symphonic leanings of other Romantic-era composers, preferring to concentrate on the more traditional operatic form. Dramatically, Verdi exhibited a technical mastery of operatic form and unsurpassed powers of characterization. The characters in his 28 operas are as complex as the characters in Shakespeare and other traditional theater. His most popular operas include *Macbeth*, *Rigoletto*, *Il trovatore* (*The Troubador*), *La traviata*, *Aida*, *Don Carlo*, *Otello*, and *Falstaff*.

In Germany, Richard Wagner advanced the majestic music drama, which combined elements from Greek tragedy and the symphonies of Beethoven into a dramatic whole that was referred to as *Gesamtkunstwerk* ("Complete Artwork"). Wagner's operas—most notably *Lohengrin* (1850), *Tristan und Isolde* (1859), and the 4-part, 16-hour *Der Ring des Nibelungen* (1869–74)—pushed the boundaries of traditional tonality and impelled the art form to a larger scale. His groundbreaking work changed the nature of opera and influenced virtually all musical forms for decades to come.

One can easily recognize Wagner's music for its power and size, requiring a huge orchestra and powerful voices that can soar over the orchestra. Wagner's music is harmonically challenging, especially for the time. His use of extreme chromaticism and shifting tonal centers led directly to the atonal music of the 20th century. Of particular note is Wagner's "Tristan Chord," the first chord used in *Tristan und Isolde*, which was emblematic of Wagner's developing harmonic sense and foreshadowed further harmonic evolution after the turn of the century.

♦**Modern Opera** In the first half of the 20th century, opera continued to be influenced by the works of the Romantic era. Most notable were the works of Richard Strauss, who bridged the Romantic and modern eras. Strauss composed intense and richly melodic works influenced in equal measure. His early operas, such as *Salome* (1905) and *Elektra* (1909), were highly dissonant works that built on Wagner's chromatic harmonies. Strauss moderated this harmonic experimentation in his later works, however. The beautifully romantic *Der Rosenkavalier* (1911) embraced a fading romanticism that starkly contrasted to the more atonal musical environment of the early 20th century.

The Romantic operas of Giacomo Puccini continued the Italian grand opera tradition of Verdi and Rossini and were marvels of characterization, sentiment, and craftsmanship. The plots of most of his operas feature a tragic female lead—the "Puccini heroine"—who usually dies at the end, thus lending a particularly romantic slant to his works. Puccini's music, while seemingly simple, is actually quite complex. His mastery of melody and genius for orchestration make his works—including *La Bohème* (1896), *Tosca* (1900), *Madama Butterfly* (1904), and *Turandot* (1926)— among the most popular and beloved in the repertoire.

At the time Puccini's works were dominating the repertory, the influences of the atonal movement were being felt in the opera world as well. Alban Berg's *Wozzeck* (1921), still the most perfomed work in this style, tells the grim story of a working-class love affair gone bad, ending in the woman's murder by her lover and his suicide. The music is unmelodic but stark and moving nonetheless.

After World War II, composers, led by Benjamin Britten, began to integrate 20th-century musical forms into the established opera form. The protagonist in a Britten opera is typically a misfit or outsider pitted against the crowd, and Britten's music reflects this 20th-century alienation in its unusual and often stark instrumentation. His most famous operas include *Peter Grimes* (1945), *Billy Budd* (1951), and *Death in Venice* (1973).

Contemporary opera is represented by composers such as Philip Glass and John Adams, who have introduced multimedia elements, political commentary, rock music, and other unconventional elements into the form. Both composers employ minimalist techniques in their work, such as constantly repeating musical patterns. Glass's operas include *Einstein on the Beach* (1976) and *Appomattox* (2007); Adams's most famous operas are *Nixon in China* (1987) and *Doctor Atomic* (2005), about the building of the atom bomb.

Day 2: The History of Dance

"Movement is the essence of life, dance its ultimate expression," wrote Walter Sorell, a leading American dance critic. Dance existed long before written language, and like all the arts, reflects the culture and time period in which it was created. Throughout history, dance has served as a means of communication, an element of religious ritual, and as pure entertainment. Nearly everywhere in the world, and in every historical period, dance has been a way of socializing. The steps from community and couples dances, such as the pavane, reel, waltz, and polka, have all found their way into theatrical dance forms.

◆**Ballet**   The origins of ballet can be found in 16th-century France. Catherine de Medici (1519–1589), an Italian noblewoman who became the queen of France, brought a group of Italian dancers and her dancing master Balthasar de Beaujoyeulx to provide entertainment for the court. The spectacle was called "Le Ballet Comique de la Reine" (The Comic Ballet of the Queen, 1581) and was based on the kind of performances given in Italy for over a century. For its first 100 years, ballet was performed by male courtiers as an amateur entertainment.

In 1661, King Louis XIV, an accomplished dancer who earned the nickname the "Sun King" from his role as Apollo—god of the sun—in "Le Ballet de la Nuit" (Ballet of the Night, 1653), established the Académie Royale de la Danse to train professional ballet dancers. Pierre Beauchamp was named the "superintendent of the king's ballets" and is credited both with developing the French ballet terminology (still in use today) and the five positions of the feet, which remain the basis for ballet instruction throughout the world. In 1669, Louis established the Académie Royale de Musique, which was run by Jean-Baptiste Lully, who created a dance academy within the school. This dance company survives today as the Paris Opera, the oldest continuously running ballet company in the world.

Following the French Revolution, the plots of ballets began to celebrate ordinary people, rather than glorifying royalty. In 1789, the choreographer Jean Dauberval created "La Fille Mal Gardée" (The Poorly Guarded Daughter), with music based on 55 popular French airs. It was the first ballet with a plot drawn from peasant life and is one of the oldest ballets still in the repertory.

In the 19th century, dance technique matured to the point where truly expressive, plot-driven works could be created. In 1832, the Italian choreographer and dancer Fillipo Taglioni created "La Sylphide" which is generally accepted as the first Romantic ballet. It featured his daughter, Marie, establishing the importance of the prima ballerina as the star. Marie popularized dancing en pointe—dancing on the tips of the toes—and by the 1860s, ballet shoes were reinforced to facilitate this skill.

By the second half of the 19th century, the center of ballet activity moved from France to Russia, where it had a long history of royal support. In the late 17th century, Czar Peter the Great introduced contemporary arts to his homeland and invited the French ballet teacher Jean Baptiste Lande to establish the first school there—the Imperial Theatre

School in St. Petersburg. In 1847, the young French dancer Marius Petipa performed at the Imperial Theater, and 20 years later became the chief ballet master. Petipa dominated the ballet scene until his retirement in 1903 and ushered in a golden age of ballet, creating 77 works, including "Don Quixote" (1869) and "La Bayadère" (1877). His most beloved, and widely performed ballets are those with scores by Peter Ilyich Tchaikovsky: "The Sleeping Beauty" (1890), "The Nutcracker" (1892), perhaps the most popular ballet in the world today, and "Swan Lake" (1895).

By the early 20th century, dance makers began to reject the artifice of 19th century plots and the highly stylized dancing that accompanied them. The most influential pioneer of this new style was Sergei Diaghilev, who brought his company, Les Ballets Russes, to Paris in 1907. Diaghilev sought out the greatest modern artists, Pablo Picasso and Henri Matisse, among them—to create sets and costumes for his dances, and he commissioned contemporary musicians, including Igor Stravinsky, Sergei Prokofiev, and Claude Debussy, to create new scores. He also nurtured the careers of great dancers and choreographers whose imprint remains on ballet today. Mikhail Fokine revolutionized ballet by eliminating the use of mime to tell the story and instead using dance movements to reveal emotion and move the story forward. His best-known works were created for Vaslav Nijinsky, who drew huge crowds in Europe with his spectacular leaps and dramatic presence. Among these were "Schéhérazade" (music by Nicolai Rimsky-Korsakov, 1910), "Firebird" (music by Igor Stravinsky, 1910) and "Petrouchka" (music by Igor Stravinsky, 1911). In 1912, Nijinsky replaced Fokine as the primary choreographer for Les Ballets Russes, creating works that foreshadowed the development of modern dance. Audiences were shocked by the sensuality of "Afternoon of a Faun" (music by Claude Debussy, 1912), and a year later, "Rite of Spring" (music by Igor Stravinsky, 1913), the story of an ancient fertility ritual in which the chosen virgin is forced to dance herself to death, which caused a riot in the theater on its opening night.

Another of Diaghilev's notable protegés was George Balanchine, a Russian dancer and choreographer who studied at the Imperial School of Ballet at the Mariinksy Theatre. Balanchine left the Soviet Union in 1923 to join Les Ballets Russes where he created 10 new works, including "Apollo" (music by Igor Stravinsky, 1928) and "Prodigal Son" (music by Sergei Prokofiev, 1929), but his greatest influence was on the growth of ballet in the United States.

Balanchine came to the United States and created the School of American Ballet, which opened in 1934. A year later, he founded a performing group called American Ballet, which, in 1948, became the New York City Ballet, one of the largest and most admired ballet companies in the world today. Balanchine created more than 150 works for the company, including a full-length version of "The Nutcracker," but his preference was for programs that included several short ballets with simple sets and costumes that enhanced the movements of the dancers.

Balanchine also created a new style of theatrical dance by incorporating elements from tap and ballet in "Slaughter on Tenth Avenue" (1936), choreographed for the Broadway musical *On Your Toes*. In Hollywood, it was Fred Astaire who began to integrate dances into movie musicals. Considered the greatest popular music dancer of all time, Astaire took his inspiration from tap, classical ballet, and ballroom dancing. In his iconic partnership with Ginger Rogers, he created memorable moments in such musical films as *Top Hat* (1935) and *Swing Time* (1936). Legendary Russian ballet star Mikhail Baryshnikov called Astaire "a genius...a classical dancer like I never saw in my life."

Gene Kelly, a versatile dancer/choreographer, combined an athletic, masculine dance style with classical ballet technique. As a dancer, he is best remembered for his soft-shoe in *Singin' in the Rain* (1952), but as a choreographer, the 13-minute ballet at the conclusion of *An American in Paris* (1951) is considered his masterpiece.

Agnes de Mille took this new theatrical dance style forward. In addition to "Rodeo" (1942) created for Les Ballet Russe de Monte Carlo, and "Fall River Legend" (1948), which had its premiere at the American Ballet Theatre, de Mille's undisputed classic work is the "Dream Ballet" from *Oklahoma!* (1943), which was followed by *Carousel* (1945). In both musicals, the dance sequences were an important element of the overall stories.

Jerome Robbins was inspired by Agnes de Mille and is undoubtedly the most successful and prolific choreographer to move between Broadway and ballet. He joined the New York City Ballet as assistant artistic director in 1948, choreographing an array of plotless, yet moving ballets, including "Dances at a Gathering" (music by Frédéric Chopin, 1969) in which the piano is onstage and the dancers interact with the pianist. At the same time, he choreographed such landmark musicals as *West Side Story* (1957), *Gypsy* (1959) and *Fiddler on the Roof* (1964).

◆**Modern Dance** In the early 20th century, dancers in America and Germany began to experiment with more "natural" movement styles. In America, one of the leaders of this new movement was Isadora Duncan (1877–1927), a Californian who created works that expressed emotion and spirituality. Duncan's pieces featured dancers in free-flowing tunics and bare feet, and although early critics considered her work vulgar, she inspired a generation of dancers and choreographers all over Europe and the United States.

At the same time, Ruth St. Denis and her husband, Ted Shawn, introduced ethnic dances to the American public. Shawn eventually established the famous Jacob's Pillow dance school in Massachusetts. One of their most talented students was Martha Graham, a dramatic dancer who was a leader in the modern dance world in the late 1920s and '30s. Her 1944 work "Appalachian Spring" (music by Aaron Copland) is recognized as one of the masterpieces of modern dance. Graham choreographed 181 works over the course of 60 years and formed the Martha Graham Company, an incubator for many formidable talents, including Merce Cunningham, Alvin Ailey, and Paul Taylor, all of whom went on to form their own major companies.

Merce Cunningham is considered one of the greatest creative forces in American dance. He was interested in movement for its own sake, and many of his pieces were performed in silence. He had a long collaboration with his partner, composer John Cage, and worked with an array of visual artists and designers. Many of Cunningham's early works featured costumes, lighting and sets by the abstract artist Robert Rauschenberg, notably "Xover" (Crossover), which included the last designs completed before the artist's death.

Paul Taylor was a soloist with Martha Graham's company, and he also performed several Balanchine ballet roles with the New York City Ballet. Taylor is known for pieces that convey the human experience, incorporating everyday gestures, and often juxtaposing humor and tragedy for effect. Among his most influential pieces are "Three Epitaphs" (featuring early New Orleans jazz music, 1956), "Duet" (music by John Cage, 1957), and "Airs" (music by George Frideric Handel, 1978). Still choreographing and teaching today, his works are much in demand by ballet and modern dance companies around the world.

Alvin Ailey studied dance with Martha Graham and acting with

Stella Adler. He formed his own company—Alvin Ailey Dance Theater—in 1958, featuring primarily African-American performers. This highly successful touring company performs the works of many pioneering choreographers of modern dance, as well as works by Ailey himself. Their signature piece is "Revelations" (1960), danced to the music of African-American spirituals.

The work of Twyla Tharp embodies the intertwining of ballet and modern dance. Tharp frequently collaborated with Mikhail Baryshnikov, and her popular ballet "Push Comes to Shove" (music by Johann Sebastian Bach, 1976) is a result of that association. Like Jerome Robbins, Twyla Tharp has created dances for Broadway and film as well as for established dance companies.

During the 1960s, new dance forms led to the postmodern dance movement, which was less technique-oriented than the work of the earlier period, and more reflective of the cultural interests of Americans at that time. In addition to creating works based on serious social issues, postmodern choreographers used dancers of varied body types and choreographed in a unisex style, so there are no traditional masculine or feminine roles.

Trisha Brown is one of the notable choreographers of this movement, known for moving dance out of the theater and into natural and urban settings, as well as exploring alternative ways of moving, such as walking in harnesses. Her piece "Set and Reset" (music by Laurie Anderson, 1983), about the choreographic process, is considered a postmodern classic.

Day 1: To Kill a King: The French Revolution

On May 10, 1774, 20-year-old Louis XVI ascended to the throne of France after the death of Louis XV, his long-reigning grandfather (1715–74). Young Louis was a devout Catholic and a quiet, unassuming man, but expected to rule as absolute monarch under the long-established principle of "the divine right of kings." Together with his beautiful wife, the Austrian princess Marie Antoinette, as well as his large retinue of relatives and favored members of the nobility, Louis lived an extraordinarily luxurious life in several elaborately appointed palaces, most notably at Versailles, just outside of Paris. The public display of the nobility's profligate lifestyle never abated despite an ever downward-spiralling French economy.

The basic cause of France's financial problems can be found in the century of almost continuous warfare and imperial overreach that began during the long reign of Louis XIV (1643–1715). During this time, France was the dominant power in Europe, but emerged deep in debt from these wars and worse, lacked a financial structure to help relieve the ever-growing burden of servicing that debt.

Nevertheless, Louis XV successfully fought several major wars on the Continent and France held its own in the overseas colonial struggles in India, China, and most importantly, North America. But the Seven Years War (1756–63)—called the French and Indian War in America—saw France's fortunes turn as the allied forces of Great Britain and Prussia were decisively victorious. In addition to losing on the Continent, France was driven from North America and India, and England became the dominant colonial power in these areas.

Humiliation at the hands of the English, a bitter rival since the 12th century, became a strong motivating factor in France's decision to help the American colonists win independence from King George III, despite the enormous debt from the most recent war. Servicing the national debt now absorbed 60 percent of all of France's tax revenues. France's military aid proved vital to the Americans, especially in the final battle of the Revolution at Yorktown in 1781, when the French fleet entrapped the British and forced their surrender.

Within three years, however, the French financial situation had reached a crisis point as repayment of war loans came due, accompanied by a decline in tax revenues. The nobility strongly resisted paying taxes, and the clergy were exempt despite the enormous wealth of the church in France. In 1786, the king's ministers drew up a plan to reform the tax system. Early in 1787, the plan was presented to a group of 144 noblemen, prelates, and local magistrates called the Assembly of Notables. When they rejected the plan, and instead proposed that a commission audit the accounts of the royal family, the king flatly refused and the assembly was dismissed. Within a year, in August 1788, the French treasury suspended payments to creditors. This bankruptcy began the end of the French monarchy. The king reluctantly agreed to call a meeting of the Estates-General for the first time since 1614, thereby tacitly acknowledging the end of his absolute authority.

◆ **1789: The Revolution Begins**   During the winter and spring of 1789, elections took place throughout France, and the Estates-General met for the first time on May 5. Over the next six weeks, events took an entirely different turn from what anyone had anticipated. In 1614, each of the three estates—nobility, clergy, and everyone else (called the Third Estate)—had one vote, so the privileged classes easily dominated the proceedings. In 1789, the leaders of the Third Estate called on the other two estates to unite with them. The nobility and clergy, however, were determined to maintain their rights and privileges. Public opinion in Paris began to play a political role as bread prices rose and small riots broke out around the city. Under the leadership of Abbé Emmanuel-Joseph Sièyes, the Third Estate asserted its power, and soon members of the clergy began to cross over to their side. On June 17, the new representative body changed its name to the National Assembly. Historians see this as the "founding act" of the French Revolution, for if the nation was sovereign, the king no longer was.

Louis XVI attempted to present his own program of reform and briefly prevented the Assembly from meeting in their accustomed place. On June 20, the delegates met in an indoor tennis court and took an oath never to disband until they had given France a constitution. This "Tennis Court Oath" strengthened their resolve, and when several days later the king ordered them to meet by estate as originally intended, they simply refused. Louis was powerless to change their minds. Now even the nobility saw that it was to their advantage to join the National Assembly; by June 27, the king agreed, essentially signaling his complete capitulation.

Over the next two weeks, the king's supporters among the nobility and the military began a troop buildup in Paris, which the people recognized as a prelude to the violent repression of the revolution and of the National Assembly. Soon small bands of discontented and hungry citizens began to ransack storage facilities for arms and flour. Many in the Paris Guard began to desert rather than be forced to attack their fellow citizens. Some joined the mobs roaming unimpeded through the city. On July 14, they stormed the Bastille (the massive state prison), killed its commander, and freed the seven prisoners held there. The rebels immediately demolished the prison, which became symbolic of the end of royal power. Bastille Day remains the most important political holiday in France.

The National Assembly now began work on the constitution it had sworn itself to produce a month earlier. Violence continued in Paris and spread to other cities as well, instilling fear in the delegates that general anarchy was approaching. In early August, a radical group in the Assembly, hoping to end the chaos, proposed an end to all the feudal rights of the nobility and the clergy. Equality of taxation and justice were accepted, and the church was deprived of the tithes that provided most of its income. Somehow these acts led to a calming of the disorder that had gripped the nation, even though it meant the end of the old order, the "ancien régime" established centuries before.

Throughout the month of August, the delegates—now calling themselves the National Constituent Assembly—devoted their energies to finishing the constitution. On August 26, they issued a Declaration of the Rights of Man and the Citizen, which contained the basic principles underlying the new constitution. These included "natural...and unalienable rights" such as "liberty, property, security," and the presumption of innocence before the law. Article III recognized that the nation is the "source of all sovereignty," an idea that directly confronted the monarchy's presumption of rule by divine right. All of these postulates reflected the thinking of the great political theorists of the Enlightenment: Rousseau, Voltaire, and Montesquieu, as well as the Englishman

John Locke. More immediately, the ideas of the Americans Thomas Jefferson and Thomas Paine (an active supporter of the French Revolution), can be readily seen in the Declaration.

In the weeks that followed, the firm outlines of a constitutional monarchy began to emerge, giving the king only limited veto powers over laws passed by the legislature. As the king hesitated to embrace the new order, the people of Paris again grew restless and then fearful, as rumors of a military buildup filled the numerous city newspapers. In early October, thousands of women marched to Versailles, broke into the palace, and confronted the queen herself with death threats, demanding that the royal family move to Paris. On October 6, the king agreed to do so and was escorted to the city by the women, followed days later by the entire Assembly.

◆**1790–92: War, Regicide, and a New Republic** The Parisian mobs may now have had the upper hand, but the Assembly continued to construct a new government with men of property in charge, as well as guaranteeing compensation to thousands who lost their privileges under the new arrangements. However, that plan was faltering on the back of collapsing tax revenues, and the threat of bankruptcy loomed once again. The Assembly's solution was to seize the lands and endowments of the church and sell them to underwrite state bonds. By July 1790, the entire structure of the church came under the jurisdiction of the state, causing further division among the people. In the spring of 1791, the pope denounced the government's actions, strengthening resistance to the revolution. The king felt threatened by the hostile mobs, despite his acceptance of the Assembly's reforms, and on the night of June 2 he and the queen fled Paris under cover of darkness, hoping to reach regions in the east where there was strong support for the monarchy. Not only were they quickly captured and returned to Paris, but a letter written by the king was found roundly denouncing the revolution. From now on, the monarchy would be seen as an enemy of the revolution.

Oddly enough, the king was saved by the completion of the constitution in September 1791. After accepting it, Louis was reinstated as king, albeit one without real power. However, the Prussian king and the Hapsburg emperor issued the Declaration of Pillnitz, which threatened military action should any harm come to the royal family of France.

The new Legislative Assembly—called when the Constituent Assembly had finished the constitution—saw this document as a deliberate provocation, and in April 1792 declared war on Austria and Prussia, despite the poor condition of the French army. A decree by the Assembly calling for reinforcements by National Guard volunteers from around the country quickly changed the situation as France's first all-citizen army gathered in Paris. Unfortunately for the king, the Prussian commander responded by threatening to destroy Paris if Louis was harmed in any way. Now the people believed the monarchy would never support the revolution. In early August, the Assembly quickly suspended the monarchy and called for a convention to draw up a new constitution based on republican principles.

As Prussian armies began to cross into France, panic gripped the nation. In Paris, fear turned to violence as more than a thousand people, alleged to be enemies of the revolution, were slaughtered. A sudden change of fortune on the battlefields at Valmy (September 20), however, brought victory to the French forces and renewed hopes for the success of the revolution.

On September 22, the new Assembly, now called the Convention, abolished the monarchy and proclaimed France a republic. Over the next two months, French armies would achieve several military successes and were now offering help to any people seeking liberty. Soon, however, the leaders of the republic realized that the presence of the king gave hope to all of the revolution's enemies. A trial before the Convention took only two days, with the king denying all of the charges of treason and opposition to the revolution. The guilty verdict was no surprise, but the sentence of death passed by only one vote. On January 21, 1793, less than four years since the meeting of the Estates-General, Louis XVI was beheaded, the first European monarch to be executed since Charles I of England in 1649. The leaders of the Convention seemed to have no idea how this act would galvanize the monarchy's supporters and in turn plunge the revolution into madness.

◆1793–95: The Reign of Terror
Within days of the king's execution, England, Spain, the Dutch Republic, and several Italian city-states joined in the struggle to defeat France. Worse, a civil war broke out in the south, in the Vendée region, as disaffected Catholics and royalists formed an army pledging to restore the monarchy. The Convention suffered its first major political division between the Girondins, who

regarded all-out war as essential to end the violence of the Paris mobs, now universally known as *sansculottes* ("without knee breeches") to distinguish them from the upper classes, and their opponents, called Montagnards ("mountainmen") because they sat in the highest benches in the Convention. The Montagnards were led by men such as the priggish, self-righteous Maximilien de Robespierre, who sided with the *sansculottes* and in June had many of the Girondins arrested.

At first, several provincial cities rebelled against the Convention's rule and the instability of the government in Paris. By the fall, the government's forces had put down the rebellion, and nearly 14,000 people were sentenced to be executed in the aftermath. The new instrument used to carry out this grisly task was called the guillotine, a word that would come to represent the next phase of the revolution.

The Convention now saw the need for terror on a wider scale as the *sansculottes* continued their mass demonstrations. Hundreds of "suspects" were arrested, and in October the queen and many of the Girondins were sent to the guillotine. The church and Christianity also came under attack, regarded as the source of all the revolution's enemies. By spring 1794, almost every church in France was closed, and most priests were in hiding. A new "revolutionary calendar" was created to replace the Christian one.

The tactical purpose of terror did result in the end of any serious opposition to the Convention, whose power was now in the hands of Robespierre and the so-called Committee of Public Safety. Between April and July 1794, Robespierre and his supporters launched the "Great Terror" to purge the nation of all those not fully committed to preserving the principles established by the revolution. Some 2,000 people were executed in this brief period, many without evidence of any kind. On the 9th of Thermidor, in the revolutionary calendar (July 28, 1794), Robespierre himself was executed as members of the Convention realized that no one was safe any longer under his rule.

The so-called Thermidoreans in the Convention acted quickly to empty the prisons of suspects, took actions to halt the power of the Paris mobs, and to reopen churches to gain the support of disaffected Catholics. Throughout 1795, the Convention worked diligently to create yet another constitution. This one relied heavily on large property owners and called for annual elections and a rotating executive made up of five men, called the Directory. When it was made public that the two legislative councils would be made up mostly of members of the Third Estate, an outraged group of royalists launched a major protest in Paris. They were soon dispersed when an army unit fired on them, an order given by a young general named Napoleon Bonaparte.

Day 2: Napoleon Bonaparte: Emperor of Europe

Born on Corsica in 1869, Napoleon Bonaparte was sent as a boy to military schools in France. At the outbreak of the revolution he returned home, hoping to join in the movement for Corsican independence from France, but his family was considered pro-French, and he was rejected by the leaders of the movement. He returned to France in 1791 and allied himself with the more radical groups in the government. In 1793, his military prowess brought him fame for the first time when, at age 24, he defeated Anglo-Spanish forces at Toulon and was immediately promoted to brigadier general. But when Robespierre and the leaders of the Terror fell from power the following year, Napoleon was imprisoned briefly, and lost his command.

At this juncture the new government of the Directory was looking to subdue the continuous unrest in Paris, and Napoleon was called back to service. His swift, unflinching attack on the royalists rioting in the streets instantly made him a hero in the eyes of the people. Napoleon himself dismissed his action as "a whiff of grapeshot," but in fact it launched his meteoric rise to absolute power in France in only five years, and to conqueror of much of Europe over the next decade.

In 1796, Napoleon was given command of the army in Italy, and within two months he won a series of victories against several city-states that were then placed under French rule. In 1798, he invaded Egypt with the intention of striking at England's possessions in India, a source of great wealth to the island nation. Although he won several quick victories on land, the English navy, led by Admiral Horatio Nelson, demolished the French fleet at the Battle of the Nile and Napoleon's plans to invade India along with it.

In 1799, Napoleon returned to France to help shore up the Directory, which had become increasingly unpopular. In November, he joined with several others to overthrow the Directory in the coup of 18 Brumaire, which established a consulate, with Napoleon as first consul. A new constitution was drawn up and approved by plebiscite, giving him extraordinary powers, which he did not hesitate to use. Almost every aspect of the government was centralized, including the collection of taxes and the financing of business through the new Bank of France, which helped to control the nation's debt and raise money for Napoleon's armies. The education system was restructured, in ways still in place today, including the *lycees*, schools for students 10 to 16. At the age of 12, male students were put on career paths, either for civil or military service. Schools for girls were also established, albeit to teach them domestic skills.

Between 1801 and 1810, Napoleon oversaw the complete revamping of the French legal system. In 1804, the famous *Code Napoléon* was established, giving France its first unified set of laws concerning the rights of citizens, including some elements from the revolution, such as equality before the law and freedom to choose one's own religion. Divorce was permitted, although the husband had the upper hand. In subsequent years, a Commercial Code, Codex of Civil Procedure, and the Code of Criminal Instruction, were all put in place, giving France the most advanced set of laws in Europe, laws that would become models for other nations throughout the 19th century.

♦**The Emperor**   Although Napoleon's domestic achievements cannot be slighted, his drive for absolute power led him to establish a secret police force that stifled dissent and increased censorship. But his popularity in France never wavered in these years, due mainly to his continued military success. In 1800, after defeating Austrian forces in Italy, at Marengo, and then in Germany, Austria was forced to sign the Treaty of Lunéville in February 1801, asserting France's rights to the Rhine, the Alps, and the Pyrenees. All of France's enemies, even England, now asked for peace.

Over the next few years, Napoleon consolidated his power and, in 1804, without any serious opposition, declared himself emperor and created a hereditary monarchy. In December 1804, Pope Pius VII officiated at a lavish ceremony in Paris at the Cathedral of Notre Dame (although it was reported that Napoleon crowned himself).

In 1804, Napoleon had himself proclaimed king of Italy and amassed a large amount of territory, thereby forcing England, Austria, Prussia, and Russia to again take up arms against him. In a series of battles over the course of a year or so, Napoleon defeated them all decisively; the Austrians at Ulm, the Russians and Austrians at Austerlitz, the Prussians at Jena, and the Russians at Friedland.

Napoleon was now the undisputed ruler of Europe as all the other powers agreed to whatever peace terms he sought. Only England remained in opposition as Napoleon's plan for an invasion collapsed in October 1805, when Admiral Nelson again destroyed the French fleet, this time at Trafalgar, off the coast of Spain. Otherwise nothing stood in Napoleon's way, so he began to install his relatives as the rulers in Spain and Italy. If he couldn't invade England, he would close off her economy by insisting the other major powers stop trading with her. This so-called Continental System helped to stir up even more resistance against France and would lead to Russian resistance.

At home, Napoleon worried that he would not have an heir to continue his dynasty, since his wife of many years, Josephine, was unable to conceive. So just as many kings had done before, Napoleon divorced her and in 1810 married Marie-Louise, daughter of the Austrian emperor, Francis I. The court was now filled with nobility mostly created by Napoleon, and whatever limitations the revolution had put on the king were not continued during Napoleon's reign.

◆**The Invasion of Russia** The first sign that French military invincibility might be ending came in Spain during the long, hard-fought Peninsula War (1808–14), which began in Portugal, a nation that had resisted the Continental System. Napoleon's attempt to install his brother as king of Spain led to a bloody, but unsuccessful, uprising. Spanish rebels were joined by the British army, who dragged the French into a protracted guerrilla war that seriously diminished French resources.

Nevertheless, when Napoleon decided to invade Russia in June 1812, he was able to raise an army of 500,000 men, the *Grande Armeé*, many from regions the French had conquered. The Russians were greatly outnumbered and so refused to engage Napoleon, but they burned crops and killed livestock until they had to fight in early September at the Battle of Borodino, which ended in a draw. On September 14, Napoleon took the city of Moscow and offered peace terms to the czar, but much of the city had been put to the torch by the Russians, which, with the impending onset of winter, meant the army could not use the city for winter quarters. As food supplies dwindled, Napoleon began his withdrawal. But it was too late. Not only did winter come early, but a retreating army of such enormous size moved very slowly, and quickly became the object of numerous cavalry attacks. Most estimates say that only 6,000 French soldiers returned home, as tens of thousands died of frostbite and disease. The drama of this campaign was vividly brought to life in Leo Tolstoy's classic, *War and Peace*, written 50 years later.

Napoleon abandoned his troops to rush back to Paris to quell any dissent. Other rulers, however, seized the moment to declare war and to form a powerful alliance against the emperor. In October 1813, Napoleon's army was crushed at Leipzig in the "Battle of Nations," but he struggled on, attempting to negotiate a favorable settlement. When the allies marched into Paris in March 1814, Napoleon abdicated and was exiled to the island of Elba, between Corsica and Italy, where he was able to live a comfortable life.

At the Congress of Vienna, allied leaders immediately restored the heir to the French throne, Louis XVIII, a serious mistake since the idea of monarchy remained very unpopular in France. Napoleon seized the moment and in March 1815, escaped from Elba, landed at Cannes, in the south of France, marched triumphantly to Paris, and immediately began to raise a large army. On June 16, his forces defeated the Prussian army at Ligny, in Belgium. Two days later, however, the allied armies under the command of Arthur Wellesley, duke of Wellington, destroyed Napoleon's army at the famous battle of Waterloo.

This time the allies exiled Napoleon to St. Helena, a remote island in the Atlantic where he spent six years essentially in solitude before he died of cancer in 1821, not yet 52 years old. Years later, in 1840, his remains were brought back to Paris and entombed in glory in the Invalides. His coffin remains on display today, where Parisians and tourists alike pay homage to the man, who for a single decade, restored France to power and glory through his genius as a military strategist, without peer in the modern world.

The Bourbon dynasty was restored once more by the Congress of Vienna, but the memory, and soon the mythology of Napoleon's glorious rule, could not be eradicated. In 1852, his nephew, Louis Napoleon, launched the Second Empire with himself as Napoleon III. His life, too, ended in ignominious defeat in 1870 when Prussia routed the French, humiliated them at the peace table, and sowed the seeds for the Great War of 1914.

Weekend 27: Energy

Day 1: Oil

When the steam engine was invented at the beginning of the 18th century, most sources of fuel worldwide were the same as they had been for centuries: wood for cooking, oil for lighting, coal for heating and industry. The advent of commercially successful steam power in 1712 allowed for machinery and engines that were larger and more capable than any machines had ever been, catalyzing the dramatic changes of the Industrial Revolution. During the 19th century, continuous improvements to steam engine design transformed factories and built railroads across Europe and the Americas. Both inventors and engineers knew, however, that steam power had significant limitations. Steam must be generated by burning fuel, usually coal, and steam engines were large and bulky to allow for a furnace. The first steam-powered locomotive, invented in 1804 by the English engineer Richard Trevethick, was so heavy it broke the rails it rode on. From the earliest days of the Industrial Revolution, engineers looked for alternatives to steam that would allow for lighter, more powerful engines.

Internal combustion provided one such alternative. For centuries, inventors had imagined and tinkered with internal combustion engines; the medieval Arab scholar Al-Jazari described twin-cylinder reciprocating pistons in 1206, and Leonardo da Vinci sketched compressionless engines in 1509. The modern combustion engine was the British inventor Robert Street's 1794 model, which used exploding gas to drive the pistons.

Finding reliable fuel in the 18th and 19th centuries was a problem. Inventors experimented with a variety of fuels including kerosene, wood, coal, natural gas, and crude petroleum. Petroleum-powered engines have since become the worldwide norm. Literally meaning "rock oil," petroleum seeps out of porous rock. Until 1857, when the first commercial oil well was drilled in Ploiesti, Romania, nearly all petroleum came from oil-saturated sand deposits called oil sands or from surface-level oil seeps. Petroleum had been known to ancient people in Asia and the Middle East, though its use as an effective engine fuel awaited

19th-century advances in chemistry. Crude petroleum burns, but not very efficiently; it must be refined and distilled to become one of several usable fuel grades, e.g. kerosene, diesel, gasoline, or jet fuel.

The birth of internal combustion engines did not mean the immediate death of coal or steam power. During this period, coal remained cheap and plentiful and continued to be used to drive large steam engines. Factories and large industrial machinery continued to use coal as the main source of fuel, and coal remains the world's most-used fuel today.

◆**Standard Oil** The first oil well in the United States was drilled in 1859 in Titusville, Pennsylvania. Early oil production focused on the distillation of kerosene, with gasoline as a discarded by-product. In 1870, the Standard Oil Company of Ohio was formed by John D. Rockefeller to refine and distribute kerosene throughout the Midwest. The company quickly grew to dominate oil production and transport throughout the country, often through aggressive competition with local companies and collusion with railroad barons who controlled distribution. In 1891, antitrust litigation forced Standard Oil out of Ohio, and Rockefeller moved the company to New Jersey, where local laws permitted companies to hold stock in other companies. This allowed Standard Oil's power and profits to spiral upward even as U.S. antitrust lawyers took aim. By 1904, Standard Oil exerted complete dominance over U.S. oil, controlling over 90 percent of oil production (at that time oil was still drilled primarily for making kerosene), but was forced by the Supreme Court to dissolve in 1911 under the Sherman Antitrust Act. The breakup resulted in 35 regional "Standards," including Standard Oil of California (which would later become Chevron), Standard Oil of New Jersey (later Exxon) and Standard Oil of New York (later Mobil).

◆**The Middle East** By the beginning of World War I, all the industrialized nations of Europe and the Americas had thriving oil markets, though the spurt of wartime industrial production caused a temporary oil shortage during 1916–17. Intense international interest in Middle East oil fields discovered in 1908 focused military and diplomatic efforts on disrupting Turkish–Ottoman control of the region and opening it to European trade and political influence. Beginning with the Sykes-Picot Agreement of 1916, several European and League of Nations actions defined French and British spheres of influence in the area and caused tensions that have carried over to today.

In the opening stages of World War I, the ruling Ottoman Turks maintained close ties with Germany while managing to suppress growing Arab unrest in the Middle East. Encouraged by British support, Arab independence movements capitalized on Ottoman entanglements to overthrow the empire during the war, but by the time the war ended, plans were already in motion to divide the area under British and French control. The Sykes-Picot Agreement of 1916 established English and French protectorates, assigning parts of modern Iraq to Britain and parts of Iran and Syria to France, arranging for access to pipelines and railways in the region. Provisions for the creation of Palestine as an area under international control, an arrangement that would prove increasingly tumultuous over time, were part of this deal.

In the wake of the war, world leaders met to decide the fate of the fallen Ottoman Empire. Prime ministers from France, Italy, Japan, and England met at San Remo, Italy, and solidified the provisions of the Sykes-Picot Agreement. Control of the Middle East and its oil were solidly in English and French hands.

◆**Saudi Arabia**   Until 1950, the United States was thought to have the largest oil reserves of any oil-producing nation. The U.S. supplied 85 percent of Allied oil during World War II, so much in fact that the U.S. became intensely concerned that the country was depleting its oil fields too quickly, and began looking for large sources of foreign oil to import.

As France and England exerted tight control over Syria, Iran, and Iraq, American speculators looked to the unproven reserves of Saudi Arabian oil fields. Geologists were increasingly convinced that Saudi Arabia sat atop an enormous supply of oil. Today, Saudi Arabian oil fields contain an estimated 25 percent of the global oil supply. So great was the U.S. government's concern over its own diminishing oil supply and its interest in Saudi oil that in 1943 President Franklin D. Roosevelt extended wartime Lend-Lease aid to the protection and upkeep of the Saudi kingdom, stating "the defense of Saudi Arabia is vital to the defense of the United States."

By the close of the Second World War, U.S. domestic consumption had nearly caught up to production. In 1945, President Roosevelt traveled to Saudi Arabia for a historic meeting with King Ibn Saud. The two met in private and no official record was kept of the conversation, though most experts agree that the meeting solidified an agreement between the United States and Saudi Arabia to trade access to Saudi oil fields for military and economic assistance. This agreement continues to affect U.S.-Saudi diplomatic and military relations today.

◆**Oil and the Cold War** The first sizable import of oil to the United States occurred in 1950, initially to supplement domestic production, though by 1958 the U.S. was consuming more energy than it produced, a development fueled by postwar prosperity and the love of automobiles. Imports made up 10 percent of U.S. oil consumption during the 1950s; a decade later it was 18 percent; in the 1970s, 35 percent. The U.S.–Saudi relationship resulted in affordable oil prices even as consumption mushroomed.

During this period, the three largest Standards (California, New York, and New Jersey), along with British-Dutch owned Royal Dutch Shell, the British-owned Anglo-Persian Oil Company (later BP), Gulf Oil, and Texaco, operated as a cartel and collectively dominated worldwide oil production and distribution, and were known as the "Seven Sisters." The initial development of the Saudi oil fields was undertaken by the Californian-Arabian Standard Oil Company (CASOC), of which Texaco was part owner. In the late 1940s, CASOC was renamed the Arabian-American Oil Company (Aramco), and gained as part owners Standard Oil Company of New Jersey and Standard Oil Company of New York. Under the wing of the Seven Sisters, Saudi Arabian oil fields increased production from 60 million barrels in 1946 to 3.1 billion barrels in 1976.

The lines connecting political, economic, and military spheres in regard to Middle Eastern oil became increasingly tangled during the Cold War. In 1960, a cartel of oil-producing nations was formed under the name OPEC (Organization of the Petroleum Exporting Countries) and originally included Iran, Iraq, Kuwait, Saudi Arabia, and Venezuela. OPEC's aim was to collectively regulate export prices and production quotas and to exert leverage against European and American pressures. By the mid-1970s, Qatar, Indonesia, Libya, the United Arab Emirates, Algeria, and Nigeria had also joined.

Meanwhile, as access to the world's largest oil supply became a strategic necessity for both the U.S. and Soviet Union, local political upheavals in the Middle East took on global ramifications. During the 1950s and 1960s, the U.S. sent a steady stream of weapons and advisers to Saudi Arabia to thwart Soviet influence in the area and ensure long-term American access to Saudi oil. When the United States sided with Israel in the 1973 Arab–Israeli War, Arab nations, including Saudi Arabia, responded with the oil embargo of 1973–74, which sent United States prices skyward and caused shortages at pumps. Furthermore, the Saudi royals nationalized Aramco assets, ending American dominance over oil fields there.

In response, the United States in 1977 created the Strategic Petroleum Reserve, which permitted the storage of 580 million barrels of oil. By 1985, the reserve held enough oil to provide a normal level of petroleum for 115 days in the absence of any other petroleum imports. The reserve proved useful in preventing additional oil price hikes during the Iraqi invasion of Kuwait in 1990. The reserve can also be used as an emergency supply of oil in case of a disaster such as Hurricane Katrina (2005), which shut down production and refining in the Gulf of Mexico for weeks. By 2010, however, the reserve had dwindled to 75 days of oil.

◆**The current picture** Domestic oil production in the United States peaked in 1972; since then, production has fallen and leveled off, though demand has continued to grow steadily. According to the Department of Energy, in 1970 the U.S. produced 9.6 million barrels of oil per day; in 2008, 5.0 million barrels a day. In terms of consumption, in 1970 the U.S. consumed 14.7 million barrels a day; 2008, 19.5 million barrels a day. As a result, reliance on foreign oil will only grow larger over time. Imports made up 55.0 percent of oil consumption in 2001; by 2010 that number reached 58.1 percent; by 2020, it will reach 66.3 percent; by 2030, 69.6 percent. In 2010, top suppliers of exports to the U.S. were Canada (2.5 million barrels a day), Mexico (1.2 million barrels a day), Saudi Arabia (1.1 million barrels a day), Nigeria (1.0 million barrels a day), and Venezuela (1.0 million barrels a day).

With the growing reliance on foreign oil comes the increasing dependence on vicissitudes of the foreign oil market. Oil prices spiked to $28.26 per barrel in 2000, retreated to $22.95 in 2001, and rebounded to $28.50 in 2003, all dramatic swings that seemed extreme at the time. On August 30, 2005, after Hurricane Katrina hit the Gulf coast, the price of oil skyrocketed to an all-time high of $70.85 a barrel, and continued to rise thereafter, crossing the $100.00 mark in January 2008 and holding near $134.00 a barrel through summer before falling sharply in the global financial upheaval late that year.

On April 20, 2010, the explosion of a BP rig in the Gulf of Mexico caused the worst oil-related environmental disaster in history. After three months, the oil well more than one mile below the surface was still spewing 60,000 gallons of oil into the Gulf each day. The financial and ecological damage will be incalculable.

Despite decades of resistance, the American people are gradually embracing the idea of widespread alternatives to petroleum power, including nuclear power—at one time thought to be the best possible source of clean, abundant, cheap energy.

Day 2: Nuclear Power

In 1938, the Italian physicist Enrico Fermi, having just been awarded the Nobel Prize, presented a paper on his work titled "Artificial radioactivity produced by neutron bombardment." In it, he described the process of slowing down neutrons and firing them at the atomic nuclei of various elements to produce radioactive isotopes. Fermi's neutrons, because they had no electric charge and since they had been slowed down, were able to penetrate the center of other atoms and change the mix of particles that made up the nucleus. The best elements to use for this experiment were the ones with relatively unstable nuclei and are found at the far end of the periodic table. The very best one was the heaviest and most unstable element found in nature, uranium.

The work was groundbreaking for atomic physicists, but unknown to most of the scientific community Fermi had actually split some of the uranium atoms and formed atoms of other, lighter elements entirely, producing nuclear *fission*, the process of forcing apart an atomic nucleus. The German scientists Otto Hahn and Fritz Strassmann built on Fermi's research and published their findings on nuclear fission in 1939.

The political implications were ominous: at the end of the 1930s, the most advanced work in nuclear physics was taking place in fascist Italy and Nazi Germany. Upon receiving his Nobel Prize, Fermi left Italy and moved to New York City to teach at Columbia University, perhaps propelled by new Italian laws discriminating against Jews, including Fermi's wife, Laura. In 1939, Germany halted all uranium exports, and it became clear to many physicists that the Nazis had begun a large-scale effort to understand nuclear fission. Also in 1939, a now-famous letter written by Albert Einstein prompted President Franklin D. Roosevelt to establish the Uranium Commission and eventually the top-secret Manhattan Project, in which Fermi would play a crucial role.

◆**The Manhattan Project** Between 1939 and 1945, the United States emerged as the leading nuclear power, as demonstrated with terrible force in the bombings of Hiroshima and Nagasaki in 1945. Manhattan Project scientists devised the most powerful weapons ever conceived and permanently changed global politics. Their research also led to the creation of the modern nuclear power industry, which today provides 2 percent of the world's power and 15 percent of the world's electricity.

The principal stages in the creation of both nuclear power and nuclear weapons are very similar. Both rely on chain reactions that occur when unstable atoms are bombarded with neutrons. These neutrons penetrate nearby nuclei and cause them to split, which—along with creating lighter elements—releases gamma radiation and frees more neutrons that in turn impact the nucleus of another atom, and so on. In very dense elements like uranium, the cumulative effect generates an incredible amount of heat and power. The main difference between the chain reactions in nuclear energy and weapons is that in nuclear power generation, the goal is the tightly controlled creation of intense heat to make steam, whereas in weapons the goal is a maximum explosive force. Both applications for nuclear fission rely on particularly unstable variants, or *allotropes*, of either uranium or plutonium. Uranium is a fairly common element (it is found in soil as often as tin), but the right allotrope of uranium needed for nuclear applications is rare in nature. Plutonium is completely synthetic and must be created from uranium. The right allotropes of both elements can be created as the by-products of the activity in nuclear reactors.

The process of using neutron bombardment to create these viable sources of either uranium or plutonium for fission use is called *enrichment*; most early reactors were designed expressly for this purpose. Fermi built the first nuclear reactor, named Chicago Pile-1, on a squash court underneath the football field at the University of Chicago in 1942. It was a mass of stacked graphite bricks that had been impregnated with uranium, and was built in a roughly spherical shape. Pile-1 served as the first draft of the X-10 Graphite Reactor built at the secret Manhattan

Project laboratory in Oak Ridge, Tennessee, the following year. The Oak Ridge reactor enriched the fuel for the bombs dropped on Hiroshima and Nagasaki.

◆After World War II The Atomic Energy Act of 1946 established the Atomic Energy Commission, a civilian-run organization that would oversee nuclear reactors and programs in the United States. Under the act, all nuclear reactors were government-owned and nuclear technology was a closely guarded state secret. In the decade following World War II, many of the resources in the nuclear community were devoted to the H-bomb race with the Soviet Union, and the attention of military strategists was already turning to unrest in South Korea. During this period, the commission oversaw production of experimental reactor prototypes for converting nuclear fission into electricity. However, most of the uranium being enriched was earmarked for weapons testing, and it was not until 1951 that experiments using nuclear reactions to generate electric power (at reactor EBR-1 in Arco, Idaho) would prove fruitful, though the electrical output was minimal.

◆Atoms for Peace In 1953, a year after the first successful hydrogen bomb test, President Dwight D. Eisenhower delivered an address before the United Nations titled "Atoms for Peace" in which he stated, "Peaceful power from atomic energy is no dream of the future. That capability, already proved, is here today." Part of Eisenhower's Atoms For Peace plan was to encourage private development of peaceful nuclear applications and to allow sharing of technical information with private companies and foreign governments. The Atomic Energy Act of 1954 widened access to previously secret data and began a period of rapid expansion of the nuclear power industry, which now had access to government reactor designs, prototypes, and technical information. The Atoms For Peace plan also called for uranium stockpiles to be monitored by an international body, eventually organized in 1957 as the International Atomic Energy Agency (IAEA). In 1956, the first commercial electricity-generating nuclear plant went online in Calder Hall, England. The first operational U.S. commercial nuclear power plant was opened in 1957 in Shippingport, Pennsylvania.

By the 1970s, several factors led to the declining growth of the nuclear power industry. First, the price of competitive fuels such as oil and coal declined as U.S. imports and production grew. Second, and more important, was the growing perception that nuclear power plants were ecologically unsafe and potentially disastrous. The nuclear accident at the Three Mile Island plant in 1979 had dramatic ramifications for the industry.

◆**Nuclear Disasters**   There have been three major nuclear disasters at commercial power plants: the 1957 Windscale fire, the 1979 Three Mile Island meltdown, and the 1986 Chernobyl explosion.

Windscale fire   The Windscale reactors near Cumbria, England, were early enrichment reactors, designed for producing allotropes of plutonium and uranium, relying on graphite core rods that had to be annealed (heated slightly and cooled) periodically. On October 10, 1957, the reactor's cooling process failed, and the rods began to superheat, fueled by the intense heat given off by the radioactive reactions. The graphite core caught fire, and in the course of battling the blaze, 20,000 curies of radioactivity were released into the atmosphere in a cloud of steam and smoke. It is estimated that radioactive iodine released into the surrounding area caused 240 cases of thyroid cancer.

Three Mile Island   While the Windscale fire originated inside the nuclear core, in the Three Mile Island, Pennsylvania, meltdown, the problem began in an auxiliary system. On March 28, 1979, feed water pumps in secondary sections of the plant failed, which affected the plant's ability to cool itself. As a standard safety measure, the turbine and reactor automatically shut down. However, during the shutdown process, a valve for coolant failed and drained the nuclear core, which began to overheat. Alarms alerted technicians to the secondary systems failures, but not to the problems in the core until it was too late. Nearly half the core melted, but fortunately the radioactive material was contained within the building. Government officials have repeatedly asserted that negligible amounts of radiation escaped the site, and that no harmful effects have been detected in people as a result.

Regardless, the Three Mile Island incident brought the U.S. nuclear power industry to a standstill. The widespread opinion that a nuclear catastrophe had only narrowly been averted fueled efforts to cast the nuclear power industry as unsafe. In addition, the falling production costs for coal and petroleum made nuclear power seem both risky and expensive. As a result, construction on nuclear power plants effectively halted, and several states enacted moratoriums on any new construction.

Chernobyl   The most famous nuclear disaster took place on April

26, 1986, at the Chernobyl Nuclear Power Plant in Pripyat, Ukraine. A power surge inside the reactor core caused it to overheat, which set off a cascade of systems failures. The superheated core caused a steam explosion that released large amounts of volatile hydrogen gas, which in turn also exploded, destroying part of the building and exposing the reactor to the outside. Once fresh air contacted the reactor core, the superheated graphite in the reactor caught fire and began to melt. The explosion and fire generated a massive cloud of radioactive smoke and steam that spread over a very wide area, including parts of nearby Belarus and Russia, and contaminated the adjacent Pripyat River, which flows toward the Ukrainian capital of Kiev.

The disastrous effects of the reactor explosion were worsened by the way the Soviet government handled the crisis. Firefighters called to battle the reactor fire were not told the smoke was radioactive, and the nearby town of Pripyat was not evacuated until the following day. The U.S. Nuclear Regulatory Commission (N.R.C.) estimates that 4,000 radiation cancer-related deaths may be traced to the Chernobyl disaster.

◆**Disposal**   Aside from safety issues, the main argument used by antinuclear activists is the issue of disposal. Nuclear reactors generate two kinds of radioactive materials: first, anything used by reactor personnel to handle, transport, or cool reactor fuel, including clothing and tools; and second, the spent fuel itself. Compared with the spent reactor fuel, the items in the first group emit very little radioactivity, and the isotopes they contain have a relatively short half-life. For spent fuel, however, disposal requires elaborate steps. The radioactive half-life of spent uranium is more than 100,000 years; there is nowhere on the surface of the planet to store it where it will become safe. To date, the United States has no permanent repository for spent nuclear fuel, and used cores are held in various temporary locations, usually onsite at nuclear plants when possible. In the 1980s, plans began for the construction of a permanent underground disposal facility at Yucca Mountain, Nevada, though the plan has met vociferous opposition and the facility has yet to be built.

Weekend 28: The Art Instinct

Day 1: Prehistoric and Ancient Art

Making art has always been an important part of human society, and the process is older, in fact, than writing or agriculture. The drive to represent the world through pictures may be innate, since wherever traces of early human settlements have been found, the sites nearly always contain works of art. In the past century, several sites were discovered in Europe—especially in France and Spain—that show a variety of prehistoric artwork. Of these, the best known are the extraordinary scenes painted around 15,000 B.C. on the walls of a series of caves at Lascaux in southwest France. The caves feature elegant multicolored murals—some over 20 yards long—of stylized but recognizable animal shapes in active poses and complex groupings. Many of the figures are outlined with black charcoal that was probably applied with moss or hair, and they are colored with mineral pigments such as ochre and iron oxide.

The Lascaux caves contain 600 individual animal figures, including horses, bulls, and stags, as well as a single human figure. Many of the Lascaux animals are drawn along the curves of the rock to suggest three dimensions, but the artists also used such sophisticated effects as layering, perspective, and a combination of frontal and profile poses.

Other important collections of prehistoric painting have been found in the Chauvet cave in France, the Altamira cave in Spain; and the Apollo 11 caves in Namibia. Many appear to have sacred or ceremonial significance and may have been drawn by group leaders to increase success on the hunting grounds, or by shamans attempting to absorb mystical powers.

♦**Egypt (2650 B.C.–331 B.C.)** Because Egyptian society was highly stratified, it produced a skilled class of artisans who created and passed down an increasingly refined style of artwork that lasted for more than 2,000 years. Artisan painters were rigorously trained to maintain consistent motifs and techniques for particular applications. Some painters worked solely to color sculptures and relief carvings, while others specialized in murals, and manuscript painters created small-scale works on papyrus. These artisans developed and mastered a variety of materials, including *distemper paint* (a combination of powdered lime and a gluelike binder) and *encaustic* (tinted wax paint colored with mineral pigments), and created very stylized and highly symbolic imagery that changed little over the years, but still allowed for individual variation.

The paintings of ancient Egypt are rarely exclusively decorative; most surviving Egyptian paintings use very formal compositions to tell narrative stories. They are symmetrical, often framed by ornate borders, and feature strong outlines filled with flat areas of bold color—especially white, black, brown, red, and blue. A distinctive innovation of Egyptian artists is the twisted perspective of human figures that places the head in profile, the torso full forward, and the legs in profile with the left foot forward. Additionally, Egyptian artists combined representational imagery with symbolic pictographs known as hieroglyphics that together related complex narratives and eventually became the basis for written language in the Western world.

After Alexander the Great invaded Egypt in 331 B.C., much of Egyptian art was overwhelmed by Hellenistic styles, although local features endured. Hundreds of small portrait paintings on wood, created in the ancient Egyptian style, have been found in the tombs of wealthy citizens of Egypt from the third century A.D.

♦Mesopotamia (4000 B.C.–331 B.C.)   In what is commonly considered the cradle of Western civilization, the land surrounding the Tigris and Euphrates Rivers hosted a succession of ancient civilizations—including the Sumerians, the Akkadians, the Hittites, the Babylonians, the Assyrians, the second Babylonian empire, and the Persian Empire. They shared a generally similar artistic style that showed a strong interest in the relationship between the natural and divine worlds. Distinctive elements include a loose compositional style and increasingly fantastical combinations of animals and humans to create winged bulls, griffins, and magnificently bearded warrior-kings. While the majority of artworks that have survived from these Mesopotamian civilizations are stone relief sculptures from palaces and small carved cylinder seals, some vases and mural fragments show refined painting techniques that emphasize stylized depictions of plants and animals as well as exaggerated renderings of human musculature and hair. As the military and trading power of the Greek city-states grew, Mesopotamian artwork began to adopt Hellenistic influences even as Greek artists borrowed themes and styles from the east.

◆**Greek Art (ca. 700 B.C.–A.D. 31)**   The art of the ancient Greeks is generally regarded as the foundation of subsequent European art, but Greek art itself was derived from that of the earlier Minoan civilization of Crete, and it was also influenced by nearby Egyptian and Mesopotamian cultures. But by the seventh century B.C., Greek artists working in vase painting, wall painting, and sculpture had developed these influences into a fully Greek style.

While artisans had painted simple geometric and symbolic motifs on pottery for thousands of years, by about 700 B.C. Greek painters created a highly workable black glaze that allowed them to decorate vases with detailed narrative scenes. These paintings were rendered as drawings and then filled in with solid color—the earliest examples are painted with the main figures silhouetted in black against the red clay, but later works (ca. 530 B.C.) were painted black with the figures left in the red color of clay. Many of the first Greek vase painters preferred to illustrate battle scenes and mythological characters like Athena, but later artists also painted commemorations of real-life events like athletic competitions and weddings and even bawdy revelries or comic scenes. The paintings feature some stylized conventions to show details such as musculature, fabric folds, and hairstyles, but also demonstrate a more naturalistic approach to composition than was used in Egypt or Mesopotamia. Greek vase painters, most of whom worked in Athens, became well known as individuals, and many different workshop traditions began to emerge, creating the beginning of the idea of the independent artistic style.

By the end of the fifth century B.C., many Greek artists had turned to wall painting with tempera and were executing complex murals, smaller works on wood panels, and even paintings on parchment, all of which allowed for greater variety of expression and a wider palette of colors than did pottery. Painters used human models to help them create more naturalistic scenes and, although none of the ancient murals survive, the names of several artists and their work are known from historical documents. Apelles was renowned for his skill in drawing and for modeling techniques that gave realistic shape to his figures; Parrhasius used spatial perspective to give the illusion of depth, making his figures stand out from their backgrounds; and Zeuxis is credited with developing the shading technique known as *sfumato*. It was said that he painted such realistic grapes that birds tried to eat them.

As Greek culture moved into the Classical (480–323 B.C.) and then Hellenistic eras (323 B.C.–A.D. 31), paintings became even less formal and more naturalistic, with dynamic poses, action-filled scenes, and more effort to accurately represent the three-dimensional world with special effects, including *chiaroscuro*—the use of contrasting light and shadow to create an illusion of depth. In Italy, however, the Etruscans (early eighth century B.C. to 510 B.C.) shunned these innovations and instead adopted the more conservative and static features shown in the Archaic Greek vases they collected. Etruscan artists adapted many of the older Greek stylistic conventions in their own pottery and tomb paintings.

✦**Roman Murals (ca. 509 B.C.–ca. A.D. 410)** As Roman power spread across the Mediterranean region, Romans readily absorbed the traditions of the Greek, Egyptian, and Etruscan cultures they had conquered. Roman leaders supported an array of civic construction projects and saw the value of including great artworks in these new buildings to promote the values and official gods of the republic. They commissioned Greek and native artists to decorate vast numbers of public buildings and private homes with sculptures, mosaic floors, and colorful murals that covered walls, ceilings, or even whole rooms. Murals were executed using both the *secco* ("dry") method of painting with watercolors on dry plaster, and the more challenging and durable *fresco* ("wet") method of applying pigment directly to wet plaster before it dries. Many fine examples of these murals remain—including some preserved in the ashes of Pompeii and Herculaneum after Mt. Vesuvius erupted in A.D. 79. They show four distinct styles of Roman wall painting. In the first, artists applied simple "faux" finishes to create flat blocks of color or to imitate the look of wood or stone; in the second, artists wrapped large murals around entire rooms and tried to extend the visual space beyond the limits of the walls with techniques that nearly achieved true linear perspective; in the third, this illusion of space was traded for flatter images confined to smaller areas and bounded by painted borders; in the fourth, these smaller images were grouped like individual paintings on a wall and executed with illusionistic painting techniques, including false frames.

Following the preferences of their Hellenistic teachers, Roman artists strove toward technical mastery in their desire to create highly naturalistic works. Even small paintings and portraits—usually made on wood using tempera and encaustic—show a nuanced approach to portraying figures in a lifelike and realistic manner. The subject matter of these paintings ranged from scenes honoring the civic gods to expansive landscapes, and from architectural scenes to elaborate interiors and still-life paintings. While some critics maintain that the Roman artists were mere imitators of the Greeks—and they did, indeed, copy many Greek works and use them as study aids—Roman painters also made several innovations, such as the development of the landscape as a painting genre and the promotion of *trompe l'oeil* paintings, which render ordinary objects as accurately as possible in order to create an illusion of three dimensions for the viewer. Unlike the celebrated Greek artists, however, most Roman painters were viewed simply as near-anonymous craftsmen for hire.

Day 2: Art in the Middle Ages and Early Renaissance

The Roman Empire was already in decline when it became a Christian empire under Constantine (ca. 274–337), who founded his capital, Constantinople, on the remnants of the ancient city of Byzantium. The geographic shift of the capital from Rome to Constantinople, and the religious shift from paganism to Christianity, provoked a massive cultural change as Christians were freed from the brutal suppression that had inhibited the early church. Constantine and his wealthy followers funded church building and missionary work throughout the region that, in turn, demanded a new style of art. The earliest Christian paintings, such as the murals in fourth- and fifth-century churches, have mostly been lost, but surviving fragments, sculptures, and mosaics from the same era suggest that they generally followed classical Hellenistic and Roman visual conventions and simply substituted New Testament subject matter. However, this was not entirely satisfactory to church leaders, and artists struggled to develop an appropriately reverent style of ecclesiastical imagery that would both honor their faith and instruct new converts.

By the early fifth century, the bishop of Rome was recognized as the primate of the church, but the repeated sackings of Rome by successive waves of barbarians left Constantinople as the political, economic and, in many ways, the spiritual capital of the empire. Freed from Roman influence, the flourishing Byzantine artists were left alone to resolve the dilemmas about how to depict Christ and the saints. These artists rejected naturalism in favor of a more lavish and allegorical approach to painting, which used stylized images with frontal poses, elongated bodies, symbolic hand gestures, large eyes, and round glowing halos. Artists intentionally made their paintings look flat and two-dimensional to remind the viewer that the image was not a representation of an earthly experience but an entry into the spiritual dimension. They generally favored simple palettes of vivid colors, often on a gold background and with specific meaning attached to each color. Most works show a formal composition with an emphasis on symmetry and with figures sized hierarchically, in order of importance. Some small *encaustic* (wax paint) paintings as well as mosaics at St. Vitale in Ravenna (completed 547) and Hagia Sophia in Constantinople (completed 537), give clear evidence of this new style. After the final collapse of the Western Roman Empire in 476, Byzantine art reigned supreme in most of the Christian world, just as Eastern Orthodoxy gained primacy in Christian belief and practice.

Byzantine painters decorated churches, illustrated manuscripts, and created paintings for individual believers, but the most characteristic product of Byzantine and later Orthodox art is the icon—a small, portable image of Christ, the Virgin and Child, or one or more saints. Icons, whether painted on folding wooden panels or combined into large altar screens, were produced in increasing quantities for churches and private chapels beginning in the seventh century and often became objects of devotion in themselves. Icons preserved the distinctively lavish features of larger Byzantine paintings and were often further gilded, heavily framed, and even encrusted with jewels. The small scale of the works encouraged artists to imbue every detail with careful symbolism, lending a rich, dense feeling to even the simplest icon. While icon painting was essentially conservative in style, there was a slow change over the centuries, and later examples show the influence of Italian Renaissance ideas of modeling and perspective.

•Celtic Painting and Illuminated Manuscripts in the Middle Ages The Celtic peoples occupied much of central and western Europe in the early first millennium B.C., with populations extending through Central Asia as far as what is now western China. Early Celtic art of the Hallstatt and La Tène cultures (eighth–fifth centuries B.C.), has much in common with the art of the Germanic peoples of northern

Europe and the Scythians of the steppe lands of Asia. It is characterized by fantastic, intertwining animal and plant designs worked on weapons, jewelry, and various utilitarian and decorative objects made of bronze, iron, or gold. In later La Tène art, Greek influence is both pervasive and totally assimilated into the Celtic "animal style."

The Celtic peoples were absorbed or displaced by the expansion of the Roman Empire and the northern Germanic tribes, surviving as intact cultures only in isolated areas of eastern Europe, Anatolia, Iberia, and westernmost Europe, including Britain and Ireland. Celtic art, especially illustrated manuscripts, reemerged in importance with the Christian conversion of Britain and Ireland in the fifth century A.D.

Few of these illustrated manuscripts have survived. The most highly regarded is the *Book of Kells*, executed on the Scottish island of Iona and preserved in Ireland after the Viking destruction of Iona in 807. Later illustrated books, including the "books of hours" popular throughout Europe from the 13th through 16th centuries, preserved many features of the Celtic manuscripts, such as decorated page borders, embellished capital letters, bold outlines, primary colors, and detailed botanical flourishes.

♦Romanesque and Gothic Painting The crowning of Charlemagne as the Holy Roman Emperor in 800 renewed the vigor of the Roman Catholic Church and eventually that of Western Christian art. Even as the Roman Church broke from the dogma and practice of the Orthodox Church, the desire to spread the Gospel to an illiterate population led Western painters away from the formal and heavily symbolic Byzantine style. Both the art and theology of western Christianity began to emphasize the suffering, Crucifixion, and resurrection of Christ through more narrative artworks. By the 10th century, newly stable feudal monarchies in northern and western Europe were wealthy enough to begin building churches and large cathedrals in what became the Romanesque style, which offered vast wall space and curving vaulted ceilings for murals. Most of these works have been lost, but many of them included scenes from the Old and New Testaments placed on opposite walls, along with a painting of Christ as the focal point of the apse. Stylistically, these murals were similar to the illuminated manuscripts of the era, and there was little attempt at creating perspective. Rather, figures and objects were sized hierarchically and simply layered to suggest their relative distance from the viewer.

As the more intellectual Gothic era emerged in the mid-12th century, a newly rich bourgeoisie joined the nobility and the church as patrons of the arts, commissioning small artworks for their own homes and private chapels. Increased literacy expanded the demand for illustrated books, and the growth of scientific and secular literature encouraged the development of secular themes in art. Even religious works were more open in style and subject matter, with looser compositions and more animated poses. Many cities formed trade guilds for painters, preserving the identity of artists more reliably than ever before, and some artists began signing their works.

In Italy, Duccio di Buoninsegna (ca.1255–ca.1318) used pigment and egg tempera to create richly gilded religious paintings and altarpieces in the tradition of Byzantine icons, but he gave his figures recognizably human gestures and expressions. His pupil Simone Martini influenced many later painters with a soft, expressive style that traded the vivid Byzantine colors and static arrangements for muted tones, dynamically posed figures, and elegant compositions. Giotto di Bodone, a native of Florence, broke further from Byzantine tradition with his masterly church frescoes that placed naturalistically conceived New Testament figures in architectural or landscape settings. Regarded as the first artist in the Gothic tradition to depict nature in a convincingly realistic manner, Giotto's art represents a crucial turning point in the progression of Western art toward the illusionism of the Renaissance. He developed an algebraic method of calculating the appropriate relative sizes of objects in his paintings and also revived the tradition of drawing figures from life. He is best known for his frescoes in the Arena Chapel in Padua, which include *The Lamentation* (1305–06), as well as small panel paintings such as *Madonna* (ca. 1310).

The Sienese painter Ambrogio Lorenzetti went further still in breaking conventions and set biblical narrative scenes in realistic Tuscan landscapes. He is best known, however, for his secular fresco cycle *Allegory and Effects of Good and Bad Government* (ca.1338–1340).

While frescoes remained an important form of painting, wooden panel paintings were developed in Italy in the 13th century, and they became the dominant form throughout Europe by the 15th century. However, manuscript painting was also very common, and the epitome of the late Gothic style is the *Trés Riches Heures*, (ca. 1413–16) an illustrated devotional book created for the Duc de Berry by the Limbourg brothers, Flemish artists working in Burgundy who were famous for their gemlike miniature paintings of medieval life.

◆**Northern Europe** In northern Europe, several artists moved beyond the Italian Gothic painters' attempts at realism. In the Netherlands, a painter known as the Master of Flémalle (possibly Robert Campin, ca.1378–1444) developed a technique of creating perspective that made his figures appear to exist in the same world as the viewer. He paid an unprecedented level of attention to ordinary objects, and his *Merode Altarpiece* (ca.1425–30) was the first known artwork to place the Annunciation scene in a contemporary domestic interior. The Master of Flémalle was also the first major artist to employ oil paints, which offered brilliant colors and allowed him to recreate the nuanced effects of light on people and objects, far more effectively than with tempera.

The other great Flemish master of the time, Jan van Eyck (1395–1441), used oils to such great effect that he is often regarded as the "Father of Oil Painting." Van Eyck brought exacting attention to human figures and fabrics, which he rendered with rich shading, deep colors, and carefully observed details. He exploited such recent inventions as the glass mirror to help him paint realistic self-portraits and to refine his perspective. Van Eyck painted religious as well as secular works, and he is credited with developing the technique of atmospheric perspective— a gradual changing of tone used to represent objects farther away in the picture space.

◆**Early Renaissance (1400–1500)** The late Gothic shift toward a more realistic style of painting continued in the Renaissance, which focused more on the immediate and tangible human experience than on an idealized afterlife. The intellectual culture of the Renaissance (literally "rebirth") looked back past the Christian era to classical Greek ideals in literature, philosophy, science, and art, so that after hundreds of years of iconographic art, naturalism and realism were again in vogue.

The trend toward realism was facilitated when the Italian architect Filippo Brunelleschi developed the mathematical method of linear perspective in about 1415. This approach, which introduced the optical trick of parallel lines receding to a vanishing point, allowed artists and architects to faithfully represent the three-dimensional world, and Brunelleschi's method was quickly taken up by other painters. Combining Brunelleschi's linear perspective with painting techniques such as modeling, the Tuscan painter Masaccio (Tommaso Di Giovanni Di Simone Guidi), produced solid-looking figures that seemed to exist in real spaces. Masaccio's use of tempera meant that his color lacked the virtuosity of van Eyck and the Master of Flémalle, but several Venetian artists, led by Giovanni Bellini, soon adopted the oil paints and rich colors favored by the northern painters.

Technical advances merged with spiritual reverence in the work of Fra Angelico, a Dominican monk whose religious frescoes and panel paintings combine a serenity of mood with precisely modeled figures and clearly defined background elements. Fra Angelico was one of Florence's most sought-after artists of the early Renaissance. He is admired for strong three-dimensional spatial compositions and is best known for fresco cycles at the Vatican and St. Peter's Basilica in Rome, as well as his fresco of *The Annunciation* (1440–50) at the monastery of S. Marco in Florence. The Tuscan painter Piero della Francesca published three treatises on mathematics and geometry, and his artwork demonstrates his exacting attention to composition and perspective. Piero's masterwork, *The History of the True Cross* (ca. 1447–1460), also includes the first nocturnal scene in Western art.

Domenico Ghirlandaio placed historical and New Testament characters in settings that combine classical architecture with contemporary domestic detail, and his exquisitely delineated outlines and masterly use of perspective recall, and often surpass, Roman *trompe l'oeil* paintings, which first attempted to fool the eye with crafty renderings of real-world objects. Secular subjects and portraits became increasingly popular in the late 15th century. The revived interest in both classical realism and pre-Christian mythology inspired Sandro Botticelli to risk the ire of the Catholic Church and paint such pagan-influenced works as *The Birth of Venus* (ca. 1480), now one of the most famous artworks in the world, which depicts a nude Venus rising from the water on a seashell.

As wealth in Europe increased and artists rediscovered Roman innovations, the stage was set for the dramatic leaps forward in the arts and humanities that would be called the High Renaissance.

Weekend 29: The European Novel

While fiction has been a part of Western culture since the time of Homer and the ancient Greeks, the modern European novel did not emerge until the early 17th century. Derived from the Italian word *novella*, the term *novel* implied the newness of the form. In other European languages, the novel is known as a *roman*, which refers to the romances of the medieval period. At its most basic level, a novel is defined as an extended prose narrative. The modern elements of the novel include characterization, plot, and theme.

The novel first appeared in Spain in the form of Miguel de Cervantes's two-volume work, *Don Quixote de la Mancha* (1605–15). Written in the picaresque (from *picaro* or "rogue") style, it depicts in episodic form the adventures of a poor, roguish hero as he travels throughout Spain, surviving by his wits. About 50 years after appearing in Spain, the novel became popular in Germany, then France, England, and much later, Russia.

Day 1: The French, German, and Russian Novel

♦**The French Novel** The first French novel to make a significant impression was Madame LaFayette's *La Princesse de Clèves* (1678), one of the earliest European novels. Originally published anonymously, and very successful upon release, the novel is set 100 years earlier, during the reign of Henry II of France. Aside from the main character, nearly every character is a historical figure. This historical novel is considered not only the first, true French novel and one of the first modern novels in Western literature, but also a precursor to the complex, psychological novel that would become popular in the 19th century.

The European Enlightenment thrived in France in the 18th century, producing legendary cultural figures such as Voltaire, Denis Diderot, and Jean-Jacques Rousseau, the philosopher and novelist whose work helped inspire the French Revolution. While most commonly remembered for his political treatise *The Social Contract* (1762), Rousseau also influenced the Romantic movement in fiction with the novel *Julie, ou la Nouvelle Héloïse* (1761). This love story was immensely popular upon release, selling out numerous editions, and inspiring such emotion in readers that Rousseau is said to have received excessive fan mail—making him one of the first celebrity authors.

The French Revolution of 1789 marked a turning point not only in the political history of France, but in the European literary tradition. The event is considered the major political catalyst of European Romanticism, the emotionally driven artistic movement dominating Europe by the turn of the 19th century. Following the French Revolution, the novel flourished in France throughout the 1800s. The novelist and literary hostess Madame Germaine de Staël, author of novels including *Corinne* (1807), advocated a new international literature of feeling. Her call was soon answered by the work of **Victor Hugo**, whose novels *Notre-Dame de Paris* (1832) (or *The Hunchback of Notre-Dame*) and *Les Misérables* (1862) remain two of the most well known works in French literature. Already a celebrated poet when he released *Notre-Dame de Paris*, Hugo achieved huge popularity with the tragic 15th-century love story of deformed bell-ringer Quasimodo and the doomed Gypsy Esmeralda. The novel was quickly translated into other European languages and even inspired the French government to restore Paris's Notre Dame Cathedral. *Les Misérables*, the story of ex-convict Jean Valjean and his adopted daughter, Cosette, was published in five volumes, and is considered one of the greatest novels in Western literature. Upon release, it received mixed reviews from critics, many of whom considered it vulgar and too sympathetic with revolutionaries. However, the novel was wildly successful and sparked social reform with its depictions of poverty and social injustice.

Hugo's contemporary and fellow Romantic **Alexandre Dumas père** became famous for his exciting, historical novels, which include *The Three Musketeers* (1844) and *The Count of Monte Cristo* (1845). Considered the most widely read French writer, his adventure stories of daring escapes and carefully plotted revenge have been translated into almost 100 languages and remain popular today. Another popular novelist of the time, George Sand (Amandine Dupin), is remembered as the first woman novelist to gain a major reputation for her fiction in France.

French fiction of the mid- to late 1800s was dominated by a series of extraordinary realistic novelists, especially **Stendhal** (Marie-Henri

Beyle). His novels *The Red and the Black* (1831) and *The Charterhouse of Parma* (1839) related vivid and unflinching tales of passion and society, marking a dramatic contrast to the Romantic literature popular at the time. Stendhal delved into the psychology of his characters and is said to have influenced the realistic and psychological novels of the late 19th and early 20th centuries. Realism was also the focus of the influential French author Honoré de Balzac, whose prolific collection of almost 100 novels, plays, and short stories is known collectively as *La Comédie Humaine*. The subject matter of this vast collection was French society following the fall of Napoleon in 1815, and he painted it in all its colors and textures, with Paris as the setting of most of his works.

Gustave Flaubert's first novel, *Madame Bovary* (1857), is considered the quintessential text of the Realism movement in French literature. The story of Emma Bovary, a doctor's wife who attempts to escape her monotonous life through a series of extramarital affairs and other indiscretions, was first published in serialized form in the magazine *La Revue de Paris* and was subsequently attacked by public prosecutors for its supposed obscenity. After acquittal at the trial, the book became a best seller and is now considered one of the greatest novels ever written.

Flaubert was a major influence on the great practitioner of French Naturalism, **Émile Zola**. Naturalism depicted humanity, often in disturbing detail, as determined by nature and environment. Zola's Rougon-Macquart sequence of 20 novels, including *Nana* (1880), examined the life of the lower classes, following two families over the course of five generations. Today, Zola is entombed at the Panthéon, along with Victor Hugo and Alexandre Dumas.

♦**The German Novel** Hans Jakob Christoffel von Grimmelshausen wrote the first German novel, *Simplicissimus* (1669). Essentially a fictionalized autobiography, it relates the author's childhood abduction into the military and his subsequent experiences in the Thirty Years War. This novel is considered one of the first of all significant modern novels, preceded only by Cervantes's *Don Quixote de la Mancha*.

Influenced by the Enlightenment and the works of Rousseau, the Sturm und Drang ("storm and stress") literary movement lasted from the late 1760s to the early 1780s. Emphasizing emotion over reason, self-expression over social norms, and celebrating nature, its greatest exponent was the novelist and dramatist Johann Wolfgang von Goëthe. While best known for his two-part drama *Faust* (1802, 1832), he also contributed to the fiction of this movement with his epistolary novel *The Sorrows of Young Werther* (1774), which was loosely autobiographical in nature.

European Romanticism arrived in Germany even before it blossomed in France following the French Revolution. Early German Romantics include the novelist Heinrich von Kleist, the most accomplished author of the newly popular form the novella; he published *The Marquise of O and Other Stories* in 1810–11, as well as numerous other works of fiction. Unlike other Romantics of the time, he focused less on nature and more on the psychology of the individual, and he often captured characters in moments of crisis and decision.

◆The Russian Novel Although the novel did not appear in Russian literature until the 19th century—much later than in Western Europe—Russia's contributions to the form over the course of the 1800s are considered among the most significant in the Western literary canon.

Nikolai Gogol is best known for his short stories and novel *Dead Souls* (1842), which he wrote in the wake of the poet Aleksandr Pushkin's death in 1837, by which he was profoundly moved. Like most of Gogol's writing, *Dead Souls* conveys social criticism through absurd humor and satire. He is considered the first Russian realist as well as a comic fantasist. A parade of prose masters followed, including Ivan Turgenev, a controversial critic of Russian society who is best known for his novel *Fathers and Sons* (1862). This novel captured the anxiety at that time over the growing generational discord that was occurring in the midst of vast social change.

Turgenev's contemporary, the brilliant novelist **Fyodor Dostoyevsky**, wrote *Crime and Punishment* (1866), *The Idiot* (1868), and *The Brothers Karamazov* (1880). Considered the culmination of Dostoyevsky's literary career, *The Brothers Karamazov* was intended to be the first book in a trilogy. However, it is *Crime and Punishment* that still resonates most deeply with modern audiences. In this novel set in 19th-century Russia, Raskolnikov, a young intellectual, ponders killing the pawnbroker Aliyona Ivanovna, not for money (although he is deeply in debt) but for philosophical satisfaction. He meets a clerk, Marmeladov, who tells him of his daughter, Sonia, a virtuous girl who has become a prostitute in order to help her family. Raskolnikov receives a letter from his mother telling him that his sister, Dounia, fired after refusing an affair with her employer, has become engaged to a wealthy businessman, and that the mother and daughter will soon be coming to St. Petersburg. Overwhelmed by the suffering around him, Raskolnikov follows through with the murder, killing Aliyona Ivanovna with an axe, and, when seen at the crime scene by her sister, kills her as well.

Raskolnikov is plagued with unease about the murders. He becomes paranoid, convinced that everyone he encounters is conspiring to make him confess. A police detective becomes convinced of his guilt but is unable to prove it. When Marmeladov dies, Raskolnikov meets Sonia and is deeply moved by the choices she has made to help her family. At Sonia's urging, Raskolnikov turns himself in and is sentenced to hard labor in Siberia. Sonia accompanies him, and Raskolnikov, at first unrepentant, becomes influenced by Sonia's selflessness and generosity, as well as by a revelatory dream, and he eventually comes to truly repent for his crime.

Dostoyevsky's contemporary **Leo Tolstoy** wrote the historical novel *War and Peace* (1865–69) and the tale of passion *Anna Karenina* (1874–77), both of which are considered among the world's greatest novels. *War and Peace* is a sweeping novel spanning the lives of several families. Combining passionate romance, a historical account of the Napoleonic Wars, and philosophical essays, the story is enormous both in length and scope. It famously opens with a party in which many of the principal characters are introduced, then focuses primarily on the lives of three people: Prince Andrei Bolkonsky, an arrogant and high-minded member of St. Petersburg's aristocracy; his friend Pierre Bezhukov, the illegitimate son of a wealthy man; and Natasha Rustov, the beautiful, spirited young daughter of a count who has lost much of his wealth.

Prince Andrei perceives the aristocratic world as lacking truth or meaning. He joins the army, and while at war, he comes to believe that battle is not a place of glory, but rather a place as empty as the society he has left behind. When Natasha meets Andrei, they quickly fall in love. However, before they are married, she is seduced by another man and, in her shame, ends her engagement. Andrei leaves for war, and

Natasha is left alone. Andrei is gravely wounded in battle, and he and Natasha are united briefly before he dies. Natasha comes to love the steadfast Pierre, who has long loved her, and the two marry. Later, Natasha's youthful brilliance fades to the drabness of an older married woman, and Pierre has found happiness in domestic life.

Anna Karenina is the story of a vibrant member of St. Petersburg's upper class who is married to the emotionally withdrawn Alexei Karenin. During a trip to Moscow, Anna meets Count Vronsky, a handsome young cavalry officer. She falls in love with him, and so must choose between a life with Vronsky, in which she would be forced to leave behind her young son, Sergei, and a life in which she would continue to languish within a loveless marriage. She chooses Vronsky, and the two eventually have a daughter together. When Anna's husband refuses a divorce, the lovers go into exile.

As the years pass, Anna becomes consumed with jealousy, certain that Vronsky no longer loves her. Vronsky, his career ruined by the love affair and now faced with Anna's increasing paranoia, withdraws. When he does not respond to a letter that Anna sends him, she commits suicide by jumping in front of a train. Only when Anna is lying on the track does she realize that her choices in life caused her to abandon what could have been true happiness.

Day 2: The English Novel, 1700–1900

In England, the novel first appeared in the 18th century with the publication of *Moll Flanders* (1722) by Daniel Defoe. Some critics, however, think that because this story of a thieving prostitute fails to depict interior consciousness—one of the basic elements of any novel—a better example is Samuel Richardson's *Pamela: Or, Virtue Rewarded* (1740). An epistolary novel, or novel written in the form of letters, it presents the character of Pamela as a model of the virtuous woman and instructs women in the proper way to behave. Richardson wrote two more novels in the same epistolary style, *Clarissa: Or The History of a Young Lady* (1748) and *Sir Charles Grandison* (1753). Henry Fielding became famous for his picaresque novels *Joseph Andrews* (1742) and *Tom Jones* (1749), which depicted the adventures of scrappy, young British rascals. For these contributions, Fielding is generally considered the first great English novelist.

At the beginning of the 19th century, two very different authors made impressions of great magnitude, bringing about a turning point in the development of the British novel. The Scottish poet and novelist Sir Walter Scott was influenced by the Romantics and is considered the father of the British historical novel. He is best remembered for his Crusade epic *Ivanhoe* (1820), though he also wrote novels set in Scottish history, along with well-plotted romances of Scottish life. His 1817 novel *Rob Roy* told the story of a legendary Scottish hero and sold out its first edition of 10,000 copies in a matter of a few weeks. His other well-known novels include *Waverley* (1814), *The Heart of Midlothian* (1818), and *The Bride of Lammermoor* (1819).

Jane Austen was a contemporary of Scott's and equally influential, though she did not achieve the public acclaim and financial success with which Scott was rewarded. Born the seventh of eight children to a minister in the lower ranks of the gentry, Austen spent her short life living quietly in the country, and her novels reflect this lifestyle. Austen wrote six novels, all of which are romantic tales of young women of her class struggling to find love and to get married. But they are also clever social commentaries and moral explorations. Austen chose to publish anonymously and therefore received little attention for her work during her lifetime. Her *Pride and Prejudice* (1813) opens with one of the best-known lines in all of Western literature: "It is a truth universally acknowledged, that a single man in possession of a good fortune, must be in want of a wife." During her lifetime, Austen published *Sense and Sensibility* (1811), *Pride and Prejudice*, *Mansfield Park* (1814), and *Emma* (1816). Her older brother and literary agent, Henry, arranged for the posthumous publication of her final two works, *Northanger Abbey* and *Persuasion* in 1817. He included a biographical note, identifying her for the first time as the author of her novels.

One year after Austen's death, Mary Shelley published one of the most popular Gothic novels ever written, *Frankenstein: or The Modern Prometheus* (1818). The daughter of the feminist philosopher Mary Wollstonecraft, and the wife of Romantic poet Percy Bysshe Shelley, she wrote the story of Victor Frankenstein, a scientist who creates and brings to life a monster made from human parts. Mary Shelley wrote the novel after spending the summer in Geneva with her husband and their friend Lord Byron. In popular culture, the name Frankenstein has come to be identified with the monster, rather than the scientist, and that monster has become a legendary character in the horror genre.

The tradition of female novelists among the gentry of the English countryside continued into the mid-19th century, with the emergence of the Brontë sisters: Charlotte, Emily, and Anne. The Brontës grew up in a family marked by both great artistic talent and great tragedy, and as young adults they each produced a novel that embraced those same Romantic, specifically Gothic, elements. In 1847, after a long search for publishers, all three sisters published successful novels, with Charlotte producing *Jane Eyre*; Emily, *Wuthering Heights*; and Anne, *Agnes Grey*. Of the three works, *Jane Eyre*, the brooding tale of an orphan who eventually finds passionate love with a man who literally has a crazy wife locked in the attic, was the most successful at the time of publication. However, all three novels were best sellers during the sisters' brief lifetimes, causing a sensation with their depictions of mental anguish and physical cruelty. *Wuthering Heights*, the tragic love story of Heathcliff and Catherine Earnshaw set upon the moors of England, is now generally regarded as one of the great classics of Western literature. All three sisters originally published their novels under pseudonyms that hid their identities as females. Like most of the characters in their novels, none of the Brontë sisters lived past the age of 40.

The trend of Romantic fiction subsided during the reign of Queen Victoria, and the satirical novel took its place as the popular fiction of the day. In 1848, William Makepeace Thackeray published *Vanity Fair*, a satire of British society. It features a heroine of sorts in Becky Sharp, a winning, though not admirable character who serves as a vehicle for attacking the upper class. Because of the novel's concern with the interior life of its characters, it is considered a forerunner of the psychological novel, a form that would grow in popularity as the 19th century progressed.

The most well known of all the Victorian satirists, and perhaps the most widely read English novelist of all time, was Charles Dickens. Also known as "Boz," Dickens created some of the most memorable, comedic, and absurd characters in the history of fiction. Most of Dickens's novels are set in the world of Victorian London, but his characters range from poverty-stricken orphans, like the title characters of *Oliver Twist* (1838) and *David Copperfield* (1850), to wealthy, vindictive recluses like *Great Expectations*'s (1861) Miss Havisham and *A Christmas*

Carol's (1843) Ebenezer Scrooge. One of the greatest characters in Dickens's literary world is the city of London itself. Dickens's novels typically feature episodic and highly sentimental plots, with many twists, turns, and cliffhangers, because like many authors of that time, his work was published in serialized form in magazines, and he had to hook readers so they would buy the next issue. Dickens's fiction was somewhat autobiographical in nature, and he frequently based characters on individuals in his life. He used his characters as vehicles for social critique, shining a light on the plight of London's poor and the consequences of industrialization. His novels were often the catalysts for real-life social reform. Dickens's other influential novels include *Bleak House* (1852–53), *Hard Times* (1854), and *A Tale of Two Cities* (1859).

The psychological novel blossomed in the second half of the 19th century, most notably through the work of George Eliot, the pen name of Mary Ann Evans. She used a male pseudonym to ensure that her work was taken seriously and to protect herself from scandal relating to her long-term relationship with a married man. She wrote eight novels, including *The Mill on the Floss* (1860), *Silas Marner* (1861), and *Middlemarch* (1872). Set in the small towns of the British countryside, her psychologically probing and highly realistic novels follow the journeys of intelligent, fully realized characters—often social outcasts——as they struggle to overcome moral challenges and live meaningful lives. Eliot's novels reflect Victorian uncertainty about religious faith, and they are highly realistic in their portrayal of the events and people of that time.

As the century progressed, the literary movements of Naturalism and Realism focused on accurately portraying the consequences of the monumental changes occurring at that time. The later part of the Victorian Age brought with it the expansion of the British Empire, the Industrial Revolution, and major breakthroughs in science, all of which created a new understanding of the world. Much of the British literature of the late 19th century, such as the work of Thomas Hardy and Henry James, reflects the loss of certainty and religious conviction that was prevalent at the time.

Thomas Hardy is remembered for both his poetry and his novels, which include *The Return of the Native* (1878), *Tess of the D'Urbervilles* (1891), and *Jude the Obscure* (1896). Like Dickens, most of his work was published in serialized form in magazines. His 1873 novel *A Pair of Blue Eyes*, in which a character is literally left hanging on the edge of a cliff in one of its original installments, is said to be the source of the term *cliffhanger*. Hardy explored the implications of the societal rules of Victorian England, and he was heavily rebuked for his sympathetic portrayal of a "fallen woman" in *Tess of the D'Urbervilles*, and his frank discussion of sexual matters in *Jude the Obscure*, which was often referred to as "Jude the Obscene." Hardy's novels are set in fictional "Wessex," his name for the region of Dorsetshire in rural, southern England. His characters are often acted upon by nature's cruel fate, and left as social outcasts.

Hardy's contemporary Henry James was born and educated in the United States but resettled in England at the age of 33. James's novels, many depicting his "international theme," are considered part of both the British and American literary canons. His plots focus on the interactions between wealthy Americans and Europeans, which were increasingly common in his lifetime, as overseas travel became easier and more accommodating. James used interior monologue, point of view, and unreliable narrators to relate stories of high-society culture clashes between the Old World and the New, which often ended in downfall. His works include *The Portrait of a Lady* (1881), *The Turn of the Screw* (1898), and *The Wings of the Dove* (1902).

Weekend 30: The Sixties

The 1960s were a time of dramatic political and cultural upheaval both in the United States and around the globe. Many date the decade's true cultural beginning to November 22, 1963, when President John F. Kennedy was assassinated in Dallas, Texas. Kennedy's shocking murder seemed to be the starting point of one of the nation's most turbulent eras, a time marked by further assassinations, urban riots, mass protests, failed presidencies, an unpopular war, and new demands for equal rights and social justice. In that sense, the tumult of the 1960s did not truly end until noon on Aug. 9, 1974, when Richard Nixon became the first U.S. president to resign his office in the wake of the Watergate scandal.

It was Kennedy himself who detected change in the air as he sought to become the nation's first Roman Catholic president in 1960. Kennedy's campaign was based on an explicit critique of the 1950s and the gray-flannel administration of President Dwight D. Eisenhower. Kennedy, as the Democratic Party's nominee, argued that it was time to get the country moving again, a sentiment that many young people—the advance guard of that giant cohort known as the "baby boom"—shared.

But in fields far removed from the campaign trail, the country was already moving in a new direction. Leading the way were thousands of ordinary African Americans who were demanding an end to blatant discrimination in the South and equal justice throughout the country. The civil rights movement was already a powerful force by the time the calendar turned from 1959 to 1960. The new decade ushered in not the movement's birth, but its maturity.

Day 1: The Civil Rights Movement

The foremost leader of the civil rights movement and one of the iconic figures of the 1960s, Dr. Martin Luther King Jr. was already a household name before the decade began. King was among the leaders of a bus boycott in Montgomery, Alabama, in 1955, and went on to found the Southern Christian Leadership Conference in 1957. On the eve of the new decade, King traveled to India to study the nonviolent tactics of the great Indian nationalist Mahatma Gandhi. King was determined to replicate Gandhi's moral leadership and civil disobedience campaigns in America, as the movement for civil rights gained momentum and publicity in the South.

In 1954, a landmark U.S. Supreme Court decision—*Brown v. Board of Education*—ruled that school desegregation was unconstitutional, beginning a systematic program of racial segregation in many cities and states. In early 1960, African Americans began to openly defy state-supported segregation, and college students in Greensboro, North Carolina, staged a sit-in at a lunch counter to protest the legally protected practice of offering counter service to whites only. The students remained seated at the counter for four days, attracting worldwide media attention and setting off similar sit-ins at segregated lunch counters throughout the South. By the end of 1960, nearly 70,000 Americans had participated in a civil rights demonstration, many of them committing acts of civil disobedience to bring attention to segregation on trains and buses, in swimming pools, and in other places of public accommodation.

As the sit-in campaign spread, another group of African-American students founded an organization called the Student Non-Violent Coordinating Committee, or S.N.C.C. The group recruited students in campuses across the nation to join the campaign against segregation, an effort that produced one of the decade's most divisive figures, Stokely Carmichael, who later argued for more aggressive tactics.

In late October 1960, as the nation prepared to go to the polls for that year's presidential election, Dr. King and 50 other demonstrators were arrested in Atlanta for taking part in a sit-in at a lunch counter. King was sentenced to four months in prison after his conviction on an unrelated charge, driving without proper license. John Kennedy called King in prison to express his sympathy; his opponent, Richard Nixon, ruined his hopes of winning over African-American voters when he declined to comment on King's arrest. Nixon lost to Kennedy in a close election two weeks later.

Kennedy's famous inaugural address, delivered on Jan. 21, 1961, contained only a glancing reference to the burgeoning civil rights movement, and even that mention was written into the speech at the last minute and somewhat grudgingly so. In a famous passage pledging America's commitment to freedom, Kennedy said the nation would defend human rights "at home and around the globe."

◆**The Challenge to Segregation**   That defense, however, took place not in the halls of the Capitol but on the streets of southern cities, and the defenders were not white men in business suits, but ordinary African Americans and their young white allies, most of them from the north. In May 1961, the Congress of Racial Equality (CORE) launched a series of confrontations on the nation's interstate bus system. CORE recruited young people, both black and white, to board buses headed south and challenge the "whites only" sections of individual bus terminals. Dubbed "Freedom Riders," the idealistic young people were set up and beaten at several stops, with police conspicuously absent.

The crisis worsened when buses were attacked in Atlanta, as mobs of civil rights opponents screamed "Kill the niggers." A federal official monitoring the ride was beaten and nearly killed. Alabama deployed National Guard troops to protect the buses, but hundreds of riders were immediately arrested when they got off the buses.

The confrontation brought an end to segregated transportation facilities in the South, but that was hardly the end of black grievances. The voting power of African Americans was severely diluted because when they attempted to vote they risked their lives and safety. The Kennedy administration and some moderate civil rights leaders supported plans to back away from outright confrontation and instead focus on voter registration and participation in 1962. But the movement for liberation could not be controlled by the nation's chief executive and its chief law enforcement official, Attorney General Robert F. Kennedy.

The University of Mississippi in Oxford was a symbol of the white-supremacist establishment. It was not segregated—it simply refused to admit African Americans. A leader of the National Association for the Advancement of Colored People (N.A.A.C.P.), Medgar Evers, was determined to bring the battle for equality to the steps of "Ole Miss," as the school was affectionately called by its all-white alumni. Evers recruited a 28-year-old Air Force veteran named James Meredith to apply to the university and, when he received his inevitable rejection, to demand justice from the nation's courts.

The stage was set for an epic confrontation in the heart of the deep South on September 30, 1962. The governor of Mississippi, Ross Barnett, was on hand to personally prevent Meredith from enrolling. Angry crowds gathered to taunt and abuse Meredith when he arrived on campus and was turned away. Insults gave way to violence, and violence provoked gunfire. Two innocent people were shot during the melee, as white mobs stormed buildings on campus.

Federal law enforcement officials escorted Meredith to campus the following day, and he was allowed to register. American public opinion supported both Meredith's courage and the White House's intervention. Segregation's supporters interpreted Meredith's victory as a bitter defeat. Several weeks later, voters in Alabama elected George C. Wallace as their new governor. In his inaugural address, Wallace vowed to support "segregation today, segregation tomorrow, segregation forever."

As this increasingly tense and violent uprising unfolded in the South, other events made their mark on the decade. John Glenn became the first American to orbit the Earth on February 20, 1962; the Students for a Democratic Society (S.D.S.) passed a manifesto in July, called the "Port Huron Statement," advocating radical change in America; and, just weeks after Meredith desegregated "Ole Miss", the Kennedy administration imposed a blockade around Cuba when it learned that the Soviets were shipping missiles to the Castro regime. The Cuban missile crisis ended in late October with the Soviets agreeing to withdraw the missiles, as well as the U.S. pledging not to invade Cuba, and to remove missiles from Turkey.

♦**Mayhem and Murder** Seeking to build on the success of confrontations at lunch counters and on college campuses, the civil rights movement stepped up protests in 1963, with a new round of sit-ins and demonstrations in Governor Wallace's home state of Alabama. Dr. King and another Southern Christian Leadership Conference leader, Ralph Abernathy, were arrested when they took part in the Alabama protests. The city's director of public safety, Eugene "Bull" Connor, regularly turned dogs and firehoses on the unarmed demonstrators, creating images of oppression that inspired worldwide sympathy for the civil rights marchers. Dr. King, imprisoned again, wrote "Letter from a Birmingham Jail," which set the moral framework for nonviolent action against immoral laws, and includes the oft-cited quotation, "Injustice anywhere is a threat to justice everywhere."

On June 11, 1963, two African-American students, Vivian Malone and James Hood, sought to enroll at the all-white University of Alabama, directly challenging the governor's pledge to support segregation forever.

Wallace blocked the entrance when one of Kennedy's assistants, Nicholas Katzenbach, tried to negotiate a peaceful registration process for the two students. Wallace read a statement denouncing the attempt, then disappeared. The two students were registered without incident, but Wallace's speech infuriated the White House. That evening, President Kennedy delivered a speech in which he declared civil rights to be a great "moral issue," and pointed out to his white audience the obstacles black children had to overcome in order to enjoy rights that whites took for granted. He urged Congress to pass a sweeping civil rights bill. The following day, Medgar Evers, who fought for his country in World War II and then again on the civil rights battlefields of Mississippi, was shot dead in front of his family. The assassin was not brought to justice for 30 years.

The civil rights movement was now one of the most powerful forces for social justice in the 20th century. Leaders called for a massive meeting on the Washington Mall on August 28, 1963. More than 250,000 people, most of them black, but joined by at least 50,000 whites, crowded in front of the Lincoln Memorial to hear Dr. King's passionate "I have a dream" speech, another iconic moment from the era of social change and mass protest. King's stirring eloquence moved many people to peaceful actions, but a black nationalist in New York City was far more militant. He called himself "Malcolm X," because his ancestral African name had been eradicated by slavery. Malcolm X derided King's speeches and strategy, demanding a more confrontational stance against white racism.

Confrontation came quickly enough, but in the form of white backlash. On the morning of September 15, 1963, militant segregationists bombed the Sixteenth Street Baptist Church in Birmingham, Alabama. Four young girls died in the blast, delivering another shock to America's self-image as a society dedicated to equality.

President Kennedy's murder on November 22 propelled Vice President Lyndon B. Johnson of Texas into the Oval Office. Many eastern Democrats were skeptical of Johnson's commitment to civil rights, but he soon made it clear that social justice and racial equality were top priorities. He renewed pressure on Congress to pass a civil rights bill as a memorial to his slain predecessor, leading to the Civil Rights Act of 1964, the most sweeping such law since Reconstruction. The act outlawed racial discrimination and segregation and gave the attorney general power to file lawsuits on behalf of those deprived of their constitutional or federally protected rights. Johnson followed up on this success a year later when he lobbied Congress to pass the Voting Rights Act of 1965, which outlawed literacy tests and other obstacles to voting. Johnson signed the bill into law in the presence of Dr. King and Rosa Parks, whose refusal to surrender her seat on a bus in Montgomery, Alabama, in 1955 helped inspire the civil rights crusade. These measures led to even more violent actions in the South. Three young civil rights workers, two of whom were white and from the North, were murdered in Mississippi in 1964, leading in turn to more militant action from S.N.C.C. and other groups.

The struggle over civil rights and race relations unfolded in the segregated South, but in August 1965, serious riots broke out in Watts, a black area of Los Angeles, that lasted six days and resulted in 34 deaths and 1,000 wounded, as well as property damages in the tens of millions of dollars. In 1967, the scene shifted to the North, as African Americans struggling against housing and job discrimination and police brutality took to the streets of Detroit and Newark. Dozens were killed, hundreds injured, and many buildings were burned to the ground. Neither city has ever fully recovered from the trauma, and the white backlash against civil rights began to gather momentum.

The worst was yet to come. On April 4, 1968, Dr. King was murdered outside a motel room in Memphis, Tennessee. The civil rights movement lost its most eloquent leader, and while the effort to attain racial justice would continue, a divided nation had begun to turn its attention to another intractable and divisive problem—the war in Vietnam.

Day 2: The Vietnam War

Like the civil rights movement, U.S. involvement in Vietnam and the rest of Southeast Asia predated the 1960s. John Kennedy's predecessor, Dwight Eisenhower, was convinced that a Communist-backed insurgency in Laos, which borders Vietnam, threatened the entire region. Kennedy deployed a small contingent of Marines to Laos in early 1961, and then followed up by sending some 2,000 troops—they were called "advisers"—to South Vietnam at the end of 1961. The South Vietnamese government, based in Saigon, was engaged in an escalating war with Communist guerillas, called the Vietcong, who were in league with the North Vietnamese government led by the charismatic Ho Chi Minh.

Vietnam had been partitioned in 1954, after insurgents defeated

France, the nation's longtime colonial ruler. The political leader of South Vietnam, Ngo Dinh Diem, ran a regime that rigged elections and stifled dissent, keeping him in power (to the embarrassment of his U.S. allies). Still, the Kennedy administration was determined to hold the line in South Vietnam, even if it meant aligning itself with a virtual dictator. The U.S. had 11,000 soldiers in South Vietnam by the end of 1962, and 16,000 by late 1963.

♦**1963** Diem's harsh treatment of South Vietnamese Buddhists led to mass protests, violent repression, and hundreds of deaths in 1963. In early November, the South Vietnamese military overthrew and murdered Diem and his brother, allegedly with President Kennedy's approval. Kennedy asked for a full review of U.S. policy in the region after Diem's murder, including options for withdrawal. He asked for the review on November 21, 1963, but was murdered the following day. His successor, Lyndon Johnson, was also determined to keep South Vietnam out of Communist control, but he also had a sweeping vision for vast domestic programs that would come to be known as the Great Society.

♦**1964** Johnson did not go to Congress to ask for a declaration of war in order to escalate the conflict, but he had the authorization he needed, thanks to a murky incident that took place in the Gulf of Tonkin off the Vietnamese coast on August 2, 1964. The U.S.S. *Maddox*, a destroyer, exchanged fire with North Vietnamese gunboats. This led to another incident two days later, when crews on the *Maddox* and another U.S. destroyer claimed they had come under attack and fired back, although those claims still remain dubious. Johnson portrayed the incident as an unprovoked attack on U.S. personnel and asked Congress to approve a resolution—which came to be known as the Gulf of Tonkin Resolution—authorizing the president to step up military operations in the region. The resolution faced no opposition in the House of Representatives and only two negative votes in the Senate.

Johnson won an overwhelming victory over Republican Barry Goldwater in 1964 and almost immediately stepped up U.S. involvement in Vietnam. Warplanes bombed targets in North Vietnam, and U.S. ground forces began to take a more prominent role in the fight against the Vietcong. More than 1,000 Americans died in combat in 1965 and another 5,000 died in 1966. Thousands more Vietnamese died in U.S. air raids over Hanoi, the North Vietnamese capital, and other targets. For the first time, American television viewers saw the war unfold in their living rooms, on the evening news, and what they saw often prompted revulsion—burned villages, maimed U.S. troops being carted from rice paddies on stretchers, and civilians mourning the deaths of children or parents.

◆**1967** The war was increasingly a flashpoint in domestic politics. Senator William Fulbright of Arkansas held public hearings on the war, giving both a platform to the war's opponents and a popular face to dissent against the war. American troops continued to pour into South Vietnam—eventually, troop strength would reach nearly 500,000. In June 1967, Johnson declared that draft boards would give top priority to conscripting young males into the army. Youthful dissent, already simmering, began to boil over, especially as the fighting became more intense. Over the next three years, college campuses around the nation were the center of continuous protests, some of which were violent. At prestigious schools such as Cornell and Columbia, students seized control of university offices and buildings, bringing police violence to the once peaceful world of academe.

A presidential election year drew close, and suddenly Lyndon Johnson looked vulnerable. Johnson's war was increasingly bogged down, despite a bombing campaign that surpassed, in pure explosive tonnage, the U.S. bombing offensives in Germany and Japan during World War II. In November 1967, Defense Secretary Robert McNamara, one of the architects of the escalation, announced his resignation. Several weeks later, an antiwar senator from Minnesota, Eugene McCarthy, announced that he would challenge Johnson for the Democratic Party's presidential nomination. McCarthy promised to bring the war to an end, but his candidacy still was regarded as a longshot; dissent was growing, but was not yet mainstream. Johnson remained a powerful figure—a wartime president around whom Americans might be expected to rally.

◆**1968** With a keen sense of timing, the Vietcong and North Vietnamese troops launched a surprise offensive in South Vietnam to coincide with the lunar new year, known as Tet. The Tet offensive in January 1968 brought the war to the streets of Saigon, the South's capital, and to the very walls of the U.S. embassy. Guerrillas murdered South Vietnamese officials by the hundreds in the city of Hue. Thousands of civilians died before U.S. and South Vietnamese forces recovered and successfully pushed back. The body count was a catastrophe for the Vietcong—they lost nearly 40,000 troops to slightly more than 1,000 American dead, but the sheer audacity of the attack disheartened Americans at home. The American news anchorman Walter Cronkite traveled to South Vietnam and reported that, contrary to the insistence of both the president and military leaders, the U.S. was caught in a stalemate and was not anywhere near victory. Meanwhile, the Pentagon asked the president to authorize deployment of an additional 200,000 troops.

Angry New Hampshire voters went to the polls on March 12 and delivered a stinging rebuke of Johnson. Although the president won the primary, McCarthy won a surprising 42 percent of the vote. Senator Robert F. Kennedy of New York, the late president's brother, entered the race only four days later, echoing McCarthy's pledge to end the war.

On March 31, Johnson added to the nation's sense of crisis when he announced that he would not seek the party's nomination. On April 4, as Americans adjusted to the possibility of peace through a change of presidents, Martin Luther King Jr. was murdered in Memphis. Senator Kennedy broke the news to an audience of African Americans in Indiana, asking them to go home and pray for their country. On June 6, Kennedy himself was murdered after winning the California primary.

•**Nixon Wins**   The nation, it seemed, was falling apart. The former vice president Richard Nixon, a voice from the Republican Party's recent past, emerged as the party's presidential nominee. Democrats chose Vice President Hubert Humphrey as their nominee during the turbulent Democratic National Convention in Chicago, where young antiwar protesters battled police in the streets and parks, providing indelible images of a nation at war with itself, as the police beat and clubbed the rampaging protestors on national television. Nixon's campaign promised that he had a secret plan to end the war, and this promise helped him defeat the Democrats, who were saddled with extensive public dissatisfaction over the war.

The change in administration in Washington did not bring the war in Vietnam to an end, but Richard Nixon did adopt a new strategy. He withdrew 25,000 troops in the spring of 1969; they were replaced with soldiers in the South Vietnamese army. Nixon hoped the "Vietnamization" strategy would allow him to de-escalate the war and still not lose it. In the meantime, he and his national security advisor, Henry Kissinger, engaged in covert diplomacy in an effort to negotiate a way out.

The public, however, grew impatient. On October 15, 1969, 7 million Americans protested the war in demonstrations around the nation. Weeks later, *The New York Times* reported that U.S. troops had slaughtered civilians in the village of My Lai. But Nixon was undeterred—on April 30, 1970, he announced that U.S. forces had invaded Cambodia in pursuit of enemy strongholds and hideouts. This escalation prompted a new series of protests, including one at Kent State University in Ohio, where National Guard troops shot and killed four students in early May.

America was divided as it had not been since the Civil War. But while protests over the Cambodian invasion continued, American troops actually were leaving Vietnam by the thousands. During the election year of 1972, fewer than 160,000 soldiers were left in Vietnam, and battlefield deaths dropped to fewer than 300 per month, as compared to nearly 10,000 in June 1968.

In February 1972, Nixon, although an ardent anticommunist, threw aside decades of U.S. policy by traveling to China to meet with that country's Communist leadership, a move, he hoped, that would help bring conflict in Southeast Asia to an end. China never responded, at least not publicly, and the war dragged on. Peace talks began in 1972 but stalled toward year's end. Weeks after winning reelection, Nixon ordered a massive bombing attack on North Vietnam's two most prominent cities, Hanoi and Haiphong. The move was bitterly criticized and prompted more large-scale antiwar demonstrations. A treaty brought the conflict between the U.S. and North Vietnam to an end on January 23, 1973. Nixon proclaimed peace with honor, even though the terms of the agreement were the same ones North Vietnam had always asked for. North Vietnam released hundreds of prisoners of war.

The war cost the lives of more than 58,000 Americans and perhaps millions of Vietnamese, and did not end with the signing of the treaty. The government of South Vietnam collapsed in the spring of 1975, eight months after Nixon's resignation, signalling complete victory for the north and a true end to the war. Its influence on American foreign policy, however, remains strong, as each succeeding president vowed that the U.S. would never lose another war. The long shadow of that defeat can be seen in Iraq and Afghanistan today, as America continues to spend hundreds of billions of dollars on war while the nation's economy sags under the burden of trillions of dollars of debt.

Weekend 31: Forms of Life

Day 1: The Animal Kingdom

Some 2,300 years ago, the Greek philosopher Aristotle collected animals, dissected them, and wrote extensive descriptions of their anatomy. He grouped together animals with similar characteristics, described the social organization of bees, the embryological development of chickens, and distinguished whales and dolphins from fish. Modern scientists point to Aristotle as the father of the scientific method. In the centuries after Aristotle's era, however, superstitions and fantasies about animals often buried facts. For example, after the fall of Rome, a book called the *Physiologus* by an unknown author examined 49 different animals (some fictional, such as the unicorn), giving each an allegorical interpretation. The *Physiologus* gained popularity as a teaching companion for the Bible and remained in widespread use for more than a thousand years.

In the 12th and 13th centuries, zoology—the study of animals and animal life—emerged as a science, driven by the work of the German scholar St. Albertus Magnus (ca. 1193–1280). Magnus rejected the superstitions associated with biology and reintroduced the work of Aristotle. In the 15th and 16th centuries, Leonardo da Vinci dissected and compared the structure of humans and animals, establishing the concept of *homology*, the correspondence of parts in different kinds of animals.

Technological advances were first applied to the study of zoology in the 19th century. In 1839, the German scientists Matthias Schleiden and Theodor Schwann used microscopes to prove that the cell is the common structural unit of all living things. This concept inspired Karl Ernst von Baer to establish the field of embryology and Claude Bernard to advance the study of animal physiology. In the 19th century, the slow acceptance of the doctrine of organic evolution pioneered by Charles Darwin came about.

Today, zoology is not confined to traditional concerns such as classification and anatomy. It is an interdisciplinary field that encompasses such studies as biochemistry, ecology, and genetics to better understand the many diverse types of animals that exist today and have existed throughout history.

◆**Animal Characteristics** Members of the kingdom animalia range in size from a few cells to organisms that weigh many tons. They share several characteristics that set them apart from other living organisms. All animals are multicellular, *eukaryotic* (their cells contain a nucleus and membrane-bound organelles—specialized subunits that have a specific function), *heterotrophic* (obtains nourishment by eating other organisms or parts of organisms), *motile* (capable of self-propelled movement), and they digest food in an internal chamber.

Almost all animals utilize some form of sexual reproduction by means of specialized reproductive cells—eggs (*ova*) and sperm. These cells fuse to form a single fertilized cell, called a *zygote*, which then divides many times to produce the millions of cells in a fully formed organism.

Unlike plants, which draw energy directly from sunlight, most animals grow by indirect use of sunlight. Animals eat plants (or other animals who have eaten plants), which have previously converted the energy of sunlight into chemical energy stored in a type of sugar called glucose. When an animal eats a plant, the sugars produced by the plant are broken down by the animal and used to help the animal grow or move. This process is known as *glycolysis*.

There are around 9 to 10 million species within kingdom animalia, divided into two major categories: invertebrates and vertebrates. About 90 percent of the world's animals are invertebrates—creatures that lack a spinal column, such as worms, mollusks, and insects. Vertebrates, which do have a spinal column or backbone, include fish, birds, amphibians, reptiles, and mammals.

◆**Invertebrates**

Sponges Species of phylum Porifera are simple multicellular organisms that spend their lives anchored to a rock or the ocean floor. They are mostly saltwater marine animals, but some species live in freshwater. Sponges have a radial symmetry with a cylindrical, globular, or irregular body. The body contains an internal skeleton of minute spicules.

Jellyfish and corals Members of phylum Cnidaria, which also includes hydroids and sea anemones, are marine and freshwater animals that have a radial symmetry with two distinct body forms: a solitary or colonial polyp and a bell-shaped, free-swimming medusa. Both types are typically fringed and have stinging tentacles with rows of "stinging cells" called cnidoblasts.

Segmented worms The annelids, phylum Annelida, have fine bristlelike *setae* on each segment that are used for locomotion. There are more than 10,000 terrestrial, marine, and freshwater species of annelids among its three classes: clamworms, earthworms, and leeches.

Mollusks Species of phylum Mollusca have a mantle, which is a fold of skin usually lining a shell, as well as a muscular foot used for motion. In many mollusks, the mantle produces a calcium carbonate external shell. There is a wide variety of species, more than 250,000 in all, including bivalves (clams, mussels, and oysters among others), snails, slugs, squid, and octopuses. They are found in virtually all freshwater, saltwater, and land habitats.

Arthropods Phylum Arthropoda is the largest animal phylum; more than 80 percent of all discovered animal species are in this phylum. The body is composed of a head, thorax, and abdomen, with three or more pairs of jointed legs. All body parts are covered by a hard exoskeleton, which the arthropod sheds when it molts. Major classes of arthropods include crustaceans (including shrimp, crabs, and barnacles), insects, centipedes, millipedes, spiders and ticks, and horseshoe crabs.

◆Vertebrates

Fish The most ancient vertebrates, fish, live in aquatic habitats, from pools and streams to oceans. They are built to move and breathe in water: all breathe through gills, have fins, and most have streamlined bodies. Beyond these similarities, however, fish are extremely diverse, and are categorized into three classes. In class Agnatha, which includes lampreys and hagfish, members are characterized by the presence of a notochord (flexible, rod-shaped body), seven or more paired gill pouches, and the absence of jaws or paired fins. Cartilaginous fishes in class Chondrichthyes, such as sharks and rays, are jawed fishes with paired fins, paired nostrils, two-chambered hearts, scales, and skeletons of cartilage rather than bone. Bony fishes (class Osteichthyes) are characterized by a pattern of cranial bones, rooted teeth, and mandibular muscle in the lower jaw. The head and pectoral girdles are covered with large dermal bones; the fin is supported with bony fin rays, and even the eyeball is supported by a ring of four small bones. All species have a lung or swim bladder. Sardines, salmon, tuna, bass, and swordfish are among the more than 29,000 species of bony fishes.

Amphibians Class Amphibia consists of four-legged vertebrates that are cold-blooded, spend at least part of the time on land, and have eggs that lack a membranous sac. Most amphibians are bound to freshwater for reproduction. Amphibian eggs hatch into larvae (tadpoles or polliwogs) that breathe with exterior gills. The larvae undergo a gradual metamorphosis into the adult, replacing the gills with lungs and developing other distinct body parts—eyelids and eardrums, for example. In frogs and toads, the tail of the tadpole also disappears. Approximately 6,000 species of amphibians exist today, including frogs and toads, salamanders, and caecilians.

Reptiles Like birds and mammals, members of class Reptilia are amniotes (animals whose embryos are surrounded by an amniotic membrane). Reptiles are thick-skinned and, unlike amphibians, do not need to absorb water. Most modern species of reptiles do not generate enough heat to maintain a constant body temperature and are thus referred to as *ectothermic* (cold-blooded). Instead, they rely on gathering and losing heat from the environment to regulate their internal temperature— moving between sun and shade, for example. Except for a few species of turtles and tortoises, reptiles are covered by scales. Most species are *oviparous* (egg-laying) and have closed circulation via a three-chamber heart. All reptiles, even aquatic species, use lungs to breathe. The approximately 7,950 species are grouped into four orders: Crocodilia (crocodiles, alligators, and caimans), Squamata (lizards, snakes, and amphisbaenids), Testudines (turtles and tortoises), and Sphenodontia (tuataras).

Birds The class Aves includes all bird species—bipedal, warm-blooded, *oviparous* (egg-laying) vertebrates that have feathers, wings, and (in most cases) hollow bones. Common characteristics include a beak with no teeth, the laying of hard-shelled eggs, a high metabolic rate, a four-chambered heart, and a light but strong skeleton. Most, but not all, birds are capable of flight. Birds range in size from tiny hummingbirds to huge ostriches and emus. There are approximately 10,000 living species.

Mammals Members of class Mammalia are characterized by the production of milk in females (lactation). Most mammals also have hair or fur, specialized teeth adapted for tearing or grinding, three small bones within the ear, and a neocortex region in the brain. Mammals are also *endothermic* (warm-blooded). Most mammals have seven bones in the neck, called cervical vertebrae. The mammalian heart has four chambers, including left and right atria (to receive blood) and ventricles (to pump blood to the lungs and body). Most mammals give birth to live young and are terrestrial in nature, although some are aquatic (such as dolphins and whales) or semi-aquatic (seals).

Mammals are organized into two major subclasses: egg-laying monotremes, such as platypuses and echidnas, and live-bearing mammals. Approximately 5,800 mammalian species have been identified, including *Homo sapiens*, the human being.

◆**Primatology** Human beings belong to the order Primates. There are about 235 species of primates, classified into two major groups: prosimians and anthropoids.

Prosimians are primitive primates, such as lemurs, pottos, and galagos. These are small- to medium-sized mammals with pointed muzzles and well-developed senses of smell and hearing. Most are nocturnal.

Anthropoids include humans, monkeys, baboons, and apes. Most have flat faces and a relatively poor sense of smell. With few exceptions, anthropoids are most active during the day.

Primates evolved from tree-dwelling ancestors, and all primates share features related to this ancestry. These include arms and legs that move more freely than those of other mammals, flexible fingers and toes, forward-facing eyes, and large brains. Nearly all primates have a full set of five fingers or toes on each limb. In many primates, the thumbs and big toes are opposable, permitting them to meet the other digits at the tips. This enables primates to grip branches, as well as pick up and handle small objects. Compared with most other mammals, primates have relatively few young. The gestational period is relatively long, as is the length of time it takes for offspring to develop. Primates have a relatively long childhood—most extreme in humans—which enables complex patterns of behavior to be passed on by means of learning.

Primates have the most highly developed brains in the animal kingdom, rivaled only by those of dolphins and whales. In particular, anthropoid primates are intelligent, inquisitive, and quick to learn new patterns of behavior. This increased brainpower not only helps primates to move about and forage for food, but also to develop social skills. Most primate species are social animals, living in groups with a defined social order.

Day 2: The Kingdoms of Life

In 2009, scientists announced the discovery of a bizarre species of fish that has lush tan and peach stripes and that bounces along the sea floor like a fist-sized rubber ball. It did not resemble any other known species of fish, and scientists were unsure what to call it. Scientists give all organisms both common and Latin names to describe their appearance and their taxonomical classification, but before a newly found organism can be named it must be successfully categorized, usually by appearance or structure. In this case, scientists were unsure whether they had found a completely new sort of fish. After studying the anatomy and DNA of this Indonesian fish, they concluded that it is closely related to frogfish of the genus *Histiophryne*. Because of its wild behavior and coloring, it was named *Histiophryne psychedelica*.

In naming the fish, the scientists used a system of *taxonomy* (scientific classification) invented in the 1700s by the Swedish botanist Carolus Linnaeus. The forerunner of Linnaeus's taxonomy was developed by Aristotle, who broadly classified animals by their characteristics and first used the terms *genus* and *species*, though his work was eventually forgotten. In Linnaeus's era, researchers around the world collected more and more different types of organisms, but no uniform system for naming them existed. Some biologists gave species long, awkward names, and different biologists commonly referred to the same organism by different names. The lack of a universal naming convention became a serious hindrance to biological study.

Linnaeus organized animals and plants on the basis of natural characteristics into a hierarchy comprising (from widest to narrowest): *kingdom, phylum, class, order, family, genus,* and *species*. Each level in the hierarchy groups similar organisms by increasingly fine degrees of differentiation. The smallest unit in the system is the species, in which members are nearly identical in genetic makeup, physical structure, and behavior. Linnaeus also developed the binomial naming system, in which each organism is referred to by genus and species, e. g. the lion is referred to as *Panthera leo*.

In Linnaeus's day, all organisms were classified in either the plant or animal kingdom, but as biologists learned more about organisms, they recognized that many are neither plant nor animal. The number of kingdoms was gradually expanded, and then a top level, *domain*, was added to the taxonomy. Today, there are three domains: Prokarya, Archaea, and Eukarya.

◆**Three Domains of Organisms** Scientists believe that the original life forms to evolve were Archaea and that early in history the Prokarya separated from them. At a later date, the Eukarya also evolved out of the Archaea.

Some "organisms" such as viruses, however, are neither living nor nonliving. Viruses are described as pseudo-living, and there is ongoing debate whether they should be placed somewhere in the taxonomy. Currently, viruses are categorized in one of two ways, either by their own taxonomic system, which includes order, family, subfamily, genus, and species, or by organizing them into one of seven groups according to the presence of DNA or RNA and their method of replication.

Domain Prokarya Discovered in the 17th century following the invention of the microscope, prokaryotes are better known by their common name, "bacteria." Bacteria resemble unicellular organisms in the domain Eukarya, but do not have a cell nucleus or any other membrane-bound organelles. Unlike similar organisms in domain Archaea, they have the sugar-polypeptide compound peptidoglycan in their outer walls. Bacteria are ubiquitous and live in almost every type of environment (there are more bacteria in your mouth than there are people on Earth). The group, which in some classification schemes is called Monera, includes both *autotrophs* (which produce their own food) and *heterotrophs* (which depend directly or indirectly on autotrophs for food).

Domain Archaea Discovered in the 20th century, archaea look like bacteria but are genetically different. As with bacteria, an archaeote's genetic material is not contained within a nucleus and there are no other membrane-bound organelles. Unlike bacteria, archaea lack peptidoglycan in the outer wall. Also, the composition and assembly of *flagella* (filaments that extend from the organism and that are used in propulsion) differ in the two groups. Archaea were once believed to live almost exclusively in extremely inhospitable environments such as hot springs and deep-sea hydrothermal vents, but they have since been discovered in almost every environment.

Domain Eukarya First classified by the ancient Greeks, eukaryotes include all unicellular, filamentous, colonial, and multicellular species; domain Eukarya encompasses everything from amoebas to humans. Eukaryotes are identified by the presence of genetic material contained within a cell nucleus delineated by a nuclear membrane, and also by the presence of additional membrane-bound organelles. There are four kingdoms in this domain: protista, fungi, plantae, and animalia.

Kingdom protista contains the simplest eukaryotes. Most are one-celled, but some species are colonial or multicellular. The algae are autotrophs; other protists—such as amoeba and paramecium—are heterotrophs. Protists live mainly in aquatic habitats.

Kingdom fungi consists of both one-celled and multicellular heterotrophs with cell walls made of chitin. They reproduce asexually by spores and sexually by conjugation. Among the best-known fungi are yeasts, bread molds, mushrooms, and puffballs.

Kingdom plantae—the plants—are multicellular autotrophs that carry out the food-making process called photosynthesis. The cells contain a large central vacuole and have walls made of cellulose. Most species live in terrestrial habitats.

Kingdom animalia—the animals—are multicellular heterotrophs, obtaining nourishment by eating other organisms or parts of organisms and digesting food in an internal chamber. Their cells do not have cell walls. Animals are capable of self-propelled movement. Some are aquatic organisms, others live strictly on land, and still others depend on both aquatic and terrestrial habitats.

◆**Kingdom plantae**   Plant species are classified by phylum based largely on three characteristics: tissue structure, seed structure, and stature. Most plants contain vascular tissue—xylem and phloem—which transports fluids. Some types of plants have naked seeds, some have covered seeds, and some do not have seeds but reproduce by spores (reproductive cells capable of reproducing without fusion with another reproductive cell). Kingdom plantae is divided into 12 phyla, which are more commonly organized into five major groups: mosses, ferns, conifers, flowering monocots, and flowering dicots.

Mosses   Mosses, liverworts, and hornworts, of the three phyla, are the only plants that lack a vascular structure for the internal transportation of fluids and nutrients. Instead, they rely on moisture from the surrounding environment. Most are small plants that thrive in moist conditions, and they reproduce by means of spores.

Ferns The category fern includes several distinct phyla—ferns, horsetails, club mosses, and whisk ferns—and totals approximately 15,000 species. They are vascular plants that transport fluids through their stem structures and reproduce by means of spores.

Conifers Slightly more evolved than ferns, conifers reproduce by means of seeds instead of spores. The seeds, however, are "naked"—not covered by an ovary. In most conifers, the seed is produced inside a conelike structure, such as a pinecone. Conifers typically have needle- or scale-like leaves with no flowers. Conifers make up the phylum Gymnospermae ("naked seed"); related phyla include maidenhair trees, cycads, and herb-like cone-bearing plants.

Flowering Monocots Monocotyledonae, a class of the phylum Angiospermophyta, are flowering plants that have a single seed leaf. There are around 30,000 monocot species, including grasses, orchids, lilies, irises, and palms. Grain-producing plants are also monocots, including wheat, oats, and corn; fruits such as dates and bananas are part of this class as well.

Flowering Dicots The vast majority of plants—some 200,000 species—make up class Dicotyledonae in the phylum Angiospermophyta. The class includes most trees, shrubs, vines, flowers, fruits, vegetables, and legumes. Their seeds grow inside an ovary, which is embedded in a flower. After the seed is fertilized, the flower falls away and the ovary swells to become a fruit. Dicots grow two seed leaves.

♦**Organisms of the Past** Scientists believe that in the early millennia of life on Earth, the variety and number of living species was vast. The earliest organisms were simple bacteria-like organisms that existed perhaps as early as 3.5 billion years ago. The fossilized organisms of widest appeal are dinosaurs, land-dwelling reptiles that evolved from reptiles called thecodonts about 225 million years ago. Scientists have named approximately 700 species of dinosaurs. The smallest was *Compsognathus longipes*, a chicken-sized dinosaur that lived about 145 million years ago. Among the heaviest was brachiosaur, which lived about 150 million years ago and weighed as much as 70 to 90 tons. The longest may have been seismosaurus, a long-necked plant eater that lived 150 million years ago and reached lengths of more than 130 feet (39 meters).

Dinosaurs are classified in two groups: Ornithischia and Saurischia. Ornithischia, or bird-hipped dinosaurs, had pelvic bones arranged like those of a bird hip, with the pubic bone bent backward. They were plant eaters with hooklike claws. This group included the duck-billed hadrosaurs, plated stegosaurids, beaked ceratopsians, and long-snouted iguanodontids.

The second group were the Saurischia, or lizard-hipped dinosaurs. Their pelvic bones were arranged like those of a lizard hip, with the pubic bone pointing forward. There were two main subgroups: Theropoda were agile hunters and included Tyrannosaurus rex, velociraptor, allosaurus, and the ancestors of modern birds; Sauropodomorpha, such as bronchiosaurus, were plant eaters with massive bodies, long tails, and front legs smaller than back legs.

Dinosaurs became extinct around 65 million years ago during a mass extinction known as the Cretaceous-Tertiary or K/T event. Scientists believe this event resulted from the collision of an asteroid with Earth, on the northwest coastline of the Yucatán Peninsula in Mexico. A crater 106 miles (170 kilometers) across formed, shooting billions of tons of matter into the atmosphere, which blotted out the Sun, caused global temperatures to plummet, plants to die, and food supplies to shrink.

Weekend 32: The Jazz Age and New Deal

Day 1: The Roaring Twenties

With the departure of Woodrow Wilson from the White House in March 1921, a new era in U.S. history began when Warren Harding, a Republican from Ohio, was inaugurated as the nation's new president. Harding's election signaled an end to the Progressive Era. He promised what he called a "return to normalcy" after the years of dramatic cultural, social, and political change that followed America's entry into World War I. Harding's campaign suggested that Americans wished to return to another time in their history, before the dizzying changes of the 20th century. Progressive Era reforms had expanded the vote to women, created greater government regulation of private industry, and stitched together the primitive beginnings of a social safety net. Harding's election indicated that Americans were tired of idealistic campaigns designed to change the world and their nation.

Although America fought on the victorious side in World War I, the immediate postwar years were a time of disillusionment in the United States. After years of steady economic growth, the country's economy fell into recession during 1920 and early 1921. Nearly 20 percent of American workers were jobless, and prices for basic consumer goods soared. Wilson's attorney general, A. Mitchell Palmer, stoked fears of a Bolshevik revolution in the U.S. and ordered the arrest of thousands of people suspected of communist sympathies. Isolationists in Congress blocked American participation in President Wilson's pet project, a League of Nations designed to arbitrate international disputes and reduce the chances of another catastrophic, global war.

Harding's policies of tax cuts, less government regulation, tighter restrictions on immigration, and a balanced budget helped create exuberance on Wall Street and prosperity on Main Street, giving the decade the moniker "The Roaring Twenties." Income taxes for the wealthy were drastically reduced, from a top rate of over 70 percent to just about 25 percent by the middle of the decade. Credit was easy, luring even the middle class to speculate in a stock market that seemed to know only one direction—up.

Americans celebrated the accumulation of wealth and the pursuit of material rewards, but unlike conditions in the Gilded Age, prosperity appeared to be more evenly distributed. People of modest means could afford the miracles of the age—cars, radios, a night at the movies. Increased leisure time allowed Americans to indulge in spectator sports, especially baseball, boxing, and college football. Nightclubs and dance halls did brisk business as many Americans, particularly in the nation's cities, flouted the 18th Amendment, which outlawed the manufacture and sale of alcoholic beverages. During Prohibition, organized crime flourished in response to demand for illegal whiskey, wine, and beer, and criminals who provided the goods, like Al Capone of Chicago, became quasi-celebrities.

Warren Harding died of a heart attack in 1923 at the age of 57. When he died, the administration that promised a return to stability was on the verge of collapse, as close presidential aides were implicated in a scheme to distribute oil drilling rights on federal land. Although Harding himself was not involved in what became known as the Teapot Dome scandal, his legacy was tainted, and his administration is considered one of the most corrupt in presidential history.

Vice President Calvin Coolidge, a terse, flinty former governor of Massachusetts, took Harding's place and presided over five years of widespread economic expansion. His administration did its best to keep out of the way of the roaring marketplace. His embrace of the status quo earned him an easy victory over John W. Davis, the candidate of a bitterly divided Democratic Party, in the 1924 presidential election.

Coolidge's election may have signaled satisfaction with business as usual, but the poll numbers were deceiving. The status quo was being challenged, especially in the nation's growing cities. Nowhere were these conflicts more visible than in New York City during the 1924 Democratic National Convention, which became a proving ground of the decade's cultural wars. An emerging Democratic power base of urban ethnics, mostly the descendants of Irish immigrants, fought a prolonged battle with Southern conservative Democrats over the participation of the Ku Klux Klan in the party, and in the party's future course. The urban Democrats were determined to nominate New York's governor, Alfred E. Smith, an Irish-Catholic product of the Tammany Hall machine, while old-school rural southerners supported William McAdoo, Woodrow Wilson's son-in-law. Smith opposed Prohibition, and was urban, Catholic, and of immigrant stock. Any one of those attributes would have made him anathema to the party's traditional Southern base. Neither side would yield; they fought bitterly over a proposal to formally condemn the K.K.K. After 103 ballots, the exhausted and demoralized delegates approved Davis, a lawyer, as a compromise presidential candidate.

During the 1920s, American cultural archetypes became more clearly defined as novelists created masterpieces such as F. Scott Fitzgerald's *The Great Gatsby* and Sinclair Lewis's *Babbitt*, which explored the shallowness and emptiness of the age's relentless pursuit of materialist wealth. The journalist H. L. Mencken became a national figure with his biting critique of the emerging American middle class, which he wrote off as the "booboise." Other writers, like Gertrude Stein, John dos Passos, and Ernest Hemingway, moved to Europe, in part to escape what they saw as the mindless materialism of their fellow Americans.

While conformity and frivolity were prominent in mainstream society, something altogether different was taking place in Harlem nightclubs, Democratic clubhouses, vaudeville dance halls, and urban sports arenas, far from the centers of commerce and cultural conformity. In those places, culture, fashion, power, and mores were challenged as young Americans began to shed the values of the late 19th century.

Evidence of disharmony amid the decade's prosperity was clear in the debates leading to the passage of a new, more restrictive immigration law in 1924. Just 32 years after a new immigration processing center opened on Ellis Island in New York, the national consensus on immigration broke down, leading Congress and Coolidge to close the nation's doors to newcomers. Asians were expressly prohibited from entering the country, while quotas severely limited European immigration. Immigrants were associated with radical ideas, including socialism.

Meanwhile, young women shed the corsets of their mothers' generation and adopted the "flapper" look—which showed off bare arms and legs—as they took possession of their sexuality as well as their new voting rights. Seeking to escape the prying eyes of their families, they flocked to dance halls where the foxtrot and the Charleston were popular. They spent evenings at the movies watching Rudolph Valentino, Mary Pickford, Greta Garbo, and Charlie Chaplin. Women also began entering colleges in record numbers, challenging the traditional notion that their place was in the home.

314 The Jazz Age and New Deal

African Americans in the South struggled to resist segregation laws passed, ironically, by Progressives in the late 19th and early 20th centuries. In the North, blacks popularized the distinctly American art form of jazz, while writers such as Langston Hughes explored the meaning of race in America at a time when members of the K.K.K. marched unchallenged through the streets of Washington, D.C. Even athletes contributed to the collapse of traditional values. While the golfer Bobby Jones exemplified old Victorian standards of modesty and fair play, baseball slugger Babe Ruth challenged the image of the hero-athlete. With his unabashed appetite, his off-the-field exploits, and his individual achievements, Ruth symbolized the new age of consumption, celebrity, and self-promotion.

Ruth may have been, pound for pound, the biggest celebrity of the age, but he was not the most celebrated. That title belonged to the aviator Charles Lindbergh, who became the first pilot to fly solo across the Atlantic Ocean, starting on Long Island on May 20, 1927, and landing in Paris the following day. "Lucky Lindy," was accorded a hero's welcome upon his return, saluted with the latest symbol of American hero-worship, a ticker-tape parade on Broadway in Lower Manhattan.

Americans from all walks of life followed the exploits of athletes, whose public profiles were raised through the new mass medium of radio, and through the explosion of mass circulation magazines and newspapers. The boxer Jack Dempsey, tennis stars Helen Willis and Bill Tilden, football coach Knute Rockne of the University of Notre Dame, and running back Red Grange of the University of Illinois transcended the games they played and became icons of American popular culture. In 1927, the New York Yankees won the World Series with a team still regarded as one of the best, if not the best, in baseball history. Led by Ruth and Lou Gehrig, the '27 Yankees remain a touchstone of American sports history, the standard by which all championship teams are measured.

These were the years associated with Coolidge and prosperity—indeed the two were intimately connected in the minds of many Americans. But as a new presidential election approached in 1928, Coolidge decided not to run for reelection. Republicans rallied behind the candidacy of Herbert Hoover, who had been secretary of commerce under both Harding and Coolidge. Hoover had gained an international reputation after World War I, when he oversaw massive efforts to feed and clothe millions of war refugees in Europe. Progressive, well-traveled, and thoughtful, Hoover was more of a successor to Theodore Roosevelt and William Howard Taft than a legatee of Harding and Coolidge. He represented change without threatening the prosperous status quo.

Democrats, on the other hand, chose to break precedent by selecting Al Smith as their candidate to face Hoover. Smith became the first Catholic to win a major party's presidential nomination, and he did so without serious opposition in his own party. Smith's nomination spoke to the party's transformation from a Southern-based, Prohibition-supporting, rural party to an urban, ethnic, working-class, wet (anti-Prohibition) party. While Smith was no radical, he supported increased government regulation and spoke as the champion of immigrants and the urban poor. Not surprisingly, given the nation's mood, Hoover soundly defeated Smith, even capturing the Democrat's home state of New York.

In a collection of short stories about life among the affluent in the 1920s, F. Scott Fitzgerald coined the phrase "Jazz Age" to describe the frantic energy of the time. Hoover's election was a sign that there was no stopping the music, that the good times would spill into the 1930s.

However, only a year later, in late October 1929, the stock market collapsed after several days of frantic sell-offs. More than $30 billion in assets were wiped out in a week. Small-time investors who dabbled in the market with borrowed money on the assumption that their stocks would only increase in value were wiped out. But so were larger and presumably more savvy investors. While stocks rallied briefly in the spring of 1930, it was only the illusion of recovery. The Dow Jones index had closed at 260 on Oct. 28, 1929; on July 8, 1932, it closed at 41.22.

Day 2: The Great Depression and New Deal

It was the worst economic catastrophe in the nation's history and the beginning of the Great Depression. The 1929 Wall Street crash brought a sudden end to the Roaring Twenties, and, eventually, to the presidency of Herbert Hoover. As the product of Progressive Era politics, Hoover believed government had a role to play in the conservation of natural resources, the protection of women and children, and the development of modern infrastructure, including the power grid. As director of postwar relief in Europe, he led an effort to address global human suffering.

When faced with the unprecedented economic meltdown, however, Hoover was overwhelmed. He believed at first that the stock market crash would lead to a short recession, just another bust in the boom-and-bust cycle of capitalism. He told a group of business leaders in May 1930 that the worst was over. In reality, it was hardly beginning. Banks began to fall by the hundreds, wiping out the savings of their depositors. In 1930, 25,000 businesses failed. Sales of consumer goods plunged. Unemployment rose to double digits and would top out at 25 percent. In some of the hardest-hit cities, nearly half of the workforce was unemployed. Millions of people took shelter in freight cars; others, evicted from their homes, lived in ramshackle communities called "Hoovervilles."

Despite being capable of addressing the blight overseas, Hoover seemed incapable of cleaning up the economic disaster at home. He believed in a balanced budget and was skeptical of calls for massive government relief projects. More than anything else, he was by nature dour and uncharismatic, hardly the sort of figure to rally the country in hard times.

Meanwhile in Albany, New York, there was an ambitious Democratic politician who spent most of his waking hours in a wheelchair—a man who had persevered in the face of an illness that might well have ended the ambitions of another, less determined figure. Franklin Delano Roosevelt was narrowly elected as governor of New York in 1928, but re-elected handily in 1930. In 1932, he set his sights on the White House. He had no ideological agenda, at least none that he articulated during his campaign. Nonetheless, he desperately wished to be president, and he saw in Hoover a very beatable opponent.

Campaigning not as a radical reformer but as a more engaged alternative to the incumbent, Roosevelt projected optimism and a can-do spirit, symbolized by his campaign theme song, "Happy Days Are Here Again." The glum, pessimistic Hoover helped seal his own fate in June 1932 when he forced the removal of jobless World War I veterans who had set up camps in Washington, demanding early payment of special bonus money due in 1945. Troops under the command of General Douglas MacArthur used tanks and bayonets to rout the veterans in a violent display that shocked millions of Americans and spoke to Hoover's cold response to the economic catastrophe. In November, Roosevelt won the presidency with 472 electoral votes to Hoover's 59.

In his inaugural address on March 4, 1933, Roosevelt famously told

Americans that the "only thing to fear is fear itself." There was no short-age of fear on that cold, gray morning in Washington. Four thousand more banks failed in January and February, wiping out more depositors. Panic-stricken Americans rushed to the banks that remained in busi-ness, hoping to withdraw their savings while they still could. Roosevelt, in one of his first actions as president, ordered a bank holiday, closing the nation's financial institutions until the panic subsided. He explained his actions on the night of March 12, 1933, in a nationwide radio address—the first of Roosevelt's famous "fireside chats." Those intimate speeches changed the relationship between the president and the American peo-ple. Radio allowed the president to bypass the print press and speak di-rectly to his constituents, a technique that every president since Roosevelt has favored.

The first 100 days of Roosevelt's administration set another prece-dent for quick and decisive action—and while he spoke bitterly about the failures of "money changers," his measures were not directed exclu-sively at those whom he blamed for the reckless speculation of the Roar-ing Twenties. He cut pensions for veterans and the salaries of federal employees. He accelerated the repeal of Prohibition. He began the cre-ation of new federal programs, starting with the Civilian Conservation Corps, which provided employment and helped conserve natural re-sources, as well as the Tennessee Valley Authority, which provided elec-trical power to the rural South. He tightened regulation of the banking industry and created price supports for farmers with the Agricultural Adjustment Act. While the economic prognosis continued to remain bleak, the flurry of activity in spring and summer of 1933 lifted the na-tion's spirits and laid the groundwork for further government action.

Americans did not look solely to Washington for a respite from their suffering. Radio, one of the miracles of the age, offered comedy, music, news reports, and so-called soap operas (mid-afternoon melodramas de-signed for a female audience and sponsored by soap companies), pro-viding a temporary distraction from unemployment and despair. Comedians who had honed their craft in vaudeville gained massive au-diences, especially Fred Allen, Jack Benny, George Burns and Gracie Allen, and Bob Hope. Hollywood transitioned from the silent movies of the Roaring Twenties to "talkies," and later experimented with color photography in the 1939 blockbusters *Gone With the Wind* and *The Wiz-*

ard of Oz. The Depression years also saw an astonishing burst of creativity in Hollywood from directors and actors whose performances created a body of work still thought of as Hollywood's golden age.

Spectator sports, particularly major league baseball, retained an important place in popular culture. Fans flocked to see stars like Joe DiMaggio, Ted Williams, and others, who replaced the fading stars of the Jazz Age. The boxer Joe Louis and Olympic champion Babe Didrickson were pioneers for African-American and women athletes, respectively.

In Washington, the Roosevelt administration drew up plans for immediate relief and for a more permanent social safety net that would greatly expand government's role in the social and economic spheres of American life. The National Recovery Administration (N.R.A.) was launched in 1933 to regulate and coordinate prices, work conditions, production, and other aspects of industrial life. While it seemed an extraordinary departure from traditional American laissez-faire economics, the N.R.A. was a variation on Woodrow Wilson's attempts to coordinate government and industry during World War I. While the N.R.A. eventually was declared unconstitutional and disbanded, other aggressive new programs were thrown together to provide short-term relief for the jobless through public works projects. The Civil Works Administration put 4 million people to work during the winter of 1933–34. The Public Works Administration spent $3.3 billion between 1933 and 1935 on projects such as sewage treatment plants, bridges, and hospitals. These programs were collectively known as the "New Deal."

Even with these efforts, however, millions were without work. Unemployment was more than 20 percent when voters went to the polls in the midterm election of 1934 to deliver a smashing victory for New Deal Democrats in Congress. Roosevelt took the election returns as a sign of public confidence in his bold new course. During the next two years, F.D.R. unveiled a new, more coordinated jobs plan known as the Works Progress Administration. The W.P.A. employed ditch diggers, carpenters, playwrights, and artists to build new schools and court buildings, stage performances of Shakespeare, and decorate the walls of firehouses and city halls throughout the nation. Designed to provide work for 3.5 million people, the W.P.A. built thousands of new structures and created a model for government spending projects all over the world.

While these programs were short-term fixes, Roosevelt had his mind on the long term as well. During the final two years of his first term, he signed the Social Security Act, which gave workers over 65 a guaranteed pension; the National Labor Relations Act, which gave federal protection to labor unions wishing to bargain collectively with employers; and new tax legislation that increased the rate for the nation's highest earners to 75 percent. The Securities and Exchange Commission was given the task of overseeing Wall Street's activities, and the Federal Deposit Insurance Corporation protected bank deposits in case of failure.

The breadth of F.D.R.'s agenda provoked bitter reactions from both the right and left. The Louisiana senator Huey Long introduced his own, more radical proposals for a new economic order, calling it "Share Our Wealth." A Roman Catholic priest named Charles Coughlin used his popular radio show to denounce F.D.R. (after supporting him at first) as a would-be dictator, incorporating virulent, anti-Semitic rhetoric in his attacks. A new organization called the Liberty League opposed what it saw as socialism creeping into the White House. But the most significant opposition to F.D.R.'s agenda came from the Supreme Court, which ruled in 1935 that the N.R.A.'s regulations were unconstitutional be-cause they regulated interstate commerce, and, the Court ruled, only Congress had that power.

Roosevelt lashed out at his foes en route to a landslide victory over Republican Alfred E. Landon in the 1936 presidential election, telling the nation that he knew his critics hated him, and, he said, he "wel-comed" their hatred. He sought a measure of revenge in his new term, proposing to expand the membership of the Supreme Court to allow for more sympathetic adjudication of further New Deal legislation. The public and even other Democrats criticized the audacious power grab, which hurt F.D.R.'s image, but retirements on the bench soon allowed him to build a friendlier court all the same.

In his second inaugural address, Roosevelt sought to remind the na-tion that even after four years of tremendous reform and effort directed by the federal government, the nation remained mired in a brutal eco-nomic malaise. "I see millions of families trying to live on incomes so meager that the pall of family disaster hangs over them day by day," he said. "I see one-third of the nation ill-housed, ill-clad, ill-nourished."

Many families remained that way deep into the 1930s, despite Wash-ington's unprecedented interventions. (Some conservative scholars continue to argue that the Depression lingered because of, not in spite of, Roosevelt's efforts.) By the spring of 1937, not long after F.D.R.'s second inauguration, the unemployment rate was about 14 percent, the lowest since the Depression started. The true figure might have been even lower, because workers on W.P.A. projects were still counted as unemployed. Roosevelt saw this success as an opportunity to retrench—he ordered a series of spending cuts, reducing the federal deficit from $2.7 billion in 1937 to $740 million in 1938. The impact was almost immediate: economic growth came to a halt, and 2 million people were thrown out of work in four months, spiking unemployment to near 20 percent. Production of steel fell from 80 percent of capacity to just 19 percent, and the Dow Jones index fell by 40 percent. By April 1938, with commentators referring to a "Roosevelt Recession," the president ordered $3.4 billion in new spending to prime the economy.

The New Deal still had some energy left. The Fair Labor Standards Act, the last major piece of New Deal legislation, established a minimum wage, set the work week at 40 hours, and mandated overtime pay for extra work. It became law in spring 1938, though historians agree that the New Deal was running out of steam by the late 1930s as the global situation grew more ominous and F.D.R. turned his attention to international matters.

It would take World War II to return the nation to full employment. As late as 1940, the Republican presidential candidate Wendell Wilkie criticized Roosevelt for the New Deal's inability to cut the jobless rate to an acceptable percentage—it was still 17 percent in 1939. In the presidential election of 1940, F.D.R. nonetheless easily won an unprecedented third term. The national economy was beginning to feel the boosting effects of government orders for tanks, airplanes, ammunition, and other war material, which were shipped to Great Britain as part of F.D.R.'s Lend-Lease Act. The United States soon put an end to mass unemployment as a war boom brought factories to full capacity for the first time in more than a decade.

While Roosevelt made it clear after the Japanese attack on Pearl Harbor on December 7, 1941, that his first goal was to win the war, he still promised to continue dramatic reform once that was accomplished. His G.I. Bill of Rights offered historic federal benefits to veterans upon their return from service. Neither he nor the New Deal, however, survived the war.

Weekend 33: English Poetry: An Overview

Day 1: From *Beowulf* to *Paradise Lost*

The earliest English poetry (written in Anglo-Saxon) celebrates the heroic deeds of kings and warriors in the period between the arrival of the Angles and Saxons in the fifth century A.D. and their conversion to Christianity in the seventh century. But this poetry does not survive in original form. The earliest recorded poems (from the second half of the seventh century) are written, like all Old English poetry, in alliterative verse form, in which sounds at the beginnings of words are repeated in each line. Some are secular paeans to kings, such as "Widstith;" others, including the nine-line "Caedmon's Hymn," are early examples of a centuries-long tradition of English Christian devotional poems. Caedmon, a Northumbrian monk, (ca. 658–80) is the first known English poet. "The Dream of the Rood" (ca. 700), in which the rood, or Christ's cross, describes its experience to the dreamer, is considered the best example of the Anglo-Saxon devotional poem. While it is often ascribed to the early English poet, Cynewulf, there is doubt as to whether he is actually its author.

Beowulf is the finest example of the Old English heroic epic, a narrative verse form depicting the deeds of a valorous hero. Written in the eighth century by an unknown author, it is set in Scandinavia and tells the story of Beowulf, who comes to the aid of his neighbors, the Danes, who are besieged by the water monster, Grendel, and his mother. Beowulf slays both Grendel and Grendel's mother after all others have failed. The epic is overlaid with Christian elements, including a judging God and a biblical lineage for the monster Grendel, but remains a celebration of courage and honor, the virtues of a harsh, pre-Christian heroic age. Later examples of heroic poems include the "Battle of Maldon" and the "Battle of Brunanburgh" (both undated).

Middle English poetry first flourished in the 14th century, although some short lyrical poems, poems of an emotionally expressive nature, appeared as early as the 12th and 13th centuries. So, too, did lyrical ballads, mostly anonymous, which were popular into the 15th century. Among these lyrics, which have themes of nature (especially of springtime), love, and Christian piety, are "The Cuckoo Song" and "Westron Wind." Numerous short ballads—narrative verse meant to be sung or spoken aloud—such as "Barbara Allen," "Lord Randall," and "Sir Patrick Spens," appeared from about 1200 to 1700.

Three other forms rose to prominence in the Middle English period. The *romance*, a narrative in which knights and other characters of chivalry are the main actors, is exemplified by *Sir Gawain and the Green Knight* (ca. 1380–1400), the story of a brave knight who must defend the honor of King Arthur and his court after its invasion by the mysterious Green Knight. The *elegy*, a poem of mourning written to commemorate the death of a person and often used as a meditation on death or life, is exemplified by *The Pearl* (ca. 1360), believed to have been occasioned by the death of the poet's daughter. The *allegory*, in which virtues or states of being are represented as persons or other objective forms, is exemplified by *Piers Plowman* (ca. 1362), which may have been written, or partly written, by William Langland, of whom little is known. The poem is an account of the Plowman's dream vision of the history of Christianity and its current, somewhat corrupted, state.

♦**Geoffrey Chaucer**   Considered the first great English poet, Geoffrey Chaucer was a Londoner who wrote in a Middle English dialect. His *Canterbury Tales*, which he began in 1386, is a narrative cycle told by 22 richly varied travelers brought together on a religious pilgrimage. It is one of the greatest works of English literature—ribald and comic in parts, yet profound and vivid in its portrayal of medieval life and character. Although Chaucer never completed this work, it develops unity and artistic resonance from the interplay among the characters, and through their tendency to respond to the stories of others in their own stories. Chaucer's other poems include the love story *Troilus and Criseyde* and *The Parliament of Fowls*.

♦**The Tudor Period**   The era of Tudor England, which began in 1485 with the accession of King Henry VII and lasted through the death of Elizabeth I in 1603, saw a modernizing of the English language, allowing it to reflect the humanist ideas and images of the European Renaissance. Fittingly, the sonnet, the 14-line form first developed in Italy, began to carve a deep impression into English poetry of the 16th century. Nearly all sonnets were love poems, often expressing disappointment or despair. The earliest English practitioners were Thomas Wyatt and Henry

Howard, Earl of Surrey, who wrote the first sonnets with an "English" rhyme scheme, which arranged the poem in three four-line sections and one two-line section, rather than the Italian pattern of eight- and six-line sections. Howard also composed the first English blank verse, unrhymed 10-syllable lines with a regular meter, usually iambic pentameter (a set of an unstressed syllable followed by a stressed syllable, repeated five times). Philip Sidney produced a similarly patterned sequence of love sonnets, *Astrophel and Stella* (ca. 1580).

During the reign of Elizabeth I (1558–1603), there was a sudden outpouring of excellent poetry and drama that remains at the heart of the canon of English literature. The greatest nondramatic Elizabethan poet was Edmund Spenser, whose romantic and allegorical *Faerie Queene* (1590–96) is one of the finest English epics and stands apart from all other 16th-century narrative poetry. Its six books are each dedicated to a courtly virtue, and its strong ecclesiastical views mark it as the first masterly English Protestant poem. Among Spenser's innovations was the nine-line stanza that is named for him. He, too, wrote a sonnet sequence, *Amoretti* (1595).

The leading Elizabethan dramatists, Christopher Marlowe and, greatest of all English writers, William Shakespeare, were also significant lyric and narrative poets. Marlowe's *Hero and Leander* (1598) retold a classical Greek love story. Shakespeare used the Roman poet Ovid as the source of two narrative poems of his early career, the mythological *Venus and Adonis* (1593) and *The Rape of Lucrece* (1594). His 154-sonnet sequence, written in the 1590s and addressed to both a young man and a woman, is the crown of that Elizabethan tradition. (See Weekend 21, "William Shakespeare.")

♦**The Metaphysical Poets**   The turn of the 17th century brought with it the reign of James I (1603–25) and introduced two new traditions in English poetry that would endure until the century's end: the Metaphysical style originated by John Donne, and the Cavalier style, embraced by the followers of Ben Jonson. John Donne created a poetry of intellectual and spiritual reaching, which in a later period was labeled "metaphysical." Donne's poetry was witty and sometimes abrupt in manner, allowing content to take precedence over form. Within his poetry, he made unusual imagistic and intellectual connections. Donne, a clergyman, wrote beautiful religious poetry including the *Holy Sonnets*, but his equally trenchant poems of physical love would inspire others who wrote in this tradition.

Other poets of the Metaphysical school included George Herbert, who approached God with more certainty than Donne, but with similar leaps of imagery. In poems such as "Easter Wings" (1633) and "The Altar" (1633), he arranged the lines on the page such that they took the shape of his subject. Richard Crashaw, a convert to Catholicism, was influenced by Italian poetry and wrote idiosyncratic, baroque, passionately devotional verse that incorporated notably Italian Catholic flesh-and-blood images.

♦**The Cavalier Poets**   Ben Jonson wrote spare, smooth lines modeled on classical poetry that are in striking contrast to those of the Metaphysical poets. Jonson's poems included satires, a celebrated tribute to a great house ("To Penshurst,"1616), and a powerful memorial to Shakespeare. But it was his lyrics addressed to women, notably "To Celia," published in 1616 ("Drink to me only with thine eyes") that influenced the casual yet polished style of the Cavalier poets. In addition to being a poet, Jonson was also a leading Jacobean playwright.

The term *Cavalier* refers to supporters of Charles I, the king beheaded in 1649 during Oliver Cromwell's Puritan Revolution, eight years after Jonson's death. The Cavalier poets modeled their work on the classical beauty of Jonson's verse. The first and finest of the Cavalier poets, Robert Herrick, was one of a group of Jonson's companions and admirers who called themselves "Sons of Ben." Herrick's lyrics, mainly short and sometimes programmatic, were often concerned with the natural things and the females that delighted him. These two subjects were often addressed in the same poem: "To the Virgins, to Make Much of Time" ("Gather ye rosebuds while ye may"); or "Corinna's Going-A-Maying." These direct addresses to women, as well as urges to "seize the day" (*carpe diem*), were repeated by later Cavalier poets. The greatest *carpe diem* poem, "To His Coy Mistress," was composed by Andrew Marvell, who wrote in both the Cavalier and Metaphysical traditions. A creator of lyrics, odes, and dialogues that married playful wit with deep significance, he has been called England's most important minor poet.

♦**John Milton** is considered one of the greatest English poets, as well as a political and religious activist and tract writer. He lived through the execution of King Charles I, Oliver Cromwell's Protectorate (for which he served as foreign secretary) and the restoration of the monarchy with King Charles II. Milton was married twice, and twice made a widower, with three daughters from his first wife surviving into adulthood. His strained marriage with his first wife led to his controversial pamphlets in favor of divorce. His tract on censorship, *Areopagitica* (1644), anticipated modern views opposing government supervision of what could be printed. Blind after 1651, he wrote some of the finest English sonnets as well as the long paired poems, *L'Allegro* and *Il Pensoroso* (1645). His towering stature rests on the long, biblically-based poems of his later years: the epics *Paradise Lost* (1667) and *Paradise Regained* (1671).

Paradise Lost is written entirely in blank verse. It begins with an invocation to a muse—a nod to classical Greek and Latin epics. Grappling with themes of predestination versus free will, Milton retells the story of humankind's original sin, embellishing heavily on the book of Genesis and relating a richly detailed story involving Satan's own estrangement from Heaven. Milton's complex and compelling portrayal of Satan is considered one of the first literary portrayals of an antihero.

The narrative begins in Hell, where Satan, once a glorious member of God's coterie, and his followers have been banished after rebelling against God. They plot revenge with a scheme to sabotage God's beloved new creations: Earth and humankind. Satan travels to Earth, meeting his offspring, Sin and Death, on the journey. God sees Satan's approach and predicts that humankind will fall from grace. God's Son offers himself as a sacrifice in their place.

Satan deceives the archangel Uriel into ushering him into Paradise, where Adam and Eve share an idyllic existence. Satan overhears Adam reiterating to Eve that God has forbidden them to eat fruit from the Tree of Knowledge. Uriel realizes his error and warns the other archangels of the imposter. Satan is discovered and evicted from Eden. God sends the archangel Raphael to caution Adam and Eve, reminding them that their own free will determines their destiny. Satan slips back into Paradise, disguised as a serpent. Finding Eve alone, he convinces her to partake from the Tree of Knowledge. Adam is horrified, but decides to join her in mutual doom. Lust is the first manifestation of their fall from God's favor. God's Son comes to Earth and tells Adam and Eve that the consequences of their disobedience will be a life of pain, toil, and eventual death. Satan returns to Hell, expecting to celebrate, but he and his followers are turned into serpents. Adam and Eve bicker, but resolve to survive by loving each other and serving God. God sends the archangel Michael to cast Adam and Eve out of Paradise. Michael shows Adam a vision of humankind's future, which will be plagued with sin and grief, but Adam also sees that God's Son will someday provide redemption. Adam and Eve sadly leave Paradise to begin an uncertain future.

Paradise Lost is considered the definitive epic poem of the English language. *Paradise Regained*, the counterpart to *Paradise Lost*, is a brief epic poem dramatizing Jesus as the epitome of Christian heroism, with a Job-like ability to constantly reaffirm faith in God and resist temptation while enduring increasingly difficult trials. The poem is structured as a series of arguments in which Satan unsuccessfully tries to tempt Jesus. Milton drew inspiration for the poem from the Book of Job and from the accounts of Jesus' temptations in the wilderness in the Gospels of Matthew and Luke.

Day 2: English Poetry: Romantics and Victorians

In the Romantic period, the focus of poetry moved away from society, toward nature and the individual expression of inner feelings. Arising in the wake of the French Revolution, Romanticism tilted to the political left, embraced nationalistic yearnings, and expressed rebellious impulses. Its poets reached beyond 18th-century restraints to commune with realities and absolute principles, such as love, beauty, and truth, which existed outside the boundaries of everyday life.

William Blake, a visionary poet-artist who, wrote both lyrics (*Songs of Innocence*, 1789; and *Songs of Experience*, 1794) and long prophetic and narrative poems. Blake was characteristically Romantic in his deep concern for economic oppression, as well as in his simple diction and use of symbolism. He is viewed as both a political revolutionary and a religious mystic. His prophetic poems include "Marriage of Heaven and Hell" (ca. 1793) and "America" (1793).

The year 1798 (marking the publication of William Wordsworth and Samuel Taylor Coleridge's collaborative effort, *Lyrical Ballads*) remains a boundary line for the Romantic movement. In a manifesto-like preface to the second edition of *Lyrical Ballads* (1800), William Wordsworth explicitly separated poetry's future from its neoclassical past, prescribing that poems should deal with "common life" in "language really used by men," and pronouncing poetry to be "the spontaneous overflow of powerful feelings." Wordsworth grew up in the English Lake District, the beauty of which inspired his poetic career. With simple diction, he described humble people and celebrated nature. Wordsworth's output includes short lyric poems, meditative odes such as "Tintern Abbey" and "Intimations of Immortality," and long poems, including the masterly, autobiographical *The Prelude*, completed in 1805 but published posthumously.

Samuel Taylor Coleridge is best known for narrative poems tinged by supernatural effects, particularly "The Rime of the Ancient Mariner," which was published in *Lyrical Ballads*, as well as "Kublai Khan" and "Cristabel," both published in 1816. He also excelled in writing more sober, meditative poems such as "Frost at Midnight" (1798) and "Dejection: An Ode" (1802). His output was constricted by physical suffering and opium addiction.

The relative brevity of the Romantic era was caused in part by the early deaths of three of its greatest poets of the second generation, George Gordon (better known as Lord Byron), Percy Bysshe Shelley, and John Keats. The eldest of these, Byron, was a notorious lover who had affairs with more than 200 women, including his half sister, and several men. He was an enormously popular writer in his own time, regarded most notably for his long narrative and satirical poems, *Childe Harold's Pilgrimage*, (1812–18) and *Don Juan* (1819–24). His "Byronic hero," the individualistic, iconoclastic immoralist, appears definitively in his tragedy *Manfred* (1817). He died in Greece at age 36 while training troops for the country's war of independence.

Shelley was a more philosophical poet who believed in the transforming power of love. Born to wealth, he was attracted to nonconformity and radical causes. He was a composer of lyrics and politically inflected poems such as "Ode to the West Wind," and his advocacy of the Romantic impulse to overcome human limitations is well expressed in the title of his great versedrama, *Prometheus Unbound* (1820), which offers the possibility of humanity's moral triumph over evil. He eloped with Mary Wollstonecraft Godwin (best known as the author of *Frankenstein*) in 1814, fleeing to France, then Italy, where he created his finest works before drowning at the age of 30.

John Keats was a poet of sensuous and emotional experience to whom life was "a vale of soul-making." He pronounced, in "Ode on a Grecian Urn," (1819) the quintessentially Romantic sentence: "Beauty is truth,

truth beauty." Yet his beautiful works also expressed the sadness that accompanies human yearning. Keats produced more great writing in a comparably brief period than any other English poet. Important early poems included "On First Looking into Chapman's Homer" and *Endymion*. In 1819, poor, sickly, and unhappily in love, he wrote an astonishing series of superior poems, including his six great odes, published in *Lamia, Isabella, The Eve of St. Agnes and Other Poems*. He also composed some of the finest English sonnets and two aborted, but celebrated "epics," *Hyperion* and *The Fall of Hyperion*. In melodious, exquisitely sensuous, beautifully phrased verse, Keats expressed the tension between the richness and sadness of physical and emotional experience. He died in 1821 at the age of 26, believing his work would never survive.

Sir Walter Scott, a Scotsman who achieved distinction as a novelist and as a narrative lyric poet, is also considered a Romantic poet. Like other Romantics, including Keats, Scott sometimes reached into the medieval past for his themes, which informed his first full-length narrative poem, *The Lay of the Last Minstrel* (1805), and his most successful poetic work, *The Lady of the Lake* (1810).

•**The Victorian Age** During the long reign of Queen Victoria, from 1837 to 1901, England was transformed into the most vigorous industrial, capitalist society ever known, and its empire gained its farthest reach. It was an age in which the population began to shift from the country to the cities, and the advance of science encroached on the ground of religious certainty. These matters roiled the poetic imagination and diversified poetic points of view.

During the Victorian age, religion was subject to experimentation, renunciation, and doubt. The dominant, longest-lived poet of the period, Alfred, Lord Tennyson, absorbed, early in his career, the age's uncertainty about material and scientific progress. Tennyson, racked by the early death of his best friend, expressed his melancholy and longing for faith in his first successful volume of poems, and later, in an extended elegy for that friend, *In Memoriam A.H.H.* (1850). Tennyson embraced faith in God and the afterlife. He found further assurance in his country's distant past, most thoroughly explored in his epic *Idylls of the King* (1859–62).

Faith and doubt were also pervasive issues for Victorian poets Robert Browning and Matthew Arnold. As a young man, Browning made the transition from atheism to belief, and he has often been misconstrued as having harbored a Pollyanna-ish certainty that, as he once wrote, "God's in his heaven/All's right with the world." In fact, he was a writer of psychological depth, keenly aware of human corruption and fully conscious of the implications of Darwin's science, whose belief in a transcendent God was buffeted from many sides. Although Arnold wrote two renowned pastoral poems, "The Scholar Gipsy" (1853) and "Thyrsis" (1865), he is considered the emblematic Victorian poet of doubt and alienation, particularly for his most famous poem, "Dover Beach" (1867), in which he spoke hauntingly of an "eternal note of sadness."

Between Tennyson and Browning, particularly, there is an obvious difference of poetic style. While Tennyson wrote within the great tradition of fluid and sonorous English verse, Browning's diction was more colloquial, his rhythms less regular, and his poetic modes more experimental, all of which traits appear in his brilliant dramatic monologues, such as "My Last Duchess" (1842). Both styles had disciples. Dante Gabriel Rossetti, for example, leader of the "Pre-Raphaelite" artistic-poetic movement (which advocated an earlier, simpler style of painting than was prevalent at the time) was a poet of rich color and smooth meter. His sister, Christina Rossetti, was a lyrical poet of strong religious sensibility. Browning's wife, Elizabeth Barrett Browning, was best known for an extended series of love sonnets, including *Sonnets from the Portuguese* (1850). Edward FitzGerald translated and revised the *Rubaiyat of Omar Khayyam* (1857–59), a selection of poems by a 12th-century Persian poet; his version, recognized for its polished beauty, quickly gained great popularity. Algernon Charles Swinburne, a Pre-Raphaelite in his early career, later became entranced by the sound of words and metrical experiment.

◆**Late Victorian and Early 20th–Century Poetry** In late Victorian times, a number of strains ran independently through English poetry. In the 1890s, one of the great novelists of the second half of the 19th century, Thomas Hardy, brought his dark but compassionate vision to the writing of lyric poetry, and over the next 30 years he developed into a major poet. He wrote poetry of plain language but stark power, including *Wessex Poems and Other Verses*, a selection of 51 poems set against the bleak Dorset landscape so often featured in his novels. In the same decade, A.E. Housman, a famous classics scholar, published a wistful and classically spare volume of lyrics, *A Shropshire Lad* (1896).

The term *decadent* refers to a school of writing, most popular in France, but present in England as well, in which art took precedence over nature. The Decadents produced poems that rejected Victorian convention and reflected the somewhat antisocial ideal of "art for art's sake." The two most important poets of the British Decadent movement were Oscar Wilde and Ernest Dowson. Dowson, the iconic English Decadent, was a sonorous, incantatory poet who characteristically expressed the loss of love, youth, and beauty, as well as a weariness with life that may have contributed to his dissipation and early death. Oscar Wilde, whose novel *The Picture of Dorian Gray* exemplifies the Decadent school's preoccupation with art and decay, looked back to the work of the Pre-Raphaelites as a model for his verse, which includes *The Ballad of Reading Gaol* (1897).

The most influential poet of the Victorian age, the Jesuit priest Gerard Manley Hopkins, is often not considered a Victorian at all. Because of his extraordinary break with the poetic traditions of his era, and because he was not published until 1918, long after his death, he is instead often grouped among poets of the 20th century. His originality included the development of an irregular "sprung" meter in which poetic feet of varying syllables are used in an attempt to mirror the rhythms of prose, a style that changed poetic rhythm; a precise diction that was partly invented; and the extensive, forceful use of alliteration.

Hopkins's verse is at times bright and at times somber. He is considered one of the language's most powerful religious poets. Like many of his predecessors, he was a master of the sonnet. Some of his best-known poems are "The Wreck of the Deutschland" (1876), "God's Grandeur" (1877), and "Pied Beauty" (1877).

◆**The End of the Victorian Age**   World War I had a profound influence on the direction of English poetry. Rudyard Kipling's patriotic poems, featuring stoically virtuous troops in India and other distant places, gave way to palpable expressions of combat experience by England's World War I poets. One of these, Rupert Brooke (1877–1915), still sang patriotically, "There's some corner of a foreign field/That is forever England;" but others, such as Wilfred Owen (1893–1918); "Anthem for Doomed Youth"), Siegfried Sassoon (1886–1967), and Isaac Rosenberg (1890–1918), wrote with darker realism and increasing bitterness. Their vivid lines, like the Great War itself, delivered a decisive finish to Victorian times.

Weekend 34: Great American Writers

Day 1: American Prose

The first serious prose work of the American colonies was William Bradford's *Of Plymouth Plantation*, a nonfiction work that told the story of the Mayflower voyage and the Pilgrims' arrival in Massachusetts. Early Colonial literature like this was usually religious in nature, but with the arrival of the Enlightenment movement of the 18th century, American literature turned toward rational and scientific concerns. Public figures such as Benjamin Franklin, Thomas Paine, and Thomas Jefferson were major contributors to the literature of the American Revolution. The novel also became a popular idiom in America at this time, especially the seduction narratives of Hannah Webster Foster, Susanna Haswell Rowson, and Charles Brockden Brown.

After the American Revolution, writers rushed to distinguish themselves from their European ancestors and to define a distinct American literary style. In the early 19th century, the novelists Washington Irving and James Fenimore Cooper furnished portraits of American lands and struggles. Irving's short story "Rip Van Winkle" (1819), which tells the story of a man from the Catskill Mountains who sleeps for 20 years and awakes confused, was a metaphor for rapidly changing life in America following the Revolution: if a citizen slept too long, he would run the risk of waking to an unrecognizable country. Cooper's series *Leatherstocking Tales* (which included *The Last of the Mohicans* in 1826) were popular adventure stories about the hazards and glories of westward expansion.

Because of the rapid progress occurring in all art forms, including literary arts, the period from 1830 to 1865 is referred to as the "American Renaissance." Influenced by European Romanticism, Transcendentalism of the mid-19th century brought European aesthetics to New World subject matter. Transcendentalism was a movement that encouraged individuals to overcome the physical trappings and societal dictates of modern life by attaining a higher spiritual level and personal relationship with God through interaction with nature. Transcendentalists rejected sin as the defining characteristic of humanity, instead embracing optimism, self-reliance, and a simpler, more spiritual existence.

◆**Transcendentalism** Transcendentalism was championed in the essays and nonfiction works of Ralph Waldo Emerson and Henry David Thoreau, both residents of Concord, Massachusetts. Considered the leader of the movement, Emerson encouraged a truly American style of literature, rejected traditional Christianity, and proposed that God is best accessed through an individual's interaction with nature. He was labeled an atheist and a poisoner of minds after giving the controversial "Divinity School Address" at the Harvard Divinity School graduation in 1838, for which he was banned from the school for 30 years. As a founding member of the Transcendental Club, he cofounded a periodical called *The Dial,* which featured other Transcendentalist thinkers. Emerson's most famous works include the essays "Nature" (1836) and "Self-Reliance" (1841).

Emerson's close friend, Henry David Thoreau, is the author of *Walden* (1854), which described the two years (1845–47) he spent in solitude as a young man in a self-made cabin by Walden Pond on the outskirts of Concord. In *Walden,* Thoreau advocates a spiritually exuberant but materially spartan and self-reliant life in nature. Thoreau rejected what he saw as the materialistic values of the changing world, and instead sought a more spiritual life by stripping away all excess. In 1849, he published "Civil Disobedience," an essay urging readers to peacefully resist and strive to improve their governments rather than submit to injustice. The essay was motivated by his opposition to slavery and the Mexican-American War and later inspired activists such as Mahatma Gandhi and Dr. Martin Luther King Jr.

Amos Bronson Alcott, another well-known Transcendentalist figure, was a close friend of Emerson and Thoreau and the father of Louisa May Alcott, author of *Little Women* (1868). One of the most popular works of children's literature ever published, the novel was loosely based on her experiences growing up with her three sisters in Concord, Massachusetts. Alcott was a feminist, and, like her father, an abolitionist. She was memorialized as "the children's friend" at her funeral.

◆**American Romantics** Like their Transcendentalist peers, the American Romantics (or "Dark" Romantics) of the mid-19th century embraced the aesthetics of European Romanticism, focusing on the emotional and psychological experience of the individual, and placing a high spiritual value on nature. However, their work was tinged with cynicism, partially a reaction against the optimism of the Transcendentalist movement. Edgar Allan Poe, Nathaniel Hawthorne, and Herman Melville explored the evil side of human nature, and the mystery and decay of the physical world.

Poe left his mark on the short story through his contributions to the American Gothic, a style of Romantic literature dealing with the realm of the supernatural. "The Fall of the House of Usher" (1839) tells the story of a woman, buried alive by her brother, who scratches her way out of her tomb; "The Tell-tale Heart" (1843) follows a narrator who kills a man, hides his dismembered body under the floorboards, and is haunted by the sound of his victim's beating heart. Poe's stories are the progenitors of modern-day horror and science fiction, and he is also widely regarded as one of the creators of the detective genre for tales such as "The Murders in the Rue Morgue" (1841).

Like Poe, the novelist and short story writer Nathaniel Hawthorne explored the toll of sin and guilt, as well as the role of the individual in society. His 1835 short story "Young Goodman Brown" follows a Puritan man in Salem, Massachusetts, who is forever disturbed after journeying into the dark forest and discovering what appears to be a witchcraft ceremony led by his neighbors. In 1850, Hawthorne published his most influential work, *The Scarlet Letter*, which tells the story of a Puritan woman shunned by her community and forced to wear a scarlet letter A on her chest as punishment for adultery.

Herman Melville's fiction draws on his adventures as a young sailor, and his early stories were heavily influenced by the European Romantic literature he grew up reading. In *Moby-Dick; or, the Whale* (1851), Melville infused an adventure narrative on a whaling ship with themes of isolation, obsession, and revenge. Beginning with one of the best-known opening lines in the English language—"Call me Ishmael."—the novel follows narrator Ishmael as he takes a job on a whaling ship with Captain Ahab, a Quaker consumed with the desire to find and kill Moby Dick, the fearsome white whale that had devoured his leg.

While many of the American Romantics and Transcendentalists

were outspoken abolitionists, abolitionist literature is more closely associated with Harriet Beecher Stowe's inflammatory novel *Uncle Tom's Cabin* (1851) and Frederick Douglass's slave narrative *Narrative of the Life of Frederick Douglass, an American Slave: Written by Himself* (1845). The sentimental nature of Stowe's prose made it accessible to a public hungry for domestic fiction; in 1851, *Uncle Tom's Cabin* sold a million copies within the year, an unprecedented literary success in the United States.

♦**Naturalism** After the Civil War, naturalism, which originated in Europe, depicted the chaos of modern life with rational, Darwin-inspired objectivity. Coming of age in the heyday of muckraking journalism, fiction writers reported on the conditions of the disadvantaged. Upton Sinclair uncovered the atrocities of the meatpacking industry in *The Jungle* (1906), and Theodore Dreiser took on the plight of the working-class immigrant in *Sister Carrie* (1900) and *An American Tragedy* (1925). Stephen Crane also explored the immigrant experience in *Maggie: A Girl of the Streets* (1893), and he changed the genre of war writing with *The Red Badge of Courage* (1895).

♦**Realism** Another group of writers known as realists attempted to capture the human condition, but instead of focusing solely on suffering and chaos, they sought to portray the immediate present, the verifiable fact, and the search for truth. With roots in journalism, Ohio-born William Dean Howells was best known for *The Rise of Silas Lapham* (1885). New York's Henry James focused on the interactions between wealthy Americans and Europeans. His psychological stories make unique use of interior monologue and point of view, with unreliable narrators usually destined for failure. His most famous works include *The Portrait of a Lady* (1881), *The Turn of the Screw* (1898), and *The Wings of the Dove* (1902). James's protégée Edith Wharton shared his fascination with the social elite. She crafted chilling and illuminating portraits of the social order in the United States, most notably in *The House of Mirth* (1905), *Ethan Frome* (1911), and *The Age of Innocence* (1919).

The realist Mark Twain (the pen name of Samuel Clemens) began his writing career as a journalist. Consequently, his work is characterized by unflinching honesty, attention to detail (including regional vernacular), and social satire. Following *The Adventures of Tom Sawyer* (1876), which was based on his own childhood on the Mississippi River, Twain achieved fame and notoriety for his *Adventures of Huckleberry Finn* (1884). Huck Finn, an adventurous and free-spirited adolescent from Missouri, rafts down the Mississippi River with Jim, a runaway slave desperate to escape to the North. The book has been frequently banned in schools and libraries since the year of its publication for both its frank language and depictions of slavery.

The California novelist Jack London wrote frontier fiction set in the icy landscape of the Klondike. His experience as a young man in the Klondike Gold Rush inspired the short story "To Build a Fire" (1902), in which a man desperately attempts to create a fire in order to stay alive. London's best-known novels, *The Call of the Wild* (1903) and *White Fang* (1906), are also set there. Sherwood Anderson explored the quiet desolation of small-town, midwestern life in his short story cycle *Winesburg, Ohio* (1919), and Willa Cather depicted frontier life on the prairies of the Great Plains in *O, Pioneers!* (1913) and *My Antonía* (1918).

♦**The Harlem Renaissance** By the 1920s, the Harlem neighborhood of New York City had become a mecca for African-American writers and musicians. An artistic movement known as the Harlem Renaissance changed the face of music, art, and literature, especially for America's burgeoning black population. Writers contributing during this era included Nella Larsen, author of *Passing* (1929), and Zora Neale Hurston, best known for her 1937 novel, *Their Eyes Were Watching God*. They gave a voice to the African-American experience, paving the way for writers like Richard Wright, Chester Himes, and James Baldwin, who depicted the racial struggles of the civil rights era, as well as present-day authors Maya Angelou, Alice Walker, and Toni Morrison.

♦**American Fiction Since 1920** During the 1920s, many American intellectuals and writers, including Ernest Hemingway and F. Scott Fitzgerald, sought refuge in Europe from what they saw as a culturally impoverished, socially repressive United States. Gertrude Stein, an American writer living in France, hosted many of these expatriates, dubbing them the "lost generation." Hemingway fictionalized their lives in his short stories and novels, including *The Sun Also Rises* (1926) and *For Whom the Bells Tolls* (1940), using his journalistic style of direct statement and concrete detail. Fitzgerald gave a voice to the libertine lost generation in *The Great Gatsby* (1925), the story of Jay Gatsby, a rags-to-riches "Roaring 20s" success story with a mysterious past. Fitzgerald later fictionalized his own life in *Tender Is the Night* (1934).

Meanwhile, southern author William Faulkner introduced stream-of-consciousness narration in his novel *The Sound and the Fury* (1929), which uses multiple points of view to depict the decay of a once-proud Mississippi family whose wealth and status have eroded. Faulkner's other well-known works include *As I Lay Dying* (1930), *Light in August* (1932), and *Absalom, Absalom!* (1937). Experiences as a manual laborer enabled John Steinbeck to authentically relate the struggles of the destitute migrant workers of 1930s California in *The Grapes of Wrath* (1939), the story of a dispossessed farm family that flees the Dust Bowl for a new life in California during the Great Depression. The voice of the disenfranchised, he is also remembered for *Of Mice and Men* (1937) and *East of Eden* (1952).

After World War II, a group of writers called the Beats rejected the conservative, postwar lifestyle and its literature which by that time had become mainstream. Instead, these writers chose to explore uncensored, spontaneous self-expression. Jack Kerouac defined this distinctly American group of artists as capable of a certain "beatitude" through altered states induced by drugs, sex, jazz, and Eastern philosophy. His book *On the Road* (1957), considered the quintessential Beat novel, depicts his adventures with fellows Beats Neal Cassady and Allen Ginsberg.

The American coming-of-age novel became a standard approach for writers over the next two decades. *The Catcher in the Rye* (1951) by J. D. (Jerome David) Salinger is the most famous work in this style. Saul Bellow, who won the Nobel Prize in 1976, had his first major success in this genre with *The Adventures of Augie March* (1953). His later novels, *Henderson the Rain King* (1959) and *Mr. Sammler's Planet* (1970) also became part of the American literary canon. So too did the works of the great writer and Russian émigré Vladimir Nabokov (notably 1955's *Lolita* and 1962's *Pale Fire*). The strange, powerful stories of Flannery O'Connor were first published in *A Good Man Is Hard to Find* (1955) and posthumously in *Everything That Rises Must Converge* (1965), securing her place in the American canon after her premature death in 1964. John Updike's tetralogy about the life of Harry "Rabbit" Angstrom, *Rabbit Run* (1960), *Rabbit Redux* (1971), *Rabbit is Rich* (1981), and *Rabbit at Rest* (1990) captured the common man's experience over three decades.

Day 2: American Poetry

In 1647, Anne Bradstreet, who came to the New World with John Winthrop, the Massachusetts Bay Colony's first governor, earned the distinction of being the first colonist to publish a book of poetry. Bradstreet's poetry is reflective of her life as a Puritan woman, focusing on domestic and religious themes. Her most famous poem, "To My Dear and Loving Husband," was published posthumously in 1678, and begins with the well-known line, "If ever two were one, then surely we." Later, the poet and former slave Phillis Wheatley earned the distinction of becoming the first published African American.

In the early 19th century, the Massachusetts-born poet William Cullen Bryant, inspired by the pre-Romantic poetry of William Wordsworth, wrote "Thanatopsis." Largely composed in 1811 when Bryant was 17, the poem praised nature as divine and inspired the Transcendentalists Ralph Waldo Emerson and Henry David Thoreau, and later, Walt Whitman. Bryant is also remembered for his poem "To a Waterfowl." Henry Wadsworth Longfellow, also born in Massachusetts and a close friend of Washington Irving, is best known for "Evangeline" (1847), *The Song of Hiawatha*, (1855), and "Paul Revere's Ride" (1861). Longfellow wrote mostly lyric poems, emphasizing rhyming patterns, and his work was celebrated in his lifetime for its musicality. Rarely autobiographical in subject matter, Longfellow's poetry instead sought to impart moral values and often explored historical legend.

Walt Whitman is among the most influential and controversial of all American poets. Influenced by the Transcendentalists, but also incorporating the photographic quality of realism, Whitman celebrated the individual, nature, and the physical world. Breaking with the poetic conventions of rhyme and meter, he used free verse to illustrate the diversity of American life, describing subjects ranging from presidents to prostitutes. By the spring of 1885, Whitman had written enough poems in this new style for a small, but complete, volume. Unable to find a publisher, he sold a house and printed the first edition of *Leaves of Grass* at his own expense. Whitman continued to revise and re-release the collection throughout his life, publishing eight more editions. Along with possibly his most famous poem "Song of Myself," *Leaves of Grass* eventually included his famous elegy to the assassinated President Lincoln, "When Lilacs Last in the Dooryard Bloomed," which he wrote upon returning from his post as a Civil War army nurse. *Leaves of Grass* is widely recognized as the most comprehensive single expression of America's democratic ideals, diverse population, and varied landscape. While Whitman became famous as the "good gray poet," he was also considered highly controversial. Under charges of obscenity, he was fired from a government position, in part due to homosexual overtones in the work, and his publisher rejected later editions of *Leaves of Grass*. Whitman himself disclaimed homosexual interpretations of his poetry, but this aspect of his life and work is commonly accepted today.

Although Emily Dickinson seldom left her Amherst, Massachusetts, home after the age of 30, she sustained a number of correspondences through numerous letters and continued to read Emerson and other Transcendentalist and Romantic poetry and prose, making spiritual and careful observations of nature in her poems. Her witty, epigrammatic style is also reminiscent of the 17th-century English Metaphysical poets, whom she admired, and her use of unlikely and highly symbolic imagery, short lines, slant rhymes, and unconventional capitalization and punctuation anticipated 20th-century modern and postmodern trends. Only 10 of Emily Dickinson's nearly 1,800 poems are known to have been published in her lifetime, but upon her death in 1886, Dickinson's family discovered 40 hand-bound volumes of poems. Many did not have titles but have become known by the opening lines, such as, "I heard a fly buzz when I died," and by poem numbers that were assigned posthumously by her publisher.

Later in the 20th century, the New England poet Robert Frost continued the tradition of using rural scenes and deceptively simple verse to explore social and philosophical questions. His catchy and oft-quoted poems granted him immense popularity in his own lifetime, as well as four Pulitzer Prizes. His most famous poems include "The Road Not Taken" (1916) and "Stopping by Woods on a Snowy Evening" (1922).

The turn of the last century brought a change in the mood of the nation and its poets. The modernists, or the "lost generation" as they were often called, reflected their generation's disillusionment with a society affected by the upheavals of war and rapid technological advancement, as well as their breathless expectation of a radically different future. This group of poets attempted to "make it new," as Ezra Pound suggested, and did so through explorative use of imagery and unconventional poetic structure. In addition to writing his own extensive opus, *The Cantos*, Ezra Pound influenced many American poets, including T. S. Eliot. Eliot's poems "The Waste Land" (1922) and "The Love Song of J. Alfred Prufrock" (1915) are among the best-known works of modernist poetry. A five-part, 434-line poem, "The Waste Land" is a collage of fragments—myths, legends, symbols, overheard voices, and cultural illusions—some in other languages, that paints a melancholy image of turn-of-the-century life in London. Several pages of explanatory notes followed the poem.

William Carlos Williams, a poet and doctor who often composed in the minutes between his patients' appointments, chose to document the local and the humble (unlike his contemporaries) rather than the foreign and exotic. Using simple language and experimental meter and structure, he let the unadorned image speak. His most famous poem, "The Red Wheelbarrow" (1923), exemplifies the Imagist philosophy of "no ideas but in things," celebrating the importance of a wheelbarrow in 16 words. Other modernist American poets include Wallace Stevens, Hilda Doolittle (H. D.), Marianne Moore, and Carl Sandburg.

The Harlem Renaissance of early 20th-century New York produced culture and artistic expression from a population previously silenced under slavery and oppression. In the vitality of this environment, a number of talented African-American poets flourished, including Langston Hughes of "The Weary Blues" (1926), Claude McKay, Countee Cullen, and Jean Toomer.

Also centered in New York City, the Beats of the 1950s formed their

own generational counterculture and rejected the modernist literature that had become mainstream by that time. Although Beat poetry
employed open forms akin to the modernists' free verse and embraced
its rebellious and controversial nature, the Beats prized spontaneous
self-expression, whereas the Modernists favored a more crafted lyri-
cism. "Howl" (1956) by Allen Ginsberg, for example, seemingly blurts
out all aspects of the author's private life—sexual encounters, drug
experiments, episodes of mental illness—in incantatory Whit-
manesque catalogs. Later mid-century poets include Elizabeth Bishop,
Randall Jarrell, John Berryman, Robert Lowell, and Robert Penn Warren, the only person ever to have won Pulitzer Prizes for both fiction
and poetry.

◆**Poetry Since 1960** The postmodernism of the late 20th century is epitomized by the work of John Ashbery, who is most famous for
his 1975 poem "Self-Portrait in a Convex Mirror." Also, the last 50
years has seen the emergence of a wide variety of poets from every
corner of the American experience, including the African-American
women Gwendolyn Brooks and Maya Angelou. Donald Hall, Charles
Simic, Sylvia Plath, and Billy Collins have all brought a truly American sensibility and use of language to a genre in need of more public
recognition. In recent years, the popularity of poetry has significantly
decreased among the reading public and new generations raised on
television, video games, and the Internet. However, over the last few
decades, American poetry has found a new incarnation in the form of
spoken word and slam poetry, which is similar in sound to the musical
genre hip-hop. Slam poetry places a high value on performance and
the use of the human voice as a poetic device and is typically focused
on issues of politics, race, gender, and the urban condition.

Weekend 35: The Human Story

Day 1: Evolution: The Theory and the Evidence

Charles Darwin, the son of a wealthy British doctor, was sent as a young man to study medicine in Edinburgh, then to Cambridge to study for the ministry. There he came under the influence of scientists and naturalists who inspired new interests in him. After a few years, his tutors suggested that he sail on a navy ship to South America, Australia, and various islands (most notably the Gálapagos, off the coast of Ecuador) to study the flora and fauna there.

Darwin's five-year voyage (1831–37) aboard the HMS *Beagle* would not only change his life, but the very way in which we understand life itself. It was on this trip that he made his first fossil discoveries, witnessed a volcanic eruption, and absorbed the concept of "deep time" explored in the recently published *Principles of Geology* by Charles Lyell. Darwin observed special adaptations organisms had for obtaining food and avoiding predators. He reasoned that organisms evolved from simpler states through what he called "survival of the fittest." Over time, he wrote, "the result of this [natural selection] would be the formation of a new species."

In 1858, Darwin was still writing a book detailing his theory of evolution when a letter arrived from Alfred Russel Wallace, an English naturalist, describing a similar theory. A few months later, Darwin presented their collaborative work at a meeting of the Linnaean Society of London, and in 1859 Darwin published *On the Origin of Species*. All 1,250 copies of the first edition were sold in one day. Twelve years later, Darwin published a sequel, *The Descent of Man*, which described how his theory applied to humans. His books sparked a scientific revolution that has made the theory of evolution a central principle of the life sciences.

The implications of that theory have provoked rancorous debate ever since, particularly from religious groups who protest that it rejects biblical teachings about the creation of the universe and does not acknowledge any role for a divine creator. It may seem ironic, then, that the man most closely associated with evolution was himself raised in a religious home and school, and was very familiar with the Bible and with Christian beliefs. Despite numerous competing theories, public protests, and efforts to ban the teaching of evolution in schools, most scientists today believe that the evidence supporting evolution is overwhelming.

◆ The Evidence

The Fossil Record Scientists today are able to accurately date fossils, the rock-bound remains of organisms from past geologic ages. When fossils are arranged along a time line, scientists can see gradual changes from simple to more complex life forms. In some cases, evolution through various intermediate forms over millions of years can be detected and compared to the present state of an organism. For example, the earliest known species of horse lived some 60 million years ago and, according to the fossil record, was less than 20 inches (50 centimeters) high at the shoulders. Successive rock layers yield fossils of increasingly larger horse species, culminating in the horses of today. As size changed, so did other aspects of the horses' anatomy: teeth became adapted to eating grass, the bones of the lower leg fused, and multiple toes evolved into a single toe surrounded by a hoof.

Comparative anatomy Organisms that are closely related, such as mammals, share similar anatomical structures. For instance, although they are used very differently, a bat's wing, a dog's foreleg, a seal's flipper, and a human's arm are composed of the same bones arranged in similar ways. All these species have a humerus bone in the upper arm, radius and ulna in the lower arm, wrist carpals, hand metacarpals, and finger phalanges. Such homologous structures, scientists believe, are explained by common ancestry. In contrast, some organisms have analogous structures that look similar externally but have different internal structures. The wings of a bat, a buzzard, and a butterfly all have the same purpose, but they are completely different in origin.

Evolutionary theory can predict which anatomical mutations might occur and which will not. For instance, because birds evolved from reptiles some 150 million years after mammals, a mutant mammal with feathers is an impossibility. However, since whales evolved from legged mammals, it is possible for a whale to be born with limbs, as does indeed occur on rare occasions.

Comparative embryology Similarities in the earliest stages of development are also evidence of common ancestry. For example, early in their embryonic development, fish, chickens, and humans all have tails (as well as gill slits and other analogous structures). In the human embryo, most of the tail vertebrae normally disappear by the eighth week in a process called "programmed cell death." Four of the tail vertebrae remain; normally they fuse to form the irregular tapering bone called the coccyx at the distal end of the spine.

The human coccyx is an example of a vestigial organ—one that appears to serve no useful function but suggests a common ancestry with organisms in which the homologous structure is functional. The coccyx is homologous to the functional tail of other primates. Similarly, the eyes of blind cave-dwelling salamanders are homologous to those of related species that live in a world of light.

Genetics and comparative biochemistry   The strongest and most direct evidence of common descent comes from genetics, a field that did not exist in Darwin's time. All living things—from human beings to bacteria—have nucleic acids called DNA and RNA, hereditary material that directs the operation of cells. What's more, the DNA molecule has the same components in every species, and even uses the same codes to carry information. Scientists have tracked evolution at the molecular level in lab experiments with certain bacteria and viruses that reproduce and mutate rapidly, and conjecture that the same process has been at work for millennia in organisms that reproduce and mutate far more slowly.

Because organisms share the same genetic material, there's a biochemical similarity in their basic processes. For example, in all known species, proteins are built from the same 20 amino acids, even though there are about 250 naturally occurring amino acids. All *aerobic* (oxygen-breathing) organisms use cytochrome c, evidence that all of these different life forms descended from a common ancestor that used this compound for respiration. Additionally, the cytochrome of cows is more like ours than that of fish, suggesting that humans and cows are more closely related than are humans and fish.

Biogeography   When Darwin was in the Gálapagos he observed 13 species of finches spread out among the islands. Each population was slightly different: some had small, thin beaks and fed on small seeds; others had larger, thicker beaks that allowed them to eat the large seeds of their home island. He reasoned that populations of a species that are separated for a long period of time, when spread out among different environments, gradually evolve along different paths.

During Earth's history, the continents have slowly changed their relative positions as a result of plate tectonics (movement of pieces, or plates, of Earth's crust), but for millions of years, all the continents were joined together in a single landmass called Pangaea. Evidence of this includes fossils of a certain fern discovered in Africa, South America, Australia, and India; unless the continents were somehow joined, there is no way the fern could have spread. The fern's descendants, like other flora and fauna, either evolved to meet their changing environments or became extinct.

◆**Dating Fossils** The scientific study of fossils began in the 17th century when the Danish scientist Nicolaus Steno noted the similarity of a modern shark's teeth to certain stony objects embedded in rock. Fossils had until then been variously attributed to the inherent characteristics of the stone, celestial origins, or "serpent tongues." *On the Origin of Species* profoundly influenced paleontologists, who began looking for ancestors of modern organisms as well as "missing links"—intermediate, transitional forms between known species. The first such link, discovered in Germany in 1861, was *Archaeopteryx*, a primitive bird with characteristics of both its flightless reptile ancestors and modern birds.

Fossils left behind by organisms of the past come in two basic types: *body fossils*, the actual remains of organisms, and *trace fossils*, the marks made by the activities of ancient organisms, such as footprints, burrows, leaf imprints, and tooth marks. The age of a fossil may be determined either by comparing the layer of rock in which it is found to the layers above and beneath to give a relative age, or by a method called *amino acid racemization*. This method compares two forms of amino acids in a fossil: the L-form, (amino acids in living things) and the D-form (those in deceased organisms). At death, the L-form racemizes, or changes, into the D-Form at a more or less steady rate. The greater the extent of racemization, the older the fossil.

◆**Human Evolution** *Homo sapiens* are, of course, a distinct species, with our own evolutionary past. The *sapiens* species (under the genus *Homo*) branched off from our genetic cousins, the chimpanzees, some 5 to 7 million years ago. Several different species of the *Homo* genus (including *Homo erectus* and *Homo neandrathalensis*—more commonly known as Neanderthals) are thought to have evolved as well, but *sapi-*

ens is now the only nonextinct species of the genus. There is not yet a consensus on which of these groups should be counted as a separate species and which as the subspecies of another. The *Homo erectus*, which lived about 70,000 to 1.8 million years ago, is considered a human ancestor; it was the first species in the *Homo* genus to walk upright, the result of adaptive traits like locking knees. The Neanderthals, on the other hand, are most likely a separate species descended from a common ancestor.

There is evidence of skull expansion and stone tool technology development in the period between 400,000 to 250,000 years ago, which mark a transition from *Homo erectus* to *Homo sapiens*. Though it is a hotly debated subject, many scientists believe that this transition occurred first in Africa, and that *Homo sapiens* gradually migrated from that continent and came to replace other species of the *Homo* genus around the globe.

Day 2: Genetics: The Blueprint of Life

Genetics is the science of heredity, hereditary transmission, and variation of inherited characteristics in living organisms. Although only formally recognized as a branch of biology at the beginning of the 20th century, the study of human genetics has helped to decode the origins of physical traits such as eye and skin color, left- and right-handedness and, more recently, susceptibility to particular diseases. The science of genetics has also overturned many erroneous preconceptions about race and human nature.

In 2006, twin girls born in the U.K. made for a puzzling headline: they appeared to be of two different races. One girl, with fair skin and blond hair, appeared northern European, while her sister had dramatically darker skin and hair. Both of their parents had racially mixed ancestry, and the girls seemed to exhibit features belonging to neither parent. If the twins had been born a hundred years ago, something would have seemed amiss, even supernatural, but modern genetics provides an explanation. A child's skin color is determined by up to seven genes, and mixed-race parents supply genes for skin types of both races. The odds that two mothers' eggs—one carrying only the genes for "white" features and one carrying only the genes for "black" features—

would be fertilized by two sperm that were exact genetic matches are a thousand to one, unlikely but not impossible.

Modern genetics began with Johann Mendel, a priest, a scientist, and perhaps most important, a lifelong gardener. Born in 1822 in what was then the Austrian Empire, he was sent as a young man to an Augustinian abbey to pursue his studies. There he took the name Gregor and taught natural sciences to high school students. Encouraged by his professors and his fellow monks, he began to experiment with garden pea plants in the monastery garden. Through careful pollination techniques and statistical analysis of some 29,000 pea plants, he developed the first clear analysis of heredity. He demonstrated that an organism's characteristics are controlled by hereditary factors, and that these factors occur in pairs. Mendel published the results of his work in 1866, but his study was criticized and virtually ignored. In 1900, 16 years after his death, scientists working independently in three countries reached similar conclusions—and discovered that Mendel had beaten them by more than 30 years. His paper "Experiments in Plant Hybridization" is now considered a seminal work in the field.

◆**Patterns of Inheritance**   When Mendel crossbred his pea plants, he kept meticulous records of certain traits of parent plants (P generation) and of first and second offspring, or filial, generations (F1 and F2 generations). The theories he developed—the principles of segregation, dominance, and independent assortment— have since been proven and today are known as basic principles of heredity.

Principle of segregation   When Mendel crossbred two parent plants from strains that always bred true to type—for example, a tall plant and a short plant—he found that the F1 generation all resembled one parent; in this case, they all were tall. However, when he allowed a plant from the F1 generation to self-pollinate, its offspring (F2 generation) were not all tall, instead having a ratio of approximately one short plant for every three tall plants.

Mendel concluded that each plant possessed two inheritance factors for height. In parent plants, the two factors were alike (tall and tall, short and short), but the F1 plants were hybrid: the two factors for the trait were different. The two factors (one tall, one short) separated when the plant produced sex cells, and only one factor from each parent was passed on to the offspring.

Principle of dominance In pea plants, there are two genetic forms (called *alleles* today) that control height: tall and short. Mendel noted that one allele for a trait may be stronger than another, in this case the tall allele. He called this the "dominant" allele, and the weaker allele the "recessive" one. In *hybrids*, plants with one of each allele, the dominant allele takes precedence; therefore, hybrid plants will necessarily be tall.

Principle of independent assortment When Mendel tracked more than one trait, he found that each trait acted in accordance with the principle of segregation; one trait did not appear to have any influence on the other trait. He concluded that each trait segregates independently of the other traits.

•**After Mendel** In the 20th century, scientists in Europe and America unlocked further information about genetic structure. Later, it was discovered that the chromosome, a single piece of coiled DNA (deoxyribonucleic acid) and the proteins that control its function, contains many genes. Genes are the basic units of inheritance. The total complement of genes carried by any organism can be thought of as the "blueprint" for that organism, the map outlining all its characteristics. This blueprint, called a *genome*, is stored in one or more chromosomes. In 1956, a Swedish group of scientists proved that humans ordinarily possess 46 chromosomes.

A crucial breakthrough in the history of genetics came in 1953, when two British scientists, James Watson and Francis Crick, determined that the DNA molecule resembles a long, twisted ladder—a shape called a "double helix." It consists of repeating subunits called nucleotides composed of simple chemicals abbreviated A, T, G, and C. These letters combine to form information that a cell can "read" and copy in order to produce proteins. Human DNA consists of around 3 billion DNA letters.

A molecule of RNA, or ribonucleic acid, also is a chain of nucleotides. But unlike DNA, RNA (ribonucleic acid) is single-stranded, and the chemicals it contains are slightly different. RNA is synthesized under the instruction of DNA, one step in the process of making proteins. Also unlike DNA, RNA exists in several forms, the best known of which are the three forms involved in protein synthesis: messenger RNA (mRNA), ribosomal RNA (rRNA), and transfer RNA (tRNA).

◆**The Genetic Code and Protein Synthesis** Between 1961 and 1967, scientists from around the world cracked the genetic code, the sequence of nucleotides in a gene (the letters described above). It's a set of instructions needed by cells for protein synthesis, spelling out the sequence of amino acids in a particular protein. The basic unit of the genetic code is the codon, a sequence of three nucleotides on a DNA or mRNA molecule that codes for a specific amino acid. For example, chromosome 11 contains the code for hemoglobin: 444 DNA letters instruct cells how to make HBB (the hemoglobin gene).

The gene can be thought of as the template for the manufacture of mRNA. This process takes place in the nucleus. The mRNA leaves the nucleus and in the cytoplasm attaches to ribosomes (made partly of rRNA). Amino acids are brought to the ribosomes by tRNA. In a process called translation, the amino acids are linked together in the order coded by mRNA to form the protein.

Mutations An alteration in an organism's genetic code is called a mutation. Such an alteration may change the order of amino acids in a protein and affect the biochemical properties of the protein. A well-known example is the replacement of A by T at the 17th nucleotide of the gene for hemoglobin, changing the codon from GAG to GTG. This single difference in the 444 DNA letters containing instructions for the hemoglobin gene wreaks havoc on the gene, resulting in the fatal blood disease sickle-cell anemia.

Non-Mendelian inheritance patterns Organisms contain many traits that do not exhibit the predictable patterns discovered by Mendel. In some cases, there is incomplete dominance; neither gene is dominant over the other. A well-known example is four-o'clock flowers. When a four o'clock plant with red flowers (RR) is crossed with a plant that has white flowers (WW), the hybrid offspring have pink flowers (RW).

Additionally, some traits have multiple alleles. An example is the major human blood alleles, of which there are three: A, B, and O. Neither A nor B is dominant over the other, but both are dominant over O. Thus, a person with type A blood may have two A alleles or an A and an O allele. A person with type B blood has two B's or BO. A person with AB blood has an A and a B, and a person with type O blood has two O alleles.

Although Mendel's principle of independent assortment states that traits are inherited independently from one another, genes on the same chromosome are usually inherited together. Certain genes are carried on the sex chromosomes. In females, who have two X chromosomes, the laws of dominance apply. Males have an X chromosome inherited from the mother and a Y chromosome from the father. The two chromosomes are not alike; there are numerous genes on the X chromosome and comparatively few on the Y chromosome. One important gene on the X chromosome codes for factor VIII, a protein needed to enable blood to clot. Lack of factor VIII results in a life-threatening condition called hemophilia. Since males have only one X chromosome, they have hemophilia if that chromosome carries the abnormal gene, but females would have to have both abnormal X chromosomes to have the disease.

◆Genetics in Medicine

Genetic Engineering The deliberate alteration, or engineering, of an organism's genetic material may involve changing the sequence of DNA letters, or moving DNA from one species to another. For example, when the human gene that directs production of the hormone insulin is inserted into the DNA of bacteria, the bacteria—and all their descendants—produce human insulin. This process has made it possible to manufacture large quantities of insulin, tissue plasminogen activator (for dissolving blood clots), several types of interferon (for treating hepatitis B and other diseases), and other substances.

Gene therapy is a method of correcting defective genes that cause disease. In the most common technique, a normal gene is inserted into the genome to supplant a dysfunctional gene. The first human gene therapy occurred in 1990, when a young girl received a blood transfusion containing billions of cells with copies of a gene she lacked. The gene enabled her body to make adenosine deaminase, an enzyme essential for a healthy immune system.

Genetic Diseases Hundreds of human diseases are caused wholly or in part by genetic errors—mutations in genes that result in physical, chemical, or mental abnormalities. If an individual inherits a mutated dominant gene or two copies of a mutated recessive gene, the result may be an inherited disease or increased susceptibility to disease. For example, Tay-Sachs disease is caused by a single recessive gene; the recessive gene must be inherited from both parents for the disease to develop.

Multiple genes may be involved in any one disease. For example, scientists have identified more than 600 cancer-related genes. The normal genes are involved in numerous different activities, but when mutated they can result in the development of a malignant growth.

Some genetic diseases, termed familial, are inherited, though their pattern of inheritance is not clear. An example is familial hypercholesterolemia, which is characterized by high cholesterol levels.

Other disorders sometimes described as genetic are not caused by abnormal genes but by defects in whole chromosomes. Down syndrome is the most familiar example; the nucleus of each body cell contains 24, instead of the normal 23, pairs of chromosomes. Fragile X syndrome is another example; it results from an abnormal number of repetitions of a normal sequence that is part of the genetic code. In some cases, genetic disease occurs because an individual receives an abnormal number of chromosomes. For example, in Klinefelter syndrome, a male is born with an extra X chromosome.

◆**The Human Genome Project**   The National Center for Human Genome Research was instituted on January 3, 1989, and with the participation of both the U.S. Department of Energy and National Institutes for Health, became the Human Genome Project in 1990, with the goal of examining and identifying the more than 20,000 genes that make up the human genome. Scientists from the European Union, Japan, and China also participate, forming together the International Human Genome Sequencing Consortium.

Teams from the U.S. and Britain completed the genome of *Caenorhabditis elegans*, a nematode worm, at the end of 1998. Scientists mapped their first plant genome at the end of 2000 with a mustard, *Arabidopsis thaliana*, a common laboratory plant for botanists. In October 2001, sequencing of the genome of the Japanese puffer fish was finished, the first fish to be mapped. The first complete draft of the human genome was completed in 2003, spurring advances in genetic medicine and biotechnology. In 2007, *The New York Times* reported that the full genome of James D. Watson had been deciphered, and in 2009, *The Times* reported that numerous low-cost technologies for decoding DNA were opening the floodgates of genetic sequencing.

Weekend 36: China

Day 1: The Mandate Of Heaven: China To A.D. 1600

Although civilization began in places such as Sumer thousands of years earlier than in China, no other place in the world can boast a continuous culture from Neolithic origins to modern times. China's imperial-bureaucratic system of government, established in the third century B.C., incorporated a merit-based civil service and remained unchanged in its essential characteristics until the 20th century.

◆**Ancient China** Agriculture in China began some 8,000 years ago, with the cultivation of millet in northern areas and of rice in the Yangtze River valley. Neolithic cultures arose in several widely scattered areas, probably reflecting considerable ethno-linguistic diversity and making significant industrial progress in the form of ceramics and finely made tools. Silk production and jade carving, both unique to Chinese culture, arose during the fourth millennium B.C.

The Chinese Bronze Age began around 2000 B.C. The production of bronze weapons and ritual vessels accompanied increased urbanization, social stratification, hereditary kingship, and other markers of advancing civilization, leading to dynastic regimes ancestral to later Chinese culture. The "Three Dynasties" (Xia, ca. 1900–1555 B.C.; Shang, ca.1555–1046 B.C.; and Zhou, 1046–256 B.C.) gradually came to dominate the North China Plain, absorbing other early cultures in a process of political, military, and cultural expansion. During the 13th century B.C., the Shang dynasty's regional dominance was enhanced by the cultivation of wheat and the use of military chariots (with associated technologies of horse breeding and management), both imported from western Asia. Also during this period, the earliest known version of the written Chinese language was used for administrative and religious purposes.

After conquering the Shang dynasty in 1046, founders of the Zhou dynasty formulated the doctrine called the "Mandate of Heaven," claiming that the conquest of an old regime by a new one was inevitable because it was empowered by the moral force of Heaven itself. This became a key element of Chinese political thought thereafter. In the early centuries of its rule (1046–771 B.C., known as the Western Zhou dynasty, because its capital was located in the western part of the royal domain, near present-day Xi'an), the Zhou kings expanded the territory under their control by appointing noble families as rulers of subordinate states. The various states, however, increasingly took power into their own hands. With a forced shift of the capital eastward to Luoyang in 771, the Zhou regime (now the Eastern Zhou, 771–256 B.C.) remained formally in power but with greatly diminished authority. A contemporary historical account (the *Spring and Autumn Chronicle*, covering the years 722–481 B.C.) describes the struggle for survival among the Zhou aristocratic states.

◆**War and Philosophy**   In the succeeding Warring States Period (481–221 B.C.), only a handful of states survived. Rulers of states used new technology (such as iron tools) and management techniques to mobilize populations for military service and state-supervised agricultural production. It was a time of population growth and increasing wealth despite near-constant warfare. As rulers looked for new sociopolitical ideas to enhance their power and security, state patronage of learning created a class of literate administrators, advisers, and teachers.

The first and most influential Chinese philosopher was Kongzi (551–479 B.C.), usually known by his Latinate name, Confucius. Confucius, along with later generations of disciples who elaborated upon his ideas (Mencius, Xunzi, and others) advocated a hierarchical society in which the ruler, aided by enlightened ministers, would serve as "father and mother of the people." The Confucians prized harmony, moderation, ritual, and historical precedent but disparaged law, which they saw as the enemy of virtue. Rival thinkers advocated strict codes of law and coercive punishments to control the populace (Shang Yang, Han Feizi); improved managerial techniques to make government more effective (Shen Buhai); frugality, universal love, and self-defense (Mozi); escapism (Yangzi, Zhuangzi); and government by a sage attuned to the rhythms of cosmic force (Laozi). In practice, government during the Warring States Period became increasingly bureaucratic and merit-based, rather than aristocratic and hereditary, as rulers adopted promising ideas and techniques from various schools of thought.

◆**Unification and Empire** The last Zhou king died in 256 B.C. without a successor, and a struggle began to reunite China's territory under a single ruler. This was accomplished by the king of the highly militarized northwestern state of Qin, whose last rival capitulated in 221. The new ruler declared himself Qin Shi Huangdi (First Emperor of Qin), coining a new title to replace the older Zhou title *wang* (king). The First Emperor undertook a number of initiatives: standardizing currency and weights and measures, confiscating and destroying most books in private hands, rebuilding and extending the Great Wall (sections of which had been built by individual states during the preceding century or so), building canals and other water control projects, and creating for himself a grandiose tomb complex that included the celebrated underground army of "terra-cotta warriors." These projects, accompanied by a harshly punitive system of laws, provoked widespread discontent. With the First Emperor's death in 210, public order dissolved in the face of palace intrigues and popular rebellions.

In 206 B.C., the commoner-turned-rebel-leader Liu Bang claimed the Mandate of Heaven and announced the founding of the Han dynasty, defeating the last of his rivals in 202 B.C. An early attempt to establish Zhou-style subordinate kingdoms proved problematic, and Han government soon returned to a centralized model, borrowing many features from the Qin administration. Under the greatest Han ruler, Emperor Wu (r. 140–87 B.C.), China expanded its territorial boundaries to the northeast, southeast, and southwest. It also defeated the aggressive Xiongnu Empire of the northern grasslands, commenced regular trade with central and western Eurasia along the Silk Road beginning around 100 B.C., and instituted a formal merit-based recruitment system for government officials. Confucianism, modified by its accommodation to bureaucratic government, was made the official state ideology, and a canon of Confucian classical writings was established as the educational basis for government service. Chinese rulers characterized their realm as the "Middle Kingdom" and "All Under Heaven"—the center of the known world and its greatest empire.

The Han dynasty fell to Wang Mang in A.D. 7 but was re-established (as the Latter or Eastern Han) in A.D. 25. The authority of the central government was weakened in the process; powerful aristocratic clans dominated much of the countryside. Brought by merchants and missionaries along the Silk Road, Buddhism arrived in China in the first century A.D., and Daoism was codified as a formal religion by the first Celestial Master, Zhang Daoling, in the second century. Rivalry between provincial aristocrats, civil servants, and inner-palace eunuchs weakened the Han government, which collapsed amid popular rebellions in A.D. 220. Thereafter, until A.D. 265, China was divided between the competing kingdoms of Shu Han, Wu, and Wei; this Three Kingdoms Period is remembered in Chinese literature and opera as a time of heroic chivalry.

China remained divided for more than three centuries, with northern areas governed by dynasties of non-Chinese ethnic groups from the grasslands (such as the Toba rulers of the Northern Wei dynasty, 386–534), while southern areas were ruled by weak and ephemeral Chinese dynasties. Despite political fragmentation, this was a culturally rich era. In particular, Buddhism and its associated arts flourished and became thoroughly assimilated into Chinese culture.

✦An Imperial Golden Age Reunification came again when Yang Jian, a general of the short-lived Northern Zhou dynasty, slaughtered the imperial family, defeated his rivals, and, in 589, proclaimed himself first emperor of the Sui dynasty. His son, Emperor Yang, attempted simultaneously to conquer Korea and build the Grand Canal linking the Yellow and Yangtze Rivers. He failed in the former and succeeded in the latter, but the combined effort depleted both popular support and the imperial treasury. The Sui dynasty was overthrown in 618 by Li Shimin, founder of the Tang dynasty.

The Tang dynasty (A.D. 618–907) is often regarded as imperial China's greatest era. Trade along the Silk Road flourished, bringing not only monetary wealth, but also cultural riches such as innovations in music and decorative arts. Women of the Tang enjoyed considerable independence. Many upper-class women were literate, owned property, played polo and other sports, and shared cultural and intellectual pursuits with men. Poetry flourished in the hands of such masters as Wang Wei, Li Bo, Du Fu, and Bo Juyi. The Tang also saw the invention of wood-block printing and gunpowder. Chang'an, the Tang capital, was one of the world's greatest cities, with a population of over 1 million and resident foreigners from many Asian and Middle Eastern countries.

The Tang projected their military power far into Central Asia, but in 751 were defeated by a Muslim army at the Talas River, west of the Pamir Mountains. Thereafter, Tang control rapidly contracted eastward along the Silk Road. A disgruntled general, An Lushan, led a military insurrection (755–63) that nearly toppled the dynasty and left it permanently weakened. Great aristocratic families again filled the power gap left by a crippled central government. A purge of Buddhist temples and monasteries in the ninth century was an attempt to replenish the imperial treasury with confiscated religious wealth, but also a manifestation of resurgent Confucianism, which disparaged Buddhism as a foreign creed. A bloody peasant rebellion (875–84) led by the charismatic Huang Chao nearly obliterated the Tang aristocracy and resulted in the deaths of millions of commoners. The dynasty collapsed in 907.

◆**China's Medieval Period** Stability returned with the founding of the Song dynasty in 960, but much of territory under Chinese control during the Tang administration was lost. The northern regions of China remained beyond the reach of the Song emperors and were ruled by non-Chinese peoples for centuries. The Liao dynasty (927–1115; ethnic Khitans) and the Jin dynasty (1115–1234; ethnic Jurchens) ruled the borderlands from a capital near present-day Beijing. The Song dynasty's capital was at Kaifeng until 1127, when Jin invasions forced a move southward to Hangzhou. Militarily weak, the Song is remembered as an era of artistic brilliance, especially for landscape painting and ceramics. Neo-Confucian scholarship flourished, eclipsing Buddhism as the focus of learning; the classical commentaries of Zhu Xi occupy a place in Chinese intellectual life comparable to the works of Thomas Aquinas in Europe. The practice of recruiting civil servants by written examinations (largely from a Confucian-educated, landowning but nonaristocratic "gentry" class) became firmly entrenched.

Both the Jin dynasty in the north and the Song dynasty in the south were crushed in the 13th century by the expanding Mongol empire of Genghis Khan and his successors. Direct Mongol rule in China was established by Genghis's grandson Kublai Khan, who proclaimed the establishment of the Yuan dynasty in 1279. But the Mongols failed to master the Chinese practice of bureaucratic government, and their habit of employing foreign administrators and tax-collectors stirred popular discontent. Marco Polo, a Venetian merchant who traveled to China in

1275 and stayed there for 17 years, may have been one such resented outsider; in his book of *Travels* he claimed to have served Kublai Khan as some sort of official. The Yuan dynasty fell in 1368 to a peasant army led by the ex-Buddhist lay brother Zhu Yuanzhang, founder of the Ming dynasty.

♦**Early Modern China** Under its vigorous early rulers, the Ming pursued an aggressive pacification policy in the northern borderlands and sent fleets of imperial "treasure ships" (seven voyages, 1405–35) under Admiral Zheng He to explore the South China Sea and the Indian Ocean. In a radical and abrupt change of policy in the mid-15th century, Ming rulers switched to a stance of defensive isolationism, rebuilding the Great Wall, and restricting foreign commerce. The Ming was an era of agricultural and commercial prosperity, rising literacy rates, and artistic creativity, but the new isolationist policy took hold just decades before the European Age of Expansion.

In 1570, the Ming emperor granted Portugal the right to establish a trading station at Macao, and in 1600 the first Jesuit missionary, Matteo Ricci, arrived in Beijing. China, which had long regarded itself as the Middle Kingdom, was experiencing the first intimations of a prolonged and difficult encounter with the rest of the world that would lead to national humiliation and the collapse of the centuries-old imperial system of government.

Day 2: Modern China: From Foreign Rule to World Power

By the early 17th century, the Ming dynasty was in severe decline with a corrupt and bloated administration unresponsive to mounting political and social problems. Peasant rebellions broke out and threatened the capital. In desperation, the Ming emperor invited Manchu warriors from the northeast to quell the disorder. The Manchus defeated the rebels, but then deposed the last Ming emperor in 1644 and proclaimed the founding of their own dynasty, the Qing.

Under a series of three long-living and hard-working emperors (Kangxi, 1664–1723, Yongzheng, 1723–36, and Qianlong, 1736–95), China enjoyed a long era of population growth, rising national income, and internal peace. Pursuing a vigorous process of subjugating the borderlands, these rulers brought the empire to its greatest extent, incorporating Manchuria, Mongolia, Xinjiang (East Turkestan), and Tibet. (The present boundaries of the People's Republic of China reflect these conquests, somewhat diminished by the loss of the Mongolian Republic and parts of Turkestan.) The Qing emperors governed China through the traditional civil service but took elaborate steps to preserve Manchu identity (the Manchus being a tiny ethnic minority in China) through regulations governing language, dress, intermarriage, and hereditary military service. European merchants were regarded by the Qing authorities as no more than a new and exotic group of "tribute-bearing barbarians" whose activities were subject to strict control; their trade was limited to the port of Canton (Guangzhou).

◆**Opium and Uprisings** Prior to the mid-18th century, European imports from China (often called "Cathay" in the West) were mainly luxury goods such as silk, lacquer, and porcelain, paid for in silver. But a growing British thirst for tea turned the China trade into a high-volume, high-value trade that increasingly drained the British economy of hard currency, as China was largely indifferent to British manufactured goods. British merchants began to press China to relax the restrictions of the Canton trade system and also began importing opium from India (under British East India Company control) to balance the trade in tea by providing an item of interest to Chinese merchants. An official trade mission (1792–94) to China under Lord Macartney was granted an audience with the emperor, but British demands for diplomatic representation and freer trade were rudely rebuffed.

Opium, brought to China by Westerners in contravention of Chinese law, was smuggled inland with the collusion of corrupt officials. Opium was sold to Chinese dealers for silver; the silver was used by British and other foreign merchants to buy tea. (The tax on tea, as American revolutionaries knew, was an important source of British Crown revenue.) Because the value of opium imports began to exceed the value of tea and other Chinese exports, by about 1820 silver was flowing out of the Chinese economy and into foreign hands. The economic consequences, combined with widespread addiction and other socioeconomic problems, alarmed the Qing court. A high official, Lin Zexu, was appointed viceroy of Canton in 1837 and instructed to put an end to the opium trade. His high-minded but undiplomatic measures to do so infuriated the foreign merchants; in 1839, British warships fired on Canton's fortifications, and in the ensuing Opium War (1839–42) China was humiliatingly defeated. The resulting Treaty of Nanking (1842) opened five additional ports to trade and removed many restrictions on foreigners' activities.

Increasing unrest in southeastern China coalesced around the figure of Hong Xiuquan, a charismatic preacher who regarded himself as the younger brother of Jesus. His Taiping ("Great Peace") movement rose in rebellion in 1851, quickly capturing the city of Nanjing and controlling much of the country's heartland. By the time it was defeated in 1864, the rebellion had been responsible for as many as 30 million deaths; other unrelated uprisings caused millions more. These rebellions left the Qing government seriously weakened. Meanwhile, the wholly avoidable Arrow War (1856–58), which began over an alleged insult to the British flag, resulted as intended in a new and more comprehensive treaty (Tientsin, 1860) that gave foreign merchants, missionaries, and others nearly unfettered access to and legal immunity in China.

◆**Foreign Domination** As the so-called Treaty Port system continued to expand, the Qing government instituted a series of "self-strengthening" measures, including training a corps of diplomats and interpreters, establishing a modern arsenal, and sending Chinese youths to study abroad. These measures proved belated and ineffective. China's weakness was exhibited in a brief Sino-French conflict in 1870 and in the Sino-Japanese War of 1894–95, both of which resulted in defeat. A group of progressive advisers to the Emperor Guangxu (r. 1875–1908) promulgated a series of far-reaching reforms in the summer of 1898, which were intended to lead to a constitutional monarchy. The reformers were, however, outmaneuvered by the conservative Empress Dowager Cixi; some were arrested and executed, and others fled abroad. The emperor himself was placed under house arrest, and the reforms were rescinded.

The xenophobic Boxer Uprising (1899–1900) was a popular movement aimed at killing or expelling all foreigners in China. ("Boxer" was the British nickname for a member of the Chinese anti-colonialist group Righteous Fists of Harmony.) A Boxer siege of the foreign embassy district in Beijing was broken by a coalition force of foreign troops in the summer of 1900, and the uprising collapsed. The resulting treaty obliged China to pay a huge indemnity to the foreign powers. The Qing government, entangled in the failed uprising, was exhausted. It attempted some reform measures to little avail, and China's ports, mines, railroads, and industries fell even further under Western and Japanese control.

◆**Revolution and Reform** Dr. Sun Yat-sen, a Cantonese trained in Western medicine, had been for some years working with overseas Chinese communities to promote a revolution aimed at transmuting China into a republic. A minor revolutionary incident in Wuhan on October 10, 1911, triggered a dominolike collapse of Qing authority. Dr. Sun hurried home from America to take charge of the newly established Republic of China, but, under foreign pressure, he was soon replaced as president by the conservative general Yuan Shikai. Under Yuan's corrupt and inept leadership, the republic quickly degenerated, and the country fell into an era of warlordism. Dr. Sun, at the head of the National People's Party (Kuomintang or KMT), led the democratic opposition from a base in Canton.

China entered World War I on the side of the Allies, sending hundreds of thousands of laborers and support troops to Europe. Citizens therefore were outraged when the 1919 Treaty of Versailles awarded former German concessions in China to Japan. A student protest demonstration on May 4, 1919, gave its name to the May Fourth Movement, which recognized language reform, educational innovation, a national debate on the roles of science and democracy, and a "rights recovery movement" aimed at nullifying a century of exploitative treaties with foreign powers.

◆**Nationalists and Communists** A tiny Chinese Communist Party (CCP) was founded in Shanghai in 1921, and with Moscow-led Communist International support, united with the KMT (now under the leadership of General Chiang Kai-shek after the death of Sun Yat-sen in 1925). The CCP rapidly gained support among urban workers but was betrayed by Chiang in 1927 in a purge designed to exterminate the party. CCP survivors fled, while Chiang's Northern Expedition (1926–28) defeated or co-opted many regional warlords and brought some semblance of unification to China once again. China's geography remained intact until 1931, when Japan, using the pretext of supposed railway sabotage, invaded and occupied Manchuria. Resistance to Japanese aggression became a touchstone of Chinese patriotism.

KMT ground and aerial attacks on the CCP's "Jiangsi Soviet" government in exile in 1933 led a desperate Communist movement to break out of the encircled base and flee to a safer area. During this famous Long March (1934–35), Mao Zedong rose to undisputed leadership of the party. From its new northwestern base in Yen'an, the CCP began to grow again, branding itself as the party of land reform and resistance to Japanese aggression. In December 1936, conflict between the CCP and KMT finally ended as Chiang was forcibly detained near Xi'an by a coalition of troops and forced at gunpoint to agree to a new United Front against Japan.

♦World War II in China Sino-Japanese hostilities, and therefore the Asian theater of World War II, began on July 7, 1937, in a small battle near Beijing. Despite tenacious KMT defense efforts, Japanese forces swept over China, controlling all its coastal provinces and most of the Yangtze River valley by the end of 1937. A pro-Japanese puppet regime under Wang Jingwei was established in Beijing, while reluctant allies Chiang and Mao pursued the war against Japan (with U.S. aid after December 1942) from bases in China's protected western territories.

The end of World War II in 1945 brought renewed CCP-KMT hostilities, despite American efforts to broker a truce. In the civil war of 1946–49, the massively armed but disorganized KMT forces were outfought by the CCP's more focused and better motivated armies. Chiang withdrew to the island of Taiwan, where he established a Nationalist government in "temporary quarters," while on October 1, 1949, in Beijing, Mao Zedong proclaimed the founding of the People's Republic of China (PRC).

♦Communist China Under Mao American political opinion strongly favored the Nationalist cause, and the intervention of the United States and China in the Korean War (1950–53) on opposing sides eliminated any chance of American recognition of the PRC. China relied on the Soviet Union for aid and advice in pursuing a twin policy of rapid industrialization and agricultural collectivization. Dissidents were encouraged to speak out in the Hundred Flowers Movement of 1956, and then purged in the Anti-Rightist Campaign of 1957–58. The Great Leap Forward (1958–60), an ill-conceived effort to accelerate

China's economic development, was a catastrophic failure, resulting in perhaps 30 million deaths from famine. His prestige damaged, Mao was forced to give way, temporarily, to the more moderate leadership of Premier Zhou Enlai and President Liu Shaoqi.

Mao struck back in August 1966, with the proclamation of the "Great Proletarian Cultural Revolution," a massive effort to rid the Communist Party of all elements not completely devoted to Mao's radical view of permanent revolution and socialist transformation. Liu Shaoqi, Deng Xiaoping, and many other high officials were demoted and, in some cases, arrested; Zhou Enlai survived in office only by scrupulously following Mao's line. Youthful Red Guards terrorized teachers, administrators, and other professionals, many of whom were sent to the countryside for long periods of "reform through labor." *The Selected Quotations of Chairman Mao* (the "Little Red Book") became the sole standard of Communist orthodoxy. Cultural life came under the puritanical sway of Mao's wife, Jiang Qing. During this period a beginning was made in Sino-American rapprochement. On February 28, 1972, President Nixon and Zhou Enlai signed the Shanghai Communique, in which each side acknowledged the other's interests in a wide range of issues. Full diplomatic recognition was established in 1979.

◆**The Post-Mao Era** The deaths of Zhou and Mao in 1976 brought an end to the Cultural Revolution. Mao's wife, Jiang Qing, and three others were arrested. This "Gang of Four" was blamed for many of the Cultural Revolution's excesses. After a period of party infighting, Deng Xiaoping emerged as China's new leader. Deng put his stamp on China's future in March 1978, with the policy of "Four Modernizations" (agriculture, industry, technology, and defense), which led to the rapid abandonment of collective agriculture and opened the door to foreign investment, joint ventures, and eventual private ownership of industrial facilities. A sometimes coercive "one child per family" policy checked runaway population growth. A bargain was struck: Chinese citizens were free to get rich as long as they did not challenge the authority of the Communist Party.

Such a challenge came in the spring of 1989, when students occupied Beijing's Tiananmen Square to rally for democratic reforms. After several weeks of inaction, party hard-liners, describing the demonstrations as a threat to public order, used military force to clear the square on the night of June 4. Hundreds of demonstrators were killed. Despite widespread international outrage, China was unrepentant and resumed its policy of political authoritarianism combined with economic liberalization.

Since the early 1990s, China has seen spectacular economic growth, often over 10 percent annually, led by an export-oriented manufacturing sector. China's cities have been transformed by new development projects. Serious problems remain, including energy and water shortages, air and water pollution, heavy production of greenhouse gases, rising personal and regional income inequalities, ethnic discontent in Tibet and Xinjiang, political stagnation, and vulnerability to world economic trends. Still, there is little doubt that China has become and will remain one of the world's dominant economic powers, with corresponding political weight in world affairs.

Weekend 37: Europe Conquers the World

Day 1: The Age of European Expansion

For over 400 years, beginning in the early 15th century, the major powers of Europe explored and colonized much of the world, bringing home vast wealth in gold, silver, and precious stones. While colonizers brought monetary and cultural riches to the mainland, they imposed their language, religion, and way of life on the indigenous peoples, many of whom were reduced to serfdom or slavery. The European conquests were facilitated by a rich heritage of seafaring and sophisticated nautical instruments, as well as superior military organization and weaponry. Motivated by a desire for riches and a sincere wish to bring Christianity to the rest of the world, many men—and later, women—willingly risked the long, dangerous ocean journey to settle in a foreign world.

◆**Portugal** In 1415, King John I of Portugal captured the town of Ceuta across the Strait of Gibraltar in Africa. His son, Prince Henry the Navigator, then sponsored voyages farther down the western coast, colonizing the Azores and the Madeiras. Traders exchanged cotton goods and metal manufactures for ivory and gold as far as the Niger River delta. These sailors replaced their rowed galleys with caravels and carracks, and used triangular sails for easier mobility. They set up the first European trading post in sub-Saharan Africa at Elmina, Ghana, in 1481. At the mouth of the Congo River, a Bantu-speaking Christian state developed under Portuguese influence after 1483.

In 1488, Bartolomeu Dias discovered an alternative route to Asia around the southern tip of Africa (which he named the Cape of Good Hope). This encouraged western Europeans to abandon the traditional route to India and the Spice Islands through the Middle East. East Asia, too, became a goal of navigation after the fall of Constantinople in 1453 seriously disrupted Silk Route trade with China.

In 1497, the Portuguese sailor Vasco da Gama began a voyage that took him around the Cape of Good Hope and across the Indian Ocean to Calicut, a major trading post on the southwestern coast of India. After da Gama's second voyage in 1502, the Portuguese established a "rosary" of more than a dozen forts, monopolizing the Indian Ocean and diverting all trade around Africa. They also established trading posts in the Spice Islands (Melaku), China, and Japan. This network also provided the route for Christian missionaries who began arriving shortly thereafter.

In the Americas, Portugal found itself in competition with its powerful neighbor, Spain. In 1494, Pope Alexander VI arranged the Treaty of Tordesillas between the two powers, which divided the world in half with a line 370 leagues west of the Azores (45°W), awarding territory to Spain west of the line and Portugal east of the line. In 1500, Pedro Cabral claimed Brazil for Portugal, which soon became an important colony in the Americas.

◆**Spain** Political unity was slow to arrive on the Iberian Peninsula, and it was not until Ferdinand of Castile and Isabella of Aragon married in 1469 that Spain was a colonizing force to reckon with. In 1492, they commissioned the Genoese merchant Christopher Columbus who, like Dias, was seeking an alternative route to India when he landed in the Bahamas. Columbus later visited Cuba and Hispaniola (modern-day Dominican Republic), where his main ship, the *Santa Maria*, was lost, then sailed to Haiti and returned to Spain in March 1493, certain he had reached the Far East. He left 39 men behind to begin a settlement on Hispaniola; they would be massacred within a year. Columbus made three more voyages, reaching mainland South America and Central America on the third and fourth trip. Determined but politically inept, he died embittered by the lack of support from his royal patrons.

Columbus's voyages were not the only Spanish conquests in the New World. As it became increasingly obvious that the New World was not a part of Asia and rather a barrier to reaching it, *conquistadores* ("conquerors") marauded the Caribbean islands and the mainland from Panama to Florida.

Spain's empire was slow to develop, but in 1520 Ferdinand Magellan sailed around the southern tip of South America, across the Pacific, bringing Spanish rule to the Philippines and the Moluccas. In 1521, conquistador Hernando Cortés conquered the Aztec Empire. When Francisco Pizarro toppled the Inca Empire in 1533, Spain acquired a stupendous world empire, the wealth of whose silver mines dwarfed the riches in the Indies.

Organized into two vice-royalties, the Spanish Empire granted *encomiendas* ("plantations") to the conquerors; although enslavement of the Indians was forbidden, the Spanish reduced them to serflike status and forced them to work for their new lords. Christian missions were immediately established with such success that more than 20 bishoprics were created by the mid-16th century. Five universities were flourishing by the middle of the 17th century.

In North America, Juan Ponce de Leon discovered Florida (1513), while conquistadors Vasco de Balboa discovered the Pacific Ocean (1513), and Francisco Coronado settled in Mexico (1535). Hernando de Soto explored much of the southern part of what became the United States (1539–42), including the Mississippi River.

In 1565, Spain claimed the Philippines in a series of campaigns, and Manila became the western terminus for a vast complex of trade. The Americas became the source of new commodities such as potatoes, cacao, tobacco, and corn. Cotton, rice, indigo, and later coffee also became cash staples, and Brazil built a thriving sugar economy.

However, disease strains from Europe devastated entire populations of the New World. As the local pool of laborers shrank, landowners increasingly relied upon African slaves. First the Portuguese, then the Dutch, English, and others encouraged states along Africa's west coast to provide them with captives that were sold for a profit as slaves in the Americas.

•**England**   In 1497, King Henry VII financed the journey of the Italian navigator John Cabot to search for a northern passage to the East. Cabot disappeared on his second voyage. Neither King Henry VIII nor Queen Elizabeth undertook any large-scale projects of exploration and colonization, but Elizabeth did encourage courtiers such as Sir Humphrey Gilbert and Sir Walter Raleigh in their early, ill-fated attempts at settlement (Roanoke Island, 1585) in North America.

Not until the Stuart dynasty did English settlement begin in earnest. Henry Hudson, backed by various patrons, made several attempts to find a northern passage from Europe to Asia in 1607–11, exploring much of the northern coast of North America. At the same time, the first successful colony was established at Jamestown in present-day Virginia in 1607. Subsequent colonies were established from Maine to the Chesapeake through grants to commercial companies and individual proprietors.

Chesapeake Bay became the center of a thriving agricultural region

based on tobacco, a crop which the natives had taught settlers to cultivate, while New England flourished as a haven for English Calvinists
known as Puritans, who fled to America to escape religious persecution.
The first African slaves arrived in Virginia in 1619, the same year the
colony established a representative government, the House of Burgesses.
A year later, the Dutch explored the Hudson Valley, founding New Am-
sterdam on the island of Manhattan, which the English would seize in
1664.

Over the course of the 17th and into the 18th centuries, English voyages followed those of the Dutch and the Spanish, which had discovered
the islands of the South Pacific: the Carolines, the Marshalls, Tasmania,
New Zealand, and Australia. Before the late 18th century, no European
colonists disturbed the indigenous peoples of these colonies, but in 1770
James Cook claimed Australia for England, which was settled as a penal
colony in 1788.

◆France　France also sent exploratory ventures to America led by
Giovanni da Verrazzano in 1524 and Jacques Cartier in 1534. However,
it was not until the 17th century that a permanent settlement was established by Samuel de Champlain, who founded New France in 1608
with a capital at Quebec on the St. Lawrence River. Champlain was the
first European to understand that success in the New World depended
on keeping peace with the Indians. His ability to do so enabled the
French to expand their settlements and foster highly profitable trade for
over a century. Missions began in 1615, but the process of converting
the Indians met with limited success. After 1642, the city of Montreal
developed around the Indian village of Hochelaga, 150 miles up the St.
Lawrence River from Quebec. Montreal became a center of the fur trade
on which the economy of New France was based.

Earlier the French had also begun colonizing the Lesser Antilles, on the
fringe of the Spanish Empire, and by 1656 they controlled a dozen of these
islands. In 1718, Jean-Baptiste Le Moyne de Bienville founded New Orleans, a strategic mainland port situated along the Mississippi River.

◆French and English Tensions in the New World　Friction between England and France in North America would gradually increase
as each nation continued to expand their holdings, especially in and
around the Ohio Valley. The same pattern was in motion across the

globe, especially in India during the latter part of the 17th century, and into the next century as well. The East India Company of England established its headquarters in Bombay in 1661 and later moved to the new city of Calcutta. The French followed in 1664, setting up a trading post at Pondicherry in 1675. Both English and French created private armies of Indian troops (sepoys) led by European officers who become de-facto rulers of large territories.

Under King Louis XIV (r. 1643–1715), the French became the dominant power in Europe and became more assertive in their overseas interests as well. During the 18th century, France and England fought a series of major wars both at home and occasionally abroad. Finally, in the Seven Years' War (1756–63), the conflict spread to India and America (where it is known as the French and Indian War). The colonists played a significant role in decisively defeating the French. In India, the British, led by Robert Clive, were also victorious in 1757, and later, when an Afghan invasion occurred, most Indian leaders sought British protection.

In India, the trend toward British domination grew between 1786 and 1813. The governors-general of the East India Company began a judicial system, gained control over the foreign affairs of most southern principalities, and entered into treaties with Persia and Afghanistan.

Day 2: Europe Colonizes the World (1650–1815)

After the Thirty Years' War ended in 1648, France dominated Europe both politically and culturally for over a century; in the Americas, however, the story was different. The British dominated North America, and the Spanish controlled Mexico, Central America, much of the Caribbean, and South America. In Africa and the Middle East, Western influence grew primarily through trade. In Eurasia, Russia and China acquired huge land empires. In South Asia, British control of India evolved slowly, while the Dutch built a colonial empire in the vast archipelago now known as Indonesia.

♦**Great Britain and North America** England's North American colonies became accustomed to self-government under their elected assemblies in a period, from the late 1600s to the 1760s, when the British government paid relatively little attention to them. The Seven Years'

War in North America became a rallying point of British colonial sentiment. The war ended with Great Britain realizing nearly all of its objectives, including bringing French Canada under British rule. When in the aftermath of the war Britain attempted to organize its vast new North American holdings in a "new imperial system," the old coastal colonies were provoked to rebellion. Their grievances included British efforts to limit settlement beyond the Appalachians, and to tax the colonists for the costs of administering British holdings.

The publication of the Declaration of Independence (July 4, 1776) initiated a war that the British found impossible to win in the face of a highly motivated colonial populace supported by French military and financial assistance. The independence of the United States of America was recognized in the Peace of Paris (1783). (See Weekend 19, "The World Turned Upside Down.")

◆**Spain and the Americas**   After about 1650, the indigenous populations of Spanish vice-royalties recovered rapidly from the disasters of the conquest period, though rule remained in the hands of the *peninsulares* from Spain or *creoles* (colonists of Spanish descent). The natives' primary contact with Spanish culture was through church missionaries and bishops, who constituted a spiritual elite. The Spanish New World colonies, with the new vice-royalties of New Granada (1717; roughly present-day Venezuela, Colombia, and Ecuador) and La Plata (1776; Bolivia, Paraguay, Uruguay, and Argentina) were governed paternalistically by Spain. Brazil prospered as a Portuguese colony and by 1800 had a population larger than that of Portugal itself.

The effect of the Napoleonic wars upon Europe's transatlantic provinces was profound. Haiti maintained its independence, gained in 1794 by a slave insurrection-turned-republican movement, despite Napoleon's attempt to re-conquer it. When Joseph Bonaparte (brother of Napoleon) ascended the throne of Spain (1808), Spanish America was thrown into confusion. Juntas loyal to the Bourbon king Ferdinand VII, led by creoles such as Simon Bolivar and José de San Martin, resisted French rule at first—but turned against Ferdinand's absolutism when he was restored to the throne. In colony after colony, the juntas fought for and won their independence: La Plata (Argentina, 1810), Chile (1818), New Granada (Ecuador, Colombia, Panama, and Venezuela, 1819), Peru (1821). In separate and more complicated developments, Mexico and Brazilian independence followed in 1822.

The Monroe Doctrine (1821) of the United States shielded the new states from Spanish repression, but nothing could protect them from their own inexperience in politics, from boundary disputes, or from the internal struggles of local leaders (*caudillos*) seeking autonomy within the new republics. Independence was followed by long periods of civil war and insurrection.

When the trade links with Spain were cut, the new states found a welcome home for their products in Great Britain. British investment fostered mining and industrial development. Following World War I, large-scale investment from the United States in industry and plantation agriculture helped fuel continued economic growth. This expansion brought social tension, as the growth of an agricultural and industrial working class added a new element to the preexisting political instability. In the 1930s, governments in Mexico, Argentina, and several other Latin American states mimicked the models of Europe. In the Caribbean, the United States played a dominant role, either as "policeman" or after 1934, "good neighbor."

◆**Europe and Africa**   In the early years of the 19th century, Britain, Denmark, and the United States abolished the slave trade. Britain actively, but not always effectively, tried to block the slave trade (still carried on by several other nations) along the African coast.

In the late 1700s, the Zulu nation of southern Africa employed trained infantry units armed with spears to establish a small empire over their neighbors. Near the southern tip of the continent, at the Cape of Good Hope, the Dutch built a Calvinist colony, which by 1815 had a population of about 80,000. The pioneering *trekboers* who founded agrarian settlements beyond the Cape found their expansion limited by the resistance of the Xhosa people, and when the colony passed from the Dutch to the British (1814), British governors attempted to halt the expansion in the name of peace.

In the first half of the 19th century, Europeans evinced only small interest in Africa. Trading forts dotted the west African coasts, while steamboats penetrated only somewhat farther inland, and missionaries began evangelizing on a small scale. "Cash crop" agriculture provided European markets with such commodities as nuts and palm products, but in this early period, the plantations tended to be domestic ventures of various African kings and chiefs. In the south, the expansion of the Zulu nation after 1818 led to disruptions that lasted into the 1850s. Meanwhile, in the Dutch colony at the Cape of Good Hope, the British ban on slavery led to the Great Trek of some 10,000 settlers into the grassy interior plateau known as the "high veld," where they came into conflict with indigenous peoples. On the east coast, the sultan of Oman moved his capital to the island of Zanzibar to better control his network of trade in cloves and slaves; the continuation of the slave trade brought increasing British estrangement from their protégé.

About 1880, a group of French projects—a railway scheme at Dakar, new trading posts on the Ivory Coast and north of the Congo River—alarmed the other powers and initiated the "scramble for Africa," which brought Britain and Portugal, and later, Germany, into a race to annex territory. The Congress of Berlin (1885) sought to bring some order to the competition, and by 1900 the entire continent had been divided among European powers, except for the colony of freed American slaves in Liberia and the ancient Christian empire of Ethiopia. Of specific interest to colonizers was the discovery of gold and diamond deposits in the republic of Transvaal, which led to Britain's conquest of the Boer republics in the Boer War (1889–1901), and the formation of the Union of South Africa (1910) which through elections, Boers soon governed.

As in other areas of the world, the natives in Africa were treated by Europeans as indentured servants, as serfs, or, in the worst cases, as slaves. Although the Congress of Berlin tried to demand that the peoples of Africa be helped to achieve dignity and freedom, this goal was rarely met. The worst atrocities, which resulted in the deaths of millions of natives, occurred in the Congo after King Leopold II of Belgium claimed the territory in 1878. Forced labor, especially in the lucrative rubber industry, and arbitrary judicial proceedings made Leopold one of the villains of colonialism.

◆**The British in India**   As Portuguese influence waned and the Dutch focused their colonial efforts on the Malay Archipelago, British commercial interests turned to India. Bombay became the headquarters of the East India Company (1661), but British gains in India were not uncontested. The French founded their East India Company in 1664 and established a trading post at Pondicherry in 1674. After the War of Austrian Succession (1746–48), French forces ruled most of southern India. But in the Indian theater of the Seven Years' War, Robert Clive roundly defeated the French. The Treaty of Paris left but a few holdings to the French, and in the aftermath, the English East India Company gained direct control of the rich province of Bengal (1764).

During this struggle, the Afghans invaded from the northwest, establishing their rule over much of northern India. Faced with a choice between Afghan and British rule, most Indian princes gravitated toward the British. Parliament's India Act (1784), which was intended to bring the company under government control and to prohibit it from interfering in Indian affairs, did not function as designed. Between 1786 and 1813, the company's governors-general created a judicial system, gained control over the foreign affairs of most southern principalities in return for British protection, and entered into treaties with Persia and Afghanistan.

The term "British Empire" probably exaggerates the degree to which Great Britain exercised direct control over India in the 18th and early 19th centuries. In reality, the company ruled directly only certain territories. There were as yet no Protestant missionaries in India, nor was India subject to the rule of British law. Indian culture was largely ignored by the British. To the majority of Indians, meanwhile, the foreigners were outside the caste system and largely irrelevant to the concerns of daily life.

The British encouraged the fiction of native rule in India while beginning to act more like a sovereign power. In the 1840s, widespread internal warfare made Britain a true imperial power and the ruling authority in India, protecting Indian princes from subversion and aggression, and then annexing their territory when their families died out. After the Great Mutiny of the *sepoys* (Indian natives in service to the British army) in 1857, Britain banished the last of the Mughals and firmly established colonial rule it called the Raj. In 1876 came the symbolic climax: proclamation of Queen Victoria as empress of India.

The British established executive and legislative councils with Indian representation, as well as courts with Indian justices sitting on the bench. Nevertheless, the ties of nationalism and anticolonialism that swept through all of Asia in the early 20th century brought a new measure of political awareness to many Indians. The Indian National

Congress, a political party established in 1885, took the first steps toward seeking independence and winning concessions from the British in 1909 and 1919. After World War I, it came increasingly under the influence of Mahatma Gandhi, whose campaigns of civil disobedience in 1921 and in 1930, presaged the postwar demands that would signal the end of British rule.

◆**The British in Australia and New Zealand**   More enduring than British influence in India, Singapore (liberated in 1819) or Burma (liberated in 1886) were Australia and New Zealand. A convict colony founded in 1788, Australia was gradually transformed by generous land grants into the Commonwealth of Australia (1901). New Zealand, similarly changed by assisted immigration and land grants, earned dominion status in 1907. Both fought loyally among Britain's allies in both of the world wars. As in the Americas, in Australia and New Zealand, the rights of indigenous inhabitants were ignored in the rush of European settlement. Aborigine rights (in Australia) and Maori rights (in New Zealand) are important political issues in both countries today.

Weekend 38: Judeo–Christian Religions

Day 1: Judaism

Judaism is the religion of the Jewish people, who, according to the Hebrew Bible, are God's chosen people. Judaism is the oldest of the monotheistic religions, which, along with Christianity and Islam, traces its origins to the biblical patriarch Abraham. Today, there are an estimated 14 million Jews in 134 countries, the great majority of whom live in the United States (5.8 million), Israel (4.1 million), and Europe (2.4 million).

◆**Scripture** Jewish religious doctrine is based on the Torah, or Law—the first five books of the Hebrew Bible, and on the Talmud, which not only contains the entirety of Jewish law but is also a significant source of Jewish philosophy, biography, literature, and folklore. The Talmud (from the Hebrew, "to teach") is important to the history of Judaism, since it explains how to interpret and apply the laws of the Torah.

The Talmud consists of two parts: the Mishnah ("repeated study"), which is the written version of the laws God gave to Moses on Mt. Sinai, and the Gemara ("completion"), which is a record of the rabbinic commentaries that followed. The writing of the Mishnah began around A.D. 170–200 and was completed in A.D. 499. The rabbi most closely associated with the Mishnah is Yehudah Ha-Nasi, a descendant of King David. The compilation of the Gemara went on for centuries, with some of the most important commentaries written in the 11th and 12th centuries by Rabbi Shlomo Yitzchaki (known to scholars as "Rashi") and Rabbi Moses Maimonides (known as "Rambam"). The first complete edition of the Talmud was printed in Italy in the 16th century. All rabbinic opinions were recorded in the Talmud, giving it a nonlinear organization. The language is often cryptic and the text includes many Greek and Persian words that became obscure over time. Scholars devote a lifetime to understanding the many opinions and arguments that appear in its pages.

The Mishnah is organized into six sections covering every aspect of Jewish law and ritual practice: Zera'im (Seeds) deals with agricultural law and the prayer service; Mo'ed (Time or Season) contains laws pertaining to religious observance, including the Sabbath and other festivals; Nashim (Women) covers all aspects of family law; Nezikin (Damages) provides guidance on civil law; Kodshim (Sacred Things) discusses ritual practices in the Temple and dietary laws; Taharot (Purity) outlines the rituals of purity.

The guidance in the Talmud does not benefit Jews alone. It offers the basis for living a wholesome life, outlines God's expectations for humankind, and prohibits idolatry, blasphemy, murder, robbery, and removing and eating a limb from a live animal.

Part of the Jewish scriptural tradition, related to but separate from the Talmud, is the body of lore known as Kabbalah. It is said that Kabbalah enables adepts to recover hidden messages encoded in particular combinations of words, letters, and numbers in the text of the Tanakh. Kabbalah is based on traditions that arose in medieval Europe, and in modern times has become popular with practitioners of New Age beliefs. However, pious Jews believe that practice of the Kabbalah should not be attempted by anyone who has not spent years becoming thoroughly familiar with the Bible and the Talmud.

◆Belief and Practice

God Like Christians and Muslims, Jews believe in a single, all-powerful God, the creator of the world. God ("YHWH, Yahweh") is most often referred to in the Scriptures as *Adonai* ("my great Lord").

Law Judaism is distinctive for its extensive body of law governing both religious conduct and daily life. Jews believe that they have a covenant with God that gives them a special and privileged position as recipients of his law and protection, and that while God guides human destiny, individuals are free to choose their actions. Failure to live in accordance with God's law is a willful sin—likewise a good life is characterized by the deliberate choice to live ethically. Jewish law consists of the Ten Commandments (given by God directly to Moses), laws established in the Torah; and by laws found in the teachings of the prophets, and the traditions and commentaries of the Talmud.

Dietary Restrictions Rules for kosher ("ritually correct") preparation and consumption of food include the exclusion of pork and shellfish, guidelines for the slaughter, butchering, and inspection of meat, and a prohibition against the intermingling of meat and dairy products. In modern times, adherence to these dietary laws among Jews varies from meticulous observance to complete disregard.

Prayer and Worship Devout Jews generally pray at dawn, noon, and dusk, and some also pray when going to bed. Traditionally, men at prayer don special clothing and objects, including a talit (prayer shawl), teffe-lin (small boxes containing handwritten passages from Scripture worn on the forehead and left upper arm), and a kippah (skullcap; yarmulke in Yiddish).

The Jewish Sabbath (day of rest) is observed from sunset Friday to sunset Saturday. On the Sabbath, many Jews assemble at synagogues for prayer and other religious observances under the leadership of a rabbi ("teacher"). A *minyan* (quorum of 10 men) is required for a public prayer service to begin.

Rites of Passage Traditionally, Jewish men are circumcised eight days after birth and are given their names on that occasion. Boys at age 13 participate in a coming-of-age ceremony called a bar mitzvah ("son of the commandment"), and in some communities a similar ritual (bat mitzvah) is performed for teenage girls. Jewish funerals emphasize purity and sanctity. The deceased are buried as quickly as possible in a plain wooden coffin, and a special prayer (the Mourner's Kaddish) is said as part of the mourning ritual.

◆**Schools and Sects** Orthodox Judaism is the most rigorous form of Judaism. Orthodox Jews strictly observe dietary restrictions and other laws, such as the prohibition of carrying burdens or operating electrical or mechanical equipment on the Sabbath. Orthodox synagogues have separate seating sections for men and women, and services are conducted entirely in Hebrew. So-called Ultra-Orthodoxy emphasizes the obser-vance of religious law in minute detail as a sign of absolute obedience to God in all things. Among the Ultra-Orthodox are various sects of Ha-sidim ("the pious"), which form self-contained communities, chiefly in Is-rael and the New York City area, with distinctive dress and a strong community life.

Reform Judaism provides a means for Jews to be thoroughly assimi-lated into wider communities while retaining a Jewish identity. Men and women worship together in vernacular languages, women may be counted in minyans and ordained as rabbis, and observance of dietary and other laws is often symbolic or entirely absent.

Conservative Judaism originated in 19th-century America as a mid-dle ground between Orthodoxy and Reform Judaism. Conservative Jews usually observe at least the more prominent dietary laws and conduct services partly in Hebrew, but Conservatism covers a range of practices. Some Conservative congregations accept the ordination of women.

◆**History** Key events in the Hebrew Bible include Abraham's journey to the Holy Land, the escape from Egyptian slavery under the leadership of Moses, and the reigns of the early kings David and Solomon. The first Temple of Solomon was destroyed in the conquest of the Holy Land by Babylon in 586 B.C. Large numbers of Jews were allowed to end their Babylonian exile in 538, and the temple was rebuilt in Jerusalem and dedicated in 516. Under the Roman Empire, a series of rebellions resulted in the destruction of the Second Temple in A.D. 70.

After this, Jews began relocating to various communities around the world, an event called the Diaspora. As the Jews dispersed, Judaism changed from a temple-centered priestly religion to one shaped and nurtured by lineages of rabbis. Many Jewish communities prospered, and Talmudic scholarship flourished. In Europe, Judaism evolved into two communities and traditions: the Sephardim of Spain and the Mediterranean lands, and the Ashkenazim of northern Europe. Both suffered centuries of periodic persecutions and expulsions, culminating in the Holocaust, the Nazi regime's attempt to eradicate the Jewish people.

Zionism is a political movement established in the 19th century by Theodor Herzl and others, dedicated to establishing a Jewish homeland. It achieved its goal with the founding of the modern state of Israel in 1948.

◆**Holidays** In the Jewish calendar, Rosh Hashanah, the first day of the seventh month, begins the civil year. Ten days later is Yom Kippur, the Day of Atonement. This 10-day period, generally in September or October, is known as the High Holy Days or "Days of Awe." A harvest festival called Sukkot, the Feast of Booths, begins five days after Yom Kippur.

Hanukkah, the Feast of Lights, celebrates the dedication of the Second Temple; it spans eight days in the ninth lunar month, generally in December.

Purim, in the 12th lunar month (usually in March), commemorates how Queen Esther averted a massacre of Jews in Persia.

Pesach (Passover), the first week of the first lunar month (March or April) recalls the escape of the Hebrews from Egypt. Its central feature is a seder, a special meal that includes a variety of symbolic foods, during which the story of the Exodus is read from the Hagaddah, a religious text.

Day 2: Christianity

Christianity, the second of the major Abrahamic monotheistic religions, centers on the problem posed by the biblical question of Adam's original sin. According to Christian belief, Jesus Christ, God incarnate, redeems all who profess faith in him of both their personal sins and humanity's essential fallen nature.

◆**Overview** Christianity began as a radical Jewish sect led by Jesus of Nazareth, who was born in Bethlehem, in Roman-occupied Judea, ca. 4 B.C. Details of his life before about A.D. 26–28 are obscure. According to the four Gospels of the New Testament, he was baptized (ceremonially bathed in sanctified water) by John the Baptist, who claimed he recognized Jesus as the Messiah (Hebrew *Mashiah*, "anointed one"), the long-prophesied savior of the Jewish people. Jesus carried out a ministry of teaching, healing, and miracles that spanned a few years. In the company of a core group of followers ("disciples") primarily in Galilee in northwestern Palestine, Jesus preached that the Kingdom of God was at hand and began to be hailed by some of his followers as "King of the Jews." He publicly rejected the legalism of the Jewish authorities called Pharisees, contending that all of traditional biblical law could be reduced to two precepts: love God with all your heart, strength, and mind; and love your neighbor as yourself. After a fateful journey to Jerusalem, he was arrested, tried, and executed by the Roman authorities who, together with members of the Jewish priestly class, were concerned with the civil and religious implications of Jesus' preaching of the Kingdom of God. According to Christian belief, Jesus rose from the dead on the third day after his Crucifixion, appeared to his disciples in various places, and then ascended to heaven. Christians believe that Jesus, the Son of God, died on the cross as an offering and sacrifice for the salvation of humankind. Those who believe in him will be saved and will have eternal life after death.

Within a few decades, Christian communities had appeared in various cities and towns in the eastern Mediterranean region and also in Rome. The achievement of turning Christianity from a small Jewish sect into a potentially universal religion was largely the work of Jesus' original disciples together with the early convert Paul of Tarsus, whose letters to various communities helped shape both the beliefs and the organization of the early church.

◆**Scripture**   Christian Bibles vary slightly among different sects but always consist of two parts. The Old Testament incorporates the Hebrew Bible, in some cases with books renamed and in different order, and in some cases with additional books. Christians generally regard the Old Testament as prophetic of the life and mission of Jesus. The second part, the New Testament, consists of 27 books, incorporating four Gospels (accounts of the life of Jesus), the Acts of the Apostles, the letters of Paul and others to early Christian communities, and the Book of Revelation. The Apocrypha includes other Gospels and additional written materials relating to the early church, but is not accepted as canonical by most Christian sects.

◆**Belief and Practice**   Although Christian churches vary greatly in structure, practice, and certain points of doctrine and faith, a few core principles are common to most.

The Trinity This fundamental Christian doctrine states that God has three natures, or exists equally in three simultaneous and inseparable personified forms: God the Father, God the Son (Jesus), and God the Holy Spirit. God the Father is the all-powerful and omniscient creator of the world, who continues to govern his creation and to regulate and judge humankind. Jesus, also called Christ (Greek for "anointed one"), is God in human form, whose death atoned for Adam's original sin. The Holy Spirit is the aspect of God through which he communicates with humankind and provides strength and guidance to believers. Believers accept that Jesus' mother, Mary, gave birth to him while she was still a virgin, having been impregnated miraculously by the Holy Spirit. (Many Christians—primarily Catholics—regard Mary as being of near-divine status herself.)

The doctrine of the Trinity has been the subject of intense debate and divergent interpretations among Christian theologians for centuries, and the way in which the doctrine is understood is one important factor separating the various branches of Christianity.

The Sacraments Many Christian traditions—especially the Roman Catholic and Orthodox churches—recognize a number of sacraments (sacred rituals). The first of these is *baptism*, the washing or immersion of persons in water to symbolically cleanse them of sin and receive them into the Christian church. In some traditions this is done soon after birth, in others, in adolescence or early adulthood. For converts to Christianity, baptism is part of the rite of conversion. The other sacraments include *confirmation*, a personal affirmation of faith and entry into full church membership; *matrimony*; *ordination*, marking a person's acceptance into the clergy; *extreme unction*, known today as "the anointing of the sick"; *confession*, in which sins are formally confessed and absolved, sometimes with the performance of penance; and the *Eucharist* (also called Holy Communion), a ceremonial sharing of bread and wine as a reenactment of Jesus' Last Supper with his disciples. Most Protestant denominations place special emphasis on baptism and Holy Communion, and have ceased to practice extreme unction and formal confession.

The Afterlife Christians believe that each human possesses an eternal soul, which after the death of the body persists in immaterial form, is judged by God, and then rewarded (in Heaven), punished (in Hell), or (in a doctrine held by Roman Catholic and some Orthodox believers but not by most Protestants) consigned to Purgatory, an intermediate step of penance and purification where souls are prepared for entry into Heaven. Most Christians believe that at some future time God will bring an end to the world in a cataclysmic event associated with the Last Judgment, when the souls of Christian believers will be reunited with their physical bodies and enter into an eternal state of heavenly bliss in the presence of God while unbelievers will be consigned to eternal damnation.

◆Schools and Sects Over the course of its 2,000-year history, Christianity has fractured into a large number of schools and sects that accept the core Scriptures and fundamental beliefs of Christianity but vary widely in particular points of doctrine and practice. Today, there are numerous Christian sects—including Lutherans, Baptists, Presbyterians, and Pentecostals—which are derived in some way from the Protestant Reformation of the 16th century. (See Weekend 24, "The Reformation of the Christian World.")

◆**History of Christianity to A.D. 800**   At the time of his death, Jesus had a small number of followers among Jews, but his teachings were not widely accepted in the Jewish community and were strenuously opposed by Jewish religious leaders. Christianity began to flourish when it ceased to be a splinter Jewish sect and embraced a mission to reach and convert Gentiles (a term embracing all non-Jews) throughout the Roman Empire. This process was associated especially with the preaching and writings of the Apostle Paul, an early post-Crucifixion gentile convert to what was beginning to take shape as Christianity. The sacred texts of Christianity came into being over a period of several generations, beginning about A.D. 50 and continuing for a century or more. The four Gospels, though associated with the names of four of Jesus' original disciples, were written after their lifetimes, probably on the basis of oral traditions. Significantly, the books of the New Testament were written in Greek rather than in Hebrew or in Aramaic (the vernacular language of Palestine), reflecting the nascent church's aspirations to grow beyond its sectarian Jewish origin to become a universal faith.

Christianity, viewed as subversive by the Roman authorities, was widely and severely persecuted throughout the Roman Empire during a period of nearly three centuries. The church during that time was in large part a clandestine organization, and many early Christians were executed for their beliefs. At the same time, Christianity began to flourish beyond the eastern frontier of the Roman Empire, across a wide swath of Asia from Mesopotamia and Persia to the regions of Central Asia along the Silk Road, and as far as India and Ethiopia. The Roman emperor Constantine I legalized Christianity in A.D. 313, and later built a new eastern capital at Byzantium (renamed Constantinople) in A.D. 330, inadvertently setting the stage for a long-term state of discord between the Roman and Byzantine churches. In 380, Christianity became the official religion of the Roman Empire by proclamation of Emperor Theodosius, initiating a period of rapid growth throughout the Mediterranean world. The head of the church at Rome had by this time assumed the title of pope and was widely recognized as the principal voice of authority within the church and as the direct heir of the apostle Peter, the first bishop of Rome.

The growth and geographical spread of Christianity led inevitably to local and sectarian differences in doctrine and practice. Church leaders tried repeatedly to reconcile these differences and impose a uniform understanding of such theological issues as the Trinity and the dual (human and divine) nature of Christ. A series of ecumenical ("universal") councils addressed these and other issues, beginning with the Council of Nicea (325) and continuing with Constantinople (381), Ephesus (431), and Chalcedon (451). The approved orthodoxy was expressed in "creeds" (concise statements of belief), notably the Nicene Creed (fifth century A.D.), which remains in wide use in Christian liturgies today.

While the ecumenical councils established certain doctrines as orthodox and condemned others as heterodox and heretical, this had the effect of consolidating belief and practice only within churches under the authority of Rome and Byzantium. The councils were not able to control, let alone extinguish, the churches deemed heretical that were outside the empire's sphere of influence. This was especially true of the Nestorian Church (named for Bishop Nestorius of Constantinople, d. 451), a Syriac-language church that was condemned as heretical in 431 in a dispute over the nature of the Virgin Mary. Others include the heresies of Gnosticism and Manichaeism in the early centuries, which were condemned and often brutally suppressed once the church had achieved political power. As late as A.D. 800, there were many more Christians in Asia than in Europe and the Byzantine Eastern Roman Empire. The Asian churches, under Islamic pressure, were in severe decline by the 12th century and exist today only as scattered and vestigial communities.

Meanwhile, the writings of St. Augustine of Hippo, notably the *Confessions* and *The City of God*, were highly influential in the developing theology of the European church. The rules of monastic life established by the Italian monk St. Benedict in the early sixth century set the European church firmly on a course of monasticism that allowed it to survive and flourish in the medieval period. *The Rule of St. Benedict* became the standard work for monks throughout Europe as the guide to communal life of work and regular prayer away from the world and free from the desires of the flesh. St. Gregory the Great (pope; 590–604) also encouraged monasticism and worked tirelessly to establish the principle of the secular and sacred primacy of the pope, making the church the most important institution of post-imperial Rome. The spread of monasteries in France and especially in Ireland and the islands off Scotland provided a refuge for scholarship in a time of secular disorder. It also had the effect of distancing the European church physically from the Orthodox patriarchs of Byzantium.

The conquest and consolidation of a great western European empire by Charlemagne had significant consequences for the church. Having gained control of France, the Low Countries, much of Germany, northern Italy, and adjacent territories, Charlemagne went to Rome in 799 to lend political support to the papacy of Leo III, and in turn was crowned Emperor of the West by Leo on Christmas Day, 800. This entwining of secular and religious authority gave rise to the later theory of the Holy Roman Empire, whereby the emperor was God's secular representative on earth, just as the pope was his spiritual representative. The pope's claim of authority to crown the emperor deeply alienated the Orthodox authorities in Byzantium and helped pave the way toward the permanent schism between the Roman and Orthodox Churches in 1054.

In the West, however, the Roman Catholic Church's power in all spiritual matters and often in secular disputes would be challenged only sporadically over the seven centuries that passed between Charlemagne's coronation and the Protestant revolt in the early 16th century. During this period the popes and bishops constructed an extraordinary organization that ruled over virtually every city, town, and village in Western Europe. The popes wielded secular power in Italy sometimes through military interventions. They would lead the call to recapture the Holy Land from the Islamic infidels, they often enforced conformity to church doctrine with extreme punishment to heretics, and by the 14th century, several popes and many bishops had succumbed to the world's temptations, as greed and lust, both for sex and for power, became commonplace. All of this would lead to what is now called the Protestant Reformation. (See Weekend 24, "The Reformation of the Christian World.")

Weekend 39: American Popular Music II

Day 1: From the Blues to Hip-Hop

♦**The Blues** Much of the music we listen to in America has its roots in other countries, but there's a uniquely American strain of music—born in African-American culture—that contributed significantly to the musical landscape of American society. The blues originated in the southern U.S. and evolved from traditional ballads that in large part had sprung from slave songs. Poor, rural African Americans in the 19th century had a rich heritage of work songs and spirituals. These vocal forms shared the use of *blues notes*—flattened notes of the normal major scale—creating a unique sound that was further defined by the use of call-and-response vocal lines.

The rural blues eventually moved to urban areas and evolved into other types of blues music. The style also migrated across race lines, giving birth to the early country music that was popular mainly in poor, white, Southern communities. In fact, throughout the 1930s, it was difficult to tell the difference between blues and country music, save for the race of the performer.

One of the primary proponents of the new urban blues was the black composer W. C. Handy, known as the "Father of the Blues." Handy was a classically trained cornetist who played in various blues bands and minstrel shows before moving to Memphis in 1909, where he lived on famed Beale Street. It was there that he wrote the song "Memphis Blues," which became a national hit. Handy, in this and similar songs, smoothed out the irregularities of the rural blues and merged it with the dance band format, thus making the new style more attractive to city audiences. After World War II, the blues migrated up the Mississippi River to Chicago and Detroit, where musicians began to amplify their music electronically. This new electric blues influenced the development of the rhythm and blues style in the 1940s and 1950s, as well as the later music we now call rock 'n' roll.

♦**Jazz** Jazz is America's homegrown classical music, a form that from the beginning was immensely popular across the country. Though different from rock or the blues, jazz often incorporates elements from both genres. It can be played over a swing beat, a rock beat, a funk beat, or a Latin beat. Any size group can play it, from a solo pianist to a big band.

The earliest form of jazz was born in New Orleans between 1885 and 1915. This type of jazz—called classic jazz, New Orleans jazz, or Dixieland jazz—grew out of the South's existing blues, ragtime, and brass band traditions. Jazz musicians, however, embellished traditional melodies, and the resulting arrangements varied considerably from one performance to the next. New Orleans jazz evolved into what was called hot jazz, a style characterized by multiple and simultaneous improvisations in which front-line instruments, most often trumpet or cornet, clarinet, saxophone, and trombone, play off one another in spontaneous counterpoint.

When it comes to the history of early jazz, one name towers over all others: cornetist and vocalist Louis Armstrong. Armstrong's small ensemble recordings of the mid-1920s with his Hot Five and Hot Seven groups revolutionized jazz music and introduced the era of the virtuosic leader. In addition to his influential trumpet playing, Armstrong also pioneered the vocal style of scat singing—improvising on nonsense syllables instead of actual lyrics. The style comes from a recording session of Armstrong's *Heebie Jeebies* album (1926), when he purportedly dropped his lyric sheet while recording and was forced to improvise lyrics. Armstrong's recordings are classics that have influenced every succeeding generation of jazz musicians.

Bix Beiderbecke (b. Leon Bismark Beiderbecke), cornetist, composer, and jazz pianist, made his mark with a style of improvisation heard on the original recordings of classic jazz standards such as "Georgia on My Mind" with Hoagy Carmichael. Other early jazz greats include the Dixieland masters Buddy Bolden (b. Charles Joseph Bolden) and Joseph "King" Oliver. Bolden was known for a loud, piercing tone that could be heard over considerable distances, and was said to be a particularly expressive player of the blues. King Oliver took Bolden's style to a new level, specializing in slow blues, and used a growling style that would influence the "jungle" style of Duke Ellington (b. Edward Kennedy Ellington). Jelly Roll Morton (b. Ferdinand Joseph La Menthe) was the most influential of the New Orleans jazz pianists, melding blues, Spanish dance rhythms, ragtime, and folk. His flamboyant originality made his compositions such as "King Porter Stomp" stand out.

During the 1930s, hot jazz evolved into swing, and most jazz groups grew into big bands. Jazz was again a dance sensation, but swing appealed to both black and white audiences. Indeed, big band swing was the popular music of its day, featuring a combination of complex arrangements, innovative improvisation, and smooth vocals by the likes of Bing Crosby and Frank Sinatra. Big bands led by white conductors enjoyed increased visibility, such as those led by Glenn Miller, Benny Goodman, Artie Shaw, and the brothers Tommy and Jimmy Dorsey. There were also several notable black big bands during the swing era, which despite racial barriers and reduced visibility were wildly popular and well respected. These included the big bands led by pianist William "Count" Basie and pianist, arranger, composer Duke Ellington.

In the late 1940s, jazz musicians began to develop a new musical approach called bebop, which used complex harmonic structures played at very fast tempos. This new music was developed primarily by the saxophonist Charlie "Bird" Parker and trumpeter Dizzy Gillespie (b. John Birks Gillespie), and was the dominant form of jazz for the next several decades. During the 1950s, an alternative and more relaxed style known as cool jazz emerged, led by the trumpeter Miles Davis, who coined the term with his 1957 album *Birth of the Cool*. Cool jazz is characterized by music lines that are generally slower and more emotionally restrained, and many recordings feature irregular phrases and harmonic key shifts.

◆**R&B and Soul** Jazz music became less popular after World War II, and a new type of music dubbed rhythm and blues (R&B) filled its place in the musical firmament. R&B merged blues harmonies with a modified swing beat, and is typically played by smaller ensembles. In its original form, and in later incarnations as soul, funk, and contemporary R&B, this music brought black culture to white audiences across America.

The driving commercial force for R&B during the 1950s was Atlantic Records, a New York-based record label founded by Ahmet Ertegün, Herb Abrahamson, and Jerry Wexler. The label was home to the industry's top R&B and soul artists, including Ruth Brown (b. Ruth Alston Weston), Ray Charles, and the Drifters. In the early 1960s, R&B gained universal popularity when it was broken down into distinct musical streams.

Motown picked up the teen-pop end of the spectrum, while soul took up the gospel intensity and high energy of the best R&B performers. What we now call the "Motown sound" sprang from the creative efforts of two men: Berry Gordy, a one-time boxing promoter and would-be songwriter, and Smokey Robinson (b. William Robinson), a singer and songwriter. Thanks to a talented staff of studio musicians—dubbed the Funk Brothers—Motown recordings had a distinctive sound that set them apart from other 1960s productions. "The Sound of Young America," as it was called, blended elements of Atlantic R&B, black gospel, and rock 'n' roll pop into a concoction that sounded great coming from the tinny car radios of the time. The success of Motown on mainstream radio showed the potential for black music to cross over onto the traditionally white pop charts, and it had a profound influence on the development of all forms of popular music.

The most popular Motown performers—the Marvelettes, Martha and the Vandellas, the Supremes, the Miracles, the Four Tops, and the Temptations—had a large base of both black and white fans. While Motown represented the most commercial style of black music in the 1960s, artists of the Memphis-based Stax label were making a less polished—but still commercial—type: soul. The Stax sound, as represented by the artists Rufus Thomas, Otis Redding, Isaac Hayes, Sam and Dave, and Booker T. and the MGs, was raw and unornamented, typically just a singer accompanied by rhythm section and a small group of horn players.

During the later 1960s, similar soulful sounds were coming from the studios in Muscle Shoals, Alabama, and New York via the venerated Atlantic label. The Queen of Soul was Aretha Franklin, who began her career singing gospel music in her father's church. Her greatest hits include "Respect" and "(You Make Me Feel Like) A Natural Woman," the latter of which was a Brill Building song written by the white composers Carole King and Gerry Goffin. If Aretha was the Queen of Soul, the Godfather of Soul was James Brown. In the mid-1960s, Brown created a highly rhythmic style of R&B called funk. Brown combined stripped-down harmonies, driving rhythms, and high-energy vocals to create a compelling—and danceable—musical mix.

◆**Hip-Hop**   In the 1970s, hip-hop music emerged from the South Bronx, New York; it was a mix of reggae dancehall, Latin *bugalu*, jazz, funk, electronic, and disco music. The first hip-hop DJ was DJ Cool Herc, a Jamaican rapper who used side-by-side turntables to extend the rhythmic sections of popular songs at parties. By the end of the 1970s, hip-hop experiments had evolved into full-length compositions, characterized by heavy use of musical samples, extended rhymes, and a dance floor oriented style. The first widely successful rap group was New York's Sugarhill Gang, whose 1979 release *Rapper's Delight* is generally credited as the breakthrough hip-hop album. It was recorded by Sugar Hill Records, which touted other early successful acts such as Grandmaster Flash and the Furious Five.

Hip-hop in the mid-1980s exploded in popularity among youth as both the dance floor successor to disco and the political follow-up to punk. As exemplified by the roster of New York-based Def Jam Recordings, hip-hop increasingly appealed to black and white listeners; Def Jam produced L. L. Cool J's debut album *Radio* in 1985, former punk band Beastie Boys' crossover smash *Licensed to Ill* in 1986, and the highly influential, critically acclaimed *It Takes A Nation of Millions to Hold Us Back* by Public Enemy in 1988.

The Golden Age By the end of the 1980s, sophisticated recording technology expanded the hip-hop sound. In New York City, where hip-hop originators had always sampled jazz sounds, groups such as A Tribe Called Quest, The Jungle Brothers, De La Soul, and Digable Planets used the medium to talk about personal and race relationships over tracks created from jazz, soul, and funk songs.

Boogie Down Productions' KRS-One (b. Lawrence Parker) became an outspoken activist for ending gang-related violence through his music, while addressing the harsher realities of gang life that would influence an emerging subgenre of hip-hop called gangsta rap. In late 1980s Los Angeles, where a full-scale gang war was taking place, hip-hop expressed political and social frustration, often sampling Californian funk, soul, and psychedelic music. The 1986 single "6 'N the Mornin'" by Ice-T (b. Tracy Marrow) is considered among the first gangsta rap recordings, which delved into the tribulations and strife of Los Angeles gang life. But it was N.W.A.'s 1988 album, *Straight Outta Compton*, that was the most influential and controversial work in the West Coast style. When Dr. Dre (b. Andre Romelle Young) released *The Chronic* in 1992, gangsta rap became mainstream, and Dr. Dre's Death Row records became the publisher for some of the most famous hip-hop albums of the 1990s.

Though mostly marginalized in hip-hop lyrics, women were also present in the recording scene. One of the earliest and most successful female groups was Salt-n-Pepa, who released their first album, *Hot, Cool, & Vicious,* in 1986, which sold 1.3 million copies and propelled the group to stardom. Rapper Queen Latifah (b. Dana Elaine Owens) released her first solo album, *All Hail the Queen,* in 1989, when she was 19 years old, and she remains one of the most recognizable hip-hop personalities into the 21st century.

By the mid-1990s, two important developments changed the hip-hop sound and industry. First, jazz and soul labels began aggressively seeking revenue for samples that had been used in hip-hop songs for a generation; as a result, the use of sampling gradually declined. Second, the increasing popularity of hip-hop music generated a more corporate industry, just as wider shifts in the music business led to an overall slump in sales.

Day 2: Folk and Country Music

Flipping through radio stations while anywhere in United States, one is bound to find some country music. As of July 2010, there were far more country radio stations—2,017—than any other musical genre, as has been the case for many years. Popular country music has a long history that begins with folk music brought to America by the first European settlers.

•**Folk Music** The word *folk* comes from the German word for "people" or "army," and was adopted in the 19th century to mean "of the common people." It was first applied to music in 1889 and referred to the combination of traditional English, Irish, and Scottish tunes that had by that time evolved into a distinctly American form in immigrant communities. Traditional fiddle rounds gave way to an American cacophony that featured household-object instruments like the washboards and clacking spoons. Lyrical stories that accompanied tunes served as an oral history of early America, and the musical patterns remain entrenched in American culture.

The first American folk music collection to have a major impact was the Texas song collector John Lomax's *Cowboy Songs and Other Frontier Ballads,* published in 1910. In 1928, the Library of Congress established its Archive of American Folk Song to preserve and promote America's traditional music. In 1933, with the support of the archive, John Lomax and his son, Alan, made a collecting trip to southern prisons. There they discovered a 12-string guitar player and singer nicknamed "Leadbelly" (b. Huddie Ledbetter), who, when they brought him north to perform, became one of the first folk stars.

Perhaps the most commercially influential folk singer was another Lomax "discovery"; a performer named Woody Guthrie. Born in Oklahoma, Guthrie was an itinerant sign painter and guitarist who gained fame as a member of the New York folk community in the 1930s. A banjo player named Pete Seeger became his close friend, and the two often performed together at union rallies and labor meetings. Guthrie was a prolific songwriter, churning out classics including "Pastures of Plenty," "Roll On, Columbia," and "This Land Is Your Land." He continued to record and perform until the early 1950s. By then, Pete Seeger was a member of The Weavers, a group that was the model for many of the popular folk groups of the late 1950s and early 1960s, such as The Kingston Trio and the Chad Mitchell Trio. Seeger is also known for penning several songs that defined the tumultuous '60s—"We Shall Overcome," adopted as the anthem of the civil rights movement, as well as "Where Have All the Flowers Gone?" and "Turn, Turn, Turn!," which helped define the Vietnam War era.

The most popular of Guthrie's followers was a young Minnesotan who took the name Bob Dylan (b. Robert Zimmerman). Dylan soon established the social-protest genre, penning such folk classics as "Blowin' in the Wind" and "The Times They Are A-Changin'." Although Dylan was a talented performer, more polished musicians such as the trio Peter, Paul, and Mary initially popularized his songs. Peter, Paul, and Mary topped the charts with both of the above titles, and they also had hits with renditions of other "folknik" compositions, like Seeger's "If I Had a Hammer" and John Denver's "Leaving On A Jet Plane." One of the best-known rock acts in the folk tradition during this era was the duo of Paul Simon and Art Garfunkel, who wrote and performed iconic songs such as "The Sounds of Silence" and "Mrs. Robinson."

The folk movement of the 1960s splintered into many smaller, more focused movements in the '70s and '80s, such as the bluegrass and old-time music revivals, as well as fusions with world music and New Age (as "new acoustic" music). In the mid-1980s, social conscience songwriting resurged at the hands of songwriters such as Tracey Chapman ("Fast Car"). During the late 20th and early 21st centuries, Top 40 performers such as Bruce Springsteen and John Cougar Mellencamp continued to rely on folk roots; Springsteen consciously emulated Woody Guthrie in the sparse songs he wrote for his albums *Nebraska* (1982) and *The Ghost of Tom Joad* (1995), and Mellencamp put together an all-acoustic band for his 1987 album, *Lonesome Jubilee*. During the beginning of the 21st century, bands in several genres, from hip-hop (such as Outkast) to indie rock (such as Sufjan Stevens) continued to incorporate the melodies and instruments of classic folk into modern albums.

♦**Popular Country Music**   Although many genres were influenced by folk music, country music is wholly derived from it. The Texas fiddlers Eck Robinson and Henry Gilliland made the first popular country recording, "Turkey in the Straw," in 1922. The following year, Okeh Records released "The Little Log Cabin in the Lane" by Fiddlin' John Carson. In 1927, Victor Records spent two weeks recording acts in Bristol, Tennessee; included in these legendary "Bristol Sessions" were the first recorded performances of Jimmie Rodgers and the Carter Family. Rodgers brought rural country music to national popularity by streamlining the music and lyrics, thus making the genre a commercially viable property. Known as the "Singing Brakeman," he cut 110 records in just six years, singing in a bluesy style with a trademark high-pitched yodel.

Country music was the staple of local radio in the mid-1920s. One of the most popular radio programs was *Grand Ole Opry*, a weekly radio show broadcast from the music hall of the same name that defined the world of country music in the 1930s and 1940s. Because of the Opry's Nashville location, the city became the hub of country music, and singers and songwriters flocked to the area, as popular musicians did to Tin Pan Alley in New York.

In the 1950s, the RCA Records producer/guitarist Chet Atkins, along with Owen Bradley, combined country and pop music in what became known as the Nashville Sound. Atkins surrounded country's traditionally simple melodies and song structures with polished pop-oriented arrangements, creating a lush sound that blended rural sensibility with urban sophistication. The country genre gained popularity, leading to a number of pop crossover hits for artists such as Jim Reeves and Patsy Cline.

By the late 1960s, the Nashville Sound had morphed into "countrypolitan," with an even heavier emphasis on pop production flourishes; most countrypolitan recordings featured multiple layers of keyboards, guitars, strings, and vocals. The producer Billy Sherrill was especially known for this style, which produced numerous crossover hits for George

Folk and Country Music 391

Jones, Tammy Wynette, Charlie Rich, and Conway Twitty, among others.

Progressive country developed in the late 1960s as a reaction against the increasingly polished sound of mainstream country music. This was a songwriter-based genre inspired by classic honky-tonk, the hard-driving beat of rock 'n' roll, and the introspective writing of Bob Dylan. Very much anti-Nashville in its sentiments, progressive country was both "roots-ier" and more intellectual than the country-pop of its day. The top progressive artists—including Kris Kristofferson, Willie Nelson, Tom T. Hall, and Jimmie Dale Gilmore—were better known for their songwriting than for their singing skills, and wrote distinctive, individual songs that pushed the boundaries of the country genre. In the 1980s, progressive country evolved into alternative country, as popularized by Emmylou Harris, Lyle Lovett, k.d. lang, and similar artists.

During the 1980s and 1990s, several artists blurred the lines between country and folk music, creating a subgenre known as country-folk or Americana. The most popular country-folk and Americana artists also fall under the singer/songwriter umbrella. The most prominent of these artists include Mary Chapin Carpenter, Steve Earl, and Lucinda Williams.

By the late 1980s, a new breed of country-pop evolved that was significantly influenced by pop/rock sensibilities, spawning crossover superstars such as Garth Brooks and Billy Ray Cyrus. A wave of male singers—dubbed "hat acts" after their ubiquitous cowboy headwear—dominated the country charts with songs that sounded more like rock than traditional country. A decade later, the emphasis had shifted to female vocalists, similarly bathed in glossy pop productions. These vocalists—most notably Shania Twain, LeAnn Rimes, the Dixie Chicks, and Faith Hill—deemphasized traditional country twang and found massive success with a mainstream audience.

◆**Western Swing, Bluegrass, and Honky-Tonk** Popular country was only one direction in which folk music developed. As the roaring '20s slowed and the Depression began to set in, a fiddler named Bob Wills and vocalist Milton Brown formed a band, popular from 1931 to 1932, called The Lightcrust Doughboys, which is often credited with creating the Western Swing sound. Born in the Texas–Oklahoma region, it's a unique combination of string band music and jazz style. The 1950s and 1960s were lean times for Western Swing, but in the early 1970s young bands such as Asleep at the Wheel began introducing a new generation to the sound. The country superstar Merle Haggard recorded an album in homage to Wills's music, and then brought the star out of retirement for his famous last session in 1973.

Developing at the end of World War II, bluegrass music drew on the earlier string band music and melded it with influences from Western Swing, cowboy, and honky-tonk. A typical bluegrass band consists of mandolin, banjo, fiddle, guitar, and bass, with a lead vocalist often complemented on the chorus by tenor and bass singers. Bill Monroe is generally called the "father of bluegrass music." His group, the Blue Grass Boys, was named for his home state of Kentucky.

Honky-tonks—small bars often located on the outskirts of rural towns—became centers of musical creation in the years following World War II. From about 1948 to 1955, the honky-tonk style, famous for lyrics about drifting husbands, lyin', cheatin', and heartbreak, became the predominant country form. The foremost honky-tonk performer was Hank Williams, whose backup combo of crying steel guitar and scratchy fiddle became the model for thousands of honky-tonk bands. The honky-tonk style reached its apex in Hank Thompson's 1952 recording of "The Wild Side of Life."

During the 1950s and 1960s, bluegrass's popularity began to spread to urban centers, with groups such as the Country Gentlemen, the Greenbriar Boys, and the Charles River Valley Boys. By the 1970s, jazz, folk, and world music influences all became part of the bluegrass style, as evidenced by eclectic mandolinist David Grisman. The 1980s saw a return to traditional bluegrass styles among younger musicians, and by the mid-1990s even Nashville renewed its interest in bluegrass music.

Weekend 40: Philosophy: The Life of the Mind

Philosophy, a word derived from the Greek meaning "love of wisdom," attempts to understand rationally, basic questions about the human condition without resorting to myth, religion, or superstition. Some of these questions are: What is truth? What is beauty? What is knowledge? What gives life meaning?

Philosophical inquiry may also be directed at specific fields of study, such as politics, science, nature, etc., but as a general field of study, it is traditionally broken down into five major branches. *Metaphysics* seeks to describe the ultimate nature of reality, and debates fundamental questions about human existence. *Epistemology*, or theory of knowledge, considers how people come to know what they know. It is the study of the nature, origins, and limits of understanding. *Logic* is devoted to understanding and expressing the rules of reasoning and inference, and originated with Aristotle. *Ethics* is the study of principles for moral human behavior. *Aesthetics* is concerned with the nature and function of art, beauty, and other sensual experiences.

Day 1: Rational Thought in the Ancient World

Many readers are familiar with the names of the most highly regarded thinkers of the ancient world, Socrates, his pupil Plato, and Plato's pupil, Aristotle. But 150 years before Socrates appeared on the scene in Athens in the mid-fifth century B.C., other thinkers had already begun to ask fundamental questions about reality and the world.

Known collectively, as the Pre-Socratics, these philosophers tried to answer questions about the fundamental makeup and structure of the world, and search for *arche*, the ultimate base substance of existence. Thales of Miletus, for example, asserted sometime around 600 B.C. that the source of all things is water, presumably because it was believed that Earth floated on water, and also because water assumes various forms as solid, liquid, and gas. Some 50 or so years later, Pythagoras founded a school of philosophy that saw in the physical world the manifestation of hidden mathematical and geometric principles. He would develop the most famous theorem of geometry related to the sides of a right triangle; he also revealed the mathematical basis for musical pitch, which is the foundation of our understanding of harmony.   Socrates and Plato were influenced by the Pythagorean belief that mathematics should be the model for true human understanding.

Throughout the fifth century B.C., Greek philosophers explored central questions of what we call natural philosophy. Heraclitus, who is credited with the idea that "you can never step in the same river twice, for fresh waters are ever flowing in," believed that existence is by nature paradoxical, and the definition of anything depends on its opposite: hot depends on cold, up on down, and so on. Empedocles believed that earth, fire, air, and water were the four natural sources of existence which reside in different proportions in all things. He also proposed that the four elements exist in constant and unchanging quantities in the universe—an early statement of the conservation of matter, a principle of Newtonian physics. Moreover, Democritus, a contemporary of Socrates, developed a complete system to explain the physical universe. Atoms, he believed, have various shapes and sizes that determine the characteristics of objects as well as the emotions and ethical character of humans. Most surprising to a reader today was their exploration of such modern philosophical questions as the concepts of "being" and "non-being" and the nature of the universe by the Eleatic School, led by Parmenides and his pupil Zeno of Elea. Their ideas about an unchanging universe are still the subject of debate today.

◆**The Sophists** In the fifth century B.C., Greek learning expanded in almost every direction. It became more and more difficult for learned men to keep up with new developments and to educate the next generation. Also, the ability to influence others through the use of rational argument was increasingly prized, mostly for arguing legal cases, but also for advancing one's political agenda in the more democratic city-states. In this environment, teachers called Sophists began to travel from town to town in the Greek-speaking world. Usually they made their living by charging fees for giving instructional speeches on rhetoric, logic, and ethics.

Of the Sophists, Progatoras, a contemporary of Socrates, was the most well known. His famous dictum that "Man is the measure of all things" emphasized the relativity of truth. Since each person is a judge of truth, the relative "correctness" of any argument depends entirely on the speaker's ability to persuade.

◆**Socrates (469–399 B.C.)** Most Athenians of his time regarded Socrates as one of the Sophists, but in fact he accepted no fees for instruction, nor was he a travelling lecturer. Socrates loathed the title, Sophist, because he regarded most of them as relativists who believed truth could be determined by the power of the argument. Socrates believed that important ethical ideas should be held to the same standard of certainty that mathematicians attain when creating a geometric proof. Truth cannot be relative or changeable.

Socrates was preoccupied with philosophical questions and he debated them frequently in public gathering places, often attracting a group of bright young men who came to listen to him and engage in dialogues with him and others. The so-called Socratic method of learning through questioning is still prevalent today. Most of what we know about Socrates' beliefs comes from the 24 dialogues written down by his disciple, Plato, in which Socrates is almost always the featured character. There is general agreement, however, that the later dialogues are more Plato's beliefs than his teacher's.

In these early dialogues Socrates is seen as searching for elementary truths such as the definition of courage (in the *Laches*), or piety (the *Euthypro*). Two dialogues deal with the imprisonment of Socrates at age 70 after the Athenian assembly convicted him of introducing false gods and corrupting the youth. In the *Apology*, Socrates gives a spirited, unapologetic defense of his life; in *Crito*, named for the old friend who visits him in prison and who tells him his friends will pay for Socrates to leave Athens, and so spare his children the pain of seeing him die. Socrates refuses on the grounds that he made an agreement as a citizen to obey the laws of Athens, and to break that agreement raises the question, still relevant today, what would happen if everyone acted in that way? In the end, Socrates famously gathered his friends and took his own life by drinking a poison made from hemlock.

◆**Plato (427–347 B.C.)** At the time of Socrates' death, Plato was still a relatively young man, but already a superb writer. His most influential works—all dialogues featuring Socrates—were written during his middle years, including the *Meno*, which attempts to find the meaning of virtue. In *Phaedo*, Plato introduces one of his central ideas, the existence of abstract objects he calls "forms" that are eternal, unchanging, and incorporeal, such as beauty, piety, justice, and courage. These forms, Plato says, should be the object of philosophical study.

In the *Symposium*, Plato praises love of all kinds, even sexual love, but the highest kind of love is one that is connected to the Form of Beauty, which may lead one to appreciate the beauty of all bodies, and eventually to a love of people's souls. Plato's firm belief that all humans have souls that exist outside of their bodies would have a great influence on Christian theology during the Middle Ages.

The theory of the forms is more fully explicated in Plato's most read work, *The Republic*, in which he posits a political community where justice is the ideal most sought after, and the people are ruled by philosophers. Some of Plato's ideas are quite radical, such as the right of women to hold political office, and the community's need to censor literature, with philosophy replacing literature as the basis of moral education.

Plato's influence on virtually all of later philosophical thought would be hard to exaggerate if only because he wrote so much more than anyone who lived before him. But one of his students who came to his school, the Academy, would also produce an enormous body of work that would be studied for centuries, down to our own day.

◆Aristotle (384–322 B.C.) Born in Northern Greece, Aristotle came to Athens when he was 17 and enrolled in Plato's Academy. He stayed for 20 years and left when Plato died. He then travelled extensively, collecting biological data wherever he went, and he took an interest in the pre-Socratics' work on the nature of matter. When Aristotle went to Macedonia he became the tutor of a young man who would become known as Alexander the Great.

Aristotle produced a massive body of work on divergent topics. Unlike Socrates and Plato, who were both focused on finding unifying principles through abstract reason, Aristotle was much more open to contemplating and understanding the complexities of nature as perceived by the senses. He opposed Plato's theory of Forms, suggesting that they are not fixed and absolute. The highest form, or "the good," means different things for different creatures. Virtue and happiness both derive from realizing one's individual nature, and thus for humans, who are highly social and adaptable, this can mean many different things. Some of the most realized humans are those who develop humanity's peculiar gift for thought and contemplation, but it would be ridiculous to expect the same virtue for any animal. Consequently, Aristotle's ethics stress discovering how to achieve personal happiness, rather than defining what correct behavior is for everyone, although in his book *Nicomachean Ethics*, he stresses virtue as the centerpiece of human happiness.

Another of Aristotle's contributions to the development of philosophy was his structured analysis of logic. He defined a *syllogism* as a logical argument consisting of a major premise, a minor premise, and a conclusion: all men are mortal; Socrates is a man; therefore, Socrates is mortal.

In his work, *Politics*, he covers many topics including why states exist, and why obtaining wealth can be worthless. He distinguishes three types of government: monarchy, aristocracy, and democracy. Although he favors democracy, he makes a strong case for a monarchy if it is highly virtuous.

Perhaps Aristotle's most widely-read work is his esoteric treatise on aesthetics, the *Poetics*. According to his analysis of tragedy, the theatrical audience experiences *katharsis* ("purgation") of the heightened emotions of pity and fear as the tragic hero, a basically good but flawed aristocrat, is brought down by his own *hamartia* ("error of judgment").

Most of Aristotle's writings were lost in the West in the early Middle Ages. Many would surface in the Arab world in the 9th century and eventually become part of university studies in Europe in the 12th century.

◆**Hellenistic and Roman Philosophy**   After Aristotle, philosophy spread out from the domain of cultured aristocrats in Athens and entered the imagination of a wider audience, one that seemed eager for a supplement to pagan religious beliefs. *Skepticism*, like all Hellenistic philosophies, took an interest in epistemology and tended to question the basis of knowledge. Pyrrho of Elis (ca. 360–ca. 275 B.C.) the most influential of the Skeptics, was the most extreme in this regard, denying even the possibility of knowledge. He believed that existence is impossible to prove, and happiness is possible only through emotional indifference to events in the apparent world. *Epicureanism*, named for Epicurus of Samos (341–270 B.C.) was essentially agnostic, professing no knowledge of any world outside of the physical one. Given the lack of a divine directive for human behavior, the Epicureans turned to personal pleasure as a source of happiness. Many have misinterpreted the Epicurean attitude toward pleasure as a ruling principle. The original Epicureans were not hedonistic. They believed that pleasure consisted in removing pain from life, resulting in tranquility. This would be best achieved by satisfying only a limited number of desires, the ones that would cause pain if not satisfied.

Stoicism was founded by Zeno of Citium (3334–262 B.C.), who was influenced by the teachings of Pyrrho, but stopped short of his radically negative theory of knowledge. Zeno's ideas were furthered by many who came later, including Chrysippus (ca. 280–207 B.C.), and the Romans, Seneca (3 B.C.–A.D. 65), Epictetus (ca. 55–ca. 135 A.D.), and Emperor Marcus Aurelius (A.D. 121–180). The Stoics believed that people are alone among all beings in their ability to understand and react to the *logos* ("reason," "word," or "sign") that orders the universe. People cannot control the world, but they can seek to understand and live by the principles that govern the world. Like the Skeptics, the Stoics sought to develop an emotional indifference to their environment, because it signaled an acceptance of the order of things.

Stoic thinkers are the source of many lasting and influential ideas, such as beliefs in the fundamental equality of all persons and the concept of natural rights. The Stoics also admired Socrates because he remained focused on universal, timeless principles despite personal hardship and eventual martyrdom. Similar ideas were later widely accepted by, and considered characteristic of, Christianity.

Day 2: From Faith to Reason

With the decline of the Roman Empire in the fourth and fifth centuries, European civilization slowly came to be dominated by a Christian world view that had no tolerance for rational skepticism. Although early Christian thinkers admired many ideas of the Greek philosophers, in the end they came to embrace divine revelation as superior to reason.

In the early 5th century, St. Augustine became the first significant Christian philosopher to base many of his ideas about God on those of Plotinus, who lived in the 3rd century and believed that the order of the universe emanated from a single spiritual entity. In Augustine's seminal work of Christian thought, *The City of God* (ca. 415), he would identify this Neoplatonist idea as a central characteristic of the God he worshipped.

◆**Scholasticism** By the 11th century the advancement of literacy and learning throughout Europe brought new rigor to the study of philosophy. St. Anselm, the archbishop of Canterbury and a powerful political figure as well, sought to show that "faith seeking understanding" could rectify the struggle between revelation and reason. His logical proofs for God's existence in *Monologium* (1070) were the first to use Aristotelian principles, opening the door to future scholars who were also loyal sons of the church.

In the 12th century, an increase in urban development led to major changes in the centers of learning, which were evolving into universities. The universities of Paris and Oxford were founded in 1150 and 1168 respectively, and their curricula began to place greater emphasis on disciplines that had come down from the Greek philosophers, such as logic and the natural sciences. Aristotle was the most influential ancient philosopher during the high Middle Ages, thanks to the appearance of new translations of and commentaries on his work from the Arab Islamic world. Chief among the Arab sources were Avicenna (980–1037), and later Ibn Rushd, known as Averroes (1126–98).

St. Thomas Aquinas was a Dominican monk whose interest in Aristotle influenced him to write a complete systematic Christian theology, The *Summa Theologica* (1267–73), based on Aristotelian principles. He constructed five arguments proving the existence of God, all based on reason. He also argued that, ultimately, both reason and revelation were viable and parallel pathways to the knowledge of God. The former is accessible only to a few, but the latter is available to all. Aquinas's work remains today a central part of Catholic philosophy.

◆**Early Modern Philosophy** During the Renaissance more philosophers would abandon religious ideas and concentrate their work on the physical world and on the behavior of men. During the 16th century, moreover, the influence of the church was significantly diminished by the attacks of the Protestant reformers. Scientific discoveries by Copernicus, and later by Galileo, helped to reveal empirical evidence about the universe that refuted many of the articles of faith held by the church.

During the 17th century the origins of a new rationality can be found in the writing of several important thinkers. The English scholar and political figure Francis Bacon was one of the first proponents of empiricism, a philosophic school that stressed sensory experience and rigorous observation as the true path to knowledge. He was extremely skeptical of any claim to knowledge based on any other authority. This approach, known as "inductive reasoning," is the basis of the scientific method of inquiry.

In France, René Descartes also sought to establish a system of knowledge that rejected the authority of the church and all previous philosophy. But Descartes did not place great trust in information obtained through the senses. In his *Meditations on First Philosophy* (1641), he maintained that the senses must be doubted, because when we dream we think we are taking in sensory information, when, in fact, we are not. He reasoned that even in the case of an evil demon's deception, the demon could not have the power to make Descartes doubt his own existence, as long as he remained a thinking being. The thinker knows his thoughts are the thoughts of a being with existence: "I think; therefore I am." On this foundation Descartes proceeded to build a rational philosophy, i.e. a philosophy based on reason, rather than experience.

Although the philosophy of Descartes and his followers became the most influential school of philosophical thought (called cartesianism) during the latter half of the 17th century, several men would lead philosophy to search for answers to more pragmatic, real-world problems. The first among these was the English scholar Thomas Hobbes, whose deep interest in how government functions led him to travel extensively to do empirical research. His many political writings include for the first time the idea that there is a "social contract" between the rulers and the ruled based on "the laws of nature." Hobbes, however, believed that because men are wicked and selfish, and life is "nasty, brutish and short," the most effective form of government is a strong monarch almost without limits. The monarch's role is to keep peace and prevent people from harming one another.

◆**The Enlightenment** Over the next century the scientists and philosophers of Europe created an age of reason, a period known as the Enlightenment. Much serious thought during this time centered on political philosophy, discussing how government and people should interact, and the role of ordinary citizens in societies governed by monarchs whose absolute powers were now being challenged in England and France, as well as in America.

In England, John Locke's *Two Treatises on Civil Government* (1690) established the idea of a social contract based on natural law, and he asserted the need for property rights and freedom of conscience. In France a half-century later Locke's work would influence the work of Charles Montesquieu whose *The Spirit of Laws* (1748) compares three types of government (republic, monarchy, and despotism) and concludes that only the separation of powers within any government can prevent tyranny.

The ideas of these two men can be clearly seen in the words and thoughts of the leaders of both the American and French Revolutions. Montesquieu was also an important member of a Parisian group of intellectuals known as the *philosophes* whose commitment to learning led them to attempt the first encyclopedia based on the rational and secular values of the Enlightenment. Under the leadership of Denis Diderot, leading writers of the period, including Voltaire and Jean-Jacques Rousseau, contributed essays. In 1772, 28 volumes were published including 11 devoted to illustrating new industrial works, and in 1780 a five-volume supplement appeared. The *Encyclopédie* was an immediate success despite attempts by the crown to censor the liberal ideas and criticisms of government and society.

Voltaire is one of the best known of the *philosophes* because of his popular writings including the novel *Candide* (1759), and his pragmatic approach to philosophy and its applications to everyday life. His famous aphorisms including "If God did not exist, he would have to be invented," and "Let us cultivate our garden" (instead of focusing on problems we can't solve) help us to understand why he became a popular leader of what was still an unpopular view of the world and of humankind.

Rousseau's sheer brilliance in many subjects made him quite famous during his lifetime, despite evidence he may have been mentally unbalanced. A central idea in his works is that humans are born innocent and corrupted by civilization, a position that contradicted Hobbes as well as the Christian belief that humans are born sinful and need redemption through Christ. In his most famous work, *The Social Contract* (1762), he insists that freedom should be the ultimate goal of society. People give up important liberties to the government in exchange for their safety and well-being but they never suspend their right to end that relationship. He did, however, support government authority when the "general will" of the people embraced the laws and traditions the government promulgated.

Through his novel *Emile* (also 1762), Rousseau applied his ideas about a state of nature to his goal of reforming education. His belief that young minds already possess a vast amount of knowledge meant that the task of educators is to draw out their potential not try to pour information into their minds. This basic idea has remained very influential among educators in the West down to the present day.

◆**Immanuel Kant** The work of this 18th century German philosopher revived some of the central questions about human knowledge addressed by Descartes and Hume, one that actually goes back to the ancient Greeks. In his *Critique of Pure Reason* (1781, rev. 1787) Kant argues that empiricism cannot answer questions about space and time yet all human beings know they exist. God, freedom, and immortality cannot be observed but morality depends on our belief in their existence. Kant's resolution of the difficulties between the rationalists and empiricists is characterized as idealism because it retains the notion that ideal metaphysical realities, such as time and space, can be known even in a world where knowledge depends on experience.

During the first half of the 19th century Kant's idealism would become a dominant element in philosophical thought. But by the end of the century his work in moral philosophy would gain prominence in the thought of many intellectuals including Nietzsche and Freud, because Kant sought to resolve the contradiction between free will and determinism. He reasoned that the individual will is necessarily determined, that is, it must be subject to some force that gives it direction. People may think that they are free to make individual choices, but that is an illusion, usually at the service of some passion of the senses. It is only when one conditions the will to follow some "ideal," or rationally determined duty, that one can know freedom. The best solution is to search for the best ideal and dedicate yourself to the service of that ideal. Kant's formulation of this idea, known as the "categorical imperative," states that one's actions should be governed by "maxims," and those maxims should be such that everyone follows them. In other words, rules that would serve everyone are the best rules to govern individual behavior, and training yourself to live by such rules is the key to freedom.

Weekend 41: The Law

One of the defining characteristics of any civilization is the nature of its legal system. Today, almost all the governments of nation-states have a written set of laws that spell out the rules of acceptable behavior, the punishment for violating those rules, as well as the procedures for settling disputes. The tradition of written law codes dates back over 2,500 years to the "cradle of civilization" in Mesopotamia. Over the centuries, two different forms of legal systems evolved in the West, the civil law and the common law. The common law, based on precedent, became the foundation of the English and American legal traditions, which were spread around the world from Australia, India, Pakistan, Bangladesh, the Philippines, Indonesia, South Korea, and Japan to Kenya, South Africa, Nigeria, and other African nations.

Day 1: Law in the Ancient World

♦**Code of Hammurabi** The earliest known figure of great legal importance is Hammurabi (1792–50 B.C.), the king of Babylonia and creator of one of the most comprehensive early codes of laws. The code, engraved on an eight-foot-tall black stone monument, is well known for its thoroughness and complexity, addressing commercial, family, labor, property, and personal injury law. But it is also known for the harsh dictum "an eye for an eye," a literal legal punishment. Many other crimes that would seem relatively minor today incurred capital punishment. Rather than attempting any of the more modern aims of the law, such as rehabilitation, the Code of Hammurabi mandated simple retribution.

♦**Law in Ancient Athens** Law began to emerge as an instrument of a more humanitarian impulse in Greece during the rule of Solon (ca. 639–ca. 559 B.C.), the Athenian general and statesman who helped lay the groundwork for democracy in Athens. Prior to Solon, the harsh laws of Draco, promulgated in 621 B.C., were in force. Under Draco's laws, most crimes, even idleness, were punishable by death (our word *draconian* comes from his name). After his election in 594 B.C., Solon instituted a milder legal regime, in which punishments were calibrated to the seriousness of the crime. Courts also took on a more powerful role under Solon's law. The Roman historian Plutarch suggested that Solon intentionally wrote laws with a measure of ambiguity in order to increase the power of the courts through interpretation—a step that foreshadowed U.S. lawmakers' proclivity to let the courts decide the application of the general provisions of statutes to specific situations. Finally, Athenian law became more democratic, as Solon reformed the existing social, economic, and political systems in Athens. Solon gave his reforms popular appeal by, among other measures, annulling all mortgages and debts, limiting the amount of land any single citizen could hold, and forbidding all borrowing that could cause a debtor to lose personal liberty.

◆**Roman Law**   Early Roman law, as stated in the Twelve Tables (ca. 450 B.C.), formed the basis for the legal systems that would later influence those of Europe and through Europe the entire world. While some of the rules contained in the Twelve Tables are nearly identical to those of the modern world, such as requiring the accused to appear before a magistrate in the initial stages of a criminal proceeding, others were rooted in their time, such as the prohibition of marriages between plebeians and patricians. Law became more sophisticated as a method of stabilizing society under Lucius Cornelius Sulla, a Roman general and dictator whose usurpation of power in 82 B.C. paved the way for the rise of Julius Caesar and the fall of the republic. His *leges corneliae* provided specific punishments for homicide, arson, the intention of killing or stealing, poisoning, and the manufacture and possession of poison. However, his rule was also marked by efforts to check the populist branches of Roman government. For example, Sulla protected the power of the Senate from populist incursions by giving it control of the courts and power over the tribunes.

The Roman Republic came to an end when Julius Caesar was given extraordinary powers after a series of dazzling military victories. The civil war that followed his assassination in 44 B.C. resulted in complete triumph for his nephew, Octavian, after he defeated Marc Antony and Cleopatra in 31 B.C. In 29 B.C., he took total control of the Roman Empire as its first emperor, with the title Caesar Augustus. (The term *emperor* derives from the Latin *imperator*, meaning victorious general.) Augustus established legal principles that would influence Western law, including clear procedures for formalizing contracts, strengthening personal property law, and the presumption that defendants were innocent until proven guilty. Augustus's legal reforms were extensive but were rooted in Roman tradition. Rome technically remained a republic governed by the Senate, but with Augustus as leading man or *princeps*.

Roman law underwent some of its most important developments under Emperor Justinian I (A.D. 483–565). Previously disparate Roman legal decisions and laws were now systematized and codified as the *Corpus Juris Civilis* (body of civil law). What was important about Justinian's Code was not necessarily what was new in it, but rather the influence that this systematic restatement of law would have on the development of future legal systems worldwide.

•**Medieval Law** In the early medieval period, the invasion of the Roman Empire by the Germanic tribes resulted in a complex coexistence of Roman and German legal systems. In general, Roman subjects of barbarian kings remained subject to Roman law, while their Germanic neighbors were subject to traditional Germanic laws and customs. Legal procedures in the early Middle Ages were heavily influenced by German customs. An accused criminal was often subjected to an "ordeal," such as being bound and thrown into water, to determine guilt or innocence. A key difference between the two systems was that Roman law retained a notion of the *rei publicae* or common good, whereas Germanic law tended to reduce every good, even justice, to a private right.

During the seventh, eighth, and ninth centuries, the Germanic tribes codified their customary law. But the influence of Roman law grew enormously after Charlemagne's establishment of the Holy Roman Empire in A.D. 800 because the Roman Catholic Church used Roman law in its tribunals, giving them a uniform system of justice throughout the West. The collapse of the Carolingian empire in the 10th century led to the emergence of feudalism, placing many disputes in the hands of the local lord whose control of the land was seen as giving him the concurrent right to administer justice.

Property law, especially in the Anglo-American legal systems, remains influenced by concepts of ownership derived from the Middle Ages. However, modern law has moved away from the medieval treatment of crime, under which harsh punishments were meted out for minor offenses (a thief, for example, might be hanged or have his eyes gouged out).

Over time, largely through the church's influence, judicial procedures on the Continent came to conform to Roman practices, including the use of torture to extract evidence in certain situations. In the 11th century, the founding of the University of Bologna in Italy, which specialized in the teaching of law using Justinian's Code as the basis of instruction, contributed to a revival of Roman law. This revival was aided by the efforts of both stronger monarchies and the church to suppress the jurisdiction of local feudal courts and to replace them with royal and ecclesiastical courts, often administered by clerics and others who had been specifically trained in Roman law.

◆**Anglo-American Law**   Anglo-American jurisdictions are said to be "common law" systems rather than "civil law" systems as found on the continent of Europe. Civil law governs society through extensive and specific codes often devised by a legislative body (the Napoleonic Code is one famous example). Common law is always evolving as scores of judges independently make legal decisions based on cases. Over time, operative legal principles in cases become clear. Thus, legal rules emerge from "case law."

After William the Conqueror invaded England in 1066, he introduced feudal concepts that had taken hold in France, and he embarked on what would become a centuries-long struggle to centralize control over justice and taxation. One result was his order to prepare the Domesday Book (ca. 1086), an inventory of all the property in his new realm. Subsequent rulers, with greater or lesser success, sought to maintain the supremacy of the royal courts, introducing new ones and modifying old ones as new situations arose. While England has never had a written constitution, it has, for centuries, relied strongly on laws and judges rather than rules handed down by divine authority. The beginnings of English constitutionalism lie in Magna Carta, the document that English barons and church elders forced King John I to sign in 1215. Magna Carta required King John to refrain from encroaching on feudal rights and to abandon the practice of waging expensive, unsuccessful wars and auctioning off church offices. Between the lines of the charter's 63 brief clauses lie the recognition of individual and communal rights inviolable by any authority. These new rights helped to form the basis of the emerging English constitution.

The development of "equity jurisdiction" under a series of lord chancellors filled the gaps in the common-law system and gave faster and more efficient justice than traditional royal courts, which had particularly inflexible procedural rules that often seemed to impede rather than facilitate justice. By the late 15th century, the supremacy of the royal courts was established, but how the different court systems were related to one another was unclear. In the early 17th century, Charles I began to collect taxes without the consent of Parliament, and soon the role of the courts became crucial as the king attempted to use them as the means of collecting taxes. In general, the traditional courts supported Parliament; and with the triumph of Parliament in the English civil wars, the supremacy of the traditional courts with their customary, non-Roman procedures was ensured.

The *common law* evolved as a coherent system under a series of jurists. Sir Edward Coke, a chief justice of the King's Bench, helped cement the common law, rather than royal prerogative, as the default law of England. Sir Matthew Hale, the lord chief justice under Charles II, helped synthesize the common law into a field of careful study. And Sir William Blackstone, a professor of law at Oxford, wrote the four-volume *Commentaries on the Laws of England* (1765–69), which conclusively demonstrated that English law was comparable to the two other grand legal systems—Roman law and the civil law of Europe.

A century later, the development of common law under the control of British and American judges was chronicled by Oliver Wendell Holmes. In his lectures and book *The Common Law* (1881), Holmes argued provocatively that the common law developed in accordance with social reality and collective desires, rather than clear moral or philosophical precepts. "The life of the law is not logic, but experience," he wrote. Holmes's approach formed the foundation for the early 20th-century legal realist movement, which understood judicial reasoning not as an abstract logical process but instead as a reflection of judges' own personal and political lives and the society of which they are a part.

◆**The Enlightenment**   Although the form and process of American law came from the British common law model, dating to the late Middle Ages, many of the ideas underpinning America's legal and political choices came from a more modern period, the Enlightenment. In the 17th and 18th centuries, philosophers began arguing for the power of rational, equality-focused, and humanistic reasoning over the inherited authority of the church and other traditional sources of law. The Enlightenment's influence on the law was therefore deep and lasting. The law now evolved to fit societies that were learning to value rational ideas and the value of individual rights, rather than the divine right of kings or the rigidity of traditional institutions. The law itself became more enlightened, more logical, more systematic, and more humane.

The familiar American rights to "life, liberty, and the pursuit of happiness," included by Thomas Jefferson in the Declaration of Independence, may be traced directly to John Locke, whose *Two Treatises on Government* (1690) helped shape the American notion of a government dedicated to protecting private property and individual liberties. Locke argued that life in the state of nature was fundamentally felicitous, and that the state was necessary only because certain people would never recognize the rights of others to "life, health, liberty, or possessions." The American dedication to natural rights and a government dedicated to protecting them borrows directly from these ideas.

In France, *The Spirit of Laws* (1748) by Charles Louis Montesquieu contained the basic notion of separation of powers to guarantee the freedom of the individual. The Founding Fathers of the United States emphasized balancing the executive, legislative, and judicial branches, an approach that can be traced directly to Montesquieu, as can their thoughtful approach to avoiding the fate of the Roman republic (the subject of a study by Montesquieu in 1734).

The American legal idea of popular sovereignty can be traced to the work of another French philosopher, Jean-Jacques Rousseau. Rousseau's political theory, found in *The Social Contract* (1762), was that people were intrinsically good prior to their involvement in a state. They traded their original sovereignty to the state in exchange for protection and social progress, so the state must recognize and obey the collective desires—the people's "general will"—on issues of political and legal significance. Such ideas stood in stark contrast to traditional monarchical or aristocratic theories of the state. They also led the Founding Fathers to base American law on the consent of the people, the limitations of the state, and the embrace of individual rights.

Day 2: The American Constitutional System

The United States possesses a highly unusual, innovative legal system as complex as it is elegant. The American legal system has several interlocking elements that are built on the Constitution itself and on federalism, which ensures that state legal systems will always have some independent authority to balance against the strength of the federal system.

The two interdependent systems share a number of elements. First, each state has explicitly incorporated the British common law as the default set of rules on matters of torts, contracts, and other basic areas of the law. Second, each state as well as the federal government has a constitution, which not only gives citizens individual rights not found in the common law but also governs the operations of the various branches of government. Third, both the states and the federal government have complex and ever-growing bodies of statutory law: rules passed by the legislature, which often supplant the common law. The growth of federal statutes (regarding labor, the environment, and consumer protection, among other matters) was one of the principal legal stories of the last 150 years. In sum, it is an enormous system with many moving parts, designed for stability rather than agility.

Constitutional Law stems exclusively from the U.S. Constitution and the constitutions of the states. In federal constitutional law, two separate documents are at work: the first five articles of the original seven in the Constitution, and the amendments subsequently added to the Constitution (including the original 10, the Bill of Rights). The first five articles deal primarily with the organization and powers of the national government, the last two with issues current in 1789.

Article I: Creates a bicameral legislature and outlines the requirements for holding office; outlines the duties and obligations of each body, especially the making of laws and control of finances.

Article II: Creates the executive branch of government with a president and vice president; describes who can hold office, and makes the president commander in chief of the armed forces.

Article III: Creates the Supreme Court and grants Congress the power to establish inferior courts, and establishes the necessity for trial by jury in all cases involving crimes.

Article IV: Requires the states to honor each other's laws and judicial decrees, and grants the citizens of each state the rights to "all privileges

and immunities" of citizens in all the states. It also guarantees that each
state will have a republican form of government and that the federal government will protect every state from foreign or domestic violence.

Article V: Provides for the ability of both houses of Congress, or the
legislatures of two-thirds of the states, to propose amendments to the
Constitution.

Article VI: Asserts that the new government would honor all public
debts incurred since 1776; and establishes the supremacy of the authority of the Constitution and national laws over state laws.

Article VII: Simply says that when nine states ratify the Constitution,
it will become the law of the land.

The men who wrote the Constitution did not realize that ratification
would require vigorous debate throughout the states and result in 10
amendments to the document before it finally became the law of the land
in September 1789. These first amendments are collectively known as
"The Bill of Rights" and several of these have become hallmarks of what
American citizens believe they mean by *freedom*, including the right to
free speech and to practice any religion they choose, or none at all
(Amendment I); the right to bear arms (II); and "to be secure in their
persons, houses, papers, and effects, against unreasonable searches and
seizures" (IV); and the right to "a speedy and public trial." (VI)

Over the last 220 years, 17 more amendments have been added, including the revolutionary 13th, 14th and 15th, passed after the Civil War,
which ended slavery and guaranteed former slaves their rights as citizens.
The 14th also prevented the government from removing the rights of any
citizen without "due process of law," helping to define the meaning of citizenship, a notable omission from the original Constitution.

◆The Court System

Federal Courts Federal courts hear cases involving federal law and
significant disputes between citizens of different states. The federal court
system has three levels: district courts, circuit courts, and the Supreme
Court. Federal district courts have jurisdiction in both civil and criminal matters. Circuit courts of appeals hear cases on appeal from district
judges' decisions. The 50 states are organized into 11 circuits, and there
are separate appeals courts for the District of Columbia and for such
specialties as federal patent issues. A circuit court will hear a case in
one of two ways: a panel, usually of three judges, may decide a case; or

an *en banc* ruling may be issued by the entire court. A panel decision may be appealed for a full *en banc* hearing. Both district judges and circuit court judges are "Article Three" judges, so called because they are formally chartered by Article Three of the Constitution and are appointed by the president and confirmed by the Senate for life terms. The third and final level is the Supreme Court, which hears most of its cases on a discretionary appeal known as a "writ of certiorari." The Supreme Court receives several thousand writs a year and accepts fewer than 150 for review, usually on issues of great legal, social, or political significance.

The Supreme Court The basic American constitutional system required interpretation and molding before it could take its present form. A strong hand was provided by John Marshall, chief justice of the United States for three decades. Marshall's extraordinary opinion in *Marbury v. Madison* (1803) established the doctrine of "judicial review," which essentially gave the Supreme Court and lower courts final power to consider and reject actions by the legislative and executive branches of government. His decision in *McCulloch v. Maryland* (1819), rejecting the argument that states could trump federal statutes and establishing congressional enactments (in this case, to launch a bank) as the law of the land, had a similar structural effect on the constitutional system.

How a Case Comes Before the Supreme Court In order for a case to be heard by the Supreme Court, at least four justices have to agree that the legal questions posed by the case merit the Supreme Court's attention. They may decide to take a case because a state supreme court or a federal appeals court has ruled on a question of federal law that the Supreme Court needs to review, or they may feel compelled to act because a lower court ruling conflicts with previous Supreme Court decisions. They may aim to provide clarity when an important point of law has been decided in conflicting ways, or to step in and rectify the situation when a lower court seriously violates the judicial process.

Once the Supreme Court has decided to hear a case, the Court solicits briefs from the two opposing sides in the form of oral and written arguments. Briefs may come from the parties involved in the case, or from federal or state governments and any persons who have an interest in the case's outcome. After all the briefs are filed, the Court hears the oral arguments, which are limited to one hour. A lawyer for each side gets a half hour, and while he or she is presenting, the justices are allowed to interrupt for questions or clarifications. These proceedings are open to the public.

State Courts Most state court systems roughly parallel the federal system, with three levels: courts of general jurisdiction, which hear all kinds of cases; intermediate appeals courts; and a state supreme court. State court systems also have courts of limited jurisdiction, which hear only certain matters, such as small claims issues. In many states, judges are popularly elected rather than appointed by the legislature or the governor.

♦Important Supreme Court Decisions Over the course of American history, the decisions of the Supreme Court have both reflected and reshaped the values and traditions of society. In addition to John Marshall's decisions, many of the most controversial have involved the power of the president, the right to privacy, and the fight for equality by former African-American slaves and their descendants. Here are just a few of them:

Dred Scott v. Sanford (1857) Dred Scott, a Missouri slave, sued for his liberty after his owner took him into free territory. The Court ruled that Scott remained a slave because the Missouri Compromise of 1820, prohibiting slavery from part of the Louisiana Purchase, violated the Fifth Amendment by depriving slave owners of their right to enjoy property without due process of law.

Ex Parte Milligan (1866) President Abraham Lincoln's suspension of some civil liberties during the Civil War was attacked in this decision, which upheld the right of habeas corpus. The Court ruled that the president could not hold military tribunals in areas where civil courts were open and functioning.

Civil Rights Cases (1883) Racial equality was postponed 80 years by this decision, which struck down the Civil Rights Act of 1875 and allowed for private segregation.

Plessy v. Ferguson (1896) The "separate but equal" doctrine supporting public segregation by law was affirmed in this ruling, which originated with segregated railroad cars in Louisiana. The Court held that as long as equal accommodations were provided, segregation was not discrimination and did not deprive blacks of equal protection of the laws.

National Labor Relations Board v. Jones & Laughlin Steel Corp. (1937) Laws protecting unions and barring "unfair labor practices" were upheld by the "stream of commerce" doctrine that employers who sold their goods and obtained their raw materials through interstate commerce were subject to federal regulation. This ruling became the basis for an expansive understanding of the commerce clause.

West Virginia Board of Education v. Barnette **(1943)** In this case, brought against a Jehovah's Witness, the Court recognized that refusing to salute the flag did not violate anyone's rights, and that the First Amendment protected the "right of silence" as well as freedom of speech.

Youngstown Sheet and Tube Co. v. Sawyer **(1952)** During the Korean War, when President Harry S. Truman seized steel plants to keep them operating despite a strike, the Court held that his action was an unconstitutional usurpation of legislative authority. Only an act of Congress, not the president's inherent executive powers or military powers as commander in chief, could justify such a sizable confiscation of property, despite the wartime emergency.

Brown v. Board of Education of Topeka **(1954)** Chief Justice Earl Warren led the Court to decide unanimously that segregated schools violated the equal protection clause of the 14th Amendment. The "separate but equal" doctrine of *Plessy v. Ferguson* (1896) was overruled.

Baker v. Carr **(1962)** Overrepresentation of rural districts in state legislatures, which effectively disenfranchised millions of voters, led the Court to abandon its traditional noninterference in drawing legislative boundaries. All states eventually reapportioned their legislatures in conformance with the "one man, one vote" doctrine.

Gideon v. Wainwright **(1963)** Reversing an earlier ruling in *Betts v. Brady* (1942), the Court held that the Sixth Amendment guaranteed access to qualified counsel, which was "fundamental to a fair trial." Gideon was entitled to a retrial because Florida failed to provide him with an attorney.

Griswold v. Connecticut **(1965)** In striking down a Connecticut law of 1879 against the use of contraceptives, the Court established a "right to privacy" that was implied by, though not specifically enumerated in, the First, Third, Fourth, Fifth, Ninth, and 14th Amendments.

Miranda v. Arizona **(1966)** Miranda's confession to kidnapping and rape was obtained without counsel and without his having been advised of his right to silence, so it was ruled inadmissible as evidence. This decision obliged police to advise suspects of their rights upon taking them into custody.

Loving v. Virginia (1967) Loving was a white man who had married a black woman and had been convicted under Virginia's law prohibiting interracial marriage. In a unanimous opinion, Chief Justice Warren struck down the law as an invidious racial classification prohibited by the 14th Amendment's equal protection clause.

Roe v. Wade (1973) In a controversial ruling, the Court held that state laws restricting abortion were an unconstitutional invasion of a woman's right to privacy. Only in the last trimester of pregnancy, when the fetus achieved viability outside the womb, might states regulate abortion— except when the life or health of the mother was at stake.

Bush v. Gore (2000) For the first time in the nation's history, the Court found itself in the position of deciding a presidential election. Vice President Al Gore filed suit in Florida to begin a recount of ballots in several counties where machines were unable to determine the voters' selection. Governor George W. Bush of Texas appealed the decision to the Supreme Court, which ruled that because there were no uniform standards for how to conduct a recount, doing so would violate the 14th Amendment's guarantee of equal protection.

Lawrence v. Texas (2003) The Court struck down a statute in Texas that made it criminal for two persons of the same sex to engage in sexual acts in private.

Hamdi v. Rumsfeld (2004) In a case that maintained judicial authority over a wartime executive, the Court ruled that the president could not deny defendants access to American courts simply by labeling them "enemy combatants." Declaring that "a state of war is not a blank check for the president," the Court said the government had deprived Yaser Esam Hamdi, an American citizen seized in Afghanistan, of his due process rights. In two companion cases, the Court ruled that non-citizens seized during military operations could not be held without access to U.S. courts.

Citizens United v. Federal Election Commission (2010) In a 5–4 decision, the Court ruled that government may not ban political spending by corporations and unions in elections. While the majority held that the decision upheld the First Amendment freedom of speech clause, the dissenters warned that corporate money would corrupt the political process. The decision overturned two recent decisions that restricted corporate and union election spending.

Weekend 42: Modern Thought

Day 1: Modern Philosophy

•**Nineteenth-century Philosophy** The greatest commonality among the various philosophical movements of the 19th century was their operation under the broad shadow of Kant. The first wave of Kantians, known as Idealists, sought to broaden metaphysics beyond Kant's very modest list of structures (such as space, time, and mathematical deductions) that guide human understanding. Growing disillusion with the hopes of the Enlightenment, coupled with the growing extravagance of the claims of the Idealists, prompted a reaction against Idealism, and against philosophy itself, in intellectual circles. By the end of the century, especially in continental Europe, philosophy became a weapon for attacking the notion that people are rational beings. Instead, according to such thinkers as Nietzsche and Freud, people merely use the guise of rationality to achieve irrationally motivated ends.

German Idealism By opening up a new space for philosophy to discuss the metaphysics of mind, Kantianism gave rise to a series of more mystical speculations about the ultimate nature of humankind and anything else that might be universal about the human experience. Georg Wilhelm Hegel extended the discussion to the point that "mind" is characterized as a universal and evolving entity. Hegel sought to determine the course of universal mind by analyzing the course of history. He concluded that universal mind is on an inexorable course toward self-awareness, although the path from ignorance to pure self-awareness is not marked by a straight line. Instead, the course of history has been a series of social upheavals marked by philosophical confusions that must be resolved before the next historical epoch can begin.

Hegel was a prolific writer for most of his life. His most famous work was his first, *Phenomenology of Mind* (1807); in 1818, he published a summary of his philosophy, *Encyclopedia of Philosophical Sciences*. One of his most influential concepts is known today as the "Hegelian dialectic," in which he asserts that one concept (thesis) generates its opposite (antithesis) and that interaction leads to a new concept, the synthesis. Hegel often coined new phrases in service to his philosophy, prompting a great deal of debate—about both his intended meaning and its value. To this day, there is very little agreement among philosophers about either, yet there is no doubt that Hegelian speculation had a strong influence on some of the great minds of the 19th century, including Kierkegaard, Marx, Nietzsche, and Freud.

Kierkegaard and Marx Søren Kierkegaard was a Lutheran theologian in Denmark who was mostly interested in the individual's relationship to God, which he viewed as parallel to the Idealists' characterization of the relationship between the individual and the universal. In works such as *Either/Or* (1843), Kierkegaard saw the various claims of the Idealists as extravagant, and he gravitated to a more skeptical view in which universals are beyond the reach of human knowledge. He saw God as an entity that humans cannot really know. Rather than languish in despair, however, Kierkegaard saw this gap in human understanding as an opportunity for faith. Kierkegaard maintained that faith is an extremely important concept undervalued in philosophical circles. In fact, it is only through faith that people can meet the various challenges they face in an irrational life filled with uncertainties.

Karl Marx accepted much of Hegel's characterization of history, but Marx sought to change the story from what he called its "fairy-tale" version into a real account of actual historical forces struggling to liberate people from oppression. Marx called his version of Idealism "historical materialism" to highlight the differences. For Marx, the key to materialism was understanding the economic forces that determine human interest. The central ideas in Marx's philosophy were that labor is an essential activity for man, and that private property represents the product of man's labor in the form of things. During production, labor is alienated from itself through the process of making commodities. The end of this alienation requires the abolishment of private property and wage labor.

In his major works, *The German Ideology* (1845), *The Communist Manifesto* (1848), both written with Friedrich Engels, and *Das Kapital, Volume 1* (1867), Marx cast history as a drama of class struggle; as new, progressive classes form, they wrestle with the old over means of production. The new ruling classes win power as society progresses and maintain their rule over the lower classes (the proletariat) through property and wages. The ultimate hope for human liberation depends on the common working people understanding their economic interests and taking control of their destiny through collective action.

Utilitarianism While Hegel's Idealism would dominate philosophical debate for the first half of the 19th century, a pragmatic philosophical strain continued to gain prominence, especially in England. In 1789, Londoner Jeremy Bentham published his *Introduction to the Principles of Morals and Legislation,* which provided the essential framework for *utilitarianism.* This moral theory asserts that any action is right if it maximizes pleasure or happiness and minimizes discomfort or unhappiness. Bentham believed that governmental social policies should be based on this idea.

Bentham's doctrines were taught to a young John Stuart Mill by his father, who schooled him at home because of the child's precocious mind. Mill's book *Principles of Political Economy* (1848) influenced radical thinkers in both politics and economics, especially in later years when socialism grew popular. In his *Utilitarianism* (1861), he sought to improve on the ideas of Bentham as well as his father by expanding the pleasure principle to include quality with quantity, advocating for the pleasures given by learning and achieving.

Mill's central idea that individuality is the key to human freedom has recently brought his works a new prominence. His most famous books today are taught in universities around the world because they deal with subject matter most relevant to our own time, and also because of Mill's insights into essential human problems that existed back then and also now. In *On Liberty* (1859), he develops the idea of the "harm principle," which holds that the only reason anyone can limit the freedom of another person is self-protection; no other reason, no matter how noble in intention, can be used to foster behavior on another unwillingly. In *The Subjection of Women* (1869), his seemingly radical positions at that time are almost all recognized today as essential rights for women in all Western industrialized nations, including the right to vote, to have unfettered access to education, and to aspire to any occupation even while raising a family.

Nietzsche As Kierkegaard had done earlier, intellectuals in continental Europe at the end of the century (such as Sigmund Freud) were taking a greater interest in the exploration of the irrational mind. Building on the thought in Arthur Schopenhauer's influential book *The*

World as Will and Representation (1819), Friedrich Nietzsche characterized philosophy as part of a grand deception designed to prevent people
from recognizing the truth about human nature.

In works such as *Thus Spake Zarathustra* (1883), *Beyond Good and
Evil* (1886), and *The Genealogy of Morals* (1887), Nietzsche asserted
that Western Judeo-Christian values were invented to subvert a prior
and more important moral order. In the world of nature, strength wins
out and weakness is eliminated. Yet Judaism and Christianity conspire
to assure people that weakness has its own strengths and that morality
is rewarded in a future life that is, in fact, nonexistent. Almost all of
philosophy has conspired with this inverted value system to justify
Judeo-Christian morality, while metaphysics is merely the creation of a
false world that proceeds according to rules people prefer, rather than
according to the laws of nature. In response, intellectual thought should
be primarily negative and antimetaphysical. Philosophical commentary
should strip away false metaphysics and expose the real physical world
in all of its naked brutality. Nietzsche's idea of a "super" man who could
stand out above "the herd" was later popularized and perverted by the
Nazis.

◆**Twentieth-century Philosophy**   Philosophy in the 20th century was dominated by what is commonly called *analytic philosophy*
(Anglo-American) and *continental philosophy* (European), but a number of individual voices, not associated strongly with any particular
school, also made significant contributions. At the turn of the century,
Henri Bergson developed a philosophy that distinguished between the
intellect, which uses reason and analysis to know the world, and intuition, which enables man to identify with entities in the world and which
provides a basis for metaphysical knowledge. Bergson shared this metaphysical inclination with Alfred North Whitehead, who promoted a
"speculative philosophy" whose primary goal was the definition of universal ideas that would explain the general nature of reality.

John Dewey, the dominant American philosopher of the early 20th
century, came from the school of Pragmatism, a descendant of Positivism
and other anti-Idealistic schools of thought. Dewey and his followers
adopted the position that reality and human responses to it were constantly evolving; in light of that state of change, philosophy's primary
task should be to find practical solutions to human problems. Dewey's

pursuit of this goal made him an influential figure in the philosophy of education in the 20th century.

Analytic Philosophy   The first major branch of analytic philosophy was *logical positivism*, which emerged at the University of Vienna in 1923. This branch was influenced heavily by the work of David Hume and the new logical system of Bertrand Russell and A. N. Whitehead. The Logical Positivists argued for a strictly scientific approach to philosophy, which was newly redefined by Ludwig Wittgenstein as "the logical clarification of thoughts," and focused in particular on the structure and use of human language. The Positivists claimed that unverifiable statements were meaningless, and thus practically all metaphysical inquiry had no value due to its purely speculative nature.

Later, however, Logical Positivists such as Wittgenstein and G. E. Moore contributed to the development of *linguistic analysis*, which focused on the language people used in daily existence instead of the rarefied and artificial language of logical positivism. Wittgenstein asserted that the ambiguous and highly contextual nature of language is what produces most philosophical problems—thus, the ultimate question of philosophy is to ask why a person uses a particular word or expression in a given situation.

Continental Philosophy   While the analytic philosophers turned their attention to language as a tool and construct of human reason, philosophers of the continental school retained a more metaphysical orientation. Elucidating on Kant's proposition that only phenomena, not things-in-themselves, are perceivable, Edmund Husserl developed the phenomenological method. His method, and the whole school of *phenomenology*, attempted to describe phenomena through intuition in the immediate moment of experience, divorced from metaphysical and scientific presumptions. Martin Heidegger, who worked with Husserl at Freiburg University, discussed phenomenology as a method of access to being. His early works did much to influence philosophers in not only phenomenology, but many other fields, including existentialism and postmodernism.

Existentialism   The last major development in 20th-century philosophy owed a direct debt to Kierkegaard's studies of human anxiety and despair. Karl Jaspers rejected the existentialist label but nonetheless worked within its boundaries, inquiring into the question of individual

Being. In his view, one's Being was revealed most clearly in extreme situations or states of mind, such as despair and suffering—occasions when the individual was confronted with the temporal nature of his or her own existence. Jean-Paul Sartre, on the other hand, embraced the existentialist label, and his literary and philosophical works are perhaps more closely associated with existentialism than any other individual. Sartre denied the existence of God, and thus the existence of any essential or preexisting human nature; people, therefore, exist in a state of total freedom and are responsible only to themselves. In most people, said Sartre, this recognition leads not to a feeling of liberation, but rather to a state of overwhelming indecision and anxiety, and subsequently to a perverse immersion in behaviors and institutions that negate that freedom and responsibility. In works such as *Nausea* (a novel, 1938), *Being and Nothingness* (1943), and *No Exit* (a play, 1944), he reached a much wider audience than any philosopher of his time.

Day 2: Psychology: Science and the Human Mind

Most people today are familiar with the meaning of such terms as *ego*, *id*, the *unconscious*, *sibling rivalry*, and *inferiority complex*. All of these had their origin just about a century ago when Sigmund Freud and his disciples promulgated a new approach to understanding the human mind and human behavior.

The intellectual origins of psychology date back to the early Greek philosophers, such as Socrates, Plato, and Aristotle, who delved into questions of human perception, motivation, and the organization of the mind. In the 17th century, philosophers also dealt with related questions. René Descartes theorized that the body and mind are two separate entities, but Thomas Hobbes and John Locke disagreed, arguing that all thoughts and sensations are physical processes occurring within the brain.

But the "birth-date" of modern psychology is believed to be 1879, when at the University of Leipzig the physiologist Wilhelm Wundt established the first laboratory dedicated to the scientific study of the mind. His progress was mirrored in the United States by William James, brother of the writer Henry James. William James offered the first academic course in psychology at Harvard University, and in 1890 he published *Principles of Psychology*, a groundbreaking work that solidified his position as the founder of American psychology. His theory of emotion and his ideas about the self and a personal identity are just two of his lasting contributions.

Other influential scholars include Herman Ebbinghaus, who pioneered the study of memory, while the American Lightner Witmer, who studied under Wundt, opened the first psychological clinic in 1896 in Philadelphia, founding the field of clinical psychology, which is concerned with the diagnosis and treatment of mental illnesses and disorders. In 1905, Alfred Binet devised the first intelligence test. This test was revised by the Stanford University psychologist Lewis Madison Terman and is now commonly known as the Stanford-Binet test. In 1912, Max Werthheimer inspired the gestalt psychology movement, which theorized that people organize the world into meaningful patterns that are essentially different from the sum of isolated sensations.

◆**Psychoanalysis** Enter Sigmund Freud, whose understanding of the mind was based on interpretive methods, introspection, and clinical observations. Few historical figures have had as much influence on modern thinking as Freud. His model of the human mind and his ideas about sexuality, repression, and the unconscious are entwined in our culture. Freud was born in Freiburg, Moravia, in 1856. He moved to Vienna when he was four years old and was associated with that city for his whole life. He pursued medicine, which was one of the few professions open to Jews, and after studying with some of the leading scientists of the day, he emerged as a forward-thinking and controversial psychologist.

Freud developed his theories while treating patients who appeared to suffer from certain ailments but had nothing physically wrong with them. He discovered that these symptoms would often disappear through the use of hypnosis, or even just through talking. In *The Interpretation of Dreams* (1889), Freud proposed that people are primarily motivated by unconscious forces, and by finding a suitable outlet for these unconscious motivations, a person could develop a more healthy personality.

In 1905, Freud published the landmark work *Three Essays on the Theory of Sexuality*, in which he concluded that sexuality is the prime mover in a great deal of human behavior. According to Freud, beginning at the youngest age, a person goes through a series of stages in which they are focused on a particular part of the body known as an eroge-nous zone. If properly stimulated at each stage, the individual reaches sexual and psychic maturity. If not, the individual fixates on a particu-lar stage, which later defines their personality type. Freud identified the stages as: oral (birth to 18 months); anal (18 months to 3 years); phal-lic (3 years to 7 years); latency (7 years to puberty) and genital (puberty to adulthood).

Freud's greatest contribution to psychology is usually said to be his psychoanalytic theory of personality, which posits that the human per-sonality is composed of three elements: the *id*, the *ego*, and the *superego*. The id is the only part of the personality that exists at birth. It is entirely unconscious and is the primary component of an individual's personal-ity. The id seeks immediate gratification and is important in early life be-cause it ensures that the needs of infants are met. However, in adulthood, it is not realistic to expect that one's desires will be satisfied immediately. The ego then, is the component of the personality that deals with reality. The ego strives to satisfy the id's desires in a manner that is acceptable in the real world. The ego develops in toddlers when they discover that they are individuals with their own wants and needs. The superego emerges around age five and is the aspect of personality that contains the morals and ideals that are acquired from parents, teachers, and society. Simply put, it is our internalized sense of right and wrong. To Freud, a balance between id, ego and superego is the key to a healthy personality.

To achieve this balance, the ego will employ unconscious psycholog-ical strategies to deal with fears, anxieties, and socially unacceptable de-sires. Known today as "defense mechanisms," the most common are: *denial* of truth or reality; *repression* of harmful or unpleasant memories; *projection* or the placement of negative or undesirable traits onto others that are actually within you; and *reaction formation*, which enables a per-son to assert ideas and emotions that are actually the opposite of how they feel.

Freud's theories dominated psychological thought in the early 20th century, although many of his followers, dubbed "Neo-Freudians," dis-agreed with his emphasis on sex as the primary motivator of behavior. Most notable was Carl Jung, who had been one of Freud's most devoted adherents. But Freud severed all relations when Jung published *Psy-*

chology of the Unconscious (1912), in which he theorized that all humans have a collective unconscious that contains universal memories (called archetypes) from their shared past. Jung also differentiated two classes of people: extroverted (outward-looking) and introverted (inward-looking), and explored how any one of the four functions of the mind—thinking, feeling, sensation, and intuition—can predominate in any given person.

Alfred Adler was another devoted follower of Freud who was savagely attacked by him when he wrote that people are motivated by feelings of inferiority (the inferiority complex) and are influenced by birth order in the family, sometimes leading to sibling rivalry.

Although both his contemporaries and subsequent generations of scientists have discredited Freud's theories of sexuality and of psychoanalysis, he revolutionized the way we think about the human mind, and he remains one of the leading intellectual and cultural figures of the 20th century. Nearly every field of study has borrowed and reinterpreted his ideas, and terms "Oedipus complex," "anal personality," and "Freudian slips" are now a part of our everyday language. In the arts, Surrealist painters, notably Salvador Dali, incorporated dream imagery into their work, and writers from Franz Kafka and D. H. Lawrence to James Joyce and Albert Camus all used Freudian motifs to explore the actions and motivations of their characters.

◆**Behaviorism** Many psychologists rejected the Freudian methods of introspection and turned their attention to the direct observation of human behavior. In 1898, Edward Lee Thorndike conducted experiments on animal learning which led him to propose the "law of effect," which states that behaviors that lead to a positive outcome are repeated, whereas those followed by a negative outcome are abandoned. In 1906, Ivan Pavlov expanded on this theory when he discovered that dogs would salivate in anticipation of food, based on the ringing of a bell before being fed. He named this form of learning "classical conditioning," in which a being comes to associate one stimulus with another. Later research found that this basic process explains how people form certain fears and prejudices.

These early studies were codified in 1913, when the animal psychologist John Watson redefined psychology as an objective branch of natural science with a goal of predicting and controlling behavior. After

Watson, the primary proponent of behaviorism was B. F. Skinner, who coined the term *reinforcement* to describe how animal and human behavior is motivated. Skinner and his followers applied these theories in a technique that came to be known as *behavior modification*.

◆**Humanistic Psychology** In an attempt to bridge the gap between the forces of the unconscious mind and the effects of reinforcement on behavior, psychologists in the 1950s and 1960s developed "humanistic psychology," a movement aimed at better understanding the conscious mind, free will, and the human capacity for self-reflection and growth.

The leader of this movement was Carl Rogers, who developed a technique known as person-centered therapy, which helped patients clarify their sense of self to aid their individual healing process. At the same time, Abraham Maslow proposed a hierarchy of needs that humans are motivated to fulfill, beginning with basic physiological needs such as hunger, thirst, and sleep, then ascending to the need for safety and security, belonging and love, and status and achievement. Once these needs are met, people strive for self-actualization, the ultimate state of personal fulfillment.

Other psychologists moved into the study of cognition, the mental processes involved in acquiring, storing, and using knowledge. The new field of cognitive psychology was based partially on the work done by the Swiss psychologist Jean Piaget in the 1920s. Piaget explored how children think and reason, and he theorized about a predictable series of cognitive states.

While many psychologists consider themselves adherents to one specific school of thought, today it is common to take an integrated approach in studying consciousness, behavior, and social interaction. This is referred to as the biopsychosocial model, which posits that all human behavior and mental processes are the products of biological, psychological, and social influences and the interactions among them.

◆**Disorders and Treatments** Researchers estimate that in the U.S., roughly 44 million adults suffer from a diagnosable mental disorder in any given year. As compared to a neurosis, which is a generally benign personality disturbance, a mental disorder will limit an individual's ability to function and enjoy life. The authoritative guide to mental illnesses is the *Diagnostic and Statistical Manual of Mental Disorders* (DSM-

IV) published by the American Psychiatric Association, which describes more than 300 different mental and addictive disorders.

◆Anxiety and Stress One of the two most common mental disorders, anxiety is defined as the inability to cope with excessive worry, fear, and apprehension.

Generalized anxiety disorder (GAD) involves constant anxiety about the routine events in one's life. It is excessive and long-lasting. Nearly 3 percent of all adults suffer from GAD.

Obsessive-compulsive disorder (OCD) involves having recurring thoughts (obsessions) and/or feeling driven to perform repetitive actions, such as hand washing (compulsions).

Panic disorder and resultant panic attacks are marked by a sudden, intense terror that causes physical symptoms such as heart palpitations, shortness of breath, chest pain, and sweating.

Phobias are persistent, intense and irrational fears, which lead to the avoidance of specific objects, activities, and situations. Claustrophobia (fear of closed spaces), acrophobia (fear of heights), and social phobia (fear of embarrassment) are some of the most common phobias.

As compared to common stress, in which the strains of everyday life affect our mood and behavior, acute stress is caused by a traumatic event that threatens serious injury or death. Symptoms include a sense of detachment, a reduced awareness of one's surroundings, and occasionally dissociative amnesia.

Anxiety and stress disorders can be treated with medications such as Valium and Xanax. They also respond well to behavioral and cognitive therapies, which help patients change their behavior through conditioning, and the development of coping skills.

◆Mood Disorders Depression is by far the most common psychological disorder today. Symptoms include feelings of sadness, hopelessness, and worthlessness, as well as changes in appetite, sleep patterns, and energy level, all lasting for two weeks or more. People with major depressive disorder lose interest in other people and experience little pleasure from normal activities.

Bipolar disorder, also known as manic-depressive illness, is characterized by mood swings alternating between the extremes of mania (an overexcited, hyperactive state) and depression. Cyclothymic disorder is a less extreme type of bipolar disorder, in which mild hypomanic and mini-depressive episodes follow an irregular course.

Depression is usually treated with a combination of antidepressant drugs and talk therapy. There are three classes of antidepressants: tricyclics and tetracyclics such as Elavil, monoamine oxidase (MAO) inhibitors such as Nardil, and selective serotonin-selective reuptake inhibitors (SSRIs), including Prozac. Electroconvulsive therapy (ECT) is often used to relieve severe depressions that have not responded to other forms of treatment. Bipolar disorder responds to a combination of antidepressants and antimanic drugs, most commonly lithium.

◆**Eating Disorders** An eating disorder is a severe disturbance in eating behavior, occurring mostly among young women in Western societies. Treatment usually involves a short-term intervention to restore body weight, as well as long-term therapy, often accompanied by the use of antidepressants, to prevent relapse.

Anorexia nervosa is characterized by a morbid fear of obesity and a distorted sense of body image. People with anorexia nervosa refuse to eat adequately or even to maintain a normal body weight.

By contrast, patients suffering from bulimia nervosa indulge in binge eating, followed by self-induced vomiting or the use of laxatives to prevent weight gain.

Weekend 43: Modernism in Art and Music

Day 1: The Shock and the New: 20th-Century Art

Increasingly pursuing their own creative ideas, artists in the late 19th century began a time of broad experimentation, beginning what is now called the Modernist period. Following the Impressionists' initial rejection of established, academic styles, rules, and attitudes about making art in the 1860s and after, European modernists supplanted the old definition of art with the new, avant-garde belief that an artist should act as a visionary and forge new cultural trends. As growing numbers of artists began to work outside the confining tastes of the Academie, they banded together into groups with shared aims, even while developing individual artistic voices. To the extent that so many artists chose to work within these groups, Modernism is unique among art periods for its profusion of manifestos and movements. Many of these movements were short-lived, but have provided lasting influence on the direction of the arts to the present day. Here are the more influential movements:

◆**Cubism**   Developed by artists Pablo Picasso and Georges Braque in the decade before World War I, Cubism sought to depict three-dimensional space in two dimensions. Cubist works such as Picasso's *Les Demoiselles d'Avignon* (1907) overlaid multiple viewpoints and divided the subject into small sections, as if the image were seen through a prism or from several vantage points at once.

◆**Expressionism**   In Germany, the Die Brücke (The Bridge, 1905) and Der Blaue Reiter (The Blue Riders, 1911) movements pushed the bounds of Expressionist painting, in which the emotional state of the artist, as shown with tactile brushwork and abstracted shapes, took precedence over the subject of the painting. Expressionists crafted some of the most radical abstract art of the period, such as Ernst Kirchner's *Five Women in the Street* (1915) and Wassily Kandinsky's *Improvisation No. 30* (1913).

◆**Dada and Surrealism**   For many artists, World War I was the final indictment of bourgeois European culture. In protest to the supposed rationality of modern culture, a group of Zurich artists started the Dada movement, which prized absurdity, nonconformity, and intuition. Dada was avowedly anti-art, which it felt had been complicit in the buildup to the war. Dada art included spontaneous performances, automatic drawing and writing, collage and cut-ups, elements of chance, presentation of manufactured or found objects as art (called "readymades"), and other procedures aimed at outraging or confounding the art establishment. Notable Dadists included Tristan Tzara, Raoul Hausmann, Man Ray, and Francis Picabia, but the most enduring figure has been Marcel Duchamp. Duchamp originally composed paintings in the Cubist style (his 1912 *Nude Descending a Staircase No. 2* is a seminal Cubist painting), but quickly evolved through several artistic ideas. He exhibited the first readymade sculptures (his 1917 *Fountain*, considered one of the pivotal artworks of the 20th century, was a factory-made urinal), developed chance art, conceptual art, installation art, and kinetic art—all trends explored by postmodernist artists in the latter half of the century.

Evolving from Dada, the circle led by the magnetic André Breton combined fin-de-siecle Symbolism with Sigmund Freud's groundbreaking work in psychoanalysis to develop Surrealism, the artistic exploration of repressed desires and the unconscious. The German painter and former Dadaist Max Ernst produced works such as *The Elephant Celebes* (1921), which features a mechanical elephant and a headless mannequin. Other surrealist artists included Joan Miró of Spain, Yves Tanguy, Jean Arp, and surrealist pop icon Salvador Dali.

◆**The New Objectivity**   As a reaction to the rise of Expressionism, a new German movement called The New Objectivity prized instead distance, form, simplicity and matter-of-factness. Several adherents would establish the most important Modernist laboratory in Europe, the Weimar-era Bauhaus school (1919–33) led by Walter Gropius. The Bauhaus valued most the marriage of form and function, practicality, and mass production. The simplified shapes and clean lines of Bauhaus designs have become iconic modernist forms, and are still widely influential today. Bauhaus instructors included well-known painters Paul Klee, Wassily Kandinsky, László Moholy-Nagy and Josef Albers, as well as the architect Ludwig Mies van der Rohe. The Bauhaus disbanded with the rise of Nazism in Germany 1933, but Bauhaus-style workshops such as the Wiener Werkstätte in Vienna and De Stijl in the Netherlands carried on the idea.

◆Art and Politics In Russia, the 1917 Bolshevik Revolution led to a short-lived explosion of artistic experimentation. In the early days of the Soviet Union, the artists Alexander Rodchenko, El Lissitzky, Vladimir Mayakovsky, and Vladimir Tatlin helped popularize a movement called Constructivism, which used psychologically charged abstraction to promote pro-revolutionary ideals. The early film pioneer Sergei Eisenstein utilized the Constructivist vocabulary in pro-revolutionary works such as *Strike* (1925) and *Battleship Potemkin* (1925), which have established a lasting standard for directorial excellence. In the 1930s Soviet Union, Joseph Stalin effected the total takeover of artistic style by the Communist Party. All art was now ordered to exuberantly support the aims of the Bolshevik revolution and the Soviet state, and artists not adhering to the new Socialist Realism style (a mishmash of heroic Realism, Expressionism, and Constructivism) were branded as conspirators. Under Stalin, the legacy of early, experimental post-revolutionary Modernism was suppressed or hidden deep underground.

In 1930s Germany, the Nazi regime expunged Modernist "degenerate art" from the cultural record of the Third Reich. Joseph Goebbels, Hitler's minister of propaganda, saw the psychologically persuasive power of Soviet-style Constructivism, however, and began using it to promote the Reich's interests. Among influential Nazi-era artists were cinematographer and director Leni Riefenstahl, whose *Triumph of the Will* (1934) and *Olympia* (1938) are still hailed as stylistic (if not moralistic) watersheds, and designer Hans Schweitzer, whose propaganda posters crystallized Nazi agitprop style.

◆The New Yorkers World War II left the European artistic scene in a dismal state. Many artists had fled or been killed, or were now living under repressive regimes. Paris, which had been the artistic nexus of the West for over a century, would never regain its former status and relatively few artists returned there after the war. Many of the leaders of prewar avant-garde movements had immigrated to New York City. Furthermore, the catastrophe of war threw the main assumptions of traditional European-style Modernism into a tailspin.

The United States emerged from World War II a financial, military, and cultural power. Many artists who had been associated with the Works Progress Administration's Federal Art Project (1935–43)—

including Jackson Pollock, Lee Krasner, William Baziotes, Willem de Kooning, Arshile Gorky, Philip Guston, and Marsden Hartley—were part of a growing group of painters living in New York City in the 1930s who took inspiration from jazz and Surrealist improvisation, and began to experiment with abstract painting.

By the early 1940s, Pollock was drawing on the muralist tradition of his teacher, the Regionalist Thomas Hart Benton, and the Mexican painter Diego Rivera to compose physical, abstract paintings on a large scale that seemed to both reflect the European history of Expressionist painting while encapsulating a new, distinctly American point of view. In Pollock's images from the 1940s, figural representation from Jungian psychotherapy gradually vanished into a chaotic haze of dripped and poured paint until, by the time of masterworks such as *Full Fathom Five* (1947), there was only a raw field of movement and action.

The style would come to be called Action Painting or more commonly Abstract Expressionism. Many Abstract Expressionist artists worked entirely intuitively, painting and repainting over the same composition until it "felt right," and deliberately leaving traces of earlier drafts in the final work. This technique is evident in key works by Dutch-born Willem de Kooning, who painted loosely representational images with impulsive-looking brushstrokes that suggested a frenzy of creation and re-creation, and also in the black-and-white paintings of Franz Kline, which went through a slow evolution to find a precise balance and rhythm.

Also among the Abstract Expressionist group were painters who tended to compose images by positioning areas of color against each other. These so-called Color Field artists included the Latvian émigré Mark Rothko, who focused on the effects of large, concentrated fields of color and subtle modulations in hue; Barnett Newman, whose paintings usually were composed of one or two vertical stripes on a contrasting background; Robert Motherwell, whose generally black-and-white paintings included stacked, totemic shapes, and Clyfford Still, whose jagged interlocking areas of color seemed to represent natural forms. These various strains of abstraction became known as the New York School.

Meanwhile, an important Southern outpost of the New York School would revive a Bauhaus-style workshop of ideas. From 1933 to 1956, North Carolina's Black Mountain College hosted some of the brightest postwar luminaries and fomented several new trends. Led by the

Bauhaus alumnus Josef Albers, Black Mountain College would host as instructors visionary Buckminster Fuller, dancer Merce Cunningham, artist/musician John Cage, poet Robert Creeley, photographer Aaron Siskind, and painters Willem de Kooning, Franz Kline, Jacob Lawrence, and Robert Motherwell, along with Bauhaus alumnus architect Ludwig Mies van der Rohe. Black Mountain College saw John Cage's first "happenings," (impromptu performances) and his development of chance music, both presaged by Marcel Duchamp's work of the 1920s. Students of the college included many of the next generation's most famous artists, including painters Robert Rauschenberg, Kenneth Noland, and Cy Twombly, and sculptor John Chamberlain.

◆**Pieces of Modernism**   As the Modernist aesthetic became more popularized via design, architecture, and advertising, a reverse trend was also taking place, as images from advertising and popular culture seeped into high art. Earlier Dadists and Surrealists incorporated popular and advertising images in their work, and a new group of artists began taking the idea further. Artists such as Roy Lichtenstein, Jasper Johns, and Andy Warhol in the U.S. and Sigmar Polke and Gerhard Richter in Europe began using logos, slogans, cartoons, and iconic popular images as subjects for paintings and sculpture. Where earlier Dadaists had been absurdist, however, the new generation of so-called Pop Artists exhibited an ironic duplicity and coolness in their work.

In 1961, the first Beat-inspired exhibition of the new Fluxus collective opened. Fluxus was a group of multidisciplinary artists who freely mixed music, art, and media works together, and included Nam June Paik (whose later sculptures composed of television sets inspired the MTV aesthetic), minimalist composer La Monte Young, and performance artists Yoko Ono and Joseph Beuys, a towering figure of postwar German art. During the same time, inspired by early pioneer Maya Deren, experimental filmmakers such as Kenneth Anger and Stan Brakhage (famous for 1964's *Dog Star Man*) drew simultaneously from Beat poetry, Symbolism, Surrealism, and Constructivism.

This new generation of artwork was meant to provoke, intrigue, and confuse. Its ambiguity signaled a new direction for the arts, and by the time Pop Art became popular in the early 1960s, many artists and critics were beginning to use the term *postmodernism* for this new movement. Modernism was begining to give way to the next era.

Day 2: 20th-Century Classical Music

If the Romantic period represented an evolution from the Classical period, the 20th century witnessed a full-fledged musical revolution. In short, high value was placed on individuality and personal expression, with the very fabric of tonality being ripped apart in the search for new and unique musical forms and sounds. Composers represent an enormous range of tastes, skills, and styles, expanding on the sophisticated harmonies of the late Romantic period with increasingly radical explorations of chromaticism and nontraditional tonalities.

♦**Claude Debussy and Impressionism** Early in the 20th century, the French composer Claude Debussy helped create a style of music in which solo and orchestral music is created from subtle blends of sound, similar to the blends of color in the paintings of Monet, Renoir, and other artists within the Impressionist movement. Like these artists, Debussy sought to express in music the impressions created by natural scenes, an intention beautifully realized in works such as *La Mer* (*The Sea*, 1905), *Prélude à l'après-midi d'un faune* (*Prelude to the Afternoon of a Faun*, 1894), and "Clair de Lune" ("Moonlight", from *Suite Bergamesque*, 1905). His interest in the music of other cultures inspired him to work with various scales besides the major and minor scales traditionally found in Western music, and to revive the whole-tone scale (a scale built entirely of whole steps), which came to define the music of the French Impressionists. Although Debussy himself resisted the idea of a "school" of Impressionism, his influence can be seen in the works of Maurice Ravel (*Bolero*, 1928, *La Valse*, 1920), Manuel de Falla (*Nights in the Gardens of Spain*, 1915), and Ottorino Respighi (*The Fountains of Rome*, 1916)

♦**The Second Viennese School** The gentle sounds of Impressionism contrasted strongly with those of *chromaticism*. A chromatic note is any note not contained within the primary major or minor scale of a composition and sounds conspicuously out of key when used against a mostly tonal backdrop. Chromatic notes became common during the Romantic era when composers such as Richard Wagner used them for special effects, but in the modern era the use of chromaticism expanded so widely that the underlying scale and tonal center became erased completely. Chromaticism was seen by its adherents as a giant, innovative leap in music, and these composers—the Austrians Arnold Schoenberg and his students Alban Berg and Anton Webern—coined for themselves the moniker the Second Viennese School to proclaim their importance (earlier Viennese luminaries, including Mozart and Schubert, apparently were the First Viennese School).

Once any and all notes became fair territory for musical writing, composers sought both ways and reasons to tame the possibilities of the new form, and by the 1920s, from atonal chaos, Schoenberg imposed order with a new kind of music called twelve-tone music. Twelve-tone music introduces each of the 12 tones of the Western chromatic scale in a predetermined order called a "tone row," which serves as the melodic line. That order becomes the basis for motifs, themes, and harmonies composed according to specific rules. Pioneering works using this method are Schoenberg's *Pierrot Lunaire* (1912), a cycle of 21 songs with texts based on the work of the French symbolist poet Albert Giraud; Alban Berg's *Violin Concerto* (1935) and opera *Wozzeck* (1922); and Anton Webern's *Das Augenlicht* (*The Light of the Eye*, 1935).

Igor Stravinsky   Russian by birth and later a citizen of both France and the United States, Igor Stravinsky's own musical journey embodied the eclectic and experimental styles of modern music. No composer in the 20th century—or perhaps, any century—worked in such diverse styles. In the ballet score *Petrouchka* (1911), written just before World War I, Stravinsky moved away from the Romanticism of the late 19th century, creating a piece that overturned the Romantic clichés of earlier ballet scores. This was followed by *Le Sacre du Printemps* (*The Rite of Spring*, 1913), which, with its unusual rhythms and unresolved dissonances, is considered an early Modernist landmark. But shortly thereafter, Stravinsky entered a neo-Classical phase, during which he began to embrace the musical forms and instrumentation of previous eras. The neo-Classical style marked a return to the classic concept that all elements of a composition should contribute to the overall structure of the piece. Stravinsky abandoned the dense chords and shifting meters of his own earlier work for a more traditional tonality—albeit one filtered through modern harmonic sensibilities. His two important symphonic works, *Symphony in C* (1940) and *Symphony in Three Movements* (1945) represent the summation of his neo-Classical principles. Other composers who worked in this style were the Russian composer Sergei

Prokofiev (*Symphony No. 1, Classical Symphony*, 1917), the British composer Ralph Vaughan Williams (*Fantasia on a Theme by Thomas Tallis*, 1910, revised 1913, 1919), and the German composer Paul Hindemith (*Sonata for Viola d'Amore and Piano*, 1922).

In the final phase of his creative life, Stravinsky turned to the twelve-tone compositional techniques of the Second Viennese School, though he adapted them in his own highly personal manner. The ballet score for *Agon* (1957) is considered his masterpiece of this period.

•**The New Nationalism** The nationalist movement in music survived from the late 19th century and found its greatest 20th-century proponents in the Hungarian composer Béla Bartók and Charles Ives of the United States, both of whom made unusually creative use of national idioms. Ives drew his inspiration from his native New England, in works that blended unconventional rhythms and harsh dissonance with familiar hymns, barn dances, and popular tunes. It was only late in Ives's life that his work was appreciated (which he had anticipated and prepared for by building a successful career in the insurance business), and in 1947 he won a Pulitzer Prize for his *Third Symphony*, after which his earlier works, such as *The Unanswered Question* (1908) and *A Symphony: New England Holidays* (1913) received more notice.

Bartók's music, as difficult as it is, has always been more frequently performed than that of Ives. Bartók drew on the folk music of Central Europe for his inspiration, and the melodies of Hungarian folk tunes and asymmetrical dance rhythms became a hallmark of his work. His six string quartets, written between 1908 and 1939, are considered the summation of his compositional style.

Other composers found "new" musical ideas by adapting the traditional folk music of their native countries into classical forms, creating nationalistic works such as Vaughan Williams's *A London Symphony* (1913), Leo Janácek's opera *Jenufa* (1904), often called "the Moravian national opera," and Aaron Copland's *Hoe Down* (1942) and *Appalachian Spring* (1944).

•**Music at Midcentury** The generation of musicians and composers who came of age after World War II showed increasing disdain for the prewar masters along with a taste for more aggressive, experimental, and radical musical ideas. Many began a wholesale interrogation of the foundations of composition: notation, tonality, harmony, rhythm, instrumentation, and even the relationships between composer and audience.

This midcentury thrust arguably begins with the French composer Olivier Messiaen's *Quartet for the End of Time* (1941), written while he was imprisoned in a Nazi camp near Gorlitz, Germany. The quartet completely overhauled the notion of time and meter, breaking off small moments into self-contained passages that each utilized their own meters and flows. After the war, Messiaen taught at the Paris Conservatory, where he instructed composers who charged off in completely new directions. Among them was Pierre Boulez, who once studied mathematics and engineering.

In the late 1940s and early 1950s, a new musical form emerged, largely due to the rivalry between Messiaen and Boulez. Boulez was already expanding on Schoenberg's rule-oriented twelve-tone method, and Messiaen went further in developing what he called total serialism: a compositional method that applied twelve-tone rules to other aspects like duration and volume. All the aspects of the individual notes were now predetermined before the composer began to write. This form is employed in Messiaen's *Scale of Durations and Dynamics* (1949). Boulez then took this form even further, expanding the twelve-tone rule that dictated that no pitch, volume, attack, or duration could repeat until the other 11 pitches, volumes, durations, and attacks had occurred. This was music at an extreme limit of rigor and structure and is exemplified by Boulez's *Le marteau sans maître* (*The Hammer Without a Master*, 1955). Other influential serial composers of the 20th century include Karlheinz Stockhausen (*Kreuzspiel*, 1951), and the American composer, Milton Babbitt (*Three Compositions for Piano*, 1947).

While serialism is intensely programmed, the American composers Earle Brown and John Cage believed that some aspects of music should be left to chance. As proponents of indeterminacy, they intentionally reduced the composer's control by basing some compositional choices on the outcome of random events, such as the rolling of dice. In Brown's *Twenty-Five Pages*,(1953), which can be played by 1–25 pianists, the score of 25 pages can be arranged in any sequence chosen by the performer(s). The most widely known of these pieces is John Cage's *4'33"*(1952), in which no sound is played at all by the musician. The point of the piece is neither silence nor a refusal to make music, but rather, it asks the audience to listen attentively to the ambient sounds of the auditorium, the hum of electric appliances, shuffling of feet and papers—the idea being that any collection of sounds, if given focus and attention, has many of the qualities of music. For Cage and his followers, the palette of sound for composition expanded well beyond those created by traditional instruments.

◆**The Late 20th Century**   In response to the increasing complexity and intellectualization of both "classical" and popular music forms, the style known as minimalism came to the fore, pioneered by two American composers, Philip Glass and Steve Reich. Philip Glass was influenced by the sitar music of Ravi Shankar and began to produce music that is hypnotic in its repetition and characterized by relatively simple melodies and rhythms. Such pieces were often played by an ensemble that included electronically amplified instruments. Examples of his early experiments with minimalism include *Strung Out* (1967) for amplified solo violin, and *Music in the Shape of a Square* (1968) for two flutes. A decade later, Glass began to write a series of orchestral works, including *Violin Concerto No. I* (1987), and operatic works such as *Einstein on the Beach* (1975).

Steve Reich's early works were created in the 1960s when he developed the technique of "phasing," in which two tape loops of music are set into motion at slightly different speeds so the tapes slowly shift "out of phase" and create new harmonies and rhythms. Reich incorporated this process into compositions for traditional acoustical instruments, notably *Piano Phase* and *Violin Phase* (both 1967).

◆**Electronic Music**   In 1948, the engineer and composer Pierre Schaeffer began to use the newly developed magnetic tape recorder to record various everyday sounds, and then combine those sounds in various ways. The result was called "musique concrete" (French for concrete music), as it consisted of "real-world" sounds, rather than the "artificial" sounds of musical instruments. Musique concrète marked the beginning of what we now call electronic music. Early composers working within this medium included John Cage, Karlheinz Stockhausen, and Herbert Eimert. The style became more prevalent (and integrated into other musical forms) as newer types of electronic instruments were developed   in the later years of the 20th century.

Weekend 44: The Earth and Its Elements

Day 1: The Earth

Speculation about the origin and composition of our planet Earth is as old as civilization itself. Most religions contain some form of creation myth, and many hold that the natural forces governing the planet are embodied by gods and spirits. In antiquity, various philosophers propounded theories of the natural world. In the sixth century B.C., Pythagoras correctly noted that the Earth is a sphere, and Aristotle offered plausible, but incorrect, theories for volcanoes, earthquakes, fossils, and other natural phenomena. Pytheas described the tides and noted that they are controlled by the Moon. By the third century B.C., Eratosthenes calculated the size of the Earth with reasonable precision

Before the Enlightenment of the 18th century, most European scientists were heavily influenced by religious belief, including the biblical story of creation. Scholars attempted to fix the age of Earth through a careful and literal reading of the Bible, concluding that creation took place about 6,000 years ago. But in the 17th century, a few scientists developed ideas that we still believe to be correct today. In 1669, the Danish scientist Nicolas Steno correctly explained fossils as the remains of long-dead organisms and introduced the idea that layers of rock, later called strata by geologists, were deposited at different times, with older layers lying below more recent ones. In Scotland in 1785, an amateur geologist, James Hutton, suggested that Earth's strata must have formed gradually. A half century later, another Scot, Sir Charles Lyell, argued strongly that one could explain geologic history perfectly well by pointing to the geological processes—the action of wind and water, earthquakes, and volcanoes—presently at work and observable on Earth. Lyell rejected the short time line derived from the Bible and proposed a much greater period for the development and evolution of Earth. Lyell's notion of a vastly great "geologic time" made possible the evolutionary theory of Lyell's good friend Charles Darwin. It provided the time scale necessary for natural selection to take place.

◆**The Formation of Earth** In 1755, the German philosopher Immanuel Kant proposed an idea that, with many adjustments by astronomers, became the basis of the modern theory of Earth's formation. He stated that Earth and the other planets coalesced from a dust cloud around the Sun. The contemporary version shows that Kant's theory was on the right track. About 4.6 billion years ago, a mass of gas and dust slowly condensed under the force of gravity into a spinning disk. This solar nebula continued to coalesce, with the Sun forming at the center of the disk, along with planets coming together out of the material in the outer regions. Earth and the other planets assembled as a result of countless collisions of smaller bodies, some mere microscopic specks and others as large as minor planets. The developing planet swept up and incorporated most of the debris in its path as it orbited the Sun, generating an extremely high temperature from the energy of all those impacts and explosions.

This violent infancy of bombardment and collision brought most of Earth's minerals to the planet, while the high temperature melted the debris. During this period, gravity drew heavier elements into the interior of the new planet, whereas lighter ones remained near the surface.

♦**Composition of the Earth**　Over the last century, geologists have discovered that the Earth is composed of five distinct layers: core, mantle, lithosphere, hydrosphere, and atmosphere.

The *core* consists of two parts—one solid, the other liquid—both thought to be a mixture of iron and a lighter element, probably sulfur or oxygen. The solid inner core begins about 2,900 miles from the surface, and the liquid outer core at about 1,800 miles from the surface.

The *mantle* makes up the bulk of the Earth—roughly two-thirds of its mass—and extends from the outer core to within about 55 miles of the Earth's surface below the higher mountains, and to within only three to five miles of the Earth's surface below some areas of the oceans. Silicon dioxide constitutes almost half of the mantle, and there is an abundance of magnesium oxide, and some iron oxide.

The *lithosphere* (formerly called the crust) is the outermost solid layer of the Earth. Under the continents, the crust varies from 19 to 55 miles in thickness, while under the oceans it is generally only three to five miles thick. Continental crust consists of granite and other relatively light rocks; oceanic crust is made up chiefly of basalt. The crust is separated from the mantle by the Mohorovicic discontinuity, or Moho.

The *hydrosphere* is the water component of the Earth and is found in all three states—solid, liquid, and vapor—on the surface, within the crust, and in the atmosphere. The overwhelming majority of Earth's water, over 97 percent, is contained in the oceans. Another 2 percent is the vast fields of polar ice and the glaciers and ice caps that exist in mountains and other high-altitude regions. The remaining portion is found in surface water—rivers, lakes, streams, etc., as well as groundwater and soil water. The abundant presence of water is, of course, what distinguishes Earth from the other planets in the solar system.

The *atmosphere* is the gaseous layer that envelops the Earth. The lower atmosphere consists of the troposphere and the stratosphere. The troposphere has an average thickness of about seven miles, although it is only five miles at the poles and as much as 10 miles around the equator. The composition of dry air at sea level is: nitrogen, 78.08 percent; oxygen, 20.05 percent; argon, 0.93 percent; and carbon dioxide, 0.03 percent. There are also lesser amounts of neon, helium, krypton, and xenon.

The stratosphere is found between seven and 30 miles out from the Earth's surface. Virtually coextensive with the stratosphere is the ozonosphere, or ozone layer, the region in which most of the atmosphere's ozone is found. Because ozone absorbs most of the Sun's ultraviolet radiation, it is vital to the continued existence of life on Earth. Beyond the stratosphere is the upper atmosphere, or ionosphere, so called because it is the layer in which atmospheric gases have been ionized by solar radiation.

◆**Plate Tectonics** This scientific theory describes the drifting and shifting of large parts of Earth's crust and upper mantle, called plates. These complex motions cause the formation of mountains and abysses. The plates move at an extremely slow pace, perhaps only a few centimeters each year, and the great distances now between them further deepen our appreciation of the length of geologic time.

In 1915, the German meteorologist Alfred Wegener became the first scientist to make a convincing case for these motions. He began with two simple observations: first, that the coastlines of some continents, such as Africa and South America, appear to fit together like the pieces of a jigsaw puzzle; second, that many land species of widely disparate continents bear striking resemblances to one another. Wegener postulated that the continents must have at one time been joined together.

Wegener gradually refined his theories and described a single, great protocontinent, which he dubbed Pangaea after the Greek for "whole Earth." This massive body was surrounded by a single vast ocean, Panthalassa, or "universal sea." For reasons he was not able to determine, Pangaea broke apart, and pieces drifted slowly into place around the globe. This theory, known as *continental drift*, states that about 300 million years ago, Pangaea broke into two main bodies. The northernmost one, encompassing modern Europe, North America, and Asia, is called Laurasia. The southern one, Gondwana-land, comprising Africa, South America, the Indian subcontinent, Australia, and Antarctica.

♦**Seafloor Spreading**　One of the unexplained parts of continental drift concerned the great mountain chains and deep trenches found at the bottom of the oceans. In 1962, the American oceanographer Harry Hammond Hess proposed that the ocean floor is created at the mid-Oceanic ridge and then spreads, widening the oceans. Sometimes the spreading pushes continents farther apart, but in some places the ocean floor plunges into deep trenches. In the early 1960s, the record of changes over long periods of time in Earth's magnetic field, as found preserved in the rock of the ocean floor and in rocks on continents, confirmed both seafloor spreading and relative changes in the positions of the continents. The most likely explanation was that Earth's crust is broken into giant plates that move with respect to one another, sometimes carrying continents along.

The action and interaction of the plates, both gradually and in occasional sudden outbursts, have created most of the familiar features of the landscape. When the leading edge of one plate meets another plate, it is called *convergence*, and this movement is largely responsible for the creation of most mountain ranges. When plates pull apart, a process called *divergence*, hot molten rock wells up into the void between them. This happens generally under the oceans; divergence causes new material to rise from Earth's interior to the crust or surface. Sometimes, the plates neither come together nor pull apart, but simply move past each other, rubbing together along the edges. These *transforms* constitute the great geologic faults such as the San Andreas Fault in western North America. Faults are breaks in Earth's crust where there is or has been movement of rock on one side of the break in relation to the other. Faults are classified according to the type of movement they exhibit—vertical, horizontal, or sideways. Faults are breaks in Earth's crust where there is or has been movement of rock on one side of the break in relation to the other. The sudden spasms of activity lead to earthquakes, tsunamis, and volcanic eruptions.

◆The Earth in Upheaval The apparent solidity and constancy of the Earth's surface prevent us from seeing the continuous activity and upheaval beneath. Just as the atmosphere can produce catastrophic phenomena such as hurricanes and gales, the lithosphere is also the site of cataclysmic events, from terrible earthquakes and volcanic eruptions to more commonplace landslides and sinkholes.

Earthquakes Tension and compression build up in the Earth's crust, particularly along faults, where large masses of rock or tectonic plates push against each other. When the pressure is suddenly released, the resulting vibrations, or seismic waves, are observed as an earthquake.

Thousands of tiny earthquakes occur annually. Most are gentle tremors, but each year a few are of moderate or greater intensity. Major earthquakes are dangerous and destructive, causing buildings or rock formations to fall, often resulting in great loss of life. In 2010, a powerful earthquake struck the island nation of Haiti, destroying the capital city of Port-au-Prince and killing more than 250,000 people, making it one of the most destructive quakes in history.

Earthquakes that occur under the oceans cause tsunamis that create enormous waves that flood coastal areas. In 2004, a powerful earthquake in the Indian Ocean caused extreme damage in India, Sri Lanka, Thailand and most of all, in Indonesia. More than 230,000 people were killed, many of them washed out to sea and never found.

Volcanoes A volcano is an opening, called a vent or fissure, in the Earth's crust through which solid rock fragments propelled by gases and lava (molten rock) escape from Earth's interior. The term *volcano* is used to describe both the vent itself and the mountain of accumulated discharged materials that builds up around it. The solid material is usually called ash or cinders when the pieces are small, but larger rocks are called bombs. When large amounts of ash, bombs, lava, or gases escape destructively, the process is called an eruption of the volcano. Volcanic eruptions can be both beautiful and horrific. History has seen untold thousands of lives lost and entire pockets of civilization wiped out by volcanic eruptions. Names such as Vesuvius, Tambora, Krakatoa,

Pinatubo, and Mount St. Helens remind us of Earth's inherent instability and destructive power. The volcano on Mt. Vesuvius in Italy erupted in A.D. 79 and covered the Roman cities of Pompeii and Herculaneum with such a thick blanket of ash that many buildings and corpses were preserved. Krakatoa, a volcanic island in Indonesia, famously erupted in 1883 with such ferocity that the explosion could be heard 2,000 miles away. It killed more than 35,000 people and nearly destroyed the island. In 2010, a volcano erupted under a glacier in Iceland, spewing ash for thousands of miles and shutting down air traffic in Europe for weeks.

Day 2: The Elements

In the late 19th century, workers in London match factories—mostly women and girls—began to suffer painful toothaches and swelling of the gums. Over time, their jawbones developed foul-smelling abscesses, which as they rotted away actually glowed a greenish color in the dark. The condition—which led to the London Matchgirls' Strike of 1888—was the result of exposure to heated fumes containing white phosphorus, and was known as "phossy jaw." The workers had tangled with the powerful chemical discovered by the German alchemist Henning Brandt in 1669. Brandt was attempting to create the fabled "philosopher's stone" by boiling urine down to a paste; instead, he discovered phosphorus, the first element discovered since antiquity.

Today, phosphorus is one of the more than 100 known elements that are the basic building blocks of the chemical world. They have taken the place of Aristotle's dictum, which surmised that all matter is composed of four substances in varying degrees: earth, air, fire, and water. A "chemical revolution" in the 18th century eventually proved the existence and importance of chemical elements. Elements are known by abbreviations of one to three letters, most often from their modern names but sometimes from earlier (especially Latin) names. For example, aluminum has the abbreviation Al, from its English name, whereas gold's abbreviation Au is from the Latin word for gold, *aurum*.

An element is defined by the number of protons—positively charged particles—in its atomic nucleus. This is the atomic number of the element, and is often represented by the symbol Z; for example, hydrogen is Z 1, iron is Z 26, and platinum is Z 78. Except for most hydrogen, an atom's nucleus also contains neutrons, which are particles with no electric charge. A given element's atoms all have the same number of protons, but the number of neutrons may differ. Atoms of the same element with the different combinations of neutrons are called isotopes of the element. For example, two isotopes of carbon are carbon-12 (six protons and six neutrons) and carbon-14 (six protons and eight neutrons). The total number of protons and neutrons of an element is the mass number of the element. In addition to the particles in the nucleus of an atom, there are negatively charged electrons, which have very little mass, in orbit around the nucleus.

The chemical activity of an element is performed by the electrons in outer orbits, called valence electrons. In chemical reactions, atoms may share electrons with one another, but not protons or neutrons. Two or more elements can join together to form a compound—a compound can be broken apart, or recombined with other compounds or elements to form new compounds. For instance, in a chemical reaction two atoms of hydrogen (H) may combine with one atom of oxygen (O) to form one molecule of water (H2O).

◆A Sampling of the Elements

Hydrogen (H; Z-1) The most abundant element in the universe (80 percent), hydrogen fuels the stars, including our Sun. The lightest of gases, it is odorless and highly flammable. It is essential to life, found in most molecules of living cells, and is a part of DNA, the bases of which are joined by hydrogen bonds. About 10 percent of human body mass is hydrogen. Hydrogen is also a component of common acids, such as sulfuric, nitric, and hydrochloric acids. Its main industrial use is in the production of ammonia for fertilizers. Hydrogen is a constituent of atmospheric water vapor, the most potent greenhouse gas.

Carbon (C; Z-6) Carbon has been known since ancient times in various forms such as coal, charcoal, peat, the soft crystal graphite, and diamond. Carbon forms very strong bonds to itself that are resistant to chemical attack, and chains of carbon atoms form compounds that are found in all living cells. Carbon represents 23 percent of human body mass, and most of our food is made up of carbon compounds. The field of organic chemistry is devoted primarily to the study of carbon compounds (of which some 20 million are known). Carbon has several isotopes, the most common of which is carbon-12, which makes up 99 percent of carbon; carbon-13 amounts to about 1 percent. (Small amounts of carbon-14 exist, which is radioactive and used to date archeological material.) Carbon is used industrially in ironmaking, printing, as activated charcoal in water treatment, and as fibers to strengthen laminates in aerospace and sports equipment. The most substantial industrial use of carbon is as fuel: enormous amounts of carbon are extracted from the earth in the form of fossil fuels, and the resultant increase in carbon in the atmosphere has contributed to higher levels of greenhouse gases in the atmosphere. In 1985, the first fullerene, a new form of carbon, was produced. Fullerenes are polyhedral (approximately spherical) molecules typically composed of 60 or more carbon atoms; nanotubes are cylindrical forms of fullerenes.

Nitrogen (N; Z-7) Nitrogen exists in many compounds and in the form of N2, an odorless, colorless, unreactive gas that composes 78 percent of the air we breathe. It is essential for life: it is part of DNA, amino acids, and nitric oxide (a body messenger). Plants require nitrogen, combined by bacteria with oxygen or hydrogen, as part of the nitrogen cycle. Commercially, nitrogen is produced by liquefication of air and is used to make ammonium nitrates for fertilizer and many other chemical compounds.

Oxygen (O; Z-8) This colorless and odorless reactive gas exists naturally as O2. It makes up one-fifth of the air and is essential for sustaining animal life through the respiratory process, which brings oxygen to the blood, and as a constituent of many important compounds in our bodies, including DNA. On Earth, oxygen is produced by the photosynthesis of carbon dioxide and water by plants. Oxygen used commercially is produced from liquefied air and is used primarily in steelmaking and chemical production; other uses include water purification and medicine. Ozone molecules consist of three oxygen atoms (O3).

Sodium (Na; Z-11) Sodium is a soft, silvery metal essential to animals; among other functions, it moves electric impulses along nerve fibers. Although discovered as an element in the 19th century, it has been known in the compounds sodium carbonate ("soda") and sodium chloride (table salt) since biblical times. Table salt is now iodized to prevent thyroid disease, and packets of glucose and salt are used in developing countries to prevent dehydration. Sodium is also an important industrial element. Sodium compounds are widely used in glassmaking, the chemical industry, and metallurgy, and in the manufacture of fire extinguishers; sodium metal is employed in chemical manufacturing, metallurgy, and street lamps.

Phosphorus (P; Z-15) In the form of phosphates, phosphorus is also essential to all living cells. Calcium phosphate is found in bones, and there are also the organophosphates in molecules such as ATP (adenosine triphosphate), which is a source of chemical energy in the body. Phosphorus itself is highly toxic. Commercial and industrial uses of phosphate include fertilizers, detergents, fireproofing, rat poison, and tracer bullets. Excess phosphates in water produce eutrophication (the growth of algae), and the use of phosphates is now regulated in many countries.

Calcium (Ca; Z-20) Essential to most living things, calcium is the most abundant metal in the human body, primarily in bone matter. In metallic form it is soft and silvery, a member of the alkaline earth metal group. Since ancient times, calcium, as calcium oxide (lime), has been mixed with sand and water to produce mortar. Calcium is now used as lime in metallurgy, chemicals, water treatment, and the production of cement. Gypsum, a hydrated calcium sulfate, is used in plaster.

Silver (Ag; Z-47) Silver has been known and worked since ancient times. It is rarely found in its metallic state; it must be mined from ore and refined, thus although more abundant than gold, silver came into use later. A principal use for silver, in which it is alloyed with copper, is in jewelry and tableware. Silver salts are used in photographic films and prints. Silver, which conducts heat and electricity very well, is widely used in the electrical industry; it also can be used as a disinfectant in medicine. It is found in the food chain in generally harmless amounts.

Gold (Au; Z-79) Gold occurs naturally in surface waters, on land, and underground in quartz veins or pyrites. The most malleable of all elements, its ready availability and easy workability made it one of the first metals used in prehistoric times. Gold's sparkling beauty and sunlike color have led people to attribute magical and religious properties to it, and has from ancient times been the basis of monetary systems. In addition to its uses in jewelry and the decorative arts, gold has electronics and aerospace applications; it is relatively unreactive and a good conductor of electricity. Gold is usually mixed with other elements to harden it. The purity of gold is measured in karats—pure gold is called

24 karat gold; an alloy of 75 percent gold is 18 karat.

Lead (Pb; Z-82) Lead is a soft, ductile gray metal that has been known and used since ancient times. It is harmful and even fatal to humans and other animals when it accumulates in the body, and for this reason many of its uses (in paints and as an additive in gasoline, for example) have been phased out. The Romans used lead extensively in water pipes and other products, and in the Middle Ages lead was added as a sweetener to wine. Current uses of lead are primarily for electrodes in vehicle storage batteries, in TV and computer screens as a shield against radiation, and in medicine as protection against X-rays.

♦Radioactivity The disintegration of certain atomic nuclei is marked by the emission of alpha particles (helium nuclei), beta particles (electrons or positrons), or gamma radiation (short-wave electromagnetic radiation). Natural radioactivity is the disintegration of naturally occurring radioactive atoms called radioisotopes. Radioactivity can also be induced by bombarding the nuclei of normally stable elements in a particle accelerator to produce radioactive isotopes.

Uranium (U; Z-92) is perhaps the best-known naturally radioactive element. It was identified in 1841, but its radioactive nature was not understood until 1896. Uranium is abundant in mineral ores and is widely mined, and is the most commonly used fuel in nuclear reactors.

Radium (Ra; Z-88) is highly radioactive and causes some of the naturally occurring radiation that can be measured all across the Earth. In metallic form, it is soft and silvery. It was widely used for luminous dials and medicinal purposes before its dangers to humans were understood. Another cause of natural background radiation of Earth is radon (Rn; Z-86). This noble (chemically inert) gas is a product of decaying uranium and other elements. It is highly radioactive; accumulations in mines and basements can be a health hazard.

Weekend 45: The Industrial Revolution

Day 1: Origins of the Modern Economic World

Between 1750 and 1900, much of the European world changed so dramatically that historians refer to those years as a revolution—the Industrial Revolution. In this period, the everyday lives of millions of people were transformed from what had been the traditional ways of farming to working in factories, mines, and offices.

In medieval Europe from the ninth to the 15th centuries, the dominant system of political and economic organization was feudalism, in which peasants offered their lords homage and service, and farmed their lands in exchange for protection. The preindustrial European economies of the 16th to 19th centuries gradually adopted a system called *mercantilism,* which evolved from the successful conquest and colonization of the Americas and large parts of Asia.

Financial innovation, first by the Dutch then the English, helped to organize the new wealth from overseas into pools of investments that fostered new business ventures as well as financing the many wars fought in the 18th century. Of more lasting value, such a money-based economy helped to fund extraordinary innovations that would produce an entirely new kind of economy.

First and foremost among these advances was the invention of an efficient and powerful steam engine in 1769 by James Watt, a Scotsman. In 1781, Watt patented a rotary engine that would be used later in factories, railroads, and ships. The steam engine provided more power to drive the many new inventions that came into existence over the next several decades including the spinning jenny and the power loom, which made England the leading textile manufacturer in the world.

The British Isles were blessed with natural harbors and a great many navigable rivers, making the movement of raw materials and finished goods within the country relatively easy. Britain's navy was, at the time, the largest in the world, so goods could be readily carried overseas as well. The numerous waterways also provided mills with power, which had promoted the development of a thriving textile industry even before the onset of factory production. Later, after the invention of the steam engine, abundant coal and iron resources were available to build and run machinery, ships, and trains.

Britain also had two human resources crucial to industrialization: markets in which to buy and sell consumer goods, and a large, mobile labor force to produce them. Many of these new workers were refugees from the dramatic changes in the agricultural sector. More food, along with advances in medicine, also meant a great many more people. Between 1720 and the early 19th century, Britain's population greatly increased. During the same period, the "enclosure" movement turned public lands into private holdings, helping to drive agricultural workers off the land and into the cities where they became the core of the workforce that made industrialization possible.

Finally, the British had the advantage of an overseas empire that provided capital for the mines that produced the fuel to run the factories that mass-produced goods, and for the railroads and steam-driven merchant ships that moved the goods. As the tools of industrial manufacturing were created, a person with money to invest could theoretically seek out the latest leading-edge inventions and develop a more efficient factory, thus stealing market share from now outdated rivals. Instead of slowly amassing wealth over a lifetime, there was now a systematic way to amass wealth relatively quickly. This new method was called *capitalism*—the investment of money in an enterprise with the objective of receiving more in return than what was originally invested.

♦**The First Economists** The economist and philosopher Adam Smith, a Scot, was the first great exponent of capitalism and the free market system. In his most famous book, *The Wealth of Nations* (1776), Smith argued that if individuals are left to pursue their self-interest without government interference, they will act, in Smith's famous words, as if "led by an invisible hand," which allocates goods and services to make the economy work to the benefit of society as a whole. Smith contended that competitive markets, where individuals pursue their own interests, could promote their freedoms and achieve the objectives of efficient production and economic growth. The ability of the market to correct itself through competition and the law of supply and demand would provide protection from harmful actions of the selfish and the greedy. From a political standpoint, Smith's *laissez-faire* (literally, "let do," but broadly meaning, "leave it alone") philosophy meant the reduction of government powers and the elimination of state regulation of the economy. Often overlooked, however, is Smith's insistence, based on strong religious convictions, that society must care for the poor and needy.

Smith believed that a free market economy would benefit everyone, not just the rich or the business classes. He favored higher wages for workers so they would not live in poverty, and he thought greater competition would bring those higher wages about. In the early part of the 19th century, however, economic liberalism came to be seen primarily as serving business interests. This change in perspective was reflected in the writings of the English economists Thomas Malthus and David Ricardo, who elaborated upon Smith's application of scientific rules in the economy, with powerful implications for the working poor and the condition of laborers.

Malthus is best known for the theory of population he presented in his *Essay on Population*, first published in 1798. According to Malthus, population increases geometrically while the food supply increases arithmetically. In other words, population always outgrows the supply of food, meaning that poverty and social unrest were inevitable. War, famine, and disease therefore were useful hindrances to unwanted population growth. The Malthusian viewpoint grew increasingly controversial over the next century, but was very influential in the early years of classical economics. Ricardo built upon Malthus's thesis in his major work, *The Principles of Political Economy and Taxation* (1817), in which he argued that the pressure of population would keep wages from rising higher than subsistence level. This "iron law of wages," as he called it, was based on the fact that when wage rates rise above subsistence levels, the number of workers quickly increases, thereby putting downward pressure on wages.

The implication of these arguments was that economics is governed by scientific laws that are unalterable; consequently, poverty is inevitable, and government policies intended to help the working poor or improve their prospects to make a good living are pointless, perhaps even injurious to the smooth functioning of the economy. Ricardo is highly regarded today more because of his theory of "comparative advantage" that encouraged free trade among nations who produced different commodities more efficiently.

Sustained by laissez-faire economics, the Industrial Revolution and the rise of capitalism brought unparalleled growth in economic output that would enhance the lives of millions, finance the building of great cities, and stimulate scientific and medical research. Moreover, the major powers of Europe were essentially at peace for the century between the fall of Napoleon and the outbreak of World War I. With capital freed from the burdens of funding large armies and navies, bankers and investors could use the new wealth to create an industrialized world.

Great Britain took the lead in creating this new world, and most of Europe quickly joined in together, as well as the new nation, the United States. Continuous improvements in transportation (e.g. the railroad, and the steamship) as well as communications (e.g. the telegraph and the transatlantic cable) helped new ideas to spread rapidly and foster even more innovation. Nations rich in natural resources, such as the United States and the newly emerging Germany, were soon in strong competition with Great Britain, but Britain's superior naval power and the riches of their far-flung empire kept them at the top.

♦**The Human Toll** As the leader of the industrialized world, Britain was examined more closely than the others for signs that not everyone was treated fairly or even humanely under the new system. The unfortunate aspects of the Industrial Revolution cannot be passed over, and sadly they are many. First and foremost was the dislocation of agricultural populations. The migration of large numbers of laborers to the urban enclaves that clustered within walking distance of the mills and factories brought extreme crowding, filth, and disease to towns and cities that were already unhealthy from a complete lack of sanitation—conditions that would only be alleviated by a series of public health acts passed in the course of the 19th century.

In the factories, many of the new machines were both clamorous and dangerous, without the safety guards required on shop equipment today. A moment's carelessness could—and often did—result in severe injury or death. The hours were long and the wages low, the work often exhausting, monotonous, and without respite as people were forced to work at the pace of the machines. Prolonged exposure to toxic substances such as mercury and lead was common, and the air in the textile factories and workshops was laden with wool and cotton fibers that the workers inhaled and ingested with their food. As the greatly increased demand for coal depleted the surface mines of the mid-18th century, those who worked the new, deeper mines were subjected to the risk of frequent cave-ins, suffocation or explosive gases, as well as black lung from breathing coal dust. According to official records, over a thousand miners were killed every year in late 19th-century Britain.

Especially dreadful was the exploitation of child labor. Many young factory workers became permanently deformed from performing repetitive tasks in unnatural postures for many hours each day, and some, whose jobs involved darting through spaces where adults would not fit, were mutilated or killed when they got too close to unfenced machinery. Children working in mines towed coal-filled carts through narrow underground passages like draft animals. Worst off were the orphans taken on as apprentices in factories for no more than the provision of shelter, inadequate clothing, and meager food rations. Subject to imprisonment if they ran away, they were, quite literally, slaves. The Factory Act of 1833—one of a series of acts that eventually brought about reform—underscores just how intolerable conditions were in its enumeration of what would be considered tolerable: children younger than nine years of age would no longer be allowed to do factory work, those ages nine to 13 were limited to working eight hours each day, and those ages 14 to 18 could work no more than 12 hours a day in the factories.

Inevitably, the changes wrought by industrialization reached beyond the factories and the mines and into people's homes. In preindustrial times, the family was the main economic unit, with productive work taking place mainly at home, either in the form of farming or the making of crafts. Husband, wife, and children all played integral roles in the single pursuit of supporting the family. As productive work moved out of the home and the earning of wages became the most tangible measure of a family's well-being, the man's job, which was usually the primary wage-earning activity, took precedence over functions performed by other family members that may have been just as essential to the family's survival. In a broader sense, more men became associated with matters external to the home, while women were increasingly confined to what was known as the "domestic sphere." The resulting change in perspective had far-reaching effects on gender roles in society over the next 150 years.

As it spread from Britain to continental Europe and the United States, the Industrial Revolution benefited society as a whole in the long run, with generally improved standards of living, more leisure time, and better health for most people. The emergence of an industrial middle class in Britain also led to electoral reforms there that extended political power beyond the nobility and the landed gentry and eventually resulted in universal male suffrage. But in the short run, the price paid in premature death, misery, and powerlessness by the working classes was high. Eventually the workers, brought together in large numbers by the growth of factories and industrial towns, overcame government opposition to organize into trade unions and protest the terrible conditions. By the 1830s and '40s, social and industrial unrest had become widespread in many places, and in some, another kind of revolution threatened.

Day 2: Marx and the Challenge to the New Order

The serious social problems caused by rapid industrialization quickly captured the attention of thinking men who had been raised with Christian and Enlightenment ideas about the dignity of man. In France, Count Claude Henri de Saint-Simon called for a society controlled by the leading industrialists and guided by men of science, who would take the place of the church. Those who were best able to organize the state for productive labor, he held, were those most fit to govern it. In his book *Le Nouveau Christianisme* (*The New Christianity*), which remained unfinished at his death in 1825, he proposed as religious doctrine the idea that all of society should organize itself for the purpose of bettering the condition of the poor.

Another French socialist, Charles Fourier, believed that poverty was the main cause of disorder in society, and that business was a source of poverty, as well as many other evils. In his first book, *The Social Destiny of Man* (1808), Fourier declared that "truth and commerce are as incompatible as Jesus and Satan." He advocated for higher wages based on the productivity of the worker and the provision of a minimum income for those unable to work. He also called for a system of cooperation in which people would live in scientifically planned communes he called "phalanxes." In them, jobs would be assigned based on individual interests, and incentives would be given for taking on the less desirable work.

At about the same time in England, a similar brand of socialism was promoted by Robert Owen, himself a very successful industrialist and philanthropist who testified against child labor before an investigating committee in Parliament, advocated for factory legislation, and organized one of the largest of the early trade unions. In his own textile mills, he raised the minimum age for workers and promoted education for young children. Central to Owen's social philosophy was his belief that people's characters were formed "for and not by" them. Poverty, in his view, was not the result of a weak character that inclined one to immoral behavior and vice—the prevailing sentiment among the industrial middle classes—rather, a weak character was the result of poverty. "Any community may be arranged in such a manner as…to withdraw vice, poverty, and, in a great degree, misery from the world." To that end, Owen set up his own experimental communities. In the early 1800s, he transformed the squalid factory town of New Lanark, Scotland, into a prosperous model community by introducing civilized working conditions, providing the workers with comfortable housing and municipal services, and setting up schools and religious meeting places, cooperative stores, and recreational facilities. Although Owen's success drew attention from social reformers from all over Europe, his attacks on the Church of England damaged his reputation, and he lost much of his influence when his planned community of New Harmony, Indiana, failed after less than three years, costing him most of his fortune.

In Germany, however, the philosophical tradition created by Kant and Hegel raised socialist ideas to an entirely different plane. In the 1840s, Ludwig Feuerbach, a leading critic of Hegel's work, insisted that the study of human life, not "Mind" as Hegel taught, should be at the center of philosophy, and that God and religion prevent humankind from appreciating its true essence and its unity as a "species." The influence of these ideas on a young student of philosophy in Berlin would change the very nature of the arguments against capitalism and industrialization.

◆**Marx and Engels** Karl Marx was born in 1818 to a middle-class family in Trier, a small city in the German Rhineland. After a rambunctious youthful life, he became a serious student of philosophy at the University of Berlin, where he received a doctorate in 1841. In 1843, he moved to Paris to take an editorial position with a new German-French journal, and there he met Friedrich Engels, who would become his lifelong friend and wealthy benefactor, supporting Marx's writing and often his family as well. The son of a German textile manufacturer, Engels had been sent to work in a Manchester, England, firm in which his father was a shareholder. Based on his observations there, as well as on official reports, he wrote *The Condition of the Working Class in England* (1845), a horrifyingly detailed account of the misery in which the industrial working class and the poor lived, and a scathing indictment of their treatment by the middle class: "I have never seen a class so deeply demoralized, so incurably debased by selfishness, so corroded within, so incapable of progress, as the English bourgeoisie," Engels wrote, "...For it nothing exists in this world, except for the sake of money." He predicted that if change did not come, the result would be a revolution "with which none hitherto known can be compared."

Marx knew that Engels would be a strong ally in the struggle he foresaw, while Engels saw immediately that Marx had a powerful mind and the will to bring his ideas to a larger audience. Marx was a contemporary of Charles Darwin, whose theory of evolution set science off into an entirely new direction, and Richard Wagner, whose operas changed the course of music history. Marx would do the same for the study of economics and history. His theory of historical materialism is based on the central idea that existence in the real world demands we deal with material things. This was clearly a break from the world of Kant and Hegel, but it also rejected as a bourgeois nicety the idea of natural rights as the basis for changing society. What mattered in history, he believed, was the "class struggle," whether between noble and serf or capitalist and worker.

According to Marx, throughout history economic systems that proved unproductive were overthrown and replaced by ones that worked more effectively. He saw capitalism in its early stages as a crucial element in ending the static feudal system that fostered a hereditary aristocracy and an oppressed class of serfs. But now in the middle of the 19th century, capitalism had matured and grown so powerful that workers had become mere commodities in the new system. The idea of "alienation" would take a central place in Western thought for about a century after Marx's use of it. *Alienation* in Marx's work means the workers feel detached from the world and are ready to be led in a cataclysmic revolution against their capitalist masters.

Marx would labor for more than 30 years, often in poverty and obscurity, to give these ideas a systematic underpinning. His early works such as *The Holy Family* (1844) and *The German Ideology* (1845), written with Engels, while not ignored, were never famous during his life;

however, they and the writing he did in newspapers and periodicals gave him stature in the socialist societies forming among the working class.

In 1847, he and Engels went to London to attend a meeting of the newly formed Communist League. Marx did well in several debates about communism, and he and Engels were asked to write in simple language the principles of the League. This commission led to the publication of *The Communist Manifesto* in February 1848. The opening and closing words of this internationally famous work give a strong sense of the urgency Marx and Engels felt about the movement they were helping to launch.

"A spectre is haunting Europe—the spectre of communism. All the Powers of old Europe have entered into a holy alliance to exorcise this spectre: Pope and Czar, Metternich and Guizot, French Radicals and German police-spies." And its more famous conclusion: "The Communists disdain to conceal their views and aims. They openly declare that their ends can be attained only by the forcible overthrow of all existing social conditions. Let the ruling classes tremble at a Communist revolution. The proletarians have nothing to lose but their chains. They have a world to win. Workers of the world, unite!"

The *Manifesto* did not produce a strong popular response at first, but its straightforward descriptions of the dire problems capitalism was causing and the solutions the growing communist movement offered, eventually made it mandatory reading for millions. At the time of its appearance, a serious economic downturn had brought misery to workers and peasants alike throughout Europe. Urban unrest soon burst into full-fledged rebellions in many major cities, including Berlin, Paris, Milan, and Prague. The political leaders of these revolutions in the spring of 1848 made demands for free speech, religious liberty, representative government, and trial by jury, that seemed outlandish to the rulers of the time. But the riots in Paris brought down the government of King Louis-Phillipe and inspired nationalist movements that would soon unite the fragmented states of Italy and Germany. By the fall, almost all of the uprisings had been suppressed, some in ruthless fashion.

Marx and Engels (as well as Richard Wagner) were caught up in this real-life revolution and were forced to flee to London, where Marx would remain for the rest of his life, and where he would write his monumental three-volume work, *Das Kapital* (Vol. 1, 1867; the other two volumes were published after Marx's death). Based on years of study in economics and history, *Kapital* contains all of Marx's best-known theories, including the "labor theory of value" and "surplus value" that in a sense turned capitalism on its head by making the worker the actual creator of capital that further enriched the capitalist who then had more power to lower the worker's wages.

In the end, Marx was wrong about many things, as virtually all influential thinkers are. But his influence has been, as the philosopher Peter Singer notes, on the order of the great religious leaders in world history. Even in societies where his communist ideas and vision of violent revolution were rejected, the political organizations that evolved over the years brought serious reform to a system based on "unfettered capitalism." The German Social Democratic Party, founded in the mid-1860s, became the largest working-class party in the world, and in France, an uprising in 1871 established the Paris Commune, hailed by Marx and Engels as the first "dictatorship of the proletariat," though it was brutally suppressed within three months. Eight years later, the creation of the Federation of the Socialist Workers of France revived the movement there, and three years after that the French Workers' Party was founded. The Fabian Society in England, founded in 1883, argued that all the programs for changing society were in place and would eventually bring about harmonious relations between workers and capitalists. This movement would evolve into the modern-day Labour Party. One could argue that all of the social welfare programs in place today had their origins in Marx's ideas.

Ironically, one of the central tenets Marx and Engels included in *The Communist Manifesto* was their belief that the uprising of the proletariat and the creation of a communist state could take place only in an advanced capitalist economy such as Germany, France, or Great Britain, but the two most successful leaders of communist revolutions, V. I. Lenin and Mao Zedong, applied Marxist ideas in nations swarming with peasants and without an urban proletariat. In the end, they and their successors twisted Marx's ideas and created violent dictatorships that caused the death of millions of people who opposed them. In time, the term *communist* became totally repugnant to most people.

Weekend 46: Poetry: An Introduction

Day 1: Poetry from the Greeks to the Middle Ages

The earliest known work of Western literature is the Babylonian poem, *The Epic of Gilgamesh*, composed around 2000 B.C., but known to us from a later version found in the library of King Assurbanipal in Nineveh (ca. 650 B.C.). It presents a mythical account of an ancient king of Mesopotamia who learns to abandon the tyranny he had imposed on his subjects. Some of the episodes in *Gilgamesh* parallel other stories in ancient literature from the Middle East, including the biblical narrative of Noah and the Flood. Ancient Egyptian literature is also rich in poetry, including love poems, hymns to the gods, and descriptions of daily life, written over a period of many centuries beginning around 3000 B.C. But the first examples of what scholars considered highly developed, complex, and sophisticated poetry, appeared around 700 B.C. in the Greek city-states.

The earliest Greek poetry survives today largely in the works of two poets, Homer, author of the great epics *The Odyssey* and *The Iliad*, and Hesiod (ca. 700 B.C.), whose work tells much about life in ancient Greece. Hesiod's poem *Theogony* is a leading source of information about the deities of ancient Greek religion, and his *Works and Days* celebrates the pleasures of agrarian and pastoral life. Greek poetry developed to include such forms as odes, lyrical poems, elegies, pastorals, and epigrams. One the most famous of the early lyrical poets was Sappho (fl. ca. 612 B.C.), the first woman poet known by name. While only fragments of Sappho's work survive, what remains are lyrical poems of a passionate and personal nature. Her work was extolled by her contemporaries and later poets and thinkers in the ancient world. Pindar (518–446 B.C.), whose work appeared during the high classical period, was considered the greatest poet of his age, famed for celebratory choral verse.

Poetry blossomed in the Hellenic Period. Theocritus (fl. 270 B.C.) invented the pastoral ode, while Appollonius Rhodius (fl. third century B.C.) wrote epic poetry in Homeric style, including the *Argonautica*, based on the ancient story of Jason and the Argonauts, heroes from Greek mythology, and their search for the Golden Fleece. Hundreds of Hellenic

Poetry: An Introduction

poems are preserved in the *Greek Anthology*, which has as its core the first-century B.C. collection *The Garland*, edited by the poet Meleager. It was augmented by a series of editors over the next millennium. Among the many poets represented in the earlier layers of the anthology are Calli-machus (ca. 300–240 B.C.), Antipater of Sidon (ca. 130 B.C.), Philode-mus (110–40 B.C.), and Lucilius (99–55 B.C.).

Roman literature prior to the first century was largely derivative of, or reactive against, Greek literature. The situation changed dramatically in the last century of the Roman Republic, with the lyric love poetry of Cat-ullus and the long expository poems of Lucretius, including *De Rerum Natura* (*The Nature of Things*).

Horace was the greatest master of Latin lyric poetry; his *Odes* and *Epis-tles* take brilliant advantage of the grammatical complexities and expres-sive possibilities of Latin. Ovid wrote amatory and erotic verse, *Amores* (*The Loves*) and *Ars Amatoria* (*The Art of Love*); his *Metamorphoses* (*Trans-formations*) are meditations on the ceaseless changes that affect gods, hu-mans, and the natural world.

•**Virgil and *The Aeneid*** (**30 B.C.**) Virgil, the greatest of the Latin epic poets, is known for his long pastoral poems, the *Eclogues* and the *Georgics*, but especially for his masterpiece, *The Aeneid*. Virgil's epic poem tells the story of the Trojan prince Aeneas and his escape from Troy as the Greeks overtook it. Modeled somewhat after Homer's *Iliad* and *Odyssey* in structure and story line, Aeneas wanders for years on his jour-ney to Italy to found the city of Rome. The poem was meant to glorify both Rome (then at the height of its power) and the emperor Augustus and was written in his time. Like Homer's tales, it is written in dactylic hexameter and imitates much of Homer's style and phraseology.

Book 1 The author invokes the Muse to tell why the goddess Juno is angry at Aeneas and his men, and causes them undue hardships during their escape from Troy and founding of the city of Rome. After several years of wandering, Aeneas's ships are shipwrecked in Carthage in north-ern Africa. They are presented to the queen, Dido. Dido asks that Aeneas tell the tale of the fall of Troy and his subsequent adventures.

Book 2 Aeneas recounts the tale of the fall of Troy; how the Greeks devised the apparent gift of a wooden horse filled with warriors and thereby entered the city. At night, after the Trojans had celebrated the vic-tory, the Greeks emerged from the structured horse and besieged and burned the town. Aeneas escaped the burning city with his father, Anchises, and his son.

Book 3 Aeneas sailed to Thrace and then to Crete, where he considered settling, but was told by Apollo in a dream not to do so and to continue on to Italy. They traveled around Greece and proceeded toward Italy, stopping at several islands for rest and nourishment. Eventually, they reached the shores of Italy, landed on the isle of the Cyclopes, and escaped after being threatened by the Cyclopes. Aeneas's father, Anchises, died on the journey.

Book 4 Dido falls in love with Aeneas and prepares for marriage. Her suitor, King Iarbas, is displeased and appeals to Jupiter, who sends Mercury to remind Aeneas of his fate to found Rome. Aeneas leaves, and Dido takes her own life.

Book 5 A storm drives Aeneas's ships to the coast of Sicily, where Acestes, a former Trojan, welcomes them. Many of those in Aeneas's band want to stay in Sicily, and they attempt to burn the ships to do so. The fires are contained, and Aeneas founds a city in Sicily for those wishing to remain. He then sets sail for the mainland with the rest of his crew.

Book 6 Aeneas pays tribute to Apollo, asking for a reprieve from their wanderings. A prophetess, the Sybyl of Cumae, alerts Aeneas that in the founding of Rome more trials are yet to come. Aeneas is accompanied by the Sybyl to the underworld to address his father. He encounters many of the Trojan heroes as well as Dido and meets his father in the land of the good, Elysium. Anchises foretells the history of Rome and its eventual greatness through Julius Caesar and Augustus.

Book 7 Aeneas and his men arrive in Latium on the banks of the Tiber River and are welcomed by King Latinus, who proposes that Aeneas marry his daughter, Lavinia, to unite the Trojans and the Latins. Latinus's wife, Amata, is enraged because she wants her daughter to wed the warrior Turnus. Aeneas's son, Ascanius, kills a favored deer. The Latins are furious and prepare for war with the Trojans.

Book 8 Worried that Turnus has many more men than he, Aeneas, alerted by the god Tiber, goes to Pallanteum, the future site of Rome, and finds allies under King Evander, an old friend of Anchises. King Evander provides 400 warriors as well as his own son, Pallas, who is to learn warfare from Aeneas. The god Vulcan forges weapons for Aeneas. The shield forged by Vulcan for Aeneas portrays many great moments in the future history of Rome, down to the battle of Actium in Virgil's own time.

Book 9 The Trojans build a wall around their camp. Turnus and his men surround it. Eventually, Turnus infiltrates the fort and kills many of the Trojans before escaping over the walls.

Book 10 At a council of the gods, Jupiter tells the feuding gods not to intervene any further. Aeneas and his warriors confront Turnus and his troops; Pallas, King Evander's son, is slain by Turnus. In a rage, Aeneas wounds the tyrant Mesentius, and, after warning his son Lausus to retreat, Aeneas kills him when he refuses.

Book 11 Amidst deep mourning for the dead, both factions realize the need for a truce. Latinus calls a council of leading citizens to discuss peace. They are close to a decision when the news arrives that the Trojans are approaching the city. Many panic, but Turnus arms himself and charges off. Camilla, a warrior maiden, tries to help Turnus in battle but is slain. Turnus retreats to the city to find help.

Book 12 A truce is arranged, but Aeneas and Turnus agree to a one-on-one battle. Aeneas is wounded by an irate Latin, and Turnus reacts by spearing many Trojans and desecrating their corpses. Venus disobeys Jupiter and heals Aeneas's wound. Aeneas rearms and eventually wounds Turnus, and when he sees that Turnus is wearing a belt stolen from Pallas's body, he kills him. The Trojans forswear their Trojan identity and unite with the Latins.

♦**Poetry in Medieval Europe** The earliest medieval European literature was written in Latin, and it predominantly expressed Christian themes. Vernacular literature first appeared ca. 800 with the now fragmentary epic in High German, *The Lay of Hildebrand*. Much of Europe's literature before the 12th century was communicated orally. Old Norse (Norwegian) oral poetry migrated to Iceland, where heroic narratives called "eddas" were written down from ca. 1100 to ca. 1350. France's national epic, the *Chanson de Roland* (*The Song of Roland*), appeared ca. 1100. Based on a historical incident, the Battle of Roncevaux Pass, in which the army of the Christian king Charlemagne was ambushed following a failed campaign in Spain, *Chanson de Roland* is the first and finest example of a *chanson de geste*, a literary form that celebrates the legendary deeds of a hero. It was followed in the next century by Spain's *Cantar del Mio Cid* (*The Poem of The Cid*) and at the turn of the 13th century by Germany's *Nibelungenlied* (*The Song of the Niebelungs*).

The Christian romance form, which recounts the heroic adventures of chivalrous knights, is based largely on British-Celtic Arthurian legend, although it also appeared in 12th-century France, where its leading practitioner was Chrétien de Troyes. In Germany, Wolfram von Eschenbach composed the great romance *Parzival* about 1220, which narrates the story of an Arthurian knight and his long quest for the Holy Grail . During this same period, lyric poetry was developed by the troubadours in southern France and spread to northern France and to Germany. In the 13th century, allegorical fable and romance arose in France, best represented by the long symbolic poem *Roman de la Rose*, a leading example of courtly literature that was written both to entertain and to teach others about the art of love.

The French lyric tradition was also picked up in Sicily, where the first sonnets are believed to have been composed in the 13th century, leading to the birth of a great Italian vernacular (Tuscan) literature. Its supreme poetic voice was the Florentine politician Dante Alighieri, creator, in the early 14th century, of one of the transcendent works of world literature, *The Divine Comedy*.

•The Divine Comedy (1310–14) This medieval poetic masterpiece was composed in the Florentine dialect in distinct terza rima (triple rhyme), near the end of the poet's life. Precisely and symbolically structured in three "canticas"—*Inferno*, *Purgatorio*, and *Paradiso*, containing a total of 100 cantos—it is a vividly descriptive, dramatic, allegorical account of the poet's journey through the Christian afterworld, inhabited by identifiable historical and contemporary figures.

It begins with the poet lost in a "dark wood," symbolic of sin, where he is rescued by the Roman poet Virgil, who guides him through the only route of deliverance, the nine circles of Hell, which descend to the center of the earth.

Inferno, with its exquisitely imagined tortures, is the most widely read section of the poem. As the poets proceed, they are blocked by a leopard, a wolf, and a lion, the first of several fierce creatures they will encounter, and must take another path into Hell's anteroom, where "the neutrals," who in life took no stand for good or evil, are attacked by wasps. Across the river Acheron, in the First Circle, or limbo, are the virtuous unbaptized, including ancient poets. Circles Two through Five are populated by those guilty of sins of incontinence–the lustful, the gluttons, the misers, and the souls who suffer for sins of anger. The Sixth Circle is occupied by heretics. Beyond, in Circle Seven, is the Plain of Fire, where the violent are tortured by fire and boiling blood. In the Eighth Circle are various fraudulent transgressors. Precipitously below the other circles is the Ninth, the Pit of Hell, where the most abject sinners, the traitors, are punished. There, trapped in ice, the giant Lucifer clenches Brutus, Cassius, and Judas Iscariot in his teeth.

Purgatorio depicts the travelers' ascent up a mountain, on the ledges of which those guilty of one of the seven great sins are purified by punishment and gradually proceed toward heaven. Atop Purgatory lies the Garden of Eden, where Virgil yields his function to the blessed Beatrice, who in life had been the object of Dante's transforming love. Their course through the nine spheres of *Paradiso*, bathed in celestial harmony and radiance, involves encounters with angels, saints, and holy warriors and culminates in the poet's ecstatic experience of the Divine.

Later in that century, another Tuscan, Petrarch, wrote a series of sonnets that became for centuries the foundation for that international verse form. His sonnets were read throughout Europe, and much lyric poetry was written in imitation of his work. Petrarch's poetry was a bridge from the Middle Ages to the Renaissance and an important factor in the development of vernacular literature. He linked Greek and Roman tradition to Christian culture and set the stage for the great flowering of poetry during the Renaissance.

Day 2: How Poetry Works

The first attempt to define poetry can be found in Aristotle's *Poetics* (ca. 335 B.C.), in which he separated poetry into *drama, lyric poetry, epic poetry,* and the *dithyramb* (a type of hymn). These distinctions were made using a number of criteria, such as the use of several elements including plot and meter, as well as the poet's intended purpose in writing a poem.

The best place to find a pure definition of poetry may be from some of history's greatest poets themselves. William Wordsworth took a truly Romantic poet's stance when he declared, "Poetry is the spontaneous overflow of powerful feelings." Samuel Taylor Coleridge, Wordsworth's colleague, famously defined prose as "words in their best order" and poetry as "the best words in the best order."

Many scholars agree that the issue of marking poetry and prose as discrete fields is a moot one; poetic prose and prosaic poetry are both common. Poetry places an emphasis on word economy. Critics generally regard the best poems as those in which every word is essential and all excess verbiage is eliminated, sometimes even articles such as "a" or "the." The Modernist poet Ezra Pound advised poets to "use no superfluous word, no adjective, which does not reveal something." Poems often use words for their aesthetic value in addition to, or even instead of, their syntactical value; as the 20th-century poet Archibald MacLeish once mused, "a poem shouldn't mean, but be."

Unlike prose, poetry often employs a variety of devices to further enhance the language, including rhyme, meter, assonance, consonance, and alliteration, among others. In addition, poetry almost always includes the deliberate breakage of lines of text, either due to metrical restraints or to achieve some artistic end.

◆**Foot and Meter**   Poems that incorporate meter use a set number of poetic "feet" per line. In English poetry, there are five basic rhythms: iambs, trochees, spondees, anapests, and dactyls; each unit of rhythm is called a "foot" of poetry. While there are many kinds of poetic feet, some are more common than others:

Iamb, an unstressed syllable followed by a stressed syllable; the iamb most closely imitates the patterns of spoken English. Iambic pentameter, which uses five iambs per line, is one of the most common types of meter, and was used almost always by Shakespeare, as in Sonnet 18:

> Shall **I** com**pare** thee **to** a **sum**mer's **day**?

Trochee, the opposite of an iamb; a stressed syllable, followed by an unstressed syllable.

> **Jack** and **Jill** went **up** the **hill** to **fetch** a **pail** of **water.**

Anapest, two unstressed syllables followed by one stressed syllable; one famous poem written in *anapestic tetrameter* (four anapests per line) is the anonymous "Visit from St. Nicholas":

> 'Twas the **night** before **Christ**mas and **all** through the **house…**

Dactyl, one stressed syllable followed by two stressed syllables; many

Greek and Roman epic poets, including Virgil and Homer, used *dactylic hexameter* (six dactyls per line; also called *heroic hexameter*) in their works. Dactylic verse is less common in English, but one well-known example is in Henry Wadsworth Longfellow's *Evangeline*:

> **This** is **for**est primeval. The **mur**muring **pines** and the **hem**locks.

Spondee, two consecutive stressed syllables; used less frequently than the others, often for emphasis. For example, in Coleridge's "Metrical Feet," the phrase "strong foot" is the spondee, used to interrupt a series of iambs:

> From long to long in solemn sort
> Slow Spondee stalks, **strong foot**!

♦Poetic Forms   The following is by no means an exhaustive list of some of the most popular and historically important poetic forms.

Ballad, originally a poem set to music; in the 19th century, it could be just a short narrative poem, often about an individual, such as Coleridge's "Rime of the Ancient Mariner."

Couplet, two successive rhyming lines; sometimes, though rarely, a poem in itself. A well-known example is from Robert Frost's "Stopping By Woods on a Snowy Evening":

> The woods are lovely, dark, and deep
> But I have promises to keep.

Elegy, a poem that mourns the death of an individual, such as Edgar Allan Poe's "Annabel Lee":

> And so, all the night-tide, I lie down by the side
> Of my darling—my darling—my life and my bride,
> In the sepulchre there by the sea,
> In her tomb by the sounding sea.

Epic, a long narrative poem that tells the stories of heroic characters and often represents critical events in the history of a race or nation; Homer's *Iliad* and *Odyssey* and Milton's *Paradise Lost* are examples.

Free Verse, a form with no regular line length or meter, intended to imitate the rhythms of natural speech. The innovator of this form was Walt Whitman, most famously in his long-form *Leaves of Grass*:

A child said, What is the grass? fetching it to me with full
  hands;
How could I answer the child?. . . .I do not know what it is any
  more than he.

Haiku, a three line, unrhymed poem in which the lines are five, then
seven, then five syllables. The form originated in Japan, where one of its
greatest practitioners was Matsuo Basho (1644–1694):

A monk sips morning tea,
it's quiet,
the chrysanthemums flowering.

Limerick, an almost always whimsical five line poem with an *aabba*
rhyme scheme. One famous practitioner is Edward Lear (1812–88), who
published poems such as "There was an Old Man of Kilkenny" in his *Book
of Nonsense*:

There was a Young Lady whose chin,
Resembled the point of a pin;
So she had it made sharp,
And purchased a harp,
And played several times with her chin.

Ode, a lyric poem dedicated to someone or something, such as John
Keats's "Ode to a Grecian Urn."

Pastoral, literally, a poem about shepherds; more generally, a poem
about rural life; may be narrative, elegaic, satirical, or dramatic. Spenser's
Shepherd's Calendar and Milton's *Lycidas* are examples.

Sonnet, a 14-line lyric poem, usually in iambic pentameter. The form
originated in 13th-century Sicily and was made famous by the Tuscan
poet Petrarch in the 14th century. Although sonnets continue to be written using various rhyme schemes, they traditionally follow Petrarchan
("Italian") or Shakespearean ("English") forms. The Petrarchan form consists of two stanzas, an octave rhymed *abbaabba* and a sestet rhymed
cdecde; the Shakespearean consists of three quatrains and a couplet,
rhymed *abab cdcd efef gg*.

❖Selected Other Poetic Terms

Alliteration, repetition of the initial consonant in a series of words:

> Peter Piper picked a peck of pickled peppers.

Assonance, repetition of the same or similar vowel sounds:

> She eats peach with speed.

Caesura, a pause or break within a line of poetry indicated by either punctuation or a natural pause in the syntax. One famous use of caesura, here by semicolon, is in Alexander Pope's "An Essay on Criticism":

> To err is human; to forgive, divine.

Consonance, repetition of the same or similar consonant sounds; for example, this line from Dylan Thomas's "A Refusal to Mourn the Death, by Fire, of a Child in London":

> Deep with the first dead lies London's daughter...

Enjambment, one line of poetry running into another unseparated by punctuation, breaking apart a phrase, as in Robert Frost's "Birches":

> When I see birches bend to left and right
> Across the lines of straighter darker trees...

Metaphor, a figure of speech comparing two unlike objects or ideas in which the writer states that one is the other. One famous example is in Shakespeare's *Romeo and Juliet*, when Romeo refers to Juliet as the sun:

> Hark, what light from yonder window breaks?
> It is the east, and Juliet is the sun.

Simile, a figure of speech comparing two unlike objects or ideas, generally using the words *like* or *as*; one example, from Edgar Allan Poe's "To Helen":

> Helen, thy beauty is to me
> Like those Nicae barks of Yore...

Stanza, a set of lines separated from other stanzas by blank space, such as a "verse" in song.

Weekend 47: Languages of the World

Human beings are unique in their use of language. Only humans have the innate, hardwired ability to employ a large vocabulary of words with a complex grammar to create language itself. Linguistic abilities are surprisingly uniform across the entire human species, and all normal human beings learn to speak the language of their native community.

Many theories exist concerning when and how language began, and because there are no fossil records related to the earliest linguistic development, the true beginnings of spoken language are lost in time. Early cultures believed that language was a gift from the gods, and the origins of language are an integral part of creation myths throughout world mythology. Ironically, the diversity of language is usually seen as a curse— a punishment for human arrogance or disobedience—a belief best exemplified by the "Tower of Babel" passage in Genesis, in the Hebrew Bible.

Although some scholars assume there was a primitive language system dating as far back as two million years, fully developed language is thought to have been an evolutionary innovation of *Homo sapiens*, which facilitated the spread of the species around the globe. Many scientists believe that at some point in their evolutionary development, humans developed larger and more sophisticated brains that allowed for the development of language, although there is no agreement on when this occurred. Richard Leakey, the noted paleoanthropologist, suggests that *Homo sapiens* did not originally possess the necessary anatomy to produce language until 300,000 years ago, while Steven Pinker, the cognitive scientist, argues that because all modern humans have identical language abilities, language must have emerged with the first appearance of modern humans about 200,000 years ago.

Language is a living thing—highly changeable in vocabulary, pronunciation, and (more slowly) grammar. Words fall into disuse; others are coined or borrowed; pronunciations change both over time and geographically, as populations disperse, or come into contact.

In 2010, Unesco identified 6,000 living languages in the world, most of which are spoken only by a small number of people. More than 3,000 languages are considered endangered, based on the number of native speakers currently living, the age of those speakers, and the percentage of children in the community who are acquiring the language. Africa currently has the highest number of languages in danger of extinction, with 250 of the continent's 1,400 languages threatened with imminent disappearance. Once a language is identified as endangered, it can be stabilized or rescued through language documentation, in which the grammar, syntax, and vocabulary are recorded and preserved; language revitalization occurs when a community takes political and educational action to increase the number of active speakers. In North America, endangered languages are primarily Native American, such as Oneida, Onandaga, Seneca, and Chinook.

Day 1: Origins and Groups

The eight most common languages—Mandarin Chinese, English, Hindi, Spanish, Russian, Arabic, Bengali, and Portuguese—are spoken by half of the world's population. Below are summaries of 15 of the world's most commonly spoken languages. English is treated separately in Day 2.

•**Arabic** Twenty-six countries around the world have adopted Arabic as an official language—more than any other language but English and French. There are approximately 280 million native speakers, and it is a second language for millions more who are familiar with Arabic through the recitation of the Koran. As with the Chinese language, spoken dialects are not mutually understandable, but Arabic speakers share a written language called Modern Standard Arabic. The main dialects are Levantine (spoken in Syria, Lebanon, Jordan, Palestine), Egyptian, Iraqi, and Moroccan. Arabic is an official language of the United Nations.

•**Bengali** is the official language of Bangladesh and India. More than 180 million people worldwide count Bengali as their mother tongue. An estimated 230 million people speak Bengali, making it the sixth most spoken language in the world.

•**Chinese** is the native language of more than 1.2 billion people, principally in China, but also in ethnic Chinese communities worldwide. Major dialects include Mandarin, also known as *guoyu* ("national language"), which is the official language of China, Taiwan, and Singapore; Guangdong (Cantonese, widely spoken in southern and southeastern China); Min (Fujian Province, Taiwan, and in Southeast Asian overseas

Chinese communities); Wu (Shanghai and nearby regions); and Hakka (southeastern China and Southeast Asian overseas Chinese communities). Although spoken dialects of Chinese are not mutually intelligible, they share the same writing system—Chinese characters, or *hanzi*, which represent words independently of their pronunciation. Chinese is also an official language of the United Nations.

◆**French** has some 150 million native speakers in France, Switzerland, Belgium, Canada, Africa, and in French overseas territories and possessions from Martinique to New Caledonia. It is widely used as a second language, especially in West Africa. French is an official language of the United Nations, and of 29 countries.

◆**German** is an official language of six European countries (Germany, Austria, Switzerland, Luxembourg, Liechtenstein, and Belgium) and the European Union. There are sizable German-speaking populations in eastern Europe, Brazil, and the United States. Native speakers total nearly 120 million.

◆**Hindi** has some 474 million native speakers in India alone, a number that rises significantly (50 million) if combined with the similar Urdu, an official language of Pakistan. Collectively, these and other closely related languages are known as Hindustani, which is also spoken in Malaysia, Singapore, Trinidad, Guyana, South Africa, Mauritius, and other countries with large expatriate Indo-Pakistani communities.

◆**Japanese** is the official language of Japan, where it is spoken by more than 130 million people, and the island nation of Palau. Significant Japanese-speaking populations are also found in Brazil and the United States. Modern Japanese employs four writing systems: kanji, hiragana, katakana, and romaji.

◆**Korean** is spoken primarily in North and South Korea, with significant Korean-speaking populations in Japan, Russia, China, and the United States. Native speakers total about 78 million people.

◆**Malay** Variants and dialects of Malay are used as an official language in Indonesia, Malaysia, Singapore, and Brunei. Although these four countries have a combined population of more than 270 million, only 40 million people claim Malay as their first language.

◆**Persian** includes Farsi, the official language of Iran, plus the closely related languages of Tajik (Tajikistan and parts of Afghanistan) and Dari (spoken by nearly half the population of Afghanistan. There are an estimated 60–70 million native speakers of various dialects of Persian.

◆**Portuguese** is spoken by 210 million people, the vast majority of whom live in Brazil, where it is an official language. Portuguese is used as an official language in only six other countries outside of Portugal, including Angola and four other countries in Africa; East Timor, an island Southeast Asia; and the special administrative region of Macau, on the southeastern coast of China.

◆**Russian** is the native language of approximately 164 million people. It is the official language of Russia, Belarus, Kazakhstan, and Kyrgyzstan. There are still significant numbers of people claiming Russian as a first language in the former republics of the Soviet Union, and approximately 114 million speak it as a second language. Russian is an official language of the U.N. and the International Atomic Energy Agency (I.A.E.A.).

◆**Spanish** is the official language of 23 countries, including Spain, Mexico, Colombia, Argentina, and many other nations of Central and South America and the Caribbean. Native speakers total about 700 million, with 100 million in Mexico alone, and including about 43 million in the United States. Spanish is also an official language of the United Nations.

◆**Tamil** is the principal language of the province of Tamil Nadu, in southeastern India and is also an official language of Sri Lanka and Singapore. There are approximately 66 million native speakers of Tamil, including the significant minority communities in the United States and Canada.

◆**Turkish Standard (Anatolian)** Turkish, plus closely related dialects and languages including Azeri, Kyrgyz, Kazakh, Türkmen, Tartar, Uighur, and Uzbek have approximately 120 million native speakers. Turkish languages are spoken across a huge span of central Eurasia, including Turkey, Azerbaijan, Kazakhstan, Kyrgyzstan, Turkmenistan, Uzbekistan, and the province of Xinjiang in northwestern China.

◆**Vietnamese** is spoken primarily in Vietnam, with sizable Vietnamese-speaking populations in the neighboring countries of Cambodia and Laos, as well as in the United States. There are approximately 86 million people speaking Vietnamese, including native speakers and those who use it as a second language.

◆**Language Families**   Languages that are related by descent from a common ancestor are said to belong to the same language family. The study of language families began in the late 18th century, when an official of the British East India Company, Sir William Jones, noticed that Sanskrit, Greek, and Latin have many similarities in vocabulary and grammar, and proposed that all three languages were derived from an extinct ancestral language, now known as proto-Indo-European. By the early 19th century, scholars began to systematically explore the similarities in languages spoken in regions from Ireland to India and from Scandinavia to Greece, and many other language families were discovered.

Language families were formed as populations migrated and became geographically separated, so that their original language divided into new but related languages, which then evolved separately.

The physical distribution of languages (now supplemented by genetic DNA studies) can be used to trace the movement of populations over the past several thousand years.

Most languages can be can be classified as members of a language family or subfamily. A few (Basque is the most famous example) are linguistic isolates, and there are also a number of hybrid forms (pidgins and creoles) that cross linguistic boundaries.

Eurasia   Indo-European embraces about 150 languages spoken by some 3 billion people worldwide. It is the most widely distributed language family— evidence of a persistent drive for territorial expansion. Indo-Europeans migrated from somewhere near the Black Sea to India, Europe, and beyond. They are believed to have originated in an area between eastern Europe and the Aral Sea, around the fifth millennium B.C.

Indo-European is made up of several subfamilies, including Indo-Iranian (Bengali, Farsi, Hindi, Pashto, Sanskrit, Sinhalese, and others); Italic or Romance (Catalan, French, Italian, Latin, Portuguese, Romanian, Spanish); Germanic (Dutch, English, German, Gothic, Icelandic, Swedish, and others); Celtic (Breton, Gaelic, Welsh, and others); Baltic (Latvian, Lithuanian, and others); Slavic (Czech, Polish, Russian, Serbo-Croatian, Slavonic, and others); and Albanian, Armenian, and Greek.

Other language families of Eurasia are:

Caucasian includes Georgian, Circassian, Chechen, and the several languages of the Kartvelian subfamily, spoken south of the chief range of the Caucasus Mountains. *Uralic* encompasses Finnish, Estonian, Hungarian, and Saami. *Altaic* includes Turkish, Uzbek, Mongolian, Manchu, and Uighur. Korean and Japanese are sometimes described as Altaic languages, but this identification is highly controversial. Despite obvious similarities, no organic link between Korean and Japanese has been proven, leading some experts to conclude that Korean is linguistically isolated, and Japanese is part of the small Koguryoic. *Sinitic* encompasses all dialects of Chinese (Mandarin, Guangdong (Cantonese), Min, Wu, Hakka, and others). *Elamo-Dravidian* includes Tamil, Malayalam, Kannada, and other languages of South India. *Austroasiatic* contains 250 languages spoken in mainland Southeast Asia, including Vietnamese, Khmer (Cambodian), Mon, and Tai. Some linguists propose that Tai and closely related languages such as Lao belong instead in the Sino-Tibetan family.

Southeast Asia and the Pacific Islands The *Austronesian* family (also called *Malayo-Polynesian*) includes several hundred languages spoken in Southeast Asia and the islands of the Indian and Pacific Oceans, ranging from Malagasy (spoken in Madagascar, off the coast of Africa) to Hawai'ian and Maori in the Pacific. Austronesians moved from southeastern China to Indonesia and then eastward to the Pacific Islands and westward to Madagascar. The family is divided into Western Austronesian and Eastern Austronesian. Western Austronesian (including Malay, Indonesian, Javanese, Tagalog, and many others) languages are spoken by more than 300 million people. The Eastern Austronesian subfamily is further divided into Micronesian and Polynesian languages.

The *Papuan* family of New Guinea, and the nearby island groups of the Moluccas and Melanesia, includes several hundred languages divided into several subfamilies, and the Australian languages of the aboriginal peoples of Australia, who were isolated from external contact for perhaps 40,000 years, are similarly divided.

Africa The languages of Africa, and the adjacent Middle East, are divided into four families:

Afro-Asiatic includes Berber, Coptic, Hausa, and the languages of the Semitic subfamily : Hebrew, Arabic, Aramaic, and Amharic. The *Nilo-Saharan* family, found in northeastern, eastern, and central Africa, includes Turkana, Masai, Dinka, Mangbetu, Efe, and the numerous languages of the Eastern Sudanic (including Nubian) and Central Sudanic subfamilies. The *Niger-Kordofanic* family is found in west, central, and southern Africa. It has two main branches, Kordofanic and Niger-Congo. The Benue-Congo subfamily group includes hundreds of languages of the Bantu sub-family (Swahili, Zulu, Xhosa, Sotho, Setsuana), reflecting a historic expansion of the Bantu peoples southward and eastward from an original homeland in the Congo basin.

Africa is home to the *Khoisan* family, which includes ancient languages (San and others) spoken by peoples largely displaced by the Bantu expansion. These languages are known for their distinctive "click" sounds.

The Americas The language families of the Americas include Eskimo-Aleut; Na-Dene (Athabascan and Navajo); and, according to the controversial theory of the late Joseph Greenberg, Amerind, which includes all other Native American languages. Other authorities divide these languages into discrete families:

Macro-Algonquian (eastern and northern woodlands and Pacific Northwest) includes Algonquin, Delaware, Cheyenne, Cree, Salish, Nootka, and Kwakiutl. *Penutian* (central and coastal California into Mexico and Central America) includes the widespread Mayan languages. *Hokan-Siouan* is widely distributed geographically, including Choctaw, Seminole, the Iroquois languages, Cherokee, Lakota, and many others. *Aztec-Tanoan* (southwestern North America and Mexico) includes Paiute, Shoshone, Comanche, Hopi, Nahuatl, and many others.

The most prominent languages of Central America, the Caribbean, and South America are Mixtecan and Toltecan (Mexico and Central America); Cariban and Arawakan (Caribbean); and Chibchan, Ge, Quechua, Aymara, Araukanian, and Tupi-Guarani (South America).

♦Pidgins, and Creoles Pidgins are simplified languages that are used for trading purposes between peoples with no common language (the word *pidgin* itself derives from the English word *business*). Pidgins can evolve into creoles, independent languages that combine features of two or more parent languages. Jamaican (with English and West African roots), Haitian (French and West African), and Hawai'ian Creole (combining Hawai'ian and English with Japanese, Tagalog, and other Asian languages) are the best-known examples.

Day 2: The English Language Today

Although English ranks only third among the world's most spoken languages, it is on its way to becoming the first truly global language—used throughout the world as the language of commerce, diplomacy, and science. English is the mother tongue for some 450 million people, and a further 1.5 billion people use it as a second language to some degree. Beginning in the 17th century, the language spread throughout the British Empire to the Americas, Africa, India, and Oceana. Today 70 countries designate English as an official language (although it does not have that status in the United States), and it is an official language of the United Nations, the European Union, Nafta, NATO, and the Organization of American States.

◆**A Brief History of the English Language** English belongs to the Germanic branch of the Indo-European family of languages, and is related to most languages spoken in Europe, Scandinavia, India, and western Asia. The story of English begins with the arrival of the Jutes, Angles, and Saxons, Germanic peoples who invaded Britain in the fifth century and divided the island nation among themselves. In Common Germanic, the Angles were called *Angli*, which later mutated to Engle, and *Engla land* soon became the name of the nation these tribes now occupied. Old English (Anglo-Saxon), which is dated from the first written documents of this period to 1066, was an amalgamation of Germanic dialects, Latin, which persisted from the time of the Roman occupation, and Norse, which was brought by the Viking invaders who arrived in force in 865. Literacy came to England when the Anglo-Saxons converted to Christianity in the ninth century.

Middle English emerged following the Norman Conquest in 1066, which brought a distinctive French influence to the language. The Normans not only introduced new vocabulary, but changed the style of writing, from a clear, easily readable hand to the more ornate Carolingian script that was used on the Continent. Norman scribes began to change the spelling of Old English as well, introducing many of the conventions that remain in the language today. For example, the Old English *cw* became *qu*, giving us *queen*, instead of *cwen*.

As Anglo-Saxon rulers were replaced by the Norman conquerors, Norman-French became the language of government and high society, and the Norman influence on the English language is still apparent, notably in the abundance of words related to the law and government: *jury*, *court*, and *parliament* are just some examples.

The Chancery Standard (CS) was developed during the reign of King Henry V (1413–1422), who ordered his government officials to use English instead of Norman-French in the course of business. CS was based on the dialects of London and the Midlands, which were the largest population centers at the time. By mid-century, CS was used in all official transactions, except by the church, which continued to use Latin, and its spread throughout the country was aided by the introduction of the printing press by William Caxton in the late 1470s.

The transition to Modern English began in the 15th century, with what is known as the "Great Vowel Shift"—a term coined in the 20th century by the Danish linguist Otto Jespersen. It refers to a major change in pronunciation that took place between 1450 and 1750. The exact cause of the shift remains a mystery, and some linguistic scholars are skeptical about its existence. One theory is that it was the result of a dramatic social change in the wake of the Black Death, which ravaged Europe from 1347 to 1351. In England, this caused a massive migration of people to the south of England, and an unprecedented mixing of social classes, who began to modify their regional vowel sounds into a standard pronunciation. Many of the peculiarities of English spelling persist from this period.

◆**Codifying the Language** In 1662, the Royal Society of London for the Promotion of Natural Knowledge appointed a committee of 22 men, including the poet John Dryden, to undertake the improvement of the English language. The committee failed in its attempt to find an appropriate arbiter of the language, and failed again in 1712, when Jonathan Swift attempted to enlist Robert Harley, the earl of Oxford, in the cause.

But finally in 1755, after eight years of work, Samuel Johnson, the great English critic and essayist, published *A Dictionary of the English Language*, which included 40,000 words, 114,000 illustrative quotations drawn from literary works dating back to the 1500s, and suggestions for proper usage. The dictionary reflects Johnson's intelligence and idiosyncratic humor. He left out words he didn't like—*gambler*, *fuss*, and *shabby*—but included words beyond the grasp of the average reader—*deosculation* (to kiss warmly), for example. His most famous definitions capture both his snobbish and self-deprecating nature:

> Oats: a grain which in England is generally given the horses, but in Scotland supports the people.

> Lexicographer: a writer of dictionaries; a harmless drudge who business himself in tracing the original, and detailing the significance of words.

It was a source of British pride that Dr. Johnson completed the dictionary almost single-handedly (he had six assistants), while the Académie Française spent 40 years, employing 40 people to publish a similar work. Dr. Johnson's dictionary dominated lexicography for almost two centuries.

In 1857, the Philological Society of London decided that existing dictionaries were inadequate and sought to reexamine the language going back to Anglo-Saxon times. In 1879, they reached an agreement with Oxford University Press and James Murray to create a new reference work that would document the language from the Early Middle English period (1150) forward. The original plan called for a four-volume work that would take approximately 10 years to complete. In the end, the final volume of what became a 10-volume work was published in 1928 under the title *A New English Dictionary on Historical Principles*, immediately becoming the definitive authority on the English language.

Because the English language is always changing, work began on updating the dictionary almost as soon as it was published. In 1933, the dictionary, renamed *The Oxford English Dictionary*, expanded to 12 volumes plus one Supplement, and after many revisions and additions, in 1989 a definitive new edition was published in 20 volumes, followed in 1992 with an electronic edition, on CD-ROM. Today, the Oxford English Dictionary Online adds new words on a regular basis, providing a continuous record of changes in our language and society.

◆**English in America** The playwright and public intellectual George Bernard Shaw famously observed at the beginning of the 20th century that the United States and the United Kingdom are "two countries divided by a common language." American English came into existence as soon as the first settlers arrived on the continent, bringing with them traditional English speech, leavened with their distinctive regional dialects. To this, they quickly added words from the local Indian languages, particularly those describing plants and animals that they had never seen before (*raccoon, moose, squash*). Within 100 years, the original English settlers were joined by the Irish, Dutch, Scandinavians, and other European colonists who built settlements in the South and Midwest, while Spanish and Mexican settlers populated the Southwest and West. The American lexicon overflows with loanwords from these languages, including *adobe*, *barbecue*, and *rodeo* from the Spanish; *cookie, freight*, and *dock* from the Dutch.

With time and distance, the differences between British English and American English became more profound, and in 1806, Noah Webster set out to establish American English as a distinctive voice, quite apart from the British standard, with the publication of *A Compendious Dictionary of the English Language*, which defined 37,000 words. His more famous *American Dictionary of the English Language*, published in 1828, was a two-volume dictionary, included 65,000 words, and was based on the principles that spelling should be practical, and that grammar should reflect the way that language was actually spoken, not according to the rules set down by "experts." The dictionary was not a commercial success, but was highly influential, and the name "Webster" has become synonymous with American dictionaries.

Americans continued to coin new words to reflect their evolving economic, political and social realities. *Ballpark, supermarket, gerrymander, gasoline* all entered the language in the 19th and 20th centuries, and in the same period, a new influx of German and Jewish immigrants taught us to *schmooze* and to eat *hamburgers*.

In 1877, Henry Sweet, an English philologist, predicted that within 100 years, American, British, and Australian English would be mutually unintelligible, but in the 21st century, because of globalization and advances in communications technology, regional variations are understood around the world.

◆New Words Dictionary publishers are always on the lookout for new words in an effort to keep the English language corpus up to date. Yet there is no formal mechanism for adding words to the English language. Neologisms—newly coined words that have not yet entered mainstream language—become popular mainly through the mass media and word of mouth. Thousands of words are coined each year, while only a few hundred achieve any kind of permanency in our vocabulary. Lexicographers often follow the use of a word for years before determining whether it deserves inclusion in a dictionary, and publishers retain panels of experts to consider the words being created within their areas of expertise. Ultimately, there are as many opinions about the legitimacy of a word as there are publishers and lexicographers.

New words most often come from the worlds of science, popular culture, business, and now, from advances in the digital world. In 1955, Vladimir Nabokov coined the word *nymphet*, in the novel *Lolita*; in 1960, the word *laser* (from *light amplification by stimulated emission of radiation*) entered the language; in 1984, *cyberspace* appeared for the first time in William Gibson's novel *Neuromancer*. New words that have made their way into dictionaries since 2000 include:

> business: *big-box; insourcing; rightsizing*
> food: *chai; locavore; olestra; turducken*
> military: *waterboarding; weaponize; WMD*
> popular culture/lifestyle: *chill pill; emo; grunge; metrosexual; plus-one; puh-leeze; supersize; unibrow*
> technology: *biodiesel; digerati; google* (as a verb); *podcast; ringtone; USB port;*

Since 1991, the American Dialect Society has designated a Word of the Year (WOTY), and the major English-language dictionary publishers followed suit. The winning words are not necessarily new, but may have taken on a new meaning or usage beyond the original, such as the 1992 WOTY *Not!*, meaning "just kidding." Some words are assimilated into the language so quickly that it seems they have always existed. The winning words in 2009 were: *unfriend*, which beat out *hashtag*, and *sexting* (from the *New Oxford American Dictionary*); *tweet*, which won over *birther,* and *shovel-ready* (from the American Dialect Society), while *Webster's New World College Dictionary* selected *distracted driving*.

Some experts argue that it takes two generations to know whether a word will have durability.

Weekend 48: Painting in the 19th Century

Day 1: American Painting

The early colonial period in America was not especially friendly to the fine arts: colonists were concerned primarily with survival, and the Puritans rejected even religious art. As a result, many of the first American painters copied 17th-century European conventions; however, as colonists sought to commemorate their new surroundings, realistic portraiture and documentary scenes became popular. Distinctively American art forms emerged by the mid-18th century.

Benjamin West was the first native-born American to study art in Europe, where he became a leading history painter. West introduced historical accuracy to neoclassical composition with works such as *The Death of General Wolfe* (1771). While painting in England, West founded the Royal Academy of Arts in 1768, where many Americans came to study. John Singleton Copley, like West, exhibited in England, but unlike West, Copley preferred to spend his days in Boston. His painstaking technique and true-to-life details in paintings such as *Watson and the Shark* (1778) made him one of the most influential painters in colonial America. Gilbert Stuart studied with West but returned to the United States, where his naturalistic approach reinvigorated the "Grand Manner" of full-length portraiture. Stuart's unfinished portrait of George Washington (1796) was engraved on the dollar bill. Another of West's pupils, John Trumbull, memorialized the Revolution and inspired generations of history painters with dramatic works such as *The Battle of Bunker Hill* (1786).

Charles Willson Peale not only painted portraits of American leaders, but was also a curator and scientist. Peale opened a museum exhibiting artwork alongside natural history specimens, and used science as a subject in works such as *Exhuming the First American Mastodon* (1808). His style of scientific naturalism, which combined neoclassical composition with precise observation, became a model for many subsequent artists.

As photographers took over the portraiture trade, American painters followed trappers and surveyors into the wilderness of the 1803 Louisiana Purchase. John James Audubon used his understanding of biology and botany to make vivid studies of birds, plants, and animals. George Catlin painted anthropological portraits and hunting scenes of Native Americans, popularizing an image of noble but endangered peoples. Both Catlin and Audubon published their paintings in books, which gave them widespread appeal.

◆**The Hudson River School** In New York's Hudson River Valley and the nearby mountains, Thomas Cole and Asher Durand were among artists painting the untamed landscape. Inspired by European Romantic painters like J. M. W. Turner and John Constable, as well as the Transcendentalist American writers Henry David Thoreau and Ralph Waldo Emerson, the Hudson River artists sought to evoke the spiritual power of the natural world. Their large and richly detailed paintings featured perspectives that contrasted the awesome grandeur of nature with the insignificance of people and their creations, as in Durand's *Kindred Spirits* (1849), which shows two gentlemen dwarfed by the trees and cliffs of the Catskills.

Dozens of painters followed the Hudson River School, but many of them went on to other subjects. Cole himself turned to allegorical paintings, including the five-canvas series *The Course of Empire* (1834–36). Frederic Edwin Church was one of several second-generation Hudson River painters whose fascination with glowing atmospheric light led to a movement called Luminism. Like Impressionism, Luminism focuses on the effects of light on a subject, generally a landscape; however, Luminism is also characterized by attention to detail and concealed brushstrokes. Church traveled widely and produced such varied scenes as *The Icebergs* (1861) and *The Heart of the Andes* (1859). The expansionist ideas of Manifest Destiny were visible in the Luminist works of German-born Albert Bierstadt, who joined several westward expeditions and returned with awe-inspiring images such as *The Rocky Mountains, Lander's Peak* (1863) and *Sierra Nevada Morning* (ca. 1890). The marine painter Fitz Henry Lane applied the warm pervasive light of Luminism to quiet, mournful seascapes.

The Hudson River painters were among the first professional artists trained in America, and public exhibitions of their works greatly influenced their countrymen's aesthetic sensibilities. Their reverent view of nature also catalyzed the conservation movement, and Thomas Moran's paintings of Yellowstone helped persuade Congress to create the National Park System in 1916.

✦**American Realism** As national optimism faded in the wake of the Civil War, Winslow Homer and Thomas Eakins developed soberly realistic styles that combined documentary objectivity with unsentimental compassion. Homer began his career producing illustrations for *Harper's Weekly*, but unlike most of the other illustrators, Homer depicted everyday camp life rather than battle scenes. Homer's development as an artist was slow but constant: over time his oil paintings became larger, his figures more solitary, and his ability to portray naturalistic detail greater. He produced scores of seascapes exploring the relationship between man and nature, like *Breezing Up* (1876), and *Lost on the Grand Banks* (1885). Known for bold, fluid brushwork and strong compositions, Homer worked extensively in watercolor and helped to popularize the medium with paintings such as *Adirondack Guide* (1894).

Thomas Eakins studied in France but derided the French Academy aesthetic as "affectation" and proclaimed truth as his highest artistic goal. Rejecting formal portraits, Eakins painted his subjects at work, as in *The Gross Clinic* (1875), which shows Dr. Samuel Gross presiding over a surgery. He also startled critics with his vigorous scenes of Philadelphia life, including wrestlers, nude male swimmers, rowers, as in *Max Schmitt in a Single Scull* (1871). In addition to painting, Eakins taught at the Pennsylvania Academy. Eakins stressed anatomy and drawing from live, nude models rather than the traditional methods of using plaster casts of antique sculptures. Eakins was a popular and influential teacher, but in 1886 was asked to resign after concerns arose about his use of nude models in mixed-gender classes. Eakins continued to teach sporadically after being dismissed, but mostly focused on his own art.

✦**Americans Abroad** Although art schools were established in Philadelphia and New York by the mid-19th century, newly affordable travel encouraged many American painters to study or work abroad among the old European masterworks. After studying painting in France, James McNeill Whistler settled in England, where he had his first success when *Symphony in White No. 1: The White Girl* (1862) was shown at the original Salon des Refuses in 1863. While Whistler's most famous painting might be *Arrangement in Grey and Black: Portrait of the Author's Mother* (1871), it was another painting that caught the attention of the public in the 1870s. In 1877, the British art critic John Ruskin attacked Whistler's painting, *Nocturne in Black and Gold: The Falling Rocket* (1874) in a scathing newspaper review. Whistler responded to this critique by suing Ruskin. While Whistler technically "won" the trial, he was awarded only a farthing and was forced to split the court costs. These costs, along with the money invested in his home, brought Whistler to bankruptcy in 1879.

Mary Cassatt was another American who studied and painted abroad. In the 1860s, Cassat joined the Impressionists in France, creating loose, intimate images of women and children. A contemporary of Cassatt, John Singer Sargent studied painting in Florence and Paris. His early work shows an interest in landscapes, but as his style and technique matured he moved toward portraiture, as in his highly controversial *Portrait of Madame X* (1884), which boldly captured its subject's haughty sexuality. His mastery of lighting is also evident in works such as *Carnation Lily, Lily Rose* (1886), which shows two young girls hanging lanterns in a garden at dusk. After 1910, Sargent gave up portraiture and devoted the rest of his life to painting murals and landscapes in watercolor, painting more than 2,000 by the end of his career.

•**The Ashcan School** Several abstract styles of painting were developed in early 20th-century Europe, but many American artists continued Eakins's legacy of truthful representations of life. The painter and teacher Robert Henri cultivated a spontaneous and unglamorous style for painting ordinary people, such as folk dancers and musicians, as well as unadorned scenes of urban life. Henri organized a 1908 show of eight New York and Philadelphia artists whose diverse styles shared themes of urban poverty and decay, winning the movement the nickname the "Ashcan School." One of the most recognizable Ashcan artists, George Bellows, is best known for his painting *Dempsey and Firpo* (1924), a rendition of a boxing match he covered for the *New York Evening Journal*. Another of Henri's later students, Edward Hopper, disavowed the loose Ashcan style, but adopted the dark undercurrents of the movement in spare, carefully composed paintings of isolated figures in commonplace settings, such as *Night Shadows* (1924), *Early Sunday Morning* (1930), *Gas* (1940), and his most famous work, *Nighthawks* (1942), which depicts four figures inside a New York diner on an otherwise deserted nighttime street.

American Scene Painting Reacting to an increasingly industrialized culture, some American painters developed a nationalistic and romanticized documentary style after World War I. Expanding the social realism of the Ashcan School, American Scene Painters created representational—if stylized—works featuring easily understandable images of rural and urban life, often inspired by social or political goals.

Influenced by the Mexican muralist Diego Rivera, many of these artists painted public murals during the Great Depression, when their images of stoic farmers and factory workers offered emotional support to the nation. Grant Wood, Thomas Hart Benton, and John Steuart Curry led a Midwestern contingent known as Regionalism, which celebrated the steadfast virtues of small towns. This sensibility is exemplified in Wood's painting *American Gothic* (1930), depicting a dour farm couple standing in front of their home, and Benton's mural series *America Today* (1930) and his murals illustrating folk songs such as *The Ballad of the Jealous Lover of Lone Green Valley* (1934).

Working outside the main trends of American art, Georgia O'Keeffe (1887–1986) became widely recognized for her semi-abstracted style and sensual flowing color in paintings of the New Mexico landscape, such as *Cow's Skull with Calico Roses* (1931) and close-up images of flowers including *Abstraction White Rose* (1927) and *Black Iris* (1926).

Day 2: Impressionism and After

Throughout the 19th century, Paris was the artistic capital of Europe, and the city's juried Salon de Paris exhibition was a crucial rite of passage for every European painter or sculptor. Sponsored by the state Academie des Beau-Arts, the Salon was not a testing ground for innovation, however. It mostly sought to preserve the tastes of the moneyed class, not to promote the ideas of freethinking bohemians that were abundant in mid-century Paris. In 1863, the Salon rejected more than 3,000 works—many of them by young purveyors of new styles—triggering an outcry widespread enough that emperor Napoleon III formed the Salon des Refuses ("Salon of Rejects") to allow the rejected artists to exhibit their works in an annex to the regular Salon. The first Salon des Refuses proved to be a turning point in the history of Western art by introducing new movements and artists to a wide audience. Included, among other now-famous paintings, were Édouard Manet's *Le Dejeuner sur l'Herbe* (Luncheon on the Grass, 1863) and James McNeill Whistler's *Symphony in White No. 1: The White Girl* (1862).

◆**Impressionism** The Salon des Refuses is generally considered the
opening bell of the Modernist period in the arts, with Manet credited as the
first Impressionist artist (though that term would not be coined until 1874).
The prevailing bohemian attitude in Paris encouraged Manet and other
artists to develop themes, techniques, and subject matter the Academie
had long prohibited: the underclass, sex, drugs, unbalanced composition,
flattened space, experiments with color and tone, and daring personal style.
The guiding motive for the Impressionists was to reinvent painting appropriate for the "modern age." Impressionists took cues from the nascent Realist movement, reflected in works by artists such as Gustav Courbet. The
Realists preferred naturalism and observation to allegory or mythology. Following the Realist lead, Impressionists painted landscapes, scenes of leisure,
and urban street scenes, always featuring contemporary settings rather than
historical narratives, and painting scenes from direct observation, often
outdoors (*en plein air*) rather than in a studio setting.

As the movement developed, distinctive approaches to both color and
composition emerged. Traditional painting had long emphasized techniques
such as *sfumato* or *chiaroscuro* to create the illusion of depth in a painting
using strong, dark, or grayish shadows, but Impressionists attempted to
rewrite the rules for color based on scientific study of the qualities of natural light on a subject. The practice of painting *en plein air* resulted in both
the increasing tendency to flatten pictorial space and use complementary
hues for shadows, both phenomena that appear to the eye under bright sunlight. In addition, many Impressionists interpreted the light and movement
of subjects in loose, abbreviated strokes, a drastic change from the classical
style of studio painting, which had long prized subtle brushwork. Impressionists also drew heavily from Asian color palettes and compositions, mimicking the elongated pictorial formats, asymmetrical compositions, and
aerial perspective found in Japanese printmaking.

Édouard Manet Manet's reputation as founder of the Impressionists
was established by two paintings that were as groundbreaking for their
controversial subject matter as for their visual feel. *Le Dejeuner sur l'Herbe*
(1863) depicts a picnic attended by two men in modern attire and a naked
woman who is staring confidently at the viewer. This odd, scandalous
scene fit nowhere in the traditional subject matter for paintings, which
had for nearly a century been concerned with allegorical or mythological
themes. Furthermore, Manet had flattened the colors and visual space of

the painting; this combination of subtle color palette and confrontational subject matter refuted both the idealized style and traditional content of academic painting. Patrons and critics at the original Salon des Refuses were disgusted, but the *Dejeuner* was an immediate sensation among artists. At the next Salon de Paris, Manet exhibited *Olympia* (1864), which depicts a naked prostitute lying on a bed while looking at the viewer, again outraging critics but energizing the Parisian cadre of experimental artists.

Camille Pissarro Impressionist paintings were mostly rejected from official exhibitions such as the Salon de Paris and were roundly criticized for looking unfinished or sloppy. Among Impressionists, Camille Pissarro was key in organizing the group to exhibit on its own, and in 1874 the Impressionist circle held the first show in which five of Pissarro's works were featured (one of which was *The Old Road to Ennery*, 1872) alongside works by Monet, Renoir, Degas, and Berthe Morisot. The show was a critical failure and in the succeeding years several of the original collective dropped out, yet Pissarro remained steadfast. By 1880, he was focusing primarily on figure studies rather than landscapes (*Young Peasant Woman Drinking Her Café au Lait*, 1881). Toward the end of his career, Pissarro experimented with Pointillism but then turned back to series paintings featuring Paris, often working on multiple canvases at the same time.

Claude Monet For many, Monet's paintings typify the visual style of Impressionism. Made *en plein air*, his paintings are composed with unblended colors and short, thick brushstrokes meant to capture specific, fleeting qualities of light. This is easily recognized in Monet's multiple series of paintings, each of which depicts the same subject in several paintings made quickly at various times of day, including those of Rouen Cathedral (1892–94), haystacks (1890–91), and water lilies (painted over 30 years beginning in 1899).

Edgar Degas In the early 1870s, Degas began to develop simplified compositions, partly under the influence of Japanese prints. Unlike his contemporaries, who were experimenting with painting *en plein air*, Degas continued to work in the studio. Between 1870 and 1873, Degas first began working on studies of ballet rehearsals and performances, including *Dance Class* (1871). In the years to follow, dancers and other performers would become one of Degas most frequently painted subjects, as in *Singer with a Glove* (1878).

Pierre-Auguste Renoir   Established as a painter of bourgeois leisure, such as in *Dancing at Le Moulin de la Gallette* (1876), many of Renoir's paintings are portraits, mostly of well-to-do women and girls, whom he painted with a characteristically cheerful palette and generally flattering compositions, as in *Two Sisters (On the Terrace)* (1881).

Mary Cassatt   The American Mary Cassatt was one of few women to be invited to exhibit with the Impressionists, first in 1879, and again in 1880, 1881, and 1886. Almost all of Cassatt's paintings feature women and children as subjects, rendered in warm colors and soft strokes. She was influential in the development of pastels as a medium, and she was known in Parisian art circles for her drawing talent and her command of asymmetrical composition. After an exhibition of Japanese artists such as Utamaro and Toyokuni in Paris, Cassatt began to shift her emphasis from form to pattern, as seen in works such as *Woman Bathing* (1890).

◆After Impressionism   As the 19th century waned, many of the original Impressionist group continued to refine the style, and the movement, which had already won credibility with the Parisian avant-garde, slowly began to gain mainstream acceptance. Younger contemporaries took advantage of the new artistic freedoms provided by the original Impressionist rebellion, and in 1884 the Société des Artistes Indépendants (Society of Independent Artists) organized, mounting its first exhibition in Paris and showing works by more than 400 artists. In some cases, these new groups and styles were an extension of Impressionist ideas, but in others, they veered off in novel directions. The key movements of this period—Post-Impressionism, Primitivism, Fauvism, Pointillism, Art Nouveau—set the stage for the dramatic evolution that would occur in the arts in the 20th century.

Post-Impressionism   Post-Impressionism generally refers to new styles that arose after the mid-1880s. Where the Impressionists had been a more or less cohesive group related by specific ideas, Post-Impressionism is better thought of as a convenient name, rather than a strict school of thought. Many Post-Impressionists pursued personal stylistic expression, rather than a common methodology or outlook.

Vincent van Gogh   By far, the most well known Post-Impressionist artist is the Dutch painter Vincent van Gogh, whose short 10-year career has nonetheless resulted in perhaps the most famous body of work of any painter of the last several hundred years. Almost completely unknown in his lifetime, van Gogh seldom exhibited and sold only a single painting. Although he used some Impressionist techniques, such as short brush-strokes and bright colors, van Gogh's paintings are considered Post-Impressionist because they portray ecstatic highs and lows, unlike most Impressionist works that sought an objective rendering of a scene. Often, van Gogh distorted space, color, and texture in his work, incorporating highly rhythmic, swirling surface patterns in his paintings, as in the famous *Starry Night* (1889), which was painted a year before his suicide.

Paul Gauguin   Often described somewhat misleadingly as a Post-Impressionist, Gauguin was a member of several movements over a short period of time, including Cloissonnism, Synthetism, and Primitivism, all of which favored bright colors, simplified shapes, and compositions that reflected an artist's emotions or opinions. Gauguin was a key proponent of Primitivism, which rejected many aspects of the Western artistic tradition and chose to emulate native styles and subjects from various developing nations. His best-known paintings were created after he abandoned his life and family in Europe and moved to Tahiti, where he used tropical palettes to depict Tahitian women, as in *Tahitian Women on the Beach* (1891) and *Motherhood* (1899).

Georges Seurat   Though inspired by the broken brushstrokes and patterned use of color popularized by the Impressionists, Seurat sought to develop a style that was more rational and scientific. Seurat studied optics and color theory, developing a method of painting in small dots of unmixed color placed close to one another, which he called Divisionism (more often referred to as Pointillism). In Pointillist paintings, colors appear to blend together as the viewer steps back from the painting. Seurat's best-known work, *A Sunday Afternoon on the Island of La Grande Jatte* (1884–85), was a triumphant vindication of his theories.

Henri Toulouse-Lautrec   In 1892, three years after completion of the Eiffel Tower crowned Paris's status as the City of Lights, the Moulin Rouge club opened its doors, setting the stage for Henri Toulouse-Lautrec's glamorously lurid, off-rhythm depictions of cancan nightlife, as in his 1892 painting *Au Moulin Rouge*. Toulouse-Lautrec is known for his paintings and posters of dancers, madames, and carousers from Parisian cabarets, and in his work, color, space, and pattern became highly distorted.

Paul Cezanne   While Cezanne used many Impressionist techniques and exhibited with them in 1874, his work focused more on the underlying structures of the objects he painted than on light qualities or observation, and he is often considered a transitional figure in the history of Western painting. By the mid-1890s, Cezanne's paintings had already exhausted Impressionism and Post-Impressionism and were exhibiting something new, a tense frisson of flattened color and space that anticipated the Cubism eventually developed by Pablo Picasso and Georges Braque. This new style, which would greatly influence later abstractionist painters, can be clearly seen in his famous depictions of Montagne Sainte-Victoire from 1898–1900.

Henri Rousseau Although he never left France nor saw a jungle, Henri Rousseau's paintings mostly depict jungle scenes and are characterized by extremely stylized shapes and Primitivist style. Self-taught and late to painting (he began painting seriously at age 40), Rousseau was often ridiculed during his lifetime, but his works, including *The Repast of the Lion* (1907), are widely popular today.

Henri Matisse First exhibiting in 1904, Matisse would become famous for his stylized, depictions of women and still lifes. His compositions and shapes became increasingly geometric and flat as in *The Dance* (1909). He would become a prominent figure in the Modernist movements of the 20th century.

◆**Art Nouveau** The libertine excesses of Parisian nightlife combined with traditional Czech printing style inspired the designer Alphonse Mucha's organic, eroticized illustrations and helped define a new style of decoration coined Art Nouveau. At once lively, stylish, and erotically charged, Art Nouveau washed over Europe under a variety of names and affected several disciplines: in France and England it was shown in the works of the designers Alphonse Mucha and William Morris and illustrator Aubrey Beardsley; in Germany, it was called Jugendstil and was evident in paintings by Egon Schiele and Hermann Obrist; in Spain, it was the funky, organic Modernisme of the architect Antoni Gaudi; in Austria it was the Viennese Secession, a group that included the painter Gustav Klimt and architects Otto Wagner and Joseph Maria Olbrich, whose Secession Hall in Vienna is an early landmark of modern architecture. Art Nouveau would captivate Europe and remain popular for roughly 15 years between 1895 and about 1910. It would be the last major movement of the 19th century, but the growing momentum of Modernism would continue to build for the next several decades.

Weekend 49: Marvels of Modern Technology

In key periods throughout history, technological innovation has been the catalyst for widespread social and economic change. The invention of the wheel, the plow, the stirrup, gunpowder, the sextant, the clock, and the steam engine are all regularly cited as such inventions that widely altered the course of human history in past centuries. Over the last 150 years, two developments emerged that have shaped the modern world in countless ways. The advent of electricity and modern transportation have remade the globe, both for business and for human comfort.

Day 1: Electricity

Almost every modern machine is electric, and nearly every human activity depends on the ubiquity of electricity. Lighting, power, transportation, washing, food storage, and long-distance communication all now depend on electricity, but a century ago, each of these activities was carried out by other means. The development of feasible electric power for home and business use transformed both urban and rural living in the late 19th century and early decades of the 20th century. In 1893, the scientist and inventor Nikola Tesla foresaw all of this in his vision of the future:

> The day when we shall know exactly what "electricity" is will chronicle an event probably greater, more important than any other recorded in the history of the human race. The time will come when the comfort, the very existence, perhaps, of man will depend on that wonderful agent.

Electricity has fascinated scientists since at least the sixth century B.C., when the Greek philosopher Thales recognized the potential for creating static electricity by rubbing together amber and wool. Ancient philosophers lacked a reliable way to generate electric current, so experimentation was limited to phenomena easily observed, such as static discharge and lightning. Without a way to reliably generate electric current, centuries passed before either deep understanding or practical applications would develop.

Throughout the 19th century, extensive experiments probed the possibilities of practical electricity: the first battery was developed in 1800, the first electromagnet in 1825, the first electric motor in 1828, and the first current-producing generator (called a dynamo) in 1831. No widely successful applications yet existed, however, to take electricity from the lab into homes or businesses. There were several problems to solve before electricity could find a crucial commercial application. First was distribution. Electricity needed to be generated somewhere by very large machines and then delivered to consumers, which demanded not only an efficient way to create and supply electric current, but also an enormous capital investment to put such a system in place. The second problem was creating a market; by the end of the 19th century, steam power was thought to be fairly efficient for most industrial applications, and there was not yet a huge demand for telegraphy or telephone, which in any case required only small amounts of electric current powered by batteries.

The solution to both of these problems was provided by the invention of the electric light bulb. By 1879, Thomas A. Edison and Joseph Swan had both improved existing designs for practical carbon-filament light bulbs powered by electric current. Early bulbs were brighter and cleaner than existing gas lamps and immediately promised both a commercial and home market for electricity. After forming the Edison Electric Light Company in 1878 with the backing of tycoon J. P. Morgan, Edison quickly began to build electric generating stations and power grids to capitalize on his invention. He opened the first commercial power plant in 1882 in downtown New York City and his business quickly grew.

♦**AC/DC: The War of Currents**   When the scientist Nikola Tesla immigrated to the United States from Croatia in 1884, all of Edison's power plants and machinery utilized direct current (DC) generators. Tesla's first stateside job was working for Edison, improving the efficiency of Edison's DC power plants. Tesla proposed that Edison use a different form of electricity: alternating current (AC). Tesla had already built and filed European patents for the first alternating current induction motor in 1883. Alternating current was clearly more efficient in generating and transmitting power over long distances (DC required large generators at least every two miles), and utilized natural fluctuations in the current's direction to provide a constant electric flow. Edison, however, felt DC was safer and that AC was commercially useless. There were likely several reasons why Edison refused Tesla's system, among them the massive investments Edison's company already had in DC patents, research, and infrastructure; also, the complex mathematical principles behind AC may have struck the pragmatic Edison as too puzzling for commercial implementation.

Tesla left Edison's company and sold his AC patents to the wealthy businessman George Westinghouse in 1888. His funding allowed Tesla to establish his own laboratory and promote AC as a more efficient alternative to DC. Edison's Electric Light Company continued to produce DC generators and systems and began an aggressive campaign to discredit Tesla's AC system. Most notably, Edison filmed and publicized executions of animals by AC to promote the idea that AC was more dangerous than DC. He also developed the first electric chair, which was powered by alternating current, and then tried to popularize the term *Westinghousing* for death by electrocution. Newspapers called the growing competition between AC and DC (and the feud between Tesla and Edison) the "War of Currents."

Meanwhile, the growing availability of commercially supplied electricity spurred inventions large and small in various countries. In Germany, Werner von Siemens created the first electric elevator in 1880 and the first electric trolley cars in 1881. In the U.S., Schuyler Skaats Wheeler invented the first electric fan in 1882. The electric sewing machine was first sold in 1889 by the Singer Sewing Co. In 1890, the first electric subways opened in London, England. The first patent for an electric escalator was awarded in 1892 to the American Jesse Reno, for a design that would later become a famous attraction at Coney Island. The first electric stove, invented by the Canadian Thomas Ahearn, was also produced in 1892.

The Chicago World's Fair of 1893, the largest American spectacle of the 19th century, provided a very public resolution to the battle between Tesla and Edison over the future of commercial electricity. The benefits of AC over DC, among them efficiency and lower cost, were widely apparent to the technological community, and Westinghouse won the bid to light and power the World's Fair at half the cost of Edison's bid. Edison refused to allow light bulbs of his design to be used by Tesla, and this provoked Tesla to invent his own, which turned out to be cheaper and more efficient. When President Grover Cleveland threw the switch at the World's Fair, he made a clear, public argument in favor of the efficiency, practicality, and safety of alternating current systems, demonstrated by an astonishing display of 130,000 incandescent lights—for most visitors, the first-ever glimpse of a large-scale installation of electric technology.

Just before the World's Fair, Tesla and Westinghouse had been awarded the contract to build a hydroelectric generating plant at Niagara Falls. The Niagara Falls hydroelectric plant went into operation in 1897, supplying AC power for homes and businesses as far away as Buffalo, New York, and proving the efficiency of AC for long-distance transmission of power. After the Niagara Falls success, the bulk of all new power contracts relied on AC technology, which quickly became the standard. Both AC and DC are in use today, with AC the norm for nearly all power delivered to homes and offices worldwide, while DC is preferred for use in transit rail systems, automobiles, and in uninterruptible power supplies like computer backup systems.

♦**Edison and Tesla** Edison's famous quote, "Genius is one percent inspiration, ninety-nine percent perspiration," helps to frame his outlook on work and innovation. After Edison's death, Tesla remarked, "His method was inefficient in the extreme, for an immense ground had to be covered to get anything at all unless blind chance intervened...just a little theory and calculation would have saved him 90 percent of the labor. But he had a veritable contempt for book learning and mathematical knowledge, trusting himself entirely to his inventor's instinct and practical American sense."

For polymath Tesla, the theoretical and mathematical underpinnings of invention were as important as the eventual practical application. The pragmatism that Tesla scoffed at, however, is precisely the trait that allowed Edison to fund an enterprise that produced utility patent after utility patent, over 1,000 by the time he died. Tesla, on the other hand, struggled to adequately finance his grand ideas and was a very poor businessman, though George Westinghouse bought many of his patents and brought them to commercial fruition. Tesla's difficult personality created problems with those he worked with and delayed popular recognition of the technology that revolutionized electric power. As he grew older, Tesla became more eccentric and difficult (probably suffering from what would now be described as obsessive-compulsive disorder); living on a small stipend at the Hotel New Yorker in New York City, he became fixated on the number three, insisting, for example, on three napkins at meals and circling buildings three times before entering, as well as becoming devoted to the pigeons that visited him.

One telling distinction between the two men is that Edison incorporated techniques of mass production into his scientific research park to produce and refine commercial and practical applications—the phonograph (1877), the duplex telegraph (1892), the lightbulb (1879), the motion picture projector (1893), to name a few—while Tesla's lab experiments mixed practical applications with arcane and visionary theory that required leaps of the imagination to understand. Among Tesla's contributions are radio (1900), remote control (1898), work on X-rays (1887–91), wireless transmission of electricity (1891), and a resonant transformer known as the Tesla Coil (1891)—all ideas that seemed, and some that still seem, somewhat fantastic.

Had Tesla been able to develop the same institutional machinery that Edison constructed at Menlo Park, New Jersey, the history of 20th-century electronics may have been significantly different. The goal of one of Tesla's most ambitious projects was unabashedly utopian: until J. P. Morgan pulled his funding, Tesla was constructing towers that he claimed would have distributed free wireless electricity to the entire eastern seaboard. Upon Tesla's death in 1943, the U.S. government's Office of Alien Property seized his files and notebooks because of his work on remote sensing (radar) and particle beams (his much-rumored "death ray"); they were later released, now belonging to the Nikola Tesla Museum in Belgrade.

◆Electricity in the 20th century Electricity spread from city to city throughout the industrialized world, bringing with it a flood of electric inventions that would quickly change both living and working conditions. The modern vacuum cleaner was invented in 1901 by the Englishman Hubert Booth, the air conditioner in 1902 (Willis Carrier, American), the residential refrigerator in 1903 (Marcel Audiffren, French), electric automobile ignition in 1911 (Charles Franklin Kettering), the television in 1925 (Philo T. Farnsworth, American), and the household toaster in 1926 (Charles Strite, American).

Electrification also brought into sharp relief the difference between industrialized city life and conditions in rural areas. Electrification was most feasible when located close to industrial centers that could supply the required capital, infrastructure, and market, and until the 1920s the ability to transmit electricity over long distances was very limited. Until the large-scale government projects of the 1930s, electrification in the U.S. was limited to urban areas; 90 percent of urban dwellers had access to electricity in the early 1930s compared to only 10 percent in rural areas.

In 1933, as a response to the Great Depression, the Tennessee Valley Authority was established to build hydroelectric dams to bring electricity to the American Midwest. In 1935, the Rural Electrification Administration, created by President Franklin Roosevelt, began an expansive program to electrify the nation's farmlands; within 15 years, electricity was available to 90 percent of farms nationwide. Also in 1935, the hydroelectric generators at the Hoover Dam went into operation, generating power for the Southwest.

By the 1950s, electrical devices were everywhere, and demand nationwide for electrical power was growing at an annual rate of 9.8 percent. Even as the U.S. population has grown, improvements in the design and efficiency of electric-powered devices has meant that power demand has slowed in growth. In the 1990s the power demand for electricity averaged 2.4 percent growth per year, and from 2000 to 2009, the growth averaged 0.9 percent per year.

Day 2: Planes, Trains, and Automobiles

A shopper in New York orders a new laptop computer from an online store. A factory in China prepares the package, which is sent literally around the globe—first by train, then airplane, then truck, then delivery van—to the recipient. The delivery takes five days. A hundred years ago this would have been unthinkable, even laughable; moving goods from factory to home was a slow, complicated ordeal. For much of the 19th century, eastern and midwestern cities had to rely on rivers and waterways to transport large quantities of goods, and areas not served by an accessible port or river could not grow. West coast cities were almost completely cut off from eastern factories by several ranges of high mountains; deliveries had to come by ship after sailing around the entire continent of South America.

In the 20th century, the growth of the network of roads, railways, and eventually airways reduced the time needed to move people and products around the country, tying together the far reaches of the United States for the first time, and allowing for the rapid growth and transformation of cities and businesses throughout the country.

◆**Trains** The first American rail tracks were laid in Boston in the early 19th century, initially to transport construction materials over very short distances. The first railroad—the 13-mile Baltimore & Ohio line—opened in 1827. Early engines and rails were modeled after designs by British engineers, who had pioneered locomotive development. As railroads expanded outward from urban centers, engineers quickly discovered that British locomotives would not serve American terrain; to traverse mountain passes between eastern cities and interior markets, more powerful engines were developed to cope with steeper inclines and cruder track.

In 1830, only 23 miles of railroad existed in the United States, but by midcentury entrepreneurs and government officials were dreaming and planning of connecting much larger sections of the country by rail. Fueled by government subsidies, generous land grants, and widespread collusion between railroad tycoons and local municipalities, a track-building boom occurred in the decades leading up to the Civil War. By 1840, 2,800 miles of railroad had been laid, and by 1850, 9,000 miles of track were in operation, as much as existed in the rest of the world combined at the time. Between 1850 and 1860, an expansion in the rail industry would more than triple the miles of railroad in the United States; by 1860, 30,000 miles of railroad had been built. In 1854, the Army Corps of Engineers undertook a massive topological survey to plan potential rail routes connecting the East with the West, and particularly to deal with traversing the formidable mountains that isolated the far western territories, and in 1862, construction began on a rail line that would connect the nation. In 1869, construction of the Transcontinental Railway was completed, uniting Omaha, Nebraska and Sacramento, California, with a single track.

In the 20 years between the completion of the coast-to-coast route and the start of World War I, rail travel in the United States tripled, and the amount of railroad track increased to 254,000 miles. At the end of the 19th century, 90 percent of passenger travel between cities in the

United States occurred by rail, and in 1920, the peak of rail travel, there were 1.2 billion riders.

The remarkable growth of American railroads during the 19th century was matched by an equally dramatic decline of passenger rail travel during the 20th, due to a key development that would shape the future of transportation in America.

♦**The Automobile**   Modern automobiles had been on the road since 1885, when the first practical, gasoline-powered car and motorcycle were invented in Germany by Karl Benz and Gottlieb Daimler, respectively. These early automobiles resembled moving sculptures—they were both hand-crafted and highly expensive. This changed with Henry Ford's assembly line innovations that produced the Model T in 1908. Ford's factories used identical, interchangeable parts, greatly improving efficiency of manufacture and lowering the price of his autos, which subsequently flooded both rural and urban roadways. The 1909 Model T sold for $850, and increasingly efficient production techniques led to lowered prices in following years. In 1909, Ford sold almost 18,000 cars; in 1915, when the price had dropped to $440 ($9,600 today), Ford sold more than 500,000, over half of all automobiles sold that year. By 1925, the price had dropped to $250 ($3,500 today), truly making the car an affordable purchase for many families. The number of registered autos in the United States hit 10 million in 1920, 20 million in 1925, and 30 million in 1938. Gasoline consumption rose with auto registrations, and by the end of World War II, 31 million American cars were using nearly 800 billion gallons of gas each year.

♦**The American Road**   In the early decades of the auto, travel by car was a short- to middle-distance affair, and usually meant travel between the city and country house or farm. A crucial piece of transportation infrastructure had yet to be constructed that would allow for long-distance car travel: reliable roads. In the early 20th century, building and maintaining roads and highways was a matter of fierce debate at all levels of government. Until the Supreme Court settled the issue in 1909, there was a widespread belief that the federal government lacked the authority to regulate roads; most roadways were state, municipal, or local projects, and the only roads under federal control were those on federal parks and lands. Early pressures to enact widespread roadway improvements came from an unlikely collection of interests:

farmers wanted federal-backed money to enable home mail delivery, bi-cyclists were hoping to improve road conditions, and of course millions of new Ford Model-T automobiles began spreading out all over the country. But even so, these groups were interested in improvements to local and farm-to-market roads, not long-distance throughways. Most long-distance travel was still conducted by railroad.

Auto trails, informal preferred routes composed of linked local roads, were the only long-distance roadways between towns. Auto trails were promoted by trade associations, and eventually numbered in a state and federal program of cataloging local routes in the 1920s, though many roads outside cities were unpaved and in varying degrees of disrepair. One notable auto trail, the Lincoln Highway, was the first coast-to-coast route, connecting New York City to San Francisco. In 1919, when the future president Dwight D. Eisenhower traveled with a U.S. Army convoy from Washington D.C. to San Francisco on the Lincoln Highway, the trip took 62 days, and the group encountered a list of troubles: bad or muddy roads, broken or unsafe bridges, inclement weather, and extremes in temperature.

Eisenhower became a key figure in the history of American transportation, when as president in the 1950s, he ended decades of incremental improvements to the patchwork of local and state roads by constructing the U.S. Interstate highway system. Eisenhower's vision for the Interstate system was initiated by a 1934 visit to Germany, where the new German Autobahn impressed him with how it allowed for rapid transportation of people and goods. In 1956, after decades of planning and rounds of negotiations with state governments over who would finance the construction, the Federal-Aid Highway Act was signed. More than 40,000 miles of Interstate highway were built under the act, crisscrossing the country in an ordered grid. North–South Interstates are numbered in increments of 10 and end in 5. I-5 runs up the Pacific coast, and I-95 runs up the East Coast. East–West Interstates are numbered ending in zero and increment by 10s; I-10 runs along the southern edge of the United States and I-90 along the northern. By the last decades of the 20th century, a uniform system of numbering Interstate exits had been adopted; Interstate exit numbers are lower in the south and west of a state and higher in the north and east. In many cases, the new Interstates incorporated sections of existing auto trails or state routes. Notably, sections of the mythologized Route 66, which connected Chicago to Los Angeles, were absorbed into I-40.

♦**The Birth of the Suburb** Except for a brief period during World War II, railway travel diminished steadily throughout the 20th century. Combined with rising rail fares, the decreasing cost of automobiles in the 1920s encouraged many Americans to choose driving over riding, and the Great Depression forced many railroad operators out of business. By the end of World War II, ridership was faltering.

The birth of the United States Interstate system would dramatically affect the fabric of American cities and towns. In the decades after World War II, families could drive quickly from new suburbs to work in the city. As a result, vast planned communities sprang up along Interstate arteries, giving birth to the American commuter and further diminishing the efficacy of rail travel. As the national landscape looked less urban and more suburban, and postwar prosperity allowed for second (and sometimes third) automobiles, the car became the primary mode of transport. Indirectly, the birth of the suburbs created the first waves of urban exodus for American cities; as middle-class families left the cities, the economic disparity between urban rich and poor became more pronounced.

By the late 1950s, travelers now had many options for long-distance travel, and increasingly, they were either driving or flying. By 1957, more passengers chose airplanes over trains for the first time, and by 1970 only 7.2 percent of all passenger travel was by rail. Partially in response, the national rail system, Amtrak, was created in 1971, though it has continually struggled to make a profit amid problems with quality, safety, and declining ridership. By 2007, there were nearly 250 million motor vehicles registered in the United States, using more than 135 billions of gas each year.

♦**The Airplane** Five years before Henry Ford sold the first Model T, two bicycle makers from Ohio, Orville and Wilbur Wright, realized centuries of dreams and aspirations with the first sustained flight of an airplane. Inventors had been working on designs for flying craft since antiquity, and in the 19th century increased understanding of physics and fluid dynamics led to working concept designs. By the 1870s, inventors in Europe had created aircraft that would temporarily remain aloft, though not under their own power and not for long. The Wright brothers took their aircraft, "Wright Flyer 1," to the windy bluffs of Kill Devil Hills on North Carolina's Outer Banks and flew it in a series of test runs in December 1903. The design of the plane incorporated engine and stability controls, and required the pilot to lay flat and exposed on the wing's surface. On December 17, after several days of near-successes, "Wright Flyer 1" took off under its own power and landed 12 seconds later after flying 120 feet.

While their first flight inaugurated a new era, it would take several decades before the dream of affordable, mass air travel would be realized. The transition from solitary pilot to jumbo jet would require decades of incremental invention.

In the early decades of the 20th century, for travelers hoping to cover long distances, train travel was still faster and less expensive than flying. In fact, early plane travel was somewhere between fairly unpleasant to miserable, depending on the weather. Today's airlines regularly fly at approximately 35,000 feet, high above mountains, clouds, and weather, but early planes regularly flew between 4,000 and 6,000 feet, had to fly around mountains, and were subject to the higher turbulence that occurs at lower altitudes. Seats were cramped and cold, and longer journeys required numerous stops for fuel or to change planes, and often involved some travel by train, since without sophisticated instruments, planes could not fly at night.

Activities such as mail service and crop dusting quickly began using airplanes, but passenger air travel developed more slowly. The first commercial airline service, the St. Petersburg–Tampa Airboat Line went into operation in 1914, shuttling a single passenger at a time across Tampa Bay, Florida.

Charles Lindbergh's solo transatlantic flight from New York to Paris in 1927 captivated the nation and made him an instant worldwide celebrity. In his plane "Spirit of St. Louis," Lindbergh made the 3,610-mile journey in 33 1/2 hours. More important, his feat set off a wave of investment in commercial flight. By 1929, investments in aviation had tripled, and new technologies, including gyroscopic instruments and automatic pilot, helped expand the range and safety of flying. In the 1930s, improvements to airplanes made air travel more affordable and comfortable. In 1933, the Boeing 247, often considered the first modern airliner, began flying with room for 10 passengers, and in 1935 the DC-3, which would serve the first true coast-to-coast routes, took to the air, carrying up to 32 passengers.

Military research and development during World War II provided extensive improvements to both aircraft design and infrastructure, not the least of which included numerous military airfields, which were sold to cities and converted into commercial airports after the war. Also during World War II, commercial airline fleets were pressed into military service, and the resulting contracts with manufacturers meant a boom in business after the war. By 1949, 16.7 million people were flying each year, and by 1954 that number had reached 35.5 million.

In the postwar decades, new airplanes sped travel and increased the number of passengers per trip. In 1958, the jet-engine Boeing 707 began flying passengers across the Atlantic, cutting New York–London travel time to six hours, and prompting many airlines to quickly replace propeller-based aircraft with jet planes. In 1970, Boeing's 747, the first "jumbo jet" went into service, carrying 450 passengers. Other jumbo jets quickly followed, including the McDonnell Douglas DC-10 and Lockheed L-1011. Prices for travel remained relatively high between 1970 and 1980, even while the number of aircraft in the skies and the number of airline passengers per year grew dramatically (108 million passengers in 1970 and 188 million in 1980). In 1978, President Jimmy Carter signed the Airline Deregulation Act, which led to declining airfares for passengers while allowing for new shakeups inside the industry. Beginning in the late 1970s, new, low-cost airlines started up, but many folded quickly, and the industry saw a period of consolidation and mergers throughout the 1980s and 1990s. According to the U.S. Bureau of Transportation Statistics, over the last 15 years, the average airfare has risen about $30 overall; prices were on a trajectory to be much higher in 2000, but fell sharply after 2001. The number of passengers reached a high of 769 million in 2007, before falling in the wake of the global economic recession beginning in 2008.

Weekend 50: Ancient Rome

The influences of ancient Roman civilization on the history of Europe, the Middle East, and Asia Minor are so extraordinary that they often overshadow the compelling story of how a small city-state on the Tiber River in Italy became the most powerful military force in the ancient world and ruler of the largest and longest-running empire in history. But it is also a cautionary tale about the deeply corrupting influence of acquiring enormous wealth through military conquest and the subjugation of foreign lands and peoples. As much as later civilizations must honor the glorious accomplishments the Roman Empire bequeathed to them, they need also to be aware of the terrible price paid by tens of thousands of people who suffered under the brutal tactics the Romans used to enforce their rule. Writing toward the end of the first century A.D., the Roman historian Tacitus gave the following speech to the leaders of the tribe who opposed the Roman conquest of Britain:

> Pillagers of the world, now they have exhausted the land by their indiscriminate devastation…neither East nor West has sated them…To plunder, slaughter, and rape they falsely give the name empire. They make a desolation and they call it peace.

Day 1: From Republic to Empire

Since no written records of Roman history exist before the third century B.C., much of what we know about the early centuries of Rome's existence is based on tradition and scholarly speculation. Romans in the early days were taught that the city was founded by the twin brothers Romulus and Remus, sons of the war god Mars and the last kings of a line descended from the Trojan hero Aeneas. When they were infants, the tyrannical ruler of the region set them adrift in a basket on the Tiber River, but they were rescued and survived when suckled by a she-wolf. The brothers later overthrew the tyrant, but while building Rome, Romulus slew his brother and became Rome's first king in the year we calculate as 753 B.C. Archaeologists have shown that Rome was founded at least a century earlier, but no one doubts that for over two centuries Rome was ruled by a series of kings, the last ones being Etruscans (ca. 610–510 B.C.).

Roman culture was greatly influenced by the Etruscans, a people of mysterious origin speaking a language still not deciphered. They would dominate the north central region of Italy for over three centuries from 800 to 500 B.C. They created a superior culture that included superb pottery works and bronze and gold craftsmanship at the highest level, as well as military innovations such as the chariot and use of iron weapons. Historians believe the Etruscans introduced the Romans to the games and chariot racing in large arenas that would become a famous element in later Roman life.

Although the Etruscan kings helped bring prosperity to the Romans and to enhance the city through the building of impressive public spaces, the leading families of Rome objected to Etruscan dominance and their interference in their governing body, the Senate. This resentment grew under the cruel reign of Tarquin the Proud, and in 510 B.C. Lucius Junius Brutus, a prominent Roman aristocrat, led a rebellion that ended Etruscan rule and began the 400-year history of the Roman republic. Another member of Brutus's family would be one of the assassins who murdered Julius Caesar for destroying that republic.

♦**The Republic, 510–264 B.C.**   By modern standards, Rome was a republic only in the sense that land-owning citizens could vote in the assemblies. Only members of the wealthy patrician class could be elected to civil or religious offices, although the plebs, or plebeians, made up the majority of citizens. The citizens elected two consuls for a one-year term to essentially command the citizen-army, and at the end of the term they resigned unless a military emergency allowed them to continue in office. At the end of their terms they rejoined the Senate, which was not an elected body but an advisory one made up of those who had held high government office.

By the middle of the fourth century B.C., the law required that one of the consuls had to be a plebeian, indicating the growing wealth and prestige of men from outside the oldest families. By this time too, the Senate had grown to about 300 members who now effectively ruled the republic by virtue of their prestige won through service to the state. Much of this prestige came from the guidance the Senate gave during the early years of continuous warfare as Rome developed a strong citizen-army to defend itself against regional enemies.

In the fifth century B.C., victories over two nearby cities enabled Rome to expand its territory by more than 80 percent. But in 390 B.C., the Roman army was soundly defeated by a tribe from Gaul, who then captured and sacked Rome itself and received a ransom in gold to leave. This humiliation appears to have convinced Rome's leaders that their future safety depended on creating allies who would help Rome defend the region from hostile invaders. Some cities joined with Rome in exchange for citizenship or military alliance. The Samnites, a tribe in south central Italy resisted, but over the course of three brutal wars from 343 to 290 B.C., the Romans not only prevailed but took control of the whole central region of Italy. At the end of these wars, the Romans also expanded northward and into Etruria and Umbria.

In 280 B.C., a Greek city in the heel of Italy called for aid against the Romans, who they feared were provoking a war. Pyrrhus of Epirus, a legendary general at the time, came to the rescue with 25,000 seasoned soldiers and 20 elephants, quickly defeating the Romans in two battles. But his losses were so great that he was forced to leave Italy, his victories and others throughout history known as "pyrrhic."

Rome was now ruler of virtually all of Italy and had at the ready an army of 700,000 men with an additional 70,000 cavalry. Not too much time would pass before it found itself in direct competition with the leading power in the western Mediterranean. The conflict that followed changed the course of Roman history.

♦The Punic Wars, 264–146 B.C.   The three wars Rome fought with Carthage over the course of more than a century were truly a struggle for survival. The term *Punic* comes from the Latin word *Punicum*, meaning "Carthaginian." Located in northern Africa near modern Tunis, Carthage was a great commercial sea power in the western Mediterranean, while Rome was a land-based power dominating most of Italy. In the end, Carthage would literally be destroyed and Rome became the most feared power in the Mediterranean world, well on her way to creating one of the greatest empires in history.

The first war (264–241 B.C.) began with the intervention of the two powers in a factional conflict on Sicily, where Carthage ruled. Fought in and around Sicily, it was primarily a naval conflict with rowed galleys used to ram, or come alongside and board opposing ships. The Romans had never been a sea power, but fearing Carthaginian power they quickly grasped the know-how of shipbuilding and were able to construct a fleet of several hundred ships large enough to carry a sizable contingent of legionnaires for hand-to-hand combat. After several victories for each side, the decisive battle took place in 242 B.C., when 200 Roman ships destroyed the Carthaginian fleet. Carthage sued for peace and was forced to give up all her possessions in Sicily.

The second war (218–201 B.C.) began after a revitalized Carthage raised a new army and established several settlements in present-day Spain. When their general, Hannibal, attacked a town that was an ally of Rome, war began again. While the Roman army was marching toward Spain, Hannibal's army of 90,000 troops and 80 elephants set out on what has become one of history's most famous marches, taking them over the Alps. Hannibal then established himself on the Adriatic coast in southeastern Italy at Cannae, a strategic point on Rome's supply line. Rome dispatched a force of 80,000 foot soldiers and 6,000 cavalry. The Roman infantry attacked Hannibal's center, which fell back in a planned, orderly retreat. Hannibal's cavalry, which were dispatched to attack the Roman flanks, were now behind the surging Roman infantry. The cavalry wheeled and turned on the inexperienced legions, which were hacked to pieces. Rome lost 50,000 troops to 6,000 for Carthage and its allies.

This devastating defeat created fear and panic in Rome, and many allies in Italy began to make peace with Hannibal. A new army was raised but, now the Roman generals avoided direct combat and resorted to hit-and-run raids on the Carthaginians and instituted scorched earth tactics, burning crops that deprived their enemy of needed food. Hannibal could never secure a final victory, and when the Roman army under Scipio Africanus invaded North Africa in 204, he was forced to return home and defend Carthage. At Zama two years later, the Romans won a resounding victory that forced Carthage to give up its possessions in Spain and turn its entire fleet of warships over to the Romans.

Despite the toll this war took on Rome's resources, the Senate and its leaders did not cease their efforts to win more power, more territory, and more wealth. Successful wars against Macedonia and then in Greece against foreign rulers there, quickly followed the end of the war against Carthage. Roman military might and pride had returned, so when the Romans realized that Carthage had once again renewed its commercial power, either fear or greed prompted the Senate to ask for a new war. "Carthage must be destroyed" became a rallying cry. In 149 B.C., Rome found an excuse to declare war and soon laid siege to the city. After one major battle outside of Carthage in 146, the Romans were overwhelmingly victorious as 60,000 Carthaginians were killed. The city was completely destroyed and plowed under. All 50,000 survivors were sold into slavery. Rome now ruled North Africa and used it as a source of much needed grain to feed its growing population.

•The Empire of the Republic By the middle of the second century B.C., the Roman republic had created an empire that included Spain, Gaul, most of Greece, the coastal regions on the Aegean Sea, North Africa, even Asia Minor. The Mediterranean was now known as *mare nostrum* ("our sea"). Roman provinces were established throughout these regions, each administered by a Roman governor and kept at peace by Roman soldiers. Taxes and booty kept the Roman treasury filled and enriched the leading families who undertook most of the military campaigns. The slave population grew with every conquest. Eventually the military leaders, who also held the office of consul responsible to the Senate, pushed for more and more expansion. Those who won great victories were given triumphal processions in Rome and regarded as exceptional heroes by the people.

The rivalry for power among the generals became so intense that within 20 years of the destruction of Carthage civil wars broke out sporadically as demagogues used their appointed power as military leaders to rule politically as well. At the end of the second century, when the consul Marius defeated Rome's enemies in North Africa and soon after in Gaul, he stayed in power for several years, a complete reversal of the traditional one-year term. In need of more soldiers due to uprisings in Italy, he also changed the laws governing who could be in the army, thereby opening the way for the poor to find a path to prosperity.

The military leader Sulla had served under Marius for a decade and won several victories. Both helped to put down the rebellion of the Italian peoples, known as the Social War (91–88 B.C.) which threatened Rome's existence. Sulla did so well he was elected consul in 88 B.C., but supporters of Marius objected and rioting ensued. Sulla marched his army into Rome, the first general ever to do so, and became a virtual dictator, murdering most of Marius's key supporters. Sulla would win more victories including an attack on Rome by the Samnites, but unrest continued after he retired.

In 73 B.C., a massive slave rebellion broke out led by Spartacus and several other slaves. At its height the slave army numbered at least 70,000 and defeated the Romans in several battles until Crassus, Rome's wealthiest citizen, took command. By 71 B.C. he had routed the rebel army. Pompey the Great, a well-known protégé of Sulla, would join in the war's final days and is known to have slaughtered thousands of slaves and crucified 6,000 survivors along the Appian Way.

•**Crossing the Rubicon** In 60 B.C., Pompey and Crassus joined with Julius Caesar, a member of one of Rome's oldest and wealthiest families, to form the First Triumvirate in order to continue the Roman expansion and to avoid destructive political rivalries. Caesar took his army to Gaul, and after a series of brilliant victories, brought the entire region under Rome's control by 51 B.C. His unwavering devotion to the men under his command won him their steadfast allegiance in the years to come. The Senate feared Caesar because he was now a popular military hero with a large veteran army, so they ordered him to give up the army and return to Rome. Caesar replied that he would if Pompey, now consul, also released his army. When the Senate refused, he led his army across the Rubicon, a small stream marking the borderline of Gaul, and made a triumphal march through northern Italy in January, 49 B.C.

Over the next five years, Caesar would defeat Pompey at the battle of Pharsalus (48 B.C., make Cleopatra queen of Egypt, stabilize Spain, Syria, and other areas of the empire, and develop a plan for administering the vast territory Rome had subdued. During his consulship he passed agrarian laws to help the people, improved their living conditions. He introduced a new calendar with 365 days (the Julian calendar would be unchallenged for 1600 years). In 44 B.C. he became dictator—supreme military leader— for life. Caesar's unlimited power now aroused jealousy and fear even among some of his close associates, and on the Ides of March (March 15), led by Brutus and Cassius, they stabbed Caesar to death in the Senate, an act that led to 13 years of civil war.

Caesar's nephew and heir, Octavian, and his protégé, Marc Antony, immediately took up arms against Brutus and Cassius, defeating them at Phillipi (42 B.C.). But Octavian and Antony could not end the rivalry between them even after Antony married Octavian's sister. By 42 B.C. Antony had fallen in love with Cleopatra, and in 37 B.C. he returned to Egypt to live openly with her as her lover. Octavian had the Senate strip Antony of his power in the East and in 31 B.C. destroyed Antony's fleet at Actium. Antony and Cleopatra committed suicide and Octavian now stood as the sole ruler of Rome.

Day 2: The Empire

Octavian is considered Rome's first emperor. Over the course of his long reign (29 B.C.–A.D. 14), he was given absolute power along with many honorific titles including *Imperator* (Commander), and in 27 B.C., *Augustus* (hence "august" or revered), a name he would be known by throughout history. He deliberately avoided ostentatious displays of his power, however, and honored the traditional government institutions of the republic.

Augustus followed Caesar's plan for the empire by securing the borders and improving the administration of the provinces. At home he made taxation more equitable and undertook many public works projects that would improve housing and beautify the city. As a military leader, he had learned the value of good roads so he set out to make improvements and expand their number throughout the empire. Augustus is usually credited with ushering in a 200-year period of peace throughout the empire. The *Pax Romana* (the "Roman Peace") was in many ways a romantic fiction since rebellions and small wars were a constant presence in those years. While Augustus was still in power the Roman army suffered one of its greatest defeats while trying to expand the empire into modern day Germany. In A.D. 9, in the Teutoburg Forest, 20,000 legionnaires were killed over three days. Rome withdrew but now knew that the borders needed to be strengthened if they were to be safe. Almost four centuries would pass before the Germanic tribes would again seriously challenge Roman power.

Upon his death, Augustus was deified as Caesar had been, but before he died he sought to create a hereditary monarchy to assure stability. The results were definitely not what Augustus had in mind. Tiberius was adopted by Augustus in A.D. 4 because he had been a very able administrator and military hero. After marrying Augustus's daughter, his path to the emperor's throne was clear. He would rule competently for more than 20 years until succeeded in 37 by Caligula, who became emperor through the intercession of the army. Historians believe a serious illness brought on his insanity shortly thereafter. His cruelties and strange behavior brought plots and murders into the palace, especially over the imperial succession. Caligula was assassinated by a tribune of the Praetorian Guard, an elite force that had protected Roman leaders for more than a century, but were formally organized by Augustus to guard the emperor. This was their first appearance in imperial politics, but not the last.

The Praetorians chose Claudius, nephew of Tiberius, to be emperor, an office he reluctantly accepted because of his fear of assassination. He ruled from 41 to 54 and succeeded in conquering Britain and creating more provinces in the East. He may have been poisoned by his fourth wife, Agrippina, and his son was murdered by her son, Nero, who became his successor. Nero's name has forever been linked to treachery and to the evils of absolute power. During his reign (54–68) Nero terrorized Rome's elite families by accusing them of plotting against him, and he murdered both his mother and his wife. When the great fire of 64 destroyed half of the city, he blamed it on a small religious sect who called themselves Christians, and launched the first persecution against them, leading to the deaths of Saints Peter and Paul. Nero committed suicide when the Praetorian Guard revolted against him.

At this juncture, the purely military underpinning of imperial power came clearly into focus. Within one year, three men became emperor by virtue of their standing with the army or the Praetorian Guard. In 69, Vespasian, a military hero who had risen through the ranks, was proclaimed emperor by his soldiers while they were in the Middle East. He marched on Rome without opposition and began a 10-year reign characterized by stability and order. His two sons, Titus and Domitian, succeeded him, thereby reestablishing the idea of a hereditary monarchy.

♦**The "Good Emperors"** Upon Domitian's death in 96, however, the Senate suddenly reasserted itself and chose Nerva, a statesman known for his honesty and fairness, to be emperor. In order to ensure stability he named his adopted son, Trajan, to succeed him. Nerva and the men who followed him are known collectively as the "Good Emperors" because they were all excellent administrators who brought stability to the empire and also to the process of imperial succession for nearly a century. One of the most admired emperors, Trajan had been born in Spain and was the first non-Italian to ascend to the throne. From 98 to 117, he launched an ambitious plan to secure restless provinces in Dacia (present-day Romania) and Parthia in Asia Minor. At home he built aqueducts, theaters, libraries, and a very large forum. Trajan personally selected Hadrian (r. 117–138) to succeed him because he knew he possessed strong leadership qualities.

Hadrian was also an excellent administrator who reformed the civil service and kept the peace at home by providing aid to the poor and staging many games and circuses. Abroad he strengthened border defenses in Germany and Britain, where he built the famous Hadrian's Wall across the northern part of the island to help protect the legions from rebellious tribes. A learned man who knew Greek and wrote poetry and music, he was typically ruthless with those who rebelled against Roman rule. Hadrian's hand picked successor, Antoninus Pius (r. 138–161) had been a highly regarded administrator in provinces in the East. Together with his chosen successor, Marcus Aurelius (r. 161–180), a 40-year period of peace and stability settled over Rome and Italy that helped to foster the arts and learning. Marcus Aurelius is remembered as a serious philosopher whose *Meditations*, based on the Stoic outlook, are still read and admired today. Known too for his benign approach to governing, he was nonetheless a serious persecutor of Christians and fought wars against the Britons, Germans, and Parthians.

◆**Decline** Most historians view the accession of Marcus Aurelius's son, Commodus, as the first sign of imperial decline. He made peace with several rebellious German tribes and devoted himself to depraved activities at home. To show off his strength, he participated in gladiatorial combat and demanded to be worshipped as a descendant of Hercules. Assassination plots again became part of the royal household until Commodus was strangled to death by a wrestler, on orders from his advisers, in 192.

Over the next century, the Roman Empire had the outward appearance of normality as a succession of nine emperors continued fighting on the borders and building monuments at home. But during this period, all of these men were chosen by the now all-powerful Praetorian Guard, often with the support of the military. Several of the emperors displayed strong military prowess, but none exhibited the skills necessary to administer the provinces, some of which fell into disarray. The sudden decline in Rome's fortunes led the emperor Diocletian (r. 284–305) to divide the empire into four sections, two in the east, two in the west, with two rulers in each section. He also reinvigorated the army and launched successful attacks on the German tribes, the Britons, and the Persians and instituted a fierce persecution against the growing Christian population. Although he assumed dictatorial power that worked for a time, the division of the empire would prove its undoing in the long run.

After 21 years as emperor, Diocletian resigned in 305, and within five years his successors became rival emperors and war ensued. Constantine emerged as sole emperor after his fabled victory at the battle of the Milvian Bridge (312) when he thoroughly defeated his rivals after allegedly seeing a flaming cross in the sky with the words "In this sign shalt thou conquer." He would soon make Christianity a legal religion in the empire, a turning point in the history of Europe.

During his long and peaceful reign (to 337), Constantine became active in church matters regarding theological questions, even presiding over the Council of Nicea, which issued the first set of standard beliefs for Christians. In 330, he moved the capital of Rome to Byzantium (present-day Istanbul), renamed it Constantinople, and dedicated the city to the Virgin Mary.

◆**Barbarians at the Gate**   Only 40 years after Constantine's death, the dismal future of the empire was foretold in a singular way. A Germanic tribe called the Visigoths had been allowed to settle within the Roman frontier region to give them protection from the oncoming Huns. The emperor Valens wanted them to disarm, and when they resisted he led an army against them, only to be killed in the battle of Adrianople (378) and his army totally defeated. Soon it was clear that the military units of Rome in the west and Constantinople in the east were not able to protect the empire. By the early fifth century the Roman emperor was forced to hire tribes to protect the borders against other tribes. In 410, the Goths sacked Rome, the first time this had happened in eight centuries. The Vandals would do the same in 455.

Only a few years before, however, the true weakness of the Roman army was revealed when the Romans were forced to employ an army of the Visigoths, led by their own general, to defeat the mighty Attila and his cavalry of marauding Huns in 451.

The year 476 is usually given as the date for the "fall of the Roman Empire" when Odoacer, leader of the Goths, deposed the last emperor in the West, Romulus Augustulus. The emperor Zeno in the East recognized Odoacer as emperor, but in 488 sent Theodoric the Great and his Ostrogoths to depose him. Theodoric became the ruler of all Italy after assassinating Odoacer, his son, and his chieftains.

◆**The Late Roman Empire**   The lapse of direct Roman rule in the West did not imply an immediate "fall" of the Roman Empire so much as a shift of Roman power elsewhere. In the city of Rome, the heir and representative of the Roman Empire was the Catholic Church. The emperor Justinian (r. 527–565) did much to revive the fortunes of the empire, but from a base in Constantinople rather than Rome itself. Maintaining a rough alliance with the Christian Franks in Gaul under their Merovingian dynasty, the emperor Justinian's armies recovered the western provinces: Vandal Africa, Ostrogothic Italy, and the Mediterranean sector of Visigothic Spain. Meanwhile, his jurists codified and preserved the whole body of Roman law that had been built up since the days of the republic. And under imperial patronage there grew up a magnificent cluster of churches whose pinnacle was Hagia Sophia in Constantinople, first constructed in 537. The city of Rome itself, however, was well launched on a centuries-long period of decline, with a shrinking population and many buildings disused or in ruins.

The cost of Justinian's efforts was great, and the defense of the West was short-lived. After Justinian's death, the empire had neither treasure nor troops enough to save much of Italy from new invaders, the Lombards. The Italian city of Ravenna kept its link with Constantinople, and Rome remained the principality of the popes. Pope Gregory "the Great" (590–604) not only organized the defense of the city but oversaw the work of converting Visigothic Spain and began the restoration of Christianity in faraway Britain through the mission of St. Augustine to Kent in 597.

◆**The Byzantine Empire**   In the east lay the empire proper, in the era after Justinian usually called the Byzantine Empire or the Eastern Roman Empire (610–1453). Its wealth and power were based in Asia

Minor, its unity dependent upon three factors: Orthodox Christianity (slowly drifting away from Roman Catholicism until the final break with Rome in 1054); Hellenistic culture and the Greek language; and Roman law and administration. Missionary ventures carried Christianity and Byzantine influence to the Serbs and Croats in the Balkans, to the Moravians and Slovaks north of the Danube, and even as far as Kievan Rus, all in the ninth and 10th centuries.

The empire was "byzantine" in the common sense of that word, a world of complex politics involving a wide variety of factors: emperors who were often weak and ineffectual; self-interested palace bureaucrats; powerful generals prone to warlordism; Orthodox prelates engaged in endless struggles with schismatic and heretical clerics; and popular political factions verging on mob rule, often linked to the fortunes of chariot-racing teams in the hippodromes. Yet the empire also prospered through trade, agriculture, and artisanal production of goods. It made brilliant cultural achievements, particularly in the ecclesiastical arts, and managed to survive, in gradually attenuating form, for more than eight centuries.

The empire, which barely held on in the East against Persia, lost large areas to the conquering armies of Islam. Between 636 and 642, Syria, Egypt, and Libya converted to Islam; in a second wave of Islamic expansion (696–711), the rest of North Africa and Spain became part of the world of Islam as well. The Mediterranean seemed on its way to becoming a Muslim lake, threatening both the Byzantine Empire and the emerging successor states to the old Roman Empire in the West.

Weekend 51: American Film

Day 1: American Film: A Brief History

Although several inventors from America, Britain, France, and Germany were working on the idea simultaneously, credit for the invention of the motion picture camera is most often given to the Thomas Edison laboratories. By 1889, Edison's assistant, William Kennedy Laurie Dickson, had synthesized Edison's ideas into a workable motion picture camera, which he called a Kinetograph. He followed the Kinetograph with a device for viewing his short films called the Kinetoscope, a peep-show box with a scope on top. One person at a time looked into the scope to watch the film.

Edison did not believe motion pictures would grow beyond a parlor amusement, so he did not bother to pay the extra $150 for an international patent to prevent European inventors from developing their own versions of the Kinetograph or Kinetoscope. Two such entrepreneurs were the Lumière brothers, Auguste and Louis, from Lyons, France, who produced their own version of the motion picture camera. Instead of being powered by electricity, the Lumières' Cinématographe was hand-cranked and weighed 16 pounds. On December 28, 1895, they held the first paid public showing of projected motion pictures in the Salon Indien in the basement of the Grand Café in Paris. Projection quickly became the format of choice for commercial showings of motion pictures around the world, since it allowed many viewers to watch the same film at the same time. The Lumière films recorded ordinary happenings and used simple titles that telegraphed the subjects of their 30-second films, such as *Workers Leaving the Lumière Factory*, *Baby's Lunch*, and *Train Arriving at the Station*.

Georges Méliès, who was already in show business when he began making motion pictures in 1896, produced films that were fairy tales or fantasy stories, such as his 1902 adventure *A Trip to the Moon*. In expanding the storytelling possibilities of the new medium, Méliès gradually increased the average length of a film to one reel—a little less than 1,000 feet, or 12–14 minutes at 16 feet per second (fps)—the standard length for a decade.

✦**Americans Take the Lead**   The first permanent movie theater in the United States was Thomas H. Tally's Electric Theater, which opened in Los Angeles in 1902. The Nickelodeon, whose name became generic for early storefront theaters, opened in Pittsburgh in 1905.

The first important American film director was Edwin S. Porter, who while working for the Edison Company, stumbled across the fundamentals of editing when he made *Life of an American Fireman* in 1903. He combined stock footage of a fire engine racing to a fire with staged shots of a mother and child trapped in a burning house, cutting back and forth between the two scenes in a way that suggested they were happening simultaneously, a technique later called parallel editing. Later that year, Porter made his masterwork, *The Great Train Robbery*, which contained simple but effective cinematic techniques, including cutting on motion, moving the camera to keep the action centered in the frame, and using diagonal compositions to exploit the depth that only the cinema offers.

Over the next decade movies became more and more popular and soon attracted serious investors to help expand the audience and filmmakers to create a new art form. David Wark (D.W.) Griffith directed his first film, *The Adventures of Dollie*, in 1908. Between 1908 and 1913 he developed and mastered the techniques that would become the basic language of film. Working in collaboration with his cameraman, Billy Bitzer, Griffith varied his scenes by distance from the camera, carefully dividing them into long, medium, and close-up shots. Each type of shot had a specific function, with close-ups carrying the most emotional weight because they could suggest what a character was thinking or feeling. In addition, Griffith added a deliberate rhythm to his edits, adjusting pace for the content of the scene. He also used a range of optical effects for transitions between shots, including the cut, the dissolve, the fade, and the iris, and he gave each effect a consistently specific function.

In 1915, Griffith directed *The Birth of a Nation*, a three-hour historical epic about the Civil War and Reconstruction. It was the culmination of his innovations in film, an exciting artistic use of his techniques that represented his complete control of the medium on a grand scale. The script was an adaptation of two explicitly racist pieces of literature by Thomas Dixon, so in addition to its important place in film history, it reveals the dismal state of race relations in the United States at that time. Griffith's film offered indefensible stereotypes of African Americans while depicting the Ku Klux Klan as the heroic saviors of a defeated South.

◆**The Rise of the American Film Industry** European moviemaking was severely inhibited by World War I, and the American film industry soon dominated the world market. The first commercial production companies, such as American Biograph, Vitagraph, and Selig, had been established in New York, New Jersey, and Chicago. The nine most powerful of these companies attempted to monopolize the production, distribution, and exhibition of motion pictures by forming a trust, the Motion Picture Patents Company (MPCC), in 1909. To escape the MPPC's oppressive business tactics, independent filmmakers moved west as early as 1911. Most of them settled in a sleepy community just outside of Los Angeles called Hollywood.

The move coincided with the development of more organized business practices, including the studio system, which was first implemented by independent producer Thomas Ince in 1912. Ince's studio near Hollywood was dubbed "Inceville." It included administrative offices, shooting stages, permanent outdoor sets, photo labs, and wardrobe warehouses—a method of operation that facilitated the efficient mass production of movies. Instead of writing, directing, and editing himself, Ince hired others who were talented in those areas to execute the tasks. He then oversaw the production of the films, retaining financial and creative control.

During this period, silent movies began to tell the standard types of stories familiar to readers of books and magazines, including westerns, slapstick comedies, romantic melodramas, and historical and biblical epics. The actors quickly became movie "stars" and the industry built large audiences for movies with the most popular ones, among them Charlie Chaplin and Buster Keaton.

A star's image was a consistent persona or archetype that an actor played repeatedly until the audience associated the actor with it. The stars were under contract to the studios, which used publicity and promotion to showcase the actors' images to attract audiences to their films. The star system became so successful that often a film's narrative, camerawork, lighting, and editing were designed around its stars. The great stars of the 1920s included swashbuckling adventurer Douglas Fairbanks Sr., Latin lover Rudolph Valentino, America's sweetheart, Mary Pickford, and sophisticated lady Gloria Swanson.

A truly revolutionary moment in film history occurred when sound was introduced in the late 1920s. The Hollywood industry was the first to successfully add synchronized sound to film. Warner Brothers studio produced several *synch-sound* musical shorts in the mid-1920s before adding a soundtrack to a feature-length film titled *Don Juan* in 1926, consisting of sound effects and orchestrated music but no spoken dialogue. The next step was to add musical performances to a feature film, which Warner Brothers did for *The Jazz Singer* (1927), starring Al Jolson. Most of the movie stars from the silent era were unable to make the transition to sound films because their voices were unsuitable to the new demands of talking and acting. Only the great comic actor Charlie Chaplin successfully resisted performing in "talkies;" *City Lights* (1931) and *Modern Times* (1936) contain synchronized sound effects but no dialogue. When Chaplin finally did speak, it was to ridicule Hitler in *The Great Dictator* (1940).

◆**The Studio Era**   After problems related to the introduction of sound were resolved, eight studios emerged to dominate the Hollywood film industry. Five of them—Warner, RKO, Twentieth Century-Fox, Paramount, and MGM—controlled the means of production, distribution, and exhibition. Together, these eight studios produced around 80 percent of the feature films released during the 1930s and 1940s, and they took in roughly 85 percent of the total income. Each studio produced about 50 feature films per year.

Despite dependence on systems, standards, conventions, and formulas—and perhaps because of them—this period produced a wide variety of highly regarded films such as *It Happened One Night* (1934), *Gone With the Wind* (1939), *The Philadelphia Story* (1940), and *Casablanca* (1942) which epitomized the glamour, craft, and appeal of Hollywood. Unfortunately, the system that perfected generic formulae discouraged formal experimentation. An exception is *Citizen Kane* (1941), co-written (with Herman J. Mankiewicz) and directed by the iconoclastic Orson Welles. With its deep-focus photography (by Gregg Toland), chiaroscuro lighting, and expressive camera angles, *Citizen Kane* looked decidedly unlike any other American film. Welles offered a dark, complex fable of American capitalism and enterprise that featured no big stars and no happy ending. The film failed at the box office and garnered little support from the industry, save an Academy Award for best original screenplay.

In 1948, the Supreme Court ruled that certain business practices utilized by the eight major studios, including vertical control and block booking, violated American antitrust laws. The ruling made filmmaking riskier for the major studies, because they no longer had a guaranteed outlet for every film. As a result, studios began making fewer films and cutting costs. The studios also let go of directors and producers, some of whom formed independent production companies, which were not under long-term contract to a studio nor directly involved with distribution. An independent producer or director found a book, play, or story to turn into a script, and then looked for interested stars, thereby putting the project and star together into one deal. This package-unit system, or independent production system, dominated Hollywood production by the mid-1950s, replacing the studio system. The major studios were still a force in the industry, but their role became that of financiers and distributors rather than producers.

◆A New Audience   Television and suburbanization altered the nature of the movie audience. In 1956, young adults and teens bought 87 percent of all movie tickets. For the first time, the industry began to seriously target the youth market, rather than focusing all of their attention on the mainstream.

Color and wide-screen technologies had been around since the silent era, but were used mainly for experiments, curiosities, and blockbusters. Now, in order to draw spectators back into the theaters, Hollywood embraced technology that offered visual experiences which audiences could not get on small black-and-white television screens. In the 1930s and after, 20 percent of films were in color, during the 1950s, 50 percent were.

Screens grew and changed shape between 1952 and 1955, when wide-screen processes were adopted by the studios. Cinerama, a wide-screen system that required three electronically synchronized cameras, was introduced in 1952. CinemaScope, introduced in *The Robe* (1953), became the wide-screen process of choice because it used conventional 35 mm film and required only a change in lens.

During the 1960s, movie attendance continued to decline; studios released fewer films per year, leading the industry to accept, even embrace, a corporate mentality. The studios no longer had a system to foster new talent, increasing the uncertainty of their future.

Hollywood's dire financial situation made it open to new ideas, even more so after the release of *Bonnie and Clyde*, *The Graduate*, and *Cool Hand Luke* in 1967. The critical and financial success of these films signaled the arrival of a "new wave" of American filmmakers. The so-called Film School Generation would follow, producing many outstanding films such as *In the Heat of the Night* (1967), *Easy Rider* (1969), *The Godfather* (1972), *Dog Day Afternoon*, *One Flew Over the Cuckoo's Nest* (both 1975), *Taxi Driver* (1976), and *Days of Heaven* (1978). These were innovative, entertaining, and daring in form and content.

◆**The Blockbuster Era** Many of the industry practices that define contemporary cinema began with *Jaws* (1975), directed by Steven Spielberg, and were cemented by *Star Wars* (1977), directed by George Lucas. Both films were action-driven narratives fueled by mechanical and special effects, which became blockbusters that attracted youth audiences and set box-office records.

In the 1980s and 1990s, studios reclaimed control of the industry. While studios continued to solicit films from small production companies and produce films in conjunction with them, they exerted more creative control over script preparation, casting, and editing. Studios continued to be absorbed by large corporations. Unlike the movie moguls of the early years, contemporary studio executives were recruited from talent agencies, the television industry, or business and marketing programs. They preferred familiar stories, formulaic genres, and projects that showcase popular stars, because those films appeal to mass audiences and inspire repeated viewings.

◆**Independent Filmmakers** The recent emergence of a large independent filmmaking community has become the main source of artistically-driven films in the United States. The success of some independent filmmakers has allowed them to straddle both independent and studio worlds. Some talented directors, such as Quentin Tarantino (*Pulp Fiction*, 1994; *Kill Bill*, 2003; *Inglourious Basterds*, 2009), the Coen

Brothers (*Fargo*, 1996; *No Country for Old Men*, 2008), Spike Lee (*Do the Right Thing*, 1989; *Inside Man*, 2006) and Steven Soderbergh (*Traffic*, 2000; *The Informant!*, 2009), began as independents and then gradually moved to big Hollywood studios, where they enjoy more creative control than most directors.

Day 2: Great American Film Directors

In 1968, the film critic Andrew Sarris published *American Cinema: Directors and Directions*, that put forth what earlier French critics called the *auteur* theory. The central idea behind the theory was that the director was the single most important person in the making of a film. Essentially it was the director's vision that stood behind the making of those films we have come to regard as essential, classic, brilliant. Several film historians have shown the flaws in this argument (notably Thomas Schatz in *The Genius of the System*, 1989) and demonstrated that the studios produced fine films, often under the guidance of the producer, and that some highly regarded directors worked very well under the studio system's restrictions. After all, *Gone With the Wind*, *The Wizard of Oz*, *Casablanca*, *All About Eve* and many others were produced by the studios and have achieved iconic status in the history of American film.

Still, the *auteur* theory has helped serious moviegoers understand that a director's body of work, when taken as a whole, can reveal a personal style and sensibility that accounts for their long-term success and the high standing of their films. Below is a short list (in alphabetical order) of 10 men with their best-known films highlighted. Anyone who takes the time to see these pictures will have a solid introduction to the most important aspects of American film.

◆**Frank Capra** Born in Sicily in 1897 and raised in California, Capra started working in movies after serving in World War I. He started directing in 1926 and made dozens of movies over the next decade. In 1934, the cheeky comedy *It Happened One Night* made stars of Clark Gable and Claudette Colbert, and won an Oscar for them as well as Capra. Capra would soon produce and direct a string of idealistic stories that featured the common man (played either by Gary Cooper or Jimmy Stewart) as hero and dupe to the rich and powerful, including *Mr. Deeds*

Goes to Town (Oscar for Best Director, 1936); *You Can't Take it With You* (Oscar for Best Picture and Best Director, 1938); *Mr. Smith Goes to Washington* (1939); *Meet John Doe* (1941), and *It's a Wonderful Life* (1946). In these films Capra stood up for the traditional values of honesty, loyalty and patriotism that some regard as corny, but which won the public's attention and affection. During World War II, he made a series of powerful propaganda films for the government, *Why We Fight* (1942, 1943).

♦**Francis Ford Coppola**   Born in 1939, he attended film school at U.C.L.A. in the mid-1960s. Coppola started as a screenwriter and by the time he was in his early 30s he had written or collaborated on more than a dozen screenplays including the smash hit, *Patton* (1970). In 1972 he directed the first of three films based on the novel, *The Godfather*, about Italian mafia families in New York. The first two won multiple Oscars and gave Coppola the clout to make his most ambitious film, *Apocalypse Now* (1979), a Vietnam war story based on Joseph Conrad's novel *Heart of Darkness*. A controversial film from the outset, it has attained a large following over the years because of Coppola's outstanding storytelling ability.

♦**John Ford**   Born Sean Aloysius O'Fearna to Irish immigrants in Maine in 1895, he went to Hollywood when he was 19 and three years later, in 1917, became a contract director at Universal Studios making westerns. At the age of 29 he directed his first western epic, *The Iron Horse* (1924). During the Depression years he made several comedies but won his first Oscar for *The Informer* (1935), a bitter story of betrayal set in Ireland; a second Oscar followed in 1940 for *The Grapes of Wrath*, based on the bestselling novel by John Steinbeck. His third Oscar-winning film was also set in Ireland, *The Quiet Man* (1952).

Ford is best known for the westerns he made beginning with *Stagecoach* (1939) which featured John Wayne. After World War II, he directed a string of extraordinary films that together forged a history of American expansion and the civilizing of the western frontier: *My Darling Clementine* (1946), *She Wore a Yellow Ribbon* (1949), *Wagonmaster* (1950), *The Searchers* (1956), and *The Man Who Shot Liberty Valance* (1962).

Alfred Hitchcock   Born in England in 1899, he was first educated by the Jesuits, an experience he later claimed caused him to make movies designed to frighten people. Hitchcock started working in film when he was 20 and five years later directed his first film in Germany where he was introduced to the techniques of Expressionism that stayed with him for his entire career. His two most famous British films, *The Man Who Knew Too Much* (1934) and *The 39 Steps* (1935) were commercial and critical successes in which Hitchcock used his trademark technique of providing the audience with information the characters do not have.

By 1940, he was working in Hollywood where he directed nine films, among them the powerful *Shadow of a Doubt* (1941) and the frightening espionage story *Notorious* (1946). During the 1950s, Hitchcock made three of his best films, *Rear Window* (1954), *Vertigo* (1958), and *North by Northwest* (1959). But his most well-known film was to be *Psycho* (1960) which featured a famous murder scene in a motel shower that is a masterpiece of film editing.

♦**Elia Kazan** A Greek immigrant from Turkey, he arrived in New York in 1913 at the age of four. Kazan was well-educated at Williams College and Yale Drama School and in the 1940s became an established stage director of major American plays by such writers as Arthur Miller and Tennesee Williams. Hollywood soon lured him west where he directed several powerful films including the first to deal with antisemitism, *Gentlemen's Agreement* (1947), which won Academy Awards for Best Picture and Best Director, and *Pinky* (1949), a realistic view of race and racial prejudice in America that still resonates with audiences today.

In April 1952, Kazan testified before the U.S. House Committee on Un-American Activities and admitted being a member of the Communist Party in the 1930s, but he also named others as members. He was now a hated man in Hollywood, but he responded by making one of the great films of all time, *On the Waterfront* (1954), the story of union corruption on the Brooklyn docks, and how a former boxer, played by Marlon Brando, broke the union's power by testifying against them. It won six Academy Awards, including Best Picture and Best Director.

Kazan followed up with a string of highly regarded films, including *East of Eden* (1955), based on John Steinbeck's novel and starring a young James Dean; *Baby Doll* (1956); *A Face in the Crowd* (1957), and *Splendor in the Grass* (1961), which marked the film debut of Warren Beatty.

◆**David Lean**   Born in England in 1908 he began working as a film editor for newsreels in the 1930s, a job he would later say taught him how to tell a story cinematically. In 1942 he worked with Noël Coward on the wartime film, *In Which We Serve*, which told a moving story about family sacrifice. After the war his directing talents developed quickly and within three years he had successfully made Coward's *Blithe Spirit*, and two films based on Dickens's classics, *Great Expectations* and *Oliver Twist*. But *Brief Encounter* (1945), the story of two married people falling in love in a train station café, would emerge as his most memorable film of this period.

Beginning in 1957, Lean worked with American as well as British studios to produce several extraordinary epics that would come to define his career. Most important were the two that won Academy Awards for Best Picture and Best Director, *The Bridge on the River Kwai* (1957), which told the story of British troops imprisoned by the Japanese in World War II, led by a strictly by-the-book commander who had them build a bridge to supply Japanese troops; and *Lawrence of Arabia* (1962), a three-hour- plus spectacular about T.E. Lawrence's role in the Arab revolution. Other lush and long films followed: *Dr. Zhivago* (1965), *Ryan's Daughter* (1970), and in 1984, the magnificent film version of E.M. Forster's *A Passage to India*, produced when Lean was 76. In 1990, he was awarded the American Film Institute's Lifetime Achievement Award, the only non-American to be so honored.

◆**George Stevens**   California born and bred, Stevens was 17 when he started in film as a cameraman. He joined RKO in 1934 and the following year directed a young Katharine Hepburn in the highly successful *Alice Adams*, a painful story about the cruelties of class relations, a theme Stevens would revive later in two of his famous works, *A Place in the Sun* (1951) and *Giant* (1956), both of which won him the Academy Award for Best Director.

Stevens directed films in a wide range of categories including the Astaire-Rogers musical, *Swing Time* (1936), the war film, *Gunga Din* (1939), the sophisticated comedy of the first Tracy-Hepburn movie, *Woman of the Year* (1942), the classic western drama, *Shane* (1953), the tragic *The Diary of Anne Frank* (1959), and the biblical epic, *The Greatest Story Ever Told* (1965). All together Stevens made 40 feature films, 15 in the silent era.

◆**Billy Wilder** Born Samuel Wilder in Vienna in 1906, he graduated from law school and in 1929 drifted into screenwriting for several German filmmakers. In 1933 he went to Hollywood and together with Charles Brackett forged a successful screenwriting career over the next decade. Their most well-known script was *Ninotchka* (1939), starring Greta Garbo. By 1942 his long career as a director began but he always continued working as a screenwriter.

By 1950 he had written and directed seven films, three of them considered classics today: *Double Indemnity* (1944), a bitter and cynical story of infidelity, lust, greed, and murder; *The Lost Weekend* (1945), which chronicles the painful descent into alcoholism of a struggling writer, won Oscars for Best Picture, Best Director, Best Screenplay and Best Actor (Ray Milland); and *Sunset Boulevard* (1950), a hard-bitten look at the movie business and its forgotten older stars and ambitious young men.

During the 1950s Wilder wrote, directed and occasionally produced a string of major films that showed his extraordinary creative talent, but now in sophisticated comedies: *Stalag 17* (1953); *Sabrina* (1954); *The Seven Year Itch* (1955); and *Some Like It Hot* (1959). In 1960, Wilder won the Academy Award for *The Apartment*, a typical Wilder film that included elements of love, sex, and money, all mingled together with humor and a healthy dollop of cynicism about the human species. This was followed by four more films including two highly regarded comedies, *Irma La Douce* (1963) and *The Fortune Cookie* (1966).

Over his long career Wilder was nominated eight times for the Academy Award for directing, but also 12 times for screenwriting (he won three: *The Lost Weekend*, *Sunset Boulevard*, and *The Apartment*). In 1986 he received a Lifetime Achievement Award from the American Film Institute.

◆**William Wyler** Like several other famous American directors, Wyler was born in Germany and came to the United States to work in the movie business. In Wyler's case it was his mother's cousin, Carl Laemmle, head of Universal Studios, who convinced the 18-year-old Wyler to start in the publicity department in New York in 1920. In 1925 he was given a chance to direct low-budget westerns and when sound arrived he began a stellar career that would last until 1970.

Over 40 years Wyler would be nominated for an Academy Award 11 times and would win three times: *Mrs. Miniver* (1942), which tells the story of an English family's struggles during World War II; *The Best Years of Our Lives* (1946), the moving account of three G.I.s returning from the war and the emotional upheaval they experience; and *Ben-Hur* (1959), the epic story of how a Jewish nobleman is persecuted by the Romans and finds hope and salvation in the Christian message. *Ben-Hur* won 11 Academy Awards.

Other well-known and critically acclaimed films were several based on famous literary works including the Brontë classic, *Wuthering Heights* (1939), Lillian Hellman's *The Little Foxes* (1941), and *The Heiress* (1949), based on a play derived from a novel by Henry James. Wyler was awarded the American Film Institute's Lifetime Achievement Award in 1976.

◆**Fred Zinnemann** Another Viennese-born (1907) giant of American film, he studied law but became very interested in movies and left for the United States to study film. By the early 1940s he had learned enough to direct several nondescript feature films. Over the next 40 years he would direct 20 more features, almost all of them highly regarded no matter what genre they represented: musical (*Oklahoma!*, 1955), drama (*The Nun's Story*, 1959), thriller (*The Day of the Jackal*, 1973).

Zinnemann's most famous film is undoubtedly *High Noon* (1952), a western starring Gary Cooper and Grace Kelly. It tells the story of a town threatened by a violent gang and defended only by a sheriff who believes his duty requires that he fight them. Famous for its attempt to tell the entire story in real time (about 80 minutes), *High Noon* was among the first 25 films chosen for the National Film Registry in 1989.

Two of Zinnemann's films would win both Best Picture and Best Director, *From Here to Eternity* (1953), a story about illicit love, adulterous love, loyalty and friendship on the eve of the attack on Pearl Harbor; and *A Man for All Seasons* (1966), based on the play about St. Thomas More whose refusal to violate his beliefs cost him his life at the hands of Henry VIII.

Weekend 52: Mathematics

Day 1: A History Of Mathematics

The roots of mathematics can be traced to ancient Egypt, China, India, and Babylonia; the discipline owes the biggest debt, however, to the ancient Greeks. Western Europeans expanded Arabic and Latin translations of Greek mathematical texts, which were developed from mathematical discoveries that predate recorded history.

◆**Early Arithmetic** It took thousands of years for the concept of numeration to evolve. The languages of many hunter-gatherer societies exhibited a "one, two, many" logic system, in which any number larger than two was simply expressed as "many." This type of system was probably the norm for much of human history, but as civilizations grew, more sophisticated mathematical systems developed to simplify trade, facilitate construction, and regulate agriculture.

The Lebombo bone, a baboon fibula etched with 29 marks, is the oldest known mathmetical artifact, dating back to 35,000 B.C. Later, Middle Eastern traders used small pieces of hardened clay as tokens to facilitate transactions. Arithmetic began as a system of manipulating tokens to determine sums and differences.

Counting boards improved on the token system by demarcating one section of a tablet for individual units, a different section for groups of 10, and a third for groups of 100s. The abacus, developed by the Sumerians around 2,700 B.C., evolved from counting boards. The Chinese adapted the abacus to their number system, forming the basis for the Hindu-Arabic numerals, which would evolve into the numbers we use today.

◆**Measurements and Geometry** Standards for length and weight existed at least 5,000 years ago. The ancient Egyptians developed techniques to measure property and restore boundaries after the annual Nile flood, and the construction of the pyramids required the ability to measure angles and make other sophisticated calculations. Mathematicians in the Old Babylonian period had relatively accurate approximations for pi and the square root of two. In a few instances, early mathematicians recognized that one idea followed logically from another—the beginnings of the formal reasoning system of mathmatical proof.

Proof became central to geometry in Greece by 600 B.C., and by 300 B.C., Euclid of Alexandria (ca. 325–ca. 265 B.C.) had organized all existing knowledge about arthimetic and geometry into a logical system. New results were proven by using a few simple rules called axioms and postulates. Euclid's work remains the basis of geometry today, although some of his reasoning has been improved upon by modern mathematicians.

◆**Algebra** While some Greek mathematical ideas followed trade routes to India, for the most part mathematics developed independently in Asia. *The Nine Chapters of Mathematical Art*, a Chinese text that dates from 200–300 B.C., contains problems solved using geometry, algebra-like manipulations, and even more advanced algorithms. The Chinese and Hindu-Arabic number systems allowed for the incorporation of innovations such as decimals and fractions (ca. A.D. 5) and negative numbers (ca. A.D. 200).

Around the third century A.D., the Greeks began using symbols to represent unknown quantities, such a the lengths of sides of geometric figures. The originator of this approach, Diophantus (ca. A.D. 210–. 290) is often called the "father of algebra." His book *Arithmetica* includes methods for solving quadratic equations using symbolic reasoning. Around the fifth century A.D., Indian mathematicians introduced a discipline related to geometry, later called *trigonometry* ("triangle measuring"). In about A.D. 800, Indian mathematicians recognized zero as a number; while seemingly a small advance, this led to the refinement of the decimal system into the flexible, place-value system in use today. In 835, the Arab mathematician Muhammed al-Khwarizmi (ca. 780-ca. 850) wrote *Al-jabr wa'l muqabalah* ("restoring and simplifying"), known in the West as *algebra*. This work introduced symbolic methods for solving quadratic equations. Later Arab mathematicians expanded on al-Khwarizmi's work, formalizing, standardizing, and proving his methods; as a result, algebra grew from a tool kit for solving individual problems into a discipline.

◆**Mathematic Renaissance** European mathematicians began to standardize symbols for operations, such as P and M for addition and subtraction, which were later improved to + and –. The need for better computation for tasks like navigation led to inventions such as the *logarithm* in 1614 by John Napier. Additionally, Renaissance painters including Leon Battista Alberti contributed to geometry with their studies of perspective. By the 17th century, algebra had developed into the complete discipline taught in high school today, and new fields of mathematics began to grow from it. *Analytic geometry*, discovered independently by Pierre de Fermat (1601–65) and René Descartes (1596–1650), merged algebra and geometry and became the basis for nearly all subsequent mathematics. Studies of perspective grew into the field of projective geometry, which freed traditional geometry from its dependence on measurement. Renaissance mathematicians also discovered the basic principles of probability, which were expanded in the 17th century by de Fermat and Blaise Pascal.

◆**The Rise of Calculus**   Ancient Greek mathematicians frequently solved problems by separating a geometric figure into tiny pieces, then recombining the pieces to find a solution. Using similar methods, mathematicians divided curved lines into a large number of small, nearly straight segments, which could then be added together to approximate the length of the curve. Such methods were used to measure all manners of irregular shapes. Analytic geometry provided a way to measure using "infinitely small" and "infinitely numerous" segments, laying the foundation for a method of problem solving now called calculus.

In 1665 and 1666, Sir Isaac Newton expanded methods of approximation to create the first version of calculus. About 10 years later, William Gottfried von Leibniz developed the same mathematical tools, but used different symbols and terminology. Although Newton circulated manuscripts much earlier, Leibniz was first to publish his findings publicly; most of the language and symbols used in calculus today derive from Leibniz.

Calculus allowed a degree of precision of measurement that was previously impossible. Mathematicians used calculus to model, measure, and predict velocities, volumes, and densities, as well as model physical phenomena and predict how changes in one variable affects others. The discipline became an indispensable scientific tool of the Enlightenment.

◆**19th-Century Reform**   Although many physical and mathematical problems were solved by calculus, some applications appeared to produce nonsensical or contradictory results. Furthermore, it was obvious that the logic of the term *infinitely small*, an essential calculus concept, was unclear. Throughout the 19th century, although the applications of calculus were largely successful, mathematicians sought to improve the theoretical underpinnings of the discipline. Bernard Bolzano formalized the definition of a "limit" in 1817, which replaced the "infinitely small" quantities of Newton and Leibniz with a more precisely defined quantity.

Geometry also experienced a revolution in the 19th century. *Projective geometry* produced alternative geometries as logical as Euclid's, but which followed different rules. This new non-Euclidean geometry greatly expanded mathematics, which no longer seemed to need a connection with observable reality.

Nineteenth-century mathematicians also looked for the simplest theoretical concepts that underlie arithmetic, algebra, geometry, and logic. Abstract algebra and symbolic logic are concerned with the implications of these underlying rules rather than physical entities. Despite the seemingly "imaginary" nature of some of these branches of study, surprising applications often followed theoretical discoveries. Albert Einstein's general relativity theory of 1916 showed that the true geometry of space may be non-Euclidean, and symbolic logic led to the binary operators that make modern computers possible.

By the late 19th century, mathematics became highly abstract. New disciplines such as set theory produced sometimes contradictory results that proved impossible to eliminate. After trying to resolve these contradictions, logicians surmised that not all problems are solvable by mathematics, and that reducing problems to arithmetic does not eliminate contradictions.

♦**Mathematics Today** These issues have not deterred mathematicians from solving old and new problems using all the tools that have been developed over the course of history. In the 20th century, applied methods of statistical inference have been developed and widely applied in computer programs, engineering, and social sciences. There have also been dramatic advances in geometry, such as the development of fractal geometry, in which patterns of smaller parts relate in complex ways to the whole. These and other modern developments in mathematics and statistics mean that, although many mathematical concepts are thousands of years old, our lives are affected by up-to-date techniques embodied in powerful computational packages.

Day 2: Branches Of Mathematics

The growth of mathematics from counting, measuring, and reasoning led to the development of a discpline with many parts. As late as the 19th century, a mathematician might have been skilled in all its branches; since the field has become so complex and diverse, however, modern mathematicians specialize.

◆**Arithmetic** The trunk from which all other branches of mathematics sprouted, arithmetic dates to before 2000 B.C. It encompasses the basic operations required to combine or divide quantities: addition, subtraction, multiplication, and division. The theoretical study of these fundamental operations is called Higher Arithmetic or Number Theory.

◆**Algebra** Algebra concerns the writing and solving of equations, which are mathematical statements that use a letter or symbol to represent an unknown quantity (called a variable). For example, the equation $2 + x = 11$ states that 2, plus an unknown quantity, equals 11. To find the solution for an equation, procedures called algorithms reduce the statement to the simple form x = (an amount); for example, by subtracting 2 from 11 in the earlier example, we are left with $x = 9$.

As equations become more complex, the algorithms become more sophisticated. Many complex equations cannot be solved with general algorithms; for such equations, there are procedures for estimating solutions and refining those estimates. Computers and graphing calculators have made the study of algebra easier and rendered some of the most complex algorithms obsolete.

Modern algebraic study focuses more on analytic geometry: the study of lines and curves on a plane that are applied as mathematical models for real-world phenomena. Modern or abstract algebra, often studied at the collegiate and postgraduate level, is not concerned with solving specific equations. Instead, this discpline deals with systems where equations obey general rules. Letters no longer necessarily represent unknown numbers but are variables that may stand for anything—numbers, points, operations, and so forth.

◆**Geometry** The Greeks, notably Euclid, established geometry as reasoning about the properties of figures, although earlier Egyptian and Mesopotamian mathematicians discovered the basic rules concerning lengths, areas, and volumes. Euclid arranged the various proofs concerning figures into a powerful axiomatic system that was the basis of geometry for the next 2,000 years. In the 1800s, mathematicians discovered a system of geometry different from Euclid's, which while originally a purely theoretical discipline, later became valuable in the study of relativity and quantum physics.

Measurement grew from geometry into its own discipline. Measurement has been used since antiquity to find lengths and weights; current applications include everything from electric current to download speed.

Topology is another discipline that evolved from geometry. The field of topology springs from deceptively simple observations: for example, although no one would confuse a square and a circle, the shapes have important similarities (both are two-dimensional, have "inside" and "outside" regions, and so forth). Topology also studies the properties of objects that are preserved despite "deformations" like squeezing or stretching. The Möbius strip, a twisted strip that has only one surface and one edge, is a classic example of the types of figures studied in elementary topology.

◆**Trigonometry** Trigonometry begins with the study of the interrelation between the sides and angles of right triangles. Given the measure of one angle and one side of a right triangle, it is easy to determine the lengths of the other sides, as they adhere to a fixed ratio. These ratios, called the sine, cosine, and tangent (terms coined in the 12th century A.D.), can be used to solve practical problems about distance and direction. Trigonometry was used in construction and navigation for centuries. Later, mathematicians discovered that the graphs of sine and cosine functions were infinite, oscillating waves. This discovery led to a host of new applications, from modeling circular motion to measuring the frequency and amplitude of electromagnetic waves. Trigonometry is also one of the most powerful tools for understanding complex, multidimensional curves.

◆**Calculus** Calculus, the mathematics of change, is used to analyze quantities that change with respect to other variables, such as velocity and acceleration. Calculus can also be used to find areas or volumes of regions bounded by curves. As arithmetic is based upon numbers and algebra on variables, calculus is based on functions, which are relationships between sets of two or more variables. The relationship between velocity and displacement (as velocity increases, so does an object's displacement from its point of origin) is a simple example of a function. In its simplest form, calculus solves two kinds of problems: the rate of change problem (called the derivative) and the area problem (called the integral). These problems are actually two sides of the same coin: the algorithms to find the derivative, when applied in reverse, can be used to find the integral. These two simple concepts have surprisingly diverse applications. The derivative can be used to find marginal cost and revenue in economics, for example, and the integral can be used to analyze anything from physical forces to population densities.

•**Discrete Mathematics** Discrete mathematics is a blanket term for the study of noncontinuous mathematical structures. While most physical phenomena can be modeled using smooth, continuous graphs (the velocity of an automobile, for example, cannot climb from 0 to 50 without briefly reaching every velocity in between), many economic, technological, or probabilistic phenomenon cannot. In modern mathematics, discrete structures have become increasingly important; the binary language of computers is one example of a discrete phenomenon. Some subcategories of discrete mathematics are:

Probability is the study of events that occur within finite systems, and the likelihood of a certain outcome. Although employed in simple dice and coin-toss problems, probability also functions importantly in fields such as meteorology and economics.

Graph Theory is the study of networks and paths, which has become an essential tool in the optimization of telecommunication networks and other systems.

Logic is the study of the relationship between true, false, and contradictory statements. Set theory, the study of finite groups of countable objects, is a subcategory of logic. True and false logic systems developed into binary on-off circuit logic that make computers possible. Other fields of discrete mathematics include cryptology, statistical theory, and game theory.

•**Chaos Theory** Beginning in the 1880s, mathematicians discovered that some systems are so complex that even tiny changes in initial conditions yielded wildly unpredictable results. Although originally these strange results were blamed on imprecision, it was later realized that this "noise" was inherent in most complex systems. Chaos theory is the study of the complexity and unpredictability of such systems.

Chaos theory has philosophical implications, as it demonstrates that some things are "unknowable" even within the structure of mathematics. Some of its concepts are part of popular culture, featured in movies such as *Jurassic Park* and *The Butterfly Effect*. While chaos theory suggests limits to the accuracy with which humans can model and predict weather patterns and economic markets, the discipline is more than the acceptance of uncertainty. Chaos theory is used to find order within seemingly disorderly systems: random phenomena such as molecular vibrations and the neurological impulses that cause epileptic seizures have been predicted using chaotic models.

•**Number Theory** Number theory (sometimes called "higher arithmetic") is the study of properties of natural numbers, or integers greater than zero. Studied for its own sake since the time of the Greek author Diophantus (ca. A.D. 200–299), number theory has recently had important applications in codes used for protecting information transmitted by computer. The study of prime numbers (numbers divisible by no other natural numbers besides themselves and one) falls under the number theory umbrella. Large prime numbers are essential in cryptology.

Number theory also encompasses the axiomatic approach to the study of simple arithmetic, formalizing the definitions and properties of basic operations such as addition. The Commutative Property of Addition, which states $a + b = b + a$, is a simple and well-known example of number theory applied to arithmetic. "New Math," a much criticized reform of American mathematics education in the 1960s, emphasized a number theory-based approach to arithmetic instruction. While New Math was deemed impractical by most experts, the theory behind it helps connect all branches of mathematics, from simple counting through the most abstract concepts.

Index

A

A-bomb. See atomic bomb
Abraham, 112, 376
Adams, John, 245
Adler, Alfred, 423
Aeneid, The, 458–60
Aeschylus, 6–7
Ailey, Alvin, 250
airplane, the, 498–500
algebra, 526, 529
alphabet, the, 141–43
American Civil War, 61–70
American film, 513–24
  blockbuster era, 518
  directors, American, 519–24
  history of, 513–18
  independent filmmakers, 518
  studio era, 516–17
American painting 429–31,
  479–82
  abstract expressionism, 429–31
  Ashcan School, 482
  Hudson River School, 480
  Pop art, 431
  Realism, 481
  scene painting, 482–83
American poetry, 337–40
American popular music,
  21–30, 383–92
  American Songbook, 21–25
  black artists, 27–28
  bluegrass, 391–92
  blues, 383
  British invasion, 29–30
  composers, 21–24
  country, 390–91
  folk, 388–90
  girl groups, 28–29
  hip-hop, 386–88
  honky-tonk, 391–92
  jazz, 383–85
  rhythm and blues (R&B), 26,
    385–86
  rock, 25–30
  singers, 24–25
  soul, 385–86
  surf music, 29
  Tin Pan Alley, 21
  wall of sound, 28–29
  Western Swing, 391–922
American prose, 331–36
  fiction, since 1920, 335–36
  Harlem Renaissance, 335
  Naturalism, 334
  Realism, 334–35
  Romantics, 332–34
  Transcendentalism, 332
American Revolution, 61, 145,
  147, 181–186, 331
American road, the 496
Americas, ancient, 219
animal kingdom, 301–05
  animal characteristics, 302
  invertebrates, 302
  primatology, 305
  vertebrates, 303
Antietam, battle of, 67
Antony, Marc, 404, 506–07

Apple, Inc., 74
architecture, Renaissance,
    179–80
Aristophanes, 110
Aristotle, 301, 396–97, 462
Arlen, Harold, 23
Army of the Potomac, 67–69
Arnold, Benedict, 185
ARPANET, 76
art. See also art, ancient; art, in
    the Middle Ages.
    20th-century, 427–31
    architecture, Renaissance,
        179–80
    early Renaissance, 279–80
    Impressionism,
    Modernism, 427–31
    painting, 19th-century, 479–88
    painting, American, 429–31,
        479–83
    painting, northern Reniassance,
        177
    prehistoric, 271–75
    Renaissance, 175–79
art, ancient, 176, 271–80
    Egyptian, 271
    Greek, 273–74
    Mesopotamian, 272
    Roman, 274–75
art, in the Middle Ages, 275–80
    Byzantine, 275–76
    Celtic painting, 276
    early Renaissance, 279
    Gothic painting, 277
    illuminated manuscripts,
        276–77
    northern Europe, 279
    Romanesque painting, 277
Art Nouveau, 488
Astaire, Fred, 24, 248

atomic bomb, 20, 88
Atomic Energy Act, 268
Atoms for Peace, 268–69
Audubon, John James, 479
Augustus. See Octavian
Austen, Jane, 287
Austria-Hungary, 11, 12
automobile, the, 496–98
Avicenna, 153

B

Babbage, Charles, 71
Bach, Johann Sebastian, 54
Bacon, Francis, 400
Balanchine, George, 247–48
ballet, 246–49, 433, 434, 485
Bartók, Bela, 434
Bauhaus, 428
Beach Boys, the, 29
Beatles, the, 29, 30, 128
Beats, the, 339
Beethoven, Ludwig van, 28,
    56–58, 244
Bellows, George, 482
Bentham, Jeremy, 417
Benton, Thomas Hart, 483
Beowulf, 321
Berg, Alban, 245
Bergson, Henri, 418
Berlin airlift, 82
Berlin, Irving, 21–23
Berlioz, Hector, 59, 243
Berry, Chuck, 27–28
Bible, the, 111–20, 373–78
    Apocrypha, 120
    Hebrew Bible, 112–115, 373,
        376, 378
    King James Version, 119

New Testament, 115–19
  Old Testament, 112–15
Bierstadt, Albert, 480
Big Bang, the, 91, 95
Black Mountain College,
  430–31
Blackstone, William, 407
Blake, William, 326
Bluegrass, 392
blues (music), 383
Boccaccio, Giovanni, 173
Bolshevik Revolution, 311,
  428, 429
Bonaparte, Napoleon. See
  Napoleon
book, the, 142–43
Bosch, Hieronymous, 178
Boston Tea Party, 182
Botticelli, Sandro, 176, 280
Boulez, Pierre, 435
Brahe, Tycho, 96
Brahms, Johannes, 58–59
Britten, Benjamin, 245
Brontë sisters, 288
Bronze Age, 217
Brown v. Board of Education,
  292
Brown, John, 65
Brown, Trisha, 250
Brunelleschi, Filippo, 179
Bryan, William Jennings, 107
Bryant, William Cullen, 337
Buddha, the, 134, 135
Buddhism, 31, 135–38, 354–55
  core beliefs, 136
  history, 135
  scripture, 136
Bull Run, battle of, 66, 67
Byzantine empire, 511–12

C

Caesar, Julius, 404, 506–07
Cage, John, 435–36
calculus, 527, 530–31
Calvin, John, 234
Calvinism, 233–34
Canaan, 45–46, 219
Cannae, battle of, 504
Canterbury Tales, The, 322
Capra, Frank, 519
Carmichael, Hoagy, 23–24
Carnegie, Andrew, 102
Carter, Jimmy, 85
Carthage, 504–05
Cassatt, Mary, 482, 486
Castiglione, Baldassare, 174
Catlin, George, 479–80
Cervantes, Miguel de, 175
Cezanne, Paul, 487–88
Chamberlain, Neville, 16, 17
Chaos theory, 531–32
Charlemagne, 382
Charles, Ray, 26, 385
Chaucer, Geoffrey, 322
Chemistry, 442–46
Chernobyl, 269–70
China, 217–18, 351–62
  ancient, 351–55
  Communist, under Mao,
    360–61
  early modern, 356
  foreign domination, 358–59
  Imperial Golden Age, 354–55
  Mandate of Heaven, 351–56
  Mao, 360–61
  Medieval period, 355–56
  modern, 356–62
  opium and uprisings, 357–58
  post-Mao era, 361–62

China (con't),
  religions, 138–40
  revolution and reform, 359–60
  Warring States period, 352
Chinese Communist Party
  (CCP), 359, 360
Christianity, 111, 112, 117,
  373, 377–82. See also New
  Testament; Reformation
  belief and practice, 378–79
  history of, 231–40, 380–82,
    508–10
  overview, 377–78
  schools and sects, 379–80
  scripture, 378
chromaticism (music), 53, 244,
  432
Church, Frederic, 480
Churchill, Winston, 16, 17, 20,
  81
Civil Rights Act, 295
Civil Rights Movement,
  291–96, 389
Civil War, American. See
  American Civil War.
civilization, 211–20
  Americas, 219
  India and China, 217
  Iron Age, 218
  Israel, 219
  Mesopotamia, 216
  Middle East, 218
  Neolithic revolution, 214
  rise of civilization, 216–220
Clark, Dick, 28
Classical music, 51–60, 432–36
  20th century, 432–36
  Baroque, 53–55
  Beethoven and the Romantic
    era, 56–60

  Classical, 55–56
  Electronic, 436
  Impressionism, 432
  Late 20th-century, 436
  New Nationalism, 434
  Renaissance, 52–53
  Romantic, 58–60
  Second Viennese School, 432–
    34
Clay, Henry, 62–64
Cleopatra, 44, 45, 404, 506,
  507
Cleveland, Grover, 106
climate change, 191–95
Clovis culture, 213
Code of Hammurabi, 403
Cohen, George, M., 21–22
Cold Harbor, battle of, 69
Cold War, the, 81–85
Cole, Thomas, 480
Coleridge, Samuel Taylor, 326,
  327, 462
Colossus (computer), 72
Comedy, 9–10
Communist Manifesto, The, 416
Compromise of 1850, 64
computing, 71–80
  business computers, 72–73
  history of, 71–75
  home computing, 73–74
  industry consolidation, 74–75
  Internet and World Wide Web,
    76–80
  supercomputers, 75
concerto, 53, 56, 57, 59, 243,
  433, 436
Confucianism, 138–40
  The Analects of Confucius,
    138–40

Confucius, 138–40, 352, 537
Congress of Racial Equality (CORE), 293
Constantine, 275, 380, 510
Constitution, U.S., 186–90, 409–10
  Articles, 409–10
  Bill of Rights, 410
  creation of, 186–90
  ratification, 189–90
Constructivism, 429
Continental Congress, 182
Coolidge, Calvin, 312, 313, 314, 315
Cooper, James Fenimore, 331
Copernicus, Nicolaus, 95, 173
Coppola, Francis Ford, 520
Counter-Reformation, the, 236–40
country music, 390–91
Credit Mobilier, 103
Crick, Francis, 347
Crosby, Bing, 24
Crusades, the, 169
Cuban missile crisis, 84, 89
Cubism, 427
Cunningham, Merce, 249
Cushing, Harvey, 159

D

Dada, 427–28
dance, 245–50
Dante Alighieri, 461–62
Daoism. See Taoism
Darwin, Charles, 301, 341–42, 343, 437, 454
Das Kapital, 455–56
da Vinci, Leonardo. See Leonardo da Vinci

DeBakey, Michael, 159–60
Debussy, Claude, 247, 432
Degas, Edgar, 485
de Mille, Agnes, 248
Deng Xiaoping, 361
Depression, Great, 315–20
Descartes, René, 460
Dewey, John, 418–19
Diaghilev, Sergei, 247
Dickens, Charles, 288
Dickinson, Emily, 338
Diocletian, 510
Directory, the, 256–57
dissonance (music), 53, 434
Divine Comedy, The, 461–62
Domino, Fats, 27
Donatello, 175
Dostoyevsky, Fyodor, 284
Dred Scot Decision, 65
Duchamp, Marcel, 428
Dumas, Alexandre, 282
Duncan, Isadora, 249
Dürer, Albrecht, 177

E

Eakins, Thomas, 481
Earth, the, 97, 437–42
  composition, 438–39
  formation of, 437–38
  plate tectonics, 439–40
  seafloor spreading, 440–41
earthquakes, 441
Edison, Thomas A., 490–93, 513
Egypt, ancient, 41–50, 270–72
  architecture, 46, 47
  art, 271–72

Egypt, ancient (con't),
cultural history of, 46–50
funerary practice of, 49
Great Sphinx, 47
hieratic, 47, 48, 141
hieroglyphics, 42, 46, 47, 48
Hyksos, 43, 46, 219
New Kingdom, 43–45
Old Kingdom, 42–43
political history of, 41–46
pyramid of Cheops, 47
religion and mythology, 48
Rosetta Stone, 41, 46, 48
Ehrlich, Paul, 158
Einstein, Albert, 226–27
Eisenhower, Dwight D., 20, 83,
268, 291, 296, 497
El Greco, 179
electricity, 489–94
elements, the (chemistry),
442–46
Eliot, George, 289
Eliot, T. S., 339
Elizabeth I, 238–39
Emancipation Proclamation, 67
Emerson, Ralph Waldo, 332,
337, 480
energy, 261–70
and the Cold War, 264
Middle East, 262
nuclear, 266–70
oil, 261–66
renewable, 195
Standard Oil, 102, 262–64
Engels, Friedrich, 146, 453–55
engine, internal combustion,
261–62
engine, steam, 261, 447

English language, 474–78
codifying, 475–76
in America, 476–77
new words, 477–78
English novel, 286–90
ENIAC, 72
environment, the, 191–200
biodiversity, 193–95
climate change, 191–95
environmentalism, 194,
196–200
global warming, 191–95
pollution, 196–99
renewable energy, 195
waste disposal, 199–200
Epic of Gilgamesh, **457**
Erasmus, Desiderius, 172
Etruscans, 502
Euripides, 9
European Expansion, 363–72
Africa, 369–70
Australia and New Zealand,
372
England, 365–66
France, 366
Great Britain and North
America, 367–68
India, 370–71
Portugal, 363–64
Spain, 364–65, 368–69
Evers, Medgar, 293, 295
evolution, 341–45
comparative anatomy, 342
comparative embryology,
342–43
dating fossils, 344
fossil record, 342
human, 344–45
Expressionism, 427

F

Faerie Queene, 323
Farnsworth, Philo T., 126
Faulkner, William, 335
Fermat, Pierre de, 491
Fermi, Enrico, 86, 266
Film. See American Film.
Fiorentino, Rosso, 178
Fitzgerald, Ella, 25
Fitzgerald, F. Scott, 313, 315, 335
Flaubert, Gustave, 283
Fleming, Alexander, 159
Fokine, Mikhail, 247
folk music, 388–90
Ford, John, 520
fossils, 342, 344
Fra Angelico, 176, 280
Francesca, Piero della, 176
Franklin, Aretha, 26, 386
Freedom Riders, 293
French and Indian War, 181
French novel, 281–83
French Revolution, the, 251–57, 281–84
  Reign of Terror, 255–56
  war and regicide, 254–55
Freud, Sigmund, 421–23, 428
Frost, Robert, 338–39, 464, 466
Fuchs, Klaus, 87

G

Galaxies, 93–94
Galen, 152
Galilei, Galileo, 91

Garrison, William Lloyd, 63
Gauguin, Paul, 487
general relativity, theory of, 224, 226–27
genetics, 345–50
  and comparative biochemistry, 343
  genetic code, 348
  genetic diseases, 349
  genetic engineering, 349
  Human Genome Project, 350
  inheritance, 346
  in Medicine, 349–50
geometry, 526–27, 529–30
German novel, 283–84
Germany, 11–20
Gershwin, George, 21, 23
Gettysburg, battle of, 68
Ghirlandaio, Domenico, 280
Gilded Age, 101–06
Gillies, Harold, 159
Giotto, 278
Glass, Philip, 245
Gogol, Nikolai, 284
Google, 79
Gorbachev, Mikhail, 85
Gould, Jay, 103
global warming, 191, 195
Graham, Martha, 249
Grant, Ulysses S., 66–70, 103, 104
Great Depression, 315–20
Greek art, 273–74
Greek comedy, 9
Greek drama, 6–10
  Aeschylus, 6–7, 9
  Aristophanes, 9, 10
  Euripides, 6–7, 9–10
  Sophocles, 6–9

Greek philosophy, 393–98
Greek poetry, 457–58
Gregorian chant, 51
Griffith, D.W., 514–15
Gutenberg, Johannes, 144

H

H-bombs. See hydrogen bomb
Hadrian (emperor), 509
Handel, George Frideric, 54,
  242, 250
Hannibal, 504
Harding, Warren, 110, 311, 312
Hardy, Thomas, 289–90, 329
Harlem Renaissance, 335, 339
Hatshepsut, 43, 44, 47
Hawthorne, Nathaniel, 333
Haydn, Franz Joseph, 55
Hayes, Rutherford B., 105
Haymarket affair, 105
Hegel, Georg Wilhelm, 415–16
Hemingway, Ernest, 313, 335
Henry VIII, 145, 178, 235,
  238, 240, 365, 524
Hideyoshi, Toyotomi, 33
Hinduism, 131–35
  core beliefs, 132
  dieties, 133
  history, 133
  scripture, 131
hip-hop, 386–88
Hippocrates, 152
Hirohito, 38
Hiroshima, 39
history, U.S.
  American Civil War, 61–70
  American Revolution, 181–86
  Civil Rights movement, 291–96

Cold War, the, 81–90
Constitution, making of,
  186–90
Gilded Age, 101–06
Great Depression and New
  Deal, 315–20
Jazz Age, 311–15
Progressive Era, 107–09
Roaring Twenties, 311–15
Sixties, the, 291–300
Vietnam War, 296–300
World Wars, 11–20
history, world
  Bronze Age, 217
  China, 351–62
  Cold War, the, 81–90
  Counter-Reformation, 236–40
  Crusades, the, 169–70
  Egypt, ancient, 61–70
  European expansion, 363–72
  French Revolution, 251–57
  Homo sapiens and the birth of
    civilization, 211–20
  Industrial Revolution, 447–56
  Iron Age, 218
  Japan, 31–40
  Mesopotamia, 216–17, 272
  Middle East, ancient, 218
  Modern economic world,
    origins of, 447–52
  Napoleonic era, 257–60
  Protestant Reformation,
    231–36
  Punic Wars, the, 503–05
  Renaissance, the, 171–80
  Revolution of 1848, 455
  Rome, ancient, 501–12
  Thirty Years War, 240
  Waterloo, battle of, 260
  World Wars, 11–20
Hitchcock, Alfred, 521

Hitler, Adolf, 15–20, 86, 429
Hobbes, Thomas, 400
home computing, 73–74
Homer, 1–5
Homer, Winslow, 481
Homo erectus, 211, 212, 344, 345
Homo sapiens, 211–14, 305, 344, 345, 467
honky-tonk, 392
Hoover, Herbert, 314–15
Hopkins, Gerard Manley, 330
Hopper, Edward, 482
Hubble Space Telescope, 91
Hudson River School, 480
Hugo, Victor, 282–83
Human Genome Project, 350
Husserl, Edmund, 419
hydrogen bomb, 88

I

Iliad, The, 1–5, 457
Impressionism and after, 483–88
    Art Nouveau, 488
    Impressionism, 483–86
    Post-Impressionism, 486–88
Ince, Thomas, 515
Industrial Revolution, the, 447–56
Internet, the, 76
Iron Age, 218
Irving, Washington, 331, 337
Islam, 161–170
    belief and practice, 163
    in Africa, 168
    in Europe, 166
    in India and Southeast Asia, 167–68
    expansion of, 166
    holidays, 165
    schools and sects, 164
    scripture, 161
Israel, ancient, 219

J

Jackson, Thomas "Stonewall," 67, 68
Jackson, Andrew, 62
James, Henry, 289, 290, 334, 420, 524
James Webb Telescope, 91
James, William, 420–21
Japan, 18–20, 31–40, 86–87. See also Sino–Japanese War; Russo–Japanese War
    20th-century, 38–40
    ancient, 31
    economy of, 40
    Edo, 33–36
    Heian Period, 32
    Meiji Period, 35–37
    Momoyama Period, 33
    samurai, 32–36
    shogun, 32–35
    Tokugawa Period, 34
    Yamato clan, 31
    in World War II, 40
Jazz, 383–85. See also Harlem Renaissance
Jazz Age, the, 311–15
Jefferson, Thomas, 62
Jenner, Edward, 155
Jesus, 111–18, 377–80
Johnson, Lyndon B., 295, 297–98

Jones, Inigo, 180
Judaism, 373–77
  belief and practice, 374–75
  history, 376–77
  holidays, 376
  schools and sects, 375
  scripture, 373–74
Jung, Carl, 422–23
Jupiter (planet), 98
Justinian, 405, 511

K

Kant, Immanuel, 402, 419, 437
Kazan, Elia, 521
Keats, John, 327–28, 465
Kelly, Gene, 248
Kennan, George, 82
Kennedy, John F., 84, 89, 128,
  291, 292, 296
Kepler, Johannes, 96
Kern, Jerome, 22
Khrushchev, Nikita 84
Kierkegaard, Søren, 416, 417,
  419
King, Martin Luther, 291, 292,
  295, 296, 299, 332
kingdoms (taxonomy), 306
  dinosaurs, 309, 310
  Domain Archaea, 307
  Domain Eukarya, 307–08
  Domain Prokarya, 307
Koran, the, 161–63
Ku Klux Klan (KKK), 313, 314
Ku Klux Klan Act, 104
Kublai Khan, 32, 327, 355, 356
Kuomintang (KMT), 359, 360

L

Languages, world, 467–78
  English, history of, 474–78
  families, 471–73
  origins and groups, 468–71
Laozi, 140
Lascaux, 212
lasers, 230
law, the, 403–14
  American Constitutional
    system, 409–14
  Anglo-American, 406–07
  in ancient Athens, 403–04
  in the ancient world, 403–05
  Code of Hammurabi, 151, 403
  Constitutional, 409–10
  court system, the U.S., 410–14
  Enlightenment, the, 407–08
  federal courts, 410–11
  How a case comes before the
    Supreme Court, 411–12
  Medieval, 405–06
  Roman, 404–05
  state courts, 412
  Supreme Court, the U.S., 411
  Supreme Court decisions, 411,
    412–14
League of Nations, 15, 17, 110,
  262, 311, 545
Lean, David, 522
Lee, Robert E., 67–70
Leiber and Stoller, 26
Leibniz, Gottfried Wilhelm,
  491
Lenin, Vladimir, 14, 458
Lennon, John, 29, 30
Leonardo da Vinci, 176, 301
Les Ballets Russes, 247

Lewis, Sinclair, 313
Lexington and Concord, battle
  of, 182
Lincoln, Abraham, 65–70
Lindbergh, Charles, 124, 314,
  499
Linnaeus, Carolus, 306
literature
  American writers, 331–40
  drama, Greek, 6–10
  Iliad and *Odyssey*, 1, 2–5
  Medieval, 460–62
  novel, English, 286–90
  novel, French, 281–82
  novel, German, 283–84
  novel, Russian, 284–86
  poetry, American, 337–40
  poetry, English, 321–30
  poetry, introduction to, 457–63
  poetry, Greek, 457–58
  prose, American, 331–36
  Renaissance, 173–75
  Roman, 458–60
  Romantics and Victorians,
    326–30
  Shakespeare, William, 201–10
Locke, John, 400–01
Loesser, Frank, 24
loose nukes, 90. See also nu-
  clear weapons.
Los Alamos, 86, 88
Louis XIV, 251
Louis XV, 251
Louis XVI, 251–55
Lumière brothers, 513
Luther, Martin, 232–33
Lyell, Sir Charles, 437

M

MacArthur, Douglas, 19, 39,
  83, 316
Machiavelli, Niccolò, 172, 174
madrigal, 52
magazines, 148–50
Magna Carta, 406
Mahler, Gustav, 60
Malcolm X, 295
Malthus, Thomas, 449
Manet, Édouard 483, 484–85
Manhattan Project, 86, 267–68
Manzikert, battle of, 168
Mao Zedong, 82, 360, 456. See
  also China, communism
  under Mao
Marcus Aurelius, 509
Marius, 505
Mars (planet), 97–98
Marshall, John, 411
Marx, Karl, 416–17, 453–56
Master of Flémalle, 279
mathematics, 525–32
  algebra, 526, 529
  arithmetic, 525, 529
  calculus, 527, 530
  chaos theory, 531
  discrete, 531
  geometry, 525, 529
  history of, 525
  number theory, 532
  topology, 530
  trigonometry, 530
Matisse, Henri, 247, 488
McCarthy, Joseph, 83
McCartney, Paul, 29, 30
McClellan, George B. Gen., 67

McNamara, Robert, 89
medicine, history of, 151–60
  from ancients to the
    Enlightenment, 151–55
  modern medicine, 155–60
Medieval poetry, 460–62
Méliès, Georges, 513
Melville, Herman, 333
Mendel, Gregor, 159, 346–47
Mercury (planet), 96–97
Meredith, James, 293–94
Mesoamerican culture, 219–20
Mesopotamia, 216–17
Messiaen, Olivier 435
Michelangelo, 177
Microsoft, 73–74
Middle Ages
  art, 275–79
  poetry, 460–62
Middle East, 262
Milky Way, 94
Mill, John Stuart, 417
Milton, John, 324–25
Milvian Bridge, battle of, 510
minimalism, in music, 436
Missouri Compromise, 62–64,
  412
modern dance, 249–50
modernism, in art, 427–31
  Abstract Expressionism, 430
  Bauhaus, 428
  Constructivism, 429
  Cubism, 427
  Dada, 427, 428
  Expressionism, 427
  New Objectivity, 428
  Pop art, 431
  Surrealism, 427, 428, 431
modernism, in music, 432–436
  electronic music, 436

  indeterminacy, 435
  minimalism, 436
  nationalism, 434
  neo-Classicism, 435
  Second Viennese School, 432,
    433, 434
  serialism, 435
  twelve-tone, 434
Montesquieu, Charles, 401
Monet, Claude, 485
Monteverdi, Claudio, 52, 242
More, Thomas, 173
Morgan, J. P., 102
Motown, 386
Mozart, Wolfgang Amadeus,
  55, 56, 242–43, 433
Muhammad, 161–63, 165, 166
music
  20th-century classical, 432–36
  American popular music, 21–
    30, 383–90
  American Songbook, 21–25
  Classical, history of, 51–60
  Folk and Country, 288–92
  opera, 241–50
  Rock, origins of, 25–30
Mussolini, Benito, 16

N

Nagasaki, 20, 39, 87
Napoleon, 57, 257–60, 283
  Code Napoléon, 258
  Directory, the, 257
  Emperor, 258–59
  Invasion of Russia, 259–60
National Association for the
  Advancement of Colored
  People (N.A.A.C.P.), 293
NATO, 82

Nazis, 15–20, 39
Neanderthals, 211, 212
neo-Classical music, 433–34
Neolithic culture, 214–15
Neptune (planet), 99
New Deal, 315–20
New Objectivity, the, 428
New Testament, 377–80
newspapers, 146–48, 150
Newton, Sir Isaac, 221–24
New York School, the, 429–31
Nietzsche, Friedrich, 417–18
Nijinsky, Vaslav, 247
Nixon, Richard, 85, 128, 196,
  291, 292, 299–300
novel, European, 281–90
  English, 286–90
  French, 281–83
  German, 283–84
  Russian, 284–86
nuclear disasters, 269–70
nuclear power, 87, 200, 228,
  266–70
nuclear weapons, 86–89
number theory, 532

O

O'Keeffe, Georgia, 483
Octavian, 45, 404–05, 506–07
  458–59
Oda Nobunaga 33
Odyssey, The, 1–5, 457
oil (petroleum), 262–65
Olmecs, 219
OPEC, 264
opera, 23, 53, 60, 123, 241–45,
  354, 433, 434
  Baroque origins, 241
  Classical, 242

modern, 244–45
Romantic, 243
Oppenheimer, J. Robert, 86
oratorio, 53
organisms, 307–09
  domains, 307–08
  of the past, 309
Osler, William, 157
Ottoman Empire, 11, 263
Owen, Robert, 452–53
Oxford English Dictionary, 476

P

Palladio, Andrea, 180
Paracelsus, 154
Paradise Lost, 324–26
Paré, Ambroise, 154
Pascal, Blaise, 173
Pasteur, Louis, 156
Pavlov, Ivan, 423
Pearl Harbor, 18, 19, 39, 320
Perry, Matthew, 35
Pet Sounds, 29
Petipa, Marius, 247
Petrarch, Francesco, 172
philosophes, 401
philosophy, 393–402
  19th-century, 415–18
  20th-century, 418–20
  analytic, 419
  ancient Greeks, 393–98
  continental, 419
  early modern, 399–402
  Enlightenment, the, 400–02
  existentialism, 419–20
  German Idealism, 415–16
  Hellenistic and Roman, 397–98
  modern, 415–20
  Pre-Socratics, 393–94

philosophy (con't),
 Scholasticism, 399
 Sophists, 394, 395
 utilitarianism, 417
physics, 221–30
 astrophysics, 225
 biophysics, 226
 Conservation Laws, 222
 geophysics, 226
 lasers, 230
 Law of Gravity, 223
 Laws of Electromagnetic
  Radiation, 224
 Laws of Motion, 221
 Laws of Quantum Physics, 225
 Laws of Thermodynamics, 224
 subatomic particles, 228
 theories of relativity, 226–27
Picasso, Pablo, 427
Pissarro, Camille, 485
planets, 96–99
plant kingdoms, 308–09
Plato, 395–96
**Poe, Edgar Allan, 333, 464,
 466**
poetry, 457–66
 foot and meter, 463
 Greek, 457–58
 how poetry works, 462
 in Medieval Europe, 460–62
 poetic forms, 464
 poetic terms, 466
 Roman, 458–60
poetry, American 337–40
**poetry, English, 175, 321–30,
 463**
 Cavalier, 324
 late Victorian and early 20th-
  century, 329
 Old English, 321

 Metaphysical, 323
 Milton, John, 324–255
 Romantics, 326
 Tudor, 322–23
 Victorians, 328–30
Pollock, Jackson, 429–30
polyphony, 51, 52, 53
Pompey, 506
Populist Party, 107
Porter, Cole, 23
Porter, Edwin S., 514
postmodern art, 431
Presley, Elvis, 26–28
Pre-Socratics, 393–94
printing press, 144–45
 influence of, 144–45
 invention of, 144
Progressive Era, the, 107–10
**Prohibition, 107, 109, 312,
 315, 317**
psychology, 420–26
 anxiety and stress, 425
 behaviorism, 423–24
 disorders and treatment,
  424–25
 eating disorders, 426
 humanistic, 424
 mood disorders, 425
 neo-Freudians, 422–23
 psychoanalysis, 421–23
Puccini, Giacomo, 244–45
Punic Wars, the, 503–05

R

R&B, 385–86
Rabelais, François, 174
radio, 121–25
 advertising agencies, 123

Columbia Broadcasting
  Company, 122
modern, 125
National Broadcasting
  Company, 122
networks, 122–25
news, 124
prime time, 124
railroads, U.S., 495-96, 498
Raphael, 177
Reagan, Ronald, 85
Reed, Walter, 157
Reformation, the, 145, 231–40
  Counter-Reformation, 236–40
  Thirty Years War, 240
Reign of Terror, 255–57
Religion
  Asia, Major Religions of, 131–
    40
  Bible, the, 111–20
  Buddhism, 135–38, 354–55
  Christianity, 377–82
  Confucianism, 138–40
  Counter-Reformation, 236–40
  Hebrew Bible, Old Testament,
    112–15
  Hinduism, 131–35
  Islam, 161–70
  Judaism, 373–77
  Koran, the, 161–63
  late Renaissance theology, 173
  New Testament, 377–80
  Reformation, Protestant,
    231–40
  Taoism, 140
Renaissance, the, 52–53,171–
80, 278–79, 399
  architecture, 179–80
  art, 175–79, 279–80
  humanism 172

  literature and ideas, 171–75,
    399
  Mannerism, 178
  music, 52–53
  painting, 175–79
  political theorists, 172
  sculpture, 177
  theology, 173
Renoir, Pierre-Auguste, 486
Revere, Paul, 182
Rhazes, 153
rhythm and blues (R&B),
385–86
Richardson, Samuel, 286
Roaring Twenties, 311–15
robber barons, 103
Robbins, Jerome, 248
Robespierre, Maximilien de,
256
Rockefeller, John D., 102, 262
Rodgers, Richard, 24
Rogers, Carl, 424
Rolling Stones, the, 30
Rome, ancient, 146, 152,
501–11
  barbarians, 510–11
  decline, 509–11
  empire, 507–11
  "Good Emperors," 508–09
  late empire, 511
  literature, 458–60
  Punic Wars, 503–05
  republic, 502
  from republic to empire,
    501–07
  Romulus and Remus, 501
Roosevelt, Franklin Delano,
18–20, 81, 316–20
Roosevelt, Theodore, 37,
108–10, 194

Rossini, Antonio, 243
Rousseau, Henri, 488
Rousseau, Jean-Jacques 281, 401, 408
Russell, Bertrand, 419
Russia, 11–16, 19
Russian novel, 284
Russo–Japanese War, 37

S

Salinger, J. D., 336
Sappho, 457
Sargent, John Singer, 482
Sarnoff, David, 121
Sartre, Jean-Paul, 420
Saturn (planet), 98–99
Saudi Arabia, 263
Schubert, Franz, 58
science
  Earth, the, 437–46
  environment, the, 191–200
  evolution, 341–45
  forms of life, 301–10
  genetics, 345–50
  mathematics, 525–32
  medicine, history of, 151–60
  physics, 221–30
  psychology, 420–26
  taxonomy, 306–10
  universe, the, 91–100
Scott, Sir Walter, 287, 328
Second Viennese School, the, 432–33
serialism, in music, 435
Seurat, Georges, 487
Shakespeare, William, 175, 201–210, 239, 323
  controversy, 204–05
  life and work, 201–03
  major plays, 205–10
  sonnets, 203–04
Shays Rebellion, 185
Shelley, Mary, 287
Shelley, Percy Bysshe, 287, 327
Sherman, William T. Gen., 68
Silk Road, 135, 353–55, 380
Sinatra, Frank, 25, 385
Sino–Japanese War, 37
Skinner, B. F., 424
slavery, in the U.S., 61–66
Smith, Adam, 448–49
Socrates, 395, 420
Solon, 403–04
sonata, 53, 57, 243, 434
Sons of Liberty, 181
Sophocles, 7–9
Soul (music), 386
Spector, Phil, 28, 29
St. Augustine, 381, 398
St. Thomas Aquinas, 399
Stamp Act, 181
Standard Oil, 262, 264
stars, 91–95
steam engine, 261, 447
Stein, Gertrude, 313, 335
Stendhal, 282, 283
Stevens, George, 522
Stowe, Harriet Beecher, 64, 333
Strauss, Richard, 244
Stravinsky, Igor 247, 433–34
Stuart, Gilbert, 479
Student Non-Violent Coordinating Committee, 292
subatomic particles, 228
Sulla, 505
Sun, the, 95–96

Sun, Yat-sen, 359
supercomputing, 75
Supreme Court, U.S., 411–12
   important decisions, 411,
      412–14
Surrealism, 428

T

Taft, William Howard, 110
Takamori, Saigo, 35,36
Tale of Genji, The, 32
Tammany Hall, 103, 312
Taoism, 140
taxonomy, 306–10
Taylor, Paul, 249
technology
   computers, 71–80
   electricity, 489–94
   energy, 201–70
   Internet and World Wide Web,
      76–80
   nuclear weapons, 86–90
   transportation, 495–500
   radio, 121–25
   television, 126–30
television, 126–30
   Cable Era, 129–30
   Commercial Television, 126–27
   Network Era, 127–29
   RCA, 126
Terra Amata, 179
Tesla, Nikola, 489–93
Thackeray, William Makepeace,
   288
Tharp, Twyla, 250
Thoreau, Henry David, 63, 332,
   337, 480
Three Mile Island, 269
Tintoretto, 179

Tojo, Hideki, 18
Tolstoy, Leo, 260, 285
Toulouse-Lautrec, Henri, 487
Trains, 495
Trajan (emperor), 508–09
Transcendentalism, 331, 332
Treaty of Versailles, 15, 16, 38,
   359
Trotsky, Leon, 14
Truman, Harry, 20, 81, 86, 87
Turing machine, 72
Turner, Nat, 62
Tutankamen, 44, 45
Twain, Mark, 334–35
Tweed, William "Boss" , 103
Twelve-tone music, 433

U

Underground Railroad, 64
Universe, the, 91–100
   Earth, 97
   galaxies, 93
   planets, 96–100
Uranus (planet), 99
utilitarianism, 417

V

Valley Forge, 184
Vanderbilt, Cornelius, 102
van Ecyk, Jan, 279
van Gogh, Vincent, 486–87
Vedas, 131–32
Venus (planet), 97
Verdi, Giuseppe, 243–44
Vesalius, Andreas, 153
Vietnam War, 296–300, 389,
   520

Virgil, 458–60
Vivaldi, Antonio, 53, 242
Volcanoes, 441
Voltaire, 401
Voting Rights Act, 296

W

Wagner, Richard, 60, 244, 432,
  454–55
Wallace, George C., 294–95
Warhol, Andy, 431
Washington, George, 61, 181,
  182, 186, 190
Waterloo, battle of, 260
Watson, James, 347, 350
Watt, James, 447
Webster, Daniel, 62
Wegener, Alfred, 439–40
Welles, Orson, 516
Wellington, duke of, 260
West, Benjamin, 479
Western Swing (music),
  391–92
Westinghouse, George, 491–92
Whistler, James McNeill,
  481–82
Whitehead, A. N., 418, 419
Whitman, Walt, 337–38, 464
Wikipedia, 80
Wilde, Oscar, 330
Wilder, Billy, 523
Wilmot Proviso, 64
Wilson, Woodrow, 14, 15, 110,
  311, 312, 318
Windscale fire, 269
Wittgenstein, Ludwig, 419

Wood, Grant, 483
Wordsworth, William, 326–27,
  337, 462
Works Progress Administration,
  318, 429
World War I, 11–15, 110, 316
  America in, 14–15
  Eastern Front, 14
  Treaty of Versailles, 15
  Western Front, 13–14
World War II, 15–20, 39, 81,
  360
  America in, 18–19
  D-Day and allied victory, 20,
  oil production during, 263
World Wide Web, 77–79
Wren, Christopher, 180
written word, the, 141–50
  alphabet, the, 141–43
  book, the, 142
  lithography, 145
  newspapers and magazines,
    146–50
  printing, 143, 145
Wyler, William, 523–24

Y

Yorktown, battle of, 181

Z

Zama, battle of, 504
Zen, 33, 34, 136
Zinnemann, Fred, 524
Zola, Émile, 283